Western Plainchant in the First Millennium

Western Plainchant in the First Millennium

Studies in the Medieval Liturgy and its Music

Edited by

Sean Gallagher

James Haar

John Nádas

Timothy Striplin

ASHGATE

Published by
Ashgate Publishing Limited
Gower House
Croft Road
Aldershot
Hants GU11 3HR
England

Ashgate Publishing Company
Suite 420
101 Cherry Street
Burlington, VT 05401–4405
USA

Ashgate website: http://www.ashgate.com

British Library Cataloguing in Publication Data
Western plainchant in the first millennium: studies in the
medieval liturgy and its music: written in honor of James
W. McKinnon
1. Gregorian chants–History and criticism
I. Gallagher, Sean
782. 3′ 222′ 00902

US Library of Congress Cataloging in Publication Data
Western plainchant in the first millennium: studies in the medieval liturgy and its music / edited by Sean Gallagher . . . [et al.].
p.cm.
Includes bibliographical references (alk. paper).
1. Church music–Catholic Church–To 500. 2. Church music–Catholic Church–500–1400. 3. Church music–Catholic Church–15th century. 4. Gregorian chants–History and criticism. 5. Catholic Church–Liturgy–History. I Gallagher, Sean, 1965–
ML3003. W388 2002
782. 32' 22' 009015–dc21 2001048706

ISBN 0 7546 0389 X

This book is printed on acid-free paper

Typeset in Times Roman by Q3 Bookwork

Printed and bound in Great Britain by MPG Books Ltd, Bodmin

In memory of James W. McKinnon

Contents

List of Plates

List of Figures

List of Tables

List of Music Examples

Contents of the Compact Disc

Gregorian Communion antiphons for Advent and Christmas (see Table 18.1, p. 456)

Track 1. *Dominus dabit benignitatem V. Ostende nobis*
Track 2. *Ierusalem surge V. Qui regis Israel*
Track 3. *Dicite pusillanimes V. Cantate Domino*
Track 4. *Ecce virgo concipiet V. Exultavit ut gigas*
Track 5. *Ecce Dominus veniet V. Beati immaculati*
Track 6. *Exultavit ut gigas V. In sole posuit*
Track 7. *Revelabitur Gloria Domini V. Ipse super maria*
Track 8. *In splendoribus sanctorum V. Donec ponam*
Track 9. *Exulta filia Sion V. Etenim firmavit*
Track 10. *Viderunt omnes V. Notum fecit Dominus*
Track 11. *Video caelos / Exiit sermo / Vox in Rama / Beatus servus*
Track 12. *Tolle puerum / Vidimus stellam / Fili quid fecisti / Dicit Dominus / Mirabantur omnes*

Roman Propers for a Nuptial Mass (see Chapter 12)

Track 13. *Deus Israel* (antiphon at the Introit), with *V. Beati omnes, Gloria Patri, V. Uxor tua sicut vitis* (Ex. 12.13)
Track 14. *Uxor tua* (Gradual responsory), with *V. Filii tui* (Ex. 12.14)
Track 15. *Alleluia. Diffusa est gratia* (Ex. 12.15)
Track 16. *In te speravi* (Offertory) and *Ecce sic benedicetur* (Communion antiphon) (Exs. 12.16–17)

Versions of the Communion antiphon *Oportet te fili gaudere* (see Chapter 14)

Track 17. *Oportet te*, seven versions (Chapter 14, Appendix, nos. A.1–A.7)
Track 18. *Oportet te*, five versions (Chapter 14, Appendix, nos. B–F)

Alleluia with sequential, Sequence, and prose (see Chapter 16)

Track 19. *Alleluia. Confitemini Domino et invocate* (Gregorian) plus sequentia / *O quam mira* (Notker) (Exs. 16.1–2)
Track 20. Sequence with prose *Carmen suo dilecto* (Notker) (Ex. 16.3)

Preface

When Jim McKinnon made known his intention to retire from active teaching, some of his colleagues and students decided to organize a symposium on chant studies in his honor, to be held in the Spring of 1999. When we learned of the illness that was to end his life, we moved the date back to January of that year.

In an expression of scholarly respect, admiration and friendship for Jim, a collective act that moved him and pleased us more than we can say, a group of the leading scholars in early chant study accepted our revised invitation. They came to Chapel Hill from all over the United States, Canada and Europe to read papers and discuss problems in chant scholarship, many of them related to Jim's work and his central interest, the rise and development of the Roman liturgy. By the time the symposium was held Jim was bedridden, but he followed the sessions on video tapes prepared daily for him, spoke through the same medium to all those in attendance, and greeted the participants as they came, one by one, to his house. We all felt that in a sense Jim had willed himself to live for this occasion (he died a month later), and for this we were grateful.

All of the papers read at the symposium are included – many of them substantially revised – in this volume; to them are added studies by several scholars who contributed essays out of respect and affection for a man whose work touched on and influenced their own scholarship.

Jim McKinnon's last book, *The Advent Project: The Later-Seventh-Century Creation of the Roman Mass Proper*, was published by the University of California Press in 2000. This magisterial volume, at once a work of definitive scholarship and an engaging read, was essentially complete before the symposium was held, thanks in part to the assistance of his student Brad Maiani. Its contents were known to a number of the participants and helped to shape the direction of the symposium, which was divided into sessions entitled 'The Formation of the Liturgy and its Music', '*Cantus et ratio* (Theory, Chant and Notation)' and 'Carolingian and Post-Carolingian Chant'.

These titles served well enough for the symposium but, as is often the case on these occasions, they were not a perfect fit. We decided to dispense with them in this volume; but the attentive reader will note a general grouping of subject matter related to the liturgy and its development (the first six chapters), to problems of notation and transmission in the chant repertory (the middle six) and to questions of interpretation and performance (the last six). Richard Crocker, who was unfortunately unable to attend the symposium, later submitted not only a paper but his own performance of early chant, contained on the compact disc included with this book.

In our judgment these papers (whose authors gracefully submitted to what we hope was not unduly intrusive editorial intervention on our part) can and do speak for themselves; they do not need capsule summaries from us. A few of the essays, conceived and written independently but interrelated in rewarding ways, read almost like consecutive book chapters. Others show what we consider the legitimately, sometimes remarkably, wide boundaries of the subject of chant research. We hope that readers will enjoy and profit from reading these essays as much as we did assembling them, and – more important – as James McKinnon did hearing them.

Our thanks go first to the contributors to this volume, whose fine work we are proud to present. One of us, Tim Striplin, himself a chant scholar, made use of his considerable computer skills to organize and format the tables, figures, and musical examples in the book. For this his colleagues in this enterprise are truly grateful. We also acknowledge with thanks the cooperative attitude and editorial expertise of Bonnie Blackburn, as well as of Rachel Lynch and her staff at Ashgate Publishing. We are indebted to the various libraries that granted permission to reproduce materials in their possession. And we thank the late James McKinnon for the unforgettable years of scholarly inspiration and collegial companionship he gave to us.

Sean Gallagher
James Haar
John Nádas
Timothy Striplin

Chapel Hill, February 2002

Abbreviations

AC	Archivio Capitolare
AfLw	*Archiv für Liturgiewissenschaft*
AfMw	*Archiv für Musikwissenschaft*
AH	*Analecta hymnica medii aevi*, ed. Guido Maria Dreves et al., 55 vols. (Leipzig: O. R. Reisland, 1886–1922)
AMS	René-Jean Hesbert, *Antiphonale missarum sextuplex* (Brussels: Vromont, 1935; repr. 1968)
BAV	Biblioteca Apostolica Vaticana
BC	Biblioteca Capitolare, Biblioteca Capitular
BL	British Library
BM	Bibliothèque Municipale
BN	Biblioteca Nazionale, Biblioteca Nacional
BNF	Bibliothèque Nationale de France
BSB	Bayerische Staatsbibliothek
BTC	*Beneventanum troporum corpus*
CAO	*Corpus antiphonalium officii*, ed. René-Jean Hesbert (Rerum ecclesiasticarum documenta, Series maior, Fontes, 7–12; Rome: Herder, 1963–79)
CCCM	*Corpus Christianorum,* Continuatio Mediaevalis Turnhout: Brepols, 1971–)
CCSL	*Corpus Christianorum*, Series Latina (Turnhout: Brepols, 1954–)
CPG	*Clavis patrum Graecorum*, ed. Maurice Geerard et al., 6 vols. (Turnhout: Brepols, 1974–98)
CPL	*Clavis patrum Latinorum*, 3rd ed., ed. Eligius Dekkers and Emil Gaar ([Turnhout:] Brepols, 1995)
CPPMA	*Clavis patristica pseudepigraphorum medii aevi*, ed. John Machielsen, 2 vols. in 4 (Turnhout: Brepols, 1990–94)
CSCO	*Corpus scriptorum Christianorum orientalium*, ed. I. B. Chabot et al. (Louvain: E. Peeters, 1902–)
CSEL	*Corpus scriptorum ecclesiasticorum Latinorum* (Vienna: Tempsky, 1866–)
CTC	*Catalogus translationum et commentariorum: Mediaeval and Renaissance Latin Translations and Commentaries*, ed. Paul Oskar Kristeller et al. (Washington, DC: Catholic University of America Press, 1960–)
DACL	*Dictionnaire d'archéologie chrétienne et de liturgie*, ed. Fernand Cabrol, Henri Leclercq, and Henri Marrou, 15 vols (Paris: Letouzey et Ane, 1907–53)

EL *Ephemerides liturgicae*
EMH *Early Music History*
GCS *Die griechischen christlichen Schriftsteller* (Berlin: Akademie, 1899–)
GR *Graduale sacrosanctae Romanae ecclesiae* (Rome: Typis Vaticanis, 1908)
GT *Graduale triplex*, ed. Marie-Claire Billecocq and Rupert Fischer (Solesmes: Abbaye Saint-Pierre, 1979)
JAMS *Journal of the American Musicological Society*
JM *Journal of Musicology*
JMR *Journal of Musicological Research*
LU *Liber usualis*
MECL *Music in Early Christian Literature*, ed. James McKinnon (Cambridge: Cambridge University Press, 1987)
MGG *Die Musik in Geschichte und Gegenwart*, ed. Friedrich Blume, 17 vols. (Kassel: Bärenreiter, 1949–86)
MGG^2 *Die Musik in Geschichte und Gegenwart*, 2nd edn, ed. Ludwig Finscher (Kassel: Bärenreiter, 1994–)
MGH *Monumenta Germaniae historica*
M&L *Music & Letters*
MMMA *Monumenta monodica medii aevi* (Kassel: Bärenreiter, 1956–)
MQ *Musical Quarterly*
NG *New Grove Dictionary of Music and Musicians*, ed. Stanley Sadie, 20 vols. (London: Macmillan, 1980)
NG II *New Grove Dictionary of Music and Musicians*, 2nd edn, ed. Stanley Sadie and John Tyrrell, 29 vols. (London: Macmillan, 2001)
NOHM *New Oxford History of Music*
OCA *Orientalia Christiana analecta*
ÖNB Österreichische Nationalbibliothek
PG *Patrologia Graeca*, ed. J.-P. Migne (Paris: Migne, 1857–66)
PL *Patrologie Latina*, ed. J.-P. Migne (Paris: Migne, 1844–64)
PLS *Patrologiae Latinae supplementum*, ed. Adalbert Hamman, 5 vols. (Paris: Garnier, 1958–1974)
PM *Paléographie musicale*
PMM *Plainsong and Medieval Music*
PO *Patrologia Orientalis*, ed. R. Graffin, F. Nau, et al. (Paris: Firmin-Didot, 1903–68; Turnhout: Brepols, 1968–)
PRMA *Proceedings of the Royal Musical Association*
RAH Real Academia de la Historia
RCG *Revue du chant grégorien*
RISM *Répertoire international des sources musicales*
SC *Sources chrétiennes*, ed. Henri de Lubac, J. Danielou et al. (Paris: Editions due Cerf, 1945–)
SB Stiftsbibliothek
UB Universitätsbibliothek

Chapter 1

Afterthoughts on *The Origins of the Liturgical Year*

Thomas J. Talley

The disciplines of musicology and liturgical history have long been intimately intertwined, but expert address to both of those has seldom been more clearly accomplished than by James McKinnon. Therefore, I was deeply honored to be invited to participate in a conference celebrating his life and work, the occasion for which this study was written. When, some six months prior to the conference, I was first approached about making a presentation, it was intimated that one reason for extending the invitation to one who is not a musicologist was Professor McKinnon's expressed appreciation of my work on *The Origins of the Liturgical Year*. That work is a historical study of the evolution of the festivals and seasons that celebrate the Christian mystery of redemption around an annual cycle. The work first appeared in 1986, and enjoyed a much-needed 'Second, Emended Edition' in 1991. While that took care of most of the more painful failures of proofreading, I now know of two minor mistakes still in the text.[1] Beyond that, years of teaching from the book and consideration of the reviews of it by others led me to undertake a more extensive revision a few years ago. That work, hardly begun, was cut short by serious attenuation of my central vision owing to macular degeneration. So when I was invited to present some material on the liturgical year to the conference, I was happy to have such an opportunity to confess some of the things I wish were different about that book.

Just to get an initial and painful problem out of the way, the book is, at least in the testimony of some, virtually unreadable. It was written, I now recognize, for the community of scholars, and could easily be made more 'reader-friendly' even within my stylistic limitations. As one example, I was asked to teach a course based on the book at Yale Divinity School in the spring of 1986, and on my first day in class I was set upon by one student who charged, 'you used a word that isn't even in the dictionary'. The offending word, I learned, was 'Quartodeciman', a term used to characterize those who kept the annual Pascha on the fourteenth day of the first month of spring, without regard to the day of the week. While I am sure the student would not suggest that our technical vocabulary should be limited to a standard desk reference dictionary, I like to think that had I been less afraid of delineating the obvious, it would have occurred to me to introduce that term more carefully. In fact, the initial discussion of the Asian custom of keeping Pascha on a fixed date, I now recognize, uses the term 'Quartodeciman' in a way that is open to the charge of mild anachronism, though no one has challenged it on that basis, so far as I am aware. In fact, the Asian fixed-date Pascha, kept on the same day as the Preparation for the Jewish Passover, 14 Nisan, came to be labeled 'Quartodeciman' only during the paschal controversy later in the second century. The Asian Christians who continued the observance of Passover did not call themselves 'fourteenthers', or Quartodecimans.

In connection with the Asian custom of observing Pascha on a fixed date, I remain dissatisfied with my introduction of the Asia Minor calendar to explain the significance of 6 April as a date still used by Montanists to determine the date of Pascha in the fifth century, according to the Constantinopolitan historian Sozomen (d. ca. 450).[2] While my description of the earlier, pre-Constantinian calendar of Asia Minor is intelligible, I believe, it is not compellingly clear. At the suggestion of a friend, Richard Norris, I prepared for the revision a table in three columns, showing: (1) the dates from 24 March through 6 April in the format familiar to us, (2) the Roman designation of those dates, counted as days before the kalends of the following month, or before the nones or ides of that month, a matter that itself needed more precise treatment, and (3) the equivalent days in the Asian month of Artemisios, numbered 1 through 14. Such a table, I hoped, would make clear how the fourteenth day of the first spring month came, after the establishment of Constantinople, to be known as 6 April. Some Asian Christians of the second century, cut off from the sages of Palestine who determined empirically whether, in a given year, the month preceding Nisan would be repeated to compensate for a lunar calendar whose twelve months fell eleven days short of the solar cycle, finally abandoned the Jewish lunar calendar. They had recourse instead to the solar calendar with which they were familiar, setting Pascha on the fourteenth day of the first month of spring in that calendar, the month sacred to Artemis and called 'Artemisios'. The understanding of this calendar of Asia Minor is critical for the interpretation of Sozomen's testimony, and of what August Strobel calls 'solar quartodecimanism'.[3]

It remains surprising to me that liturgical scholarship (my own included, for too long) has been, for the most part, so unconscious of the significance of that calendar. The resource on which I depended for treating of that calendar was E. J. Bickerman, *The Chronology of the Ancient World*, but the calendar was given more detailed treatment by Theodor Mommsen in an essay I was able to locate at Dumbarton Oaks only after the second edition of *Origins* was in press.[4] Fundamentally Julian, this Asian recension, established in 9 BC, took the birthday of Augustus on 23 September, the ninth day before the kalends of October, as its New Year's Day, the first day of a month called Kaisar (or Kaisarios), and so began each month nine days prior to its Roman equivalent. This made the Roman 24 March, the ninth day before the kalends of April, the first day of Artemisios in Asia Minor, and the fourteenth day of that first spring month, a solar equivalent to the Jewish Day of Preparation of the Passover, the day of the crucifixion, corresponding to the Roman 6 April. After the founding of Constantinople, the Roman calendar was adopted, and its designations displaced the old Asian calendar designations. This redesignation did not erase significant dates from memory, but translated them into the Roman terminology. So it is, for example, that the tenth-century Typikon of Hagia Sophia preserved in MS Hagios Stauros 40 in the Jerusalem patriarchal library still notes that 23 September is New Year's Day, τὸ νέον ἔτος.[5] This is why Sozomen's Montanists reckoned Pascha from 6 April, the Roman redesignation of 14 Artemisios.

Roland Bainton, to whose work we all owe a debt that will not soon be discharged, was unaware of this, and, convinced that 6 April was not a significant solar date, supposed that the date mentioned by Sozomen was computed back nine months from 6 January (a date for the nativity that Bainton took to have been adopted from a pagan festival, to arrive at the date of Christ's conception, often identified with that of his death).[6] As I hope will become clear shortly, that reverse computation from the nativity date to the date of the conception leaves unexplained the identification of the dates of the conception and death of the Lord. I shall be concerned shortly to accuse myself of a similar flaw of argument in another context. In any case, 6 April is not, as Bainton believed, a day of no solar significance, but the translation into Roman terminology of what had been designated the 14th day of the first month of spring in Asia Minor, a solar calendar equivalent to the lunar 14 Nisan, the Preparation of the Passover, and the day of the crucifixion according to the chronology of the Fourth Gospel.

Also in need of more explicit treatment is the difference between that Asian paschal date, 14 Artemisios, later known as 6 April, and the Western dating of the crucifixion to Friday, 25 March, in the year that would come to be designated AD 29. While both dates, 6 April and 25 March, would be associated with the crucifixion, they were not two different answers to the same question, but answers to two different questions. The question in Asia Minor was, 'how can we observe Passover on the fourteenth day of the first month when we don't know which month is first because the rabbis decide that *ad hoc*?' The question at Rome was, I suspect, 'how can we reasonably keep the death dates of the martyrs if we do not know the date of the Lord's death, which they emulate?' Committed to ending the fast of Pascha on Sunday, the West did not seek a standing solar equivalent to the biblical date, but rather sought to know the year of the Lord's death and the Julian date of the Preparation of the Passover, 14 Nisan, in that year. The Asian question was liturgical, the Western was historical.

However, this distinction between a historical date and that of a liturgical festival is not a simple matter, and some dates arrived at as historical can become liturgical observances. Our earliest source for the observance of the nativity on 25 December, the almanac assigned to the Chronographer of 354, gives a list of martyrs' memorials that begins with a notation against the eighth day before the kalends of January, 25 December, *natus Christus in Betleem Iudeae*.[7] That table of liturgical festivals of fixed date makes no mention of 25 March nor does it mention the day of the Lord's passion. That was not an observance of fixed date, but was moveable, and always on Friday. Nonetheless, the *Fasti Consulares* in that almanac do assign the passion to the consulates of the two Gemini, AD 29: 'His consulibus Dominus Iesus Christus passus est, die Veneris, luna quartodecima'.[8] The same list assigns the nativity of Christ to the consulates of Caesar and Paul, AD 1. Both are recorded as historical dates, but only the nativity became a festival of fixed date.

Epiphanius reports some Quartodecimans who observe Pascha on 25 March, and we shall return to that shortly. It would be unwise, however, to leap to the supposition that wherever we encounter a calendrical note assigning the death or even the resurrection of the Lord to 25 March, as happens in some later medieval calendars, we have run across a wild strain of solar Quartodecimanism. Sources that clearly end the paschal fast only on Sunday nonetheless insist that the Lord died on 25 March. By the fourth century, many of these sources will assign his conception to the same day, but this cannot be taken as testimony of a liturgical feast of the Annunciation.

I mentioned above Bainton's failure to account for the identification of the dates of Christ's death and conception. I now recognize that I made that more difficult than it needed to be through a serious tactical blunder in Part II of my work, by its treatment of Christmas before dealing with the Epiphany. While the introduction of some Talmudic material identifying the birth and death dates of the patriarchs provided a somewhat broader base for the introduction of Duchesne's computation hypothesis, it provided no rationale for the identification of Christ's conception and death dates. Duchesne had argued that the dates of Christ's death and conception were reckoned to be the same because a symbolic number system is intolerant of fractions. This determination of the conception date, he continued, would allow the computation of the nativity date nine months later, on 25 December (counting from 25 March) or 6 January (counting from 6 April).[9]

When we look rather at the Asian fixed-date Pascha, it becomes clear that, as the only annual feast of Christ in the second century, Pascha celebrated the entire mystery of redemption, including the incarnation as well as the death and resurrection of the Lord. Such a paschal homily as the *Peri Pascha* of Melito of Sardis testifies to the inclusion of the conception in the womb of the Virgin among the themes of the festival, focused in the first instance upon the Lord's passion and death. The date of that festival, eventually known as 6 April, had enabled the setting of the birth date nine months later, on the date known to Clement of Alexandria as 11 Tybi, the Egyptian equivalent to the Roman 6 January, although other scholars have read this passage of Clement's *Stromateis* to place the nativity on 18 November. This revised reading of *Stromateis* I.21.145–6 was the most brilliant achievement of Roland Bainton's doctoral research on Basilidian chronology, and seems to have gone unnoticed until he recast it in his article 'The Origins of Epiphany'. One could wish for parallel evidence setting the birth on 6 January from Asia itself, but the spread of that date to Egypt by the end of the second century is all the more impressive in view of Alexandria's Sunday Pascha, as opposed to the fixed-date Pascha in Asia.

Some argument has been generated by my not well-disguised preference for Duchesne's computation hypothesis, setting the birth date nine months after the date of Christ's death and conception, over the more long-standing 'History of Religions' hypothesis that saw the birth date as taken from a pagan festival. Both remain hypotheses, and both continue to find adherents. But the inadequacy of the 'History of Religions' explanation is much more evident in the case of 6 January than for 25 December. Further, in light of the paschal homily of Melito, we can see clearly how the incarnation came to be associated with the day of the Lord's death as a subsidiary theme in a unitive paschal liturgy. But that association is not so easy to understand in the case of the Western historical date for the passion. In Asia the incarnation and the passion were themes in a liturgical celebration of the entire mystery of redemption. One can imagine such an identification of the dates of conception and death being applied subsequently to the Western historical date for the passion. It is more difficult to account for that identification without reference to the Asian paschal liturgy. The Asian Quartodeciman observance on 25 March, reported by Epiphanius,[10] may have led to the assignment of the conception to that date, if its supporters, like earlier Quartodecimans, celebrated the entire mystery of redemption at Pascha, including the incarnation with the passion and resurrection. The assessment of his testimony, however, would still be dependent upon such an argument as can be made from second-century Asian preaching at a Pascha nine months before 6 January. That is why I deeply regret addressing the history of Christmas before exploring the festival of the Epiphany. The argument is much more compelling if we look first at the Epiphany, nine months after the paschal liturgy that took note of the conception of the Lord, along with his death.

As for Christmas itself, the 'History of Religions' hypothesis is more impressive, since we have a definite festival on the nativity date itself, *Dies natalis solis invicti*, and can date its establishment to the reign of Aurelian, and to the year AD 274. By that time, however, the assignment of the passion to 25 March was already well established at Rome and in Africa, being reported in works of Hippolytus, as well as in the treatise *Adversus Iudaeos* usually attributed to Tertullian, and in *De Pascha computus*, the Pseudo-Cyprianic (and possibly North African) opusculum dated to AD 243. While evidence for treating 25 March as also the date of the conception appears only in the following century, the foundation for the computation of the nativity date to 25 December was already in place before Aurelian established the feast of *Sol Invictus* on that date, traditionally but not astronomically recognized as the winter solstice. Dom Anselme Davril, who translated my book for its French edition, has been more bold than I was, and suggests in a separate essay that Aurelian's establishment of the Birthday of the Invincible Sun on 25 December was influenced by the Christian celebration of the nativity of Christ on that day.[11] I know of no evidence that would refute that suggestion, but I must confess that Père Davril is more personally secure than I.

In fact, having heard complaints that my pleading of Duchesne's computation of Christmas from 25 March in a later summary presentation was one-sided, not allowing for any influence from the Roman festival, I think I am now prepared to strengthen my quotation of Duchesne in *Origins*. He said, 'I would not venture to say, in regard to the twenty-fifth of December, that the coincidence of the *Sol novus* exercised no direct or indirect influence on the ecclesiastical decisions arrived at in regard to the matter.'[12] I still see no reason to suppose that it was Aurelian's festival that led Christians to date the nativity to 25 December. Christians already had the means of arriving at that date; but that would be a significant date only if based on what was taken to be the historical date of the passion, identified with the date of the Lord's conception. The emergence of a liturgical festival on that date could well have been influenced by the general population's celebration of the return of the Sun. It is clear that Christmas appeared well before any feast of the Annunciation on 25 March, and the liturgical observance of the passion was not on that date, but always on Friday. We may suppose, then, that the reckoning of 25 December as date of the nativity received from popular solar celebration the impetus that made it a liturgical festival, without implying that the feast was only a Christian adaptation of the pagan festival of *Sol Invictus*.

In that regard, I now regret that, having presented the views of some of the proponents of the 'History of Religions' hypothesis, I failed to pay particular attention to the essay that has, perhaps, done more than most to popularize that argument, 'The Origin of Christmas', by Oscar Cullmann. There, among other matters, he argued that it was a syncretist Constantine, still in the throes of the solar piety in which he grew up, who changed the date of Christ's birth from 6 January to 25 December. He wrote: 'The analogy of Sunday, which certainly became the official holy day under Constantine, seems to make it probable that it was as early as Constantine, and through his influence, that the festival of Christ's birth was changed over to December 25th, the great festival of the sun. Christ's birth was now linked up with the sun on December 25th in the same way as his resurrection with Sunday (the day of the sun).'[13]

Cullmann's assessment of the role of Constantine, I now recognize, deserved more serious address. I was at first convinced by the revisionist views of Robin Lane Fox that consideration of Constantine's pagan past would amount to whipping a dead horse. However, arguments with some of my colleagues have convinced me that the old horse is far from dead, and my brief address to the role of Constantine in connection with the establishment of Christmas at Constantinople was, in effect, thrown away. Therefore, in 1987, I published 'Constantine and Christmas', a short essay that tried to detail the extremely limited presence of Constantine in the city of Rome, his impatience with the ingrained conservative paganism there, and his foundation of a new imperial capital at Byzantium as a city where his Christian sentiments could find more complete expression.[14] Against that background, the fact that the nativity of Christ was never celebrated in Constantinople on 25 December during Constantine's lifetime seems to be a sufficient response to the claims of Cullmann. I regret, however, that this material was developed only in a subsequent publication and not in the book itself. As for the date of the establishment of Christmas, I remain impressed by the argument of Brunner[15] and others that it antedates the Donatist schism and, with that, the accession of Constantine. The possibility that it originated in North Africa rather than at Rome continues to be enticing, but unresolved.

In 1991, Robert Taft published an extended review of *The Origins of the Liturgical Year*. Toward the end of that almost embarrassingly appreciative review, his love of the truth finally took over, and he asserted that my treatment of the preparatory season for the feast of the nativity, especially as regards the Eastern Church, was woefully inadequate. By that time, even I knew that he was right, having finally come by the dissertation of Father John Moolan published in India in 1985.[16] If my original manuscript was already in press by the time of that publication, it remains true that Father Moolan's work is not mentioned in the second edition either. In fact, it was only a chance meeting with him that brought the publication to my attention and, by his gracious gift, to my hand. His dissertation richly supplies the data on the East Syrian season of Annunciation to which I did not have access.

In Syria by the middle of the fifth century, homilies of Antipater of Bostra reveal memorials of John the Baptist and the Blessed Virgin on the two Sundays preceding the nativity. The calendar of the great liturgical reformer of the seventh century, Išo-Yabh III of Adiabene, shows this Annunciation period extended to four Sundays among the East Syrians, and later West Syrian calendars extend the period to six Sundays, as is now the case with the East Syrian Chaldean rite as well. These commemorate the annunciation to Zechariah, the annunciation to Mary, the visitation to Elizabeth, the nativity of the Baptist, the revelation to Joseph, and the expectation of the nativity of the savior, with the reading of the genealogy from Matthew. The period is known as the season of Annunciation (*Subôro*), and that seems to be the meaning behind the term used for the six Sundays before Christmas at Milan, *De exceptato*.[17]

However, it was what did not come up in Father Moolan's dissertation that opened my eyes to what is probably the most regrettable feature of my own treatment of the time before Christmas. He makes no reference to the discipline of fasting, a monastic initiative that I took as the basis for my treatment of Advent. Considering that the Byzantine rite maintains a fast of forty days before Christmas with nothing like a liturgical season, nor any interruption of the course reading in progress, it becomes clear that the liturgical season and the disciplinary fast are separable and need to be treated separately, however much they may have coincided in Western history. While it seems unlikely that I shall undertake the methodical lectionary analysis that such a study of the seasons of Annunciation and Advent would require, it is comforting to know that this interest continues to be pursued by my friend and colleague Neil Alexander, once my student but now more often my teacher.

As regards the major fast that we know as Lent, the suggestion that this fast of forty days began, not as a fast before Easter, but one following Epiphany has been perceived, I suppose, as the most novel aspect of the argument of the book. Here, however, I must reiterate that the basic insight was in no way my own, but that of René-Georges Coquin. It was he who, in a paper at the liturgical studies week of the Institute Saint-Serges in 1965, presented the trail of evidences for such a fast following the Epiphany celebration of Christ's baptism, a trail stretching from Origen in the third century to Abu 'l-Barakat in the fourteenth.[18] The only item I have added to that dossier is the Mar Saba Clementine Fragment, containing the 'secret gospel of Mark', studied so extensively and problematically by the late Morton Smith, to whom I owe much. It was that one item that suggested the later reconstitution in the Byzantine liturgy of the Alexandrian Markan cursus for the fast, no longer following Epiphany but now preceding Holy Week. There, however, the 'secret gospel' has vanished, and its account of the raising from the dead and subsequent initiation of a youth at Bethany, a gospel kept secret at Alexandria, and read only at the conferral of baptism, has been replaced with its only canonical parallel, the raising of Lazarus in the Fourth Gospel on the final Saturday. It is from that same gospel that one also read the account of the entry into Jerusalem on the following day, as Alexandria had read the Markan account of the entry on the Sunday after the baptismal day. Such, at least, is my reconstruction.

When and how that shift happened is one of many things that remain in the dark for me. If there is any truth in my argument, then this Alexandrian pattern was adopted and adapted at Constantinople prior to 383, the year in which Egeria reports reenactments of the raising of Lazarus and the triumphal entry at Jerusalem, reenactments that I have argued are paraliturgical events reflecting the liturgy of Constantinople. Chrysostom, who preached on the Saturday of Lazarus and speaks of Palm Sunday in the same sermon, already sees these days not as the end of a Markan cursus for the forty days, but as standing at the head of Holy Week. There is no mention in that sermon of the baptism on the Saturday of Lazarus that looms so large in the Typika of the ninth and tenth centuries, and vestigially still today.

I placed that sermon during Chrysostom's episcopate at Constantinople rather than at Antioch, on the basis of a text from Severus of Antioch in the sixth century that implies that Palm Sunday was a recent development there. Issue has been taken with that placement of Chrysostom's sermon by Pauline Allen. She would place the sermon at Antioch, though she does not refer to the evidence I offered from Severus. In a 1994 Festschrift honoring the seventieth birthday of Charles Laga, Allen presented evidence from the sixth-century patriarch Eutychius that does refer to baptism on the Saturday of Lazarus and calls the practice προφωτίσματα, 'the illumination beforehand'.[19] That term, which occurs also in the title of a sixth-century sermon of Leontius in manuscripts from the ninth and following centuries, shows that the conferral of baptism on the Saturday of Lazarus has come to be regarded as a prolepsis of paschal baptisms.

All this suggests to me that the Byzantine adaptation of the Alexandrian Lenten program was very early. In light of Coquin's further argument that the fast of forty days was set prior to the paschal fast as a dimension of the settlement of the paschal question at the Council of Nicaea,[20] one could well imagine that this Lenten course reading of Mark, ending with the Johannine accounts of the raising of Lazarus and the Entry into Jerusalem on the Saturday and Sunday before Great Week, is as old as the liturgical tradition of Constantinople itself. Still, there is no known evidence of baptism on the Saturday of Lazarus at Constantinople prior to the fragment from Eutychius in the sixth century, adduced by Allen. Citing my hypothesis, she expresses wonder at the absence of evidence of such baptism at Constantinople prior to 383. I, too, wonder what spoor of the Alexandrian baptismal day lay embedded in the documents that guided the Byzantine liturgists, and how that memory was transmitted in their own documents. We have learned, I believe, that liturgical documents and the mode of their transmission through generations of copying can be as important a vehicle of liturgical tradition as liturgical practice itself. Further, nothing in Egeria suggests that the Saturday of Lazarus was known to be a baptismal day, and we must leave open the possibility that it became so in fact only after Chrysostom's episcopate. Even so, an Alexandrian source, remote or proximate, seems likely.

All that said, as regards my abandoned revision of *The Origins of the Liturgical Year*, I must admit that I have made no further advances toward supporting the complex and admittedly hypothetical argument of Part III of that book. That failure only intensifies my gratitude for the rather generous reception accorded my treatment of the Byzantine Lent. My work of revision, while it lasted, was largely occupied with a projected Part IV dealing with the cult of the saints, a quite separate matter from the closely integrated cycle of seasons, but of equal antiquity. Indeed, the earliest of the martyrologies, the *Martyrdom of Polycarp*, shows already in the second half of the second century all the principal elements that will be involved in the liturgical *cultus* later, about as early as any clear evidence we have for the Christian Pascha. The development of the veneration of saints, from the honoring of martyrs to the rich tapestry of the varieties of holiness that is acknowledged in the calendar today, is a fascinating topic that has already, thankfully, received expert treatment, to which my preliminary studies found nothing to add.

There is, of course, the possibility that further mastery of technological aids might one day renew my resolve to return to the revision, and that possibility has recently been enhanced by Professor Alexander's consent to collaborate in that enterprise. Failing all these, as my central vision continues to fail, I am content to leave the work where it is, making my own once again the wise words of E. J. Bickerman: 'knowledge is required to produce a work of scholarship, but only ignorance gives the courage to publish it'.[21]

Notes

1 Thomas Talley, *The Origins of the Liturgical Year* (2nd emended edn, Collegeville, Minn.: Liturgical Press, 1991). On p. 3, a reference to Mark 14: 21 should be Mark 14: 12 and on p. 150, a reference to 'the synod at Tarragone' should be to the synod at Saragossa.

2 Sozomen, *Historica ecclesiastica*, VII.18. English text in *Nicene and Post-Nicene Fathers*, 2nd ser., 2 (Grand Rapids, Mich., 1989), 389.

3 August Strobel, *Ursprung und Geschichte des frühchristlichen Osterkalenders* (Berlin: Akademie-Verlag, 1977), 373.

4 E. J. Bickerman, *The Chronology of the Ancient World* (2nd edn, London: Thames & Hudson, 1980); Theodor Mommsen, 'Die Einführung des asianischen Kalendars', in *Gesammelte Schriften*, v (1908), 518–31.

5 *Le Typicon de la Grande Eglise: Ms. Saint-Croix no 40, Xe siècle*, ed. Juan Mateos, 2 vols (OCA 165–6; Rome: Pontificium Institutum Studiorum Orientalium, 1962–3), i, 42.
6 Roland Bainton, 'The Origins of Epiphany', in *Early and Medieval Christianity: The Collected Papers in Church History*, i (Boston, 1962), 22–38, at 34.
7 *Chronographus anni CCCLIIII*, ed. Theodor Mommsen (MGH *AA* 9/1; 1892), 71.
8 Ibid., 57 (Nativity on previous page).
9 Louis Duchesne, *Christian Worship, its Origin and Evolution: A Study of the Latin Liturgy up to the time of Charlemagne* (London: Macmillan, 1949), 263–4.
10 Epiphanius, *Panarion* 50.1.18; Epiphanius, *Panarion haer. 34–64*, ed. Karl Holl, rev. Jürgen Dummer (Berlin: Akademie-Verlag, 1980), 246.
11 Anselme Davril, 'L'Origine de la fête de Noël', *Renaissance de Fleury: La revue des moines de Saint-Benoit*, 160 (1991), 9–14.
12 Duchesne, *Christian Worship*, 264.
13 Oscar Cullmann, *The Early Church* (Philadelphia: Westminster Press, 1956), 32.
14 'Constantine and Christmas', *Gratias Agamus: Jubilee Volume of Studia Liturgica*, 17 (1987), 191–7.
15 Gottfried Brunner, 'Arnobius eine Zeuge gegen das Weihnachtsfest?' *Jahrbuch für Liturgiewissenschaft*, 13 (1936), 178–81.
16 John Moolan, *The Period of Annunciation–Nativity in the East Syrian Calendar: Its Background Place in the Liturgical Year* (Kottayam, Kerala: Paurastya Vidyapitham, 1985).
17 *DACL*, s.v. 'Annonciation (fête de l')'.
18 The documents adduced by Coquin include Origen's tenth homily on Leviticus, the fourth-century Canons of Hippolytus, a Coptic papyrus codex of the fifth or sixth century, the tenth-century Annals of Eutychius, a letter of Macarius, Bishop of Memphis in that same tenth century, and *The Lamp of Darkness*, by the fourteenth-century encyclopedist of Coptic Church practice, Abu 'l-Barakat. See René-Georges Coquin, 'Les Origines de l'Epiphanie en Egypte', in B. Botte, E. Mélia et al. (eds), *Noël, Epiphanie: Retour du Christ* (Lex Orandi, 40; Paris: Cerf, 1967), 139–70.
19 Pauline Allen, 'Reconstructing Pre-paschal Liturgies in Constantinople: Some Sixth Century Homiletic Evidence', in A. Schoors and P. Van Deun (eds), *Philohistôr: Miscellanea in honorem Caroli Laga Septuagenarii* (Louvain: Peeters, 1994), 217–28.
20 René-Georges Coquin, 'Une Réforme liturgique du concile de Nicée (325)?' *Comptes rendus, Académie des Inscriptions et Belles-lettres* (1967), 178–92.
21 Bickerman, *The Chronology of the Ancient World*, 7.

Chapter 2

The Desert, the City and Psalmody in the Late Fourth Century

Joseph Dyer

In 1994 James McKinnon published an article, 'Desert Monasticism and the Later Fourth-Century Psalmodic Movement', in which he charted the monastic background of the flowering of enthusiasm for psalm singing that coursed through Eastern Christianity as the fourth century came to its close.[1] The existence of this 'psalmodic movement', which he portrayed with such vividness, is less remarkable than the idea that the way of life implied by the name 'desert monasticism' might have contributed to such a popular musical and devotional exercise. The monks who retreated to the sands of Egypt in Late Antiquity sought uninterrupted solitude and a more intimate relationship with their Creator, not the opportunity to sing psalms with other monks. On certain occasions desert ascetics did sing psalms, either alone or in common, but I believe that they had far less influence on the 'later fourth-century psalmodic movement' than did communities of ascetics in the urban centers of Late Antiquity.[2] McKinnon did not by any means neglect this aspect of the development, but I would place in somewhat higher relief the role that urban monastic foundations played in stimulating the striking enthusiasm for psalmody first evident in the East before its rapid spread westward. Though questions still remain unanswered about the musical form (responsorial vs. antiphonal) of this psalmody, a topic covered, if not entirely resolved, in many specialized studies,[3] I believe that some conjectures can be made about what the chanting of psalm verses might have sounded like at this remote period. All of this can be best understood by first examining the early history of monasticism in Egypt, the motivations that drew so many to the desert, and the life led by those who had decisively renounced the secular society of their day.

The Flight into the Desert

One of the most remarkable phenomena of fourth-century Christianity was the departure of thousands of men and a considerable number of women, primarily in Egypt but also in Syria, Palestine and throughout Asia Minor, for inhospitable, uninhabited 'deserts'.[4] This development fascinated the Christian world of Late Antiquity, and it continues powerfully to attract the attention of scholars today.[5] About the year 285 the legendary Antony heard in church the reading of Jesus' challenge to the rich young man: 'If you would be perfect, go, sell what you possess and give it to the poor, and you will have treasure in heaven' (Matt. 19:21). Antony did just this and took up a solitary existence in the desert east of the Nile. Both his departure and that of thousands more into the Egyptian desert over the following century and a half were motivated by a desire for disengagement from society. Many retreated to the desert on the outskirts of a village, but others penetrated into the 'deep desert', unimaginably remote from all human company except for the few ascetics with whom they shared their lonely habitat.

The motivation for this wholesale abandonment of the home village and the society of family and friends has been variously explained. Not all of the first monks were inspired by religious impulses, and a few were antisocial misfits. Peter Brown has emphasized the stressful, even contentious, aspects of Egyptian village life, escape from which to a solitary, celibate existence meant relief not only from these tensions but also from pressing societal responsibilities (with their attending economic burdens) to perpetuate the family.[6] Some historians argue that at least a few of the 'dropouts' were farmers fleeing from debt or from the oppressive taxation imposed by Roman authorities.[7] Whatever role social and economic factors might have played, the deprivations of living on the fringes of civilization might not have been significantly worse than the poverty left behind in the villages. The religious persecutions of the late third century probably made the desert an attractive alternative to martyrdom. After the public profession of Christianity had ceased to be dangerous, fervent souls sought escape from the tepidity of a generation of lukewarm Christians in a life of asceticism that, under the changed circumstances, could be now regarded as a type of living martyrdom.

The strongest impetus for Christian *anachoresis* (separation from society) as a mode of life was demonstrably religious.[8] But departure for the desert entailed virtually complete detachment from Christianity, largely an urban religion at the time, into an environment in which institutional public worship, ecclesiastical structures and theological speculation were irrelevant and even unwelcome. One of the most celebrated monastic aphorisms counseled monks to flee women and bishops: the former a danger to chastity and a seduction to social entanglement, the latter a danger to monastic serenity with their sometimes importunate offers of sacerdotal ordination.

The bishops, on the other hand, could not so easily ignore the monks. So powerful was the presence of an autonomous monasticism in fourth-century Egypt that even successive bishops of Alexandria, Athanasius and Cyril, had to go to great lengths in securing the allegiance of the monks in a land proliferating with heterodox Christian beliefs.[9] Eventually, conflicts over the teachings of Origen, which appealed mainly to Greek-speaking monks of intellectual background, divided monastic communities. Monks also became entangled in the Christological controversies of the time with their inextricable links to imperial politics. All of this disturbed the tranquility of monastic detachment, and the decisions of the Council of Chalcedon (451), called to resolve these theological questions, led to further rifts in the Egyptian monastic communities.

Three modes of desert monasticism, each with distinctive characteristics, manifested themselves toward the end of the third century. A very few hardy individuals attempted pure *anachoresis*, an absolutely solitary existence in the forbidding desert, a hermit-like isolation that was well nigh impossible without external support. The vast majority of Egyptian monks, however, lived a semi-anchoritic existence. They spent most of the week in their cells alone or in the company of one or two other monks or disciples, joining with nearby brethren for prayer and a common repast only on weekends. This usually included the Eucharist, celebrated either by a local priest or by a monk who had accepted ordination. In Upper Egypt there flourished the very different institution of cenobitic monasticism. Thousands of monks joined together in communities organized by the charismatic Pachomius and his successors. These amounted to genuine 'cities' in the remoteness of the desert.

The cell was the world of a semi-anchoritic monk. There he confronted both the demons who inhabited the desert and those that lodged within his own soul. Boundaries between the physical world and the often malevolent spirit world hovered perilously close to each other in the desert. Demons, real or imagined, constituted an ever-present threat. Hallucinations – heightened no doubt by extreme sensory deprivation and a level of malnutrition that bordered on starvation – must have made these demonic predators seem terrifyingly real.[10] Yet monks were warned by their spiritual fathers of the dangers to be encountered upon leaving the cell, particularly if motivated by the state of boredom the monks knew as *acêdia*, a distaste for things spiritual and a sense of isolation from God. The perfection of the 'contemplative life', as preached by Evagrius Ponticus (346–99), himself a monk of the Egyptian desert, was a solitary state in 'total isolation from the material universe and therefore from other men'.[11] However achieved, the goal of the monk was *apatheia*, freedom from domination by the passions, a prelude to contemplation, the higher stages of which were a gift of God and a sign of the monk's union with him. In sum, desert monasticism carried within itself a highly individualistic proclivity that emphasized severe personal asceticism and personal engagement with God in contemplation, not salvation attained in community.

Contemporary Sources

The flight to the desert and separation from the 'world' (defined as all those possessions and attachments, even if good in themselves, that diverted the soul from union with God) was such a remarkable phenomenon that it did not pass unnoticed by contemporary chroniclers. Although virtually none of the renowned abbas of the desert left any literary testaments, their visitors preserved a copious record of the wisdom and experience of the desert.[12] The principal sources of documentation exist not only in their original languages, usually Greek or Coptic, but also in complete or partial translations into Latin, Coptic, Syriac, Georgian or Armenian. In some cases these 'visitors' passed many years in one or another of the monastic settlements; others came briefly to drink at the font of Egyptian monasticism and pass on some of its lore. They recorded what they learned from their spiritual guides in the form of 'sayings', either exact quotations or anecdotes that exemplified a moral or ascetical point.

The earliest source of substantial information about Egyptian desert monasticism is the celebrated *Life of Antony*. This influential biography of the monastic pioneer par excellence was written by Athanasius (ca. 296–373), archbishop of Alexandria, a year after its subject's death in 356.[13] Antony's monastic career spanned many decades, and his fame drew numerous disciples seeking instruction and guidance. Once his years of solitary combat with demonic powers were concluded, he provided support to leading churchmen in the defense of orthodoxy. From a literary standpoint, Athanasius' biography of Antony established the anecdotal tone that was to pervade subsequent monastic literature of this edifying type.

Two broad surveys of Egyptian monasticism date from a slightly later period. The anonymous *History of the Monks in Egypt* (though written in Greek, often cited as the *Historia monachorum in Egypto*) records a journey down the Nile made by a group of seven monastic travelers about 394/5.[14] Visiting individual abbas and semi-anchoritic monastic settlements, the travelers were impressed by the enormous numbers of monks who had populated the desert. Within a few years, Western monks were introduced to the *Historia monachorum* by the Latin translation of Rufinus (345–410), who supplemented the text with information drawn from his own personal experiences in Egypt.[15] Another 'history' consists of short biographical notes about the leading Egyptian ascetics. Its author, Palladius, received his monastic initiation in Palestine before taking up the life of a monk in Egypt, first outside of Alexandria and later at Kellia, but his health forced him to renounce the arduous life of a desert ascetic. Palladius was requested by Lausus, chamberlain at the court of Theodosius II in Constantinople, to set down a record of his knowledge of Egyptian monasticism. This he did in the so-called *Lausiac History*, written about 419 or 420.[16] Neither of these treatments is quite what a modern reader would expect from a historical narrative. Their purpose was not to establish an exact chronology of a momentous social and religious movement but to provide awesome inspirational examples for those who might wish either to follow in the footsteps of the fabled ascetics or to admire their virtues from afar.

Valuable information about the spirit and discipline of Egyptian monasticism is transmitted by John Cassian (360–435), who had known Palladius in Constantinople and had traveled with him to Rome to defend John Chrysostom. Born about 360 probably in Scythia (present-day Romania), Cassian became a monk at Bethlehem before spending about fifteen years among the Egyptian ascetics, mainly at the remote desert of Scetis (see below).[17] He ultimately settled in Gaul, founding two monasteries near Marseilles, one for men (St. Victor) and the other for women (St. Savior). Bishop Castor of Apt (419–26) requested Cassian to compose a work on monastic discipline and spiritual guidance for the members of a cenobitic community he had founded. Cassian's *De institutis coenobiorum* took as its focus not the extravagant exploits of the semi-anchoritic abbas but the monastic life lived in community.[18] As he admits in the preface to the *Institutes*, Cassian moderated the rigorous ideals of desert monasticism in view of the practical requirements of cenobitic monasticism, the prevailing form in Gaul and the West.[19] Cassian's synthesis conflated observances with which he was directly familiar with ones about which he had only secondhand information, sometimes filtering both through his personal perspective. Cassian's other major work, the *Conferences*, focuses entirely on the teachings of the venerated abbas whom he and his companion Germanus had met while living and traveling in Egypt.[20] The twenty-four conferences expound at length the teaching of renowned ascetics on various topics of the spiritual life: discretion (Conf. 2), the changeableness of the soul and evil spirits (Conf. 7), and prayer (Conf. 9 and 10).

The largest corpus of material that illuminates the world of desert monasticism is found in the collections of anecdotes and spiritual advice known as the 'Sayings of the Fathers' (*Apophthegmata patrum*). Called by a modern scholar 'the most important single source for our knowledge of the monasticism of fourth- and fifth-century Lower Egypt', the 'Sayings' consist of about 1,600 anecdotes and aphorisms that transmit spiritual guidance along with biographical information liberally spiced with legend. It is generally believed that the Sayings were written down about the middle of the fifth century, possibly in Palestine. The abbas who have been identified extend from Antony and his later contemporaries to those who inhabited the settlement at Scetis just before its decline in the mid-fifth century.[21] The sources mentioned earlier (*Historia monachorum in Aegypto*, *Lausiac History*, Cassian's *Institutes* and *Conferences*, etc.) draw on material preserved in the Sayings, presumably while they were in a state of oral transmission. Two principal collections have been preserved: (1) an alphabetical series organized according to the name of the abba who delivered the teaching, followed by a series of anonymous Sayings, and (2) a systematic collection, in which the Sayings are arranged by topic.[22] The Sayings are not exclusively (as the name might suggest) pithy advice or puzzling conundrums. They often teach by example or merely pass on the lore of the desert to new recruits or to those who read them in translation far from the Egyptian deserts.

The Monastic Deserts of Egypt

The single term 'desert monasticism' thus obscures the varieties of ways in which the ascetic vocation was realized in fourth-century Egypt. Given the rather eccentric personalities who sought refuge in the sandy wastes, that should hardly be surprising. In Lower (i.e., northern) Egypt there were three different semi-anchoritic 'deserts', each with a distinctive profile. The northernmost monastic settlement was the mountain of Nitria, so called because of the presence of nitrate deposits in the vicinity. Founded about 315 by Amoun, it was located about sixty kilometers southwest of Alexandria on the edge of the 'Great Desert' (πανέρημος).[23] The model of life followed by the monks there, whose number Palladius estimated at 5,000 (almost certainly an exaggeration), was semi-anchoritic. Each of the monks inhabited his own 'cell', a self-standing structure with one or two rooms, and, as Palladius says, they followed 'different ways of life, each as he can or will'. Sometimes two or even three monks lived together.[24] The dwellings of the Nitrian monks were spread across the desert without any special plan. While the Greek text of the *Historia monachorum* claims that they were spaced far apart ('so that no one should be recognized from afar, or be seen easily, or hear another's voice'), Rufinus' Latin version claims that they were 'set near each other' (*vicina sibi*).[25] Given the fact that Rufinus passed many years in this monastic settlement, it is difficult not to give him the benefit of the doubt. In principle, the monks kept to their cells during the week, but visiting another monk was not discouraged. Only on Saturday and Sunday did the entire community gather for a common synaxis and Mass.[26]

As Nitria became more and more crowded, some of its inhabitants evinced restlessness for a greater solitude. A suitable site was chosen by the revered Antony while on a visit to Nitria, probably in 338.[27] This settlement, Kellia (the cells), was situated about twenty kilometers to the southwest in a more forbidding environment. There the individual cells were placed at greater distances from each other than at Nitria. (Rufinus says of the distance between the hermitages at Kellia, which he visited in 374, what the original Greek *Historia monachorum* claimed about Nitria.) Some monks lived four to six kilometers distant from the single church that served the loosely organized, semi-anchoritic settlement for the weekend synaxis. On Saturday afternoon the monks gathered for the *agape*, followed by a communal synaxis that lasted through the night and into Sunday morning, at which time the Eucharist was celebrated by the single priest in their midst. Palladius estimated that about 600 monks lived at Kellia during the time he was a monk at Nitria.[28] Apart from the possibility of visiting after the daily meal, eaten in the cell at the ninth hour, they had no contact with each other during the week. The prayer observances of the individual monks and the structure of the weekly communal synaxis at Nitria and Kellia were probably similar, but no substantial evidence survives to establish their content.

Yet further into the desert, the third monastic settlement, Scetis, located seventy kilometers southwest of Nitria, was founded by Macarius about 330.[29] Fewer monks were able to sustain the hardships of this site (among them, however, John Cassian), and fewer travelers disturbed its solitude. The monastic travelers whose adventures are recounted in the *Historia monachorum* did not venture into this place, said by their Latin translator, Rufinus, to be 'in eremo vastissima positus'.[30] Despite the remoteness of the site – even today the location of a few flourishing cenobitic monasteries – the influence of the Scetis tradition resonated widely in the monastic world. As noted earlier, most of the abbas quoted in the Sayings had ties to Scetis, and several of the spiritual mentors to whom John Cassian attributes the teachings conveyed in the *Conferences* dwelt there.

Another group of very important monastic 'cities' in the desert were the eleven monasteries founded by Pachomius (d. 346) in the Thebaid region of Upper (i.e., southern) Egypt. Pachomius, born a pagan, began his monastic career, as was the custom, under the tutelage of an elder hermit, Palemon, but was eventually drawn to his true vocation as the founder of cenobitic monasticism. He established his first permanent community at Tabenessi; others quickly followed until the monasteries in the region that embraced the Pachomian *koinonia* (community) sheltered thousands of monks and nuns. They lived in strictly organized communities ruled by a superior, following rules formulated by Pachomius and codified by his successor Horsiesios.[31] Armand Veilleux has emphasized how radically the Pachomian *koinonia* differed from the isolated lives led by the monks of Lower Egypt: 'Groupés autour d'un père spirituel ou autour d'une église, ces anchorètes demeurent des anchorètes. Le cénobitisme fondé en Égypte par Pachôme sera autre chose.'[32] Among the followers of Pachomius and his successors spiritual perfection was not sought in the isolation of the cell but in a shared life of work and prayer.

Meditation and Psalmody in Egyptian Monasticism

Though the desert monks were perhaps the first to prize the psalms as Christian prayer, they used them in ways peculiar to their own system of spirituality.[33] Very few passages in the contemporary historical sources or the Sayings refer to 'psalmody', and the activity might not always have been audible![34] In view of the wealth of evidence about monasticism that has survived from the fourth and fifth centuries, the amount of attention given to the singing of psalms seems small indeed. Crucial to understanding the singing of psalms in the monastic world of Late Antiquity is an understanding of the terminological distinctions made by writers of the time. Modern English translations of the original texts cannot always be relied upon for careful discrimination in this regard. While psalmody forms the primary focus of the present chapter, it cannot be understood fully apart from the monastic practice of 'meditating' on scriptural passages.

Monastic 'meditation' was not an intellectual exercise that pondered the meaning and implication of a sacred text, as the term is generally understood today.[35] Rather, it involved the very slow vocalization of a memorized scriptural passage, producing a sound something like a muted rumble or hum, particularly if several monks were meditating simultaneously.[36] One of the Sayings records that bystanders were able to hear the abba Achilas while he was meditating, apparently on a single phrase (λόγον), 'Do not fear, Jacob, to go into Egypt.'[37] Cyril of Scythopolis (ca. 525–after 557) mentions several times in his biography of the monk Sabas that he followed a practice of 'reciting Davidic psalms to himself'.[38] While 'recitation' was applied to this practice, an alternative term, 'rumination', is even more suggestive, since it conjures up the image of an animal that chews the cud – an evocative parallel to the monk who 'chews over' the words of Sacred Scripture in order to digest their meaning and make them part of himself.[39] Though sound was produced, it bore little relationship to anything we would identify as music. Meditation in common did not, moreover, imply coordination: each of the monks carried out the exercise independently.

Monks meditated on the psalms during work, a fact attested by Cassian in his admiring description of the Egyptian ascetics: 'manual labour is incessantly practised by them in their cells in such a way that meditation on the psalms and the rest of the Scriptures is never entirely omitted'.[40] Meditation on the Scriptures (not only the psalms, of course) could be performed while sitting quietly in the cell or traveling from place to place. In fact, Pachomius insisted that the brethren meditate on biblical texts as they moved from one activity to another.[41] Constant recitation of psalm verses encouraged the monk to 'treat them in his profound compunction of heart not as if they were composed by the prophet [David] but as if they were his own utterances and his own prayer'.[42] Augustine was requested by a colleague, Bishop Aurelius of Carthage, to correct the notion held by some of his monks that they should devote themselves exclusively to prayer and not engage in manual labor. Augustine responded with *De opere monachorum*, in which he asked: 'What, therefore, hinders the servant of God working with his hands from meditating on the law of the Lord and singing to the name of the Lord most high?'[43] (Note the distinction Augustine makes between meditating and singing.) Meditation was so profoundly spiritual an exercise that demons, who were said to be able to sing psalms when they disguised themselves to tempt a monk, were never said to 'meditate'. The best they could do was 'remember passages from the Scriptures' or 'chatter from the Scriptures'.[44] Meditation can also be related to the ancient habit of always reading aloud, even to oneself. A connection between the two may exist in an injunction in the *Procatechesis* of Cyril of Jerusalem. Before the ceremony of exorcism that preceded baptism he charged the virgins to 'sing or read, but without noise, so that their lips may speak, but others may not hear'.[45] A similar injunction is addressed to married women. Of course, Cyril may have intended merely to keep them quiet!

'Psalmody' differed from meditation, since it implied a more 'musical' rendering of the text, whatever that might have meant in the world of the Egyptian desert.[46] The singing of psalms could be a daily ritual carried out by the monk alone in his cell or by a group of monks at a communal synaxis. The plural, 'psalmodies', occurs with some frequency in Greek, perhaps signifying that a series of psalms was chanted. Although psalmody seems to have been esteemed among the desert monastics, the Egyptian sources yield none of the extravagant praise expressed by the Church Fathers.[47] When mentioned, psalmody is passed over quickly without elaboration or the provision of details about its musical execution.

One of the rare passages in the literature of the Egyptian desert that goes beyond merely mentioning psalmody is an evocative scene in the *Lausiac History* about the daily prayer time of the Nitrian monks. Palladius, who lived at Nitria for three years before transferring to Kellia, placed himself in the role of an observer rather than a participant: 'at about the ninth hour one can stand and hear the psalmodies (ψαλμωδίαι) issuing forth from each cell and imagine that one is high above in paradise'.[48] Since Palladius implies that he heard the psalmody coming from several cells (one or at most two monks in each cell), they could not have been so far apart, a point that seems to confirm Rufinus' observation about their proximity in his Latin version of the *Historia monachorum*.[49] (The Greek original, it will be remembered, claims that the cells were separated by considerable distances.) One can only imagine how the sound of all the monks within earshot singing *different* psalms might have transported Palladius symbolically to paradise, but it could hardly have done so on the strength of its aesthetic appeal!

When a monk received a visitor in his cell, he and his guest would perform the 'office' (of psalmody) together. The *Lausiac History* narrates the encounter between the celebrated Antony and a would-be disciple, an elderly man later known as Paul the Simple. Palladius mentions that Antony 'intoned a psalm which he knew, and when he had sung it twelve times, he prayed twelve times', and then '[he] prayed twelve prayers and sang twelve psalms'.[50] Usually its content is left undetermined, but the 'office of the twelve psalms' is several times mentioned in a way that takes for granted that it would be familiar.[51] Palladius transmits another anecdote about a certain Elpidius, who lived in a cave near Jericho. He ate only on the weekend and 'stood up all night singing psalms'.[52] The story implies that Palladius himself and other monks joined with Elpidius in this nocturnal psalm chanting. Here again, however, one cannot be sure that all the monks chanted the words in unison.

Not all chanting of the psalms was solitary. The daily private psalmody of the monks of Lower Egypt in their cells was replaced on the weekend by a communal synaxis: each of the monks took turns in chanting one or more of the psalms. Cassian describes this kind of synaxis in book 2 of the *Institutes*, and Rufinus says in his additions to the *Historia monachorum* that 'the brothers [at Scetis] conducted themselves as usual, all being seated while one of them said a psalm and the rest either listened or made the response'.[53] In the Pachomian communities there was a daily synaxis that brought together all the monks of the monastery from the houses of thirty to forty monks into which the community was divided. The prescriptions for this daily morning office in the *Regulations of Horsiesios* make no mention of the singing of psalms. Instead, the office consists of a succession of prayers, frequent tracing of the sign of the cross on the forehead, and the recitation of 'holy words' from the Scriptures.[54] This recitation by a single monk of memorized texts paralleled the meditation he would have practiced by himself. In the communal context the brethren could 'overhear' the ruminated words. A similar daily synaxis took place toward evening in the individual houses where the monks retired at the close of the day.[55] Though memorized psalm verses might have been recited at either of these synaxes, nothing in the text of the *Regulations* distinguishes their performance from ordinary prose texts. Armand Veilleux points out that the words used elsewhere to describe individual 'meditation' (μελετᾶν and ἀποστηθίζειν) are here used in conjunction with a communal liturgy.[56]

Only on Sunday morning does the Pachomian monastic legislation for the monks' office specify the *singing* of psalms. The one who chants (not *recites*, as on other days of the week) the psalm verses on Sunday must be a housemaster or one of the senior members of the community. The members of the house whose turn it is to perform weekly service (e.g., distributing the rushes or palm fronds for plaiting, organizing work, seeing to the needs of the individual houses) may not on this account be absent from this synaxis 'and not responding to the psalmist'.[57] The response itself, whether a prolongation of the final syllable sung by the psalmist or a recurring psalm refrain, is not further specified. It has been argued that the honor reserved to the elders of singing the psalm verses on Sundays does not necessarily mean that psalmody was neglected during the week.[58] Several of the Pachomian Precepts (8, 127–2, 141–2) do indeed mention psalmody without specifying who is to lead it. For example, the injunction that 'one shall not neglect the times of prayer and psalmody, whether he is on a boat, in the monastery, in the fields, or on a journey' implies that any monk could lead psalmody.[59] From this regulation applying to special circumstances it cannot be construed that, if one of the brethren recited a psalm text at the daily morning or evening synaxis during the week, it would be treated any differently from a non-psalmic text. Sunday was a different matter. The conclusion is inevitable that the genuine singing of psalms had only a restricted share in the prayer life of the Pachomian *koinoni*a.

Choral psalmody had no place in the Pachomian synaxis – except insofar as the monks responded chorally to the singer of the psalm verses on Sunday. It might have been employed in processions, however. The First Greek Life of Pachomius describes the funeral exequies for the deceased monk Eron: 'the brothers spent the whole night in vigil around his corpse, singing psalms and reading [= reciting] until the first light of dawn appeared. Then, on the Sunday of joy, the body having been prepared, he [abba Theodore] buried him while the brothers sang psalms.'[60] The singing of psalms during processions connected with the burial of deceased brethren became a tradition of the Pachomian *koinonia*.[61] In this special case, the singing of the verses is not restricted to the elders as it is at the Sunday synaxis, but no brother may sing the verses without authorization from a superior. As the body is carried to the cemetery, the brothers 'shall not neglect to respond, but maintain unison', an instruction similar to the one that governs the Sunday morning synaxis.

The Bohairic Life of Pachomius describes vividly the visit of Bishop Athanasius of Alexandria, a friend and admirer of the Egyptian monks, to the Thebaid.[62] Apa Theodore, Pachomius' successor, led a large delegation of monks, '*reciting* all together from the words of the Holy Scriptures and the Gospels' to meet the archbishop. Athanasius was himself accompanied by an entourage that included 'monks from various places who were chanting psalms and canticles'. After greetings had been extended, 'the brothers, a hundred men strong, preceded [the archbishop] singing psalms' to the church in the city of Smoun. The text clearly distinguishes 'recitation' from the singing of psalms, but one cannot determine whether the monks (exceptionally) chanted all of the words of the psalms together or whether only one of them did so, to which the others responded, as was the custom at the Sunday synaxis.

Anselme Davril searched the *Apophthegmata patrum* for references to psalms, of which he found only thirty-seven.[63] This relatively small number might not be entirely indicative of the place the Psalter played in private meditation and the weekly monastic synaxis at Scetis, source of most of the

Sayings, but the paucity of references cannot be entirely devoid of implication. Not all of the texts, moreover, point unmistakably to the *singing* of psalms. Davril's study confirms, however, that the psalms fulfilled several functions in the teachings of the desert fathers. They served both as texts for meditation and as texts suitable for some kind of musical rendition, whether or not a sung response is implied, for a monk often performed his psalmody alone. Meditation on the psalms, not singing them, seems to be implied in about ten of the Sayings identified by Davril. For example, it is reported of Isidore, a priest-monk of Scetis, that he and a disciple recited two psalms; then the venerable abba continued to recite (presumably also psalms) from memory for an entire day! Many of the references to the apparent singing of psalms collected by Davril (about fifteen in all) are at best ambiguous. Never is there any reference to responsorial or antiphonal psalmody, the forms so closely identified with the 'later fourth-century psalmodic movement'.

Monks seem to have stood for the singing of the office psalms, while meditation could be done in any posture. In one of the more unusual anecdotes among the Sayings, the abba Serapion makes an appointment with a prostitute, then asks if he could first complete his office. He began the Psalter, and after a while the woman, deeply moved, stood and began to pray (sing?) with him, presumably adopting the same posture as Serapion.[64] The psalmist of the Pachomian Sunday morning synaxis also stood, as did the mysterious angelic visitor who, according to a celebrated legend, resolved the question of the number of psalms (twelve) that should constitute the monastic morning and evening office.[65] Posture, rarely mentioned in connection with the psalms anyway, is not by any means an infallible guide. In the final analysis, one is forced to conclude that the very paucity of references to psalmody in the literature of the desert renders it highly unlikely that the Egyptian monks had a significant role in the popularization of psalmody in the late fourth century.

Monastic Views of Music

Hostile monastic attitudes toward any kind of sensual pleasure would not have made an exception for music, including the singing of psalms. The idea that music could lead to compunction and receptivity to grace was as foreign to the desert mentality even as it seemed obvious to the Fathers who extolled the 'fourth-century psalmodic movement'.[66] Given the virtual absence of critical statements about singing or the seductive power of music in the desert literature,[67] it may never have constituted a threat. Whatever 'psalmody' meant to the semi-anchoritic monks of Nitria, Kellia, Scetis, or to the cenobites of the Thebaid, it never reached a musical level that attracted notice or provoked condemnation from the severe defenders of monastic discipline. Significantly, however, music figures in the story (one of the Sayings in the alphabetical series) of a 'certain Roman monk' who retired to Scetis from a career as a high imperial official. A visiting monk, who regarded his host's modest living style as excessively indulgent, was reminded that the Roman patrician had given up 'music and kitharas'. Instead, he says, 'I say the twelve psalms [during the day] and the same at night'.[68] The use of the verb 'to say' (λέγω) may not be unduly significant: the contrast intended is probably not between singing and speaking but rather between the lavish music of secular society and the sober, unpretentious psalmody of the monk.

Two other anecdotes in the monastic 'sayings' tradition that evince pronounced hostility to music seem to be somewhat exceptional.[69] Neither can be dated exactly, and both contain anachronisms that preclude an early dating, yet both demonstrate antagonistic feelings toward music placed in the mouths of venerable Egyptian abbas. The first anecdote was included in the *Plerophoria* (Testimonies and Revelations) of Bishop John of Maiûma, written in Greek between 512 and 518.[70] In this anecdote Abba Silvanus responds to a young brother whose soul is troubled because of his captivation with the latest musical innovations. He complains that 'when I rise at night, I struggle much [in the psalmody], and I say (λέγω) no psalm without an *echos*, and I am not able to overcome my weariness'.[71] The elder monk responded by denouncing singing altogether: 'the true brother does not sing, for singing stiffens and hardens the heart and does not permit the soul to experience katanyxis [compunction]'. Worse still, the brother confesses: 'Abba, from when I [began to] live in solitude I sang the akolouthia of the kanon [verses of the biblical canticles?] and the hours and the things [τὰ] of the octaechos.' Such behavior merely confirms the abba's suspicions, and he reminds the young man that the venerable fathers of old, Paul the Simple, Pambo and Apollo, did not sing such things, and that singing (ᾆσμα) 'has already dragged many down to the baser things of the world (εἰς τὰ κατώτατα τῆς γῆς); . . . [it] is a thing for people of the world, and that is why the people come together in the churches'. Silvanus' message could not be clearer: music may be attractive to laymen and women in the cities, but monks should have nothing to do with a studied musical treatment of the sacred texts. Such can never produce the simplicity and contrition that must permeate the soul of a monk. The mention of the octoechos and suspicion that the 'kanon' may be the later Byzantine poetic form raise serious questions about the dating of the received text.[72] While the story may have a foundation in reality, it has passed through the hands of a redactor since the publication of the early sixth-century *Plerophoria.*

Another story, supposedly a 'saying' of the Nitrian abba Pambo (d. 385/90) takes a similar point of view.[73] A young disciple of the master had been sent to Alexandria to sell wares produced by the monks. He stayed at a xenodochium (hostel) maintained by the church of St. Mark, as would be expected of a traveling monk, and he could not help listening to the troparia and canons sung by the choirs of the church. Saddened that monks did not sing these, he questioned 'Pambo' and was quickly informed that such things had no place in the life of the monk:

> What katanyxis, what tears come from troparia? When someone stands in church or in his cell and raises his voice the way cattle do? For if we stand in the presence of God, it should be with great compunction and not with haughtiness. For

> indeed monks did not come to this desert so that they could stand before God and behave haughtily, sing songs (ᾄσματα) and melodies (ἤχους), shake their hands and stamp their feet.

Though the anachronistic allusion to troparia and kanons betrays that the anecdote cannot possibly record the exact words of Pambo, the passage reveals later monastic views of the corrupting power of music here attributed to a respected abba. In his closing words to the disciple, 'Pambo' makes a point of denouncing non-scriptural texts: 'they will rip up the Sacred Scriptures and compose troparia [in their place]'. The anecdote thus takes aim at not one but two developments perceived as objectionable by its monastic author. Singing could contribute nothing to the fulfillment of the monastic vocation, and the insertion of non-scriptural texts had to be even less desirable. Ambivalence towards texts of recent invention (troparia and kanons) was by no means confined solely to monastic circles.

This monastic musical dossier may be complemented by an often overlooked Western text, part of a document known as the *Consultationes Zacchaei et Apollonii.* The *Consultationes* are a fictitious dialog between a pagan philosopher (Apollonius) and Zacchaeus, a Christian who answers the philosopher's searching, but not necessarily hostile, questions. Its provenance is uncertain (Gaul or Africa), but it can be dated to the end of the first decade of the fifth century and hence from the period when the 'psalmodic movement' was in full swing.[74] Chapter 6 of book 3 is entitled 'Quae consuetudo psallendi orandique sit, vel unde monachis haec praecepta venerunt' (What the custom of singing and praying is and whence these precepts came to monks). Apollonius questions whether the 'cantandi studium' is idle (*otiosum*) for monks.[75] He objects that attentiveness suffers in singing ('et adtentior in ipsa supplicatione sit raritas') and wonders whether 'the divine majesty should be fittingly honored more by serious praises than by mere elegance' (et divinam maiestatem seriis potius laudibus quam facetis deceat honorari). Zacchaeus agrees that seriousness of intention must receive primary emphasis, but he argues that those who beseech the Lord with frequent petitions will all the more swiftly receive their requests: 'Amen dico vobis, si non dabit propter amicitiam, dabit propter inportunitatem' (cf. Luke 11:8). While merit might avail little, persistence *will* pay off! Zacchaeus supports this arguably self-serving philosophy with the conventional scriptural exhortations to constant prayer, a common topos in monastic literature of the fourth and fifth centuries.[76] He asserts, furthermore, that the Hebrew Scriptures attest many times to divine approbation of singing and that the sacred text itself confirms that praise and prayer offered to God can only be enhanced by song. Zacchaeus explains, furthermore, that the singing of psalms affords special benefits:

dum in hac mentium oblectatione et fidei honor et alacritas crescit animorum, interque saeculi ac professae inquietudinis curas laeta	while in this spiritual delight both the honor of the faith and their own spiritual zeal increase; meanwhile joyous grace dispels the cares of the

exigit gratia, quod obtinere non praevalet tristior disciplina.[77]	world and of manifest disquiet – something a harsher discipline cannot accomplish.

The theme that music can be a powerful aid to devotion recurs with frequency in the patristic literature, often justified by the argument that a difficult teaching can thus be made more attractive ('severa blandis permiscens'). It is thoroughly exceptional to find such an idea expressed in a monastic context.

The Western monastic rules generally do not go beyond stating the obligation to sing the psalms devoutly and with understanding, fixing certain prayer times as part of the monastic horarium, or legislating the number of psalms to be sung at a given office.[78] A few Western monastic texts go beyond this reticence, however. The Rule of Macarius placed restrictions on the exercise of musical skill and craftsmanship: 'let no one pride himself in his skill or in his voice . . . in the monastery let no one practice a craft, except him of proven faith'.[79] The Rule of Paul and Stephen, one of the most problematical of the rules with respect to its dating, cites the passage from the Augustinian *Praecepta* that forbids the singing of anything that is not specifically ordained to be sung. Then it proceeds to admonish that 'the Lord requires from us the sacrifice of obedience rather than of victims; nor does he take pleasure in striving for artistic singing as much as in the observance of the commandments and purity of heart'.[80] Jerome warned the monk Rusticus about the proper performance of psalmody: 'sweetness of voice is not required but a proper mental disposition; as the Apostle writes, "I will sing with the spirit, I will sing with the mind also"'.[81] In general, distrust of musical skill as a distraction from monastic values, particularly the danger to humility, was not an uncommon theme in either Eastern or Western monasticism.

Psalmody and Urban Monasticism

A close link between desert monasticism and the 'psalmodic movement' that pervaded Christian urban centers around 400 cannot be either inferred or established. While the extraordinary ascetic feats of the desert solitaries captured the popular imagination, their conception of 'psalmody' bore little resemblance to what was happening in the urban milieux of the Christian East. The liveliness of the popular psalmody described by patristic authors of the late fourth and early fifth centuries is foreign to Egyptian monastic literature. Though the 'sayings' attributed to Pambo and Silvanus cannot in their transmitted form be authentic, they draw the line between what might be acceptable in the cities and what desert monks could allow themselves. If monastics can lay claim to any responsibility for the promotion of the 'later fourth-century psalmodic movement', one must look to the urban ascetics of the East who had close ties to local church structures and episcopal authority. The history of early urban monasticism, a less flamboyant lifestyle than that of the desert fathers, attracted less attention in Late Antiquity, as it has in modern studies of monastic history. What follows can thus be considered only a preliminary survey that awaits completion based on future research into urban monasticism of the fourth and fifth centuries.

Urban monasticism took many forms: individual ascetics living by themselves or as part of a family group, married couples living as brother and sister, communities of men or women leading lives of prayer and penance, and genuine monastic communities ruled by the equivalent of an abbot or abbess. Widows, sometimes discouraged from remarrying even if they had the opportunity, formed another recognizable group within the Christian community. Their lives centered on the church, as did those of the 'virgins', whether young, unmarried girls or (more likely) those who had chosen (or were able to choose) a life of celibate asceticism and were supported either by their families or by the local church, often in return for a pastoral ministry.[82] None of these urban monastics chose to leave their home and retreat into the desert in order to devote themselves to a life of prayer.

The distinction between the monasticism of the desert and that of the city was well established and widely recognized by the late fourth century. In one of the earliest polemical writings after his conversion, *De moribus Ecclesiae catholicae et de moribus Manichaeorum* (388), Augustine held up the lives of orthodox ascetics as an antidote to Manichaean excesses.[83] He distinguished between recluses who inhabited the 'desertissimas terras' and cenobitic monks, who joined 'in communem vitam castissimam sanctissimamque'. Judging from Augustine's description of their regimen, these were communities whose governance resembled that of the Pachomian model. They must have lived some distance from inhabited areas, because Augustine distinguishes them from 'a laudable race of Christians . . . who live in the cities [but] aloof from ordinary life'.[84] Augustine notes the presence of a *diversorium* (i.e., monastery) at Milan presided over by a learned priest. He says little about it, because his purpose of attacking Manichaean ascetic practices was best served by describing the strict fasting observed in several Roman monasteries, most likely including some of the women's communities that had been directed by Jerome while he was in Rome. These Roman communities were of humbler profile than Jerome's aristocratic retreats, since Augustine points out that, 'according to Eastern custom' ('Orientis more') and the example of the apostle Paul, they worked to support themselves (unlike the Manichaean 'elect', who depended entirely on others to supply their needs).

The same distinction between urban ascetics and those who separated themselves geographically from life in the towns and villages is noted by Zacchaeus in the *Consultationes*. He observes that, paradoxically, those who live in the cities nevertheless inhabit 'places apart',[85] keeping to a regular schedule of daily prayer times and nocturnal vigils. The dawn never finds them sleeping: 'their morning devotion constrains them to offer praises to God'.[86]

The urban monastics of Palestine, Syria and Cappadocia were thoroughly integrated into local ecclesiastical structures.[87] Those who lived in community had their private devotions, but they often joined the rest of the laity in regular attendance at the Eucharist and at public times of prayer (Vigils, Lauds and Vespers) in the churches. The types of asceticism practiced in Syria were very varied. They ranged from the most antisocial isolation to what would now be called an urban apostolate.[88] In Cappadocia strong encouragement for the ascetic life practiced in community came from Basil, elected bishop of Caesarea in 370. He had visited the principal monastic sites as far away as Egypt and had spent time as a solitary at one of his family's estates. The urban ascetic communities nurtured by Basil are to be identified with the 'people' (λάοι) who appear in the famous letter he wrote to the clergy of Neocesarea, defending the psalmody of his church. James McKinnon quoted an extensive passage from this important source in 'Desert Monasticism'.[89] Why Basil should have needed to defend the singing of psalms, or the observance of vigils, or whether the passage testifies to the introduction of antiphonal psalmody at Caesarea are questions as frequently asked as they are difficult to resolve.[90]

In the present context the question is not 'what' but 'who'. Basil says that 'the people arise at night and go into the house of prayer; . . . and finally getting up from prayer they commence the singing of psalms'. These 'people' are not ordinary members of the laity, but devout urban ascetics living the common life, whom Basil regarded as Christians devoted to carrying out fully and completely the authentic mandate of the Gospel. For this reason he eschewed conventional monastic terminology here as in his ascetical writings generally.[91] Basil's description fits a monastic vigil quite well, but the company seems to sit for the psalmody. They then divide into two groups, singing to each other (ἀντιψάλλουσιν ἀλλήλοις), then they meditate on the Scripture. Afterwards, one person leads another round of psalmody, to which all respond.

A unique source because of its length and attention to detail is the record of a visit to Egypt and the Holy Land undertaken ca. 381–4 by the adventurous Spanish nun Egeria. Its very singularity has made it a primary source for historians in many disciplines, especially the history of the liturgy.[92] The remarkable Egeria was an indefatigable traveler, constantly astounded at her good fortune to be visiting the fabled sites associated with Jewish history or the ministry of Jesus and the places hallowed by martyrs who perished in the persecutions. Almost everywhere she went, she found monks as custodians of the shrines built over the holy sites. Our pilgrim did not usually remain long enough to learn much about their synaxes, but when she arrived at Jerusalem, she recorded in considerable detail the liturgical observances at all of the churches and shrines linked to Jesus' last days on earth and his appearances after the Resurrection.

In addition to the throngs of pilgrims and permanent residents of Jerusalem, there seem to have been two distinct groups of local ascetics who participated in the singing of the liturgy and the chanting of 'hymns' during the frequent processions. The first group is divided into *monazontes* and *parthenae* ('as they are called here', Egeria adds), who come every day before cockcrow to the Anastasis, the church built over the site of the Holy Sepulchre.[93] The constituency of a second group of ascetics, called by Egeria 'aputactitae', is less easy to determine. This name, applied to both men and women living in cenobitic communities, was not restricted solely to Jerusalem. Egeria mentioned them first on her visit to the tomb of St. Thecla, located near Seleucia (Isauria), the center of a semi-anchoritic settlement. The female *apotactitae* there were under the direction of Marthana, a woman Egeria had met earlier in Jerusalem.[94] It would seem that the *apotactitae* embraced a more severe regimen of fasting and self-discipline than other monastics. At Jerusalem, they were expected to fast all year long, with the exception of Paschaltide, eating only one meal a day.[95] Egeria mentions the singing of hymns, psalms, and antiphons with considerable frequency in her descriptions of the Jerusalem liturgy. The psalm responses might not have been an obstacle for a polyglot congregation of pilgrims if the refrains were simple enough, but the resident communities of ascetics were the ones who supplied the psalmody for vigils and other offices. One would suspect that some role in the singing of 'antiphons' was reserved to these communities as well.

Collaboration between, and the distinctive roles of, urban ascetics and ordinary layfolk is revealed in Gregory of Nyssa's touching description of the funeral of his sister, Macrina, who died in 379.[96] The preparation of the body for burial was accompanied by 'the psalmodies of the virgins mixed with lamentations'. When some of the laity arrived, they did not engage in the singing of psalms, which they would not have known, but in 'hymnody'. This continued through the night after the manner of vigils at the shrines of the martyrs. By dawn expressions of grief by the ever increasing crowds began to disturb the virgins' psalmody, which had resumed. Gregory restored order by joining the laywomen to the choir of virgins and the men to the cohort of monks (*monazontes*), 'arranging everything so that the psalmody of each was unified, euphonious and harmonious, just like the singing of a single choir, blended and well-ordered thanks to the unison of all'.[97] The role of each group could not be clearer. The urban ascetics, female and male, knew how to sing the psalms from daily usage. Left to themselves, the people sang 'hymns', whatever these may have been. If the singing at Macrina's funeral were to continue with (responsorial?) psalmody, the laity had to be assisted by the more practiced assemblies of monks and nuns, presumably in the chanting of refrains in response to the psalm verses sung by members of the ascetic communities.

An understanding of urban monasticism in Eastern centers may cast a new and different light on a famous passage in the *Confessions* of St. Augustine. Augustine was profoundly moved by the music he heard at Milan, which he described as a 'mode of consolation and exhortation, with the brethren singing together with great earnestness of voice and heart'.[98] He dated its origin to a confrontation that took place in 386 between Bishop Ambrose and the empress Justina, an Arian sympathizer. Ambrose and Augustine's mother Monica gathered in the cathedral with the 'pia plebs', fearing the worst.[99] As encouragement, the singing of hymns and psalms 'according to the custom of the East' ('secundum morem orientalium partium') was introduced. This practice, according to Augustine, 'has been retained from that time until the present and imitated by many, indeed by almost all your congregations throughout the rest of the world'.

The numerous interpretations to which this brief passage has been subjected generally suppose that Augustine had a very specific musical form of *psalmody* in mind, when in fact the statement links hymns with the psalms. It was long thought that Augustine here referred to the introduction of antiphonal psalmody to the West, but the introduction of responsorial psalmody has been put forward as the likeliest interpretation of the passage.[100] McKinnon interpreted the episode as the first appearance of the all-night psalm vigil in the West. To this plausible explanation I would contribute an additional nuance. Augustine mentions only in passing that his mother and the others kept vigil in the church – the beleaguered may have had little option but to do so![101] As to the identity of those who stood close by their bishop, it does not seem likely that many of the ordinary citizenry would have placed themselves in danger over a theological controversy that was scarcely new at the time and would continue to agitate the Christian world for many years to come. Perhaps the real novelty (Augustine's term is *mos*, custom) imported from the East was the involvement of urban monastics (Augustine's 'fratres' and 'pia plebs') in the kind of sung office described by Basil, Egeria and Gregory of Nyssa.[102] Ambrose himself, in a letter describing the same event, used the term 'brethren', but without indicating that he thought anything musically novel or unusual happened that tense night.[103] The date of the 'stand-off' between bishop and empress is consistent with the introduction of a cathedral office entrusted to urban ascetics. In addition, the episode confirms the leading role of urban ascetics in the singing of psalms as the fourth century came to its close.

The Letter of Athanasius to Marcellinus on the Psalms

Having established the identity of the chief proponents of the 'later fourth-century psalmodic movement', we may turn our attention to the manner in which the psalms might have been rendered in song. In this regard, a letter addressed by Athanasius, archbishop of Alexandria, to a certain Marcellinus contains several interesting distinctions.[104] Athanasius forgoes the allegorical explanations of Scripture favored by the Alexandrian school, and instead guides Marcellinus to a reading of the psalms adapted to the needs of personal devotion. The identity of the recipient cannot be determined, but Marie-Josèphe Rondeau has pointed to aspects of the letter, principally the vocabulary, that ostensibly indicate the recipient to have been a monk.[105] The reverse seems at least as likely to me: that Marcellinus was a devout layman or a cleric seeking to deepen his understanding of Scripture. In the opening paragraph of the letter Athanasius congratulates Marcellinus for maintaining his *askesis* in the midst of his tribulations. This word has a monastic flavor, but Athanasius says that he learned from the bearer of the letter containing Marcellinus' request that he was especially devoted to the reading of the Psalter. It is difficult to believe that Athanasius would have singled out this fact if he were addressing a monk, of whom it could be expected that he knew most of the Psalter by heart.

More than half of the letter (sections 14–26) is devoted to Athanasius' explanation (or that of the 'learned old man' whose wisdom he claims to transmit) of how each psalm – apart from the strictly messianic-prophetic ones – could be used as personal prayer according to one's circumstances. The person who prays the psalm 'recognizes [the psalmist's words] as being his own words, and the one who hears is deeply moved, as though he himself were speaking, and is affected by the words of the songs, as if they were his own songs'.[106] Then, in a passage filled with philosophical and musical terminology, Athanasius proposes that the singing of psalms is an expression of the harmony of soul and body. This Platonic concept of *harmonia* is reiterated several times, probably because Athanasius knew that it would be convincing to a man of Marcellinus' learning. 'The harmonious reading of the psalms is a figure and type of such undisturbed and calm equanimity of our thoughts (τῶν λογισμῶν ἀταραξίας). . . . So also the Lord, wishing the melody of the words to be a symbol of the spiritual harmony in a soul, has ordered that the odes be chanted tunefully and the psalms recited with song.'[107] Thus psalmody has a profound moral efficacy: 'beautifully singing praises, [the singer] brings rhythm to his soul and leads it, so to speak, from disproportion to proportion'.[108] Athanasius reminds Marcellinus repeatedly that this 'harmonization' of the human person is the purpose for which the psalms are sung and not merely for esthetic pleasure, even though some of the 'simple' might erroneously believe that 'the psalms are rendered melodiously for the sake of the ear's delight'.[109] This sounds not like a monastic exhortation to avoid every type of musical adornment, but the advice of a bishop in whose diocese the 'psalmodic movement' had taken hold.

Even more interesting for our purposes, however, is the distinction Athanasius makes between two manners of publicly 'reading' scriptural texts. The law, the prophets, the historical books and all of the New Testament should be proclaimed 'with continuity' (εἴρηται [from ερῶ; say, speak, proclaim] κατὰ συνέχειαν), while the words of the psalms, odes and canticles demand a different treatment, described by Athanasius as κατὰ πλάτος ('with expanse'). Athanasius assumes, incidentally, that the psalms will in fact be sung 'with melodies and strains' (μετὰ μέλους και ᾠδῆς), despite the potentially ambivalent verb λέγεσθαι (to say).[110] As prayer texts, the psalms are to be distinguished in their public rendering from the historical books of the Hebrew Scriptures: 'the book of psalms is like a garden containing things of all these kinds [law, prophecy, etc.], and it sets them to music, but also exhibits things of its own that it gives in song along with them'.

A passage from the *Confessions* of Augustine (354–430) has more than a little relevance in this context. Augustine wrote the *Confessions* between 397 and 400, nearly a quarter-century after Athanasius' death. In book 10 he struggled with his ambivalent reactions to the seductive beauty of sacred music. Augustine cited with admiration the practice of Alexandria, but he must have had little direct information about the way psalms were sung there during Athanasius' episcopate. That much is evident from Augustine's own words: 'and safer it seems to me *what I remember was often told me* concerning Athanasius, bishop of Alexandria, who required the reader of the psalm to perform it with so little inflection (flexu) of voice that it was closer to speaking (pronuntianti vicinior) than to singing (canenti)'.[111] Perhaps this is another way of expressing Athanasius' κατὰ πλάτος. Augustine's admittedly second-hand (but not necessarily inaccurate) report seems consistent with Athanasius' words to Marcellinus. It appears to recognize, furthermore, a threefold distinction for the public recitation of sacred texts: (1) cantillation for the historical and prophetic books of the Hebrew Scriptures, (2) a more musical chanting applicable to the psalms and (3) an even more expansive mode of delivery recognizable as genuine singing for other texts. Augustine's report suggests also that Athanasius strove to temper the extravagance of secular cantors, bringing them in line with the sober monastic customs that he so admired.

The first term used by Athanasius (συνεχής; continuous, unbroken) to distinguish the rendition of the historical from the lyrical books of Scripture recurs in Boethius' *De institutione musica*. Boethius classifies voices (or more likely melodies), distinguishing between a *vox* that is συνεχής and one that is διαστηματική.[112] According to Boethius, the former applies to 'speaking or reciting a prose oration', thus necessitating a relatively rapid presentation of the text in which 'the voice hastens not to get caught up in high and low sounds', a definition that probably corresponds to Athanasius' use of the same term two centuries earlier. Boethius' διαστηματική category, on the other hand, implies genuine singing in which the melody takes precedence, 'wherein we submit less to words than to a sequence of intervals forming a tune [*modulis*]', and thus most probably a more elaborate musical delivery than Athanasius had in mind for the singing of psalms. Boethius also refers to a third, intermediate vocal style, a *tertia differentia* identified and taught by the otherwise unknown Albinus: 'such as when we recite heroic poems not in continuous flow as in prose or in a sustained and slower moving manner as in song'.[113] This 'intermediate' manner (not given a special term by Boethius) might be the equivalent of the κατὰ πλάτος style, which found favor with Athanasius for the singing of psalms. If so, Boethius' description helps to clarify its meaning to some extent. Boethius returns to the topic later in *De institutione musica* (5.5) in a discussion of 'Ptolemy's opinion concerning differences between sounds'. Here he seems to be concerned with refining the interpretation of διαστηματική, more particularly the difference between discrete melodic pitches ('discretae . . . veluti colores inpermixti') and a tonal continuum (compared to a rainbow by Ptolemy) in which the boundaries between pitches are not clearly defined.

John Cassian and Monastic Psalmody

John Cassian's writings about Egyptian monastic prayer practices and psalmody were directed to inhabitants of cenobitic monasteries in Gaul. In the *Institutes* Cassian informed his Gallic readers that he was transmitting an accurate description of the 'Egyptian office', but he actually conflated material drawn from a number of Egyptian monastic sources. Robert Taft connected this 'somewhat idealized Egyptian office' with the monastic settlement at Scetis.[114] For Cassian the singing of psalms was the centerpiece of what a monastic office should be. His description of the Egyptian office reveals something about the way the psalms were sung, and it suggests that the practices of Egypt and Gaul were not dissimilar.

In his version of a famous monastic anecdote known as the 'rule of the angel', Cassian recounted the experience of a group of abbas who met 'in the early days of the faith' to fix the number of psalms to be recited daily at the evening and nocturnal monastic synaxes. Some of the more fervent brethren had argued for sixty or more psalms. Finally, they interrupted their 'pious dispute' to celebrate the evening office. The result was not quite what they anticipated:

cotidianos orationum ritus volentibus celebrare, unus in medium psalmos domino cantaturus exurgit. Cumque sedentibus cunctis, ut est moris nunc usque in Aegypti partibus, et in psallentis verba omni cordis intentione defixis, *undecim psalmos* orationum interiectione *distinctos contiguis versibus parili pronuntiatione cantasset* . . .[115]	and, as they wished to celebrate the daily rites of prayer, one rose in their midst to sing psalms to the Lord. While they were all seated, as is the custom in the land of Egypt, concentrating on the words of the singer with all their heart, he sang eleven psalms with successive verses evenly pronounced and separated by prayers . . .

Cassian says very clearly that the psalm was sung, but he adds that the successive verses were rendered 'parili pronuntiatione'. Does this imply a mode of unadorned singing of the psalms similar to Athanasius' κατὰ πλάτος of a generation earlier, to Albinus' *tertia differentia*, and to the Western psalm tones attested only centuries later? Such simple formulae could easily have survived oral transmission intact over long periods of time. As someone who had spent his entire life in monastic circles, Cassian was no friend of musical elaboration that distracted from the ascetic core of monastic discipline. He criticized monasteries in which 'some have decided that twenty or thirty psalms ought to be recited each night, and that these ought to be prolonged by the melodies of antiphons and the addition of certain rhythms'.[116] He objected therefore not only to the multiplication of psalms (and the danger that those praying them would be less attentive to the meaning of the words) but equally to ambitious (at least from his perspective) musical embellishment. What kind of 'prolongation' Cassian had in mind is not clear; perhaps it was a response to the psalmist like those made at the Pachomian Sunday synaxis.

Conclusions

I have tried to refocus the connections between early monasticism and the wave of interest in singing the psalms evident in many urban centers in the Christian world around the year 400. The main sources of information about this urban 'psalmodic movement' are the writings of the Fathers, not the literature of the desert. Almost all of the Fathers, with the exception of Ambrose, had some personal monastic experience, yet the phenomenon they describe cannot be easily linked to the world of desert monasticism, whether practiced on the sands of Egypt or in the hills of Syria. The monastic 'lifestyle' of the desert did not support communal psalmody. In Lower Egypt psalmody was something the monk did alone in his cell and its level of musical development was rudimentary, probably very like the *in directum* method in which the psalm text continued from beginning to end without interruption. Only the Pachomian Sunday synaxis and the description by John Cassian of a gathering at which an angelic psalmist chanted twelve psalms in succession while the assembled monks listened in silence give evidence of monastic communal psalmody. In the first case there is a response; in the second there is none, save for the 'alleluia' response to the twelfth psalm.

Whatever visitors brought back from the monastic deserts of Nitria, Kellia and Scetis, it was not a model for popular singing of the psalms. For this, we must direct our attention to urban centers: Antioch, Constantinople, Jerusalem and other cities in the Near East and Asia Minor. Urban ascetics, male and female, who lived in a close relationship to the cathedrals of their home cities or who had taken up residence in the vicinity of the graves of famous martyrs, took an active part in popularizing psalmody. A clearer picture of their involvement might well emerge from a more thorough understanding of the history of urban monasticism in Late Antiquity. While one can perhaps arrive at an impressionistic appreciation of monastic meditation, the musical characteristics of the fourth-century psalmodic movement are much more difficult to assess. The information is fragmentary at best: the distinctions made by Athanasius, Augustine's impression of Alexandrian psalmody and the comments of Boethius. These reveal, nevertheless, something about the musical style of ancient psalmody, called by Basil the Great 'the work of the angels . . . a spiritual incense'.[117] It might not have been far removed from the Western psalm 'tones', chanted by European monks and canons, not only in the cities but also in the remote monastic establishments that duplicated the isolation of the (unmusical) Egyptian desert.

Notes

1 James McKinnon, 'Desert Monasticism and the Later Fourth-Century Psalmodic Movement', *M&L* 75 (1994), 505–21. The groundwork for this article (and the basis for future research by other scholars) was laid in the collection of source material *MECL*.

2 The statement that psalmody is a 'defining characteristic of monasticism at this time' is probably true of urban monastics. See James McKinnon, 'The Book of Psalms, Monasticism, and the Western Liturgy', in Nancy van Deusen (ed.), *The Place of the Psalms in the Intellectual Culture of the Middle Ages* (Albany: State University of New York Press, 1999), 59–89, esp. 49–50.

3 See esp. Robert Taft, *The Liturgy of the Hours in East and West: The Origins of the Divine Office and its Meaning for Today* (Collegeville, Minn.: Liturgical Press, 1986; 2nd rev. edn, Collegeville, Minn.: Liturgical Press, 1993); Paul F.

Bradshaw, *Daily Prayer in the Early Church* (Alcuin Club Collections, 63; New York: Oxford University Press, 1983).

4 A 'desert' might be located on the fringes of a village. The monastic settlement on the 'mountain' of Nitria southwest of Alexandria was actually only a few feet above the level of the Nile. Syrian ascetics lived only a healthy walk from inhabited areas.

5 Among the many general surveys of monastic beginnings, see especially García M. Colombás, *El monacato primitivo*, 2 vols (Madrid: Biblioteca de autores cristianos, 1974–5); Jean Gribomont, 'Monachisme', *Dictionnaire de spiritualité* (1932–94), x/2, 1535–47 ('Naissance et développements du monachisme chrétien'); Karl Suso Frank, *Frühes Mönchtum im Abendland*, 2 vols (Zurich: Artemis-Verlag, 1975); J. C. O'Neill, 'The Origins of Monasticism', in Rowan Williams (ed.), *The Making of Orthodoxy: Essays in Honour of Henry Chadwick* (Cambridge: Cambridge University Press, 1989), 270–87; Karl Heussi, *Der Ursprung des Mönchtums* (Tübingen: Mohr, 1936; repr. Aalen: Scientia, 1981); Peter Hawel, *Das Mönchtum im Abendland* (Freiburg im Breisgau: Herder, 1993); Susanna Elm, *Virgins of God: The Making of Asceticism in Late Antiquity* (Oxford: Oxford University Press, 1994); Vincent Desprez, *Le Monachisme primitif: des origines jusqu'au concile d'Ephèse* (Bégrolles-en-Mauges: Abbaye de Bellefontaine, 1998). McKinnon ('Desert Monasticism') drew principally on Derwas James Chitty, *The Desert a City: An Introduction to the Study of Egyptian and Palestinian Monasticism under the Christian Empire* (Oxford: Blackwell, 1966). See also the source material gathered in Adalbert de Vogüé, *Histoire littéraire du mouvement monastique dans l'Antiquité*, 5 vols. (Paris: Editions du Cerf, 1991–), i (1991), 356–85; ii (1993), 384–96; iii (1996), 391–405; iv (1997), 393–409; v (1998), 404–14.

6 Peter Brown, *The Making of Late Antiquity* (Cambridge, Mass.: Harvard University Press, 1978), 81–101; id., *Society and the Holy in Late Antiquity* (London: Faber & Faber, 1982); and id., *The Body and Society: Men, Women, and Sexual Renunciation in Early Christianity* (New York: Columbia University Press, 1988). Some of the conclusions of these studies are summarized with the author's accustomed elegance in the chapter 'Asceticism: Pagan and Christian', in *The Cambridge Ancient History*, xiii: *The Late Empire, A.D. 337–425*, ed. Averil Cameron and Peter Garnsey (Cambridge: Cambridge University Press, 1998), 601–31.

7 See Naphtali Lewis, *Life in Egypt under Roman Rule* (Oxford: Clarendon Press, 1983). Not a few scholars would downplay the 'tax evasion' impulse as a primary motivation for recourse to the desert. For further background see Roger S. Bagnall, *Egypt in Late Antiquity* (Princeton: Princeton University Press, 1993).

8 Many aspects of the life adopted by the earliest Christian monks resembled the disciplined, ascetic mode of life cultivated by Greco-Roman philosophers of Late Antiquity, most notably the Neoplatonists (Plotinus, Porphyry, Proclus and Iamblichus) and their followers. See Heussi, *Der Ursprung des Mönchtums*, 292–8, and the works of Peter Brown cited above, n. 6. A bibliography of pagan Greek asceticism may be found in Tomas Špidlík, Michelina Tenace and Richard Cemus, *Questions monastiques en Orient* (Rome: Pontificium Institutum Studiorum Orientalium, 1999), 13–14.

9 C. Wilfred Griggs, *Early Egyptian Christianity from its Origins to 451 C.E.* (Leiden: E. J. Brill, 1990), 146–69.

10 The temptations of St. Antony have been a frequent subject in the visual arts. Paul Hindemith evoked them musically in the third movement ('Die Versuchung

des heiligen Antonius') of the symphony *Mathis der Maler*. The arrival of divine aid is symbolized, somewhat anachronistically, by the eucharistic sequence *Lauda Sion salvatorem*. The plot of Jules Massenet's opera *Thaïs* contrasts the sensual allurements of the city (Alexandria) with the monastic detachment of the desert.

11 Thomas M. Gannon and George W. Traub, *The Desert and the City: An Interpretation of the History of Christian Spirituality* (New York: Macmillan, 1969), 40. An excellent brief introduction to Evagrius' thought may be found in *Evagrius Ponticus: The Praktikos and Chapters on Prayer*, trans. John Eudes Bamberger (Spencer, Mass.: Cistercian Publications, 1981), pp. lxxi–xcvi.

12 The sources and bibliography are cited in Johannes Quasten, *Patrology*, iii: *The Golden Age of Greek Patristic Literature* (Utrecht: Spectrum, 1966), 146–89.

13 *Vie d'Antoine*, trans. Gerhard M. Bartelink (SC 400; Paris: Editions du Cerf, 1994); *The Life of Antony and the Letter to Marcellinus*, trans. and ed. Robert C. Gregg (New York: Paulist Press, 1980). The Latin translation of Evagrius of Antioch (before 374) is reproduced in *PG* 26: 837–976. Athanasius would have had occasion to recount stories of Antony and other Egyptian ascetics during his travels in the West while exiled from his see.

14 *Historia monachorum in Aegypto*, ed. André Marie Jean Festugière (Brussels: Société des Bollandistes, 1961); trans. Norman Russell, *The Lives of the Desert Fathers: The Historia monachorum in Aegypto* (Kalamazoo, Mich.: Cistercian Publications, 1981).

15 Rufinus' Latin translation of the *Historia* can be found in *PL* 21: 387–462. That Rufinus supplemented the transmitted Greek text seems more logical than the supposition that he had access to a fuller Greek textual tradition of the *Historia*, as proposed by Jean-Claude Guy, 'Le Centre monastique de Scété dans la littérature du ve siècle', *Orientalia Christiana periodica*, 30 (1964), 129–47 at 138–42. Rufinus' additions are included in an appendix to Russell's translation; Rufinus' text forms the basis of the translation in Helen Waddell, *The Desert Fathers* (London: Constable, 1936), 55–80. Heussi (*Der Ursprung*, 154–8) describes the itinerary in detail but doubts its reliability as the accurate record of a voyage. In the introduction to *The Lives*, trans. Russell, Benedicta Ward argues persuasively for its authenticity.

16 I have used the edition of Joseph Armitage Robinson, *The Lausiac History of Palladius* (Texts and Studies, 6/1–2; Cambridge: Cambridge University Press, 1898); trans. Robert Meyer, *Palladius: The Lausiac History* (Westminster, Md.: Newman Press, 1965).

17 The most recent evaluation of Cassian's life and works is Columba Stewart, *Cassian the Monk* (New York: Oxford University Press, 1998). Still of value, however, are Michel Olphe-Gaillard, 'Cassien (Jean)', *Dictionnaire de spiritualité*, ii, 214–76; Jean-Claude Guy, *Jean Cassien: vie et doctrine spirituelle* (Paris: P. Lethielleux, 1961); and Owen Chadwick, *John Cassian* (2nd edn, London: Cambridge University Press, 1968). A recent review of biographical information about Cassian that resurrects the argument that he was a native of Gaul is Karl Suso Frank, 'Johannes Cassian über Johannes Cassian', *Römische Quartalschrift für christliche Altertumskunde und Kirchengeschichte*, 91 (1996), 183–97.

18 *Johannis Cassiani De institutis coenobiorum et de octo principalium vitiorum remediis*, ed. Michael Petschenig (CSEL 17; Vienna: F. Tempsky, 1888). This text is reproduced with a French translation by Jean-Claude Guy as *Institutions cénobitiques* (SC 109; Paris: Editions du Cerf, 1965); trans. Edgar Charles Sumner

Gibson, *The Institutes of John Cassian* (New York: The Christian Literature Company, 1894). Following a more recent translation (*John Cassian: The Monastic Institutes, consisting of On the Training of a Monk and The Eight Deadly Sins*, trans. Jerome Bertram [London: Saint Austin Press, 1999]): 'I shall not be concerned to weave in stories of miracles and portents, . . . since they would only move the readers to wonder, rather than to improve their life' (p. 5).

19 'Illam sane moderationem opusculo huic interserere praesumam, ut ea quae secundum Aegyptiorum regulam seu pro asperitate aerum seu pro difficultate ac diversitate morum inpossibilia in his regionibus vel dura vel ardua conprobavero, . . . aliquatenus temperem.' (However, I shall be so bold as to introduce into this work some moderation of the original Egyptian rule, which I deem too harsh and impossible in these parts, because of the coldness of the climate or for sheer difficulty or strangeness.) *Instit.* praef. 8–9; CSEL 17: 6–7; SC 109: 30–32; trans. Bertram, 6. Like so many reformers, Cassian attributed venerable age to practices that he promoted as the norm; see Adalbert de Vogüé, 'Les Sources des quatre premiers livres des Institutions de Jean Cassien: introduction aux recherches sur les anciennes règles monastiques latines', *Studia monastica*, 27 (1985), 268–73.

20 John Cassian, *Collationes*, ed. Eugène Pichery (SC 42, 54, 64; Paris: Editions du Cerf, 1953–9); trans. Boniface Ramsey, *John Cassian: The Conferences* (New York: Paulist Press, 1997). A selection (nos. 1, 9, 10, 11, 15, 18, 19) is printed in Owen Chadwick, *Western Asceticism* (Philadelphia: Westminster Press, 1958), 190–289.

21 An earlier version of the Greek systematic collection was translated into Latin by the deacon (later pope, 556–61) Pelagius and the subdeacon John, who may himself have become pope as John III (561–74). Owen Chadwick has translated sections 1–17 of the seventeenth-century Rosweyde edition (*PL* 73: 855–1022) in *Western Asceticism*, 33–189. It is interesting to speculate how the monastic inclinations of the young patrician Gregory, later Pope Gregory the Great (590–604), might have been influenced by this translation. Even Evagrius' methodical treatise on asceticism, the *Praktikos*, closes with a few 'Sayings of the holy monks'; Evagrius Ponticus, *The Praktikos and Chapters on Prayer*, 39–41.

22 Graham Gould, *The Desert Fathers on Monastic Community* (Oxford: Clarendon Press, 1993), 4. The original text of the alphabetical collection of the *Apophthegmata Patrum* has been printed in *PG* 65: 72–440. The systematic collection has begun to be published: *Les Apophtegmes des pères du désert*, ed. and trans. Jean-Claude Guy, i (chs. 1–9) (SC 387; Paris: Editions du Cerf, 1992). For an English translation see *The Sayings of the Desert Fathers: The Alphabetical Collection*, ed. and trans. Benedicta Ward (Kalamazoo, Mich.: Cistercian Publications, 1975), and the same translator's *The Wisdom of the Desert Fathers* (Oxford: S. L. G. Press, 1975). The Sayings have been published in French translation by the Abbey of Solesmes (Sablé-sur-Sarthe) under the editorship of Dom Lucien Regnault in the series *Les Sentences des Pères du désert: Série des anonymes* (1985), *Collection alphabétique* (1981), *Nouveau recueil, apophtegmes inédits ou peu connus* (2nd edn, 1977), *Receuil de Pélage et Jean* (2nd edn, 1976), *Troisième recueil et tables* (1976). Very useful evaluations are Jean-Claude Guy, 'Les *Apophthegmata Patrum*', in *Théologie de la vie monastique: études sur la tradition patristique* (Théologie, 49; Ligugé: Aubier, 1961), and id., *Recherches sur la tradition grecque des Apophthegmata patrum* (Brussels: Société des Bollandistes, 1962). See also Lucien Regnault, 'Les

Apophtegmes en Palestine au ve–vi^e^ siècles', *Irénikon*, 54 (1981), 320–30; repr. in *Les Pères du désert à travers leurs apophtegmes* (Sablé-sur-Sarthe: Abbaye Saint-Pierre de Solesmes, 1987). On the complex questions of transmission see Ferdinand Cavallera, 'Apophtegmes', *Dictionnaire de spiritualité*, i, 765–70.

23 Desprez, *Le Monachisme primitif*, 277–8, 286 ff. See Gabriele Giamberardini, 'Kellia' and 'Nitria', *Dizionario degli istituti di perfezione*, ed. Guerrino Pelliccia and Giancarlo Rocca, 9 vols. to date (Rome: Edizione Paoline, 1974–), v, 342–6 and vi, 303–5. The use of the term 'mountain' is of course relative – the locale might not be more than a few feet above the level of the Nile.

24 *Lausiac History* 7; ed. Robinson, 25; trans. Meyer, 40; this fact is corroborated in Rufinus' translation of the *Historia monachorum* 21 (*PL* 21: 413).

25 *Historia monachorum* 20.7; ed. Festugière, 120; trans. Russell, 106; Rufinus, *Historia monachorum* 21 (*PL* 21: 413).

26 Though 'synaxis' (assembly) seems to imply a gathering of monks, it is frequently used to signify the 'office' performed by a monk praying alone in his cell at fixed hours.

27 Life of Antony 34; *PG* 65: 85–8; trans. Ward, 7. Details about the site are drawn from Antoine Guillaumont, 'Histoire des moines aux Kellia', in id., *Aux origines du monachisme chrétien: pour une phénoménologie du monachisme* (Bégrolles-en-Mauges: Abbaye de Bellefontaine, 1979), 151–67, repr. from *Orientalia Lovaniensia periodica*, 8 (1977), 187–203. The archeological finds all date from a later period in the settlement's history.

28 *Lausiac History* 7.2; ed. Robinson, 25; trans. Meyer, 40.

29 Guy, 'Le Centre monastique'. A trip to one of the extant monasteries of the Wadi Natrun, the location of ancient Scetis, inspired Robert Taft's 'Praise in the Desert: The Coptic Monastic Office Yesterday and Today', *Worship*, 56 (1982), 513–36. On the history and present flourishing of monastic life there see Matta el-Meskeen, *Coptic Monasticism and the Monastery of St. Macarius: A Short History* (Cairo: Monastery of St. Macarius Scetis, 1984). Father Matta was himself responsible for the restoration of monasticism at this venerable site.

30 *Historia monachorum* 23, ed. Festugière, 130–31, trans. Russell, *The Lives of the Desert Fathers*, 113 ('It is a very perilous journey for travelers'). The Latin translation of Rufinus supplements the original with the translator's own observations (*PL* 21: 387–462 at 453; trans. Russell, 152–3). See also Gabriele Giamberardini and D. Gelsi, 'Scete', *Dizionario degli istituti di perfezione*, viii, 1023–30.

31 *Pachomian Koinonia*, trans. and ed. Armand Veilleux, 3 vols. (Cistercian Studies, 45 [Lives], 46 [Chronicles and Rules], 47 [Instructions, Letters, etc. of Pachomius, Theodore, Horsiesius]; Kalamazoo, Mich.: Cistercian Publications, 1980–2). The classic elucidation of prayer in the Pachomian *koinonia* is Armand Veilleux, *La Liturgie dans le cénobitisme pachômien au quatrième siècle* (Rome: Herder, 1968). The nature of the Pachomian *koinonia* is explored in Philip Rousseau, *Pachomius: The Making of a Community in Fourth-Century Egypt* (Berkeley: University of California Press, 1985).

32 Veilleux, *La Liturgie*, 175.

33 For Western examples see Joseph Dyer, 'The Psalms in Monastic Prayer', in Nancy van Deusen (ed.), *The Place of the Psalms*, 49–89.

34 One cannot always be sure what musical implications can be read into an ancient text when it refers to 'psalmody' or uses the verb 'to psalm'. Nor does 'psallere' (ψάλλειν) necessarily imply the singing of the biblical psalms, though this is most often the case.

35 Emmanuel von Severus, 'Das Wort "Meditari" im Sprachgebrauch der Heiligen Schrift', *Geist und Leben*, 26 (1953), 365–75; Heinrich Bacht, *Das Vermächtnis des Ursprungs: Studien zum frühen Mönchtum* (Wurzburg: Echter Verlag, 1972), 244–64 ('"Meditatio" in den ältesten Mönchsquellen'); Fidelis Ruppert, 'Meditatio — ruminatio: Zu einem Grundbegriff christlicher Meditation', *Erbe und Auftrag*, 53 (1977), 83–93. This word is particularly subject to misunderstanding in English editions of monastic literature.

36 A later European monastic source, the Life of John of Gorze by Arnulf of Metz, compared its sound to the buzzing of bees: 'et in morem apis psalmos tacito murmure continue revolvendo' (*PL* 137: 280).

37 Achilas 5 (*PG* 65: 125), in *The Sayings*, trans. Ward, 25.

38 Cyril of Scythopolis, *Lives of the Monks of Palestine*, trans. Robert M. Price (Kalamazoo, Mich.: Cistercian Publications, 1991), nos. 18, 51, 73 (pp. 110, 152, 187).

39 'Si enim ea quae saepissime audistis cum iucunditate, in ore cogitationis ruminastis, nec oblivione tanquam in ventre sepelistis.' Augustine, *Enarr. in ps.* 59.1 (*PL* 36: 713).

40 *Instit.* 3.2; CSEL 17: 34; trans. Gibson, 213. The Pachomian monks were expected to 'recite something from the Scripture' while going from one activity to another.

41 Cf. Evagrius Ponticus: 'When you go to manual labor, let the mouth sing psalms (ἡ γλῶσσα ψαλλέτω) and the mind pray'; *Capita Paranetica* 80 (*PG* 79: 1256), as quoted in Bacht, *Das Vermächtnis des Ursprungs*, 262.

42 'Ita incipiet decantare ut eos [psalmos] non tamquam a propheta compositos, sed velut a se editos quasi orationem propriam.' *Conf.* 10.4; CCSL 13: 304; John Cassian, *The Conferences*, trans. Ramsey, 384.

43 'Quid ergo inpedit servum dei manibus operantem in lege domini meditari et psallere nomini domini altissimi?' (cf. Pss. 1: 2 and 12: 6); *De opere monachorum* XVII.20; CSEL 41: 564–5; *MECL* 387. 'Servus dei' was an Augustinian term for a monk; see John Kevin Coyle, *Augustine's 'De moribus ecclesiae catholicae': A Study of the Work, its Composition, and its Sources* (Fribourg: University Press, 1978), 220. For a newer critical edition see *De moribus ecclesiae catholicae et de moribus Manichaeorum libri duo*, ed. Johannes Bauer (CESL 90; Vienna: Hoelder-Pichler-Tempsky, 1992).

44 *Vie d'Antoine*, ed. Bartelink, 25.1 (μνημονεύουσι τῶν ἀπὸ τῶν γραφῶν λέξεων), SC 400: 204; trans. Gregg, *The Life of Antony*, 50; see also *Vie d'Antoine* 39.5 (λαλοῦντες ἀπὸ τῶν γραφῶν), SC 400, 242, trans. Gregg, 61. For other passages in the Life of Antony see 19.2 (SC 400: 186) and 55.4 (SC 400: 282), trans. Gregg, 45 and 73. The monks inspired by Antony's long speech are said to inhabit cells (*monasteria*) 'filled with divine choirs, singing, meditating' (ταλλόντων, φιλολογούντων), *Vie d'Antoine* 44.2; neither of the translations (SC 400: 254 or Gregg, 64) renders this nuance.

45 *St. Cyril of Jerusalem's Lectures on the Christian Sacraments: The Procatechesis and the Five Mystagogical Catecheses*, ed. and trans. Frank Leslie Cross (London: S. P. C. K., 1951), 9 and 49.

46 But cf. Epiphanius 3: 'The true monk should incessantly have prayer and psalmody *in his heart*' (*PG* 65: 166).

47 *MECL passim*; a glance at the index indicates how frequently the topic of the psalms and their singing was addressed by the Fathers.

48 *Lausiac History* 7; ed. Robinson, 26; trans. Meyer, 41.

49 Rufinus was more impressed by the 'silentium ingens' of Kellia in his translation of the *Historia monachorum* (*PL* 21: 444).

50 *Lausiac History* 22.6 and 8; ed. Robinson, 72; trans. Meyer, 78–9. The Jerusalem monk Adolus stood at night on the Mount of Olives 'singing psalms and praying' (καὶ ψάλλων καὶ προσευχόμενος), *Lausiac History* 43.1; ed. Robinson, 130; trans. Meyer, 43. Subsequently, it is mentioned that Adolus would go from cell to cell, waking the brethren for prayer and 'sing with them one or two antiphons' (καὶ καθ' ἕκαστον οἶκον συμψάλλων αὐτοῖς ἕν ἢ δεύτερον ἀντίφωνον). *Lausiac History* 43.3; ed. Robinson, 130; trans. Meyer, 120. The text uses the singular αντίφονον – should ἕν be emended to πρῶτον (i.e., first or second antiphon)? This might be the unique appearance of the word 'antiphon' in the Egyptian monastic literature outside of Cassian, who was writing for a Western audience.

51 Macharius 34, *PG* 65: 277; *The Sayings of the Desert Fathers*, trans. Ward, 114. Of the two verbs used in this anecdote in conjunction with the psalms, one (βάλλω) might conceivably be interpreted to mean 'to meditate', but it is followed immediately by ψάλλειν.

52 *Lausiac History* 48.2 (ψάλλων); trans. Meyer, 131.

53 'Moris est autem inibi, sedentibus cunctis, ab uno dici psalmum, ceteris vel audentibus vel respondentibus'; *Historia monachorum* 23 (*PL* 21: 454). The use of 'vel' does not necessarily imply that the monks would have had an option *either* to listen *or* to respond: they did both successively. Cf. Cassian *Institutes* 2.5; CSEL 17: 22; trans. Gibson, 207.

54 *Reg. Hors.* 12; *Pachomian Koinonia*, ii, 198–201. A nightly recitation in the cell preceding the synaxis is mentioned in *Reg. Hors.* 17, *Pachomian Koinonia*, ii, 202.

55 Taft, *The Liturgy of the Hours*, 62–5; there would seem to be an extra sign of the cross inserted after the Our Father in the outline on p. 64.

56 Veilleux, *La Liturgie*, 308.

57 Precepts 15–16; *Pachomian Koinonia*, ii, 147–8; also Veilleux, *La Liturgie*, 313–15.

58 See Frans Kok, 'L'Office pachômien: *psallere, orare, legere*', *Ecclesia orans*, 9 (1992), 70–95.

59 Precepts 142; *Pachomian Koinonia*, ii, 166.

60 First Greek Life 147; *Pachomian Koinonia*, i, 404; Veilleux's English translation omits the first reference to psalmody present in the Greek text. The same episode is reported in the Bohairic (a dialect of Coptic) Life 205 (*Pachomian Koinonia*, i, 257), but without mention of psalmody.

61 Precepts 127–8; *Pachomian Koinonia*, 164.

62 The Bohairic Life of Pachomius 201; *Pachomian Koinonia*, i, 249–51. Cf. *MECL* 294.

63 Anselme Davril, 'La Psalmodie chez les pères du désert', *Collectanea Cisterciensia*, 49 (1987), 132–9. Davril also cites passages from the *Lausiac History* and Cassian's *Institutes* and *Conferences*. His intention is to show the frequent convergence of psalmody and prayer.

64 Serapion prayed the *entire* Psalter, at the conclusion of which the woman fell to the ground. From the alphabetical collection (*PG* 65: 413–16; *MECL* 126).

65 'Unus in medium psalmos domino cantaturus exsurgit.' Cassian, *Instit.* 2.5; CSEL 17: 22, trans. Gibson, 207. For a discussion of the 'rule of the angel' see Joseph Dyer, 'Monastic Psalmody of the Middle Ages', *Revue bénédictine*, 99 (1989), 41–74, esp. 47–52.

66 How very different is the opinion of Abbot Smaragdus of St. Mihiel: 'Multi enim reperiuntur qui cantus suavitate commoti, sua crimina plangunt, atque ex ea parte magis flectuntur ad lacrymas, ex qua psallendi insonuerit dulcedo suavissima'; *Diadema monachorum* 2, as cited in Jean Leclercq, 'Culte liturgique et

prière intime dans le monachisme au moyen âge', *La Maison-Dieu*, 69 (1962), 39–55 at 42–3.

67 McKinnon, 'Desert Monasticism', 508.

68 Abba of Rome, *PG* 65: 388; *The Sayings of the Desert Fathers*, trans. Ward, 176.

69 Johannes Quasten, *Music and Worship in Pagan and Christian Antiquity*, trans. Boniface Ramsey (Washington, DC: National Association of Pastoral Musicians, 1983; originally pub. 1930, 2nd edn, 1973), 94–7 and 118–19.

70 PO 8: 180; F. Nau, 'Les Plérophories de Jean évêque de Maiouma', *Revue de l'Orient chrétien*, 3 (1898), 232 ff. On John of Maiûma see Joseph-Marie Sauget and Tito Orlandi, 'John of Maiûma (John Rufus)', *Encyclopedia of the Early Church*, ed. Angelo di Berardino, trans. Adrian Walford, 2 vols. (New York: Oxford University Press, 1992), i, 244–5. Only fragments (of a later redaction?) of the Greek original remain; there is also a later Syriac version of the tract.

71 In addition to the Quasten–Ramsey translation, there is an English translation of the entire text in John Gale, 'The Divine Office: Aid and Hindrance to Penthos', *Studia monastica*, 27 (1985), 13–15; also in Irénée Hausheer, *Penthos: The Doctrine of Compunction in the Christian East*, trans. Anselm Hufstader (Kalamazoo, Mich.: Cistercian Publications, 1982), 106–7.

72 Milos Velimirovic, 'Christian Chant in Syria, Armenia, Egypt, and Ethiopia', in *NOHM*, ii, ed. Richard Crocker and David Hiley (2nd edn, Oxford: Oxford University Press, 1990), 3–9.

73 This text is better known, having been published in the first volume of *Scriptores ecclesiastici de musica sacra potissimum*, ed. Martin Gerbert, 3 vols. (St. Blasien, 1784; repr. Milan: Bollettino Bibliografico Musicale, 1931; Hildesheim, Olms, 1963), i, 1–4. Michael Bernhard has published a Latin translation found in Monte Cassino, Biblioteca dell'Abbazia, MS 318 that omits the mention of kanons and troparia that would have been unintelligible to a Western audience and concludes with apocalyptic pronouncements: *Clavis Gerberti: Eine Revision von Martin Gerberts Scriptores ecclesiastici de musica sacra potissimum (St. Blasien, 1784)* (Munich: Verlag der Bayerischen Akademie der Wissenschaften, 1989), 1–3. (It is interesting to note that this document regards 'opus dei' as grammatically invariable: 'quia ociosus semper fui in opus dei' [5].) See also Egon Wellesz, *Byzantine Music and Hymnography* (2nd edn, Oxford: Clarendon Press, 1961), 171–4. I have not had access to Otto Wessely, 'Die Musikanschauung des Abtes Pambo', *Anzeiger der Österreichischen Akademie der Wissenschaften. Philosophisch-historische Klasse*, 89 (1953), 42–62.

74 The text (*CPL* 103, there listed under the *spuria* of Firmicius Maternus) was edited by Germain Morin (1935); this has been superseded by the edition of J. L. Feiertag, *Questions d'un païen à un chrétien: Consultationes Zacchaei christiani et Apollonii philosophi*, 2 vols (SC 401–2; Paris: Editions du Cerf, 1994). Vogüé ('Consultationes Zacchaei et Apollonii') dates the work 'poco dopo 411' and notes the author's high esteem for the monastic life (eremitic and cenobitic) in *Dizionario degli istituti di perfezione*, ii, 1695–6. See also Pierre Courcelle, 'Date, source et genèse des Consultationes Zacchaei et Apollonii', *Revue d'histoire des religions*, 146 (1954), 174–93.

75 'Otium' took on a pejorative connotation in monastic literature; see Jacques Biarne, 'Le Temps du moine d'après les premières règles monastiques d'Occident (IV–VIe siècles)', *Le Temps chrétien de la fin de l'Antiquité au Moyen Age: IIIe–XIIIe siècles; Paris, 9–12 mars 1981* (Paris: Editions du Centre national de la recherche scientifique, 1984), 103. Cf. Basil, Reg. 34 (*Basili Regula a Rufino latine versa*, ed. Klaus Zelzer (CSEL 86; Vienna: Hoelder-Richler-Tempsky, 1986), 109.

76 Benedict of Aniane quoted a passage from St. Augustine (*In Evang.* 'Ubi duo vel tres . . .') in his *Concordia regularum* 25.11: 'opus est itaque ut quod postulat vocis sonus obtineat sedulitatis affectus' (*PL* 103: 921).

77 *Questions* 3.6, ed. Feiertag, SC 402: 208.

78 Psalmody is mentioned as part of the discipline of the monastic horarium. For an orientation to the rules see Adalbert de Vogüé, *Les Règles monastiques anciennes (400–700)* (Turnhout: Brepols, 1985), and id., 'Regole cenobitiche d'Occidente', *Dizionario degli istituti di perfezione*, vii, 1420–28 (in English as 'The Cenobitic Rules of the West', *Cistercian Studies*, 12 (1977), 175–83); a useful brief summary may be found in Biarne, 'Le Temps du moine', 100–102.

79 *Regula Macarii* 19 ('nullus se in sua peritia neque in voce exaltet') and 30 ('ut intra monasterium artificium non faciat ullus, nisi ille cuius fides probata fuerit'), in *Early Monastic Rules: The Rules of the Fathers and the Regula Orientalis*, ed. Carmella Vircillo Franklin et al. (Collegeville, Minn.: Liturgical Press, 1982), 46 and 50; also *Les Règles des saints pères*, ed. Adalbert de Vogüé, 2 vols. (SC 297–8; Paris: Editions du Cerf, 1992), 297, 380 and 389. The prideful monk-craftsman is admonished in the Rule of Benedict, 57.1–3; see *RB 1980: The Rule of St. Benedict in Latin and English with Notes*, ed. Timothy Fry et al. (Collegeville, Minn.: Liturgical Press, 1981), 264–5. The story is told of Pachomius that he ordered his disciples to make the pillars of an oratory crooked lest too great pleasure be taken in its beauty (*Paralipomena* 32; *Pachomian Koinonia*, ii, 55–6). Veilleux agrees with Chitty (*The Desert a City*, 119) that this legend was intended to explain the condition of a misshapen building that had settled into the sand because of a defective foundation.

80 'A nobis dominus magis oboedientiae quam victimarum sacrificium quaerit; nec cantilenae artificiorum studium, quantum observantiam mandatorum et cordis munditiam delectatur.' *Regula Pauli et Stephani. Edició critica i comentari*, ed. J. Evangelista M. Vilanova (Montserrat: Abadia de Montserrat, 1959), ch. 14, p. 114; there is a French translation in Vincent Desprez, *Règles monastiques d'Occident (IVe–VIe siècle): D'Augustin à Ferreol* (Bégrolles-en-Mauges: Abbaye de Bellefontaine, 1980), 355.

81 'Non dulcedo vocis sed mentis affectus quaeritur, scribente apostolo: psallam spiritu, psallam et mente'; Ep. 125, *Ad Rusticum monachum* 15; CSEL 56: 134 (*MECL* 328).

82 Female asceticism is the subject of Elm, *Virgins of God*, esp. 331–72 ('Athanasius of Alexandria and Urban Asceticism'), and figures in Brown, 'Asceticism: Pagan and Christian'. A comprehensive study of their role in urban liturgical life would be desirable.

83 Coyle, *Augustine's 'De moribus ecclesiae catholicae'*, esp. 295–7.

84 Ibid., 297.

85 'Locis primum remotioribus habitant, etiamsi in urbibus degunt.' *Consultationes* 13; SC 402: 184.

86 'Numquam praeterea diei falluntur adventu, sed strenuos semper pallentis aurorae tempus exsuscitat, atque ad offerendas deo laudes devotio matutina compellit.' *Consultationes* 16; SC 402: 184.

87 In this less studied aspect of monastic history I am indebted to Jean-Miguel Garrigues and Jean Legrez, *Moines dans l'assemblée des fidèles à l'époque des pères (IVe–VIIIe siécles)* (Paris: Beauchesne, 1992).

88 The poet, theologian and exegete Ephrem the Syrian (ca. 306–73) chose such a ministry, though after his death monks sought to claim him as one of their own. See Frédéric Rilliet, 'Ephrem the Syrian', *Encyclopedia of the Early Church*, i, 266–67; Garrigues and Legrez, *Moines dans l'assemblée*, 44–8.

89 'Desert Monasticism', 513–14; also *MECL* 139. The assembly alternates the two by now familiar monastic practices of singing psalms and meditating on scriptural texts (μελέτην τῶν λογίων), a nuance that is not reflected in the *MECL* translation: 'intensifying their carefulness over the sacred text'.

90 The situation recalls that of Augustine defending a certain Carthaginian practice against the tribune Hilary; see Joseph Dyer, 'Augustine and the *Hymni ante oblationem*: The Earliest Offertory Chants?' *Revue des études augustiniennes*, 27 (1981), 85–99.

91 '[Basile] ne veut considérer ses frères en ascéticisme que comme des chrétiens logiques avec eux-mêmes'; see Jean Gribomont, 'Le Monachisme au IVe siècle en Asie Mineure de Gangres au Messalianisme', *Studia patristica*, 2 (1957), 400–25 at 413. On their identity see also Juan Mateos, 'L'Office monastique à la fin du IVe siècle', *Oriens Christianus*, 47 (1963), 53–88, esp. 85–6. Peter Brown has emphasized the effect of 'the drastic rite of baptism', often delayed to mature years, as initiation to a celibate life of personal asceticism; see 'Asceticism', 618.

92 *Ethérie: Journal de voyage*, ed. and trans. Hélène Pétré (SC 21; Editions du Cerf, 1971); this has been re-edited by Pierre Maraval (SC 296; Paris: Editions du Cerf, 1982); English translation and annotation by George E. Gingras, *Egeria: Diary of a Pilgrimage* (New York: Newman Press, 1968). Several passages are translated in *MECL* 242–54.

93 *Journal* 24.1, SC 21: 188 (SC 296, 234); trans. Gingras, 89. Previously, Egeria used the normal Latin term 'monachi' for the monks she encountered in her travels, but 'monazontes' seems to have been the term favored at Jerusalem, a convention that she scrupulously preserves. Subsequently, the word is used to signify both men and women ascetics.

94 '. . . and so, after spending two days there seeing the holy monks and the *apotactitae*, both men and women, who live there . . .'; *Journal* 23.3 and 6; SC 21: 184 and 213 (SC 296: 226 and 230); trans. Gingras, 87 and 213 (n. 255); see also A. Lambert, 'Apotactites et Apotaxamenes', *DACL*, i, 2604–26.

95 'Consuetudo enim hic talis est, ut omnes qui sunt (ut hic dicunt) aputactitae, viri vel feminae, non solum diebus quadragesimarum, sed toto anno, qua manducant, semel in die manducant.' *Journal* 28.3; SC 21: 214 (SC 296: 264); trans. Gingras, 101. If any of the *aputactitae* could not abstain from from all food on the weekdays of Lent, a feat undertaken by the *hebdomadarii* (27.9; SC 21: 214, SC 296: 244; trans. Gingras, 100), they were permitted to eat in the evening on certain weekdays.

96 *Vita* 33; *Grégoire de Nysse: Vie de Sainte Macrine*, ed. Pierre Maraval (SC 178; Paris: Editions du Cerf, 1971), 246–8; *MECL* 152. Basil the Great was also her brother.

97 μίαν ἐξ ἑκατέρων εὔρθμόν τε καὶ ἐναρμόνιον καθάπερ ἐν χοροστασίᾳ τὴν ψαλμῳδίαν γίνεσθαι παρεσκεύσα διὰ τῆς κοινῆς πάντων σύνῳδίας εὐκόσμως συγκεκῆαμένην, *Vita* 33; SC 178: 248.

98 'Non longe coeperat Mediolanensis ecclesia genus hoc consolationis et exhortationis celebrare magno studio fratrum concinentium vocibus et cordibus.' *Confessions* 9.7.15; CCSL 27: 141–2, *MECL* 351.

99 'Excubabat pia plebs in ecclesia mori parata cum episcopo suo, servo tuo. Ibi mater mea . . .' (The pious people kept watch in the church, prepared to die with their bishop, your servant. There my mother . . .). This sentence was omitted from the translation in *MECL* 351.

100 Helmut Leeb, *Die Psalmodie bei Ambrosius* (Vienna: Herder, 1967).

101 This might be supported by the statement made thirty-six years later by Ambrose's biographer, Paulinus of Nola, that 'antiphons, hymns and *vigils* first

began to be celebrated in the church of Milan'. Paulinus' mention of antiphons is now regarded as anachronistic and perhaps his statement about vigils should be interpreted with caution.

102 The role of urban monastics in the development of a fixed office may be deduced from the table in Suso Frank, ΑΓΓΕΛΙΚΟΣ ΒΙΟΣ: *Begriffsanalytische und begriffsgeschichtliche Untersuchung zum 'engelgleichen Leben' im frühen Mönchtum* (Münster in Westfalen: Aschendorff, 1964), 80–81.

103 'Cum fratribus psalmos in ecclesiae basilica minore diximus' ('we recited psalms with the brethren in the minor basilica of the church'). Ep. 20.24 (CSEL 82: 123; *MECL* 292). Interestingly, Ambrose makes no reference to the novelty that Augustine found so striking. Cf. George Lawless, *Augustine of Hippo and his Monastic Rule* (Oxford: Clarendon Press, 1987), 40: 'Augustine depicts eremitic and cenobitic life without using the words "hermit", "cenobite", "monk", or "monastery". Persons pursuing "so exalted a peak of sanctity" are called "holy men", "brothers", "people who serve god" – words which in this context clearly designate a structured ascetic life.' See *De moribus ecclesiae catholicae* 1.31.66; ed. Coyle, 294–5.

104 Marcellinus had requested a guide to the psalms that he could study while recovering from illness. For the Greek text and a Latin translation see *PG* 27: 11–46; the letter has been translated into English with annotations by Gregg, *Athanasius: The Life of Antony and the Letter to Marcellinus.*

105 Marie-Josèphe Rondeau, 'L'Epître à Marcellinus sur les psaumes', *Vigiliae Christianae*, 22 (1968), 176–97, and ead., *Les Commentaires patristiques du psautier (IIIe–Ve siècles)*, 2 vols. (Rome: Pontificium Institutum Studiorum Orientalium, 1982, 1985), i, 79–80.

106 *Vie* 11, trans. Gregg, 109. Cf. *Vie* 12: 'And it seems to me that these words become like a mirror to the person singing them, so that he might perceive himself and the emotions of his own soul, and thus affected, he might recite them . . . therefore, when someone sings the third psalm, recognizing his own tribulations, he considers the words of the psalm to be his own'; trans. Gregg, 111. Cf. the words of Cassian: 'ita incipiet decantare ut eos [the psalms] non tanquam a propheta compositos, sed velut a se editos, quasi orationem propriam profunde cordis conpunctione depromat, vel certe ad suam personam aestimet eos fuisse directos', *Conf.* 10.11.4; trans. Ramsey, *The Conferences,* 384. See also Dyer, 'The Psalms in Monastic Prayer', *passim.*

107 Letter to Marcellinus 28, *PG* 27: 40; trans. Gregg, 124–5. The Sceptic philosopher had as his goal the achievement of a state of *ataraxia*, a peace of mind not disturbed by conflicting opinions; see Sextus Empiricus, *Against the Musicians*, ed. and trans. Denise Davidson Greaves (Lincoln: University of Nebraska Press, 1986), 17–18.

108 Letter to Marcellinus 28–9, *PG* 27: 39–41; trans. Gregg, 124–5.

109 Letter 27, *PG* 27: 37–40; trans. Gregg, 123. Cf. a statement in the collection known as the *Canons of Basil*: 'Those singing psalms at the altar shall not sing with pleasure' (canon 97; *MECL* 266).

110 Curiously, the same phrase is used by Athanasius to describe how the devil attempted to deceive Antony by 'pretending to sing psalms with melodies' (ψάλλειν μετ' ᾠδῆς); *Vie* 25; SC 400: 204, trans. Gregg, 50.

111 This is perhaps the best-known text reflecting Augustine's anguished uncertainty about the power of music (*Confessions* 10.23.49–50; *MECL* 352): 'a passage unique among the church fathers for its aesthetic introspection'. It is familiar to American students of music history from an excerpt in Donald J. Grout and

Claude V. Palisca, *A History of Western Music* (5th edn, New York: Norton, 1996), 27. The same phrase, attributed to the psalmody of the 'primitiva ecclesia', is repeated by Isidore, *De ecclesiasticis officiis* 1.4; *PL* 83: 742.

112 *De institutione musica* 1.12, ed. Gottfried Friedlein, *Anicii Manlii Torquati Severini Boetii De institutione musica libri duo* ... (Leipzig: B. G. Teubner, 1867), 199; trans. Calvin M. Bower, *The Fundamentals of Music* (New Haven: Yale University Press, 1989), 20; cf. the related passage in 5.6, borrowed from Ptolemy. This chapter uses the term εμμελὴς, also in Athanasius, Letter 28 ('the harmonious reading of the psalms'). See Nicomachus, *Enchiridion* 2, in *Musici scriptores Graeci*, ed. Karl von Jan (Leipzig: Teubner, 1895–9), 238. The same terminology was borrowed by Regino of Prüm, *De harmonica institutione* 9 (*Scriptores*, ed. Gerbert, i, 237). The *Quatuor principalia* (14th c.) also employs Boethius' Latin equivalents: 'vox continua' and 'vox cum intervallo suspensa'; in *Scriptorum de musica medii aevi nova series a Gerbertina altera*, ed. Edmond de Coussemaker, 4 vols. (Paris: Durand, 1864–76), iv, 204.

113 Calvin Bower observes that Albinus, whose works have not survived, is also cited by Cassiodorus (*Institutiones* 2.5.10). The third type is also mentioned in Martianus Capella, *De nuptiis* 9.937.

114 On the office of Cassian's *Institutes* see Taft, *The Liturgy of the Hours*, 96–100, and Dyer, 'Monastic Psalmody', 41–52. For an edition and English translations of the *Institutes* see above, n. 18.

115 *Instit.* 2.5–6; CSEL 17: 21–2; *MECL* 338.

116 'Quidem enim vicenos seu tricenos psalmos et hos ipsos antiphonarum protelatos melodiis et adiunctione quarundam modulationum debere dici singulis noctibus censuerunt.' *Instit.* 2.2; CESL 17: 18; *MECL* 336.

117 ψαλμὸς τὸ τῶν ἀγγέλων ἔργον ... τὸ πνευματικὸν θυμίαμα. *Homilia in psalmum* 1; *PG* 29: 213.

Chapter 3
Monastic Reading and the Emerging Roman Chant Repertory

Peter Jeffery

The Psalmodic Movement

In a series of thoughtful articles,[1] James W. McKinnon outlined the main features of what he calls a 'psalmodic movement' that took place in the early church: 'an unprecedented wave of enthusiasm for the singing of psalms that swept from east to west through the Christian population in the closing decades of the fourth century'.[2] Two kinds of evidence survive to document this movement. Most numerous and often most detailed are the many sermons of the period, authored by the most distinguished bishops and ecclesiastical leaders of the late fourth and early fifth centuries. Less numerous but more diverse are the writings associated with the monasticism of the same period, an emerging new movement that called lay people out of mainstream society into communities of ascetic withdrawal and unceasing prayer. It is a commonplace that, as the conversion of the Roman Empire ended the persecution of Christians, monasticism emerged to replace martyrdom as a model of heroic Christian devotion – and central to this model was psalmody.

From the sermons we learn that the psalms were often sung responsorially; that is, a soloist sang the psalm a verse at a time, and the congregation responded to each verse with a fixed refrain. This was done in a variety of liturgical contexts that probably included the first half of the eucharistic service or Mass, as well as the evening and night services of the Divine Office. But we also learn of a certain ambiguity that pervaded this practice. On the one hand, the responsorial psalms were treated as readings: they had the same status as the liturgical proclamation of other sections of the Bible, so that a sermon could be based on the psalm of the day just as on any other segment of the Old and New Testaments. 'The individual who chanted the psalms was called a *lector* [reader], not a *cantor* [singer], and . . . he was not a professional musician, but rather an adolescent boy, presumably of the pre-clerical state', that is to say a youthful member of the minor order of readers.[3] It is as if reading and psalmody were not clearly distinct activities, and in fact preachers often used words for 'sing', 'say' and 'read' interchangeably.[4] On the other hand, this should not be taken to mean that the psalms were merely read aloud in a speaking voice. Indeed they were musical enough to discomfit the scrupulous: in the famous passage from St. Augustine's autobiographical *Confessions*, he remembered the powerful effect this psalmody had had on him as a new convert, directly addressing God: 'The delight of the ear drew me and held me firmly, but you unbound and liberated me. . . . However, when I recall the tears which I shed at the song of the Church in the first days of my recovered faith . . . I vacillate between the peril of pleasure and the value of the experience', dreading the power of music to move the senses beyond the control of reason, yet recognizing that 'by the pleasure of hearing the weaker soul might be elevated to an attitude of devotion'.[5]

Augustine's remarks are often cited as the paradigmatic example of a uniquely Christian other-worldliness that denied the goodness of natural pleasures, but in fact they owe far more to ancient philosophy than to the thought-world of the Bible. Mistrust of music's emotional power is at least as old as Plato, who would have severely restricted the types of poetry and song available in his ideal republic: musical performances, after all, sprang from inspiration and feeling rather than from reason and learning, and such performances used emotional means to incite audiences to imitate the irrational and immoral behavior of flawed heroes, or of anthropomorphically hedonistic and violent gods.[6] Plato's antipathy was evidently magnified further when Cicero rewrote the *Republic* in Latin; though most of that text is lost, an ancient reader tells us that Cicero 'reviles music and censures it as inferior'.[7] Cicero's more negative attitude would have been shaped by his Stoicism, for the Stoics identified virtue so completely with rationality that they thought 'all the passions' or emotions 'should be completely extirpated from human life', as 'forms of false judgement or false belief'. The Stoic ideal therefore held up 'a picture of the radical detachment of the Stoic sage, the detachment that greets slavery and even torture with equanimity'. As Cicero himself notoriously remarked, a father who receives news that his child has died should respond with a dispassionate, 'I was already aware that I had begotten a mortal'.[8] This radical philosophy had a profound impact on ethical thinking in the late antique world, including Jewish and Christian morality,[9] and Augustine (d. 430), who had been a teacher of rhetoric before becoming a Christian and a bishop, knew his Cicero well.[10] But he came to disapprove of rhetoric for much the same reason he was suspicious of music: as an art that aimed at emotional manipulation, rhetoric could be 'used to give conviction to both truth and falsehood' when practiced outside of a moral framework.[11] In fact Augustine's critique of rhetoric contrasted it specifically with the truth of the psalms.[12]

In spite of all this, Augustine's ultimate acceptance of psalm-singing was not purely pragmatic. Though he recognized the advantages of what his contemporary St. John Chrysostom (d. 407) called 'melody blended with prophecy',[13] Augustine also knew that music and the other arts could draw one upward from a worldly, corporeal reality to a higher, spiritual plane: 'The beauty of the world, like the great song of some ineffable musician, rushes outward into the eternal contemplation of the splendor which is rightly worshiped as God.'[14] Augustine's own sermons are, in fact, the most extensive source of information regarding the psalmody of this period, and in them he makes it very clear that the musical rendition of the psalms was morally acceptable.

> Among all the things that delight, righteousness [*justitia*] itself should delight you more. Not that the other things should not delight, but it should delight more. For certain things naturally delight our weakness, as food and drink delight the hungry and the thirsty; as that light delights which is poured out from heaven by the rising sun, or which shines from the stars and the moon, or which on earth is lit in the lamps that console the darkness of the eyes. A singing voice [*canora vox*] delights, and a most sweet song [*suavissima cantilena*]. A good odor delights; even whatever pertains to some enjoyment of the flesh delights our sense of touch. And of all these things, which delight us in the bodily senses, some are lawful. For these great spectacles of nature delight the eyes, as I said, but the spectacles of the theaters also delight the eyes. The former are lawful, the latter unlawful. A sacred psalm sweetly sung [*Psalmus sacer suaviter cantatus*] delights the hearing, but the songs [*cantica*] of the actors also delight the hearing – the former lawfully, the latter unlawfully. Flowers and aromas and such creations of God delight the sense of smell, but the incense offerings on the altars of demons also delight the sense of smell – the former lawfully, the latter unlawfully. . . . Let righteousness delight, so that it may conquer even the lawful delights, and prefer righteousness to that delight in which you delight lawfully.[15]

It was McKinnon who first pointed out that the late fourth-century enthusiasm for musical psalmody was contemporaneous with the late fourth-century enthusiasm for monasticism, and he sought to connect the two. 'The defining characteristic of monasticism at this time was psalmody; no invocation of the monastic way of life could fail to mention it', he wrote. 'Monastic psalmody had an overwhelming effect upon the Church in the later decades of the fourth century' as 'monastic spirituality became the standard for the church as a whole'.[16] The monastic literature on early psalmody seems to describe a wide range of liturgical usages and psalmodic practices, some associated with the individual exercises of particular solitaries or hermits, others with the cenobitic communities that flourished in the Egyptian desert. Though the practices were hardly uniform, they at least shared the basic principles governing what modern liturgical historians call the 'monastic office': the biblical ideal of 'unceasing prayer', expressed in a daily round of services with the recitation of long series of psalms, and an austere, ascetic approach suitable for those who had fled the world, eschewed clerical ordination, and embraced poverty.[17] However, in the cities of the late Roman empire, beginning perhaps in Syria and Cappadocia, there were also communities of 'urban monks' who, while accepting the same principles, also participated in and helped to shape the worship of the ordinary townspeople, what liturgiologists call the 'cathedral office'. The ideals of this type of worship were somewhat different: it was performed by ordained clergy and lay people in a hierarchical relationship, in contrast to the rough egalitarianism of early monasticism, originally a lay movement. And instead of aspiring to 'unceasing prayer', this type of worship emphasized the divisions of time: the daily alternation of light and darkness, the weekly recurrence of the Lord's Day (Sunday), the annual feasts of the liturgical year.[18]

But the monastic and cathedral approaches to worship were already interacting and even merging in the fourth century. Thus McKinnon went beyond pointing out circumstantial coincidences, by making two more specific proposals: the psalmodic movement may have begun when the offices of urban monks began to be admired and attended by the general public, so that monastic psalmody inspired congregational psalmody. More particularly, there may have been a kind of cross-fertilization when the two kinds of offices, monastic and cathedral, came into closest proximity with 'the rise of the popular psalmodic vigil',[19] celebrated through much of the night, leading into the early morning service of Lauds at dawn. Such services, with both monks and laity participating, are described for example by Egeria, the Latin pilgrim whose account of her stay in Jerusalem details the entire liturgical year celebrated there in AD 383.

> Each day before cockcrow, all the doors of the Anastasis [i.e., the Church of the Holy Sepulchre] are opened, and all the *monazontes* [i.e., monks] and *parthenae* [i.e., nuns], as they are called here, come down, and not only they, but also those lay people, men and women, who wish to keep vigil at so early an hour. From that hour until it is light, hymns are sung [*dicuntur*] and psalms responded to, and likewise antiphons; and with every hymn there is a prayer.

A few priests and deacons were on hand to say the prayers 'with every hymn and antiphon', but it was only at dawn, when 'they start to sing the morning hymns', that the bishop arrived with the rest of the clergy to begin the cathedral office.[20]

The Spread of Responsorial Psalmody

The practices of Jerusalem were widely respected and imitated, so that the Holy City probably had a role in the dissemination of monastic–congregational psalmody.[21] At any rate, the geographic and chronological progression of the 'psalmodic movement' can be plotted to some extent, showing a mid-fourth-century origin in the East, and a late fourth-century expansion to the West. 'There is a traceable chronology in these events that enables one to observe the enthusiasm for psalmodic vigils moving from East to West in the 370s and 380s.'[22] Apparent references to psalmody and psalmodic vigils appear by the mid-fourth century in writings of St. Athanasius of Alexandria (ca. 296–373),[23] though the musicality of the performances seems still to have been somewhat restrained. It is difficult to evaluate the historical accuracy of the rumor that, Augustine reported, 'was often told me concerning Athanasius, bishop of Alexandria, who required the reader of the psalm to perform it with so little inflection of voice that it was closer to speaking than to singing'.[24] It may be simply a conflation of two historical memories: (1) that musical psalm performance had developed relatively recently, mostly after Athanasius' death in 373, and (2) that Athanasius, through his promotion of monastic spirituality, was nonetheless one of the original figures in the psalmodic movement, even if its development toward more musical performances came after his time. In fact Athanasius was also the author of what is arguably the first major treatise on the uses of the psalms in Christian worship and life, his 'Epistle to Marcellinus on the Interpretation of the Psalms'.[25] Along with much general information on the reasons for reading the psalms, the Epistle includes long lists identifying specific psalms for use on particular occasions – lists that could easily have been expanded into a primitive liturgical book. Thus the work stands as a preface to the earliest copy of a liturgical psalter, in the Codex Alexandrinus, one of the oldest manuscripts of the complete Bible in Greek.[26] The Book of Psalms in this fifth-century codex must have been copied from an early psalter for liturgical use, because it is supplied not only with Athanasius' preface but with other protoliturgical material: an appendix of fourteen odes or canticles, including an early text of the *Gloria in excelsis Deo*;[27] a list of psalms to recite at each of the twenty-four hours of the day, according to an Egyptian monastic form of the Divine Office; and a list of 150 titles providing Christian interpretations for each the psalms, ascribed to Eusebius, the fourth-century church historian.[28]

A generation later, we can witness the spread of the psalmodic movement to Asia Minor, in the writings of the Cappadocian fathers. Sermons of St. Basil the Great (ca. 330–79) and St. Gregory of Nazianzus (329/30–389/90) refer to psalmody in conjunction with biblical readings, and during night vigils.[29] Basil's brother, St. Gregory of Nyssa (ca. 330–ca. 395), seems at first to have had little awareness of the psalmodic movement, for in his youthful, probably unfinished treatise on the titles of the Psalms, he makes comparisons with the music of the spheres and the singing of the heavenly host, but alludes only briefly to actual singing by Christian congregations.[30] Yet he too left us sermons that quote from liturgical psalmody,[31] and his life of St. Macrina (ca. 327–80), his and Basil's sister, describes the psalmody of the family monastery in which she lived her life.[32] In fact the most detailed written description of a monastic psalmody vigil up to that time describes the practice of this very community. It occurs in a letter that Basil wrote in 375 to the clergy of Neocaesarea (modern Niksar near the Black Sea), defending their monastery in Cappadocia (farther south in eastern Turkey) against a charge of innovation. After outlining recognizable examples of responsorial, direct and even alternating or antiphonal psalmody, Basil insists that these practices 'are in full accord and harmony with all the churches of God', but mentions only places to the south and east: Egypt, north Africa, Palestine, Syria, Arabia, and Babylon (= modern Iraq). Psalmody like this was not in use, it would seem, in Neocaesarea to the north (where Basil's critics lived), or even in Constantinople to the west, to say nothing of the Latin-speaking world.[33] Indeed Athanasius' Western contemporary, St. Hilary of Poitiers (ca. 315–367/8), seems as yet untouched by the new kind of psalmody, though he himself was a composer of hymns.[34]

One important episode in the spread of responsorial psalmody to the West is dramatically described by Augustine himself. His autobiographical *Confessions*, written about the year 397, dates the adoption of Eastern-style psalmody in Milan to about 386, a year before he was baptized by St. Ambrose, the bishop of Milan. Ambrose and his flock had barricaded themselves in the church of St. Lawrence in the city, to prevent the troops of the Arian empress Justina from forcibly returning it to her recently expelled co-religionists. Anxious and sleepless, Ambrose's embattled followers evidently spent the night singing 'hymns and psalms . . . after the manner of the Eastern regions, lest the people be worn out with the tedium of sorrow [*maeroris taedio*]. The practice has been retained from that time until today and imitated by many, indeed by almost all [Christian] congregations throughout the rest of the world'.[35] Though there is no detailed description of the new practice in this famous passage, a later passage in the *Confessions* describes both the singing of a responsorial psalm and a recollection of one of Ambrose's hymns.[36]

Ambrose's own account of the same event is more laconic: 'That entire day was spent in our sorrow', he wrote to his sister shortly afterward, using the same word as Augustine (*maeror*) to describe the sorrowful mood. 'I was not able to return home, because soldiers surrounded the basilica, keeping it under guard. We recited [*diximus*] psalms with the brethren in the lesser basilica of the church',[37] suggesting that the congregation simply joined in with the nocturnal monastic psalmody that 'the brethren' would have been performing anyway. A sermon that Ambrose delivered during these events, quoted in the same letter to his sister, actually cites one of the responsorial refrains the congregation had sung: 'At the morning office, as you will recall, brethren, there was read [*lectum est*] what we sing in response [*respondemus*] with great sorrow of spirit: "O God, the heathen have come into thy inheritance".' (Ps. 78: 1 [79: 1]).[38] Relating the refrain text to the particular occasion, Ambrose interpreted the 'heathen' (*gentes* or 'nations') as the mercenary soldiers of the imperial army, ethnically Gothic and doctrinally Arian, who had surrounded the building in which he was then preaching. Another of Ambrose's sermons from this episode mentions the stirring effect of his own metrical hymns: 'They also say that the people are led astray by the charms of my hymns. Certainly; I do not deny it.'[39]

Ambrose's words do not imply that any dramatic innovations were just taking place, as Augustine recalled. Yet detailed study of Ambrose's entire corpus of writings seems to indicate that none of his many references to congregational responsorial psalmody need be dated before 386.[40] The fact that another letter of Ambrose quotes a psalm refrain in Greek may be a further suggestion of the Eastern origin of responsorial practice.[41] While Augustine's recollection, therefore, was entwined with his memory of a highly emotional moment that happened to coincide with his own experience of conversion and preparation for baptism, Ambrose's more sober account is consistent with the more general trend perceived by McKinnon: a new type of psalmody that was gradually working its way west through many channels. As a major stopover on the pilgrim itinerary to and from Jerusalem, Milan was well positioned to be a key center for the Western diffusion of Eastern psalmody.[42]

The Legacy of the Psalmodic Movement

But if Augustine is our chief witness to the western spread of the new psalmody, he also seems to represent its historical peak. After him, sermons referring to liturgical psalmody peter out. In a thorough search of Augustine's extant sermons, McKinnon found nineteen that unequivocally or probably quote the refrains of responsorial psalms that had been sung at the same service, shortly before the sermon was delivered, though only rarely can we tell whether this service was a morning Mass or Eucharist, an evening Office or Vespers, or a late-night vigil. Many more sermons refer to psalmody less explicitly, so that the full dossier of evidence consists of over 150 sermons citing over half the psalms.[43] Augustine's ample testimony is supported by the sermons of other Western preachers of roughly the same period, who died in the first decades of the fifth century: the bishops St. Chromatius of Aquileia (d. 407), St. Nicetas of Remesiana (r. 370–ca. 414), and St. Maximus of Turin (d. between 408 and 423), as well as the priest St. Jerome, who headed a Latin-speaking monastery in Bethlehem from 386 to his death (419–20).[44] With the passing of this generation, however, enthusiasm for the practice seems to have begun to wane. Congregational responsorial psalmody is mentioned less often in the sermons of the next generation, though preachers like St. Peter Chrysologus of Ravenna (d. ca. 450)[45] and Pope St. Leo the Great at Rome (see below) testify that it did continue toward mid-century. By the sixth century, sermons referring to liturgical psalmody have become rare, and after the sixth century they cease altogether. That is why, even when texts known to have been sung in the fourth century re-emerge in the medieval chant repertories, it is usually not possible to document uninterrupted usage all the way back to the fourth century.

The responsorial psalm readings of Augustine's eucharistic service bear an obvious resemblance to the Gregorian genre known as the Gradual or *responsum gradale*, and to homologous forms in other traditions such as the Byzantine prokeimenon. All were performed in close proximity to the epistle, Gospel and sermon, and a small but significant minority of psalm texts cited in the fourth- and fifth-century sermons actually reappear as Graduals in the medieval chant sources. For at least one, Psalm 117 [118] with the refrain *Haec dies* (from verse 24), there is a nearly continuous record of evidence attesting to its use at Easter Mass, from Augustine's time down to the notated medieval sources. For this text and a few others, the diverse medieval traditions share certain similarities of mode and melodic shape, suggesting relationships to a common melodic antecedent.[46] But despite such intriguing cases of apparent continuity, McKinnon prudently warned that often 'there is a powerful argument for discontinuity. . . . In Augustine's sermons we witness no more than the uncertain beginnings of a tendency to associate the same epistle, psalm or Gospel with a particular date in the liturgical year. The liturgical year itself was in an embryonic state.'[47]

Even more problematic are questions about how the psalmody of Augustine's generation may have been related to other genres of medieval chant. For instance, McKinnon found it hard to see how the Gregorian Alleluias could have derived from responsorial psalms, even though there is evidence that the word 'alleluia' was commonly used as a responsorial psalm-refrain.[48] Other Mass chants of apparently responsorial origin – the Tract, the Offertory[49] and the Communion[50] – pose difficult questions of their own. Even less explored is whether the responsorial psalmody of the fourth-century

Vespers and vigils may be related to the great responsories of medieval Matins, and such alleged Eastern counterparts as the Byzantine kathismata and hypakoai.[51]

Thus we are faced with a major historical difficulty. As the original fervor of the psalmodic movement waned, it seems, so do the primary sources describing psalmody:

> By the middle of the fifth century all the great church fathers had passed from the scene and with them the flow of commentary on liturgical chant. . . . This is true of the West especially, where there is a gap in the sources corresponding roughly to the period of the so-called Dark Ages. Monastic rules such as St Benedict's great exemplar constitute something of an exception; they provide us with an outline of the monastic office, but we must await the beginning of the eighth century and the *Ordines Romani* for similar information on the Roman Mass. This interim period – broadly considered that extending from the patristic period to the Carolingians – is one of special challenge to the music historian.[52]

This historical 'gap in the sources' is the main subject of the present article. Just prior to the gap we have the psalmodic movement, with congregations, apparently inspired by monasticism, singing responsorial refrains to psalms that can also be preached upon as readings. Yet when the familiar medieval chant repertories emerge about the eighth century, chants are clearly a distinct genre separate from the readings, performed by a clerical schola, seemingly with less involvement from the congregation. How do we trace the transition from one to the other?

One popular response has been outright skepticism. In the mid-twentieth century, a generation of scholars argued forcefully that, in fact, there was little if any real continuity: that Gregorian chant as we know it from medieval sources actually represented a decline or departure from the original populist ideal of the psalmodic movement. Surely the old congregational music must have been simple, a kind of folk song that scarcely resembled the highly melismatic Graduals of Gregorian chant. And surely the processes that created the melismatic choral chants represented a turning away from the popular songs we read about in Augustine's sermons, in the direction of a regrettable medieval vogue for 'virtuosity'. At a time when many in the church were calling for an *aggiornamento* with the modern world – a world marked by unprecedented levels of literacy and the expansion of democratic political systems – it was natural to call for a return to the apparently more popular and inclusive psalmody of Augustine's time: this, as much as the change from Latin to vernacular, became the justification for the general abandonment of Gregorian chant in modern Catholic worship, in favor of the 'folk Mass' and other experiments that mimic contemporary pop culture.[53]

Influential as this skeptical answer was, it was never actually tied to specific times and places by means of documented historical research. Such a thing seemed hardly possible in view of the chronological gap McKinnon pointed out. Yet there is a pathway through the darkness, a direct developmental line from the popular psalmody of the fourth century to the liturgical choir of the eighth. To find it, one must resist the temptation to impose modern agendas on the past, and look instead at the ideal of psalmody itself. We must ask, that is to say, what the promoters and practitioners of psalmody in the fourth century and later thought its essential purposes were. Following their testimony across the centuries, we can observe changing approaches to the reading of texts that take us through a series of dichotomies: (1) An original tension between 'psalm as reading' and 'psalm as song' grew into an exegetical confrontation, as an early tradition of studying the psalms as allegorical 'history' conflicted with a monastic approach to the psalm as an ethical 'mirror' reflecting the individual soul. (2) After centuries of pressure from the Christian intelligentsia, the old pedagogy based on Homer, Vergil and the literature of classical antiquity gave way to a new Christian curriculum, in which the Psalter was the first text used to teach beginning readers. But at the same time, with the social and political collapse of the Roman world, literacy itself became more difficult to acquire, and thus more restricted to monastic and clerical contexts. The composition of new sermons became rare, and the older sermons became holy writings themselves, collected into anthologies both for delivery by preachers and for private study by monastics. (3) This led to a situation in which learning to read the psalms became an essential part of monastic and clerical formation, with the result that the Psalter was perceived as a model or training ground for individual prayer (humans addressing God), distinct from the rest of the Bible, which only invited or provoked a prayerful response (God addressing humans). As a result, daily chanting of the psalms became a monastic and clerical obligation, of a completely different character from the readings of the rest of the Bible. Psalmody became an activity distinct from liturgical reading, and sermons no longer made reference to the psalm texts. That is why the history of liturgical chant after the fifth century cannot be traced through sermons. Instead, we will have to turn to other types of sources, some of which have rarely or never been employed in musicological research.

The Ideals of the Psalmodic Movement

Remarkably, those who looked back to fourth-century psalmody as an ideal to be recovered in the twentieth century rarely made much of a text that, prima facie, would have strongly supported their case, for it insists that the participation of the lay congregation is mandatory. This is an apocryphal work known as the 'Vision of St. Paul' (*Visio Pauli*), purporting to describe the Apostle's journey through Heaven and Hell (cf. 1 Cor. 12: 1–5). The work probably dates from the year 388, and thus to the period of the psalmodic movement; it is so deeply rooted in the thought-world of Athanasius and early monasticism that the author seems likely to have been 'a Greek-speaking Pachomian monk from a monastery near Alexandria'.[54] In fact the text seems to have been particularly popular among monks,[55] and it was even cited in Latin in the sixth-century monastic Rule of the Master, written within the Roman orbit and a major source of the classic Rule of St. Benedict.[56]

In the *Visio*, said to be one of the sources of Dante's *Divine Comedy*,[57] Paul is shown encountering many Old Testament figures, and there is a lot of singing throughout. But the anonymous author's views on music become most explicit in his description of King David. In chapter 28, the writer associates psalm-singing with the ethical life, perhaps even the monastic life. In the first part of chapter 29, an even more glorious place is awarded to those unlettered individuals who, not knowing the Bible or the psalms, behaved in accordance with what they had heard, seemingly in the liturgical readings and psalmody. Beginning with the paragraph I will here call 29b, the traveler sees David himself leading a responsorial Alleluia in Jerusalem, and is told that the Mass is never to be celebrated without psalmody, the earthly shadow of this heavenly worship. After some bogus Hebrew etymologies that stand in their own long tradition,[58] the angelic guide condemns those who are present at psalmody but do not join in,[59] mercifully exempting those who are prevented by age or infirmity:

> 28. And again he carried me near the river of oil on the east of the city. And I saw there men rejoicing and singing psalms, and I said, 'Who are those, my lord?' And the angel said to me, 'These are they who devoted themselves to God with their whole heart and had no pride in themselves. For all those who rejoice in the Lord God and sing psalms to the Lord with their whole heart are here led into this city.' 29. And he carried me into the midst of the city near the twelve walls. . . . And turning round I saw golden thrones placed in each gate, and on them men having golden diadems and gems; and I looked and I saw inside between the twelve men thrones placed in another rank which appeared to be of greater glory, so that no one is able to recount their praise. And I asked the angel and said, 'My lord, who is on the throne [*sic*]?' And the angel answered and said to me, 'Those thrones belong to those who had goodness and understanding of heart, yet made themselves fools for the sake of the Lord God, as they knew neither Scripture nor psalms, but mindful of one chapter of the commands of God, and hearing what it contained, they acted with much diligence and had a true zeal before the Lord God, and the admiration of them will seize all the saints in the presence of the Lord God, for talking with one another they say, "Wait and see how these unlearned men who know nothing more have merited so great and beautiful a garment and so great glory on account of their innocence."'
>
> [29b.] And I saw in the midst of this city a great altar, very high, and there was someone standing near the altar whose countenance shone as the sun, and he held in his hands a psaltery and harp, and he sang saying, 'Alleluia!' And his voice filled the whole city; at the same time, when all they who were on the towers and gates heard him, they responded, 'Alleluia!' so that the foundations of the city were shaken; and I asked the angel and said, 'Sir, who is this of so great power?' And the angel said to me, 'This is David; this is the city of Jerusalem, for when Christ the King of Eternity shall come with the assurance of his kingdom, he again shall go before him that he may sing psalms, and all the righteous at the same time shall sing responding "Alleluia!"' And I said, 'Sir, how did David alone above the other saints make a beginning of psalm-singing?' And the angel answered and said to me, 'Because Christ the Son of God sits at the right hand of his Father, and this David sings psalms before him in the seventh heaven, and as it is done in the heavens so also below, because a sacrifice may not be offered to God without David, but it is necessary that David should sing psalms in the hour of the oblation of the body and blood of Christ: as it is performed in heaven, so also on earth.' 30. And I said to the angel, 'Sir, what is Alleluia?' And the angel answered and

said to me, 'You ask questions about everything.' And he said to me, 'Alleluia is Hebrew, the language of God and angels, for the meaning of Alleluia is this: *tecel cat marith macha*.' And I said, 'Sir, what is *tecel cat marith macha*?' And the angel answered and said to me, '*Tecel cat marith macha* is: Let us all bless him together.' I asked the angel and said, 'Sir, do all who say Alleluia bless the Lord?' And the angel answered and said to me, 'It is so, and if any one sing Alleluia and those who are present do not sing at the same time, they commit sin because they do not sing along with him.' And I said, 'My lord, does he also sin if he be hesitating or very old?' And the angel answered and said to me, 'Not so, but he who is able and does not join in the singing you know as a despiser of the Word, and it would be proud and unworthy that he should not bless the Lord God his maker.'[60]

Immediately afterward, the Apostle and his mentor depart for a tour of the infernal regions, with their terrifying array of eternal punishments.

Why was psalmody so important that it was a sin for those present to refrain from joining in? If we recall the likely monastic background of the rigorist author, we can look for an answer to St. Athanasius, the patriarch of Alexandria who was one of the original promoters of the monastic movement. According to his 'Letter to Marcellinus on the Interpretation of the Psalms', the Psalter was unlike the rest of the Bible, in that its words could be applied directly to oneself:

And furthermore, there is also this paradox in the Psalms: In the other books [of the Bible], what the saints say, and what [the books] may say about them – these things readers apply to those about whom they are written. Likewise, those who listen [to the Bible being read] consider themselves different from those about whom the Word speaks, so that they come to imitate the deeds that are told only to the extent of marveling and desiring to emulate them. By contrast, however, he who takes up this book [i.e., the Psalter] goes through the prophecies about the Savior with admiration and adoration, as is customary in the other Scriptures. But the other psalms he reads as being his own words. And the one who hears [rather than reads] assents as if he himself were speaking, and is sympathetically affected by the words of the songs [ᾠδῶν] as if they were his own. . . . No one would ever utter the words of the patriarchs as his own, nor would anyone dare to imitate and to say Moses' own words. . . . Indeed it is clear that one who reads the [other biblical] books utters the words not as his own, but as the words of the saints and those who are presented in the text. But contrariwise, the paradox: apart from the prophecies about the Savior and the nations, he who says the Psalms is uttering the rest as his own words, and each sings [ψάλλει] them as if they were written about him, and he accepts them and goes through them not as if another were speaking, nor as if signifying about someone else. But he handles them as if he is speaking about himself. . . .

And it seems to me, that to the one singing (ψάλλοντι) these [psalms], it becomes like a mirror, so that in them he might perceive both himself and the emotions (κινήματα) of his soul, and thus affected, he might recite (ἀπαγγέλλειν) them. For in fact he who hears the reader receives the song that is said (λεγομένην τὴν ᾠδὴν) as being about him, and either convicted by his conscience, being pierced (κατανυγεὶς), he will repent, or, hearing of hope in God, and of the succor available to believers – how this kind of grace exists for him – he exults and begins to give thanks to God. Therefore, when someone sings the third psalm, [for example,] recognizing his own tribulations, he considers the words in the psalm to be his own . . .[61]

Thus the psalms, like no other book of the Bible, offered a unique opportunity to read oneself into the Scriptures, and this made psalmody ideally suited to promote the more personal and heartfelt spirituality that monasticism promoted. This monastic way of reading or hearing the psalms as a 'mirror' in which to see oneself, however, contrasted with a different tradition of interpretation that was already old, and had deeper roots in late antique hermeneutical techniques. The older approach involved ascribing the words of the psalms, not to oneself, but to one of the characters in the Bible. Thus the exegete's task began with identifying the speaker of each passage in the text. St. Hilary of Poitiers, Athanasius' Western contemporary who had not yet encountered the psalmodic movement, describes this method at the beginning of his psalm commentary:

> The first thing in understanding the psalms is to be able to discern by what person, or about whom, one should understand the things which may be said. For the makeup [of the Psalms] is not uniform and undifferentiated, as if they didn't have diverse authors and genres. For we frequently find that the person of God the Father is accustomed to be represented in them, as in the eighty-eighth psalm when it says: 'I exalted a chosen one from my people. I have found David my servant, in holy oil I have anointed him. He has invoked me, "You are my father and the guardian of my salvation." And I will put him, my firstborn, on high above the kings of the world' (Ps. 88: 20–21, 27–8 [89: 19–20, 26–7]). But [we find] the person of the Son introduced almost as much, as in the seventeenth: 'A people that I have not known has served me' (Ps. 17: 45 [18: 44]), and in the twenty-first: 'They have divided my garments among them and for my clothing they cast lots' (Ps. 21: 19 [22: 18]).
>
> But now the same principle teaches that this first psalm cannot be understood either from the person of the Father or from the person of the Son: 'But in the law of the Lord was his will and in his law he will meditate day and night' (Ps. 1: 2). . . . But indeed now when it says 'But in the law of the Lord was his will', no person of the [Trinity] is shown speaking of himself, but rather [someone] preaching the blessedness of another [person], namely of him – that is of the man – whose will is in the law of the Lord. Therefore the person of the prophet [David], in whose mouth the Holy Spirit speaks, is now to be recognized, teaching us through the ministry of his mouth to recognize a spiritual sacrament.[62]

This approach has been dubbed 'prosopological exegesis' by one modern scholar, after the Greek word that originally meant 'face', then 'mask', then 'character in a drama'.[63] Its first major exponent was the third-century exegete Origen, in many respects the founder of Christian biblical studies. Origen himself was heavily indebted to older Alexandrian methods of textual study, which had been developed by both Jewish and non-Christian gentile writers.[64] But the roots of prosopological interpretation can already be found in the New Testament, where a variety of Old Testament passages are put forward as predictions or foreshadowings of the Christ to come.[65] Athanasius' approach may have been somewhat new, on the other hand, at least in its emphasis on the psalms. When the mirror simile was used in the New Testament, it was applied to the Bible as a whole:

For if someone is a hearer of the word and not a doer, he is like a man who observes the face he was born with in a mirror; for he observes himself and goes away, and immediately he forgets what he was like. But one who peers into the perfect law, the law of freedom, and perseveres – being not a hearer who forgets but a doer who acts – he will be blessed in what he does.[66]

If additional polysyllabic neologisms were desirable, we might dub the practice of seeing oneself in the Scriptures 'eisoptrological exegesis' (from the Greek word for 'mirror') in contrast to 'prosopological exegesis'. But in fact it was not the mirror metaphor that dominated early writings on the monastic approach to the psalms. What early monastic authors emphasized was the reader's emotional reaction to seeing his own reflection: *compunctio* – the prick of conscience or sting of remorse that one should feel on seeing one's sinful state revealed in the inspired text. As Athanasius put it, 'convicted by his conscience, being pierced, he will repent'. We can read more about this in the work of St. John Cassian (d. ca. 433), the leading Western monastic writer of Augustine's generation, and thus a contemporary of the psalmodic movement:

But it is, I say, largely up to us whether the character of our thoughts improves and whether either holy and spiritual thoughts, or earthly and carnal ones, increase in our hearts. Therefore we practice the frequent reading of and constant meditation on Scripture, so that we may be open to a spiritual point of view. For this reason we frequently chant the psalms [*idcirco decantatio crebra psalmorum*], so that we may continually grow in compunction. For this reason we are diligent in vigils, fasting, and praying, so that the mind which has been stretched to its limits may not taste earthly things but contemplate heavenly ones. When these things cease because negligence has crept in again, then, it is inevitable that the mind, by the accumulated filth of the vices, will soon turn in a carnal direction and fall.[67]

One can perceive an ascending sequence in this passage, beginning with 'frequent reading of and constant meditation on Scripture', moving to 'frequently chanting the psalms', leading to more intense 'vigils, fasting, and praying'. That these represent three points on a continuum can be seen from the word Cassian used for 'chanting', *decanto*. It can mean simply 'sing', but it can also refer to recitation or monotonous, droning repetition, such as we might call 'singsong' in English.[68] Cassian's choice of this word thus reminds us that the psalms were, first of all, a favorite section of the Scriptures, which the monk studied Latin diligently in order to read, and endlessly repeated in order to memorize. This experience by itself could lead to the next step of feeling compunction, and onward from there to the state of prayer:

... Taking into himself all the dispositions of the psalms, [the monk] will begin to repeat them [*decantare*] and to treat them in his profound compunction of heart, not as if they were composed by the prophet [David], but as if they were his own utterances and his own prayer. Certainly he will consider that they are directed to his own person, and he will recognize that their words were not only achieved by and in the prophet in times past, but that they are daily borne out and fulfilled in [the monk himself] ... When we have the same disposition in our heart with which each psalm was sung or written down [*decantatus uel conscriptus*], then we shall become like its author, grasping its significance beforehand rather than afterward. That is, we first take in the [emotional] power [*uirtutem*] of what is said, rather than the [intellectual] knowledge [*notitiam*] of it, recalling what has taken place or what does take place in us in daily assaults [of temptation] whenever we reflect on them. When we repeat them [*decantantes*] we call to mind what our negligence has begotten in us, or our diligence has obtained for us, or divine providence has bestowed upon us, or the enemy's [i.e., Satan's] suggestion has deprived us of, or slippery and subtle forgetfulness has taken away from us, or human weakness has brought upon us, or heedless ignorance has concealed from us. For we find all of these dispositions expressed in the psalms, so that we may see whatever occurs as in a very clear mirror and recognize it more effectively. Having been instructed in this way, with our dispositions for our teachers, we shall grasp this as something seen [for ourselves] rather than [merely] heard [about], and from the inner disposition of the heart we shall bring forth not what has been committed to memory but what is inborn in the very nature of things. Thus we shall penetrate its meaning not through the written text [*textu lectionis*] but with experience leading the way. So it is that our mind will arrive at that incorruptible prayer . . . [that] is not only not laid hold of by the sight of some image, but [that] cannot even be grasped by any word or phrase. Rather, once the mind's attentiveness has been set ablaze, it is called forth in an unspeakable ecstasy of heart and with an insatiable gladness of spirit, and the mind, having transcended all feelings and visible matter, pours it out to God with unutterable groans and sighs.[69]

Yet it would be a mistake to think that Cassian had in mind nothing more than the rote drill of the classroom. For the truly musical rendition of the monastic office could also contribute to motivating compunction, going beyond the effect of the words alone:

But who, endowed with whatever experience, could satisfactorily explain the very different types of compunction, with their origins and causes, by which the mind, ardent and enkindled, is moved to pure and fervent prayers? By way of example we shall propose a few of these to the extent that, with the Lord's illumination, we are able to recall them at present. Sometimes, while we have been singing [*decantantibus nobis*], the verse of some psalm has offered the occasion for fiery prayer. Now and then the melodious modulation of a brother's voice [*canora fraterna uocis modulatio*] has excited insensible minds to intense prayer. We know as well that the distinction and gravity of the cantor [*distinctionem grauitatemque psallentis*] have contributed a great deal to the fervor of those in attendance.[70]

The words of the psalm, the melody of a brother's voice, the prestige and moral example of the song leader – all can excite the feeling of compunction that leads to prayer. How different from Augustine's ambivalence over the emotional impact of music! And clearly the monk Cassian, like the bishop Augustine, heard the psalms performed with genuine musicality, not merely spoken recitation.

Was Cassian unusual in this respect? There is after all a tradition, at least in Greek monastic literature, that monks rejected musicality and ecclesiastical hymns as obstacles to *katanuxis* (the Greek word for 'compunction').[71] But recent research has nuanced the traditional view: the sources tend to be of late or doubtful date, so that the anecdotes and sayings cannot be securely ascribed to the individuals who are said to have uttered or occasioned them. Moreover, the monks to whom such opinions are attributed were of the most rigorously ascetic type, the anchorites or solitaries of the desert, not the cenobites who lived in monastic communities. As the Rule of the Master makes clear, anchoritic monasticism was the most advanced form, suitable only for those who had gained many years of experience in a monastery as cenobites.[72] And the anchorites who are recorded as rejecting hymnody were motivated by multiple concerns, upholding an ideal of psalmody as the unending, solitary recitation of scriptural texts by laymen who eschewed ordination and had departed civic life for the desert. It was not simply to music, but to the entire complex of the 'cathedral office' that they objected, with its hierarchy of ordained personnel, its non-scriptural hymns and chants, its choirs and congregational song. But though these heroes of renunciation spoke for the whole monastic movement, their prescriptions cannot be assumed to apply to all monasteries, particularly those urban communities that participated in the liturgical life of the cities.[73] Cassian too was aware that, among the many divergent arrangements for the night office that he knew of, there were 'some persons who have felt it appropriate each night to recite twenty or thirty psalms – and these prolonged with the tunes of antiphons and the addition of certain melodies'. But his objection was not that these performances were too musical, or even too long, only that they did not correspond to the Egyptian model that Cassian himself advocated.[74]

The psalmodic movement, then – that is the surge of popularity for psalm-singing in the late fourth and early fifth centuries – was motivated not only by monastic practices, but by a monastic way of reading the psalms, applying them to oneself as if looking into a mirror. This collided with the 'prosopological' approach that bishop preachers had already been using, in which psalm passages were interpreted by identifying the speaker with a biblical personage – God, Jesus, David, etc. – like characters in a drama.

The tension between these two types of exegesis found its ideal synthesis in the greatest preacher of the age, the most important witness to the psalmodic movement itself, St. Augustine. In dozens of sermons on the psalms, Augustine combined both types of exegesis, utilizing the Pauline doctrine of the Church as the mystical body of Christ: the belief that the united community of all Christians forms a corporate entity of which Christ is the spiritual head: 'For just as the body is one and has many members, and all the members of the body, though many, are one body, so it is with Christ. . . . Now you are the body of Christ and individually members of it.'[75] Therefore Augustine understood the Psalter as expressing 'the whole Christ [*totus Christus*]'. In other words, it could be interpreted as referring both to the individual figure of Jesus and to the body of believers assembled in his Church:[76]

> Certainly, we have sung [*cantavimus*] this: 'I will extol you, Lord, for you have upheld me, nor have you let my enemies rejoice over me' (Ps. 29: 2 [30: 1]). If we have learned from the Holy Scriptures who our enemies may be, we recognize the truth of this song [*cantici*]. But if the prudence of the flesh deceives us, so that we

> no longer recognize those against whom we are in contention (cf. Eph. 6: 12), [then] we find in the very opening lines of this psalm a question we cannot solve. For whose voice do we suppose is it that praises God and gives thanks and exults and says: 'I will extol you, Lord, for you have upheld me, nor have you let my enemies rejoice over me'? First let us consider [that it is] the Lord himself, who, since he deigned to become human, was able to apply these words to himself, not unfittingly, as a prophetic foretelling. Since he was human, he was also weak; since he was weak, he was also someone who prayed. For what we have just heard, when the Gospel was read, was how he withdrew from his disciples even into the desert, to which they followed after him and found him. But having withdrawn, 'he was praying there', and it was said by the disciples who found him, 'People are looking for you'. But he responded, 'Let us go preach in other places and towns, because this is what I came for' (Mark 1: 35–8). . . .
>
> Perhaps this voice is not that of our Lord Jesus Christ, but that of mankind itself, of the universal Church of the Christian people, because in Christ all men are one man, and the unity of Christians is one man. Perhaps it is this man, that is the unity of Christians itself, that says, 'I will extol you, Lord, for you have upheld me, nor have you let my enemies rejoice over me.' But [if it is] about them [i.e., all Christians], how is it true? Are not the Apostles included [in the unity of all Christians]? Are not those [also included] who were cut down, are not those who were whipped, are not those who were killed, are not those who were crucified, are not those who were burned alive, not those who fought against beasts, [the martyrs] whose memories we celebrate? But when people did these things to them, did they not rejoice over them? How is it, therefore, that even the Christian people are able to say: 'I will extol you, Lord, for you have upheld me, nor have you let my enemies rejoice over me'?
>
> We shall understand this if we first see the title of the psalm. For it has: 'Unto the end, a psalm of a canticle, at the dedication of the house, of David himself' (Ps. 29: 1 [30: title]). In this title is the entire hidden meaning, and all hope of resolving this question. The house that is now being built will be dedicated at some future time. For now the house – that is the Church – is being built; afterward it will be dedicated. At [that] dedication will appear the glory of the Christian people, which is now hidden. Now enemies rage . . . Job was tried; the devil was confuted. . . . The martyrs were killed, but judged themselves to have conquered [their] persecutors. . . .[77]

From the way the sermon repeats the words 'I will extol you . . .', which are introduced by 'we have sung', we infer that this may have been the text of the responsorial refrain that was sung with the psalm, before the Gospel reading that is also quoted in this sermon. The psalm text can be understood as being spoken by Christ in his human nature.[78] Or it can be understood as being spoken by the whole Christian people,[79] including those currently living on earth, but also the martyrs in heaven. Thus to be present in Augustine's worship, hearing the verses of a psalm and singing the refrain, is to be united with all other Christians throughout history and with Christ himself. Since many members of Augustine's flock could not read for themselves, in fact, this aural performance was their main way of experiencing the Bible. The readings, the psalms, and the preaching were not mere instruction, but a profound spiritual event in which the Divine presence was made real through the medium of sound:

We sang, brethren, 'God will come manifestly, our God, and he will not be silent' (Ps. 49: 3 [50: 3]). The Scripture has foretold that God, Christ, comes to the judgment of the living and the dead. For when before he came to be judged, he was hidden; when he comes to judge, he will be manifest. . . . Therefore he will come manifestly, and he will not be silent. . . . Now if he were silent, Scripture would not speak. The reader goes up [to read], and he is not silent. The preacher speaks: if he speaks truly, Christ speaks. If Christ were silent, I would not be saying these things to you. Nor is he silent through your mouth, for when you were singing, he was speaking. He is not silent; the task is that we hear, but with the ear of the heart, for it is easy to hear with the ears of the flesh. We should hear with those ears that the Teacher himself asked for when he said, 'He who has ears to hear, let him hear' (Matt. 13: 9). For when he was saying these things, who stood before him without ears of flesh? All had ears, yet few had them; not all had ears of hearing, that is of obeying.

. . . How terribly was it spoken by the prophet Ezekiel. I believe you have used your ear, I believe you have heard how he said, '. . . This people will not hear you, because it does not hear me' (Ezek. 3: 5–7). What does it show, except that God himself was speaking through the prophet? But because in the same prophetic words we are especially frightened, that is, [we] leaders [of the church] whom he put [here] to speak to his own people, in those words we see first of all our own face. For it is shown to us, in the sounding of the reader, as a mirror where we examine ourselves. And we have examined ourselves; examine yourselves. Look, I am doing what I heard there.[80]

Reading through Augustine's approximately 500 surviving sermons,[81] one can gain a vivid mental picture of what these services looked like. 'The reader goes up' to read from a high place. He carefully picks his way through the written letters, grouping them into syllables to be sure he pronounces them accurately. The congregation chimes in, enthusiastically and repeatedly, and then Augustine, seated in his bishop's chair, explains the meaning of it all, using the impressive rhetorical skills of a highly trained orator, yet translating the message into terms anyone can understand. The listeners, feeling united with their savior and their co-religionists throughout history, find themselves on the threshold of eternity, the heavenly life of the eschatological Jerusalem, in which they will know God without any intermediary, even that of the sacred text itself:

Every teaching that is given out in this entire time will pass away. For thus says the Apostle, 'Knowledge will be destroyed, and prophecy will be laid aside . . . for we know in part, and we prophesy in part, but when what is perfect comes, what is in part will be laid aside' (1 Cor. 13: 8–10). . . . A book [*codex*] will be read to us there, or a sermon will be preached, just as one is being preached to you now. Therefore [the Word] is preached now so that it may be kept there; therefore it is divided by syllables now, so that there it will be contemplated whole and entire. The word of God will not be absent there, but nevertheless [it will] not [be present] through letters, nor through sounds, nor through books [*codices*], nor through a reader, nor through a preacher. How, then? Just as 'in the beginning was the Word, and the Word was with God, and the Word was God' (John 1: 1). . . . Such a word will we contemplate, for 'the God of Gods will appear on Zion' (Ps. 83: 8 [84: 7]). But when will this be? After [our] pilgrimage, when the way is finished. . . .

> [When] the loud noise [*strepitus*] of the Tullian voice sounds [*sonat*], [when] Cicero is read – it is some book [*liber*], a dialogue of his, either his or Plato's or some other such person's – do the unlearned hear, the weak of little heart? Who would dare expect such a thing? . . . [On the other hand,] who hears the sound of a psalm and says, 'It is too much for me'? Look, now when the psalm sounds, certainly there are hidden mysteries. Yet it sounds in such a way that children delight to hear it, and the unlearned draw forward to the fountain, and the satiated erupt in psalm-singing [*psallendo*]. . . .
>
> Remember, dear ones, while there may be one utterance of God extended to all in the Scriptures, and one Word may sound through the many mouths of the saints, that while it is God with God in the beginning, there it does not have syllables, because it does not have divisions of time. Nor should this surprise us, for because of our weakness he descended to our halting sounds [*particulas sonorum*], when he descended to take on the weakness of our flesh (John 1: 14).[82]

Augustine's principle, the unity of all Christians living and dead in one body, can lead to a certain confusion of roles that makes it difficult to reconstruct the performance practice as carefully as we might like. In the following example, Augustine is surely speaking of a psalm that was actually rendered in the liturgy, for the words 'which now you have heard sung to you' shows the congregation listening to the singing reader. The congregational refrain is not explicitly identified, and lines like 'one may sing, or many may sing' suggest it did not matter who actually did the singing. But the same psalm is subsequently referred to as 'the things we have read', reflecting the usual ambiguity between singing and reading, but also implying that somehow the whole congregation was itself the reader. 'These who are exulting sing the things we have read', that is, the martyrs in heaven, but then the congregation is told that, 'looking' into the text as if into a mirror, it can see itself as one with the martyrs, who are the actual singers of the psalm from a prosopological perspective. Thus the congregation's own voice can be said to be in the psalm as well, and the assembled people can sing the apparent refrain that is properly spoken by the martyrs, 'If the Lord had not been with us' (Ps. 123: 1 [124: 1]):

> Well have you known, dearest brethren, that 'A Song of Degrees' is a song about our [own] ascent, and this same ascent is not an ascent of the body to be done with the feet, but an ascent of the heart to be done with the affections. . . . And therefore this psalm, which now you have heard sung to you, has 'A Song of Degrees' written above it: that is its title. Therefore those who are going up sing. Sometimes they sing as one, sometimes as many, because the many are one, and Christ is one, and in Christ the members of Christ make one with Christ, and the head of all these members is in heaven. But the body, though it labors on earth, is not cut off from its head, for the head looks down from above, and consoles the body. . . . Therefore either one may sing, or many may sing, and the many men are one man because he is a unity. And Christ, as we said, is one, and all Christians are members of Christ. . . .
>
> These who are exulting sing the things we have read; these exulting members of Christ sing this psalm. And who exults here [on earth], except in hope, as I said? Let this same hope be certain to us, and exulting let us sing. For those who sing are not strangers to us, or else our voice is not in this psalm. Hear thus as you have

> heard yourselves; hear thus as you have noticed yourselves in the mirror of the Scriptures. For when you pay attention to the Scriptures as a mirror, your face rejoices. When, in the exultation of hope, you find yourself similar to certain members of Christ, the members who sing these things, you will also be among these members, and you will sing these things. Why therefore do they sing these things with rejoicing? Because they have gone out. Therefore there is hope in what they sing. For when we are here and on pilgrimage, we have not yet gone out. Certain members have gone before us, from this body to which we also belong, and they are able to sing in truth. And this the holy martyrs sing, for they have already gone out, and are in exultation with Christ, to receive bodies already incorrupt, the same which at first were corruptible, in which they suffered pains, which to them will become insignia of righteousness. Therefore we in hope, they already in reality, sharing the love of their crown, and desiring such life as we do not have here, and are not able to have there unless we have desired it here, let us all sing together, and let us say, 'If the Lord had not been with us'. For they have looked back on certain tribulations which are past, and have considered in that place already, constituted both in blessedness and in security, from what they have passed, to what they have come. And because it was difficult to be delivered from thence, unless the hand of the liberator was present, they said in joy 'If the Lord had not been with us'. So they began to sing; they have not yet said from where they have gone out, so great is their exultation: 'If the Lord had not been with us'.[83]

The text of the psalm, in fact, invites joining in on this verse as a refrain:

> If the Lord had not been with us, let Israel now say –
> If the Lord had not been with us when men rose up against us,
> surely they would have swallowed us alive. . . . (Ps. 123 [124]: 1–3)

Thus Augustine's preaching united the two methods of exegesis in such a synthesis that the same psalm could function as both reading and song, could refer to biblical characters or to the congregation itself. One must grasp all this to understand what became of the psalmodic movement and the congregational responsorial psalmody it advocated. For change certainly came. Congregational singing did not disappear during the Middle Ages, but somehow its ideal shifted, so that it was no longer the psalmodic proper chants but rather the chants of the Mass ordinary that were urged on the faithful.[84] What made this change possible were social and historical trends that transformed the monastic uses of psalmody, both within the liturgy and without. To see how that happened, we must turn our attention to the earliest evidence of chant at Rome.

The Psalmodic Movement at Rome

Did the psalmodic movement make itself felt in Rome? How and when did it arrive there? My answer begins with an apparent direct link to the Milan of Augustine and Ambrose, a man who may have heard the new Eastern psalmody of 386, and who seems to have been responsible for bringing it to Rome. This was Pope Celestine I (reigned 422–32), who is credited in the sixth-century *Liber pontificalis* with introducing psalmody into the first part of the Roman Mass, where formerly only the Epistle and the Gospel had been read. That this most likely refers to responsorial psalmody in connection with the readings has been argued elsewhere.[85] The evidence that Celestine may have spent time in Ambrose's Milan comes from the only surviving fragment of a sermon attributed to him, in which he claims to recall Ambrose leading the congregational singing of his hymn *Qui regis Israel*, so closely based on Psalm 79 [80]. The sermon was apparently given at a synod held in Rome as a preparatory step toward the third ecumenical council, which met at Ephesus in AD 431, and which Celestine did not personally attend. The Council of Ephesus was held to condemn the theological position of Nestorius, then patriarch of Constantinople, who had objected to the practice of calling the Virgin Mary 'Mother of God':

> But Saint Celestine . . . preached in the sight of God and of all, asserting that his own understanding was confirmed by the preeminent bishops of our [western] province. He openly expounded this to have been the understanding of Damasus, Ambrose and Hilary. For he said in that Council, 'I remember that Ambrose of blessed memory, on the birthday of Our Lord Jesus Christ, made all the people sing [*canere*] to God with one voice, thus, "Come, Redeemer of the nations, show us the offspring of the Virgin, let the whole world admire, [for] such an offspring befits God".'[86]

The authenticity of this passage is not beyond question, for its only source is Arnobius the Younger, who wrote about a generation after Celestine. Yet Arnobius could have been an eyewitness if, as is believed, he was one of the monks who fled to Rome from northern Africa about 430, to escape the depredations of the Vandals. It may be more likely that Arnobius knew the sermon from a written copy, but it was not quoted by any other writers we know of, including the writer of the *Liber pontificalis* account of Celestine's reign; we can therefore regard the *Liber* and Arnobius as two independent witnesses to Celestine's knowledge of liturgical singing.

In any case, responsorial psalmody was certainly known at Rome in the generation after Celestine, for it is mentioned in the earliest extant substantial corpus of Roman sermons – those of Pope Leo I the Great (r. 440–61), who had been a deacon under Pope Celestine. The one chant text to which Leo refers unmistakably is the verse from Psalm 109 [110], 'Tu es sacerdos in aeternum' ('You are a priest forever'). Leo quotes this in two sermons delivered in different years on the anniversary of his own episcopal consecration; the more explicit of the two says the following: 'Hence also, beloved, it was not for our own elation but to the glory of Christ the Lord that we sang the Davidic psalm with consonant voice [*consona uoce cantauimus*]. For he is the one about whom it was said prophetically, "You are a priest forever according to the order of Melchizedek"' (Ps. 109: 4 [110: 4]).[87] This chant must have had a certain stability, being sung on the same occasion in at least two different years. Yet any attempt to show that it survived into the medieval Roman chant repertories will founder amid too many uncertainties. The text, of course, can be found within the refrain of the medieval Gradual *Juravit*

Dominus: 'The Lord has sworn and he will not repent, you are a priest forever according to the order of Melchisedek' (Ps. 109: 4 [110: 4]). But Leo's remarks do not suggest that he knew the refrain in this longer form. In the earliest Gregorian chant manuscripts, the Gradual is assigned to the feasts of the sainted popes Felix, Clement and Gregory, but different Graduals are assigned to the feasts of other popes, such as Sylvester, Xystus and Urban.[88] In the Old Roman manuscripts, on the other hand, the Gradual texts for feasts of popes are distributed differently, and *Juravit* is assigned to the feast of Popes St. Fabian and St. Mark, as well as St. Gregory and the Common of Priests.[89] Remarkably, there is no feast of Pope St. Leo the Great in either group of manuscripts. It seems unlikely, then, that the medieval *Juravit* is directly descended from the chant to which Leo referred; it seems more likely to be an independent composition derived from the same psalm and by the same exegetical route – perhaps by someone who had knowledge of Leo's sermons.

Unfortunately, none of Leo's other psalm quotations describes actual psalm-singing unequivocally. Psalm 21 [22] is cited in five sermons for Passion Sunday and the following Wednesday (i.e., Wednesday in Holy Week), and this is the psalm that provided the Tract for Palm Sunday, *Deus Deus meus*. The coincidence is uniquely Roman, for this psalm was assigned to Good Friday in Jerusalem and in the non-Roman Western traditions we know of.[90] But Leo never states that this psalm had actually been read or sung at the service in which the sermons were delivered, whether by soloist, congregation or choir. Again, in one of Leo's sermons for the beginning of the Lenten fast, Leo cites the psalm verse *Jacta cogitatum* (Ps. 54: 23 [55: 22]), which is also the refrain of the Gregorian and Old Roman Gradual for the day after Ash Wednesday. But he gives no reason to suppose this text was chanted either, and again the wording is somewhat different from that of the medieval Gradual.[91]

Similar ambiguity pervades other Roman sermon texts from approximately Leo's time. A sermon for the service of the Reconciliation of Penitents on Holy Thursday, one of a set of three delivered by an anonymous Roman archdeacon in the presence of an unidentified pope, says, 'For they hear and do what the prophet said, "Confess to the Lord for he is good."'[92] This implies that the text 'Confitemini domino quoniam bonus' had actually been read or sung earlier in the service, though it does not unquestionably assert it; in any case it is not specified which of the four psalms that begin with this verse was intended.[93] Yet the possibility that the singing of this psalm verse was a regular part of this service would seem to be strengthened by the fact that the same text figures even more prominently in another set of three anonymous sermons for the reconciliation service, of unknown provenance.[94] Even here, however, we are not explicitly told that the text was sung, nor does the psalm occur in later Roman sources of the ritual for readmitting baptized sinners to church membership. At the equivalent ceremony in the so-called Gelasian Sacramentary of the seventh century, there is only one brief statement by the deacon rather than an entire sermon; verses of several psalms are quoted, but not this verse. Probably none of the quoted psalms was sung that day, for the rubric at the beginning of the service reads, 'Eodem die non psallitur', apparently meaning, 'there is no psalmody on this day'.[95] Neither is there any trace of a *Confitemini* text in the reconciliation services outlined centuries later in medieval pontificals.[96]

However, there is a psalm commentary from approximately Leo's time in which the reconciliation ceremony is linked to Psalm 105 [106], the first of the four psalms that begin with the *Confitemini* verse. As the commentary shows, this psalm is the most appropriate of the four for use in a penitential context, because it also includes the verse 'we have sinned with our fathers, we have acted unjustly, we have committed iniquity'.[97] The author of this commentary is Arnobius the Younger, the same Roman monk who preserved for us the fragment of Celestine's sermon.[98]

The psalm commentary of Arnobius is, in fact, full of references and allusions to the liturgical psalmody of his time, so that for our purposes he is the most important Roman writer of the fifth century.[99] His commentaries are not sermons comparable to Augustine's, intended for the public liturgies of the city; they are much shorter, and seem to have been intended not for oral delivery, but for reading by Arnobius' fellow monks.[100] Yet Arnobius reveals much about the interpretive background that determined the ultimate liturgical assignments of many psalm texts in the Roman chant traditions. 'Arnobius is especially valuable for his allusions to the use made of certain psalms and other biblical passages in the liturgy of Rome in the first half of the fifth century', Germain Morin pointed out almost a century ago.[101] These include the singing of Psalm 148 and possibly 62 [63] in the daily morning office, and of Psalm 117 [118] on Sundays, all of which remained in the Roman and Benedictine cursus of Office psalms.[102] Besides that, Morin found similarities of vocabulary and wording with the *Te Deum* and a number of other Roman chant and prayer texts, particularly those associated with St. Agnes, Rome's most prominent virgin martyr.[103] There are also references to the *Sursum corda*,[104] the *Deus in adjutorium*,[105] the teaching of the Creed to the catechumens,[106] the singing of Psalm 41 [42] at their baptism,[107] and the first Alleluia that the white-robed neophytes sang, just after they emerged from the baptismal font during the great vigil of Easter.[108]

In this commentary, we can recognize an early form of the medieval approach to exegesis, in which there were multiple levels of textual interpretation.[109] Arnobius began with the historical sense, by which the psalms represented episodes in the life of David, Moses and other Old Testament figures.[110] Above it was the mystical sense, by which the psalms foretold or foreshadowed the events of the New Testament, and the moral sense, the highest of all, 'so that we may do what we sing'.[111] One might expect that the historical and mystical senses would reveal the most continuity with the tradition of 'prosopological' interpretation, while the moral would derive from the 'mirror' approach. But in fact it is the moral sense that leads Arnobius to an expanded range of prosopological identifications, so that in the psalms he finds Adam and Job, even Judas and the Devil.[112] In fact Arnobius goes beyond the characters of the Bible, finding allusions to the major Roman saints – a fact that is particularly interesting if, as some believe, he also authored some important hagiographical writings.[113] For example, Arnobius relates the text of Psalm 111: 9, 'Dispersit dedit pauperibus' ('He distributed and gave to the poor') to the Roman deacon St. Lawrence, renowned for his charity to the poor.[114] The same text occurs as both Introit and Gradual for the vigil of Lawrence's feast,[115] and in a sixth-century mosaic in the church of St. Lawrence Outside the Walls, where Lawrence is buried (see Pl. 3.1).[116] Clearly we have here a local tradition of interpretation that links a particular psalm verse with an important local saint. But what is the origin of what? Did Arnobius in the fifth century and the artist of the sixth-century mosaic already know some prototype of the chants for Lawrence's vigil? Or were Arnobius and/or the mosaic the sources from which some later cantor created the Introit and Gradual?

The same issue occurs with Psalm 138 [139], which Arnobius applies to St. Peter, the chief martyr and apostolic founder of the Roman church. This does not seem to have been a common interpretation outside of Rome, yet this psalm is the basis of the Introit and Offertory *Mihi autem nimis*, sung on the vigil of and feast of St. Peter, the feasts of St. Paul and St. Andrew, Peter's

Pl. 3.1 Arch mosaic from San Lorenzo fuori le mura, Rome, showing the deacons St. Lawrence (left) and St. Stephen (right) holding books containing psalm texts that were sung at their liturgical feasts. At the far left is the donor of the mosaic, Pope Pelagius II (r. 579–90), the immediate predecessor of Pope St. Gregory I. Photo: Scala/Art Resource, New York

brother, and the feast of the apostles Simon and Jude.[117] Again, was Arnobius influenced by a contemporary custom of singing this psalm at celebrations of Peter and Paul, or were the chant texts created at a later period, perhaps under the influence of Arnobius' commentary? While a full evaluation of Arnobius' witness remains to be made, it seems clear that Arnobius stands closer than most patristic writers to the milieu in which at least some of the Gregorian texts were established. Presumably this was the environment of the Roman monasteries, many of which, clustered about the seven great basilicas of the city, served a primary function of carrying out the liturgy of the capital.

If Arnobius does indeed bring us close to the fifth-century Roman chant, it is particularly noteworthy that he is one of the earliest Western writers to use the word *antiphon*, though he does so figuratively, without clearly indicating what liturgical practices he associated with this term. In the doxology closing his remarks on Psalm 26 (right column), Arnobius paraphrases a verse of the psalm (left column); the Holy Spirit then 'responds in antiphon' with a paraphrase of this and the succeeding verse:

Psalm 26: 13–14 [27: 13–14]	*Arnobius*
I believe I will see the good things of the Lord in the land of the living	But I who despise these [heretics], *I believe* that I may see *the good things of the Lord in the land*, not of the dead, but *of the living*.
Await the Lord and act manfully, and your heart will be comforted, and hold out for the Lord[118]	To these things the Holy Spirit responds in [an] antiphon: 'If, therefore, you believe you *will see the good things of the Lord in the land of the living, await the Lord; act manfully, your heart will be comforted, and hold out for the Lord*', who reigns forever and ever. Amen.[119]

It is of course possible, though unconfirmed, that Arnobius was quoting an actual antiphon or psalm refrain, but it seems more likely that the dialog between the soul and the Holy Ghost is simply meant to resemble the kind of alternation one might hear in the psalmody. However, the expression 'respondit in antiphona' raises the question whether Arnobius recognized a clear distinction between antiphonal and responsorial psalmody, though such a distinction had already been made in a monastic source of the preceding century, the so-called *Ordo monasterii*, which from early times has been transmitted as a kind of preface to the monastic Rule of St. Augustine.[120] Debate continues as to whether this text may have been known to Augustine himself or to monastic communities he founded, but there are suggestions that it was known in Italy, if not in Rome itself.[121] Whether Arnobius knew it we cannot say.

One other source that may be connected to fifth-century Rome, even if indirectly, is the earliest series of *Tituli psalmorum*, explanatory titles written over the psalms in certain manuscripts of the Bible. Following the tradition of prosopological exegesis, these titles typically identify the personage who is allegorically understood to be the speaker of the psalm: Christ, the Church, the apostles or the prophet David, for example. Six series of this sort circulated in the Western church, variously derived from the writings of Jerome, Origen and Cassiodorus; there was also a Latin version of the titles ascribed to Eusebius in the Codex Alexandrinus. But the oldest series, attested in an Irish manuscript of the sixth century, as well as many Anglo-Saxon and Continental manuscripts of the eighth through twelfth centuries,[122] witnesses more clearly than the others to an early time when liturgical psalms were still treated as readings. For certain psalms, that is, the title includes information about the occasion when the psalm was read, or about the other books of the Bible that were read with it. Some of these reflect traditions that helped shape the Roman chant repertory, though they were also known elsewhere: the title of Psalm 90 [91], 'The voice of the Church to Christ; to be read at the Gospel of Mark where Christ is tempted', parallels the fact that all the Roman proper Mass chants for the first Sunday in Lent are drawn from this psalm, which is quoted in the Gospel of the day: Matthew's story of the Temptation of Jesus in the desert.[123] Again, the title of Psalm 41 [42], 'It is the voice of Christ before baptism', recalls the Gregorian Tract *Sicut cervus*, sung before the baptisms performed at the Easter and Pentecost vigils.[124] Thus a relationship to the developing Roman chant tradition is plausible, and the Irish and Anglo-Saxon provenance of most of the important manuscripts is arguably consistent with this.[125] On the other hand, there are also points of difference with the Roman and Gregorian chant repertories. The association of Psalm 2 with the nativity Gospel from Luke,[126] and of Psalms 22 [23] and 31 [32] with baptismal ceremonies,[127] can be documented in early liturgical traditions – but only from places other than Rome. The linkings of Psalm 44 [45] with the Queen of the South mentioned in Matthew 12: 42, and of Psalm 47 [48] with the new Jerusalem of Apocalypse [Revelation] 21: 9–27, are not so easily localized.[128] Whatever these stray liturgical rubrics are vestiges of, they represent the end of a tradition; in later series of psalm titles the liturgical information was edited out or smoothed over.[129]

Our two major Roman writers, Leo and Arnobius, are also transitional figures. Leo's sermons are much less likely than Augustine's to be based on – or even mention – the liturgical psalms. Arnobius' commentary, not meant for preaching, is closer than Augustine's to the multilayered medieval approach to exegesis. The psalmodic movement, in short, was running out of steam, even while the fifth-century sources seem somewhat less removed from the chant repertories of the Middle Ages.

The Sixth Century: Patristic Compilations

With Leo and Arnobius we are in the middle of the fifth century; perhaps the oldest *Tituli psalmorum* take us back that far as well. But it was in the sixth century that something changed, and sermons that treat congregational responsorial psalmody among the readings come to an end. The last major homilist to comment on liturgical psalmody was Caesarius of Arles (born 469/70, in office 502–42),[130] by whose time the context of preaching had changed noticeably. 'Caesarius was the first of the well-known patristic preachers who was active under barbarian rule, and who spoke to a public that, for the most part, lacked traditional rhetorical education.'[131] His sermons aim at a simpler and more direct language than Augustine or Leo used, and they provide vivid pictures of his illiterate, half-pagan, superstitious congregation. Many of Caesarius' sermons, moreover, borrow, excerpt or revise sermons by Augustine and other early writers. In fact Caesarius advocated the novel position that, given the great pastoral need and the wide geographic dispersion of Gallican congregations, the right to preach should no longer be restricted to bishops, but extended to priests and deacons as well. Since both the rhetorical and the theological learning of these lower clergy was widely mistrusted, Caesarius edited collections of sermons for them to read in church, mixing his own work indiscriminately with excerpts and revisions of earlier writers, particularly Augustine.[132] The broad dissemination of these collections did at least as much to confuse modern textual critics as it may have done to uphold standards of parish preaching in his own time.[133]

Yet Caesarius was hardly the only one reusing Patristic writings in this period. A certain Eugippius, who brought the body of St. Severinus from the Danube to Naples and there built a monastery around the tomb, compiled extracts from Augustine and other writers into a monastic 'rule'.[134] The commentary entitled *Breviarium in psalmos*, which is actually assembled from the writings of Jerome, may have been compiled by John, the Roman deacon who wrote an important tract on the Roman baptismal liturgy, perhaps the same man who became Pope John I (r. 523–6).[135] The sixth century, in fact, was a time of massive and widespread recycling of texts written in the fourth and fifth centuries, and this indicates that the older texts were acquiring a new status: what had originally been sermons or expositions of the sacred Scriptures were now becoming primary sources, holy writings in their own right.[136] This higher status is made explicit in one of the most influential writings of the sixth century, the Benedictine Rule: it is the first document to mandate that the sermons and commentaries of the Church Fathers were to be read at Matins alongside the Bible itself: 'And let books of divine authority, both of the Old and of the New Testaments, be read during the vigils, but also expositions of them, which were made by renowned and orthodox catholic fathers.'[137] Benedict's insistence that the authors be well known and orthodox catholic testifies to a concern that emerged in the wake of the new trend: not every older author could achieve the more exalted status now being accorded to the great Church Fathers of the past. The extant literature had to be sifted, with those eligible for approval distinguished from those that were not. The same spirit motivates the Pseudo-Gelasian decree, a sixth-century document falsely ascribed to Pope Gelasius I (492–6), which purports to outline the Roman view on what could safely be read in church – even though this extensive 'bibliography' of approved and unapproved writings may have achieved its final form outside Rome.[138] The author of Benedict's rule, in fact, seems to have been informed by the decree or something like it, for in reusing substantial excerpts from his main source, the Rule of the Master, he scrupulously excised all the quotations from apocryphal and questionable writings that he found therein, including the *Visio Pauli*.[139] The next logical step would be taken in the seventh-century monasteries that served St. Peter's basilica in Rome, with the creation of the homiliary, a liturgical book in which patristic sermons were arranged according to the feasts and seasons in which they were to be read.[140]

This is one of the reasons, then, that sermons of the kind McKinnon studied did not continue through to the eighth and ninth centuries, giving us an unbroken chain of evidence for liturgical psalmody from the time of the 'psalmodic movement' down to the Middle Ages. Skill in preaching was itself becoming scarce, and original sermons were being replaced by compilations of authoritative texts from the past. For evidence of psalmody in the sixth century, therefore, we must turn away from homiletics, toward the growing literature of anthologies and commentaries assembled from older material. To do so is to recognize that this kind of literature includes the immediate antecedents of the medieval antiphoners and books of chant.

One such document is a pseudonymous letter, purportedly from St. Jerome to his nun correspondents Paula and Eustochium. There are two recensions: the later one, like some of Jerome's genuine correspondence, stands as a preface to the Psalter in two manuscripts of Gallican provenance.[141] In the tradition of Athanasius' 'Epistle to Marcellinus', which was never translated into Latin nor circulated in the West, this document of pseudo-Jerome proposes uses for many of the psalms – some strictly liturgical, others hardly so. For example, Psalms 19 [20], 34 [35] and 72 [73] are described here as 'per ieiunium' ('for the fast'); the latter two are in fact sources of some important Lenten chants.[142] Psalm 109 [110], which supplied the Gradual *Tecum principium* for Christmas midnight Mass, is here called 'de natale domini'.[143] Psalm 90 [91] 'oratio nocturni temporis', had wide use as an evening psalm and was a part of daily Compline.[144] Psalm 33 [34], 'oratio ad [*or*: ante] altare', was a popular source of Communion chants.[145] Many other assignments, however, are clearly suggestions for private, non-liturgical, prayer, such as Psalm 131 [132] 'de lamentatione', 25 [26] 'de tribulatione inimicorum' ('when troubled by enemies'), 102 [103] 'ut creatura creatorem laudet' ('that the creature should praise the creator'), 81 [82] 'dum intras ad alienigenam' ('when you enter a foreign land'). Some are ambiguous, such as Psalm 50 [51], 'ut peniteatur homo' ('that one should do penance').[146]

The differences between the two recensions suggest the later one was more 'liturgical', even though some of these could also be interpreted as simple corruptions: whereas the earlier text recommends Psalm 9 'ut laudes ante deum fundantur' ('that praises should be poured out before God'), the later one identifies it as 'ut laudes in Te Deum' ('as praises at the Te Deum').[147] Psalm 6 'de vigiliis in grabatto' ('on vigils in bed') seems meant for private prayer in bed, while the later text 'de vigiliis aut in grabatto' ('on vigils or in bed') seems to offer a choice between that and a more formalized vigil service. Psalms 22 [23] and 31 [32] are listed in the later recension (but not the earlier) as 'ante baptismum', in agreement with the oldest series of *Tituli psalmorum*. The assignment of Psalm 48 'ad Jonam prophetam' (only in the later recension) is harder to pin down, though the book of Jonah was often read during Holy Week.[148]

In short, this forged letter of Jerome appears to represent a time when traditional or customary liturgical associations of the psalms were being recorded in texts that served as supplements to the biblical Psalter. The formation of a full liturgical book, a psalm lectionary or antiphoner, is only a logical step away. It is reported that Gennadius of Marseille actually compiled a book of biblical readings and psalm refrains about the year 480,[149] and indeed a sixth-century fragment of such a book has been published as 'the oldest liturgical book of the Western church'.[150] In the East, Jerusalem had had a book of this sort since the early fifth century.[151]

The outstanding sixth-century example of a compilation that recycles earlier sermon material is a work that clearly derives from a Roman milieu. This is the expansive *Expositio Psalmorum* by Cassiodorus (485–ca. 580), the longest psalm commentary to survive from the Patristic period. Though it may actually have been penned during Cassiodorus' stay at Constantinople in the 540s, its Roman character is unmistakable. Cassiodorus' text is an important witness to the Roman text of the Latin Psalter, and its dedicatee should probably be identified with Pope Vigilius (reigned 537–55).[152] Cassiodorus' avowed purpose was to rework Augustine's sermons on the psalms, and his indebtedness to Augustine is indeed considerable, though the resulting synthesis amounts to an original work that draws on numerous other Christian and non-Christian classical writers.

A layman who would eventually retire to a quasi-monastic life, Cassiodorus was well aware that the psalms were sung in the liturgy, and he made a number of references to this practice. The use of psalms in the daily cycle of offices is described twice.[153] Liturgical uses are indicated for a few psalms,[154] and references are made to Ambrosian hymns.[155] Yet his commentaries are no sermons. Helpful as it might be to one preparing to sing or preach on the liturgical psalms, this is a book to be read not in church, but in the library or the classroom. A pedant rather than a preacher, this author of the Middle Ages' most popular bibliography, and of a treatise on spelling, had his own theory of the relationship of Christianity to pagan learning: it was the Scriptures that contained all knowledge, and it was from them that the pagan masters of the seven liberal arts plagiarized their disciplines.[156] Thus Cassiodorus' Psalm commentary is a kind of massive introduction to secular knowledge, particularly the arts of the trivium: it is full of definitions and etymologies from the study of grammar, and it identifies in the texts of the psalms numerous rhetorical schemata and dialectical topics and syllogisms. Short disquisitions on the arts of the quadrivium are also scattered about, and marginal signs in the manuscripts were intended to help the reader locate these places by serving as a kind of index.[157] The end result was 'to make of Augustine's treatise a textbook of sacred and secular learning and an introduction to the spiritual life and liturgy of monasticism'.[158]

There was a good reason for this; the Psalter had by this time become the first book that people learned to read, the basic textbook of Christian Latin culture, as Cassiodorus himself clearly stated:

> The significance of the Psalter, therefore, is that through it one enters the holiness of Divine Law. For novices do not start from Genesis, nor from the Apostle [Paul], nor is the holy authority of the Gospels attempted at these early stages. But let the Psalter be the fourth book of divine authority, so that novices first beginning the Holy Scriptures [can] nevertheless make a proper start at reading from there.[159]

For some time Christians had felt uncomfortable with the classical educational curriculum based on the epics of Homer and Vergil, in which multitudes of pagan gods are as unable to restrain their passions for violence and sex as are the human characters. This feeling had been well expressed in Cassian's *Conferences*, composed as a series of dialog between himself and the wisest monks in Egypt. It includes an extensive discussion on the study of the Bible, in the midst of which Cassian grows discouraged:

> Upon hearing these things I was at first very moved by a hidden compunction, and then I groaned deeply and said: 'All these things that you have discussed at great length have brought upon me a greater despair than I had previously endured. For, besides those general captivities of the soul by which I have no doubt that the weak are afflicted from without, there is a particular stumbling block to salvation that comes from the knowledge of literature which I seem to have acquired to a slight degree. In this respect the insistence of my teacher and the constant attention paid to reading have so weakened me that now my mind, infected as it were with those poems, meditates even during the time for prayer on the silly fables and narratives of wars with which it was filled when I was a boy and had begun my studies. The shameless recollection of poetry crops up while I am singing the psalms or asking pardon for my sins, or a vision of warring heroes passes before my eyes. Daydreaming about such images constantly mocks me, and to such an extent does it prevent my mind from attaining to higher insights that it cannot be gotten rid of even with daily weeping.'[160]

Such feelings are difficult to appreciate in our age of widespread secular literacy, but in other societies where literacy is a high-prestige activity restricted to a narrow part of the culture, one can similarly observe that all reading and all books tend to draw people back toward the milieux where reading is most central.[161]

In his *De Doctrina Christiana*, Augustine himself had already proposed a new Christian curriculum in which the Bible would supplant the classical authors. By the time of Cassiodorus more than a century later, this hope was becoming a reality, and the study of the psalms was becoming the same thing as the acquisition of basic literacy – one therefore encountered the psalms and the first liberal arts of grammar and rhetoric at the same time. But there was more at stake than this. Learning to read by means of the psalms provided a firm foundation not only for general education, but specifically for progress toward studying the more difficult books of the Bible, in order to grow in the

Christian life. For Cassiodorus, the pagan knowledge of classical antiquity was not worth studying apart from this goal:

> For these [rhetorical and dialectical figures of speech], when they gleam in the Divine Scriptures, are certain and very pure. But when they come to the opinions of men and to more inane questions, they are troubled by the meaningless ramblings of debates, so that what is always firmly true here is frequently rendered uncertain elsewhere. So also our tongue, when it sings psalmody [*psalmodiam canit*], is adorned with the nobility of the truth – but if the words are turned to absurd fables and blasphemies, it is excluded from the honor of uprightness. As the apostle James said, 'With the same mouth we bless God the Father, and with the same mouth we curse a man, who was made in the image and likeness of God' (James 3: 9).[162]

Thus in the same period that new sermons on the psalms were becoming scarce, the psalms were taking on a new role as the central text in elementary education, and the most important corpus of sermons on the psalms, left behind by Augustine, was reworked into a massive pedagogical work, almost an encyclopedia of the liberal arts. But just as the psalms were becoming the portal to literacy, literacy itself was becoming harder to obtain. Opportunities for education were growing fewer, and the educational process was becoming intertwined with the process of monastic formation.

The Sixth Century: The Monasticizing of Education

Reading had always been central to monastic life: monks not only had to read texts in liturgical celebrations, but were expected to spend part of each day in private, spiritual reading: *lectio divina*.[163] But this too was changing. Cassian's threefold pattern began with 'the frequent reading of and constant meditation on Scripture, so that we may be open to a spiritual point of view'. To Cassian and other early monastic writers, meditation had meant oral, murmured recitation to support memorization of the texts, and monks were admonished to do this during all physical activities: walking, working in the kitchen, carrying out agricultural or handicraft labor to support the monastery, and any other tasks. This led naturally enough to Cassian's next step, 'frequently chanting the psalms [*decantatio crebra psalmorum*], so that we may continually grow in compunction'. And compunction was the spur to being 'diligent in vigils, fasting, and praying, so that the mind which has been stretched to its limits may not taste earthly things but contemplate heavenly ones'.

In the Italian monasteries of the sixth century, however, the practice emerged of having one brother read aloud while the others worked.[164] Individual murmuring during work activities was no longer recommended in monastic rules, as the emphasis shifted to another ancient principle: 'Monks ought to cultivate silence at all times.'[165] Meditation was no longer a way of keeping the mind preoccupied during manual labor, but became associated specifically with a monk's own reading, which in turn was coming to be seen as study aimed at preparing one to take part in the liturgy.[166] Thus the Rule of St. Benedict admonishes, 'Let [the time] that remains after Vigils be devoted to meditation by brothers who need [to learn] something of the psalter or the readings',[167] as if 'meditation' were synonymous with 'study'. Thus the foundation was laid for the medieval understanding synthesized in the twelfth century as 'lectio–meditatio–oratio–contemplatio', which could be paraphrased, 'Reading leads to thoughtful reflection, which leads to prayer, which leads to mystical experience.'[168]

Outside the monasteries, however, the ability to read was becoming rarer and more difficult to attain, the ability to write even more so. The situation can be observed in the writings of Pope Gregory I the Great, whose reign (590–604) brought the sixth century to a close. The twin declines – in general literacy among the laity, and in the composing of original sermons by the clergy – are both evident in a letter of the year 602, which Gregory wrote to a subdeacon John of Ravenna.[169] Disturbed that a certain Abbot Claudius had circulated inaccurate notes taken from Gregory's oral preaching, Gregory authorized John to descend on the monastery, confiscate all the monks' notes, and send them to Rome, even at the risk of physical danger to himself. Furthermore, John was to tell his own bishop Marinianus to stop reading Gregory's commentary on Job at the vigils, because it was not suitable for people of low education. As Gregory put it, 'it is not a popular work, and to rude listeners it causes more obstruction than [spiritual] progress. But tell him that he should have comments on the psalms read at the vigils, for they especially would instruct the minds of worldly people to good deeds.'[170] Thus it seems that even the bishop of a see as important as Ravenna was no longer composing his own sermons, but reading sermons by other people – and that Gregory, one of the most literate people of his age, thought beginners should start with the psalms. Ironically, Gregory's commentary on Job is the only text mentioned in the letter that still survives – it is the great Magna Moralia, the most important example of an entire book interpreted according to the moral sense of exegesis.[171] But the texts that Claudius hoped to save from oblivion have indeed been lost.[172] Though extant commentaries on the first book of Kings (= 1 Samuel) and the Song of Songs have been ascribed to Gregory by some,[173] Gregory's remarks on the book of Proverbs, the Heptateuch (Genesis through Judges) and most of the prophets do not survive at all, nor do we have any psalm commentaries by the namesake of Gregorian chant.[174]

Moreover, many of Gregory's extant sermons clearly were not intended for the general public. Those on Job, as Gregory stated in his letter, were actually monastic conferences, delivered to an advanced, specialist audience that systematically worked its way through biblical books chapter by chapter. However, his sermons on Ezekiel bear an interesting dedication to the same Marinianus of Ravenna, in which Gregory says that they were delivered 'in the presence of the people [*coram populo loquebar*]' eight years earlier, but that at the urging of 'the brethren [*petentibus fratris*]' Gregory had gone back to the stenographic transcriptions made at the time [*notariorum schedas requirere studui*] and corrected them, even though he felt reluctant to circulate his own work since it did not measure up to the standard of Augustine's and Ambrose's writings.[175] It was probably uncorrected transcriptions of this sort that Claudius had been using.

The extant sermons of Gregory that were most clearly intended for an ordinary lay congregation are the forty sermons on the liturgical Gospel readings, evidently delivered at papal Mass in the stational churches of Rome.[176] These never mention chant texts or liturgical psalmody, as if such texts no longer had the status of readings suitable for preaching upon.[177] It is not preaching itself that has changed – Gregory's sermons were focused on the scriptural readings as much as Augustine's were – but the perception that, whatever psalms may have been sung, they were no longer readings, but now only chants.

Thus, just when the labor of Church leaders over several centuries had finally succeeded in replacing classical pedagogy with a Christian curriculum, beginning with the psalms as the primer for acquiring basic literacy, economic and social forces conspired to make that literacy very difficult to obtain, with high levels of erudition increasingly rare even among the non-monastic clergy. As a result, fewer churchmen composed their own sermons, so that we can no longer rely on sermon literature as a source of historical evidence regarding the liturgical psalmody. But psalmody was changing too. Where the Psalter had once been one of the most accessible books of the Bible, and a book particularly applicable to an individual's spiritual life, it was now the first stage in a monk's preparation for liturgical worship and Bible study. It would not be surprising if such changes also had some effect on the liturgy. Historians of monasticism, in fact, do believe that a change took place during the sixth century.

The Sixth Century: Liturgical Changes

The original Egyptian practice for monastic psalmody is described in detail in Cassian's other major work, the *Monastic Institutions*. In the monasteries of Egypt that Cassian had visited, the psalm was recited by a soloist, much as if it were a reading. Sometimes the monks joined in by singing the word 'alleluia' as a response. At the end of the psalm, everyone stood in silent prayer, then prostrated in silence, then stood again; this last time the reciter prayed aloud on behalf of all, giving rise to the term *collecta* or collect, meaning a prayer spoken by a liturgical leader that in effect collects into one the prayers of the entire assembly.[178] This Egyptian practice seems to have been widely followed in the West, at least in part due to the influence of Cassian himself, and several series of collects to be said after the office psalms still survive.[179] The practice seems to show that, for Cassian, the psalms were still biblical readings more than they were prayers. Listening to them, even joining in on the refrain, prompted feelings of compunction, which motivated the monk to pray silently, individually, and then even to lie on his face before getting up again for the communal prayer. 'Just as, at the Mass, the psalm was above all understood as a reading, so in the prayer of the hours it was first heard as a word from God, calling forth prayer in response, and offering to this prayer not only materials and suggestions, but even models.'[180]

By the time of the Benedictine Rule in the early sixth century, however, the practice seems to have been breaking down. Choral psalmody was beginning to replace solo psalmody, the period of silence after each psalm was being curtailed, and the collects are never clearly mentioned by Benedict, though he may have known of them.[181] Alongside these changes was a shift in the understanding of the purpose of psalmody. The monk no longer listened to a lone speaker or reader of the psalm, as one would to a reading, and then responded with silence, prostration and prayer. He no longer mumbled the psalms during his daily work, but studied them during periods set aside for reading. Having trained himself to internalize the psalms completely, the monk at worship now sang them with his own lips. 'Thus a sort of revolution was wrought in the psalmody from the time of Cassian to that of the Master. Instead of being primarily a message from God to man, it has become chiefly man's homage to God. . . . [T]he hearers of the word of God have been changed into those who sing his majesty.'[182] The psalm itself was now the prayer, providing the words by which humans addressed God, rather than the divine word to which humans listened. The daily recitation of the psalms was even coming to be understood as a duty he owed to God; 'duty' is, after all, the original meaning of the word 'officium' or office.[183] Thus as the psalms became the basis of training in literacy and spirituality, their liturgical performance changed as well. From the monastic exegesis of imagining oneself in the psalms, the monk now felt obliged to become himself the very speaker of the psalms.

For Benedict's disciple and hagiographer[184] Pope Gregory the Great, at the end of the sixth century, the newer understanding has become superimposed on the old. Performing the texts of the psalms was still a kind of Scripture study, giving one access to the 'mysteries of prophecy or the grace of compunction'. Yet it was now also a 'sacrifice of praise', that in itself offered direct contact with God. As Gregory says in the introduction to his sermons on Ezekiel:

> But sometimes the spirit of prophecy is absent from the prophets. It is not always available to their minds, so that when they do not have it, they will recognize that they have it as a gift when they do have it. Thus Elisha, when he prohibited the Shunamite woman from being torn away from his feet by the servant Gehazi, said, 'Let her be, for her soul is in bitterness, and the Lord has concealed it from me and has not indicated to me [what she wants to know]' (4 Regum [2 Kings] 4: 27). So also, when Jehoshaphat questioned him about future events, and the spirit of prophecy was absent from him, he had a musician [*psalten*] brought, so that the spirit of prophecy would descend and fill his soul with the [knowledge of] things to come (4 Regum [2 Kings] 3: 15). For through the sound of psalmody [*vox enim psalmodiae*], when it is done with the intention of the heart, a path to the heart is prepared for the almighty Lord, so that he may pour out into the intent mind either the mysteries of prophecy or the grace of compunction. Whence it is written, 'A sacrifice of praise will honor me, and in that [sacrifice] is the path in which I will show him the salvation [*salutare*] of God' (Ps. 49: 23 [50: 23]). For the Latin word 'salutare' [i.e., salvation] is 'Jesus' in Hebrew. In the sacrifice of praise, therefore, Jesus is the path in which we are shown [salvation], because while compunction is poured forth through psalmody [*psalmodiam*], a way is made for

> us in the heart, by which it arrives at Jesus in the end – as he himself speaks concerning his showing of himself, saying, 'Whoever loves me will be loved by my father, and I will love him, and I will manifest myself to him' (John 14: 21). Hence also it is written, 'Sing to the Lord, say a psalm to his name, make a path to him who ascends above the sunset, the Lord is his name' (Ps. 67: 5 [68: 4]). For he ascends above the sunset who trampled down death by rising again. When we sing to him, we make a path so that he may come to our heart and inflame us by the grace of his love.[185]

Here Gregory has followed the Latin Vulgate in calling Elisha's musician a 'psaltes'. This Greek word, which originally meant 'harpist',[186] is used to render the Hebrew מְנַגֵּן (*mənaggēn*), 'one who plays a stringed instrument'.[187] Both words could also refer to singing with the accompaniment of a plucked-string instrument. But since the book known in Hebrew as תְּהִלִּים (*Təhillîm*; 'praises') had been renamed Ψαλτήριον or Psaltery in Greek, the Greek verb ψάλλω, ψάλλειν ('to pluck') and its Latin borrowing *psallo*, *psallere* also came to mean 'to sing psalms', and in the Greek church ψάλτης became the most common term for an ecclesiastical cantor.[188] It is in this last sense that Gregory understood the passage, helped by the fact that, though the Hebrew and Greek say in effect that the spirit of prophecy came upon Elisha 'while the plucker plucked', the Vulgate literally says that this happened 'while the psaltes sang' (*cumque caneret psaltes*). Though the verb *cano* can also refer to the sounding of instruments (e.g., 'while the harpist played' or 'sang and accompanied himself'),[189] Gregory clearly understood that Elisha's musician was not (or not merely) plucking strings, but singing psalms.

What is truly new here, however, is the vocabulary: previously the phrase 'sacrifice of praise', which occurs only three times in the Psalms,[190] had been applied to Christian life and worship more generally.[191] The earliest writer to apply this expression to psalmody as such seems to have been Cassiodorus, who also seems to have been the first Latin author to make extensive use of the Greek loanword *psalmodia*.[192] Thus, after the mid-sixth century, psalm-singing was no longer simply a category of Bible-reading, but had become an act of worship in itself, with its own names. What this meant in musical terms can be seen in the other early text that uses the phrase 'sacrifice of praise' with this special meaning. This is the somewhat obscure monastic rule of Paul and Stephen, written in some unidentified sixth-century monastery near Rome.[193] The community here clearly included monks who were only just learning to read from the Psalter, who were studying individually under more experienced mentors, and who were forbidden to share in the one daily meal unless they could recite their assigned passage from the psalms. The community as a whole clearly spent much time in the chanting of the office.[194] In this monastery, the line distinguishing chants from readings was as sharply drawn as the line between canonical scripture and unapproved unorthodox texts:

> Let no one presume to sing [*canere*] in this congregation, or meditate or say responsories or antiphons that are not taken from the canonical scripture, as some are accustomed to do, with the sound composed for their own pleasure. Nor may

> anyone dare to meditate on any things of this sort [received] from a visiting guest, without the permission of the prior. Nor may they disdain the maturity of simplicity and truth for straying, variable doctrine – ensnared, as it were, by sweet absurdities – and, bound in the shackles of shallowness and idleness by the sounds of song [*cantilenae sonos*], either hasten to flee from our congregation by the persuasion of the devil, or to despise all inside the monastery, puffed up as if by a singular knowledge. Instead it behooves us to imitate the sane and simple apostolic doctrine and grace of our fathers, to stabilize the heart and subdue behavior with discipline. And we ought to sing [*cantare*] those things which, as blessed Augustine says, are so written that they may be sung [*cantentur*]. But those things that are not so written we may not sing [*cantemus*]. Nor should [any things] be said in his praise in any way other than that in which the Lord himself commanded them through his prophets and apostles to be manifested to men. Nor may we change those things which are to be sung [*cantanda*] into the manner of prose [*in modum prosae*], and as if into [one] of the readings [*lectionum*], or by our presumption turn into tropes and the art of song [*in tropis et cantilenae arte*] those things which are so written that we use them in the order of readings. For we should offer to God a sacrifice of confession and praise such as he himself commanded [us] to offer to him: from us he seeks a sacrifice of obedience more than of victims, nor is he delighted by study of the artifices of song [*cantilenae artificiorum studium*] as much as by observance of the commandments and purity of heart.[195]

It is ironic that this sharp distinction between chants and readings was justified by appeal to the authority of Augustine himself, in whose time the genres were not clearly distinct. The reference is to a text that occurs in three distinct writings: (1) the *Praeceptum*, that is, the core document in the monastic rule ascribed to Augustine; (2) the corresponding section in the Augustinian rule for nuns, known as *Regularis informatio*; and (3) a letter Augustine wrote to a monastery of women who had asked him to remove their superior. Instead of granting this request, Augustine laid down many rules designed to restore peace and harmony; a few of these had to do with the worship:

> Apply yourselves to prayers at the appointed hours and times. Let no one do anything in the oratory except what it was built for and also takes its name from, so that, if some want to pray outside the appointed hours, if they have the opportunity, those who wanted to do something else there will not be an obstacle. When you pray God with psalms and hymns, let what is expressed with the voice be pondered in the heart, and do not sing [*cantare*] anything except what you read is to be sung [*cantandum*]. But what is not written so that it may be sung [*cantetur*], should not be sung.[196]

It is not clear precisely which document provided the original setting for this text, or precisely what Augustine had in mind here. We have no information about the nuns' quarrel except what we can infer from his letter. But his command is a purely negative one: 'Sing only what you are supposed to sing, and nothing else.' As reinterpreted in the Rule of Paul and Stephen, it is made to support something that Augustine did not intend, an absolute distinction between sung chants and spoken readings.

For Augustine the fundamental distinction was not between psalmody and reading, but between singing and praying; thus he could not have understood psalmodic chant to be a type of prayer, as Gregory later would: in ordinary human experience, Augustine believed, speech has the twofold function of communicating new information (*docere*) and calling forth the memory of what is already known (*commemorare*). Prayer, however, even when uttered aloud, fails to fulfill these two functions of speech, because it is speech addressed to God, who already knows everything, and thus can neither be informed nor reminded. True prayer, therefore, actually takes place in the hidden silence of the interior mind, silence that focuses our attention on truth just as the rests in a piece of music or the shadows in a painting call attention to the underlying order and structure of the artistic plan.[197] Thus for Augustine, song could never be anything more than a way of performing texts – at most, the beauties of music may attract the listener's attention to the words, and thus 'elevate the weaker soul to an attitude of devotion'. But the melody is not the prayer. That is why Augustine's advice to the nuns begins 'When you pray God with psalms and hymns' or 'in psalms and hymns' (*psalmis et hymnis cum oratis Deum*), not 'when you pray psalms and hymns to God' (*psalmos et hymnos cum oratis Deo*). Prayer is so different from music that it is more like the rests than like the sound.

But in the monastery of Paul and Stephen, as for Gregory, the singing of psalms was an offering or a sacrifice in itself. This is important because, though we do not even know who Paul and Stephen were, we can document – as we cannot for Gregory himself! – that they had some sort of relationship to the emerging repertory of Roman chant. This occurs in another chapter of their rule, which focuses on the singing of the *Opus Dei* ('God's Work'), the Benedictine name for the Divine Office:

> Let God's Work ... be said with consonant voice [*consona uoce dicatur*], with discipline and the fear of God. Not abruptly, as someone might want, with the excuse of his work or occupation, [so that] a junior [monk] presumes to jump in ahead of the senior [monk], and to get ahead of him with immature haste – and the divine work, which ought to be done with fear, is by impudent boldness sung [*psallatur*] foolishly and not wisely (cf. Ps. 46: 8 [47: 7]). For by such a practice the still-unformed minds and throats of some brothers cannot be brought back to harmony [*consonantiam*] within the oratory, except by the strong bridle of violent disciplinary measures. Therefore we exhort in simple charity that this vice of usurpation be cast away from you: for 'God is the hearer of all' such people, 'he sent his angel and brought me from my father's flocks'.[198]

The quotation is easily recognized as coming from the Roman/Gregorian responsory *Deus omnium exauditor*, unlike the vague allusions to liturgical responsory texts that have been perceived in the Benedictine Rule.[199] It is clear from the wording that the quotation comes from the liturgical text and not from its source, the apocryphal Psalm 151.[200] Indeed, the authors' disapproval of non-canonical texts makes it seem more likely that they did not even recognize the source. Thus it is hard to escape the conclusion that the community for which the Rule of Paul and Stephen was written was familiar with some form of the Roman chant repertory, indeed a more developed form of it than Benedict knew. If so, then we have managed to trace a historical path from the psalmodic movement of Augustine's time to medieval chant, and to medieval Roman chant at that.

Conclusion

Obviously, much more remains to be done before this sketchy and oversimplified outline is filled in. But the general direction for research can be pointed out. The historical 'gap in the sources' between the fifth century and the eighth is real, for sermon evidence ceases in the fifth and properly liturgical texts begin in the eighth. However, this lack of sources is not due to accidents of preservation. The phenomenon we are interested in, liturgical chant, experienced significant transformations during this period, and these changes inevitably made a difference in the kinds of evidentiary tracks that could be left behind on the historical record. To trace its development during the period of the 'gap', therefore, we must unearth the kind of evidence that does exist, and learn to interpret it correctly. In broad outline, what we will find is this: while the reading and singing of the psalms probably had a place in Christian worship from the beginning, the rise of monasticism in the fourth century provoked a renewed interest in psalm-singing, at first in the East, but spreading to the West by the 380s. The psalmodic movement brought with it a new, more personal way of reading the psalms, and this was doubtless part of its appeal. The monastic method of applying the psalm texts to oneself, as though scrutinizing one's inner life in a spiritual mirror, conflicted with the more traditional method of reading the psalms as if they were spoken in the 'voice' of various biblical characters. But the tension between the two was held in balance at least by St. Augustine, the greatest preacher of the age. It is mainly from his sermons and those of his contemporaries that we can still learn about the psalmodic movement, the interpretations that linked particular psalms to specific feasts, and the interactions between reader and congregation that included responsorial performance. In doing so we are taking advantage of the fact that the psalms were still being thought of as readings from the Bible, even while they were also songs. It was their status as readings that caused them to be mentioned so frequently in the sermons.

This state of affairs weakened over the course of the fifth century, however. Sermons like those of Pope Leo the Great were less likely to mention the liturgical psalms, and by the sixth century even many bishops were recirculating sermons of Augustine's generation rather than composing their own. As a result, sermons cease to be an important source of information about the development of liturgical psalmody after the mid-fifth century. Instead, commentaries and monastic sources become more important, notably those of Arnobius the Younger, in whose work we see an early form of the medieval approach to exegesis, which distinguished multiple 'senses' of Scripture. Arnobius' work is of particular value to us because his interpretations are often echoed in the medieval Roman chant traditions, presumably reflecting a close relationship to the monasteries of the city wherein these traditions were formed.

As Christianity more thoroughly pervaded late antique culture, the traditional pedagogy based on classical authors was replaced by a Christian curriculum that began with the psalms. From the sixth century on, learning to read meant learning to read the psalms, and thus the Psalter became the gateway to more advanced reading of the Bible and other religious texts. At the same time, however, the political and socio-economic collapse of the ancient world meant that fewer people had access to education, so that reading became a largely monastic activity, and learning to read became a central part of monastic formation and training. '[D]uring the centuries when societal and ecclesiastical collapse and confusion made anything except physical survival seem like a luxury, monasticism virtually alone provided the context within which some Christians could cultivate the knowledge of scripture and the life of penance and prayer that prepared the believer for more special forms of immediate contact with God in this life.'[201]

Because many monks learned to read as part of their monastic training, rather than coming to the monastery already literate, the liturgical performance and function of the psalms also began to change. In the fourth century, the liturgical psalms were recited by soloists, and the other monks responded with prostration and silent prayer; in effect the psalm was a special type of biblical reading. Outside the liturgy, monks studied and memorized the psalms by repeatedly murmuring them during manual labor and other activities; the learning of the psalms promoted feelings of compunction, or sorrow for one's sins, and compunction was an incentive to pray. In the sixth century, however, at least in central Italy, a greater emphasis on monastic silence, and the use of designated readers during periods of labor, meant that the murmuring stopped. Monks studied the psalms and other writings in order to inspire thoughtful reflection as a way to prayer, and as preparation for the liturgical office, which was now the major venue for oral recitation of the psalms. Instead of listening to a lone reciter, all the monks now joined in on each psalm; perhaps the ancient reciter's role developed into the medieval job of starting the choral psalmody by intoning its opening words. In any case psalmody itself changed from being a category of reading to a category of prayer. The prayers following each psalm withered away as no longer necessary, and the psalm itself was reinterpreted as a spiritual sacrifice, an offering the monk owed to God. The rendition of the psalms had been melodic and musical at least since the psalmodic movement, in the time of Augustine and Cassian. But by the time of Pope Gregory the Great, the psalms had become chant, a category quite separate from the liturgical readings. This is marked by the emergence of a special vocabulary for psalm performances, including the Greek loanword *psalmodia* and the identification of psalmody with the biblical *sacrificium laudis*. It was the hegemony of a monastic approach to the psalms, and not some undocumentable mania for 'virtuosity', that led to the medieval dominance of monastic and clerical choirs and the erosion of congregational singing – and only through theological *ressourcement*, aimed at recovering the early church's contrasting models of musical worship, will the stoics and anchorites, mystics and virtuosos of today be able to cooperate in solving the problems plaguing liturgical music in our time.

For students of chant history, the way to trace a path through the 'gap' from the 'psalmodic movement' to the Middle Ages is the study of monastic sources, understanding the changing ideals of reading and singing that determined the transition from responsorial congregational reading to monastic *psalmodia*. Among the results we can expect is a much-needed 'change' in 'the hagiographic context of the question' of Gregory's 'involvement in the development of Roman liturgy and chant'.[202] We should not expect to find confirmation of medieval claims that Pope Gregory compiled an antiphoner or founded a schola cantorum – probably he did neither. But if the knowable history of Roman chant in the sixth through eighth centuries parallels the history of Roman monasticism, Gregory is right at the center of it. As a promoter of monks in general and Benedict in particular, as an important biblical exegete, and as the most prolific Roman writer of this period, Gregory contributed much to shape the intellectual world in which Roman chant developed. It is that world that we must imaginatively reenter if we seek the origins of the psalmody that bears his name.

Notes

1 Beginning with James McKinnon, 'The Fourth-Century Origin of the Gradual', *EMH* 7 (1987), 91–106.
2 James McKinnon, 'Desert Monasticism and the Later Fourth-Century Psalmodic Movement', *M&L* 75 (1994), 505–21 at 506.
3 James McKinnon, 'Liturgical Psalmody in the Sermons of Saint Augustine', in Peter Jeffery (ed.), *The Study of Medieval Chant, Paths and Bridges, East and West: In Honor of Kenneth Levy* (Rochester, NY: Boydell & Brewer, 2001), 7–24 at 15. See also McKinnon, 'The Fourth-Century Origin', 104–6.
4 McKinnon, 'The Fourth-Century Origin', 102, 104.
5 *Confessions* 10.33.49–50. *MECL* 352, pp. 154–5. For improved text and commentary of Augustine's remarks, see Augustine, *Confessions*, ed. James Joseph O'Donnell, 3 vols. (Oxford: Clarendon Press, 1992), i, 138–9, iii, 218–20. For a complete English translation, see Saint Augustine, *Confessions*, trans. Henry Chadwick (Oxford: Oxford University Press, 1991), this passage, 207–8.
6 *Republic* 377A–403C, 522A, 595A–608B. Plato was already developing this view, which he ascribed to Socrates, in his early works *Ion* and *Apology* 22B–C. Among the many available translations is *The Collected Dialogues of Plato including the Letters*, trans. Edith Hamilton and Huntington Cairns (New York: Pantheon, 1961, repr. Princeton: Princeton University Press, 1980), 8, 215–28, 623–48, 754, 819–33.
7 This is the assessment of the Greek music theorist Aristides Quintilianus, whom Thomas Mathiesen would place in fourth-century Antioch, thus roughly contemporary with Augustine. See Mathiesen, *Apollo's Lyre: Greek Music and Music Theory in Antiquity and the Middle Ages* (Lincoln, Neb.: University of Nebraska Press, 1999), 521–3, 546. While most of Cicero's *De re publica* is lost, the final section, known as *Somnium Scipionis*, 'the dream of Scipio', survived with multiple commentaries, and played an important role in the development of the idea of the 'music of the spheres'. See ibid., 617–18.
8 Martha Craven Nussbaum, *The Therapy of Desire: Theory and Practice in Hellenistic Ethics* (Princeton: Princeton University Press, 1994), 357–8, 366, 363.

The problem of how the logical mind should relate to the emotional heart is, of course, a perennial one, but much research published in the past twenty years has legitimated scientific study of the relationships of cognition and emotion. See, for example, Joseph P. Forgas (ed.), *Feeling and Thinking: The Role of Affect in Social Cognition* (Cambridge and Paris: Cambridge University Press and Editions de la Maison des Sciences de l'Homme, 2000).

9 For example, the Hellenistic Jewish writing known as 4 Maccabees, which is included in the Old Testament of the Eastern church but not of the Western, recounts in great detail the torture of an entire family of Jewish martyrs, citing their extraordinary equanimity and self-control in support of a philosophical argument that 'devout reason is sovereign [αὐτοδέσποτος] over the emotions' (1: 1). For a translation with some commentary see *The Harper Collins Study Bible: New Revised Standard Version with the Apocryphal/Deuterocanonical Books*, ed. Wayne A. Meeks et al. (New York: Harper Collins, 1993), 1814–37.

10 See A. Curley, 'Cicero, Marcus Tullius', and N. J. Torchia, 'Stoics, Stoicism' in *Augustine through the Ages: An Encyclopedia*, ed. Allan D. Fitzgerald et al. (Grand Rapids, Mich.: William B. Eerdmans, 1999), 190–93, 816–20; *The Cambridge Companion to Augustine*, ed. Norman Kretzmann and Eleonore Stump (New York: Cambridge University Press, 2001), 5, 32–5, 160, 195–9, 227. On the impact of Stoicism more generally, see Marcia L. Colish, *The Stoic Tradition from Antiquity to the Early Middle Ages*, ii: *Stoicism in Christian Latin Thought through the Sixth Century* (Leiden: E. J. Brill, 1985), 142–238; Troels Engberg-Pedersen, *Paul and the Stoics* (Westminster: John Knox, 2000).

11 Augustine, *De doctrina christiana* 4.4, ed. and trans. R. P. H. Green (Oxford: Clarendon Press, 1995), 196–209 at 197. This issue too was an ancient one, discussed already centuries earlier in Plato's *Gorgias*. See Paul Woodruff, 'Rhetoric and Relativism: Protagoras and Gorgias', in *The Cambridge Companion to Early Greek Philosophy*, ed. A. A. Long (Cambridge: Cambridge University Press, 1999), 290–301. Translations of a number of ancient texts on the subject of good and bad rhetoric will be found conveniently in *Ancient Literary Criticism: The Principal Texts in New Translations*, ed. D. A. Russell and Michael Winterbottom (Oxford: Clarendon Press, 1972), for example, Seneca's views on 362–7.

12 *Confessions* 3.3.6; 4.2.2; and esp. 9.2.2–9.4.11, in O'Donnell's edition, i, 25, 33, 103; ii, 160–62, 206–8; iii, 75–101. Chadwick, 38, 53, 155–62.

13 St. John Chrysostom, *MECL* 164. See also McKinnon, 'Desert Monasticism', 516–19. For a more extended excerpt, see Oliver Strunk, *Source Readings in Music History*, rev. edn, ed. Leo Treitler with McKinnon et al. (New York: Norton, 1998), 123–6. On Chrysostom's sermons as evidence for his liturgical practices, see Franz van de Paverd, *Zur Geschichte der Messliturgie in Antiocheia und Konstantinopel gegen Ende des vierten Jahrhunderts: Analyse der Quellen bei Johannes Chrysostomos* (OCA 187; Rome: Pontificium Institutum Studiorum Orientalium, 1970).

14 '. . . universi saeculi pulchritudo . . . uelut magnum carmen cuiusdam ineffabilis modulatoris excurrat . . . in aeternam contemplationem speciei qui deum rite colunt'. Augustine, *Epistolae* 138.5, ed. Alois Goldbacher (CSEL 44; Vienna: Tempsky, 1904), 130. See Carol Harrison, *Beauty and Revelation in the Thought of Saint Augustine* (Oxford: Oxford University Press, 1992), 24–31, 67–81, 170–71, 186–7.

15 *Sermo 159*, *PL* 38: 868–9.

16 James McKinnon, 'The Book of Psalms, Monasticism, and the Western Liturgy', in Nancy van Deusen (ed.), *The Place of the Psalms in the Intellectual Culture*

of the Middle Ages (Albany: State University of New York Press, 1999), 43–58 at 50.

17 Michael Marx, 'Incessant Prayer in Ancient Monastic Literature' (diss., Rome: Facultas theologica S. Anselmi de Urbe, 1946); Paul J. Konkler, 'Unceasing Prayer' (Thesis, Jesuit School of Theology at Berkeley, 1977); Cipriano Vagaggini (ed.), *La preghiera nella bibbia e nella tradizione patristica e monastica* (2nd edn, Milan: Edizioni Paoline, 1988), esp. the following articles: G. Penco, 'La preghiera nella tradizione monastica', 263–324; P. Tamburrino, 'Dottrina ascetica e preghiera continua nel monachesimo antico', 325–70; and Roberta C. Bondi, *To Pray and To Love: Conversations on Prayer with the Early Church* (Minneapolis: Fortress Press, 1991).

18 See Paul F. Bradshaw, *The Search for the Origins of Christian Worship: Sources and Methods for the Study of Early Liturgy* (Oxford: Oxford University Press, 1992), 185–92; Robert Taft, *The Liturgy of the Hours in East and West: The Origins of the Divine Office and its Meaning for Today* (2nd rev. edn, Collegeville, Minn.: Liturgical Press, 1993), 31–56 and throughout; James McKinnon, 'The Origins of the Western Office', in Margot Fassler and Rebecca Baltzer (eds), *The Divine Office in the Latin Middle Ages: Methodology and Source Studies, Regional Developments, Hagiography, Written in Honor of Professor Ruth Steiner* (New York: Oxford University Press, 2000), 63–73; Peter Jeffery, 'Eastern and Western Elements in the Irish Monastic Prayer of the Hours', ibid., 99–143.

19 McKinnon, 'Desert Monasticism', 512.

20 *MECL* 242–3; McKinnon, 'The Book of Psalms', 50–54; Taft, *Liturgy of the Hours*, 48–55. For the latest translation and commentary, see *Egeria's Travels*, ed. John Wilkinson (3rd edn, Warminster: Aris and Phillips, 1999), 142–3. On the date of Egeria's visit to Jerusalem, see *Egérie: Journal de Voyage (Itinéraire)*, ed. and trans. Pierre Maraval (SC 296; Paris: Editions du Cerf, 1982), 27–39. It remains controversial how Egeria used the terms 'hymn', 'psalm' and 'antiphon' or recognized distinctions of genre.

21 Peter Jeffery, 'The Lost Chant Tradition of Early Christian Jerusalem: Some Possible Melodic Survivals in the Byzantine and Latin Chant Repertories', *EMH* 11 (1992), 151–90; id., 'The Earliest Christian Chant Repertory Recovered: The Georgian Witnesses to Jerusalem Chant', *JAMS* 47 (1994): 1–39; id., 'Rome and Jerusalem: From Oral Tradition to Written Repertory in Two Ancient Liturgical Centers', in Boone (ed.), *Essays on Medieval Music in Honor of David Hughes*, 207–47.

22 McKinnon, 'The Book of Psalms', 53.

23 *MECL* 102.

24 *MECL* 352 (see n. 5 above).

25 *CPG* 2097. *MECL* 98–100.

26 London, BL, Royal MS 1 D V–VIII. On the significance of the manuscript see: P. Batiffol, 'Sinaiticus (Codex)', *Dictionnaire de la Bible*, ed. F. Vigouroux, v (Paris, 1928), 1783–6; Bruce Metzger, *Manuscripts of the Greek Bible: An Introduction to Greek Palaeography* (New York: Oxford University Press, 1981), 86–7; id., *The Text of the New Testament: Its Transmission, Corruption, and Restoration* (3rd enlarged edn, New York: Oxford University Press, 1992), 46–7.

27 See James Mearns, *The Canticles of the Christian Church Eastern and Western in Early and Medieval Times* (Cambridge: Cambridge University Press, 1914), 7–25; *Septuaginta* 10: *Psalmi cum Odis*, ed. Alfred Rahlfs (Göttingen: Vandenhoeck & Ruprecht, 1931), 341–65.

28 *PG* 23, 66–72, not listed in *CPG*, but see: Marie-Josèphe Rondeau, *Les Commentaires patristiques du psautier (IIIe–Ve siècles)*, i: *Les Travaux des Pères grecs et latins sur le psautier* (OCA 219; Rome: Pontificium Institutum Studiorum Orientalium, 1982), 71–2; Alice Whealey, 'Prologues on the Psalms: Origen, Hippolytus, Eusebius', *Revue bénédictine*, 106 (1996), 234–45.

29 *MECL*, pp. 64–73.

30 Gregory of Nyssa, *In inscriptiones Psalmorum* 1.3.17–25, 1.9.115–22, in *Gregorii Nysseni Opera*, v, ed. J. McDonough (Leiden: E. J. Brill, 1962), 30–31, 65–9. For a translation see *Gregory of Nyssa's Treatise on the Inscriptions of the Psalms*, trans. Ronald E. Heine (Oxford: Clarendon Press, 1995), 88–92, 120–23.

31 For example, his Easter sermons cite the Easter gradual/prokeimenon, Ps. 117 [118]: 24; see *Gregorii Nysseni Opera*, ix, ed. G. Heil et al. (Leiden: E. J. Brill, 1967), 249, 279, 310. For translations with extensive discussion of the liturgical background, see *The Easter Sermons of Gregory of Nyssa: Translation and Commentary*, ed. Andreas Spira and Christoph Klock (Cambridge, Mass.: The Philadelphia Patristic Foundation, 1981). Gregory's sermons for Ascension Day and Pentecost begin by saying that there is a psalm verse for every feast and occasion. See *Gregorii Nysseni Opera*, ix, 323–7, and vol. x/2, ed. Friedhelm Mahn et al. (Leiden: E. J. Brill, 1996), 287–92.

32 *MECL* 151–2.

33 *MECL* 139. For extended discussion, see Benoît Gain, *L'Eglise de Cappadoce au IVe siècle d'après la correspondance de Basile de Césarée* (OCA 225; Rome: Pontificium Institutum Studiorum Orientalium, 1985), 168–87.

34 *MECL*, pp. 121–5. The hymns are described at *CPL* 463, where, however, the following edition is not cited: Walter Neidig Myers, 'The Hymns of Saint Hilary of Poitiers in the Codex Aretinus: An Edition, with Introduction, Translation, and Notes' (Ph.D. diss., University of Pennsylvania, 1928).

35 *Confessions* 9.7.15. O'Donnell, i, 109; iii, 109–12. Chadwick, 164–5. On the date of the *Confessions*, see O'Donnell i, pp. xli–li; *MECL* 351. For discussion see McKinnon, 'Desert Monasticism', 513–15.

36 *Confessions* 9.12.31–2. O'Donnell, i, 116–17; iii, 140–43. Chadwick, 175–6.

37 Partially translated in *MECL* 292, p. 131; for the Latin, see *Sancti Ambrosii Opera*, 10/3, ed. Michaela Zelzer (CSEL 82; Vienna: Hoelder, Pichler, Tempsky, 1982), 123.

38 *MECL* 291; for the Latin, see CSEL 82: 120.

39 *MECL* 298; CSEL 82: 105.

40 Helmut Leeb, *Die Psalmodie bei Ambrosius* (Vienna: Herder, 1967), 111–13. On the dating of Ambrose's sermons on the psalms, see Hans Jörg Auf der Maur, *Das Psalmenverständnis des Ambrosius von Mailand: Ein Beitrag zum Deutungshintergrund der Psalmenverwendung im Gottesdienst der Alten Kirche* (Leiden: E. J. Brill, 1977), 11–16.

41 I am not as certain as Leeb, *Die Psalmodie*, 59–60, that the refrain Ambrose cited in Greek (combining Ps. 44: 3 [45: 2] with Isa. 52: 7) could not have been sung in Greek by Ambrose's Latin-speaking congregation.

42 Thus the *Itinerarium Burdigalense*, dating from the year 333 (*CPL* 2324) outlines a land route from Bordeaux to Jerusalem via Arles, Milan, Aquileia and points east including Constantinople and Antioch, returning by sea to Capua (near Naples), then continuing by land through Rome to end at Milan. The work is edited by P. Geyer and O. Cunz in *Itineraria et alia Geographica* (CCSL 175–6; Turnhout: Brepols, 1965), 1–26.

43 McKinnon, 'Liturgical Psalmody in the Sermons of St. Augustine', esp. 20–24. For examples, see *MECL* 353–7, 362–74.

44 For the most relevant quotations from Nicetas and Jerome, see *MECL*, pp. 134–45. Examples from Chromatius, Maximus and others are cited in Jeffery, 'The Lost Chant Tradition of Early Christian Jerusalem'.

45 F. Sottocornola, *L'Anno liturgico nei sermoni di Pietro Crisologo: Ricerca storico-critica sulla liturgia di Ravenna antica* (Cesena: Centro studi e ricerche sulla antica provincia ecclesiastica ravennate, 1973), 65–75.

46 Jeffery, 'The Lost Chant Tradition of Early Christian Jerusalem'.

47 McKinnon, 'Liturgical Psalmody in the Sermons of Saint Augustine', 17–18.

48 James McKinnon, 'Preface to the Study of the Alleluia', *EMH* 15 (1996): 213–49. For examples from Augustine, see *MECL* 362, 363, 370 and 373.

49 Joseph Dyer, 'Augustine and the *Hymni ante oblationem*: The Earliest Offertory Chants?', *Revue des études augustiniennes* 27 (1981), 85–99; id., 'The Offertory Chant of the Roman Liturgy and its Musical Form', *Studi musicali*, 11 (1982), 3–30.

50 For indications that the Communions were originally responsorial, see: Willibrord Heckenbach, 'Responsoriale Communio-Antiphonen', in Detlef Altenburg (ed.), *Ars Musica, Musica Scientia: Festschrift Heinrich Hüschen* (Cologne: Gitarre und Laute, 1980), 224–32; Thomas H. Schattauer, 'The Koinonicon of the Byzantine Liturgy: An Historical Study', *Orientalia Christiana Periodica*, 49 (1983), 91–129.

51 I hesitate to agree fully with much of what Juan Mateos has written in 'La Psalmodie: ses genres', in his *La Célébration de la parole dans la liturgie byzantine: étude historique* (OCA 191; Rome: Pontificium Institutum Studiorum Orientalium, 1971), 7–26, particularly his identification of the great responsories with the Byzantine kathismata and hypakoai (25). The repertory of the Byzantine psaltikon and asmatikon preserve prokeimena for Vespers that can claim at least a liturgical parallel to the Western office responsory; see Gisa Hintze, *Das byzantinische Prokeimena-Repertoire: Untersuchungen und kritische Edition* (Hamburg: Verlag der Musikalienhandlung Wagner, 1973), 12–19, 123–81. Yet to be examined is a significant repertory of hypakoai from the early chant repertory of Jerusalem, preserved in the Georgian Iadgari. For an introduction to this source see Jeffery, 'The Earliest Christian Chant Repertory Recovered'.

52 *MECL*, p. 171.

53 The two most important spokesmen for such views were Joseph Gelineau and Helmut Hucke. See my remarks in *Re-envisioning Past Musical Cultures: Ethnomusicology in the Study of Gregorian Chant* (Chicago: University of Chicago Press, 1992), 76–86, 112–15, and my 'Communication', *JAMS* 49 (1996), 175–9, esp. 177–8. A record of what happened at the official level by one of the people most involved in it is Annibale Bugnini, *The Reform of the Liturgy 1948–1975*, trans. Matthew J. O'Connell (Collegeville, Minn.: Liturgical Press, 1990), 885–914. It is only fitting to point out that, in our many private conversations on these matters, James McKinnon was always a model of charity, which is more than I can say for myself.

54 Kirsti Barrett Copeland, 'Mapping the Apocalypse of Paul: Geography, Genre and History' (Ph.D. diss., Princeton University, 2001), 178. On the date, see pp. 21–5.

55 Over 300 manuscripts and fragments survive in various languages; see Peter Dinzelbacher, 'Die Verbreitung der apokryphen "Visio Pauli" im mittelaltelichen Europa', *Mittellateinisches Jahrbuch*, 27 (1992), 77–90. The Greek historian Sozomen, in his *Historia ecclesiastica* 7.19.10, ed. Joseph Bidez and

Günther Christian Hansen in *GCS* 50: 331 (Berlin: Akademie, 1960), says that the book is 'commended by most monks'. See Copeland, 'Mapping', 25–35, 170–71.

56 *Regula Magistri* 34:10. See *La Règle du Maître*, ed. Adalbert de Vogüé, 3 vols. (SC 105–7; Paris: Editions du Cerf, 1964–5), i, 214–15, ii, 188–91; on the Roman background of the Master, see i, 225–33. For an English translation from Vogüé's text, see *The Rule of the Master*, trans. Luke Eberle and Charles Philippi (Kalamazoo, Mich.: Cistercian Publications, 1977), 198.

57 *Apocalypse of Paul: A New Critical Edition of Three Long Latin Versions*, ed. Theodore Silverstein and Anthony Hilhorst (Cahiers d'orientalisme, 21; Geneva: Patrick Cramer, 1997), 17–18, 21.

58 For other interpretations of the word 'Alleluia' see: Donatien De Bruyne, *Préfaces de la bible latine* (Namur: Auguste Godenne, 1920), 66, 76–7; Charles Wright et al. in *Collectanea Pseudo-Bedae*, ed. Martha Bayless and Michael Lapidge (Dublin: School of Celtic Studies, Dublin Institute for Advanced Studies, 1998), 251–4.

59 The 'psalmodic movement' certainly had its opponents. Among them was a certain Hilarus, against whom Augustine wrote a Tract, unfortunately lost. See *MECL* 385; Dyer, 'Augustine and the *Hymni ante oblationem*'.

60 From 'The Apocalypse of Paul (Visio Pauli)' in *The Apocryphal New Testament: A Collection of Apocryphal Christian Literature in an English Translation*, ed. J. K. Elliott (Oxford: Clarendon Press, 1993), 631–3. For Latin texts, see *Apocalypse of Paul,* ed. Silverstein and Hilhorst, 128–35. For an English translation of the (shorter) Greek text, see *The Ante-Nicene Fathers: Translations of the Writings of the Fathers down to A.D. 325*, ed. Alexander Roberts and James Donaldson (Buffalo: The Christian Literature Company, 1886; many reprints), 578. For some Armenian texts, see *Ecrits apocryphes sur les apôtres: traduction de l'édition arménienne de Venise*, i, ed. Louis Leloir (Turnhout: Brepols, 1986), 124–5, 146, 167–8. For an English translation of the Coptic, see Copeland, 'Mapping', 208–9. For another account of an Alleluia, sung before the Gospel, in an apocryphon attributed to Matthew, see *Apocryphal New Testament*, ed. Elliott, 522–3.

61 *Epistula ad Marcellinum de interpretatione Psalmorum* 12. *PG* 27: 21–4. I have modified the translation published on pp. 109–11 of: Athanasius, *The Life of Antony and the Letter to Marcellinus*, trans. Robert C. Gregg (New York: Paulist Press, 1980), 101–29 nn. 144–7; see also Ignasi M. Fossas, 'L'epistola ad Marcellinum di Sant'Atanasio sull'uso del salterio: studio letterario, liturgico e teologico', *Studia monastica*, 39 (1997), 27–76.

62 Hilary of Poitiers, *Tractatus super Psalmos* 1.1–3, ed. J. Doignon (CCSL 61; Turnhout: Brepols, 1997), 19–20. 'Principalis haec in psalmis intellegentia est, ex cuius persona uel in quem ea quae dicta sint intellegi oporteant, posse discernere. Non enim uniformis et indiscreta eorum est constitutio, ut non et auctores habeant et genera diuersa. Inuenimus enim in his frequenter personam Dei Patris solere proponi, ut in octogesimo et octauo psalmo, cum dicitur: "Exaltaui electum de plebe mea. Inueni Dauid seruum meum, in oleo sancto unxi eum. Ipse inuocauit me: Pater meus es tu et susceptor salutis meae. Et ego primogenitum ponam eum, excelsum super reges terrae." Personam uero Filii in plurimis fere introduci, ut in septimo decimo: Populus, quem non cognoui, seruiuit mihi; et in uicesimo primo: Diuiserunt uestimenta mea sibi et super uestem meam miserunt sortem. Nunc autem primum hunc psalmum uel ex persona Patris uel ex persona Filii non posse intellegi res ipsa absolute docet: . . . At uero nunc cum dicitur: SED IN LEGE DOMINI FVIT VOLVNTAS EIVS ET

IN LEGE EIVS, nulla Domini persona de se loquentis ostenditur, sed alterius potius beatitudinem, eius scilicet uiri, cuius in lege Domini uoluntas sit, praedicantis. Persona atque prophetae, cuius ore spiritus sanctus loquatur, nunc esse noscenda est officio oris eius ad cognitionem nos sacramenti spiritalis erudiens.'

63 Rondeau, *Les Commentaires patristiques du psautier*, esp. vol. ii (OCA 220, 1985). See also: André Rose, *Les Psaumes: voix du Christ et de l'église* (Paris: P. Lethielleux, 1981); Balthasar Fischer, *Die Psalmen als Stimme der Kirche: Gesammelte Studien zur christlichen Psalmenfrömmigkeit*, ed. Andreas Heinz (Trier: Paulinus-Verlag, 1982); *Le Psautier chez les Pères* (Strasbourg: Centre d'Analyse et de Documentation Patristiques, 1994); Günter Bader, *Psalterium affectuum palaestra: Prolegomena zu einer Theologie des Psalters* (Tübingen: J. C. B. Mohr [Paul Siebeck], 1996).

64 David Dawson, *Allegorical Readers and Cultural Revision in Ancient Alexandria* (Berkeley: University of California Press, 1992).

65 For example, Matt. 21: 4–5, 42–4; 22: 41–6; Luke 4: 16–30; John 19: 23–4, 28–37; Acts 8: 30–38; 1 Cor. 10: 1–5. The Epistle to the Hebrews is full of examples.

66 James 1: 23–5. For the other New Testament mirror metaphor, see 1 Cor. 13: 12.

67 *Conlationes* 1.17.2, ed. Michael Petschenig (CSEL 13; Vienna: C. Geroldi Filium, 1886, 26–7; ed. Pichery (SC 42, 1955), 98–9. Translation from John Cassian, *The Conferences*, trans. and annotated by Boniface Ramsey (New York: Paulist Press, 1997), 56–7.

68 Synonyms include 'semper repetere', 'iterare', 'recitare ad nauseam' and 'deblaterare', according to *Thesaurus linguae Latinae*, v (Leizpig: Teubner, 1910), 117–18.

69 *Conlationes* 10.11.4–6; *Conferences*, trans. Ramsey, 384–5.

70 *Conlationes* 9.26.1–2, ed. Pichery (SC 54, 1958), 62; translation adapted from Ramsey, *Conferences*, 346.

71 The Greek term has, however, a much more complicated etymology than the Latin: H. Greeven, 'κατανύσσω, κατάνυξις', *Theological Dictionary of the New Testament*, iii (Grand Rapids, Mich.: Wm. B. Eerdmans, 1965), 489–503; *A Patristic Greek Lexicon*, ed. G. W. H. Lampe (Oxford: Clarendon Press, 1961), 713; *Thesaurus linguae Latinae*, iii (1906–12), 2171–5.

72 *Regula Magistri* 1.3–5; *La Règle du Maître*, ed. Vogüé (1964), i, 328–30. The text is repeated in the Benedictine Rule, which is heavily dependent on the Rule of the Master. *La Règle de saint Benoît*, ed. Adalbert de Vogüé and Jean Neufville, 7 vols. (SC 181–6; Paris: Editions du Cerf, 1971–7). For this passage see SC 181 (1972), 436–8. An English translation from the Vogüé–Neufville text is *RB 1980: The Rule of St. Benedict in Latin and English with Notes*, ed. Timothy Fry et al. (Collegeville, Minn.: Liturgical Press, 1981).

73 For a traditional account of this topic, see Johannes Quasten, *Music and Worship in Pagan and Christian Antiquity*, trans. Boniface Ramsey (Washington, DC: National Association of Pastoral Musicians, 1983), 94–9, 117–20. A more thoughtful, nuanced assessment is Stig Simeon Frøyshov, 'La Réticence à l'hymnographie chez des anachorètes de l'Egypte et du Sinaï du 6 au 8 siècles', in *L'Hymnographie: Conférences Saint-Serge*, 46, ed. A. M. Triacca et al. (Rome: CLV, 2000), 229–45. On the later date of some of the most widely quoted stories, see McKinnon, 'Desert Monasticism', 508; Jeffery, 'Eastern and Western Elements', 102, 135, n. 14.

74 Cassian, *De institutis coenobiorum* 2.2, ed. Michael Petschenig (CSEL 17; Vienna: F. Tempsky, 1888), 18: 'quidam enim uicenos seu tricenos psalmos et hos ipsos antiphonarum protelatos melodiis et adiunctione quarundam modulationum debere dici singulis noctibus censuerunt'. For an interpretation of the 'certain

melodies', see Jürgen Raasted, 'Die Jubili Finales und die Verwendung von interkalierten Vokalisen in der Gesangspraxis der Byzantiner', in *Griechische Musik und Europa: Antike – Byzanz – Volksmusik der Neuzeit*, ed. Rudolf M. Brandl and Evangelos Konstantinou (Aachen: Alano Verlag, Edition Herodot, 1988), 67–80, esp. 79; id., 'The "Laetantis adverbia" of Aurelian's Greek Informant', in *Aspects de la musique liturgique au Moyen Age*, ed. Christian Meyer (Paris: Editions Créaphis, 1991), 55–66, esp. 64. Both articles refer back to Raasted, *Intonation Formulas and Modal Signatures in Byzantine Musical Manuscripts* (Monumenta musicae Byzantinae: Subsidia, 7; Copenhagen: Munksgaard, 1966), 158.

75 1 Cor. 12: 12, 27. See also Col. 1: 18–24, 2: 9–19; Eph. 1: 23, 2: 16, 4: 4–16, 5: 23–30.

76 See Michael Fiedrowicz, *Psalmus vox totius Christi: Studien zu Augustins 'Enarrationes in Psalmos'* (Freiburg im Breisgau: Herder, 1997). Tarsicius van Bavel, 'The "Christus Totus" Idea: A Forgotten Aspect of Augustine's Spirituality', in *Studies in Patristic Christology: Proceedings of the Third Maynooth Patristic Conference, October 1996*, ed. Thomas Finan and Vincent Twomey (Dublin: Four Courts Press, 1998), 84–94.

77 *Enarratio 2 in Psalmum 29* 1, 5–6, in *Enarrationes in Psalmos*, ed. Eligius Dekkers and Johannes Fraipont, 3 vols (CCSL 38–40; Turnhout: Brepols, 1956), i, 173–4, 177–8.

78 A similar interpretation probably lies behind the uses of this text in the Roman chant traditions as the antiphon *Exaltabo te Domine* for Matins on Ascension Day and as the refrain of the Gradual *Exaltabo te Domine* on Wednesday in Passion week: *CAO* 3, no. 2755, p. 213; *AMS*, no. 70, pp. 84–5; Paul F. Cutter, *Musical Sources of the Old-Roman Mass: An Inventory of MS Rome, St. Cecilia Gradual 1071; MS Rome, Vaticanum latinum 5319; MSS Rome, San Pietro F 22 and F 11* (Neuhausen-Stuttgart: American Institute of Musicology, 1979), no. 73, pp. 120–21.

79 Such an interpretation may explain the Roman use of this text as the Offertory *Exaltabo te Domine* for Ash Wednesday: *AMS*, no. 37, pp. 50–51; Cutter, *Musical Sources*, no. 38, p. 81. The text is also used in a rare antiphon for the Office of the Dead, where it is understood as being spoken by the departed soul: *CAO* 3, no. 2756, p. 214.

80 *Sermo 17*, in *Sermones de Vetere Testamento*, ed. Cyril Lambot (CCSL 41; Turnhout: Brepols, 1961), 237–8.

81 About 400 authentic sermons are listed in the most recent enumeration, E. Rebillard, 'Sermones', in *Augustine through the Ages*, 773–92, esp. 774–89. However, this does not include another 100 or so that were incorporated into Augustine's commentaries on the Psalms and the Gospel and Epistles of John. See M. Cameron, '*Enarrationes in Psalmos*', A. D. Fitzgerald, '*Epistulam Johannis ad Parthos tractatus, In*' and Fitzgerald, '*Johannis evangelium tractatus, In*', ibid., 290–96, 310–11, 474–5.

82 *Enarratio in Psalmum 103*, sermo 3.3, 4; sermo 4.1. CCSL 40: 1500–1501, 1502, 1521.

83 *Enarratio in Psalmum 123*, sermo ad populum 1, 3. CCSL 40: 1825–7. In this passage the word *canto, cantare* is used for 'singing' throughout.

84 Jacques Froger, 'Les Chants de la messe aux VIIIe et IXe siècles', *Revue grégorienne*, 26 (1947), 165–72, 218–28; 27 (1948), 56–62, 98–107; 28 (1949), 58–65, 94–102; Dmitri Conomos, 'Change in Early Christian and Byzantine Liturgical Chant', *Studies in Music from the University of Western Ontario*, 5 (1980), 49–63; Burckhardt Neunheuser, 'The Relation of Priest and Faithful in the Liturgies of Pius V and Paul VI', in *Roles in the Liturgical Assembly* (New York: Pueblo,

1981), 207–19; Edward Foley, 'The Song of the Assembly in Medieval Eucharist', in Lizette Larson-Miller (ed.), *Medieval Liturgy: A Book of Essays* (New York: Garland, 1997), 203–34; Frederick R. McManus, 'From the *Rubricae Generales* and *Ritus Servandus* of 1570 to the *Institutio Generalis* of 1969', in Kathleen Hughes (ed.), *Finding Voice to Give God Praise: Essays in the Many Languages of the Liturgy* (Collegeville, Minn.: Liturgical Press, 1998), 214–42.

85 Peter Jeffery, 'The Introduction of Psalmody into the Roman Mass by Pope Celestine I (422–432): Reinterpreting a Passage in the *Liber Pontificalis*', *AfLw* 26 (1984), 147–65. My interpretation of the word 'antiphonatim' in this text is supported by a fourteenth-century chronicler: Thomas Ebendorfer, *Chronica pontificum Romanorum*, ed. Harald Zimmerman (Munich: MGH, 1994), 145.

86 Arnobius Junior, *Conflictus cum Serapione* 2.13, in *Arnobii Iunioris Opera omnia*, ii: *Opera minora*, ed. Klaus-D. Daur (CCSL 25A; Turnhout: Brepols, 1992), 112; see also *MECL* 395; *CPL* 1654. The quote is from St. Ambrose's hymn *Intende qui regis Israel*; for full text see Walther Bulst, *Hymni antiquissimi LXXV Psalmi III* (Heidelberg: F. H. Kerle, 1956), 43; *Ambroise de Milan: Hymnes: Texte établi, traduit et annoté*, ed. J. Fontaine et al. (Paris: Editions du Cerf, 1992), 263–301.

87 Leo Magnus, *Tractatus 3 in Natale Eiusdem*, in *Sancti Leonis Magni Romani Pontificis Tractatus septem et nonaginta*, i, ed. Antoine Chavasse (CCSL 138; Turnhout: Brepols, 1973), 10. The other sermon that mentions this psalm is *Tractatus 5 in Natale Eiusdem*, CCSL 138: 23.

88 *AMS*, pp. 26–7, 42, 166–7, 42–3, 20–23, 144–5, 122–3.

89 Cutter, *Musical Sources*, 64 (St. Fabian), 257 (St. Mark; a different Gradual on 311), 348 (the Common of Priests), 73 and 279 (St. Gregory).

90 In the Roman usage of Leo's time, the Sunday before Easter was Passion Sunday and focused on the liturgical reading of the Gospel accounts of the Passion. The non-Roman Western churches, following the usage of Jerusalem, celebrated this day in part as marking the triumphal entry of Jesus into Jerusalem before his Passion. As the Roman rite became hybridized with Frankish and Gallican usages, the Sunday before Easter became known as Palm Sunday and the name Passion Sunday was moved back to the previous Sunday, producing the standard late medieval nomenclature. However, the Mass of the Sunday before Easter retained its Passion-themed chants, including the Tract based on Psalm 21 [22]. The palm procession was simply tacked on in front of it. See A. G. Martimort et al. (eds), *The Church at Prayer: An Introduction to the Liturgy*, iv: *The Liturgy and Time* (new edn, Collegeville, Minn.: Liturgical Press, 1983), 70–71, 75; Adrien Nocent, 'La Semaine sainte dans la liturgie romaine', in Anthony George Kollamparampil et al. (eds), *Hebdomadae Sanctae Celebratio: Conspectus Historicus Comparativus* (Rome: CLV, 1997), 277–310, esp. 302–6. Sermons witnessing to the reading or singing of this Ps. 21 [22] in connection with the Passion celebration include one of Maximus of Turin (d. 408 or 423; CCSL 23: 112–15) and five by Augustine (*PLS* 2: 543–5; CCSL 38: 121–34; CCSL 39: 1163; CCSL 40: 1494; CCSL 36: 138). The Jerusalem practice of performing this psalm in the afternoon service on Good Friday (precisely the time when Jesus was on the cross) is attested in the 380s by Egeria (CCSL 175: 81, SC 296: 288) and St. Cyril of Jerusalem (*PG* 33: 804–5, 828). The use of verse 19 [18] as the responsorial refrain at Jerusalem is attested in the early fifth-century Armenian lectionary: *Le Codex arménien Jérusalem 121*, ed. A. Renoux, 2 vols. (PO 35, fasc. 1; 36, fasc. 2; Turnhout: Brepols, 1969, 1971), see esp. PO 36: 284, 292; the eighth-century Georgian lectionary: *Le Grand Lectionnaire de l'église de Jérusalem (V*[e]*–VIII*[e] *siècles)*, ed. Michel Tarchnischvili, 2 vols. in 4 (CSCO 188–9, 204–5;

Louvain: Secrétariat de Corpus Scriptorum Christianorum Orientalium, 1959–60), see CSCO 188: 101; 205: 111, and the Greek typikon of 1122: 'Τυπικὸν τῆς ἐν Ἱεροσολύμοις Ἐκκλησίας' [Typikon of the Church in Jerusalem; in Greek], Ἀνάλεκτα Ἱεροσολυμιτικῆς Σταχυολαγίας' [Collections of Gleanings from Jerusalem], ed. A. Papadopoulos-Keramefs, ii, 1–254 (St. Petersburg: B. Kirschbaum, 1894; repr. Brusssels: Culture et Civilisation, 1963), 137, 158 in the G authentic mode. The spread of this usage to other Eastern centers is attested in the oldest Syriac lectionary (fifth or sixth century), F. C. Burkitt, 'The Early Syriac Lectionary System', *Proceedings of the British Academy* (1921–3), 301–38, esp. 309; the tenth-century typikon of Constantinople: *Le Typicon de la Grande Eglise: Ms. Saint-Croix no 40, Xe siècle*, ed. Juan Mateos, 2 vols. (OCA 165–6; Pontificium Institutum Studiorum Orientalium, 1962–3), ii, 80; and the Byzantine prophetologion: *Prophetologium*, ed. Carsten Höeg and Günther Zuntz (Monumenta musicae Byzantinae: Lectionaria, 1; Copenhagen: Munksgaard, 1939–81), i/4, 405–6. The use of verse 17 [16], 'They have pierced my hands and my feet', as refrain is also attested at Jerusalem ('Τυπικὸν', ed. Papadopoulos-Keramefs, 150) at terce, in the plagal E mode; and in the Ambrosian chant repertory on Good Friday: *Manuale Ambrosianum ex codice saec. XI olim in usum canonicae vallis Travaliae*, ii: *Officia totius anni et alii ordines*, ed. M. Magistretti (Milan: Ulrico Hoepli, 1904), 31, 44, 55. Augustine seems to have known a refrain that combined both verses (see sermons above). In the Roman traditions, the performance of a substantial portion of the psalm on the Sunday before Easter takes the form of the Tract *Deus Deus meus*: *AMS*, no. 73; Cutter, *Musical Sources*, no. 77. A similar usage occurs in the two branches of Mozarabic chant: see *Antifonario visigótico mozárabe de la Catedral de León*: *edición del texto*, ed. Louis Brou and José Vives (Barcelona: Centro de estudios e investigación S. Isidoro, 1959), 273; *Liber misticus de cuaresma y pascua (Cod. Toledo, Bibl. Capit. 35,5)*, ed. José Janini (Toledo: Instituto de Estudios Visigótico-Mozárabes, 1980), 89–90. Usage on Holy Saturday is attested in the East Syrian and Coptic rites: A. Rücker, 'Die wechselnden Gesangstücke der ostsyrischen Messe', *Jahrbuch für Liturgiewissenschaft*, 1 (1921), 61–86, see esp. 74; *Le Lectionnaire de la semaine sainte; texte copte édité avec traduction française d'apres le manuscrit Add. 5997 du British Museum*, ed. Oswald Hugh Ewart Burmester (PO 24, fasc. 2; 25, fasc. 2; Paris: Firmin-Didot, 1933–9), see 25/2, 356, 371, 429–33. An anonymous Irish sermon seems to indicate the psalm was performed after the Gospel on Holy Thursday: see André Wilmart, *Analecta reginensia: extraits des manuscrits latins de la reine Christine conservés au Vatican* (Vatican City: Biblioteca Apostolica Vaticana, 1933; repr. 1966), 34, 38. Note also the remarks of Cassiodorus (CCSL 97: 208): 'Iste psalmus est quem nobis paschali munere sollemniter decantat ecclesia.'

91 CCSL 138A: 252–3; *AMS*, no. 38; Cutter, *Musical Sources*, no. 39. For another possible case (CCSL 138A, 587) see McKinnon, 'Liturgical Psalmody in the Sermons of St. Augustine', 17 n. 32.

92 'Audiunt enim et faciunt quod propheta dixit: *Confitemini domino quoniam bonus* est.' Archidiaconus anonymus romanus, *Sermo 2 ad reconciliandis paenitentibus*, ed. F. Heylen, CCSL 9: 359–60; *CPL* 238.

93 This same first verse is shared by Pss. 105 [106], 106 [107], 117 [118] and 135 [136].

94 Pseudo-Augustine, *Sermones Mai 171–173* (*PLS* 2: 1266–74). No author is proposed on p. 148 of *CPL*. However, *CPPMA* 1: 1780–82, reports an opinion that the unknown author can also be credited with other extant sermons, including sets of three for the Traditio Symboli – the ceremony in which the

Creed was taught to catechumens in preparation for baptism (1022–4) – and on the anointings of the baptismal service (1117–19), as well as one on Christmas (903) and one possibly for Easter (894). It is proposed that the author may have been a sixth-century Italian bishop, and the fact that the baptismal ceremonies included a washing of feet suggests the archdiocese of Milan. See Edward Yarnold, *The Awe-Inspiring Rites of Initiation: The Origins of the R[ite of] C[hristian] I[nitiation of] A[dults]* (2nd edn, Collegeville, Minn.: Liturgical Press, 1994), 30–31, 121–3.

95 *Liber sacramentorum Romanae aeclesiae ordinis anni circuli*, ed. Leo Cunibert Mohlberg et al. (Rome: Herder, 1960), 55; see also the deacon's speech on 56–7.

96 Instead, we find Ps. 33 [34] taking a central role in the rite: *Le Pontifical romano-germanique du dixième siècle*, ed. Cyrille Vogel and Reinhard Else, ii (Vatican City: Biblioteca Apostolica Vaticana, 1963), 59–67; *Le Pontifical romain au moyen âge*, i: *Le pontifical romain du XII*[e] *siècle*, ed. Michel Andrieu (Vatican City: Biblioteca Apostolica Vaticana, 1938), 214–19.

97 Ps. 105 [106], 6: 'peccauimus cum patribus nostris iniuste egimus iniquitatem fecimus'.

98 *CPL* 242. *Arnobii Iunioris Opera omnia*, i: *Commentarii in Psalmos*, ed. Daur, 162–6.

99 On what can be learned of Arnobius' identity and biography, see CCSL 25, pp. xi–xiv. Besides the author's interest in Pope Celestine, other indications that he wrote from a Roman point of view are: (1) his generally pro-papal views on the controversial heresies of the time, particularly his opposition to the local Roman schism of the Novatianists (see pp. xvi–xvii), and (2) his unusually strong anti-Jewish attitude, suggesting he lived in a place with a substantial Jewish community. Rome was such a place; see Leonard Victor Rutgers, *The Jews in Late Ancient Rome: Evidence of Cultural Interaction in the Roman Diaspora* (Leiden: E. J. Brill, 1995). On Novatianism, see E. Amann, 'Novatien et novatianisme', *Dictionnaire de théologie catholique*, ed. A. Vacant et al., xi (Paris: Letouzey, 1931), 816–49; Tables générales 3 (1972), 3327–8.

100 That Arnobius envisioned readers rather than listeners is made clear in the preface to CCSL 25: 3, and in the commentary on Ps. 40 [41], CCSL 25: 59. That he is addressing fellow monks is clear from the commentaries on Pss. 140 [141] and 141 [142], CCSL 25: 238–41. See also the commentary on Ps. 105 [106], CCSL 25: 165.

101 'Arnobe le jeune', in Germain Morin, *Etudes, textes, découvertes: contributions à la littérature et à l'histoire des douze premiers siècles* (Maredsous: Abbaye de Maredsous, and Paris: A. Picard, 1913), 309–439 at 365.

102 CCSL 25: 87, 187, 253–4. For other attested uses of these psalms in various traditions of the Office, see Taft, *Liturgy of the Hours*, 394–5.

103 Morin, 'Arnobe', 363–8.

104 Part of the dialog that begins the Preface, leading into the Sanctus at Mass. See the commentary on Ps. 120 in CCSL 25: 205.

105 The versicle from Ps. 69: 2 [70: 1] that is said at the beginning of each office hour. See the commentary on Ps. 51 [52], CCSL 25: 75. A lengthy discussion of this verse, advocating its meditative repetition throughout the day, will be found in Cassian's *Conlationes* 10.10.2–13 (CSEL 13: 297–302; SC 54: 85–90); *Conferences*, trans. Ramsey, 379–82.

106 See the commentary on Ps. 9, CCSL 25: 11.

107 CCSL 25: 60. This psalm is the source of the Holy Saturday Tract *Sicut cervus*. *AMS*, no. 79; Cutter, *Musical Sources*, no. 83; see also n. 124 below.

108 See the commentary on Ps. 104 [105], CCSL 25: 162. The corresponding chant in the Roman and certain other Italian traditions, however, takes its verse *Confitemini domino* from Ps. 135 [136]. *AMS*, no. 79; Cutter, *Musical Sources*, no. 83. See also Kenneth Levy, 'The Italian Neophytes' Chants', *JAMS* 23 (1970), 181–227; and id. '*Lux de luce*: The Origin of an Italian Sequence', *MQ* 57 (1971), 40–61.

109 The classic work of Henri de Lubac, *Exégèse médiévale: les quatre sens de l'écriture*, 2 vols. in 4 (Théologie 41, 42, 59; Paris: Aubier, 1959–64), is now available in English as: Henri de Lubac, *Medieval Exegesis: The Four Senses of Scripture*, 2 vols., trans. Marc Sebanc and E. M. Macierowski (Grand Rapids, Mich.: William B. Eerdmans; Edinburgh: T. & T. Clark, 1998–2000). See also Susan K. Wood, *Spiritual Exegesis and the Church in the Theology of Henri de Lubac* (Grand Rapids, Mich.: William B. Eerdmans; Edinburgh: T. & T. Clark, 1998).

110 See Pss. 50 [51], 73 [74], 89 [90], for example (CCSL 25: 71–4, 107–8, 133–5).

111 'id quod canimus faciamus'. From the commentary on Ps. 61 [62], CCSL 25: 86. See also the commentaries on Pss. 3, 40 [41], 88 [89] (CCSL 25: 5, 59, 131).

112 See the commentaries on Pss. 1, 37 [38], 40 [41], 51[52] (CCSL 25: 4, 52, 59, 75).

113 Cebrià Pifarré, *Arnobio el Joven y la cristología del 'Conflictus'* (Montserrat: Publicacions de l'Abadia de Montserrat, 1988), 42–9.

114 CCSL 25: 177–9.

115 *AMS*, no. 135; Cutter, *Musical Sources*, nos. 149a, 244a.

116 There are many published photographs, for example: Walter Oakeshott, *The Mosaics of Rome from the Third to the Fourteenth Centuries* (Greenwich, Conn.: NY Graphic Society, 1967), pl. 77, pls. 79–82. The book held by St. Stephen says 'Adesit anima mea' (Ps. 62: 9 [63: 8]), incipit of antiphon texts used for both Lawrence and Stephen. *CAO* 3, nos. 1271–2. Oakeshott's discussion (pp. 17–18, 145–6), misreads the inscription in Stephen's book.

117 *AMS*, pp. 136–7, 138–9, 168–9, 162–3; Cutter, *Musical Sources*, pp. 220, 222, 291–2, 272, 317, 258, 311, also for the Common of Apostles in MS F 22, pp. 336–7.

118 'credo uidere bona Domini in terra uiuentium. Expecta Dominum et uiriliter age et confortetur cor tuum et sustine Dominum.' *Le Psautier romain et les autres anciens psautiers latins*, ed. Robert Weber (Rome: Abbaye Saint-Jérôme; Vatican City: Libreria Vaticana, 1953), 52.

119 'Ego autem qui haec contemno, *credo* quod uideam *bona domini in terra* non mortalium, sed *uiuentium*. Ad haec respondit in antiphona spiritus sanctus: Si ergo credis *uidere bona domini in terra uiuentium, expecta dominum; age uiriliter, confortetur cor tuum, et sustine dominum*, qui regnat in saecula saeculorum. Amen.' See the commentary on Ps. 26 [27], CCSL 25: 35.

120 *CPL* 1839a. *CPPMA* 2: 3592. The critical edition is in *La Règle de saint Augustin*, i: *Tradition manuscrite*, ed. Luc Verheijen (Paris: Etudes augustiniennes, 1967), 148–52. Verheijen's text is reprinted and translated in George Lawless, *Augustine of Hippo and his Monastic Rule* (Oxford: Clarendon Press, 1987), 74–9. On the questions of date and authorship see Lawless, 167–71. On its place in the history of the office, see Taft, *Liturgy of the Hours*, 94–6.

121 Lawless, *Augustine of Hippo*, 170; Germain Morin, 'L'Ordre des heures canoniales dans les monastères de Cassiodore', *Revue bénédictine* 43 (1931), 145–52.

122 Pierre Salmon, *Les 'Tituli Psalmorum' des manuscrits latins* (Rome: Abbaye Saint-Jérôme; Vatican City: Libreria Vaticana, 1959), 55–74; Bonifatius Fischer, 'Bedae de titulis psalmorum liber', in Johannes Autenrieth and Franz Brunhölzl

(eds), *Festschrift Bernhard Bischoff zu seinem 65. Geburtstag* (Stuttgart: A. Hiersemann, 1971), 90–110, tables 2–6.

123 'Vox Ecclesiae ad Christum. Legendus ad evangelium Marci ubi temptatur Christus.' Salmon, *'Tituli Psalmorum'*, 67. Oddly, the psalm title cites the Gospel of Mark, which barely mentions the temptation; compare Matt. 4: 1–11 with Mark 1: 13. The Matthew reading occurs at the beginning of Lent in non-Roman traditions also, both Eastern and Western. See, for example, the table in *Le Lectionnaire de Luxeuil (Paris, ms. lat. 9427): édition et étude comparative*, ed. Pierre Salmon, 2 vols. (Rome: Abbaye Saint-Jérome; Vatican City: Libreria Editrice Vaticana, 1944, 1953), i, pp. cviii–cix; Adrien Nocent, *The Liturgical Year*, ii: *Lent*, trans. Matthew J. O'Connell (Collegeville, Minn.: Liturgical Press, 1977), 222, 228, 232.

124 'Ante baptismum vox Christi est.' Salmon, *'Tituli Psalmorum'*, 61. Perhaps the exegete imagined Christ reciting this psalm prior to his own baptism by John, recounted in Matt. 3: 1–17 and parallels. Use of this psalm at baptism is attested by Zeno of Verona (CCSL 22: 51, 70, 188, 202), Augustine (CCSL 38: 460 'sollemniter cantatus hic psalmus, ut ita desiderent fontem'), Jerome (CCSL 78: 542–4, titled *In psalmum 41 ad neophytos*), Cassiodorus (CCSL 97: 387, 'Et ideo hodieque hunc psalmum boni desiderii suasorem atque institutorem baptizandis congrue decantat Ecclesia'). The sixth-century Egyptian papyrus lectionary fragment published in Herbert John Mansfield Milne, 'Early Psalms and Lections for Lent', *Journal of Egyptian Archaeology*, 10 (1924), 278–82, assigns this psalm to the fifth Sunday of Lent, a scrutiny day of preparation for baptism (p. 281, with 2 Cor. 2: 16 and Matt. 11: 25). The Roman Tract is already mentioned in the seventh-century 'Gelasian' sacramentary; see *Liber sacramentorum*, ed. Mohlberg et al., 72. The mosaics in early Christian baptisteries sometimes depict this psalm. See Ejnar Dyggve, *History of Salonitan Christianity* (Oslo: Aschehoug, and Cambridge, Mass.: Harvard University Press, 1951), 33, 43, and figs. II.4–II.7, II.13, II.25, and esp. II.29 and II.30 following p. 48; Djordje Mano-Zissi, 'La Question des différents écoles de mosaïques gréco-romaines de Yougoslavie et essai d'une esquisse de leur évolution', *La Mosaïque gréco-romaine* (Paris: Editions du Centre Nationale de la Recherche Scientifique, 1965), 287–95 and plates ff., see esp. 292–3 and pl. 21; Lucien De Bruyne, 'La Décoration des baptistères paléochrétiens', in *Miscellanea liturgica in honorem L. Cuniberti Mohlberg*, i (Rome: Edizioni liturgiche, 1948), 200–202; H. C. Puech, 'Le Cerf et le serpent: note sur le symbolisme de la mosaïque découverte au baptistère d'Enchir-Messaouda', *Cahiers archéologiques*, 4 (1949), 17–60. See also André Rose, 'Les Psaumes de l'initiation chrétienne I. Les psaumes ou versets psalmiques utilisés dans l'église occidentale', *Questions liturgiques et paroissiales*, 47 (1966), 279–92; 48 (1967), 111–20; Auf der Maur, *Das Psalmenverständnis*, 118–27, 333.

125 See the list of sources in Salmon, *'Tituli Psalmorum'*, 47–51. The earliest manuscript, however, is the sixth-century Irish psalter of St. Columba. Despite the long-standing Irish antagonism to Roman liturgical customs, the fact that the Columba MS contains the Vulgate ('Gallican') text of the psalter, and that later Irish Gallican psalters contain the Roman series of canticles, could be made the basis of an argument that the early Irish church received its psalter from Rome. See my article 'Eastern and Western Elements', 103–4, 135.

126 'Legendus ad evangelium Lucae. Vox Patris et apostolorum et Christi. Ad caput scribendum.' Salmon, *'Tituli Psalmorum'*, 55. Uses of Ps. 2 in a Christmas context are attested in Jerusalem: *Le Codex*, ed. Renoux (PO 36), 214, 216; *Le Grand*

Lectionnaire, ed. Tarchnischvili (CSCO 188: 9, 13. Constantinople: *Le Typicon*, ed. Mateos, i (OCA 165), 152; Hintze, *Das byzantinische Prokeimena-Repertoire*, 102–3. The Mozarabic rite: *Antifonario*, ed. Brou and Vives, 94. An anonymous sermon for Christmas shows this psalm being sung along with an alleluia that takes its verse from Ps. 71: 6 [72: 6]: Pseudo-Augustine, *Sermo Mai 199* (*PLS* 2: 1285–6). According to *CPPMA* 1: 1807, the sermon is 'antiquus et africanus', suggesting a milieu close to Augustine's time and place.

127 The *titulus* for Ps. 22 [23] is 'Vox ecclesiae post baptismum', for Ps. 31 [32] 'Post baptismum vox paenitentium'; Salmon, *'Tituli Psalmorum'*, 57, 59. The singing of Ps. 22 [23] after baptism was an ancient Milanese practice mentioned more than once by St. Ambrose (CSEL 73: 63, 107; CSEL 32/2: 430), and the tradition appears to survive in the chant *Dominus regit me*, sung while leaving the baptistery toward the end of the Ambrosian Pentecost vigil. See Yarnold, *The Awe-Inspiring Rites*, 87–8, 143–5; Peter Jeffery, *A New Commandment: Toward a Renewed Rite for the Washing of Feet* (Collegeville, Minn.: Liturgical Press, 1992), 15–18; *Manuale Ambrosianum*, ed. Magistretti, 271. In southern Italy this psalm was taught to the catechumens during Lent, prior to baptism, as witnessed in a sermon of uncertain authorship (*Morin Sermo 30*, *PLS* 4: 825–31, *CPL* 915). The preceding sermon in this group is about the teaching of the Creed to the catechumens (*Morin Sermo 29*, *PLS* 3: 821–5). See 'Evêque anonyme du ve siècle: recueil de XXX homélies', in Morin, *Etudes*, 37–8. Ps. 31 [32] was sung in Hagia Sophia at Constantinople as the newly baptized left the baptistery to return to the church. At Milan it served the same function in the piece *Alleluia alleluia alleluia ℣Beati quorum remissae sunt iniquitates*, sung while leaving the baptistery for Mass at the end of the Easter vigil. See *Le Typicon*, ii, ed. Mateos (OCA 166), 88–9; *Manuale*, ed. Magistretti, ii, 211.

128 'Legendus ad evangelium Matthei, de regina Austri. Propheta pro Patre de Christo et Ecclesia dicit', and 'Legendus ad Apocalipsin Johannis. Figura Ecclesiae Hierusalem futurae.' Salmon, *'Tituli Psalmorum'*, 61–2. The Apocalypse was, however, often read during the Easter season.

129 See the second and third series of titles in Salmon, *'Tituli Psalmorum'*, 81–93, 100–13. Both preserve the Nativity reference in Ps. 2 and the baptismal association of Ps. 22, but with weaker implications of liturgical usage: 'Ad nativitatem Christi pertinet' and 'De baptismatis sanctificatione', in the second series, for example.

130 Felix Raugel, 'Saint-Césaire, précepteur du Chant gallican', in *International Musicological Society: Bericht über den siebenten Internationalen musikwissenschaftlichen Kongress Köln 1958*, ed. Gerald Abraham et al. (Kassel: Bärenreiter, 1959), 217–18.

131 R. Collins, 'Caesarius von Arles', *Theologische Realenzyklopädie*, vii (1981), 531–6 at 534.

132 William E. Klingshirn, *Caesarius of Arles: The Making of a Christian Community in Late Antique Gaul* (Cambridge: Cambridge University Press, 1994), 9–15, 146–51, 231–5; T. O'Loughlin, 'Caesarius of Arles', and E. Rebillard, 'Sermones', in *Augustine through the Ages*, 115–16 and 773–92, esp. 791.

133 R. Etaix, 'Nouvelle Collection de sermons rassemblée par saint Césaire', *Revue bénédictine*, 87 (1977), 7–33; Réginald Grégoire, *Homéliaires liturgiques médiévaux: analyse de manuscrits* (Spoleto: Centro Italiano di Studi sull'Alto Medioevo, 1980), 393–422.

134 *CPL* 676, 1858a. *CPPMA* 2: 3645. See the articles collected in Adalbert de Vogüé, *Le Maître, Eugippe et Saint Benoît: recueil d'articles* (Hildesheim: Gerstenberg, 1984), 337–431.

135 *CPL* 629, 950. *CPPMA* 2: 2357. See Morin, *Etudes*, 59–60; Helmut Boese, *Die alte 'Glosa Psalmorum ex Traditione Seniorum': Untersuchungen, Materialien, Texte* (Freiburg im Breisgau: Herder, 1982), 70–72; R. Aubert, '334. Jean Diacre', *Dictionnaire d'histoire et de géographie ecclésiastiques*, xxvi (1997), 1466.

136 Aimé-Georges Martimort, 'La Lecture patristique dans la liturgie des heures', in Giustino Farnedi (ed.), *Traditio et progessio: studi liturgici in onore del Prof. Adrien Nocent, OSB* (Rome: Pontificio Ateneo S. Anselmo, 1988), 311–31.

137 'Codices autem legantur in vigiliis divinae auctoritatis, tam veteris testamenti quam novi, sed et expositiones earum, quae a nominatis et orthodoxis catholicis patribus factae sunt.' *Regula Benedicti* 9: 8, see *La Règle de saint Benoît*, ed. Vogüé and Neufville, ii, SC 182 (1972), 510–13.

138 *CPL* 1676. On the dating see Eduard Schwartz, 'Zum Decretum Gelasianum', *Zeitschrift für neutestamentliche Wissenschaft*, 29 (1930), 161–8.

139 See *La Règle de saint Benoît*, ed. Vogüé and Neufville, i, SC 181 (1972), 143–8, 270–71, and n. 56 above.

140 Grégoire, *Homéliaires liturgiques médiévaux*; Raymond Etaix, *Homéliaires patristiques latins: recueil d'études de manuscrits médiévaux* (Paris: Institut d'Etudes Augustiniennes, 1994).

141 *CPL* 633; *CPPMA* 2: 900, 2362. What is evidently an earlier form of the text is published in *PL* 30: 305–6 (315–16 in some editions). The later recension occurs as a preface to the Psalms in Paris, BNF lat. 15176, and Paris, Bibliothèque Ste-Geneviève, 8–10; it is published in De Bruyne, *Préfaces de la bible latine*, 62–3.

142 In fact the texts form something of a block at the junction between Passion Week and Holy Week. From Ps. 34 [35] we have the Graduals *Pacifice loquebantur*, *Exsurge domine et intende*, *Ego autem*, the Introit *Judica domine nocentes* and the Communion *Erubescant*, which occur on successive weekdays (Friday in Passiontide, Monday and Tuesday in Holy Week). On the Sunday that interrupts this sequence, Ps. 72 provides the text of the Gradual *Tenuisti manum*. *AMS*, pp. 86–7, 90–91; Cutter, *Musical Sources*, pp. 123, 127–30.

143 *AMS*, no. 9, pp. 12–13; Cutter, *Musical Sources*, no. 10.

144 The use of Ps. 90 [91] as a daily evening psalm is also mentioned by Caesarius (CCSL 103: 32) and Cassiodorus (CCSL 98: 835).

145 Ps. 33, with verse 9 as refrain [34: 8], seems to have been the usual Communion psalm at Jerusalem, where it is cited by Cyril of Jerusalem (SC 126: 168–70), and Jerome *In Esaiam* 2.5.20 and 7.19.18 (CCSL 73: 77, 284). It survives in the Communion of the Byzantine Liturgy of the Presanctified: see Neil K. Moran, *The Ordinary Chants of the Byzantine Mass*, 2 vols. (Hamburg: Karl Dieter Wagner, 1975), i, 170–74, ii, 201–3. In the West, the use of this psalm at Communion is attested by Cassiodorus (CCSL 97: 298–9, 303); the Irish Stowe Missal: *The Stowe Missal*, ed. George F. Warner, ii (London: Harrison & Sons, 1915); and in the Mozarabic rite, where the usual rubric for Communion antiphons, *ad accedentes*, suggests Ps. 33: 6 [34: 5]. M. Férotin, *Liber ordinum mozarabicus: le Liber ordinum en usage dans l'église wisigothique et mozarabe d'Espagne du cinquième au onzième siècle* (Paris: Firmin-Didot, 1904; repr. Rome: Edizioni liturgiche, 1996), 241–2. Cf. *PL* 85: 564–5. In the Roman traditions, of course, this psalm is the source of the Communion *Gustate et videte*: *AMS*, no. 180; Cutter, *Musical Sources*, no. 136.

146 As the most important of the seven penitential psalms, this Ps. 50 [51] saw extensive use in both liturgical and private contexts. Sometimes it was featured at the beginning of Lent: *Le Codex*, ed. Renoux (PO 36), 238; *Le Grand Lectionnaire*, ed. Tarchnischvili (CSCO 188), 49; Burkitt, 'The Early Syriac Lectionary', 306, 309. This practice survived in the Ambrosian psalmelli *Domine*

labia mea ℣ *Miserere* for Quinquagesima and *Redde mihi laetitiam* ℣ *Miserere* for the first Sunday in Lent: *Manuale*, ed. Magistretti, ii, 119, 135. It has also been used on Good Friday at Jerusalem (after the reading of the Passion Gospel Luke 23: 32–49) and in the Mozarabic rite (with an antiphon derived from Luke 23: 42): 'Τυπικὸν', ed. Papadopoulos-Keramefs, 137; *Antifonario*, ed. Brou and Vives, 274. As a daily psalm of the morning Office it was used in the Roman rite, and in the rite of Constantinople, among others: see Jeffery, 'Eastern and Western Elements', 132; *Le Typicon*, ed. Mateos, i (OCA 165), pp. xxiii–xxiv. It was also a daily morning psalm in monastic usage; see Adalbert de Vogüé, 'Les Sources des quatres premiers livres des Institutions de Jean Cassien: introduction aux recherches sur les anciennes règles monastiques latines', in Adalbert de Vogüé, *De saint Pachôme à Jean Cassien: études littéraires et doctrinales sur le monachisme égyptien à ses débuts* (Rome: Cento Studi S. Anselmo, 1996), 373–456, esp. 425–6.

147 This reading is plausible because, in the tradition followed by Irish monasteries on the Continent, there were antiphons and other texts used to supplement the *Te Deum*. See Jeffery, 'Eastern and Western Elements', 115, 120, 122–3.

148 For examples in the Beneventan tradition, see Thomas Forrest Kelly, *The Beneventan Chant* (Cambridge: Cambridge University Press, 1989), 132, 156–60. Ambrose's letter to his sister, cited above in n. 37, also speaks of reading the book of Jonah in the week preceding Easter, as the *competentes* preparing for baptism were being taught the Creed.

149 *MECL* 398.

150 *CPL* 1947. *Das älteste Liturgiebuch der lateinischen Kirche: Ein altgallikanisches Lektionar des 5./6. Jhs. aus dem Wolfenbütteler Palimpsest-Codex Weissenburgensis 76*, ed. Alban Dold (Hohenzollern: Kunstverlag Beuron, 1936).

151 It survives in the oldest form of the Armenian lectionary: *Le Codex*, ed. Renoux.

152 *CPL* 900. Cassiodorus, *Expositio Psalmorum*, ed. M. Adriaen, 2 vols (CCSL 97–8; Turnhout: Brepols, 1958). For a study of his exegetical method see Reinhard Schlieben, *Cassiodors Psalmenexegese* (Göppingen: Kümmerle, 1979). For a complete and annotated English translation, see *Cassiodorus: Explanation of the Psalms*, trans. P. G. Walsh, 3 vols (New York: Paulist Press, 1990–91).

153 CCSL 97: 5, 98: 1132. See James J. O'Donnell, *Cassiodorus* (Berkeley: University of California Press, 1979), 173 n. 44.

154 Ps. 33 [34] at Communion and perhaps at baptisms, CCSL 97: 303, 298–9; Ps. 90 [91] as an evening psalm, CCSL 98: 835; Ps. 21 [22] at the reading of the Passions, CCSL 97: 208; Ps. 41 [42] at baptism, CCSL 97: 387. There are also discussions of the word 'alleluia', for example at CCSL 98: 942–3, 956–7.

155 Ambrose's Epiphany hymn *Illuminans altissimus* is cited at CCSL 98: 689; his Christmas hymn *Intende qui regis* at CCSL 97: 95 and 98: 652; and the Pseudo-Ambrosian *Bis ternas horas* at CCSL 98: 899, 1132. *Ambroise de Milan: Hymnes*, ed. Fontaine, 335–59, 263–301.

156 See the commentary on Ps. 6, CCSL 97: 73.

157 See the list in CCSL 97: 3. For the major texts on music, see CCSL 97: 9, 293, 299; CCSL 98: 750, 881. Significant passages that are not marked with the marginal sign include CCSL 97: 414, 581.

158 O'Donnell, *Cassiodorus*, 175. O'Donnell's chapter on the *Expositio Psalmorum* (131–76) is a good introduction to this massive work.

159 'Psalterii quoque proprium est quod per eum legis diuinae sanctitas introitur. Non enim tirones incohant a Genesi, non ab apostolo, non inter ipsa initia auctoritas euangelica sancta pulsatur; sed, licet psalterium quartus codex sit

auctoritatis diuinae, primum tamen tirones incohantes scripturas sanctas, inde legendi faciunt decenter initium.' CCSL 97: 22.

160 *Conlationes* 14.12 (CSEL 13: 413–14; SC 54: 199); *Conferences*, trans. Ramsey, 516–17. For a more complex look at the 'problem' of pagan literature, see Sabine MacCormack, *The Shadows of Poetry: Vergil in the Mind of Augustine* (Berkeley: University of California Press, 1998).

161 For example, 'no social arena is as suffused with literacy on Nukulaelae as religion. The religious service is the only regular occasion in most Nukulaelae Islanders' weekly routine during which they read from a book, and carrying a Bible to church is a must (a hymnal is optional but desirable). On Sunday mornings . . . much good-natured bantering takes place over who will get to take the family's Bibles to church, since there usually aren't enough copies for every adult and child. . . . Some Nukulaelae Islanders also bring to church books that are not generally used there, like an English Bible (a high prestige commodity), copies of religious pamphlets gleaned from various sources, or other printed materials of no obvious religious relevance, which they may or may not open during the service.' Niko Besnier, *Literacy, Emotion, and Authority: Reading and Writing on a Polynesian Atoll* (Cambridge: Cambridge University Press, 1995), 116.

162 *Expositio Psalmorum*, Praefatio 15. CCSL 97: 19.

163 J. Rousse, H. Sieben and A. Boland, 'Lectio divina et lecture spirituelle', in *Dictionnaire de spiritualité ascétique et mystique, doctrine et histoire*, ed. Marcel Viller et al., ix (1975–6), 470–510; E. von Severus and A. Solignac, 'Méditation I', ibid., x (1977–80), 906–14; J. Leclercq, 'Lectio divina', *Dizionario degli istituti di perfezione*, v (1978), 561–6; J. Biarne, 'La Bible dans la vie monastique', in *Le Monde latin antique et la Bible*, ed. Jacques Fontaine and Charles Pietri (Paris: Beauchesne, 1985), 409–29.

164 Adalbert de Vogüé, '"Lectiones sanctas libenter audire": silence, lecture et prière chez Saint Benoît', *Benedictina*, 27 (1980): 11–26; repr. in Vogüé, *Le Maître, Eugippe et Saint Benoît*, 610–25, esp. 16–17 = 615–16.

165 *Regula Benedicti* 42.1. See *La Règle de saint Benoît*, ed. Vogüé and Neufville, ii, SC 182: 584; see also 6.1–8 on *taciturnitas*; ibid., i, SC 181: 470–72.

166 Adalbert de Vogüé, 'Les Deux fonctions de la méditation dans les Règles monastiques anciennes', *Revue d'histoire de la spiritualité*, 51 (1975), 3–16; repr. in Vogüé, *Le Maître, Eugippe et Saint Benoît*, 807–20.

167 *Regula Benedicti* 8.3: 'Quod uero restat post uigilias a fratribus qui psalterii uel lectionum aliquid indigent meditationi inseruiatur.' *La Règle*, ed. Vogüé and Neufville, ii, SC 182: 508.

168 Though this aphorism was often attributed to both Augustine and Bernard of Clairvaux, it is actually by Guigo II, Abbot of Chartreuse (*PL* 184: 475–84), who died probably in 1188. See *Prier au moyen âge: pratiques et expériences (V^e–XVe siècles): Textes traduits et commentés*, ed. Nicole Bériou, Jacques Berlioz and Jean Longère (Turnhout: Brepols, 1991), 308–12. For a complete English translation see Guigo II, *The Ladder of Monks: A Letter on the Contemplative Life and Twelve Meditations*, trans. Edmund Colledge and James Walsh (Garden City, NY: Doubleday Image Books, 1978; repr. as Cistercian Studies Series, 48 (Kalamazoo: Cistercian Publications, 1981)). For more on medieval monastic prayer and contemplation in general, see Thomas Merton, *The Climate of Monastic Prayer* (Shannon Irish University Press, 1969).

169 Gregory, *Registrum epistularum* 12.6, ed. Norberg, CCSL 140A: 974–7.

170 'quia non est illud opus populare et rudibus auditoribus impedimentum magis quam prouectum generat. Sed dic ei ut commenta psalmorum legi ad uigilias

faciat, quae mentes saecularium ad bonos mores praecipue informent.' CCSL 140A: 975–6.

171 *CPL* 1708. *CPPMA* 2: 2231.

172 'Praeterea quia isdem carissimus quondam filius meus Claudius aliqua me loquente de prouerbiis, de canticis canticorum, de prophetis, de libris quoque regum et de eptatico audierat, quae ego scripto tradere prae infirmitate non potui, ipse ea suo sensu dictauit, ne oblivione deperirent, ut apto tempore haec eadem mihi inferret et emendatius dictarentur. Quae cum mihi legisset, inueni dictorum meorum sensum ualde inutilius fuisse permutatum.' CCSL 140A: 974.

173 *CPL* 1709, 1719; cf. *CPPMA* 2: 2290, 2230. See the editors' introductions to CCSL 144, ed. Verbraken (1963), and SC 351, ed. Vogüé (1989). However, Vogüé has since come to the conclusion that the commentary he edited is not Gregory's work after all; see his 'La *Glossa Ordinaria* et le commentaire des rois attribué à Grégoire le Grand', *Révue bénédictine*, 108 (1998), 58–60; and F. Clark, 'Authorship of the Commentary *In 1 Regum*: Implications of A. de Vogüé's Discovery', ibid., 61–79.

174 The commentary on Proverbs ascribed to Gregory is probably not his: *CPPMA* 2: 2225, 2290. A commentary on the seven penitential psalms has been ascribed to both Gregory and Cassiodorus, but is actually by Heribertus de Reggio Aemilia (d. 1092): *CPL* after 1721, *CPPMA* 2: 2126, 2291.

175 *CPL* 1710. Cf. *CPPMA* 2: 2288. For the dedication to Marinianus, see CCSL 142: 3, ed. Adriaen (1971). For more on Marinianus, see *Prosopographie chrétienne du bas-empire*, ii: *Prosopographie de l'Italie chrétienne (313–604)*, ed. Charles Pietri and Luce Pietri (Rome: Ecole française, 2000), ii, 1401–7.

176 *CPL* 1711, *CPPMA* 2: 2289. Now at last newly edited by Raymond Etaix in *Gregorius Magnus: Homiliae in Evangelia* (CCSL 141; Turnhout: Brepols, 1999). On the audience see J. McClure, 'Gregory the Great: Exegesis and Audience' (D.Phil. diss., Oxford University, 1979).

177 However, some of these Gospels actually supplied texts for medieval liturgical chants, notably the Gospels of Easter Week that are so central to the famous Old Roman Vespers that took place in the Lateran baptistery. Because some of the antiphons of these Vespers draw their texts from the same Gospel readings on which Gregory preached, we can recognize that at least these chants are deeply rooted in early liturgical traditions going back through Gregory. Yet we cannot affirm that the chants already existed in Gregory's time, because he does not explicitly mention them. See John K. Brooks-Leonard, 'Easter Vespers in Early Medieval Rome: A Critical Edition and Study' (Ph.D. diss., University of Notre Dame, 1988).

178 *De institutis coenobiorum* 2.7–9 (CSEL 17: 23–5); also ed. Guy in SC 109 (1965), 70–74; Taft, *Liturgy of the Hours*, 58–62; F. Kok, 'L'Office pachômien: *psallere, orare, legere*', *Ecclesia orans*, 9 (1992), 69–95; Vogüé, 'Les Sources', 409–11. On the vocabulary for postures at worship, see Elisabeth Kasch, *Das liturgische Vokabular der frühen lateinischen Mönchsregeln* (Hildesheim: Gerstenberg, 1974), 213–37. On the collect see Albert Blaise, *Le Vocabulaire latin des principaux thèmes liturgiques*, rev. A. Dumas (Turnhout: Brepols, n.d. [ca. 1965]), 191 n. 1.

179 *CPL* 2015. André Wilmart, *The Psalter Collects from V–VIth Century Sources (Three Series)*, ed. Louis Brou (London: Harrison & Sons, 1949). Brou's introduction (pp. 10–16) outlines the evidence regarding the liturgical performance of such collects up to the Rule of the Master. See also Louis Brou, 'Où en est la question des "Psalter Collects"?', in *Studia patristica*, ii: *Papers Presented to the Second International Conference on Patristic Studies Held at Christ Church,*

Oxford, 1955, pt. 2, Texte und Untersuchungen, 64 (Berlin: Akademie-Verlag, 1957), 17–20, esp. 18–19. On the date of the collects and some possible relationships with Cassiodorus and the Rule of the Master, see Christine Mohrmann, 'A propos des collectes du psautier', *Vigiliae Christianae*, 6 (1952), 1–19; repr. in ead., *Etudes sur le latin des chrétiens*, iii: *Latin chrétien et liturgique* (Rome: Edizioni de storia e letteratura, 1965), 245–63.

180 Adalbert de Vogüé, 'Le Psaume et l'oraison: nouveau florilège', *Ecclesia orans*, 12 (1995), 325–49 at 349.

181 Adalbert de Vogüé, *La Règle de Saint Benoît*, v: *Commentaire historique et critique* (SC 185; Paris: Editions du Cerf, 1971), 577–88; id., 'Psalmodier n'est pas prier', *Ecclesia orans*, 6 (1989), 7–32; id., 'Le Psaume et l'oraison'; Joseph Dyer, 'The Singing of Psalms in the Early Medieval Office', *Speculum*, 64 (1989), 535–78; id., 'Monastic Psalmody of the Middle Ages', *Revue bénédictine*, 99 (1989), 41–74.

182 Vogüé, *La Règle de Saint Benoît*, vii: *Commentaire doctrinal et spirituel* (Paris: Editions du Cerf, 1977), 218, as translated in: A. de Vogüé, *The Rule of Saint Benedict: A Doctrinal and Spiritual Commentary*, trans. John Baptist Hasbrouck (Kalamazoo, Mich.: Cistercian Publications, 1983), 147.

183 Vogüé, *La Règle*, vii, 206–21, trans. Hausbrouck, 139–49.

184 For appreciations of the relationship see Aelred Sillem, 'St Benedict (c. 480–c. 550)', and D. H. Farmer, 'St Gregory and St Augustine of Canterbury', in Farmer (ed.), *Benedict's Disciples* (Leominster: Gracewing, 1980; repr. 1995), 21–40, 41–51.

185 *Homiliae in Hiezechihelem Prophetam* 1.1.15 (CCSL 142: 12–13). See also G. Penco, 'La preghiera presso il monachesimo occidentale del secolo VI', and B. Calati, 'La preghiera nella tradizione monastica dell'alto medioevo', in Vagaggini (ed.), *La preghiera*, 469–512 and 513–611, esp. 481, 557–9.

186 That is, one who plays a triangular-framed string instrument (a harp or psaltery) by plucking the strings with the fingers rather than a plectrum; see Mathiesen, *Apollo's Lyre*, 235–7, 270–86. Note that in medieval Europe the word 'psaltery' came to have a different meaning, referring to a zither-like instrument. See Howard M. Brown and Joan Lascelle, *Musical Iconography: A Manual for Cataloguing Musical Subjects in Western Art before 1800* (Cambridge, Mass.: Harvard University Press, 1972; repr. 1998), 75. The Greek Septuagint translation of the Jewish Bible does not use ψάλτης in this verse but ψάλλων.

187 Older dictionaries suggested or implied that the Hebrew root *ngn* was related to *ng'*, 'to strike, touch', implying plucking with the fingers (as with the Greek word) rather than using a plectrum: F. Brown, S. R. Driver and C. A. Briggs, *The Brown-Driver-Briggs Hebrew and English Lexicon* (Boston: Houghton, Mifflin, 1906; repr. Peabody, Mass.: Hendrickson, 1996), 618. More recent dictionaries refrain from such speculation, however: F. Zorell et al., *Lexicon Hebraicum Veteris Testamenti* (Rome: Pontificium Institutum Biblicum, 1984), 4; L. Koehler, W. Baumgartner, et al., *The Hebrew and Aramaic Lexicon of the Old Testament*, trans. and ed. M. E. J. Richardson et al., ii (Leiden: E. J. Brill, 1995), 668. Ernest Klein, *A Comprehensive Etymological Dictionary of the Hebrew Language for Readers of English* (New York: Macmillan, 1987), 404 offers an Akkadian antecedent for *ngn'*, and an Aramaic cognate for *ng'*, suggesting that the two are not closely related.

188 G. Delling, 'ὕμνος, ὑμνέω, ψάλλω, ψαλμός', *Theological Dictionary of the New Testament*, viii (1972), 489–503; Lampe, *Patristic Greek Lexicon*, 1539–40; J. Lust et al., *A Greek-English Lexicon of the Septuagint*, ii (1996), 523; Albert Blaise, *Dictionnaire latin-français des auteurs chrétiens*, ed. Henri Chirat (Strasbourg:

Librairie des Méridiens, 1954; repr. Turnhout: Brepols, n.d.), 681–2; *Le Typicon*, ed. Mateos, ii (OCA 166), 328–29.

189 *Thesaurus linguae Latinae*, iii (1906–12), 263–72.

190 Ps. 49 [50]: 14, 23; 106 [107]: 22; 115 [116]: 17. Outside the Book of Psalms, it is found in Tobit 8: 19.

191 Thus in Augustine's *Enarrationes in Psalmos* the phrase 'sacrificium laudis' is usually applied to Christian life or worship in general (CCSL 38: 590–93, 597–9, CCSL 39: 653, 928, CCSL 40: 1663–4, 1938, 1946; see also *Sermo 68*, *PL* 38: 435), but sometimes more explicitly to prayer (CCSL 39: 1335, CCSL 40: 1453, 1577, 1656) or to hymn-singing, probably understood figuratively (CCSL 38: 427–28, CCSL 40: 2177). In a sermon attributed to Maximus of Turin the sacrifice of praise is understood as referring to martyrdom (*PL* 57: 711). In some early Mass prayers it is applied to the Eucharist: *Corpus Praefationum*, ed. Eugenio Moeller (CCSL 161A; Turnhout: Brepols, 1980), no. 693, p. 204; *Corpus Orationum*, ed. Eugenio Moeller et al. (CCSL 160F; Turnhout: Brepols, 1995), nos. 4693a–b, pp. 189–90. Robert J. Daly, *Christian Sacrifice: The Judaeo-Christian Background before Origen* (The Catholic University of America Studies in Christian Antiquity, 1; Washington: Catholic University of America Press, 1978), shows that in Greek writers through the third century there was no particular correlation between psalm-singing and notions of sacrifice.

192 For 'sacrificum laudis' see *Expositio Psalmorum* 26.6, 49.1, 49.14, 49.23, 106.1, 106.22 (CCSL 97: 238–9, 441, 447, 451–2; CCSL 98: 973, 979). For 'psalmodia' see the quote given above at n. 162, the first of many cases in the *Expositio*. My views on the usage of these terms prior to Cassiodorus and Gregory are based on searches of *Patrologia Latina Database* (online). In March 2001, information was available at www.chadwyck.co.uk.

193 The work is dated to the second half of the sixth century, 'from the Roman region', in Vogüé, *Le Maître, Eugippe et Saint Benoît*, 753, 762–3. *CPPMA* 2: 3700.

194 *Regula Pauli et Stephani: Edició crítica i comentari*, ed. J. Evangelista M. Vilanova (Montserrat: Abadia de Montserrat, 1959); on the chanting of the Office, see 145–67.

195 Ibid. 14, pp. 113–14.

196 Translated from the letter, item (3); see Augustinus, *Epistola* 211 (CSEL 57: 361). For the two monastic rules see Lawless, *Augustine of Hippo*, 84–5, 111; on the date, background and interrelationships see ibid., 152–4; *La Règle de Saint Augustin*, ii: *Recherches historiques*, ed. Verheijen, 125–74. On the possibility that Augustine intended to forbid the singing of apocryphal or non-canonical texts, see Adalbert de Vogüé, *Histoire littéraire du mouvement monastique dans l'antiquité*, i: *Le Monachisme latin*, 3: *Jérôme, Augustin et Rufin au tournant du siècle (391–405)* (Paris: Editions du Cerf, 1996), 84–5.

197 See Augustine's *De Magistro* 1.1 (ed. Daur, CCSL 29: 157–8) and *De Genesi ad litteram, imperfectus liber* 5.25 (*PL* 34: 229). For discussion of these and many other passages see Brian Stock, *Augustine the Reader: Meditation, Self-Knowledge, and the Ethics of Interpretation* (Cambridge, Mass.: Belknap Press of Harvard University Press, 1996), 7, 120, 147–52, 238–9. Many other Augustinian writings on this topic are discussed in Timothy Maschke, 'St. Augustine's Theology of Prayer: Gracious Conformation', in Joseph T. Lienhardt et al. (eds), *Augustine: Presbyter Factus Sum* (Collectanea Augustiniana; New York: Peter Lang, 1993), 431–46. On Augustine's philosophy of knowledge and language, see Gerard O'Daly, *Augustine's Philosophy of Mind* (London: Duckworth, 1987); *The Cambridge Companion to Augustine*, 148–204.

198 *Regula Pauli et Stephani*, 112–13.

199 Not very conclusive are the apparent reminiscences of Lenten responsories alleged in Anselmo Lentini, *Il Ritmo prosaico nella regola di S. Benedetto* (Montecassino, 1942), 100–101.

200 This is the responsory *Deus omnium exauditor*; see *Regula Paula et Stephani*, 58–9, 113. Vilanova cited the text from the Gregorian monastic antiphoner of Hartker, but it also occurs in the Old Roman tradition: *CAO* 4 (1970), no. 6430; *Biblioteca Apostolica Vaticana, Archivio S. Pietro B 79: Antifonario della basilica di S. Pietro (Sec. XII)*, 2: *Fac-simile*, ed. Bonifacio Giacomo Baroffio and Soo Jung Kim, 2 vols. (Rome: Torre d'Orfeo, 1995), fols. 124^{v}–125. On the apocryphal Ps. 151, see *Septuaginta* 10: *Psalmi cum Odis*, ed. Rahlfs, 339–40; *Harper Collins Study Bible*, 1749–51; S. C. Pigué, 'Psalms, Syriac (Apocryphal)', *The Anchor Bible Dictionary*, ed. David Noel Freedman et al. (New York: Doubleday, 1992), 536–7; Peter Flint, 'Psalms, Book of: Apocryphal Psalms', and J. Sanders, 'Psalms Scroll', in *Encyclopedia of the Dead Sea Scrolls*, ed. Lawrence H. Schiffman, James C. VanderKam et al. (Oxford: Oxford University Press, 2000), ii, 708–10, 715–17.

201 Bernard McGinn, *The Presence of God: A History of Western Christian Mysticism*, i: *The Foundations of Mysticism* (New York: Crossroad, 1991), 132.

202 James McKinnon, 'Gregory the Great', *NG II*, x, 376–7.

Chapter 4
Songs of Exile, Songs of Pilgrimage

Nancy van Deusen

'Upon the rivers of Babylon, there we sat and wept: when we remembered Sion: On the willows in the midst thereof we hung up our instruments. For there they that led us into captivity required of us the words of songs. And they that carried us away, said: Sing ye to us a hymn of the songs of Sion. How shall we sing the song of the Lord in a strange land?'[1]

How can one sing at all in exile is the real question. The psalm goes on to speak of Jerusalem: 'If I forget thee, O Jerusalem, let my right hand be forgotten. Let my tongue cleave to my jaws, if I do not remember thee: If I make not Jerusalem the beginning of my joy.' Psalm 136 succinctly and evocatively sets forth the most important aspect of exile, namely, that acculturation is out of the question. To paraphrase: If I forget thee, O Jerusalem, let my right hand forget why it is attached to my body; let me be rendered speechless, let me, by the loss of memory concerning my homeland, be rendered ineffectual and useless. If I forget my true homeland, let me be put to shame.

Strong words indeed, and subject to interpretation. The psalm formed the catalyst for conversations between James McKinnon and myself, both for its emotional and liturgical content, and for the contrast it formed with the 'Gradual Psalms' that precede it.[2] We were certainly not alone in discussing this particular psalm. Hundreds of years of commentary, in words, in visual image and, as we will also see, in a close combination of text and music, attest to the fact that this psalm could be read in diverse ways, with many different points of emphasis. All of the figures delineated clearly in the text – the *figura* of harp, or of musical instrument, of the ancient polarized cities of Babylon and Jerusalem, the singers of the songs of the Lord, and their audience, and Babylon herself, personified as a whore, a harlot, by Daniel and John in their apocalyptic revelations of both the Old and New Testaments – could be connected by means of numerous analogies, and applied, finally, to life as it is lived in the world. The psalm, in a sense, defies time, since it brings together, almost with lyricism, past, present and future. Even the willow trees are important here, because one could make something of the wood – the cross of Christ, for example, uniting Old and New Testaments, the Babylonian Captivity and the Crucifixion of Christ.

The entire 136th Psalm could be interpreted historically, of course, since the Jewish people had been conquered, carried into captivity in Babylon, and also dispersed throughout the nations; tropologically, since the psalm gave, in a sense, some practical advice as to what to do and think if one should find oneself in such a situation; eschatologically, as one contemplated the return, ultimately, of God's people to their eternal home and the destruction of the enemies of the people of the Lord; and, perhaps most of all, since one has come to expect analogical language within the Psalms, it could be read allegorically, in that a meaning, not immediately apparent on the surface of the text, was signified, as one applied oneself and persevered to the *hidden* interpretation. The city of Jerusalem was seized upon as an example – repeated throughout the medieval period – of all four modes of interpretation: it was a historical city, and therefore could be interpreted in the historical, literal, mode; it refers allegorically to God's people; it is a tropological metaphor for behavior; and it was understood to refer to the heavenly city of God, the place of rest and respite for believers.[3] All modes of interpretation, of course, used the same word, Jerusalem; yet, through diverse *figurae* of speech and thought, *differentiae* were perceptible, indicating different *modi*.[4] Hence, on many levels, we see the significance of this psalm of exile, and a stream of interpretation flowing from it, as, one after the other, commentators explored both superficial and especially hidden interpretations.

From late antiquity – or the early Christian period – onwards, through centuries of what is conventionally considered to be the 'medieval' period, commentators did just that. They sorted out the multiple meanings of Psalm 136, as do some illuminators. I have selected three visual interpretations from the tradition of Psalter illustration. The 136th psalm was not by any means illuminated in every Psalter, nor, apparently, was there any set program for its visual interpretation. It is illustrated more often in Byzantine sources than in medieval Latin Psalters – a difference that would be worth exploring. In the principal illustrations of the Latin tradition,[5] we notice various and diverse *figurae*, including the *figura* of instrument.[6] The Psalter illustrations in these manuscripts do not belong to the program that occurs most frequently, not only in Latin Psalters but those of the Byzantine tradition as well. This series includes: (1) David as king, musician, writer of the Psalms, conflated with the image of Christ; (2) David rebuked by Nathan the Prophet; (3) Moses crossing the Red Sea; (4) Moses receiving the Law; (5) Hannah at prayer; (6) Hannah and Samuel; (7) Isaiah at prayer; (8) Hezekiah's life lengthened; (9) Jonah in the whale, coughed up, and at Ninevah; (10) Christ crucified; (11) Christ and the miracle of the fig tree; (12) John the Baptist preaching; (13) Christ and the last judgment; (14) Sinners in hell; (15) Virgin Mary and Child. The illustrations obviously pair psalms with both Old and New Testament significance, prophecy and fulfillment, Old Testament figures such as Hezekiah and New Testament figures such as John the Baptist. The illustrations given as examples here, however, form another exception: while the city/concept of 'Babylon' is not an uncommon subject for manuscript illumination, by far the larger number of examples are appended to the book of Revelation, the Apocalypse, especially Rev. 17: 1–4.[7]

There are other sources of interpretation for this psalm as well. Augustine, for example, was preoccupied, apparently for his entire life, with a comparison of the two cities mentioned in the psalm, Babylon *versus* Jerusalem, eventually writing *The City of God*, a work on which he said he spent fifteen years. He wrote at least three commentaries on Psalm 136, either as portions of sermons that he delivered to his congregation in North Africa (as bishop of Hippo), or as *enarrationes*, that is, elucidations, commentaries on the psalms. Here is one set of his commentaries on the passage quoted at the outset of this study:

> Therefore, dearly beloved, give your attention to the river of Babylon. The river of Babylon is all one loves that is transient. Whatever it is that one loves, strictly speaking, one cultivates, that is to say, one's mind is occupied, and one's will is taken up with what one loves, to the exclusion of other things. One desires what one loves, and returns again and again to it. In this particular case, that is, the transient river of Babylon, what one loves, cultivates, and desires is not the stable foundation of Jerusalem (*fundamentum Jerusalem*) but the flowing river of Babylon, a river that passes away and carries everything with it, including one's treasure.[8]

Augustine goes on to the phrase 'We hung up our harps on the willows in our midst' (*In salicibus in medio eius suspendimus organa nostra*). It is interesting here, by the way, that a specific musical instrument, *harp*, has been introduced into the King James Version, while Augustine's Latin translation uses the much more general term for instrument, *organa*. We know that Augustine had several Latin translations of the psalms at his disposal, and he apparently used them all, drawing upon a certain word in a certain context for the exact nuance of meaning he needed.[9] Augustine continues that the citizens of Jerusalem have as their instrument the Scriptures, the precepts of God and God's promises (*scripturas Dei*, *praecepta Dei*, *promissa Dei*) as well as their meditation upon a glorious future – that is, their own reward at the end of time. But in the midst of the city of Babylon, all they can do is hang up these instruments (the word of God, the precepts, and the promises of God concerning the future) on trees. Now these trees in the middle of Babylon, writes Augustine, are patently without fruit, perfectly ineffectual; these trees – and especially in this place – bring absolutely nothing good out of their position, planted as they are right in the middle of Babylon. There is nothing good to be expected from this situation. All the branches are sterile. So it is with those who are greedy, avaricious, venal, sterile in good works, just like the citizens of Babylon.[10]

It was a subject that got Augustine going, since the connection to the New Testament, the Gospel of John, and the words of Christ reported in the fifteenth chapter of that Gospel would have been clear: 'I am the true vine; and my Father is the husbandman. Every branch in me, that bearest not fruit, he will take away: and every one that beareth fruit, he will purge it, that it may bring forth more fruit. . . . I am the vine; you the branches: he that abideth in me, and I in him, the same beareth much fruit: for without me you can do nothing.'[11] In *The City of God*, Augustine, in his pastoral role as bishop, delved still further into the topic of Babylon, not only as the city of transience but a city of confusion. He compares and relates Babylon not only to the tower of Babel (hence, he thinks, the name) but also to the city of Athens, where:

> philosophers went milling around with their groupies, each one belligerently propounding his own persuasions, some saying that there is only one world, some saying that it began, others that it had no beginning, some saying it will come to an end, others, that it will go on forever, some saying that the world is ruled by divine intelligence, others that it is driven by fortuitous chance.

And he concludes:

> Tell me, has any people, senate, or person with any power or authority in the ungodly city ever bothered to examine these and the other almost innumerable results of philosophical wrangling with a view to approve and accept certain fixed principles and to condemn and reject all contentions to the contrary? Is it not the case, rather, that the ungodly city has, without the smallest degree of critical discrimination, taken all these scrapping ideas from here, there, and everywhere, clutching them in pell-mell confusion to her bosom? . . . No wonder, then, that this earthly city has been given the name of Babylon, for Babylon means confusion. Actually, their diabolical king does not care a straw how many contradictory opinions Babylon harbors or how her people squabble over them, so long as he goes on in possession of them and all of their errors – a tyranny they deserve by reason of their enormous and manifold ungodliness. How differently [here Augustine refers to Ps. 136] has that other commonwealth of people, that other City, the people of Israel, to whom was entrusted the word of God, managed matters! No muddle-headed mixing of true prophets with false prophets there![12]

We have seen, then, that there is much to be got out of this particular psalm. In fact, what we have here is, succinctly expressed, a considerable number of the major preoccupations, not only of Augustine throughout his long and immensely productive life, but of many other writers from late Antiquity through the Middle Ages. Let us review what we have so far: the *figurae* or delineatory figures of speech and thought of: (1) *waters* of Babylon, (2) memory of the *homeland*, *Zion*, (3) *harps* hung up (or musical *instrument*, *organum*, *organa*), (4) *trees*/willow/wood in the middle of *Babylon*, (5) *Jerusalem*, (6) *Babylon*, (7) comparison of home city *versus* city of exile, (8) familiar songs *versus* strange city/country, (9) *Jerusalem* as joy. Commentators, in text and image, selected among these sharply delineated constructs for pen, mind and memory. In his selection, throughout his commentaries, as well as in *The City of God*, Augustine is looking specifically for connections made between Old and New Testaments, and he finds them. For Augustine, the psalm formed a bridge, a consciously constructed transition between the Old and New Testaments. This is a subject to which we will return.

Cassiodorus, writing in the sixth century, was well acquainted with Augustine's psalm commentaries. He quotes them, but he also has much more to say, beginning with his *expositio* on the 136th psalm. Let us take note of what constructs Cassiodorus selects and what he makes of them. Here is a quotation from the beginning of his commentary on this psalm, designated as a 'hymn' since the psalms were considered to be the hymns of the Old Testament: 'Considering, then, this hymn cannot be said by those rejoicing, but is to be sung with sad compunction.'[13] Sad songs, then, these songs in exile, writes Cassiodorus, and he continues:

> And here we have the historical mode, given by God, who has designated Jerusalem, as a unified entity, a 'vision of peace' (*visio pacis*). Here then, in the present, much pressure must be endured, and the slander of those who err, in humility, afflicted, having hope in a future eternal life, a hope that renews those who have been subjugated, and are under subjugation. This is quite in contrast to Babylon, a diabolical city, full of confusion, a city that flourishes here, is full of superficial, ephemeral exuberance, and is also full of pride – all swelled up – since the corruption of this world is watered by a mighty river (*hic florida, superba, laetissima est, quae istius saeculi vitiis tamquam magnis fluminibus irrigatur*).[14]

Cassiodorus goes on to the passage translated as 'How shall we sing the song of the Lord in a strange city?' He writes:

> What then can be done with a sweet musical instrument, when bitter times of life are occupied with lamentation? Here indeed, the historical mode is tranferred to a spiritual or tropological mode. We hang up (*suspendimus*) our instrument, when we bring together all of the grace communicated within Scripture. This is then our instrument in exile, the accumulated grace that is present within the psalter all collated together with the joy we have in the hope of eternal life.'[15]

Although Cassiodorus is obviously aware of Augustine's commentary on the 136th psalm – he quotes Augustine repeatedly in his own commentaries – his contribution to the interpretation of the psalms is quite different since he focuses upon the concept of *figura*, a delineatory construct made primarily within intellection and the mind. He compares and conflates here the unified *vision* of peace, God's city of Jerusalem, with the unified *instrument* of grace, a composite of all the elements conjoined within the entire Psalter. This unified 'instrument', he explains in another context, is God's instrument. The psalter as an instrument is brought together with the composite of 'the means and expression of grace' within the New Testament. The instrumental quality of this patently *musical* instrument is that the Psalter functions as an instrument to unite both Old and New Testaments, the historical city of Jerusalem with the eschatological city of the eternally redeemed, at the end of time, the New Jerusalem, constructed for the imagination in the New Testament Book of Revelation.

This concept of the Psalter as an instrument was a topic to which Cassiodorus returned. What came out of this instrument was a subject he approached in the introduction to his commentaries on the psalms, categorizing the diverse songs that issued from the Psalter, and, finally, discussing what each of the strings signified. All the strings of the Psalter gave forth together sound that was sweet to the taste, as well as delicious both in anticipation and recollection. Cassiodorus' 'strings' are: (1) the prophetic 'string', (2) psalm titles that gave the names of diverse authors of the psalms, (3) explicits, that is, what is mentioned in the final phrase at the end of each psalm (*in finem*), (4) a definition of the psalterium, and how all the psalms together formed an instrument (*quid sit psalterium, vel psalmi quare dicantur*), (5) a clarification of 'psalm' (*quid sit psalmus*), (6) clarification of 'song' (*quid sit canticum*), (7) 'psalmsong' (*psalmocanticum*), (8) 'songpsalm' (*canticumpsalmum*), and so on to the eleventh, the 'diapsalm' (*diapsalma*). All of these strings together then give forth praise to God, concludes Cassiodorus.[16]

Let us look closely at one of Cassiodorus' 'strings', the *canticumpsalmum*, the songpsalm *psalmocanticum*, the plainsong. Cassiodorus writes: 'What then is a psalmsong? A psalmsong was sung by a chorus as a society of voices in acclamation, preceded by instrumental music, followed then by divine words.'[17] Keeping in mind that 'psalm' signifies 'instrument', the medieval sequence, within the Mass celebration, was sung between the Alleluia, with its psalm verse (the 'instrument'), and the reading of the Gospel. Furthermore, it appears from presentation in manuscripts that the sequence, either part or whole, was never sung by a solo voice.[18] In addition, Cassiodorus places the *psalmocanticum*, together with both an incipit or title and a closing explicit, *in finem*, then repeats this close relationship of *psalmocanticum* to title. One need not look at many sequences in medieval liturgical manuscripts containing music to notice that the sequence is almost always preceded by a title, especially in Germanic cultural regions, during the earlier Middle Ages.[19] But there are other reasons in addition to its position between Alleluia and Gospel reading for regarding the sequence as the 'song of the Lord in a strange country' – the psalmsongs of exile to which Psalm 136 refers. Let us look more closely at an example of this 'psalmsong', *Mittit ad virginem non quemvis* (Ex. 4.1).

Although this sequence has been edited from a fifteenth-century manuscript (commonly known as Gran, Cathedral Library, MS I 3) from the cathedral of Esztergom, the primary episcopal see of Hungary, one would be able to find it in a large number of manuscripts, since it was sung all over Europe for at least five centuries. In regarding the entire sequence, one notices first that the music and text seem to move 'in place', that one appears to be going nowhere. Step by step, sometimes up, sometimes down, nearly all of the syllables and notes equidistant from one another, the sequence seems to move along steadily, without perceptably approaching a goal. At least this is the way it appears for a while, with the mode distinguished by the tones emphasized; then in the middle of the sequence (verses 7–8) the melody becomes a good deal higher, remains there, and seems to use other musical space, or the tones reiterated by a different musical mode. The thick, compact text, which appropriates various Latin expressions in an intense manner of speaking that is full of allusions to a shared biblical background in both Old and New Testaments, ends (verse 12) with the phrase 'Ut post exilium fruamur gloria sanctorum omnium, amen' ([Pray for us], that after exile, we may have the enjoyment of glory in company with the saints). The music and text together suggest exactly what the sequence is about, namely, transition, exile, moving in place, but, for the moment, going nowhere. How typical must be that feeling, for the exile – a perception of being nowhere, certainly not at home, and not having yet arrived. How ingenious is this sequence in conveying, with such sophistication, that point of view. One also learns from the music itself – music that is clear and plain – the theological message: we *suspended* our harps; how shall we sing the song of the Lord in a strange country?

This sequence is not a unique example, but rather one that is typical of this genre, consisting largely of allegories, one after the other (the allegorical interpretational mode), concluding with a final line that almost invariably expresses the safe arrival of the people of God, in company with other believers, before God: *gaudeamus, et sanctis in patria* (we praise, and are joyful along with the saints in the homeland); direction or passage leading to this arrival: *auctor, ad te transire* (author to you we move), *a beata, transfer ad celestia* (the blessed are transferred to heaven), *duc ad celestis* (lead [us] to heaven), *nos his ducant ordinem* (leading us in order), *adornatum transduxit ad propria* (adorned, led to the right place); or making the point of exile even more explicitly: *angelorum transfer post exilium* (transferred [by angels into heaven] after exile).[20]

What can be made of this? Just as the emigré, the refugee, the outcast, even the cosmopolitan – all varieties of not being where one belongs – constitute, to a certain extent, anomalies, so the sequence stands out among the other constituent parts of the Mass liturgy throughout the Middle Ages. The sequence is outside the accustomed, the generally true, the conventional practice. Nearly all the parts of the Mass ceremony fit together, sometimes in amazing and stunning ways, biblical excerpts, primarily from the Psalms, but also from the prophetic books of the Old Testament, such as Isaiah. In other words, the Book of Psalms was carefully divided into many chunks, all approximately the size of what one could sing or speak in a single breath, and placed together, almost like blocks of musical building material. These excerpts from the Psalms or prophets, placed together, constituted all of the items of the Mass Proper: the Introit, Gradual, Alleluia, Offertory and Communion. Both the make-up of the individual excerpts and the manner of placing them together were the same for all the categories of the Mass Proper. But not the sequence. The sequence is not formed from bits of either the Old or New Testaments, but is, rather, a composed psalmsong of transition between the two. Naming in the Middle Ages also differentiates the Introit, Gradual, Alleluia, Offertory and Communion, since they are all *cantus*, whereas the sequence is either *sequentia*, *pro sequentia* (or prosa [proSa], or, as we have seen, a *canticumpsalmum*, a songpsalm.

The sequence is, on as many levels as possible, a song of transition: it is sung between the Alleluia (which is reminiscent of the Old Testament since it uses one of the two or three Hebrew words preserved within the Mass ceremony) and the Gospel reading. Both text and music are utterly unlike any of the other portions of the liturgy. This ceremonial placement, as well as its unique, completely recognizable text–music relationship, was fixed throughout the entire medieval period, defying liturgical change and geographical difference. Our first manuscripts containing both musical notation, or music *figurae*, and sequence texts appear around 875, and sequences are still to be found in large collections, particularly in Central Europe, sometimes also with vernacular words, in the later part of the sixteenth century.[21] There are over 3,000 sequences, in as many manuscripts from 875 to around 1600, all over Europe – from Spain to the British Isles, from Palermo to Hamburg, from Paris to Prague, and Berlin to Budapest.

Ex. 4.1 Sequence *Mittit ad virginem non quemvis angelum* (Esztergom, Cathedral Library, MS I 3), fols. 378r–379v; *AH* 54: 296

10
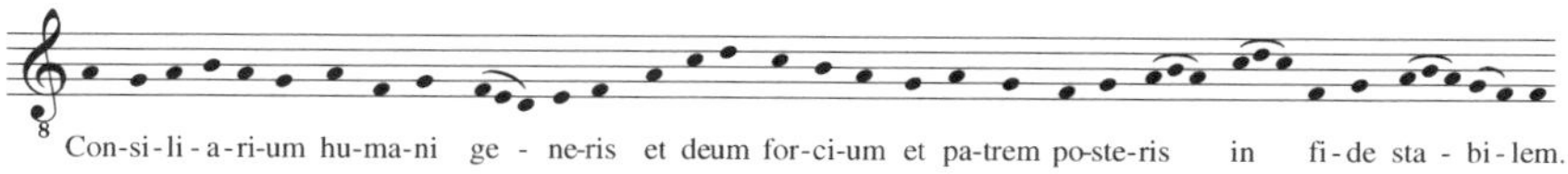
Con-si-li-a-ri-um hu-ma-ni ge - ne-ris et deum for-ci-um et pa-trem po-ste-ris in fi-de sta - bi-lem.

11

Qui nobis tri-bu-at pec-ca-ti ve - ni-am re-a-tus di-lu-at et do-net pa-tri - am in ar-ce sy - de-rum.

12
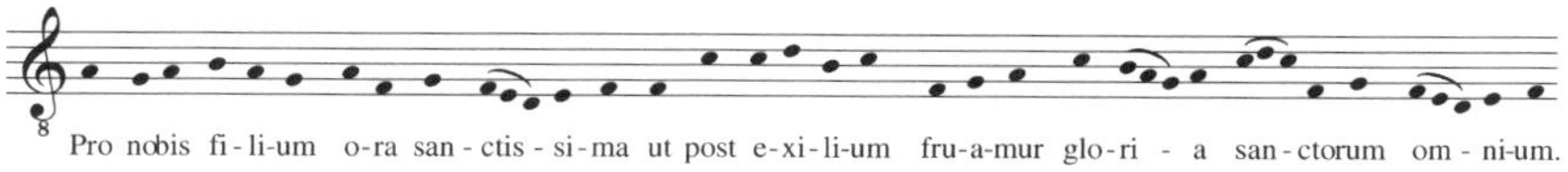
Pro nobis fi-li-um o-ra san - ctis - si-ma ut post e-xi-li-um fru-a-mur glo-ri - a san-ctorum om - ni-um.

A - - - - - men.

In other words, its liturgical stability, that is, its fixed place between Alleluia and Gospel reading at the mid-point of the Mass, in preparation for the Eucharist, identified the sequence and gave it recognizability to those who either sang sequences or heard them sung on a regular basis (that is, everyone attending services in Europe for approximately 800 years). We can see how the sequence made the points of transition and connection between the Alleluia and Gospel reading by verbal reference directly invoking the theme of transition, by mixed musical modes, and by mixed musical-textual (syllabic setting) style. Using the psalms as a model, the sequence displayed many features in common with them, such as varying overall length; conceptual as well as musical parallelism between lines; and copious use of the allegorical interpretational mode. Finally, as with many psalms, the sequence closed with the eschatological mode of textual interpretation, the topos of the Christian's presence before God in unified company.[22]

David, the primary psalm writer, is the key figure for medieval interpretation of the Scriptures and in bridging the gap between the old and the new. He is the universal celebrant, dancing, singing and playing before the Lord, not as a member of the priestly caste but by his own choice. An Old Testament figure, he nevertheless personifies a 'new liturgy' based on will, not duty. The central concern of the medieval psalm commentaries was to extend and elucidate, with examples, the relationship between Old and New Testaments. In the majority of sequence texts, just this link between Old and New Testaments, made by the psalms and reinforced, explained and interpreted in medieval commentaries, is fashioned not only textually but also musically by the sequence within the context of the Mass.

There is an internal logic for placing the sequence at just this place, for its central themes are those that have roots in the Old Testament, and resolution and clarification in the New Testament. These themes include the prophets' predictions linked to Christ (*Qui regis sceptra*), the serpent and Eve related to

Mary the mother of Christ (*Dicat exsultans omnis creatura*), the creation and the God-Man (*Nato canunt omnia*), David with Christ (*Fulgens preclara rutilat*), the Law of Moses with the inner 'Law' of grace (*Alleluia, dic nobis quibus*), Old Testament heroes of faith united with the saints by Christ's sacrifice (*Grates salvatori ac regi*), and the synagogue consolidated with the *ecclesia* or Christian believers (*Carmen suo dilecto*). There are many examples for each category, and many other classes of connection between the Old and New Testaments as well.[23] Poised between prophecy and culmination, between announcement and fruition, placed between birth and final fulfillment, the sequence occupies the space between goals – the song of the Lord in a strange country. This interval between goals also occupies the space of this present life.

That music exists to make plain the inner realities of life was not only a commonplace in the Middle Ages, it formed the basis of the medieval – as well as Renaissance and Early Modern – position of music as an art of material and measurement. In this case, the sequence within the Mass discloses what it really means to be an exile, that is, *in transitu*, on one's way.

Writing in the twelfth century, Hugh of St. Victor, no doubt himself an emigré, thought that it was good to be exiled from one's homeland, because one thus appreciated the reality of human existence more fully and completely. We are in exile, he wrote, as wayfarers, removed from our homeland.[24] In literally thousands of ways the sequence makes and reinforces this point through seven hundred years. How shall we sing the songs of the Lord in a far country? A medieval answer: one can sing the 'psalmsong' of exile, the sequence.

Notes

1 Douay-Reims-Challoner translation. Cf. the Vulgate version: 'Psalmus David, Jeremiae. Super flumina Babylonis illic sedimus et flevimus, Cum recordaremur Sion. In salicibus in medio eius, Suspendimus organa nostra; Quia illic interrogaverunt nos, qui captivos duxerunt nos, Verba cantionum; Et qui abduxerunt nos: Hymnum cantate nobis de canticis Sion. Quomodo cantabimus canticum Domini in terra aliena?' *Biblia sacra iuxta Vulgatam Clementinam*, Nova Editio (Madrid, 1977). The psalm closes with the sentence that, understandably, has generated difference within the commentary tradition, and would seem to be difficult to interpret: 'Blessed be he that shall take and dash thy little ones against the rock.'

2 These are Pss. 121 [122] through 133 [134]. The psalms fascinated James McKinnon and provided a point of departure for his writing as well as personal ruminations. See, for example, McKinnon, 'The Book of Psalms, Monasticism, and the Western Liturgy', in Nancy van Deusen (ed.), *The Place of the Psalms in the Intellectual Culture of the Middle Ages* (Albany: State University of New York Press, 1999), 43–58, an article published shortly before his death that summarizes his lifelong consideration of the psalms. The article begins: 'It is hardly an exaggeration to say that the Western medieval liturgy consisted in the public singing of the Psalter. The entire cursus of 150 psalms was chanted each week in the Office, and the five principal sung items of the Mass – the introit, gradual, alleluia, offertory, and communion – all came into existence as psalms, even if the responses and antiphons

that accompanied the original psalms eventually achieved a musical prominence beyond that of their progenitors. We may be inclined to take this overwhelming psalmic presence for granted, but we should not; it was by no means inevitable.' This statement, emphasizing the formative and ubiquitous impact of the Psalter, forms the basis for the study presented here. Its significance not only for the medieval liturgy but for the verbal communication of underlying thought-priorities as well makes it a particularly appropriate topic for a volume of essays published in memory of Professor McKinnon.

3 The use of the city of Jerusalem was a commonplace in the Middle Ages, as well as a pedagogical device for teaching the four modes of scriptural interpretation. See Henri de Lubac, *Exégèse médiévale: les quatre sens de l'écriture*, 2 vols. (Paris: Aubier, 1959–64), ii, esp. 644–9. But common as the allusion to Jerusalem was, 'Babylon' too was used as a didactic tool to expose the interpretative potential of a text. See, for example, the *Didascalicon* of Hugh of St. Victor, who explores the potentiality of the city of Babylon for disclosure not only of the historical sense involving time, place and event, but of personification, revealing internal, characteristic, qualities: 'For although the Lord threatened the one city of Babylon through the prophet Isaias, nevertheless, while speaking against that city he passed from this species, or specific group of mankind, to the genus or mankind in general, and turned his speech against the whole world. Surely, if he were not speaking against the entire world he would not have added later the following general remark: "And I will destroy all the earth and will visit the evils of the world, . . ." In the same way, after he has charged the world in the person of Babylon, he once more turns to things that have happened specifically to it.' See *The Didascalicon of Hugh of St. Victor: A Medieval Guide to the Arts*, trans. J. Taylor (New York: Columbia University Press, 1961), 123–4. The notes related to the interpretative senses are of particular lucidity and value, especially n. 1 to Book Five, p. 219. The *Didascalicon* was written, so far as we know, in Paris in the late 1120s and was apparently greatly influential, as attested by nearly one hundred extant manuscripts from the twelfth to the fifteenth centuries, preserved, as Taylor notes, across Europe from Ireland to Italy, from Poland to Portugal (introduction, p. 4).

4 This is an important conceptualization that was made clear, perhaps most of all, in music, that is, the *differentiae* indicated by prominent, delineatory *figurae* that differentiated *modi* one from another, using exactly the same tones or musical material.

5 These are: Stuttgart Psalter (Stuttgart, Württembergische Landesbibl. Biblia folio 23), fol. 132$^{r–v}$; Harley Psalter (London, BL Harley 603), fol. 70^{r}; Utrecht Psalter (Utrecht, Universiteitsbibl. MS 32), fol. 136. Cf. Ernest Theodore DeWald, *The Stuttgart Psalter, Biblia folio 23* (Princeton: Pub. for the Department of Art and Archaeology of Princeton University, 1930); William Noel, *The Harley Psalter* (Cambridge: Cambridge University Press, 1991) and Suzy Dufrenne, *Les Illustrations du psautier d'Utrecht: sources et apport carolingien* (Paris: Ophrys, 1978), with its extensive bibliography, not only concerning the Utrecht Psalter, but covering Psalter illustration in general. See also Dufrenne, 'L'Illustration médiévale du psautier', in *Actes du colloque de l'Association des médiévistes anglicistes de l'enseignement supérieur publiés par les soins d'André Crépin sur les techniques narratives du Moyen Age* (Amiens: U.E.R. de langues et cultures étrangères, 1974), 59–72.

6 Cf. James McKinnon, 'Musical Instruments in Medieval Psalm Commentaries and Psalters', *JAMS* 21 (1968), 3–70, a pivotal study of this topic; and Tilman

Seebass, *Musikdarstellung und Psalterillustration im früheren Mittelalter*, 2 vols. (Bern: Francke, 1973).

7 Cf. Henri Omont, 'Manuscrits illustrés de l'Apocalypse au IXe et Xe siècles', *Bulletin de la Société française de reproductions de manuscrits à peintures*, 6 (1922), 80 ff. Psalter illustration is a minefield, mainly due to a lack of criteria, order and consistency with regard to what is included and what is left out – even inconsistency concerning what is included under the category of 'Psalter illustration'. Different types of manuscripts are considered together as a hodge-podge of sources in order to survey a specific attribute, subject or program. In fact, one of the most inconvenient aspects of the Psalter illustration literature in general is that the texts, that is, specific psalms, are in many cases unidentified, in a consideration of similarities with respect to feature and shape. Visual aspects are obviously the priority, whereas *figurae* of text and *figurae* of illustration would have been, for a medieval readership, coequivalent and complementary. Despite this, the connection between Old and New Testament made by, and within, the psalms themselves is also maintained in illuminations.

8 Augustine, *Enarrationes in Psalmos* 136.3, on v. 1, ed. Eligius Dekkers and Johannes Fraipont (CCSL 40; Turnhout: Brepols, 1965): 'Tamen, carissimi, adtendite flumina Babylonis. Flumina Babylonis, sunt omnia quae hic amantur et transeunt. Nescio quis amavit, verbi gratia, agriculturam ipsam exercere, inde ditescere, ibi occupare animum, inde percipere voluptatem; adtendat exitum, et videat illud quod amavit non esse fundamentum Ierusalem, sed fluvium Babylonis.'

9 Pierre-Patrick Verbraken, 'Le Psautier des tropistes', in Gunilla Iversen (ed.), *Research on Tropes* (Stockholm: Almquist & Wiksell, 1983), 65; as well as Arthur Allgeier, *Die altlateinischen Psalterien: Prolegomena zu einer Textgeschichte der Hieronymianischen Psalmenübersetzungen* (Freiburg im Breisgau: Herder, 1928).

10 *Enarrationes in Psalmos* 136.6, on v. 2: '*In salicibus in medio eius suspendimus organa nostra*. Habent organa sua cives Ierusalem, scripturas Dei, praecepta Dei, promissa Dei, meditationem quamdam futuri saeculi; sed cum agunt in medio Babyloniae, organa sua in salicibus eius suspendunt. Salices ligna sunt infructuosa; et hoc loco ita posita, ut non aliquid boni possit intellegi de salicibus; alibi autem forsitan potest. Modo ligna intellegite sterilia . . . Sicut sunt homines cupidi, avari, steriles in opere bono; ita cives Babyloniae, ut etiam ligna sunt illius regionis, ex istis voluptatibus verum transeuntium pascuntur, tanquam rigata a fluminibus Babyloniae.' See Nancy van Deusen, 'The *Cithara* as *Symbolum*: Augustine *vs* Cassiodorus on the Subject of Musical Instruments', in ead. (ed.), *The Harp and the Soul: Essays in Medieval Music* (Lewiston, NY: E. Mellen Press, 1989), 201–55, esp. 240 ff.

11 John 15: 1–2, 5. Cf. Matt. 3: 8.

12 Augustine, The City of God, trans. G. G. Walsh et al. (1949, repr. New York: Doubleday, 1958), 370, 410 f.

13 'Considerandum est autem quoniam hymnus iste non a gaudentibus dicitur, sed sola dolorum compunctione cantatur.' Cassiodorus, *Expositio psalmorum*, ed. M. Adriaen, 2 vols. (CCSL 97–8; Turnhout: Brepols, 1958), ii, 1230. Note the specific use of *hymnus* and *cantatur*, that is, 'is to be sung'. In another context, in his introduction to his entire commentary on the psalms, Cassiodorus states that the psalms are the hymns of the Scriptures, with the total Psalter forming the totality of an instrument. See also G. Zinn's introduction to van Deusen (ed.), *The Place of the Psalms*.

14 'Duas enim civitates in hoc mundo esse crebra lectione comperimus: una est Domini, quae dicitur Ierusalem, id est visio pacis. Ista hic pressuram patitur et multis malis irruentibus sauciatur: humilis, afflicta, spem habens in illa aeterni-

tate quae numquam novit defectui subiacere. Econtra diaboli civitas, quae Babylonia dicitur, cuius interpretatio significat confusionem, hic florida, superba, laetissima est, quae istius saeculi vitiis tamquam magnis fluminibus irrigatur . . .'.

15 '[2.] *In salicibus in medio eius suspendimus organa nostra*. Hic doloris exaggeratur acerbitas, quando delectationem suam, qua se populus poterat consolari, velut non necessaria suspendebatur arboribus. Quid enim illic agerent organa dulcia, ubi tempora vitae amaris erant lamentationibus occupata? Verum haec historia ad spiritalem intellegentiam transferatur . . . Talibus ergo viris organa nostra suspendimus, quando communicata gratia de scripturarum divinarum lectione conferimus. Ipsa sunt enim nostra organa, quae et psalmodiae gratiam praestant et alterna nos collatione laetificant. *In medio eius*, Babyloniae civitatis dicit, non fluminis, quia necesse est in medio mundi sit sanctissimus Christianus, quamvis ad superna animo videatur esse translatus.' Cf. van Deusen, 'The *Cithara* as *Symbolum*', 240–42.

16 Cassiodorus, *Expositio psalmorum* (*praefatio*), i, chapter headings: 'Caput I: De prophetia, II: Cur in psalmorum titulis quasi auctorum nomina diversa reperiantur; III: Quid significet *in finem*, quod frequenter invenitur in titulis; IV: Quid sit psalterium vel psalmi quare dicantur; V: Quid sit psalmus; VI: Quid sit canticum; VII: Quid sit psalmocanticum; VIII: Quid sit canticumpsalmum; IX: De quinquefaria divisione; X: De unita inscriptione titulorum; XI: Quid sit diapsalma; XVII: Laus Ecclesiae.'

17 'Quid sit canticumpsalmum. Canticumpsalmum erat, cum choro ante canente, ars instrumenti musici in unam convenientiam communiter aptabatur, verbaque hymni divini suavis copula personabat.' *Expositio psalmorum*, i, 13.

18 Wolfram von den Steinen assumed that the sequence was sung by alternating choruses (see his *Notker der Dichter und seine geistige Welt*, 2 vols. (Bern: A. Francke, 1948, repr. 1978), 81, 83, 109, 118, 134, 141, 161, 294); and although it is plain that a strong tradition exists for this point of view, there is also even more persuasive textual evidence, since nearly all of the sequences end with an explicit that brings to expression the concept of the Christian believer before God in the presence of a society or whole company of angels and saints. Anagogical terms to this effect, such as *cives*, *cunctae partes*, *camenas*, *congregatio fidelis*, *coniubilando coeli angelica* and countless other expressions of 'society' not only abound, but constitute an essential aspect of the sequence's identity. See Nancy van Deusen, 'Sequence Repertories: A Reappraisal', *Musica disciplina*, 48 (1994), 191–222.

19 An overview of the entire manuscript transmission, with complete catalog of over 3,000 manuscripts, as well as text and music incipits of all of the sequences will soon be available in Nancy van Deusen, *The Medieval Latin Sequence, 900–1600: A Catalogue of the Manuscript Sources*, 4 vols. (forthcoming). The conclusions presented in the present study are based on research undertaken for the preparation of these volumes. In this context, it is remarkable that Notker, to whom a *liber hymnorum* of sequences has been attributed, working in the monastery of St. Gall in the second half of the ninth century, undoubtedly knew Cassiodorus' psalm commentaries, as there was a complete set in St. Gall; he was, of course, intimately acquainted with the psalms themselves. One can be certain that Notker knew Cassiodorus' 'canticumpsalmum' as well as its function, and I believe that he wrote his sequences as songpsalms. As support for these deductions, see Cassiodorus, *Expositio psalmorum* 1: x (manuscript transmissions of Cassiodorus' psalm commentaries; St. Gall, Stiftsbibliothek MSS 200, 201, 202 (ninth century) contain the complete Cassiodorus *Expositio psalmorum*); Peter W. Tax, *Notker Latinus: Die Quellen zu den Psalmen 1–150*, 3 vols (Tubingen: M. Niemeyer,

1972, 1973, 1975) and Nancy van Deusen, 'The Use and Significance of the Sequence', *Musica disciplina*, 40 (1986), 1–46.

20 See van Deusen, 'The Use and Significance of the Sequence', for further examples of explicits that make this point, in the eschatological mode, of the people of God before God, a point that forms an appropriate *copula* to the reading of the Gospel. The Gospels are included in the New Testament for the purpose of delineating just how one might achieve that status, that is, presence, unashamed, before God. Thus the sequence also reveals a concern through many centuries for appropriateness and logic within the *ductus* of the Mass, that is, *modulatio*.

21 Again, the forthcoming overview of sequence transmission, van Deusen, *The Medieval Latin Sequence, 900–1600*, will correct many erroneous impressions created by the volumes of the *Analecta hymnica* and perpetuated throughout the twentieth century, such as 'Victorine' sequences as 'late' sequences, a classification that does not take into account the sequence collections of Central Europe.

22 Some examples of psalm explicits are: 15: 11, 'Thou hast made known to me the ways of life, thou shalt fill me with joy with thy countenance: at thy right hand are delights even to the end'; 16: 15, 'But as for me, I will appear before thy sight in justice: I shall be satisfied when thy glory shall appear'; 22: 6, 'And thy mercy will follow me all the days of my life. And that I may dwell in the house of the Lord unto length of days'; and many explicits, such as 113: 18, 'But we that live bless the Lord: from this time now and for ever.' One notices, however, what appears to be a conscious alteration from first person singular, typical for the psalms, to the first person plural that is consistent for sequence explicits throughout the medieval period.

23 Cf. *Analecta hymnica medii aevi*, ed. Guido Maria Dreves et al., 55 vols. (Leipzig: O. R. Reisland, 1886–1922): *Qui regis sceptra*: vii, 31, liii, 8; *Dicat exsultans omnis creatura*: liii, 12; *Nato canunt omnia*: vii, 49, liii, 41; *Fulgens preclara rutilat*: vii, 57, iii, 62; *Alleluia, Dic nos (nobis) quibus*: vii, 73, iii, 69; *Grates salvatori ac regi*: liii, 92; *Carmen suo dilecto*: liii, 96.

24 Hugh of St. Victor, *Didascalicon*, III: xix (trans. Taylor, 36 ff.), in which Hugh observes that the perfect lover of philosophy considers the whole world as a place of exile.

Chapter 5

The Geography of Martinmas

Alejandro Enrique Planchart

The present study deals primarily with the evolution and transmission of the different formularies for Martinmas. Two earlier studies have dealt with these Mass formularies. The first is an article by Dom Guy Oury,[1] in which the emphasis is on a simple inventory of all the chants in a large number of sources.[2] Dom Oury's study is thorough and most useful. He has indeed found virtually all the chants for the different Masses for St. Martin in all the Western rites with the exception of the Beneventan, which escaped his notice; but the context of the Mass formularies in each source, and the nature of the recombinations of pieces from source to source and from one geographic area to another, are not considered by him except very much in passing. The other is Martha van Zant Fickett's dissertation on Martinmas chants, a careful and insightful work where the emphasis is primarily on a close analysis of the music itself, particularly in the case of Aquitanian Masses for the saint.[3]

Saint Martin, bishop of Tours in the fourth century and the father of monasticism in Gaul, became within a relatively short time one of the most widely revered saints of the early Middle Ages. His festival was celebrated throughout Christendom, appearing in most of the early liturgical documents from every Western rite – Ambrosian,[4] Beneventan,[5] Gallican,[6] Gregorian,[7] Mozarabic,[8] and Roman.[9] In the West Martin shared the day of his festival, 11 November, with an earlier soldier-saint who was also widely revered, the Libyan martyr Mennas, buried some fifteen kilometers south of Alexandria, where a small town, Karm abu Mina, grew around the basilica that Emperor Arcadius (395–408) built upon his tomb.[10] The Evangeliary of 645 and the Gregorian Sacramentary mention Martin's Mass after Mennas, which might indicate that his was the more recent feast. In the East the importance of Mennas caused the feast of St. Martin to be celebrated on 12 November in the Byzantine rite and on 10 November in the Coptic rite.[11] The shift of Martin's feast to 12 November is also attested by the Würzburg Evangeliary.[12] This occasionally created some confusion since this day is also the feast of St. Martin Pope and Martyr.[13]

In Rome itself – a city that did not normally take well to ultramontane saints – Martin's cult was established from the early sixth century on. Pope Symmachus (498–514) built a basilica dedicated to St. Martin near that of St. Silvester.[14] A monastery of St. Martin became associated with the basilica of San Pietro in Vaticano in the late seventh century and played a considerable role in the liturgical life of the basilica.[15] According to Ordo 36, an account of Roman ordination ceremonies perhaps written by a Frankish cleric, it became the custom for the pope to ordain the bishops in the oratory of St. Martin.[16] Finally, a freestanding altar dedicated to St. Martin stood in the passage that connected the rotunda of St. Andrew with that of St. Petronilla in old St. Peter's (see Fig. 5.1).

In a number of essays leading to his book *The Advent Project*, James McKinnon has made a brilliant argument for his view that about a century and a half after the establishment of the cult of St. Martin in Rome, namely in the late seventh century, the Roman *schola cantorum* embarked upon an ambitious musico-liturgical program that resulted in the rationalization of the church year and the creation of a complete set of Propers for the feasts of the Temporale and the Sanctorale. The Propers for the different feasts were arrived at, according to this view, partly by imposing an order upon whatever fund of traditional texts and chants was already in existence, and more importantly by the systematic creation of a large body of new works.[17] It was this body of text and music that was transmitted to the North under the early Carolingians and became what is known today as the basic layer of Gregorian chant, supplemented in the North by other texts and music, some new and some perhaps traditional, to cover those festivals celebrated in Francia but not in Rome.

It would stand to reason that if Martinmas was celebrated in Rome in the sixth and seventh centuries, Propers would have been assigned to it by the clerics of the *schola cantorum*, and that such Propers would have been, when transmitted to the North, associated with that feast. They did not need to be specific to the feast since McKinnon has demonstrated that in the sanctoral part of the Advent Project we meet with what he has called a proto-*commune sanctorum*. McKinnon also developed a simple test of whether a given festival had Roman Propers before its transmission to the North, namely textual identity in Roman and early Frankish sources. Sensibly he used as his sources for this test the Lateran Gradual, Vatican City, BAV Vat. lat. 5319, and the Mont-Blandin *antiphonale missarum* in Hesbert's *Sextuplex*.[18]

St. Martin's feast fails this test spectacularly. The Lateran Gradual has only the Propers for St. Mennas, who is not provided with a single unique chant. The Mass for St. Martin, however, is present, though partially illegible, in the twelfth-century Roman Gradual Vatican City, BAV San Pietro F 22. The Roman Propers for 11 November are given in Table 5.1.

The transmission of the Mass for 11 November to the North shows a number of discontinuities. The situation in the sources for Hesbert's *Sextuplex* is shown in Table 5.2. Hesbert calls attention to what he deems the not very coherent testimony for this Mass in the early manuscripts.[19]

Let us first consider St. Mennas. Four of the five manuscripts that contain a Mass for 11 November show a rubric for him and the Introit *Os iusti* found in the Roman sources. The Roman Gradual, in contrast, is to be found in none of the northern sources, which show two different Graduals among them. Leaving aside the Alleluia, three of the four sources that show the Introit found in Rome agree on the Offertory, *Desiderium animae*, but in the case of the Communion, even though four sources agree on a Communion, it is not that found in Rome for St. Mennas. It is interesting to note that the Gradual indicated in Compiègne, Senlis and Corbie is that which the later Roman

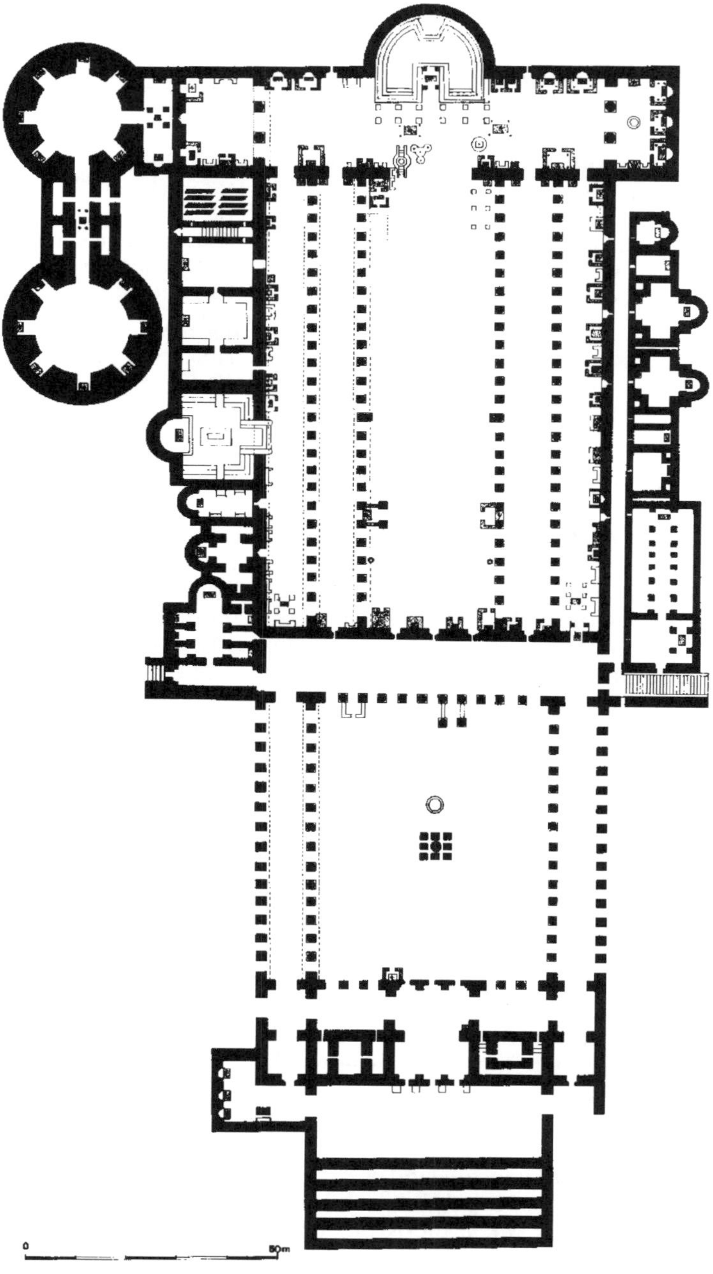

Figure 5.1 Plan of Old St. Peter's

Table 5.1 Roman Propers for the Masses of 11 November

In both sources only incipits are given.

Vat. lat. 5319	*San Pietro F 22*
Mense Novembris Dies VI [*recte* XI]. s Menne	**Sancte Menne**
IN Os iusti meditabitur	IN Os iusti meditabitur
GR Beatus vir	GR Beatus vir
AL Iustus non conturbabitur	AL Iustus non conturbabitur
OF Desiderium animae	OF Desiderium animae
CO Laetabitur iustus	CO Laetabitur iustus
	Sancti Martini
	IN Sacerdotes tui
	GR Inveni David
	AL Disposui
	OF Inveni David
	CO [no longer legible]

manuscript assigns to the Mass of St. Martin. But the illegible Communion in this manuscript was most likely drawn, as are all the other Propers for St. Martin in BAV San Pietro F 22, from the pool of chants grouped on fols. 94v–97r under the rubric *In commemoratione sacerdotum*, which do not include the Communion *Magna est* found in the Frankish manuscripts.

In the case of St. Martin the discontinuity between Rome and the earliest northern sources is total. The only point of contact would be if the Communion in San Pietro F 22 were *Fidelis servus*, found in Compiègne and in the pool of Communions *In commemoratione sacerdotum* in San Pietro F 22. Concerning this feast in the manuscripts of the *Sextuplex*, Hesbert rightfully concluded that the Mass transmitted by the northern manuscripts, with the exception of Monza, from which we have nothing beyond the Gradual, is by and large a Mass for a martyr and thus for St. Mennas, which makes, in his view, the double rubric in Corbie a suspect case.[20] Still, as he noted, the Offertory *Inveni David* is primarily used for confessors rather than martyrs, and it may well be that the presence of Martin's feast on 11 November, and his importance to the Franks, might have begun a process of contamination in this case.

The Mass for St. Martin that the Maurist fathers report as having been in the Compiègne Antiphoner (there is now a lacuna at this point) is already a Mass for a confessor and much closer, in terms of its Propers, to what would become the Mass for St. Martin in the late Middle Ages. It has, however, two Offertories, the first one shared by other confessors and eventually part of the *commune confessorum* and a second entirely specific to St. Martin, which again indicates some possible conflation in the compilation of this Mass.

The discontinuity between the Roman and early Gregorian Masses for St. Martin, given the presence of a feast of St. Martin in the Roman Evangeliary of 645 and what the history and archeology of St. Peter's Basilica appear to tell us about the cult of St. Martin in Rome, has two probable consequences for our

Table 5.2 Mass Propers for 11 November in the early Gregorian chant books

Mont-Blandin	*Senlis*	*Corbie*
III Idus Novembres Natale Sancti Mennae	**III Idus Novembris Natale Sanctae Menne**	**III Idus Novembres Natale Sancti Mene et Sancti Martini**
IN Os iusti Ps. Noli aemulari	IN Os iusti Ps. Noli aemulari	IN Os iusti
GR Gloria et honore V. Et constituisti	GR Inveni David V. Nihil proficiet	GR Inveni David
	AL Alleluia V. Inveni David	
OF Desiderium animae	OF Desiderium animae V. Vitam petiit V. Laetificabit eum	OF Desiderium animae
CO Magna est gloria	CO Magna est	CO Magna est
Compiègne [lacuna][a]	*Monza*	*Rheinau*
[St. Mennas] [IN Os iusti] [GR Inveni David V. Nihil proficiet] [OF Gloria et honore] [CO Magna est]		No sanctoral
[St. Martin] [IN Statuit eit dominus] [GR Os iusti meditabitur V. Lex dei eius] [OF 1 Veritas mea] [OF 2 Martinus igitur] [CO Fidelis servus]	**In Natale Sancti Martini** GR inveni David V. Nihil proficiet	

[a] The manuscript has a lacuna here, but *AMS*, pp. xx and cix, gives the liturgy reported by the Maurists, who saw the manuscript before the folios containing this mass were lost.

understanding of this Mass. First of all, from the admittedly late evidence of the manuscripts it is possible that St. Martin was venerated at St. Peter's but not at the Lateran before the twelfth century, when Pierre Jounel notes that Martin has entered the calendar of the Lateran,[21] and thus the Roman Mass for him in San Pietro F 22 may or may not be a late Mass. This may also indicate a varied reaffirmation of one of Bruno Stäblein's main theses concerning the transmission of the Roman chant to the North, namely that what was sent to Pepin and Charlemagne was essentially a papal liturgy, which may not have included some festivals important not only in the titular churches, but even in some of the Constantinian basilicas other than the Lateran.

Since a Mass for St. Martin apparently did not travel to the North with the Roman Propers, at least in the eighth century, the development of this

Mass north of the Alps would be a matter of adaptation of Roman materials and the addition of northern chants, some of which might have been newly composed in the eighth and ninth centuries and later, and some of which might be relics of older local traditions. In light of McKinnon's recent work it might be that what we have in the St. Martin liturgy is a first reaction of local Francian cantors to the new style of Gregorian chant. However this may be, the development of the Mass for St. Martin seems to differ along broad regional lines; it might be useful to examine the different traditions.

We may begin by examining the tradition represented by the German and Swiss manuscripts, also including in this case the Graduals from Monza, which in many respects reflect the East Frankish tradition as well. Table 5.3 gives the Mass for St. Martin in a representative group of tenth- and early eleventh-century East Frankish sources. As is usual for the East Frankish tradition, the Mass for St. Martin in these sources is quite stable, and remains so to the end of the Middle Ages. It is the closest, in terms of its repertory, to the Mass found in San Pietro F 22, with which it shares the Introit, Offertory and perhaps Communion (since the Propers for St. Martin in San Pietro F 22 are all not only taken from the pool *in commemoratione sacerdotum* but are either the first or second chant for each category in that pool, and the two Communions found in the German manuscripts are in fact the first and second Communions of the series in San Pietro F 22). Thus it is possible that this tradition reflects what was the old Mass for St. Martin in Rome, but we cannot be absolutely certain. There was some seepage of the St. Gall tradition into the Roman manuscripts, not only in the well-known presence of Notkerian *versus ad sequentias* in the Lateran and the Santa Cecilia Graduals, but also in one of the most unexpected places for such seepage to occur, the Easter Sunday Introit. In the Santa Cecilia Gradual the Introit appears with its usual psalm verse and a verse *ad repetendum*, but the text of the latter, despite the psalm tone to which is set, is not a psalm verse at all but rather

Table 5.3 Mass for St. Martin in tenth- and early eleventh-century East Frankish sources

Bamberg lit. 6 (Bamberg) *Einsiedeln 121 (Einsiedeln)* *Kassel 15 (Regensburg)* *St. Gall 339 (St. Gall)* *Tübingen 15 (Minden)*	*Graz 807* *(Klosterneuburg)*	*Monza 75 (Monza)* *Monza 76 (Monza)*
IN Sacerdotes tui	IN Sacerdotes tui	IN Sacerdotes tui
GR Ecce sacerdos	GR Ecce sacerdos	GR Ecce sacerdos
V. Non est	V. Non est	V. Non est
AL —	AL Iuravit dominus	AL — (75) AL Amavit eum dominus (76)
OF Inveni david	OF Inveni david	OF Martinus igitur obitum suum
CO Domine quinque talenta	CO Beatus servus	CO Beatus servus

the text of an Introit trope from the St. Gall repertory.[22] Still, from McKinnon's work on the evolution of the Propers it is clear that the more likely possibility is that the German sources, particularly those of St. Gall, reflect in this case the Roman tradition of the Mass for St. Martin and that this tradition was connected with St. Peter's Basilica rather than with the Lateran. This view of the locus of the cult of St. Martin in Rome agrees with the archeological evidence of the presence of an altar to him in the old basilica and the historical evidence of the existence of a monastery of St. Martin connected with St. Peter's in the seventh century. The one oddity in Table 5.3, the Offertory in the Monza Graduals, comes precisely where one would expect it, in an enclave of the German Gregorian tradition virtually next door to St. Ambrose's Milan and surrounded by churches that followed a number of different traditions – as will be seen when we examine the north Italian sources for Martinmas. Apart from the Alleluia, the Offertory is the most variable section of these liturgies and it is there where we find the Monza Mass for St. Martin reflecting not the German tradition but rather one of the many traditions of the north of Italy.

The picture presented by northern France, the Rhineland and England is also relatively coherent. The situation in a number of early sources from these regions is summarized in Tables 5.4 and 5.5, to which we might add the Mass for St. Martin that the Maurist fathers reported in the Compiègne Antiphoner from Table 5.2. The Introit and the Communion in Chartres, BM 47 may represent a further stage in the conflation of the Masses of St. Martin and St. Mennas indicated by the rubric in the Corbie Antiphoner. What eventually happened, of course, was the displacement of St. Mennas by St. Martin in the liturgies of ultramontane Europe (given the particular national importance of St. Martin for the Franks). Reading Tables 5.4 and 5.5 from left to right we see the stabilization of the Mass for St. Martin in northern France and England. The changes are localized and are a function of both space and time. Corbie or St. Denis, Cambrai, Nevers and Prüm have largely the same Mass, some of which is echoed in the sources from Winchester. The changes in the Winchester sources are symptomatic of changes over time. The Old and New Minsters in Winchester were originally in such proximity that the chanting in one of them could be heard in the other, according to a chronicler, but the repertory in Oxford, Bodl. Lib., Bodley 775 probably reflects the liturgy of the mid-tenth century,[23] while that of Le Havre, BM 330 reflects the post-conquest liturgy at the end of the eleventh century. Predictably, the *Graduale Sarisburiense* published by Frere[24] lines up with the sources from northeast France and the Rhineland. The one oddity that cannot be readily explained is the appearance in the later of the two manuscripts from Nevers, Paris BNF lat. 1235, of the Gradual *Iuravit dominus* instead of *Domine praevenisti*, which had become nearly universal in the region in the late eleventh century.

The manuscripts from Nevers and Prüm (Paris, BNF lat. 9448) on the Continent, and from Dublin and St. Albans across the channel, are witnesses of a different development, one that first made its appearance in the second Offertory in the lost folios of the Compiègne Antiphoner, namely the presence of an entirely new set of Propers uniquely specific to St. Martin. All of these have texts derived not from the Bible but largely from the writings of Martin's friend and first biographer, Sulpicius Severus.[25] This Mass was trans-

Table 5.4 Mass for St. Martin in sources from northern France and the Rhineland

Chartres 47 (Chartres)	*Mont-Renaud* (Corbie? St-Denis?)	*Cambrai 60* (Cambrai)	*Paris 1235 and 9449* (Nevers)	*Paris 9448* (Prüm)	*Darmstadt 1946* (Echternach)
			Mass of the day	**First Mass**	**Mass of the day**
IN Os iusti	IN Statuit ei	IN Statuit ei	IN Statuit ei	IN Statuit ei	IN Ecce sacerdos
GR Ecce sacerdos V. Non est inventus	GR Os iusti V. Lex dei eius	GR Domine praevenisti V. Vitam petiit	9449: GR Iuravit dominus V. Dixit dominus 1235: GR Domine praevenisti V. Vitam petiit	GR Domine praevenisti V. Vitam petiit	GR Statuit illi V. Fungi sacerdotio
AL — oratione	AL —	AL Statuit dominus	AL Martinus abrahe	AL Iustus ut palma	AL Hic in
OF Inveni david stabilita	OF Veritas mea	OF Veritas mea	OF Veritas mea	OF Veritas mea	OF Beatus vir V. Ideo
CO Magna est	CO Domine quinque	CO Beatus servus	CO Beatus servus	CO Beatus servus	CO Collaudabunt
			Mass of the Vigil (Paris 1235 only)	**Second Mass**	
			IN O beatum virum	IN O beatum virum	
			GR Ora pro nobis V. Dum sacramenta	GR Ora pro nobis V. Dum sacramenta	
			AL Hic martinus	AL Hic martinus	
			OF Martinus igitur	OF Martinus igitur	
			CO Martinus abrahe	CO Martinus abrahe	

abrahe	CO Martinus abrahe

Table 5.5 Mass for St. Martin in sources from the British Isles

Oxford 775 (*Winchester, Old Minster*)	*Le Havre 330* (*Winchester, New Minster*)	*Graduale Sarisburiense*	*Oxford 892* (Dublin)	*London 2. B. IV*
IN Statuit ei dominus	IN Statuit ei dominus	IN Statuit ei dominus	IN Statuit ei dominus[a] IN O beatum virum	IN O beatum virum
GR Iuravit dominus V. Dixit dominus	GR Inveni david V. Nihil proficiet	GR Domine praevenisti V. Vitam petiit	GR Domine praevenisti[a] V. Vitam petiis GR Ora pro nobis V. Dum sacramenta	GR Ora pro nobis V. Dum sacramenta
AL Beatus vir – martinus	AL Beatus vir – martinus	AL Hic martinus	AL Hic martinus AL O martine AL Martinus episcopus	AL Hic martinus
OF Inveni david	OF Veritas mea	OF Veritas mea	OF Veritas mea[a] OF Martinus igitur	OF Martinus igitur
CO Fidelis servus	CO Magna est	CO Beatus servus	CO Martinus abrahe sinu	CO Martinus abrahe sinu

[a] = Incipit.

mitted with some consistency in a number of regions, including Aquitaine, eastern Spain and northern Italy.[26] Typical of this development is the proliferation of Alleluia settings; while the sources give a new Introit, Gradual and Communion, we have five different Alleluias, some of them simply set to one of the known melodies but others apparently entirely new. There is, however, no simple correspondence between the specific Mass for the saint and the Alleluias with unique melodies. The Alleluia in Paris 1235 and presumably in Paris 9448 uses the melody of the *Alleluia. Posuisti domine*, no. 47 in Schlager's catalog,[27] while that in the Winchester books has a unique melody.

The position of the Mass specific to St. Martin in Nevers and Prüm is what liturgical historians have usually considered a symptom of an old liturgy being displaced, either by being transferred to the vigil of the feast in Nevers, or by being copied as a doublet – and without music at that – in Prüm. We need to look no further than the case of the *aliae missae* in the Beneventan books for examples of this. Its appearance in Oxford, Bodl. Lib., Rawl. C. 892, in contrast, is that of an imported liturgy that is replacing what by the late twelfth century has become the formulary from the *commune sanctorum* used in England and Ireland for St. Martin.

The situation in Echternach, on the other hand, is absolutely unique. The Mass for St. Martin sung there in the eleventh century survives only in the Echternach Sacramentary-Antiphoner; it is used only for St. Martin and no concordance from any other establishment has ever been found. The texts for all of the Mass chants are derived from a single book of the Bible, Ecclesiasticus, beginning with the Introit *Ecce sacerdos magnus*,[28] and are therefore scriptural.[29] The existence of this Mass is also reflected obliquely in the repertory of the Echternach troper copied about a century after the Sacramentary-Antiphoner, Paris, BNF lat. 10510. That manuscript contains a modest series of proper tropes (largely Introit tropes) for the entire liturgical year. Each of them has a rubric for a specific feast and only one has a rubric pointing to a *commune sanctorum*: it is the trope *Divini fuerat* to the Introit *Statuit* and it follows immediately the tropes for St. Willibrord, whose feast is 7 November. Now *Divini fuerat* is one of the most widespread tropes for St. Martin, and Martinmas, on 11 November, would in any calendrically oriented book follow closely the feast of St. Willibrord, so there is no doubt that in the model for Paris 10510, and thus quite possibly at Echternach before the composition of the special Mass *Ecce sacerdos magnus*, a Mass beginning with *Statuit* was sung. In any event, *Divini fuerat* in Paris 10510 is provided the rubric *De uno confessore*.[30] The Mass *Statuit*, sung for St. Martin in northern France and the Rhineland, made some further inroads into the German areas. Tropers from Mainz (London, BL Add. 19768), Heidenheim (Oxford, Bodl. Lib., Selden supra 27) and St. Emmeram (Munich, BSB clm 14083, also with a trope for *Sacerdotes domini*), have tropes to *Statuit*, and the Moosburg Gradual (Munich, UB 2° 156) has no Mass for St. Martin at all in the Gradual itself, which follows All Saints with St. Cecilia, but it has tropes to *Statuit* specifically indicated for St. Martin in the troper.[31] On the other hand, Munich, Kremsmünster 309, Munich, BSB clm 14322, and Bamberg, Staatsbibl. lit 5 show instead tropes for the Introit of the German tradition, *Sacerdotes domini*.

If the second Offertory in the Mass for St. Martin in the Compiègne Antiphoner was copied by the main hand, something we can no longer determine, then at least part and possibly all of the Mass *O beatum virum* for St. Martin using Sulpicius Severus as the source for its texts was in existence by the ninth century. The origins of this Mass probably do not lie in the north. In Nevers, as noted above, it is assigned to the vigil of St. Martin, while in Prüm it follows the main Mass for the feast and is left entirely without musical notation. Its adoption in England is both late and transient, in that even at St. Albans it was replaced by the common of a confessor by the end of the thirteenth century. The earliest fully notated source I have found for it is the idiosyncratic Gradual from Saint-Michel de Gaillac, Paris, BNF lat. 776, where it is the first Mass for St. Martin. The situation in the Aquitanian sources, given in Table 5.6 below, is both complex and interesting.

The version of the first Mass in Paris 776 has a trait suggesting that in it we have a version that may be the closest to the early form of the Mass. It consists of a unique reading of the Offertory *Martinus igitur*, with three verses instead of two. The first two verses have exactly the same text but with different melodies (see Ex. 5.1). This is the kind of trait that would easily be lost in transmission, and indeed none of the other recensions of the Mass known to me has it. In the Graduals of Toulouse (London, BL Harley 4951) and St. Yrieix (Paris, BNF lat. 903) this Mass appears, as in Nevers, for the vigil instead of the day, and with a second Communion that, though psalmodic, is not part of the Gregorian repertory. At first it would seem as if the same situation is found in Paris 776, all the more so because the Mass for St. Mennas intervenes between the two Masses for St. Martin, so that at least the order of the Masses agrees with what we encounter in Toulouse, St. Yrieix and Nevers as well as with the older traditions of the *Sextuplex*, where St. Mennas is the main saint of 11 November. But the rubrics of Paris 776 tell a different story. While in Toulouse and St. Yrieix the first Mass is clearly labeled as a vigil Mass, the rubrics in Albi are as follows: fol. 119^{v}, III IDUS NOVEMBRIS NL SCI MARTINI EPI for the first Mass, fol. 120^{r}, EODEM DIE SCI MENNE MARTIRIS for the Mass of St. Mennas, which consists of nothing but incipits except for the *Alleluia. Haec est martyr quem coronavit*,[32] and the rubric for the second Mass for St. Martin, also on fol. 120^{r}, reads ALIU IN SCI MARTINI OFFICIUM. The rubrics in Paris 776, together with the extra Offertory verse, lend weight to the view that this Mass is indeed the oldest Aquitanian Mass for St. Martin, which is in the process of being shifted to the vigil, and that Paris 776 is our best witness for it. It retains both the older rubric as a Mass for the day and the extra Offertory verse even though its place in the manuscript is already that of a Mass for the vigil. This is, in fact, the only way of making sense of the order of the Masses for St. Martin and St. Mennas in Paris 776.

The construction of this Mass shows it to be a mixture of dependence upon some Gregorian models and a good deal of original material. Fickett provides a careful analysis of each of the movements,[33] and it is interesting to note the extent to which the composition of this Mass follows, *mutatis mutandis*, what McKinnon has discovered about the nature of the Proper repertories in *The Advent Project*.[34] It is as if the Frankish musicians who compiled this Mass knew that the Introit and the Communion were to have their own

Ex. 5.1 The Mass *O beatum virum* in Aquitaine (Paris, BNF lat. 776, fols. 119^{v}–120^{r})

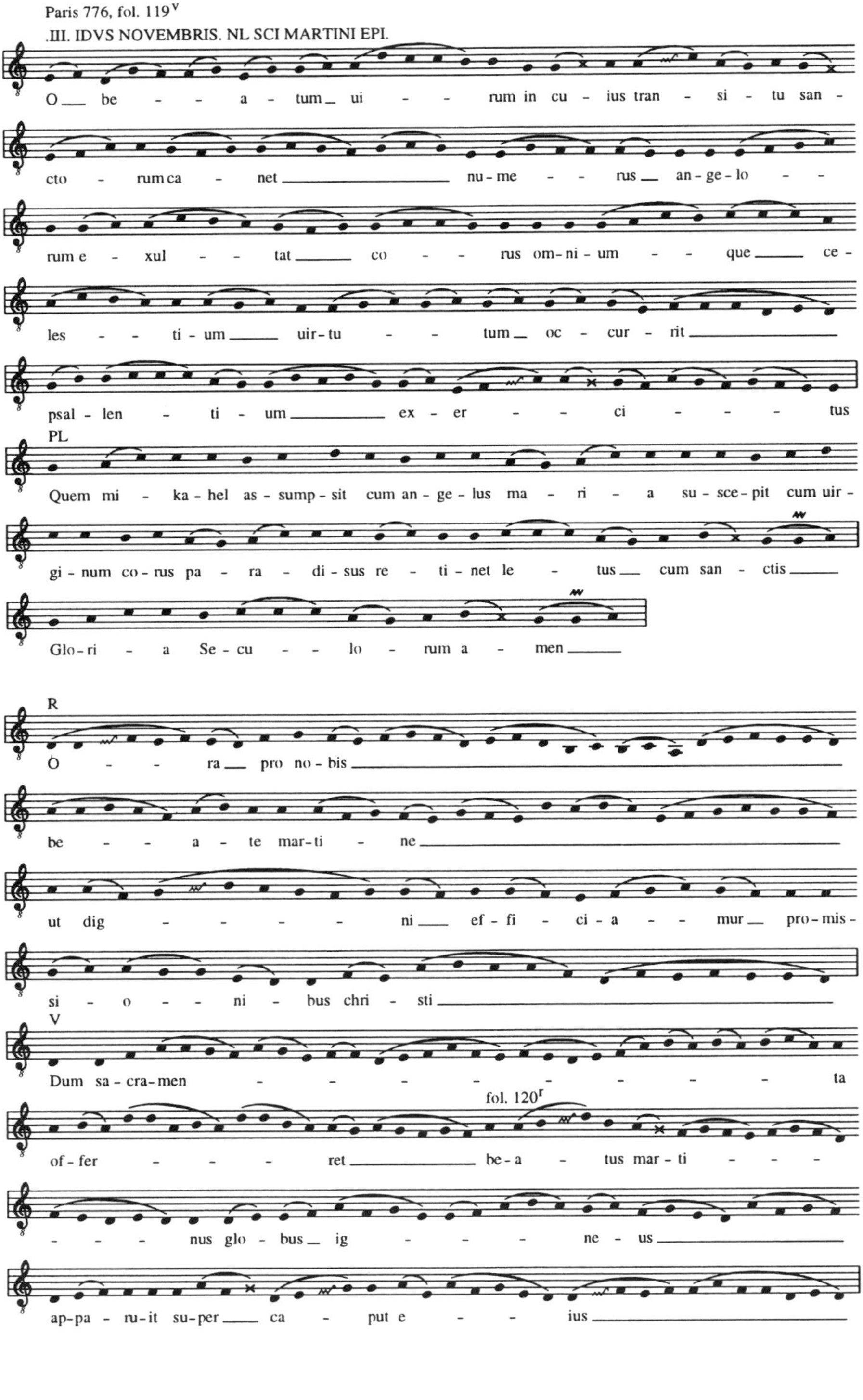

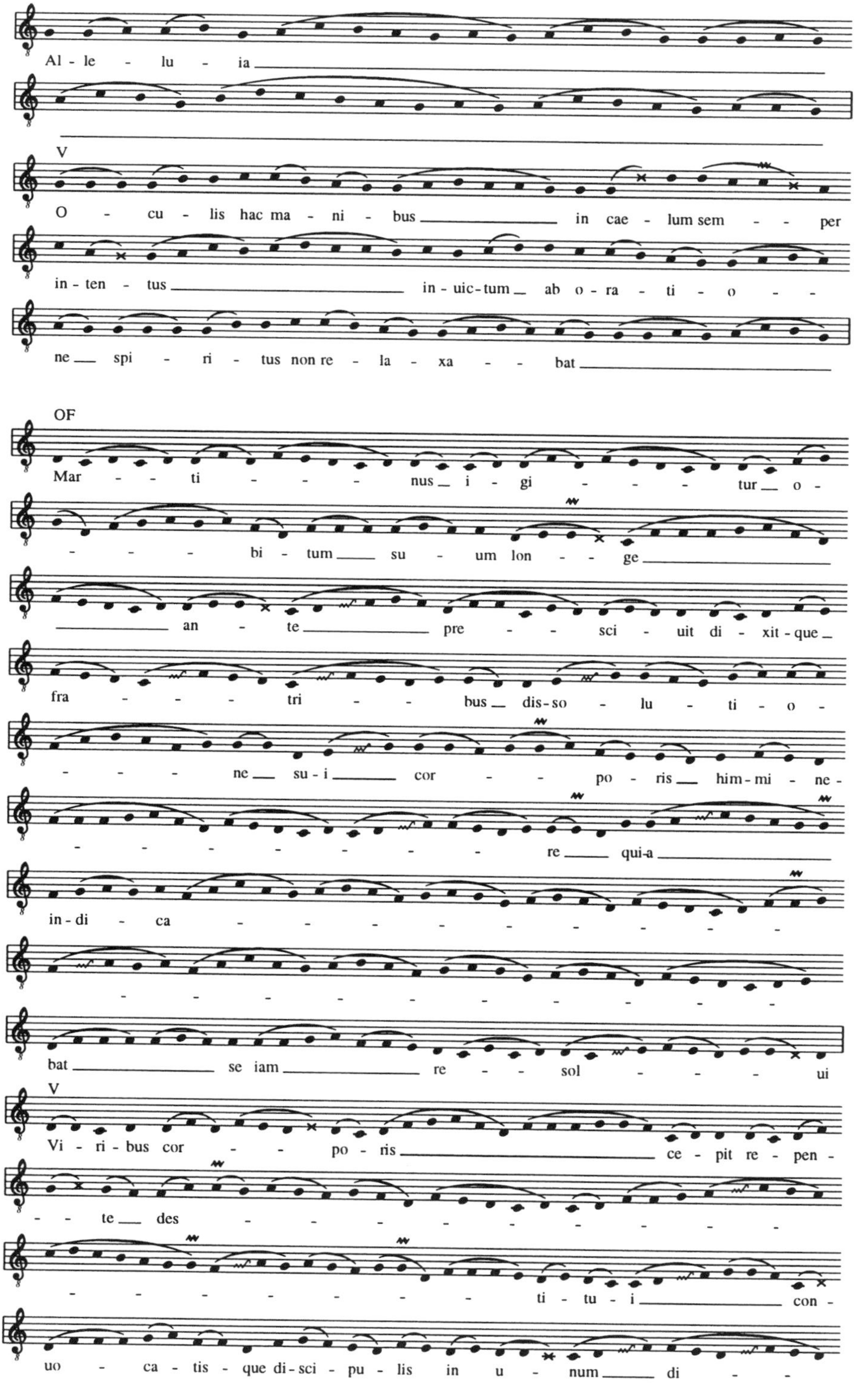
Al - le - lu - ia
V
O - cu - lis hac ma - ni - bus in cae - lum sem - - per
in - ten - tus in - uic - tum ab o - ra - ti - o - -
ne spi - ri - tus non re - la - xa - - bat
OF
Mar - - - ti - - - - nus i - gi - - - tur o -
- - - bi - tum su - um lon - - ge
an - te pre - - sci - uit di - xit - que
fra - - - tri - - bus dis - so - lu - ti - o -
- - - ne su - i cor - - po - ris him - mi - ne -
- - - - - - - re qui - a
in - di - ca - - - - - - - - -
bat se iam re - - sol - - - ui
V
Vi - ri - bus cor - - po - ris ce - pit re - pen -
- - te des - - - - - - - - -
- - - - - - ti - tu - i con -
uo - ca - tis - que di - sci - pu - lis in u - num di - -

xit - - que dis-so - lu - ti - o - - - - nem su-i
cor - - po - ris him-mi - ne - - - - - - re
V
Vi-ri - - bus
cor - po - - - - ris ce-pit re - pen - te de - sti - - tu - i
con - uo-ca - tis-que di - sci - pu - - lis in u - num
In - di - - - ca - [bat]
V
Mar - ti - - - - - - - - - - -
- - - - - - nus e - pi - - - - - -
sco - - pus mi - gra - uit a se-cu - - lo ui-uit
in chri - sto gem - - ma sa - cer - do-tum
Qui-a in-di - ca-[bat]
CO
Mar-ti - - nus a - bra - he si - nu le - tus ex - ci - pi-tur
mar-ti - - nus hic pau - - per et mo - - di - - cus
cae-lum di ues in - gre - di - - - - tur ym-nis
cae-le - sti - bus ho - no - - - - - - ra - tur
Glo - ri - a se-cu - - lo-rum a - - men Cae-lum di - [ues]

melodies.[35] The Gradual *Ora pro nobis* is an adaptation of the Gregorian *Constitues eos*,[36] while the Offertory *Martinus igitur* is largely an independent work in terms of the respond but in the verses it contains borrowings from three Offertories, the Frankish *Stetit Angelus* (i.e., *Viri galilei* and *Custodi me* are the verses?) and *Viri galilei*, and the Gregorian *Custodi me*.[37]

The Toulouse Gradual presents us with three Masses for St. Martin's Day. The first is a common Mass for confessors except for the Alleluias specific to Martin. Elements of it are found in the Masses for St. Martin in northern France and in England, but the specific constellation of elements finds no exact parallel elsewhere. A second Mass is very close to the first, but with an Introit specific to Martin and a different Gradual for a confessor, found for St. Martin otherwise only in sources east of the Rhine. The third Mass is also a common Mass for a confessor with three Alleluias that are specific to St. Martin. The Mass for the day in the Gradual of St. Yrieix is, for all intents and purposes, a conflation of the second and third Masses in the Toulouse Gradual. It shares the Introit and Gradual with the second Mass, Alleluias 3–5 (in reverse order), Offertory and Communion with the third Mass, and adds three further Alleluias, all of which are specific to Martin. Much of this material is also present in the second Mass in Paris 776. The differences in the repertory of all three manuscripts as far as this Mass is concerned suggest that it had a young and not entirely stable tradition in the first half of the eleventh century. Both of these Masses, in fact, appear to have a relatively unstable tradition, with a higher percentage of melodic variants than one encounters in the Gregorian repertory even though they survive in a relatively narrow group of sources. Both Masses are a complex combination of adaptation of Gregorian melodies and completely new material.[38]

This second Mass for St. Martin in Paris 776 has, apart from the Alleluias, only one purely Martinian piece, the Introit *Ecce sacerdos magnus Martinus*. Fickett shows to what extent the Introit shares the tonal strategy of the Frankish responsory *Martinus abrahae sinu*, making it less of an independent melody than *O beatum virum*.[39]

Examples 5.1 and 5.2 give both of the Aquitanian Masses specific to St. Martin, transcribed from Paris 776.[40] The music of the new pieces, that is, those which are not contrafacts, approaches that of the Roman-Frankish Gregorian repertory, but occasionally shows traits that suggest that the cantors who produced these pieces had come across the new music of the early *sequentiae* and their proses as well as whatever melos existed in southern French liturgical chant before the arrival of the Gregorian repertory. In addition there are an unusually high number of small melodic and notational variants among the three manuscripts, variants that one does not normally encounter in the Gregorian repertory of these three sources – which belong, after all, to the same liturgical and notational tradition and were copied within less than a century of each other. This again suggests that we are dealing here with a tradition that was not only younger than that of the Frankish recension of the Gregorian chant, but one that did not have the juridical weight of the Gregorian repertory.

The Mass in Paris, BNF lat. 1132, a Gradual copied at St. Martial after the abbey was taken over by the Cluniacs, is also largely a conflation of the second

Ex. 5.2 The Mass *Ecce sacerdos magnus Martine* in Aquitaine (Paris, BNF lat. 776, fol. 120r)

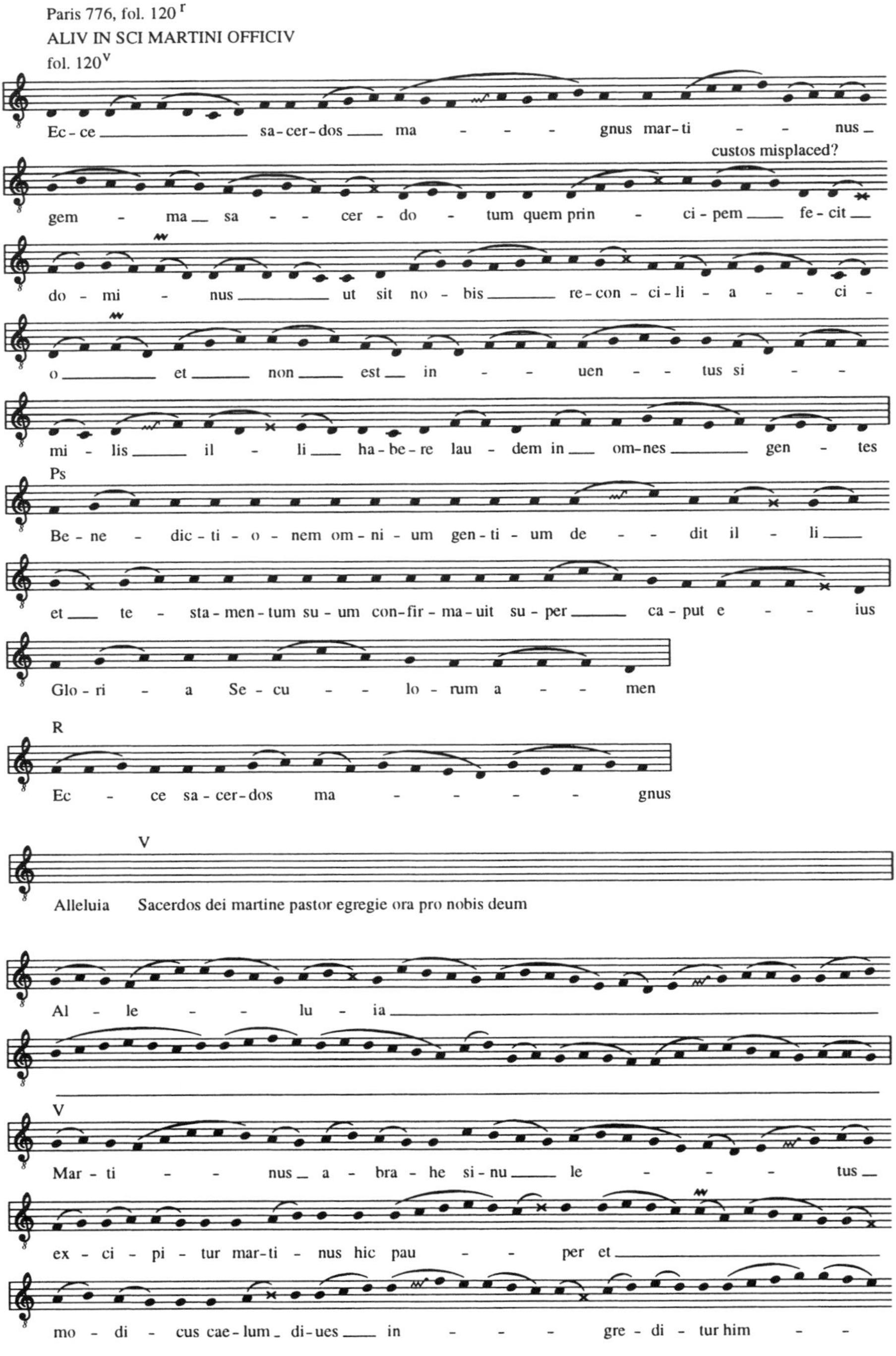

nis
Repeat of iubilus
cae-le sti - bus ho - no ra - tur
Al - le lu ia
Melisma up to * repeated in Paris 903
*
V
Mar - ti nus si gni po-tens ful - go -
re uir - tu tum ip-se re
ver - be - rat as - tra et in pa ce
Repeat of iubilus
san - cto - rum om - ni - um con - ser - tus est
From * to the end of the iubilus not in MS, reconstructed from fol. 12v *
Al - le - lu - ia
V
These two neumes one step too high in MS
Mar-ti - nus hic pau - per et mo - di - cus
* *
cae - lum di
Repeat of iubilus
ues in - gre - di tur

1) Passage indicated by *___* probably should be repeated, MS has enclosed it within two 'd' signs.

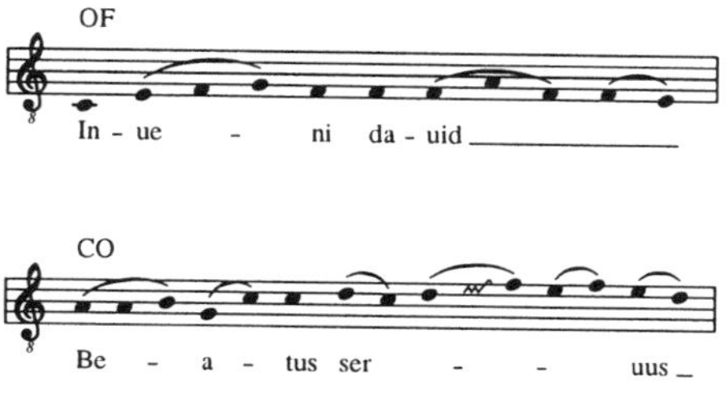
OF
In - ue - ni da - uid
CO
Be - a - tus ser - uus

and third Masses in Toulouse with a new and different Communion, *Semel iuravi*. It may well be that the Cluniacs, whose opposition to tropes is well known, were also not particularly well disposed toward local Propers. I had access to no Gradual or missal from St. Martial itself earlier than Paris 1132.

The evidence of the Aquitanian tropers is, however, interesting. These sources do not include the Gradual and very rarely the Alleluia, but from the cues to the Introit, Offertory and Communion tropes give us a sense of which Propers were used for a given feast. Almost without exception they all indicate the Introit *Statuit ei dominus* for St. Martin. The exception itself is both interesting and puzzling. Paris, BNF lat. 1118, the immense collection of tropes, *prosulae*, *sequentiae* and proses copied somewhere in southwest France at the very end of the tenth century, provides incipits for the Gradual and the Alleluia as well; it thus transmits essentially the third Mass of the Toulouse Gradual with the Alleluia *Tu es sacerdos* instead of the multiple Alleluias found in the Toulouse Gradual. But between the last Introit trope for *Statuit* and the trope to the *Gloria in excelsis*, we meet the rubric ALIUM OFFICIUM (fol. 97^{r}), followed by the entire Introit *Ecce sacerdos magnus Martinus* and its psalm incipit, without tropes. There is not a single other instance of an entire Introit copied in Paris 1118, much less one without tropes, so it is not surprising that Günther Weiss thought he was dealing here with an immense trope to the psalm verse,[41] but the rubric is unequivocal and the music agrees entirely with the Introit as found in Paris 776, Paris 903 and Harley 4951. The presence and function of this Introit in Paris 1118 remain inexplicable unless we assume that the scribe was actually compiling the manuscript from a number of different sources and constructing the admittedly very complex liturgical series of Paris 1118 on the spot.[42]

Apart from this exception, neither the Introit *O beatum virum* nor *Ecce sacerdos magnus Martinus* is to be found in the Aquitanian trope collections. This is particularly curious in the case of the St. Yrieix Gradual, which as Table 5.6, shows, does not have *Statuit* as the Introit for St. Martin, but which in the troper section shows no fewer than three tropes for the Introit *Statuit* assigned to St. Martin. The Offertory *Veritas mea*, with no Communion, turns up in Paris, BNF lat. 1240, implying at least the use of this Offertory at St-Martial de Limoges a century or so before the copying of Paris 1132, since the St. Martin tropes are in the hand of the main troper of Paris 1240. It may also be worth noting that the Offertory trope for St. Martin in Paris 1240, *Iamque pura pio*, is unique to this source (it also appears without music for St. Martial, whose earliest trope repertory seems to have been built upon borrowings from St. Martin).[43] Returning to *Veritas mea*, it appears as well in the oldest section of Paris, BNF lat. 1084 in an ambiguous context. This manuscript gives for St. Martin a common trope to the Offertory *Posuisti domine* and its verse *Magna est*, followed by a trope to the Communion *Beatus servus*. Immediately after this we encounter two tropes for the verses of the Offertory *Veritas mea*, but without a cue to the Offertory itself, only to the verses, followed by a trope to the Communion *Domine quinque talenta*. All these pieces were left without music. The remaining Aquitanian tropers are unanimous in assigning the Offertory *Posuisti domine* and the Communion *Beatus servus* to St. Martin. This suggests that there was an older tradition in southern France of assigning the Offertory *Veritas mea* to St. Martin, a tradition consonant with that found in the older northern French and Rhenish manuscripts. This was replaced by the use of the Offertory *Posuisti domine*, a Frankish Offertory that may have originated in Cluny, according to Dom Hourlier,[44] and that makes its earliest recorded appearance in two of the *Sextuplex* antiphoners for St. Gorgonius, a minor Roman martyr whose relics were translated ca. 760 to Gorze by Chrodegang.[45] *Posuisti domine* was used in the tenth century as an Offertory for martyrs and confessors, appearing widely in the late tenth century as an Offertory for St. Stephen.[46] In southern France it was shared by St. Martin and St. Stephen, while *Veritas mea* was assigned almost uniquely in the tropers to St. Martial after its lone appearance for St. Martin in Paris 1240.

Before leaving the southern French tradition for St. Martin it may be well worthwhile to suggest that the use of the common of confessors Mass for St. Martin in this region might have been influenced by the desire to sing tropes on his feast, and that the repertory of tropes for St. Martin in the Aquitanian sources is virtually entirely imported from elsewhere, where the more specific Masses *Ecce sacerdos magnus Martinus* and *O beatum virum* were not used. Indeed, given the liturgical use of this Mass in Paris 776 as compared not only with the other Aquitanian Graduals but with those in the North, the origin of both Masses would seem to be in Aquitaine itself. The spread to Spain, noted by Dom Oury, of the Introit *Ecce sacerdos magnus Martinus*[47] is not surprising given the enormous inroads that the Aquitanian repertory made into the Iberian peninsula.[48] The transmission of some of these pieces to northern Italy follows the pattern of transmission of Aquitanian tropes to that region detailed in my own studies and those of James Borders.[49] On the other hand, the late adoption of the Mass *O beatum virum* across the English channel as the main Mass for St. Martin in a few places is one of these cross-cultural currents that have no clear explanation right now.

The situation for Martinmas in the Italian peninsula is far more complex than in any of the other regions. Only a very small view of it is afforded by Tables 5.7 and 5.8. The diversity in the Italian sources parallels aspects of the Italian repertory of tropes and sequences well known to scholars, and often explained by the large number of different currents and traditions that one meets in Italy, particularly in the north. I included the Monza Graduals in the table of the German tradition (Table 5.3), but indeed they have the Offertory of the French Mass, albeit without any of the verses. The variability of the Mass for St. Martin reaches an extreme in certain regions of northern Italy. The manuscripts from Aquileia and Cividale, which usually line up with those of the Abbey of St. Gall in Moggio and the Basilica of San Marco in Venice, transmit, as they often do, an almost pure German liturgical tradition, but in Moggio and San Marco the Western Mass for a confessor, with Alleluias specific for St. Martin, obtains. The manuscripts from Bobbio present a curiously incoherent tradition. The earliest, Turin, Bibl. Naz. Univ., G.V.20, gives us the Mass for St. Martin in the German tradition; Turin, Bibl. Naz. Univ., III.17, from the late twelfth century, gives instead a West Frankish Mass for a confessor with a specific Alleluia (compare it, for example, with the Mass in Paris 1132). As one can see from Table 5.7,

Table 5.6 Mass for St. Martin in Aquitanian sources

Paris 776 (Gaillac)	*Paris 903* (St. Yrieix)	*London Harley 4951* (Toulouse)	*Florence Ashb. 62* (southern France)	*Paris 1132* (St. Martial – Cluniac)
First Mass	**Mass of the Vigil**	**Mass of the Vigil**	**Mass of the Day**	**Mass of the Day**
IN O beatum virum	IN O beatum virum	IN O beatum virum		
GR Ora pro nobis	GR Ora pro nobis	GR Ora pro nobis		
V. Dum sacramenta	V. Dum sacramenta	V. Dum sacramenta		
AL Oculis ac manibus	AL Oculis ac manibus	AL Oculis ac manibus		
OF Martinus igitur obitum	OF Martinus igitur obitum	OF Martinus igitur obitum		
V. Viribus corporis 1	V. Viribus corporis 1	V. Viribus corporis 1		
V. Viribus corporis 2				
V. Martinus episcopus	V. Martinus episcopus	V. Martinus episcopus		
CO Martinus abrahe sinu	CO Martinus abrahe sinu	CO Martinus abrahe sinu		
		CO Iuravit dominus		
		Mass of the Day		
		IN Statuit ei dominus		
		GR Iuravit dominus		
		V. Dixit dominus		
		AL Tu es sacerdos		
		AL Martinus episcopus		
		OF Veritas mea		
		CO Beatus servus		

Table 5.6 (continued)

Paris 776 (*Gaillac*)	*Paris 903* (*St. Yrieix*)	*London Harley 4951* (*Toulouse*)	*Florence Ashb. 62* (*southern France*)	*Paris 1132* (*St. Martial – Cluniac*)
Second Mass	**Mass of the Day**	**Second Mass**		
IN Ecce sacerdos/martinus	IN Ecce sacerdos/martinus	IN Ecce sacerdos/martinus	IN Ecce sacerdos/ martinus	
GR Ecce sacerdos (incipit)	GR Ecce sacerdos magnus	GR Ecce sacerdos magnus	GR Ecce sacerdos magnus	
	V. Non est inventus	V. Non est inventus	V. Non est inventus	
	AL Iste sanctus digne	AL Tu es sacerdos	AL Martinus abrahe sinu	
AL Sacerdos dei (no music)	AL Sacerdos dei martine			
AL Martinus abrahe	AL Martinus abrahe sinu			
AL Martinus signi potens	AL Martinus signi potens			
AL Beatus vir sanctus	AL Martinus hic pauper			
AL Martinus hic pauper	AL Hic martinus pauper			
OF Inveni david (incipit)	OF Posuisti domine	OF Veritas mea	OF Inveni david	
CO Beatus servus (incipit)	CO Beatus servus	CO Beatus servus	CO Euge serve	
		Third Mass		
		IN Statuit ei dominus		IN Statuit ei dominus
		GR Invenit david		GR Inveni david
		V. Nihil proficiet		V. Nihil proficiet
		AL Martinus hic pauper		AL Hic martinus pauper
		AL Martinus signi potens		
		AL Martinus abrahe sinu		
		OF Posuisti domine		OF Veritas mea
		CO Beatus servus		CO Semel iuravi

Table 5.7 Mass for St. Martin in northern Italian sources

Rome Angelica 123 (Bologna)	*Vercelli 146, 160, 161 (Vercelli)*	*Pistoia 119, 120 (Novalesa, Pistoia)*	*Padua A. 47 (Ravenna)*	*Vatican lat. 4770 (Abruzzi region)*	*Piacenza 65 (Piacenza)*
First Mass					
IN Statui ei dominus[a]	IN Statuit ei dominus	IN Statuit ei dominus	IN Statuit ei dominus	IN Ecce sac./martinus	IN Statuit[a]
GR Inveni david[a]	GR Inveni david	GR Inveni david	GR Ecce sacerdos	GR Ora pro nobis	GR Inveni david[a]
V. Nihil proficiet[a]	V. Nihil proficiet	V. Nihil proficiet	V. Non est inventus	V. Dum sacramenta	V. Nihil proficiet[a]
AL —	AL Iuravit dominus	AL Beatus vir/martinus	AL Iuravit dominus	AL Hic martinus pauper	AL Hic est sacerdos
				AL Serve bone et fidelis	AL Serve bone[a]
OF Veritas mea[a]	OF Inveni david	OF Veritas mea	OF Veritas mea	OF Martinus igitur	OF Veritas mea[a]
CO Beatus servus[a]	CO Fidelis servus	CO Fidelis servus	CO Beatus servus	CO Martinus abrahe	CO Fidelis servus[a]
Second Mass					
IN O beatum virum					
GR Inveni david[a]					
V. Dum sacramenta					
AL Sanctae trinitatis					
AL Beatus vir/martinus					
OF Inveni david[a]					
OF Martinus obitum					
CO Domine quinque[a]					

Turin 20 (*Bobbio*)	*Turin 17* (*Bobbio*)	*Turin 18* (*Bobbio*)	*Modena 7* (*Forlimpopoli*)	*New York* *Morgan 797* (*northern Italy;* *Padua?*)
IN Sacerdotes domini GR Inveni david V. Nihil proficiet AL Amavit eum OF Inveni david CO Beatus servus	IN Statuit ei dominus GR Inveni david V. Nihil proficiet AL Hic martinus pauper OF Veritas mea CO Beatus servus	IN Beatus martinus GR Dixerunt discipuli V. Invadent enim AL Amavit eum AL Iuravit dominus OF O virum ineffabilem CO Sacerdos dei martinus	IN Beatus martinus GR Dixerunt discipuli V. Invadent enim AL — OF Veniens miles CO Cumque venerat	IN O beatum virum GR Ora pro nobis V. Dum sacramenta AL Beatus vir/martinus OF Martinus igitur CO Martinus abrahe
Berlin 40608 (Venice)	*Udine 234* (Moggio)	*Udine 2* (Diocese of Aquileia)	*Cividale 56, 58, 79* *Vatican Ross. 76* (Cividale, Aquileia)	*Ivrea 60* (Pavia)
IN Statuit ei dominus GR Ecce sacerdos V. Non est inventus AL Beatus vir/martinus OF Inveni david CO Domine quinque	IN Statuit ei dominus GR Ecce sacerdos V. Non est inventus AL Beatus vir/martinus AL Martinus episcopus OF Inveni david CO Domine quinque	IN Statuit ei domini GR Inveni david V. Nihil proficiet AL Iuravit dominus AL Amavit eum OF Veritas mea CO Domine quinque	IN Sacerdotes domini GR Inveni david V. Nihil proficiet AL Iuravit dominus OF Veritas mea CO Beatus servus	IN Statuit ei dominus GR Ecce sacerdos V. Non est inventus AL Martinus episcopus OF Inveni david CO Beatus servus **Second Mass** IN Beatus martinus GR Dixerunt discipuli V. Invadent enim AL Beatus vir/martinus OF O virum ineffabilem CO Sacerdos dei martinus

[a] = Incipit.

Table 5.8 Mass for St. Martin in southern Italian sources

Benevento 40 (Benevento, Santa Sofia)	*Benevento 39 (Benevento, San Pietro in Benevento)*	*Benevento 33, 34, 35, 38 (Benevento) Vatican lat. 6082 (Montecassino)*	*Vatican Ottob. lat. 576 (Bari region) Baltimore 6 (Canossa)*	*London Egerton 857 (Benevento)*
First Mass	**First Mass**			
IN Statuit[a]	IN Statuit[a]			
GR Ecce sacerdos[a]	GR Ecce sacerdos[a]			
AL Disposui[a]	AL Disposui[a]			
OF Veritas mea[a]	OF Veritas mea[a]			
CO Beatus servus[a]	CO Beatus servus[a]			
Second Mass	**Second Mass**			
IN Beatus martinus	IN Beatus martinus	IN Beatus martinus	IN Beatus martinus	IN Beatus martinus
GR Dixerunt discipuli	GR Dixerunt discipuli	GR Dixerunt discipuli	GR Dixerunt discipuli	GR Dixerunt discipuli
V. Invadent enim	V. Invadent enim	V. Invadent enim	V. Invadent enim	V. Invadent enim
AL Oculis ac manibus	AL Oculis ac manibus	AL Oculis ac manibus	AL Oculis ac manibus	
AL Beatus vir/Martinus	AL Beatus vir/martinus	AL Beatus vir/martinus		AL Beatus vir/ martinus
	AL Martinus episcopus			
	AL Elegit te dominus			
		OF Martinus semet (only in 6082)	OF Martinus semet (only in 576)	
OF O virum ineffabilem ineffabilem	OF O virum ineffabilem	OF O virum ineffabilem	OF O virum ineffabilem (only in Bal 6)	OF O virum ineffabilem
V. O beatum virum	V. O beatum virum	V. O beatum virum		
		V. Martinus semet (35)		
		V. Brachia nobilium (35)		

Table 5.8 (continued)

Benevento 40 (Benevento, Santa Sofia)	*Benevento 39 (Benevento, San Pietro in Benevento)*	*Benevento 33, 34, 35, 38 (Benevento) Vatican lat. 6082 (Montecassino)*	*Vatican Ottob. lat. 576 (Bari region) Baltimore 6 (Canossa)*	*London Egerton 857 (Benevento)*
OF Martinus igitur	OF Martinus igitur			
V. Martinus semet	V. Martinus semet			
V. Brachia nobilium	V. Brachia nobilium			
CO Sacerdos dei	CO Sacerdos dei	CO Sacerdos dei	CO Sacerdos dei	CO Sacerdos dei
Third Mass (Beneventan)				
ING Stolam iocunditatis				
GR Ecce magnum				
V. Dispersit dedit				
OF Martinus abrahe				
CO Dixerunt discipuli				
CO O quantus luctus				

[a] = Incipit.

a form of this Mass could be found in Bologna, Vercelli, Novalesa, Pistoia, Pavia, Ravenna and Piacenza, and also from the evidence of the Italian tropers in Mantua, Nonantola and Volterra. But as we turn to Turin, Bibl. Naz. Univ., F.IV.18, also from the twelfth century but most likely earlier than Turin III.17, we find yet a third liturgy, namely a specific Mass for the saint largely with non-biblical texts. The Alleluias in this Mass, however, use biblical verses, which is a reversal of the commonly encountered situation where it is the Alleluia alone that has a text specific to the saint in question. The situation becomes more complicated when we look at the tropes for St. Martin in Bobbio, because Turin G.V.20 has the Introit *Sacerdotes domini*, but assigns no tropes to it, even though some German manuscripts (though not those in the St. Gall tradition) show a number of tropes connected with it and with the feast of St. Martin.[50] Similarly Turin III.17, with the Introit *Statuit*, has no tropes for the Mass of St. Martin, but Turin F.IV.18, which has the Introit *Beatus martinus*, has one of the oldest and best-known Introit tropes for the saint, *Martinus meritis virtutum*,[51] cued, however, to the Introit *Statuit*, which is not used in this manuscript for St. Martin. The situation, with the three manuscripts in approximate chronological order, is then as follows:

Turin G.V.20	Introit: *Sacerdotes domini*	no tropes
Turin F.IV.18	Introit: *Beatus martinus*	trope *Beatus martinus meritis*, cued to *Statuit ei*
Turin III.17	Introit: *Statuit ei*	no tropes

It is interesting that the existence of the Introit *Beatus martinus* seems to have contaminated the text of the trope itself in the Italian tradition. In the tropers from Novalesa, Piacenza and Mantua, as well as in Turin F.IV.18, the opening of the trope has been expanded from *Martinus meritis virtutum et stemmate pollet*, a competent if mouse-brown hexameter, into *Beatus Martinus meritis virtutum et stemmate pollet.*[52] In every instance, however, the version of the trope beginning *Beatus martinus meritis* is cued to the Introit *Statuit*. The only source that cues it to the Introit *Beatus martinus obitum suum* is the troper of Rome, Bibl. Angelica 123, which gives the uncontaminated version of the trope. Further, even though the Gradual in Angelica 123 has two Masses for St. Martin, one of which is largely a Martinian Mass, neither one of them uses the Introit *Beatus martinus*. Thus the witness of the troper in Angelica 123 is in itself inconsistent with the gradual in exactly the opposite direction of the situation in Turin F.IV.18. Since it is only in Turin F.IV.18 where the variant form of the trope exists in close proximity to the Introit *Beatus martinus*, I am inclined to believe that the origin of that variant is Bobbio.

The case of the transformation of *Martinus meritis* into *Beatus martinus meritis* brings to mind what may be another echo of an Introit in later music. In St. Gall Martin was never provided with tropes, and his Mass began, as it did throughout the entire German region except for the Rhineland, with the Introit *Sacerdotes tui domini* and continued with the Gradual *Ecce sacerdos magnus*. Notker, at the start of his sequence for Martin, reacts to the Mass text in a manner similar to that in which, as Calvin Bower showed, he reacted to the Mass texts in the Easter cycle of Sequences in the sense that the

Sequence begins by telling us who the great priest is of whom the Introit and Gradual have sung, *Sacerdotem christi martinum cuncta per orbem canat ecclesia*.[53] In a sense Notker's piece reinterprets the previous two Propers heard in the liturgy, creating a progression of specificity from *Sacerdotes tui domine* to *Ecce sacerdos magnus* and to *Sacerdotem christi martinum*.

I will return to the Mass beginning with *Beatus martinus* shortly, but it is to be noted that the second Mass in Angelica 123 is clearly related to the Aquitanian Mass for St. Martin with which it shares a number of pieces. The second Offertory, *Martinus obitum*, is really a different piece from the better-documented Offertory *Martinus igitur obitum suum* found in Aquitaine and in other Italian sources, and the second Communion, *Domine si adhuc* is also a specifically Martinian work, which I have yet to find in another source and which forms a pair with the Offertory *Martinus obitum*. Closer to the southern French Mass is the liturgy for St. Martin in New York, Pierpont Morgan Lib. 797, a North Italian gradual of uncertain provenance (perhaps from Padua?) with a notation reminiscent of that of Piacenza, BC 65. Similarly, the Introit *Ecce sacerdos magnus martinus* found in the very old-fashioned Abruzzi Missal in the Vatican (Vatican City, BAV Vat. lat. 4770) is documented elsewhere only in southern France. Thus it is apparent that the French Masses for St. Martin found their way to Italy very early on.[54]

In contrast to the various combinations of specifically Martinian pieces and the common of confessors that one finds in northern Italy, the sources that preserve the Mass beginning with *Beatus martinus* seem to transmit a stable constellation of chants that travel together. In the north it appears in Pavia in the early eleventh century and in Bobbio in the twelfth. Only in the Gradual from Forlimpopoli is the relative stability of the set of chants for this Mass breached; the Offertory and the Communion, even though they are specifically Martinian works, have not turned up in any other source available to me.

The probable source for this Mass is southern Italy. Table 5.8 shows that the south Italian manuscripts transmit this Mass with remarkable unanimity as the 'Gregorian' Mass for St. Martin, even though in Benevento, Arch. Cap. 39 and 40 it is preceded by the incipits of the Mass that St. Martin shares with a number of other confessors.[55] There can be little doubt, however, that the Mass beginning with *Beatus martinus* is the main south Italian Mass for him, since it is the only one in the other Beneventan and Cassinese sources.[56] The music for the south Italian Mass for St. Martin is given as Ex. 5.3.

As I noted in connection with the Aquitanian Mass, the Introits specific to St. Martin are never provided with tropes north of the Alps and, with the exception of the assignment of *Martinus meritis virtutum* as a trope to *Beatus martinus* in Angelica 123, the same applies to Italy north of Rome.[57] South of Rome, however, all the Beneventan Graduals transmit a set of varied tropes for *Beatus martinus*,[58] and the Montecassino troper Vatican City, BAV Urb. lat. 602 transmits yet another, although this last one has remained irrecoverable from that source.[59] However, it may yet turn up. Indeed what is probably the lost trope that precedes it in the manuscript has recently been found by Thomas Kelly on a leaf in Beneventan script in Lanciano, and he has most kindly sent me a color slide of it.

The Mass shows in a few places the south Italian taste for the repetition of large-scale melodic patterns, as in the *Alleluia. Beatus vir sanctus martinus.* The overwhelming majority of the sources for this Alleluia are Italian, but as Schlager indicates, it is found in Paris 776, Paris 1084 and the two Winchester Tropers.[60] But only in Italian sources are the repetitions quite as worked out, and the Beneventan sources all include the prosula *Summe Martine*, found elsewhere only in Angelica 123. This may be a case of an Aquitanian melody reworked in Italy or one of the few cases of an Italian melody finding its way to the north, as is the case with a few of the tropes in Winchester.[61]

An unusual work in the south Italian Mass is the Offertory *O virum ineffabilem*; it has an extravagantly low tessitura reaching down to *gamma ut*, but its melody is stable in all sources and those with lines and clefs present it at the same very low range (see Ex. 5.3). Fickett shows that the respond is based upon the Gregorian Offertory *Dextera domini*, one of a number of second-mode melodies usually transmitted with an *a* final which the Beneventan manuscripts transmit with a *D* final.[62] As Fickett shows, the modeling continues through the verse *O beatum virum*, based on the verse *In tribulatione* of *Dextera domini*. She notes that Benevento, AC 34 does not have the verse *In tribulatione* as part of *Dextera domini*,[63] but this may reflect, as so much else in Benevento 34 does, the influence of Montecassino. The Offertory, for the third Sunday after Epiphany, is missing from Benevento, AC 38, 39 and 40 but is present, with the verse *In tribulatione*, in Benevento, AC 35, fols. 9^{v}–10^{r}.

The Offertory of the Beneventan manuscripts presents the most complex situation in the tradition of this Mass. As Table 5.8 indicates, Benevento 39 and 40 have two Offertories, *O virum ineffabilem* with the verse *O beatum virum*, and *Martinus igitur* with the verses *Martinus semet* and *Brachia nobilium*.[64] Benevento 34 and 38 have only the first Offertory, Benevento 35 has the first Offertory with its own verse and both verses of the second,[65] and Vatican City, BAV Vat. lat. 6082 has *Martinus semet*, rubricated as an Offertory – as the *first* Offertory for St. Martin – followed by *O virum ineffabilem*. Given the tradition in the carefully copied Benevento 39 and 40, it would appear that the version in Benevento 35 may be the result of the scribe losing concentration and not entering the respond for *Martinus igitur*, but the rubric for *Martinus semet* in Vat. lat. 6082 suggests that at least this verse had an independent tradition.

In the case of *Martinus igitur* we have no way of knowing if the Aquitanian Offertory preceded the Italian one or if it was the other way around. Chronologically the earliest source for either one is Benevento 33, but whoever produced the later version clearly knew the earlier one. Still the two pieces are different. The antiphons share a general melodic strategy but fill in the details very differently. Curiously enough, given the south Italian love for melodic repetition, the extended double neuma at 'indicavi' in the French melody finds no echoes in the Italian version. The very rough similarity of the antiphons disappears entirely in the verses, where the two traditions do not even share the same text.

The melos of most of the music for the Martinian pieces on both sides of the Alps reflects an awareness of the Gregorian style, and some of it is based upon Gregorian models; still, much of this music remains subtly different from Gregorian chant. It is hard to tell at this point if these differences are a reaction to the Gregorian style or if they reflect echoes of an earlier

Ex. 5.3 The Mass *Beatus Martinus* in Benevento (Benevento, AC 40, fols. 135v–138v)

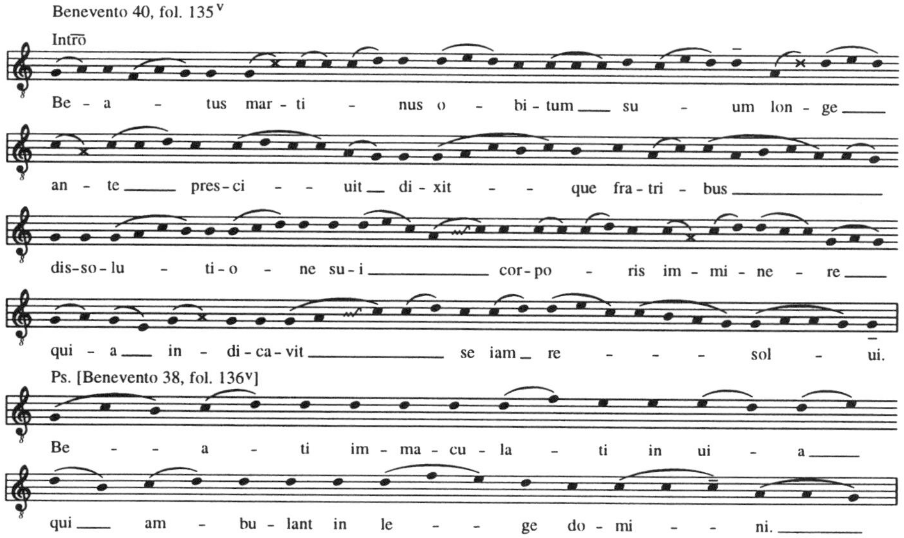
Benevento 40, fol. 135v
Intrō
Be - a - tus mar - ti - nus o - bi - tum su - um lon - ge
an - te pres - ci - - uit di - xit - - que fra - tri - bus
dis - so - lu - ti - o - ne su - i cor - po - ris im - mi - ne - re
qui - a in - di - ca - vit se iam re - - - - sol - ui.
Ps. [Benevento 38, fol. 136v]
Be - - - a - ti im - ma - cu - la - ti in ui - a
qui am - bu - lant in le - - ge do - mi - - - ni.

For the psalm Benevento 40 has *Beati immacula* underneath the music for the opening and the close of the verse.

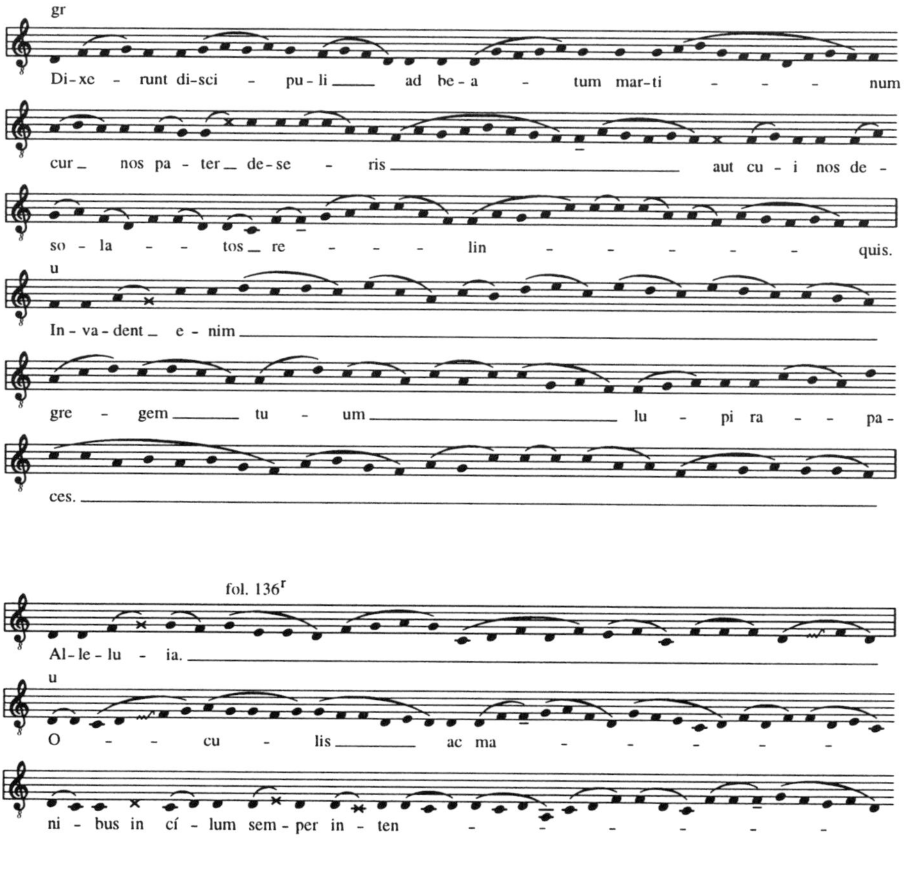
gr
Di - xe - runt di - sci - pu - li ad be - a - tum mar - ti - - - - num
cur nos pa - ter de - se - ris aut cu - i nos de -
so - la - - tos re - - - - lin - - - - - - quis.
u
In - va - dent e - nim
gre - gem tu - um lu - pi ra - - pa -
ces.
fol. 136r
Al - le - lu - ia.
u
O - - cu - lis ac ma - - - - - -
ni - bus in cí - lum sem - per in - ten - - - - - -

The prosula is copied after the melisma

fols. 136^{v}-137^{v}: Sequences, *Candida contio melos* and *Gloriosa dies adest*

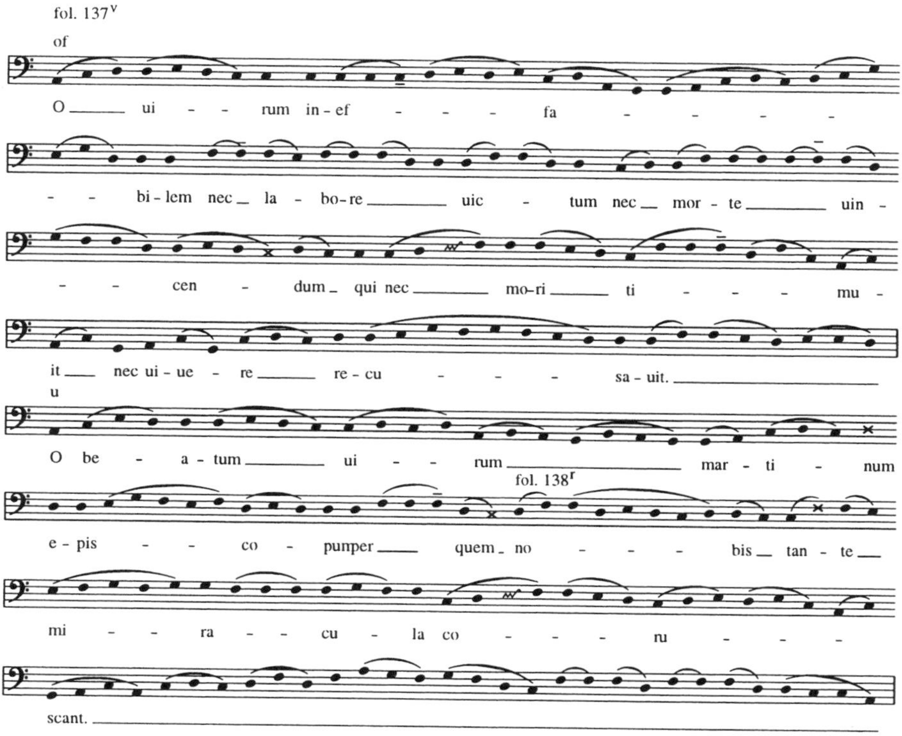
fol. 137v
of
O ui - - rum in - ef - - - - fa - - - - -
- - bi - lem nec la - bo - re uic - tum nec mor - te uin -
- - cen - dum qui nec mo - ri ti - - - - mu -
it nec ui - ue - re re - cu - - - - sa - uit.
u
O be - a - tum ui - - rum mar - ti - num
fol. 138r
e - pis - - co - pumper quem no - - - bis tan - te
mi - - ra - - cu - la co - - - - ru - - - -
scant.

of
Mar - ti - - nus i - gi - - - tur o - bi - tum
su - - um lon - ge an - - te
pres - - ci - uit di - xit - que fra - - tri - bus
(MS sic)
dis - so - lu - ti - o - - nem sui cor - po - ris
im - mi - ne - - - - re qui - a
in - di - ca - - - - - - - - - -
bat se iam re - sol - - uit.

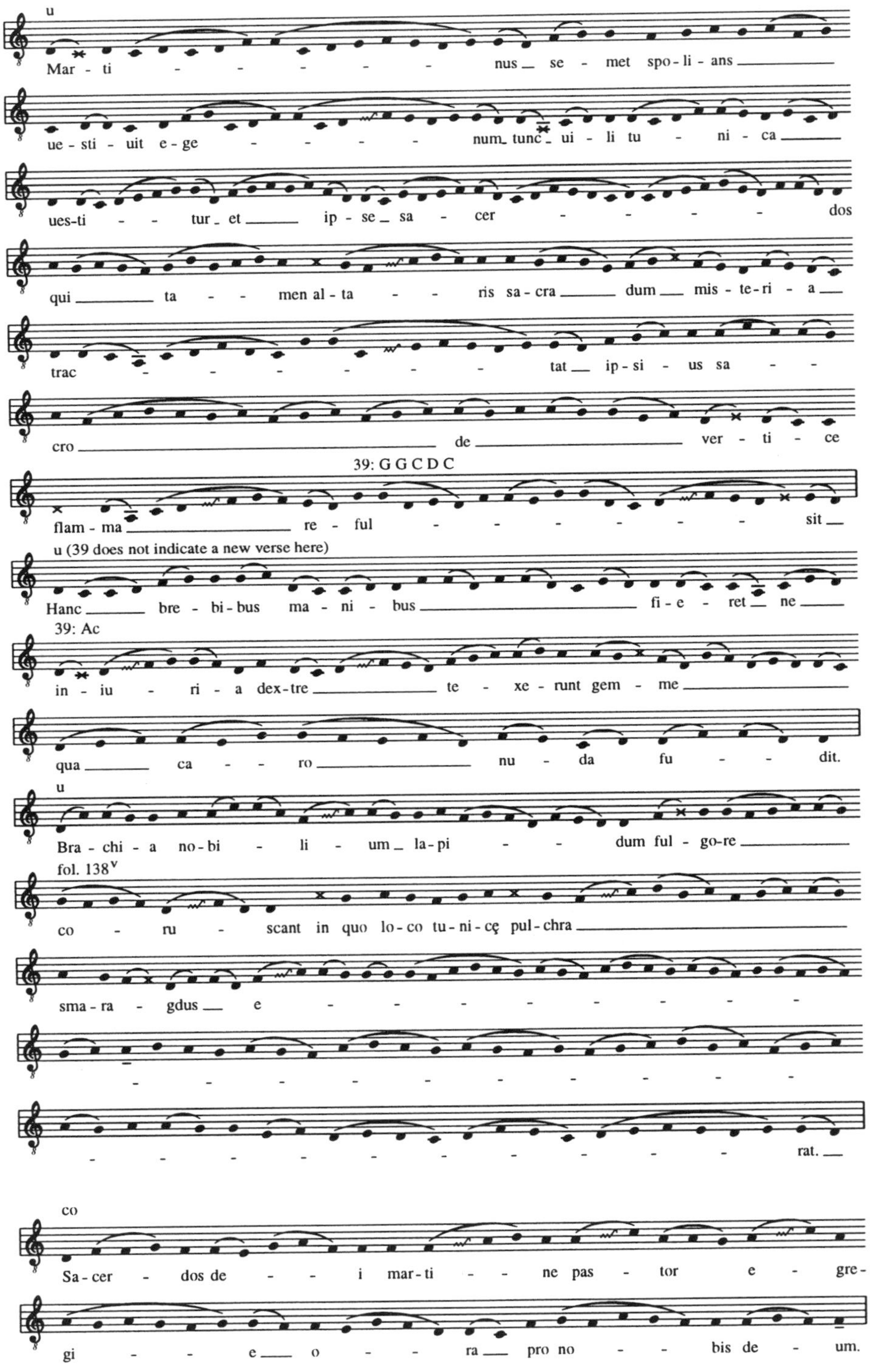
u
Mar - ti - - - - - nus se - met spo - li - ans
ue - sti - uit e - ge - - - - - num tunc ui - li tu - ni - ca
ues - ti - - tur et ip - se sa - cer - - - - dos
qui ta - - men al - ta - - ris sa - cra dum mis - te - ri - a
trac - - - - - - - tat ip - si - us sa - -
cro de ver - ti - ce
39: G G C D C
flam - ma re - ful - - - - - - sit
u (39 does not indicate a new verse here)
Hanc bre - bi - bus ma - ni - bus fi - e - ret ne
39: Ac
in - iu - ri - a dex - tre te - xe - runt gem - me
qua ca - - ro nu - da fu - - dit.
u
Bra - chi - a no - bi - li - um la - pi - - dum ful - go - re
fol. 138v
co - ru - scant in quo lo - co tu - ni - cę pul - chra
sma - ra - gdus e - - - - - - - - -
- - - - - - - - - - -
- - - - - - - - - - rat.
co
Sa - cer - dos de - - i mar - ti - - ne pas - tor e - gre -
gi - - - e o - - ra pro no - - bis de - um.

tradition. The Introit *Beatus martinus* is full of the sunlit melodic grace one finds in a large number of other south Italian pieces with a G final (which is not so often found in the Gregorian repertory, although the Roman cantors clearly knew of it since it can be heard in the Introit *In virtute tua*). This relationship to Gregorian style appears even in the Ambrosian Ingressa for St. Martin, *Dispersit dedit pauperis* (Ex. 5.4a), which has a scriptural text.[66] In sharp contrast, the melos of the Beneventan Ingressa *Stolam iocunditatis* (Ex. 5.4b) strikes the ear forcefully as a very different kind of music from all of the other examples. The Ingressa is adapted from Ecclesiasticus 6: 32,[67] and the verse of the Gradual has the same psalm text as the Ambrosian Ingressa, but the rest of the Beneventan Mass is non-biblical.

In any event, the tally of specifically Martinian pieces is quite impressive. I count three Introits; one Ingressa; four Graduals, one of them with Beneventan chant; nine Alleluias; six Offertories, one of them with Beneventan chant; and six Communions, two of them with Beneventan chant. And this does not take into account the Mass in the Echternach antiphoner or the Ambrosian and Mozarabic liturgies that Martin shares with other saints, nor the dozens of tropes to Gregorian Introits, Offertories and Communions that can be shown to have originated for St. Martin and were then borrowed for other confessors, such as St. Martial and St. Swithun. The textual source for most of the specifically Martinian Propers is not the Bible but rather the writings of Sulpicius Severus, which of course also provided much of the text for the majority of the pieces for St. Martin's Office. The music of the Martinian Masses is for the most part a very far cry, even in the Communions, from the concise elegance and poise of such pieces as the Christmas Communion *In splendoribus sanctorum* (which I view as the masterpiece of the cantor McKinnon has called 'The master of the re-fa advent lyrics'). Most of the Martinian pieces are quite beautiful, but also in many ways wild and overgrown, something I wish to think reflects the spirit of Martin himself, whose deeds and thoughts were often the despair of his fellow bishops and the Roman rulers. Further, given the homely nature of Martin, and despite Severus' literary merits and, let us say it, his pretensions, it is also fitting that much of the text of his liturgy comes out, when all is said and done, from someone's letter to his mother-in-law.

In the end, Martin – snubbed by the Lateran singers of the Roman *schola cantorum*, perhaps because of his being a saint from beyond the Alps and because his *cultus* in Rome had grown on the wrong side of the river – had his revenge, and not until the late Middle Ages' infatuation with St. Nicholas and St. Catherine is there quite the amount of music and poetry devoted to any other saint comparable with the early burst of works, coming from both north and south of Rome, that we have for him.

Notes

1 Dom Guy Marie Oury, 'Formulaires anciens pour la messe de Saint Martin', *Etudes grégoriennes*, 7 (1967), 21–40.

2 Given the extensive collection of sources Dom Oury uses, there are some surprising lacunae. Apart from Benevento, BC 33 and 34 and Vatican City, BAV

Ex. 5.4 Ambrosian and Beneventan *Ingressae* for St. Martin: (a) *Antiphonale Missarum Mediolanensis* (1935), 381; (b) Benevento, AC 40, fol. 138v

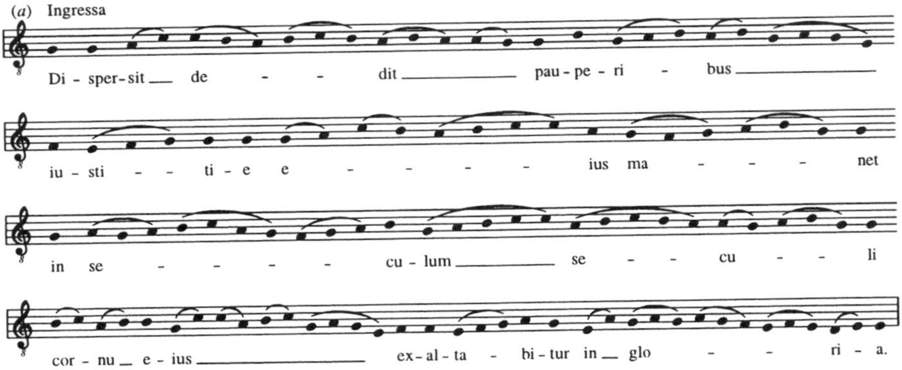

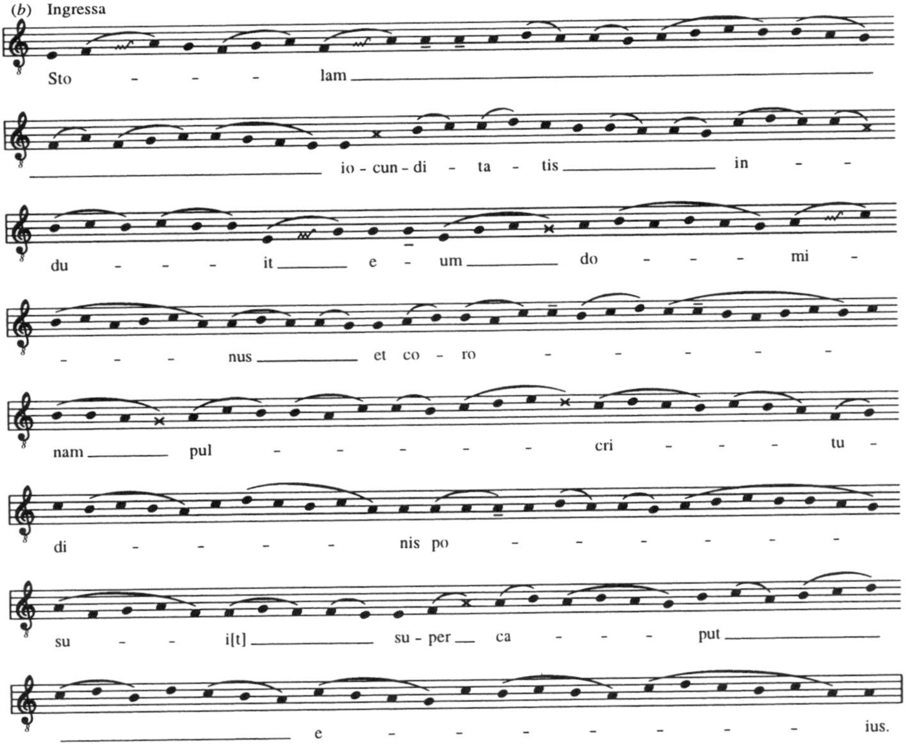

Vat. lat. 6082, none of the south Italian manuscripts was consulted, and in dealing with the Aquitanian Masses and some of the north Italian traditions the evidence of the tropers was not examined.

3 Martha van Zant Fickett, 'Chants for the Feasts of St. Martin of Tours' (Ph.D. diss., Catholic University of America, 1983).

4 *Das Sacramentarium Triplex: Die Handschrift C 43 der Zentralbibliothek Zürich*, ed. Odilo Heimig (Liturgiewissenschaftliche Quellen und Forschungen, 49; Corpus Ambrosiano-Liturgicum, 1; Münster: Aschendorff, 1968), 250. See also *Manuale Ambrosianum ex codice saec. XI olim in usum canonicae vallis Travaliae*, ed. Marco Magistretti, 2 vols (Milan: Ulrico Hoepli, 1904; repr. Nendeln, Liechtenstein: Kraus Reprint, 1971), ii, 1–5.

5 *Benevento, Biblioteca Capitolare 40, Graduale*, ed. Nino Albarosa and Alberto Turco, with essays by A. Thibaut, R. Fischer, and T. F. Kelly (Padua: Linea editrice, 1991), fols. 138^{v}–139^{r}; and *Les Témoins manuscrits du chant bénéventain*, ed. Thomas Forrest Kelly (PM 21; Solesmes: Abbaye Saint-Pierre, 1992), 215–16.

6 *Missale Gothicum (Vat. Lat. 317)*, ed. Leo Cunibert Mohlberg (Rome: Herder, 1961), 112–13.

7 *AMS*, no. 164.

8 *Antifonario visigótico mozárabe de la catedral de León*, ed. Louis Brou and José Vives, 2 vols (Barcelona: Centro de estudios e investigación S. Isidoro, 1959), i, 407–12.

9 It is mentioned in the Evangeliary of 645. See Theodor Klauser, *Das römische Capitulare Evangeliorum* (2nd edn, Munster: Aschendorff, 1972), 40–41. Klauser's Type Π Evangeliary gives the date for St. Martin as 12 November. The same date appears in the Type Δ Evangeliary (Roman, ca. 740; see Klauser, 87). Only in the Type Σ Evangeliary (Roman, ca. 755; see Klauser, 125) do Mennas and Martin share the same day. One could think that the earlier two Evangeliary types refer not to the feast of St. Martin of Tours, but to that of St. Martin Pope, but the Gospel assigned every time is the same. See also BAV San Pietro F 22, fol. 85^{v}.

10 The basilica and the town had disappeared by the fifteenth century; see J.-M. Sauguet and M. C. Celletti, 'Menna', *Bibliotheca sanctorum*, 12 vols. (Rome: Istituto Giovanni XXIII nella Pontificia Università lateranense, 1961–70), ix, cols. 324–43.

11 Pierre Jounel, *Le Culte des saints dans les basiliques du Latran et du Vatican au douzième siècle* (Rome: Ecole française de Rome, 1977), 309.

12 Germain Morin, 'Liturgie et basiliques de Rome au milieu du VIIe siècle', *Révue bénédictine*, 28 (1911), 296–330, at 316 and n. 7.

13 Cf. n. 9 above.

14 Christian C. F. Hülsen, *Le chiese di Roma nel Medio Evo: cataloghi ed appunti* (Florence: L. S. Olschki, 1927; repr. Hildesheim: G. Olms, 1975), 382.

15 Guy Ferrari, *Early Roman Monasteries: Notes for the History of the Monasteries and Convents at Rome from the V through the X Century* (Vatican City: Pontificio Istituto di archeologia cristiana, 1957), 230–40. It is perhaps worth remembering that John the Archcantor of St. Peter's in Rome, sent to England to teach the Roman chant to the English, was the abbot of the monastery of St. Martin connected with the basilica. See Bede, *Opera historica* , with trans. by J. E. King, 2 vols. (Loeb Classical Library, 246; Cambridge, Mass.: Harvard University Press, 1930), ii, 96–103 (Liber IV, cap. 18).

16 Michel Andrieu, *Les Ordines Romani du haut moyen âge*, 5 vols. (Louvain: Spicilegium Sacrum Lovaniense Administration, 1956–65), iv, 147–8.

17 James McKinnon, 'Preface to the Study of the Alleluia', *EMH* 15 (1996), 213–49; 'Properization: The Roman Mass', *Cantus Planus: Papers Read at the Sixth*

Meeting of the International Musicological Society Study Group, Eger, Hungary, 1993, ed. László Dobszay (Budapest: Hungarian Academy of Sciences Institute for Musicology, 1995), 15–22; 'The Eighth-Century Frankish-Roman Communion Cycle', *JAMS* 40 (1987), 179–227; 'The Fourth-Century Origin of the Gradual', *EMH* 7 (1987), 91–106; 'The Roman Post-Pentecostal Communion Series', *Cantus Planus: Papers Read at the Fourth Meeting of the International Musicological Society Study Group, Pécs, Hungary, 1990*, ed. László Dobszay (Budapest: Hungarian Academy of Sciences Institute for Musicology, 1992), 175–86; 'Vaticana Latina 5319 as a Witness to the Eighth-Century Roman Proper of the Mass', *Cantus Planus: Papers Read at the Seventh Meeting of the International Musicological Society Study Group, Sopron, Hungary, 1995*, ed. László Dobszay (Budapest: Hungarian Academy of Sciences Institute for Musicology, 1998), 401–11; and *The Advent Project: The Later-Seventh-Century Creation of the Roman Mass Proper* (Berkeley: University of California Press, 2000).

18 McKinnon, *The Advent Project*, 245–6.

19 *AMS*, p. cix.

20 *AMS*, pp. cix–cx.

21 Jounel, *Le Culte*, 308.

22 The piece in question is *Hodie resurrexit dominus*; cf. the edition in *Tropes of the Proper of the Mass from Southern Italy, A.D. 1000–1250*, ed. Alejandro Enrique Planchart [Pt. 1]. Beneventanum troporum corpus, 1 (Madison, Wis.: A-R Editions, 1994), 87.

23 Oxford, Bodl. Lib., Bodley 775, as Andreas Holschneider has shown, is a late copy of an exemplar from the third quarter of the tenth century; see his *Die Organa von Winchester: Studien zum ältesten Repertoire polyphoner Musik* (Hildesheim: Olms, 1968), 24–7.

24 *Graduale Sarisburiense*, ed. Walter Howard Frere (Plainsong and Mediaeval Music Society; London: Bernard Quaritch, 1894; repr. Farnborough: Gregg Press, 1966).

25 For the writings of Sulpicius Severus concerning St. Martin in an English translation see Sulpicius Severus et al., *The Western Fathers*, ed. F. R. Hoare (London: Sheed & Ward, 1954; repr. New York: Harper, 1965).

26 See Tables 5.6 and 5.7a. In addition to sources listed in those tables, the Mass is transmitted in manuscripts listed in Tables 5.4–6 for the Mass *O beatum virum*; it also appears complete in Langres, Grand Séminaire 312, Lucca, BC 608, Madrid, RAH Aemil. 51, Madrid, Palacio Real 429, Oxford, Bodl. Lib. 366; Paris, BNF lat. 10511; Perugia, BC 21, Rome, Bibl. Vallicelliana C 52, St. Petersburg, Saltykov-Shchedrin Publ. Lib., O.v.I.6; Toledo, BC 35.10.

27 Karlheinz Schlager, *Thematischer Katalog der ältesten Alleluia-Melodien aus Handschriften des 10. und 11. Jahrhunderts, ausgenommen das ambrosianische, altrömische und alt-spanische Repertoire* (Munich: W. Ricke, 1965).

28 This, of course, is not the text *Ecce sacerdos magnus martinus* found in some of the Martinian Masses elsewhere, but rather the text that has survived in the modem chant books as the Gradual *Ecce sacerdos magnus*.

29 The texts are available in Oury, 'Formulaires', 32–3. A facsimile of the entire manuscript (Darmstadt, Hessische Landes- und Hochschul Bibl., 1946) is available in *Echternacher Sakramentar und Antiphonar*, ed. Kurt Staub, P. Ulveling and F. Unterkircher, 2 vols (Graz: Akademische Druck- und Verlagsanstalt, 1982). The St. Martin Mass appears on fols. 232^{v}–233^{r}.

30 Alejandro Enrique Planchart, *The Repertory of Tropes at Winchester*, 2 vols. (Princeton: Princeton University Press, 1977), ii, 167.

31 Fols. 116^{r} (gradual) and 253^{r} (troper); facsimile in *Moosburger Graduale: München, Universitätsbibliothek, 2° Cod. ms. 156*, ed. David Hiley (Tutzing: Hans Schneider, 1996).

32 Schlager, *Thematischer Katalog*, no. 27, verse r: *Hic est vere martyr*. Schlager omits the occurrence in Paris 776 for St. Mennas.

33 Fickett, 'Chants for the Feasts', 19–22, 33–9, 44–54 and 63–4.

34 McKinnon, *The Advent Project*, proposes that Introits and Communions received individual melodies, Graduals made far more use of contrafacts and model melodies, and the Offertories, particularly in their verses, were closer to the Graduals in their formulaic construction. These ideas are presented in the summaries of the chapters for each genre but a general summary of them may be gleaned from pp. 362–72.

35 Fickett, 'Chants for the Feasts', 20–22, compares the Introit *O beatum virum* with a third-mode responsory with interesting but not wholly convincing results.

36 Ibid., 36–7.

37 Ibid., 50–54; see also Ruth Steiner, '*Holocausta medullata*: An Offertory for St. Saturninus', in Peter Cahn and Ann-Katrin Heimer (eds), *De musica et cantu: Studien zur Geschichte der Kirchenmusik und der Oper – Helmut Hucke zum 60. Geburtstag* (Musikwissenschaftliche Publikationen: Hochschule für Musik und Darstellende Kunst Frankfurt am Main, 2: Hildesheim: Olms, 1993), 263–74 at 274.

38 A detailed analysis of the variants would go well beyond the limits of this study, but a very sensible analysis of the music for these Masses appears in Fickett, 'Chants for the Feasts', 15–71.

39 Ibid., 23–5. As Fickett notes, the first to have called attention to some of the formal and melodic connections between Introits and the responds of the Great Responsories was Helmut Hucke, 'Das Responsorium', in Wulf Arlt, Ernst Lichtenhahn and Hans Oesch (eds), *Gattungen der Musik in Einzeldarstellungen: Gedenkschrift Leo Schrade* (Bern: Francke, 1973), 144–91, esp. 189–90.

40 The versions in Paris 903 are easily available in PM 13.

41 *Introitus Tropen*, i: *Das Repertoire der südfranzösischer Tropare des 10. und 11. Jahrhunderts*, ed. Günther Weiss (Kassel: Bärenreiter, 1970), no. 85.

42 There is a good deal of evidence for scribal initiative in Paris 1118, but it has yet to be fully set forth and explained. See Alejandro Enrique Planchart, 'On the Nature of Transmission and Change in Trope Repertories', *JAMS* 41 (1988), 215–49 at 224–5.

43 The relationship between St. Martial and St. Martin in the Aquitanian tropers is extremely complex and some of the borrowing may go both ways.

44 Jacques Hourlier, Review of Alejandro Planchart, *The Repertory of Tropes at Winchester*, in *Etudes grégoriennes*, 17 (1978), 231–2. The presence of the Offertory in two of the manuscripts of the *Sextuplex*, however, would suggest that it predates Cluny.

45 *AMS*, p. cvi and no. 148; Jounel, *Le Culte*, 286.

46 Planchart, *Repertory of Tropes*, i, 95–100.

47 Oury, 'Formulaires anciens', 33.

48 The dependence of Spanish sources on the Aquitanian tradition has never been fully examined, but a good sense of it can be gathered from Miquel Gors i Pujol, 'Les Tropes d'introït du graduel de Saint-Félix de Gérone', in *Corpus troporum*, viii: *Recherches nouvelles sur les tropes liturgiques* ['Huglo Festschrift'], ed. Wulf Arlt (Stockholm: Almqvist & Wiksell, 1993), 221–9. My own indices of the manuscripts Vich, Museo Episc. 105 and 106 reveal that over 90 percent of their repertory is Aquitanian in origin.

49 Alejandro Enrique Planchart, 'Italian Tropes', *Mosaic*, 18/4 (1985), 11–32, and 'Notes on the Tropes in Manuscripts of the Rite of Aquileia', in Graeme M. Boone (ed.), *Essays on Medieval Music in Honor of David G. Hughes*

(Cambridge, Mass.: Harvard University Press, 1995), 333–69. See also *Early Medieval Chants from Nonantola, Parts I–II*, ed. James Borders (Madison, Wis.: A-R Editions, 1996).

50 German-region manuscripts with tropes for St. Martin are as follows: Bamberg, Staatsbibl. lit. 5; Munich, Kremsmünster 309; Munich, BSB clm 14083 and clm 14322 with tropes to *Sacerdotes domini*. Munich, UB 2° 156; Oxford, Bodl. Lib., Selden supra 27; Paris, BNF lat. 9448; and London, BL Add. 18768 with tropes to *Statuit*.

51 For a pan-European concordance of this piece see Planchart, *Repertory of Tropes*, ii, 172–3.

52 Novalesa: Oxford, Bodl. Lib., Douce 222; Piacenza: Piacenza, BC 65; Mantua: Verona, BC 107.

53 Calvin Bower, 'The Origin and Fate of Notker's Easter Week Cycle', paper read at the Forty-Fourth Annual Meeting of the American Musicological Society (Minneapolis, 1978). I am indebted to Professor Bower for a copy of this work.

54 This is very similar to what happened with the *sequentia* for *Exsultet elegantis*, which appears to have reached Italy in a very early version no longer found in any of its French sources. See Planchart, 'An Aquitanian *Sequentia* in Italian Sources'.

55 Note that in northern Italy this Mass, with the exception of the Alleluia, is that for St. Martin in the Ravenna Gradual (Padua, BC A. 47), which has an uncommon number of connections with the south Italian repertory.

56 The examples given in Table 5.8 represent a small sample of the sources for the Mass *Beatus martinus* south of Rome. All the Mass books in Beneventan script I have examined transmit it.

57 It should be remembered that the gradual itself in Angelica 123 has the Introit *Statuit* for St. Martin, which is the Introit normally troped by *Martinus meritis virtutum*.

58 See *Beneventanum troporum corpus*, ed. Planchart, i/1, 9–12 and i/2, 6–15, for an edition of the tropes and for evidence that at least one of the tropes, *Gentis linguae*, was used in Pistoia in connection with the Introit *Statuit*.

59 The trope is a three-verse piece beginning with the initials Q, O and P. See Alejandro Enrique Planchart, 'Fragments, Palimpsests, and Marginalia', *JM* 6 (1988), 293–339 at 324.

60 Schlager, *Thematischer Katalog*, no. 396.

61 This is the case for the tropes *Admirans vates proclamat*, *Nos sinus ecclesiae . . . esse* and *O quam clara nites*; see Planchart, *The Repertory of Tropes*, i, 197–8 and ii, 192–3.

62 Fickett, 'Chants for the Feasts', 52–6.

63 Ibid., 52 n. 1.

64 In Benevento 40 alone there is a verse mark at the phrase *Hac* [*Ac*] *breuibus* of the verse *Martinus semet* not found in any of the other sources.

65 Benevento 35 shows a period and a capital at *Brachia nobilium* but no verse mark.

66 For the Ambrosian Masses of St. Martin see Oury, 'Formulaires', 38–9. Interestingly, The entire Ambrosian and Mozarabic Masses for St. Martin, given ibid., 36–9 are based largely on biblical texts; the exceptions are the Ambrosian Offertory for the Mass of the day, *Beate Martini meritum*, which reads like a Collect, and the transitorium for the day, *Sancti Martini magna est festivitas*.

67 It is probably mere coincidence, but the entire Lotharingian Mass for St. Martin in the Echternach Antiphoner is taken from Ecclesiasticus.

Chapter 6

Style and Structure in Early Offices of the Sanctorale

David Hiley

James McKinnon's magnificent achievement in mapping out stages in the development of the Proper of the Mass evokes more than admiration for that work in itself. It gives one hope that other areas of the chant repertory may prove susceptible to similar methods of investigation and inspires one with courage to attempt the task. The chants of the Divine Office, to which the following remarks are addressed, offer a particularly daunting challenge, since their number is so great and their transmission relatively late. To realize how arduous the work will be one has only to think of the wide discrepancies between the earliest comprehensive source of office chant texts, Hesbert's manuscript 'C' (Paris, BNF lat. 17436, mid-ninth century), and other early manuscripts. In this chapter I offer a few observations about features of structure and musical style that may help toward keeping one's bearings while exploring the territory.[1]

I begin in the year 1052, in Regensburg, at the Benedictine monastery of St. Emmeram. Pope Leo IX is present for the canonization of one of Regensburg's greatest bishops, Wolfgang. This Leo is none other than Bruno of Egisheim/Toul, born 1002, Pope 1049–54, composer of the plainchant office *Gloriosa sanctissimi* for St. Gregory (and other offices). The music for a new office for Wolfgang has been composed by Hermannus Contractus of the Reichenau (1013–54). Example 6.1 gives one of the larger antiphons from the Wolfgang office. The office is hardly known, although its existence was recognized over a hundred years ago, and a transcription was published by Franz Stein in 1975.[2] Only two of the many offices composed by Hermannus appear to have survived, the other one being that for St. Afra. A facsimile of one source of the Afra office was published by Wilhelm Brambach, Peter Wagner quoted an example from it, and recently Karlheinz Schlager published an article about it and discussed the shorter antiphons in it.[3] But Hermannus is still better known as a theorist than as a composer, and opinions such as that expressed by Urbanus Bomm and quoted by Hans Oesch in his study of 1961 are still current. Bomm reckoned that 'Hermann's Historia de sancta Afra falls far short of the spiritual distinction of [his] Salve regina melody.'[4] Oesch had obviously not looked at the Afra office properly and did not know about the Wolfgang office at all.

Example 6.1 – closely comparable with the antiphon quoted by Wagner – is a remarkable piece in many respects. One striking feature is the way in

Ex. 6.1 Antiphona ad Magnificat *Gaudeat tota* from 1st Vespers of the Office of St. Wolfgang (canonized 1052), composed by Hermannus Contractus (1013–54) (Munich, BSB clm 14872)

which the tonal space within which the melody moves is clearly divided into segments bounded by the finalis, upper fifth and upper octave. It is a particularly clear demonstration of features that have been noticed by several scholars in many chants of this period. Moreover, it has not gone unremarked that these melodic characteristics seem to correspond to a new trend in music-theoretical writing of the time, where modality is defined in terms of scale segments, namely the fourth below the finalis, the fifth above it, the fourth between the upper fifth and the upper octave, and even the fifth above that. In the introduction to their new edition of antiphon melodies in the series Monumenta Monodica Medii Aevi, 5, László Dobszay and Janka Szendrei say that 'in antiphons in the newer style . . . the mode is not a sum of motivic elements but is rather a general tonal framework ('scale') for melodic motions. . . . To "compose" . . . became a . . . procedure helped by theoretical categories and by musical notation. Invention was now influenced by the theoretical definition of the modes.'[5] This is just one example of many such statements in the chant literature.

Hermannus' antiphon *Gaudeat tota* is nevertheless an extreme example of this tendency in chant composition. Because his theoretical writings are well known – or at least the fact that he was a theorist is well known – the connection between practice and theory seems fairly clear cut in his case. It would be wrong to attribute great influence to Hermannus' music-theoretical writings, and I would not necessarily argue that he is a seminal figure. But at least at St. Emmeram's in Regensburg his writings were known. The connections between St. Emmeram's and the Reichenau were of many decades' standing. Wolfgang himself had been a novice at the Reichenau. A former cantor of the Reichenau, Burchard, was abbot of St. Emmeram's at the time when a new plainchant office was composed for St. Emmeram himself, by the Regensburg monk Arnold, about twenty years before the Wolfgang office was created. And Hermannus' ideas are reflected in the music theory treatise of Wilhelm, monk of St. Emmeram and later abbot of Hirsau in the Black Forest. Wilhelm presumably sang in the first performance of the Wolfgang office by Hermannus Contractus.[6] For example, the diagram 'Figura tropicae dispositionis' in Wilhelm's treatise is the perfect illustration of how the tonal space was divided up. The scale segments are indicated by semicircles with inscriptions defining position and range. The horizontal lines are named for the four basic tonalities: protus, deuterus, tritus and tetrardus, whose structural keystones are marked on the same lines, for example, tetrardus with keynotes *D–G–d–g*. In the top part of the diagram it is explained how the 'tropi' are composed from the appropriate keynotes ('chordae') and the scale segments that lie between these. The latter are defined as species of the fifth (diapente) or fourth (diatessaron), according to the succession of tones and semitones in each of them.[7] It goes almost without saying that the chants in the Wolfgang office are arranged in the numerical order of the modes.

Although, as already indicated, Hermannus' chants are extreme examples of their type, they are by no means alone in the way they explore tonal space. Wherever one looks in the eleventh century, one comes across chants exhibiting similar tendencies. In this respect the twelfth century is then, generally speaking, a time of consolidation, and in any case the new poetic type of office with rhymed, accentual verse makes its appearance at the end of the century; the one for Thomas of Canterbury, presumably written straight after his martyrdom in 1170, seems to be one of the earliest examples. But did it all begin in the eleventh century? How far back can it be traced? To answer these questions there seems little alternative to checking through the saints' offices covered by Hesbert's *Corpus antiphonalium officii* (*CAO*), in order to put a marker on those sets of chants exhibiting the newer stylistic features. It will be recollected that Richard Crocker, for one, has already been over similar ground, in his study of the antiphons in one of the *CAO* sources, the twelfth-century antiphoner from St. Denis, Paris, BNF lat. 17296.[8] Working through the other *CAO* sources is necessary in order to gain an idea of the wider patterns of transmission and locate other interesting offices not in the St. Denis book.

Of particular interest are groups of chants that have a good chance of being composed as a set – as a 'project', to borrow James McKinnon's useful term – especially those exhibiting the more modern melodic characteristics mentioned above. There is no space here to report on a sophisticated analysis of the type to which Richard Crocker treated us. I draw attention to just one telltale feature, the way in which the upper octave of a chant is handled, that is, the note one octave above the finalis in the authentic modes and one fifth above the finalis in plagal modes. Is that top note reached at all? Is it touched upon simply as an upper neighbor-note? Or does it function as a melodic goal of real structural importance?

The way Hesbert presents the contents of his twelve chosen manuscripts in *CAO* I–II is no doubt the best possible in the circumstances, but when the manuscripts diverge in their choice of pieces it is not always easy to assess the possible relationships between them. It is easier to work with tables where the chant incipits are set out in a different way (see Tables 6.1–3).

This makes it easier to see where the manuscripts have the same pieces but in a different order, or where they have quite different pieces. The manuscripts represented are the twelve of Hesbert plus the Mont-Renaud manuscript (CO = Corbie) and the Old Roman antiphoner (OR). The next step would be to include other ninth-century witnesses – the Metz tonary and Amalarius' antiphoner, as far as it can be reconstructed – and then other tenth-century sources: that is, the Albi manuscript and the table of office chants in Paris, BNF lat. 1240. And then one can start adding in sources from the CANTUS project, and so on as the need arises and time allows.

The tables make it easier to identify sets of chants that have established themselves as a group and one can then start to analyze them from whatever point of view one chooses: text, possible Roman or other origins, melody type, and so on. Such tables emphasize graphically the relatively high agreement among sources in their choice of antiphons for Lauds and their concentration on a nucleus of responsories for Matins. The biggest divergences always occur in the series of antiphons for Matins, and in many cases it is clear that whatever archetype may have existed in, say, the early ninth century, it did not include Matins antiphons. In fact, even when manuscripts have different selections of Lauds antiphons, and one suspects that other pieces have been drafted in or newly composed, they are stylistically usually of an older type. The only feasts of the Sanctorale where there are obviously divergent traditions between sources at Lauds are those listed in Table 6.4. This means that most feasts of the Sanctorale show a more or less uniform selection of Lauds antiphons in older styles.

Bold type indicates the presence of sets of Lauds antiphons in what I continue to call modern style. And it may be seen that they are all associated with a modern numerical office, either continuing the numerical series of Matins antiphons (Gregory, the Annunciation, Mary Magdalene[9]) or supplementing one (Nicholas). It will immediately be obvious that only later feasts not represented in the older *CAO* sources have these modern sets of antiphons. I have divided the feasts between two columns to make this clear. Those in the second column are later or localized traditions of chants. I should point out that I have not included in this survey some local saints with a very limited distribution. I shall mention a few of these cases later. In order not to miss anything I have noted a number of series 'with modern tendencies', that is, where the antiphons are, stylistically, borderline cases. I shall not enlarge the discussion of these here, since similar cases will come up among the Matins antiphons.

Table 6.5 gives information for Matins antiphons (some series are omitted because of lack of access to the Benevento antiphoner L; a number of eccentric items, additions to otherwise stable series, have also been omitted). Although I had expected to find many more numerical offices than Richard Crocker noted in the St. Denis antiphoner, this turned out not to be the case. From the scarcity of offices listed here in bold type one can see immediately how restricted the distribution of these offices was. Furthermore, as far as their musical style goes, they are often not more progressive than many non-numerical offices. Naturally, the designation 'old' covers several different layers, which I have not even attempted to distinguish. The ideal key to all analysis of this sort is the recently published antiphon edition by László Dobszay and Janka Szendrei, organized according to melody types.[10] Sorting out the items in the 'old' category according to their melodic types and families, and collating the melodic evidence with the liturgical, is all work for the future. So is the matter of the respective Roman and Frankish contributions.

Even a generous interpretation of the criteria fails to elicit many chants that might be designated as modern. Example 6.2 gives the antiphons from the numerical office of Holy Innocents in the *CAO* manuscript G, some of which are also in *CAO* manuscript S. Very few aim for the upper octave with any conviction (see the phrases marked with brackets).

It is therefore clear that the move to compose numerical series and, less often, pieces in the more modern style was a very limited one before the eleventh century. In fact one must turn to much more local cults in order to find examples. When and where? It is important to note that the feast of All Saints, absent from C but represented in books of the next century, has no numerical sets or modern pieces. And, as Richard Crocker pointed out, neither does the St. Dionysius office, nor the others that may date back to the time of Hilduin (814–40) at Saint-Denis.[11] Then we have the three offices

Table 6.1 Matins responsories for Holy Innocents

For tables 6.1–6.3 sigla are as in *CAO*, plus Corbie (CO) and the Old Roman antiphoner (OR). Other abbreviations are:

*	incipit only	x	single antiphon, not part of a series
L	responsory at Lauds	+	'cum reliquis' from Commune Sanctorum
L-Ab	Antiphona ad Benedictus	c	Antiphona ad cantica
a	alternative series		

	C	*G*	*B*	*E*	*M*	*V*	*H*	*R*	*D*	*F*	*S*	*L*	*CO*	*OR*
Sub altare dei audivi voces	1	1	1	1	1	1	1	1	1	1	1	1	1	1
Effuderunt sanguinem sanctorum	2	2	2	2	2	2	2	2	2	4	2	3*	2	
Adoraverunt viventem	3	3	3	4	3	3	3	3	4	5	3	2	4	5
Isti sunt sancti qui passi sunt	4	4	4	6	4	4	4	4	5	10	4	4	5	4
Ecce vidi agnum stantem	5		6				6	11	10	8	9	12	9	
Ambulabunt mecum in albis	6	7					9	6	8	2			7	
Istorum est enim regnum	7													
Centum quadraginta quatuor	8	9	9	9	6	9	10	12	11	12	12	8	13	2
Viri sancti	9*												11*	
Tradiderunt corpora	10*												12*	
Verbera carnificum	11*													
Hec est vera fraternitas	12*													
Sancti mei qui in isto	13*													
Cantabant sancti canticum		5	5	7		6	5	5	L	3	5	5	8	
Isti sunt sancti qui non inquinaverunt		6	7	8	5	5	7	7	6	7	6	6	6	
Fulgebunt iusti sicut lilium		8												
Coronavit eos dominus			8				11	10			7	11		
Exultabunt sancti in gloria				3										
Letamini iusti et exultate				5										
Hi empti sunt ex omnibus						7						11		
Ex ore infancium						8								
Sub throno dei omnes sancti							8	9	3	11	10		3	
Hii sunt qui cum mulieribus								8						
Sancti et iusti in domino								L						
Hodie matryrum flores									7					
Vox in Rama audita est									9	6				3
Vidi sub altare dei animas										9		9		
Concede nobis domine											8			
Sci tui domune benedicent											L			
Vidi turbam magnam												7		
Isti qui amicti sunt stolis albis												10		
Absterget													10*	6*

Table 6.2 Lauds antiphons for Holy Innocents

Sigla are as in *CAO*, plus Corbie (CO) and the Old Roman antiphoner (OR). For abbreviations see Table 6.1.

	C	*G*	*B*	*E*	*M*	*V*	*H*	*R*	*D*	*F*	*S*	*L*	*CO*	*OR*
Herodes iratus [est] occidit	1	1	1	1	1	1	1	1	1	1	1	1	1	1
Angeli eorum semper vident	2	2				2				2	2		2	4
Vox in Rama audita est	3	5	3	3	3	3	3	3	3	3		3	4	
Sub throno dei omnes sancti	4	4	4	4	4	4	4	4	4	4	4		5	5
Cantabant sancti canticum	5	3	5	5	5	5	5	5	5	5	5	4	6	
A bimatu et infra			2	2	2		2	2	2		3	2	3	2
Hi empti sunt ex omnibus												5		
Sinite parvulos venire ad me														3
L-Ab														
Sinite parvulos venire ad me	1						2							
Laverunt stolas suas	2				2									
A bimatu et infra occidit	3													
Ambulabunt mecum in albis	4				3									1
Hii sunt qui cum mulieribus	5			1	1	x	1	x		x	x	1	x	
Innocentes pro Christo	6	x*		3								2		
Hi empti sunt ex omnibus	7													
Hi sunt qui venerunt ex			x	2										
Clamant clamant clamant				4										
Splendent Bethleemitici									x					
Vox in Rhama audita est														2

Table 6.3 Matins antiphons for Holy Innocents

For abbreviations see Table 6.1.

	C	*G*	*B*	*E*	*M*	*V*	*H*	*R*	*D*	*F*	*S*	*L*
In lege domini fuit voluntas	1											
Predicantes preceptum domini	2			a2*			2					
Voce mea ad dominum	3											
Fili hominum scitote quia	4			a3*			3					
Scuto bone voluntatis	5		2*	a4*			4					
In universa terra gloria	6			a5*			5					
Iustus dominus et iustitias	7											
Habitabit in tabernaculo tuo	8						6					
Sanctis qui in terra sunt	9		3*	a6*			7	x*+				
Herodes videns quia illusus		1									1/10*	
Christus infans non despexit		2										
Arridebat parvulus occisori		3										
Norunt infantes laudare deum		4									13	
Erigitur itaque infantium etas		5									14	
Dignus a dignis laudatur		6									15	
Dicunt infantes domino		7										
Licuit sanguine loqui		8									9/11*	
Vindica domine sanguinem		9	5				12					
Secus decursus			1*	a1*		1	1	x*+				
Hec est generatio querentium			4*	7			8					
Sinite parvulos venire ad me				1		2				9	6	3
Angeli eorum semper vident				2					3			4
Ambulabunt mecum in albis				3		8			2	c*		7
Innocentes et recti pro Christo				4								
Adoraverunt viventem				5								
Ex ore infantium [deus] et lactentium				6		6				4		5
Beati quos elegisti domine				8			11					
Laverunt stolas suas				9		5			c	12		8
A bimatu et infra				a7		4						
Clamaverunt iusti				a8			10					

	C	*G*	*B*	*E*	*M*	*V*	*H*	*R*	*D*	*F*	*S*	*L*
In paucis vexati in multis						3						
Sanguis scorum martirum						7						11
Vidi turba magna ex omnibus						9						
Letamini in domino et exultate							9					
Innocentum passio Christi							c					
Hi sunt qui cum mulieribus									1			
Fulgebunt iusti sicut sol									4			
Stabunt iusti in magna									5			
Ecce merces scorum									7			
Viri sancti gloriosum									8			
Iustorum anime in manu									9			
In circuito tuo domine lumen									10			
Vindica domine sanguinem									11			
Beati eritis cum vos									12*			
Novit dominus vias innocen-										1		
Rex terre infremuit adversus										2		
Deus iudex iustus iudica nos										3		
Iudicabit domins pupillo										5		
Quis ascendet aut quis stabit										6		
Innocentes adheserunt mihi										7		
Inter innocentes lavabo										8		
Mendaces et vani dum										10		
Filio regis datum est iuditium										11		
Novit dominus viam iustorum											2	
Clamant clamant clamant											3	
Arridebat parvulus occisorum											4	
Dabo sanctis meis locum											5	
Reddet deus											7*	
O beata lactantium gloria											8	
Ecce vidi agnum stantem											12	
O quam gloriosum											c	
Sub throno dei omnes sancti												1
Acceperunt divinum												2
Clamant ad dominum innocentes												6
Innocentes (. . .?)												9*
Coronavit eos dominus												10

Table 6.4 Sets of Lauds antiphons where sources diverge

Sigla as in *CAO*. Boldface indicates antiphons in modern style.

CAO	Older, universal tradition/ *later or local tradition*	Lauds antiphons
46	*Vincentius*	series *Assumptus ex eculeo* G E M D F non-numerical, some with modern tendencies series *Dum pateretur beatus Vinc.* L not checked
50.4	*Gregorius*	series *Beatus Gregorius natione* B H L non-numerical, old series *O admirabile beati Gregorius* D non-numerical, old **series *Gregorius vigiliis confectus*** R numerical, modern (continuation of Matins series)
50.5	*Benedictus*	various divergent series C B H R D F S L, non-numerical, old supplementary series of Benedictus antiphons in F *O beati viri Benedicti* also almost all old
51	*Annunciatio BMV*	**series *Quando venit ergo sacri*** R numerical, modern (continuation of Matins series) series *Post partum virgo inviolata* F put together from older material
91	Philippus et Iacobus	divergent series (non-numerical), one or two with modern tendencies
100	Iohannes et Paulus	eccentric series *Dominum tibi preponimus* in L not checked
101	Petrus et Paulus	series *Petrus et Iohannes ascendebant* C M D non-numerical, old series *Petre amas me pasce oves* B E H R L non-numerical, old series *Beatus Petrus apostolus vidit* F non-numerical, some with modern tendencies
102.5	*Maria Magdalene*	**series *Una sabbati Maria Magdalena*** R numerical, modern **series *Annua Magdalene recolentes*** D numerical, modern series *Maria ergo unxit pedes Iesu* L not checked
105	Hippolytus	two overlapping series, C B F M H R / D F CO both old
115	Omnes Sancti	series *Scimus quoniam diligentibus* B M R S non-numerical, old series *Vidi turbam magnam quam* E (V) F non-numerical, old
120.2	*Nicholaus*	**series usually starting *Beatus N. pontificatus/lis*** B E R D F S L *not* numerical, modern but (non-numerical) monastic extensions in R and D F not modern

Table 6.5 Sets of Matins antiphons where sources diverge

Sigla as in *CAO*. Boldface indicates antiphons in modern style.

CAO	Older, universal tradition/ *later or local tradition*	*Matins antiphons*
5	Lucia	none
20	Stephanus	series *Beatus vir qui in lege* C commune series *Hesterna die dominus* B E M V H R L non-numerical, old **series *Beatus Steph. iugi*** G S CO (D) numerical, some modern
21	Iohannes Evangelista	series *In omnem terram* C and E commune series *Qui vicerit faciam* B V H R (L) , non-numerical, old **series *Iohannes apostolus et evangelista*** G B E M V (D) F S CO numerical, most modern
22	Innocentes	similar commune selections C E H other (mostly) commune selections D; S **series *Herodes videns quia illusus*** B (S) numerical, some modern series *Novit dominus vias innocentes* F non-numerical, old
44	Sebastianus	mostly derived from Lauds, non-numerical, old
45	Agnes	series *Discede a me pabulam mortis* almost universal, partly drawn from commune, non-numerical, old
46	*Vincentius*	**series *Sanctus Vincentius a pueritia*** E (secular) expanded in D F, numerical, mostly modern (ed. Crocker 459–63) series *Satis est laudabile* L not checked
48	Purificatio BMV	series starting *Benedicta tu in mulieribus* and variants and extensions all old
49	Agatha	series usually starting *Ingenua sum et expectabilis* non-numerical, old
50.4	*Gregorius*	**series *Gregorius ortus Rome*** (secular), expanded in R, numerical, modern series *Gregorius papa inclitus patre* D non-numerical, old series *Beatus Gregorius urbis Rome* L not checked
50.5	*Benedictus*	series *Fuit vir vite venerabilis gratia* in various mutations, all monastic C H R D F S L, non-numerical, old
51	*Annunciatio BMV*	**series *Missus est angelus Gabriel*** continuing *Ingressus angelus ad Mariam* R numerical, modern series continuing *Ave Maria gratia plena Dominus* F mostly drafted in from elsewhere, non-numerical, mostly old

Table 6.5 (continued)

CAO	Older, universal tradition/ *later or local tradition*	*Matins antiphons*
91	Philippus et Iacobus	no regular series
92	Inventio Crucis	series *Adoremus crucis signaculum* S (Inventio) non-numerical, mostly old
110	Exaltatio Crucis	series *Ecce crucem domini fugite* F (Exaltatio) non-numerical, mostly old
98	Marcellinus et Petrus	none
99	Iohannes Baptista	series *Priusquam te formarem in utero* almost uniform, non-numerical, old; extensions also old
100	Iohannes et Paulus	series *Iohannes et Petrus martires* in L not checked
101	Petrus et Paulus	series *In omnem terram exivit sonus* C commune
		series *Petrus et Iohannes ascendebant* B E V H R F L non-numerical, old
		series *In plateis ponebantur infirmi* M D F S numerical, modern
102	Paulus	series *Qui operatus V. Qui me seg.* almost uniform, non-numerical, old
102.5	*Maria Magdalena*	series *Ingressus Iesus domum Sym.* R non-numerical, some modern
		series *Cum discubuisset Dominus* L numerical, mostly modern
102.6	Inventio Stephani	**series *Luciano venerabili presbitero*** D F S L numerical, some modern
103	Laurentius	series *Quo progrederis V. Beatus L. dixit* fairly uniform distribution, non-numerical, old
105	Hippolytus	series *Valerianus tradidit* D (cf. C) non-numerical, old
106	Assumptio BMV	series (somewhat variable) starting *Exaltata es sca Dei genetrix* non-numerical, old
		series *Ecce tu pulchra es amica mea* V (second series) numerical, *not* modern (cf. Nativ. BVM)
		other possible series (S L) not checked
107	Symphorianus	none
108	Decollatio Iohannes Bapt.	two series *Iohannes Baptista arguebat* and *Audivit Herodes tetrarcha* in V not checked
109	Nativitas BMV	series *Celeste beneficium introivit* E not checked
		series *Gloriose virginis Marie* V not checked
		series *Ecce tu pulchra es amica mea* R numerical, *not* modern (cf. V at Assumpt. BVM)

Table 6.5 (continued)

CAO	Older, universal tradition/ *later or local tradition*	*Matins antiphons*
		series *Hodie nata est beata virgo* F numerical, *not* modern
111	Mauritius	series *Quanta excolendus est* E D F non-numerical, old
112	Cosmas et Damianus	none
113	Michael	series *Stetit angelus* non-numerical, old (extensions in D F also old)
114	*Dionysius*	series *Sanctus Dionysius qui tradente* C V H R D F CO non-numerical, old
115	Omnes Sancti	usual series *Novit Dominus viam iustorum* B E M V H R F S L non-numerical, old
		series *Letentur omnes qui sperant* E not checked
		series *Adesto Deus unus omnipotens* D compiled from various other offices
116	Martinus	series *Martinus adhuc caticuminis* C B E M V H R S L non-numerical, old
		series *Sanctus Martinus obitum* D F CO non-numerical, old
117	Bricius	none
118	Cecilia	series *Cecilia virgo Almachium* non-numerical, old
119	Clemens	no series
120	Andreas	series (various) beginning *Vidit Dominus Petrum et Andream* all non-numerical, old extensions in D old
120.2	*Nicholaus*	**series *Nobilissimus siquidem*** B E R D F S L numerical, modern
		monastic extras in R and D F respectively not modern, though D F group preserves modal order
121	Thomas	overlapping series E V S L not checked
90.5	Evangelistae	**series *Convocatis Iesus duodecim*** D F S L numerical, *not* modern

Ex. 6.2 Matins antiphons for Holy Innocents in numerical modal order (Utrecht, Universiteitsbibl. 406 [3.J.7])

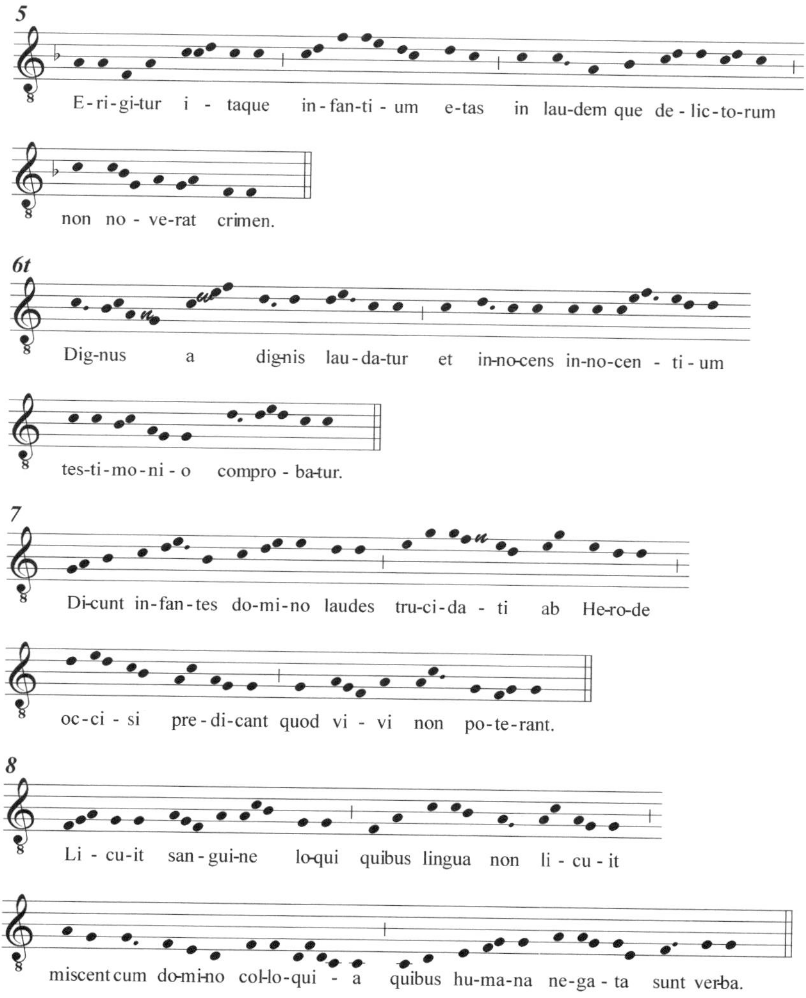
5
E-ri-gi-tur i - taque in-fan-ti - um e-tas in lau-dem que de - lic-to-rum
non no - ve-rat crimen.
6t
Dig-nus a dig-nis lau-da-tur et in-no-cens in-no-cen - ti - um
tes-ti-mo-ni - o compro - ba-tur.
7
Di-cunt in-fan-tes do-mi-no laudes tru-ci-da - ti ab He-ro-de
oc-ci - si pre-di-cant quod vi - vi non po-te-rant.
8
Li - cu-it san-gui-ne lo-qui quibus lingua non li - cu - it
miscent cum do-mi-no col-lo-qui - a quibus hu-ma-na ne-ga - ta sunt ver-ba.

Ex. 6.3 Selected antiphons from the Office of St. Gallus, composed by Ratpert of St. Gall, ca. 900 (Karlsruhe, Badische Landesbibl. Aug. LX)

8

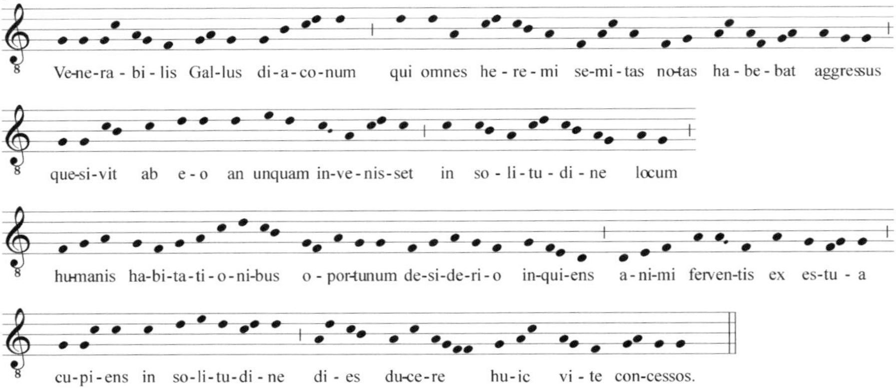
Ve-ne-ra - bi - lis Gal-lus di-a-co-num qui omnes he - re - mi se-mi - tas no-tas ha - be - bat aggressus
que-si-vit ab e - o an unquam in-ve - nis-set in so - li - tu - di - ne locum
hu-manis ha-bi-ta-ti-o-ni-bus o - por-tunum de-si-de-ri-o in-qui-ens a-ni-mi ferven-tis ex es-tu - a
cu-pi-ens in so-li-tu-di - ne di - es du-ce-re hu-ic vi - te con-cessos.

7

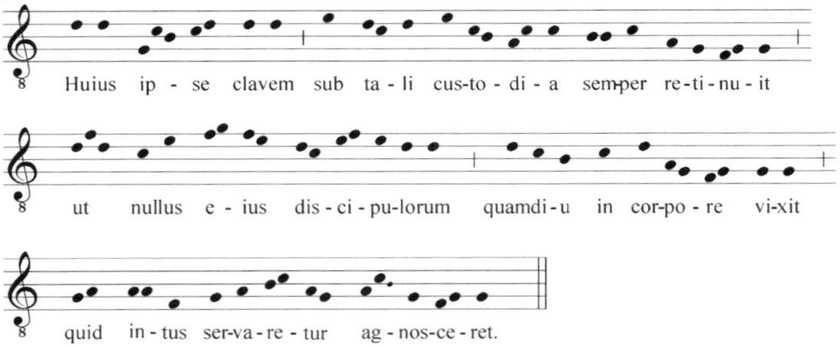
Huius ip - se clavem sub ta - li cus-to - di - a sem-per re-ti-nu-it
ut nullus e - ius dis - ci - pu-lorum quamdi-u in cor-po - re vi-xit
quid in - tus ser-va - re - tur ag - nos-ce - ret.

8

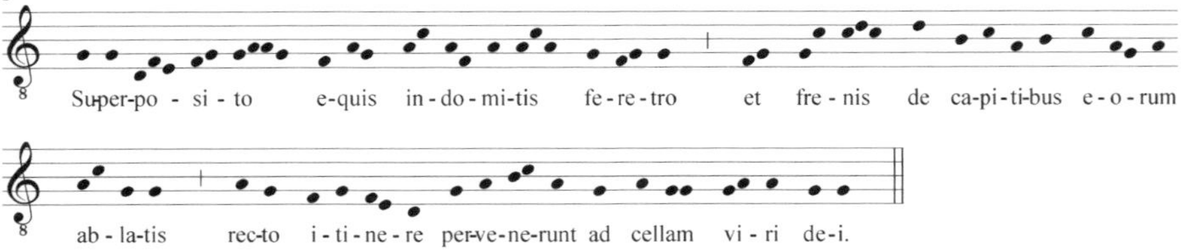
Su-per-po - si - to e-quis in - do - mi-tis fe - re - tro et fre - nis de ca-pi-ti-bus e - o - rum
ab - la-tis rec-to i - ti - ne - re per-ve-ne-runt ad cellam vi - ri de-i.

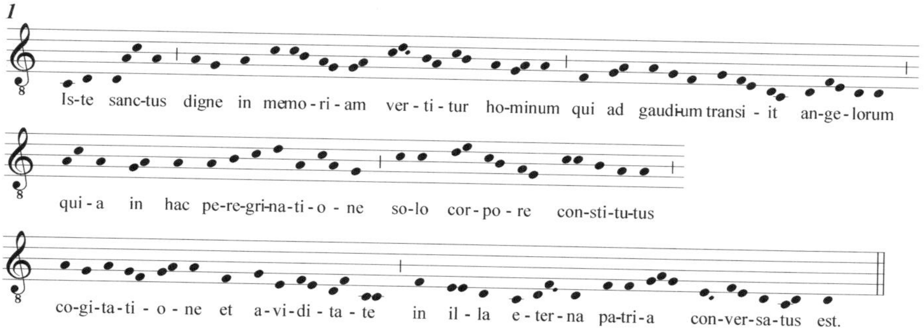
1
Is-te sanc-tus digne in memo-ri-am ver-ti-tur ho-minum qui ad gaudi-um transi - it an-ge-lorum
qui - a in hac pe-re-gri-na-ti - o - ne so-lo cor-po - re con-sti-tu-tus
co-gi-ta-ti - o - ne et a-vi-di - ta - te in il - la e - ter - na pa-tri-a con-ver-sa-tus est.

attributed to Stephen, archbishop of Liège, born about 850, educated at Metz and in the palace school, archbishop from 901 to 920. The offices for the Holy Trinity, for Lambert and for the Invention of Stephen are all numerical but rarely explore the upper tetrachord or pentachord systematically. Hucbald's numerical cycle of Matins antiphons *In plateis*, for St. Peter, presumably written about the same time, is much more consistent in this respect.[12]

Now, although the Hartker antiphoner has the Trinity office, it ignores the Invention of St. Stephen, as do most books from the eastern half of Europe. And looking back at the list of numerical offices, and those with stylistically more modern pieces, the relative lack of interest in East Francia is quite noticeable. It is therefore no surprise to find that the office of St. Gallus composed by Ratpert about 900 is not numerical.[13] Most of its antiphons are very restrained in style, but one or two pieces are more adventurous. These are given in Ex. 6.3.

One other example should not be overlooked, and this takes us back into the area of North France and Lotharingia at the beginning of the tenth century. A proper office of St. Cuthbert, with hymn and Mass as well, was composed 'probably by a clerk from the Low Countries' (Hohler), for the court chapel of King Athelstan of England (924–39) or his father Edward the Elder (899–924).[14] The earliest notated source, London, BL Harley 1117, dates from the late tenth century. This is a numerical office, and several of the chants exploit tonal space in the 'progressive' way highlighted above. It is, moreover, a partly versified office. Thus three of the characteristics that make the Trinity office of Stephen of Liège so important for its date are also present in the Cuthbert office: verse text, modal order and progressive musical style. Seven antiphons from this office are given in Ex. 6.4.

It seems clear, therefore, that the new feeling for tonal space is evident principally in the new numerical offices, but that not all items of the latter exhibit this stylistic feature. As far as antiphons are concerned, therefore, the

Ex. 6.4 Selected antiphons from the Office of St. Cuthbert, early ninth century (Worcester, Cathedral Chapter Library, F 160)

1

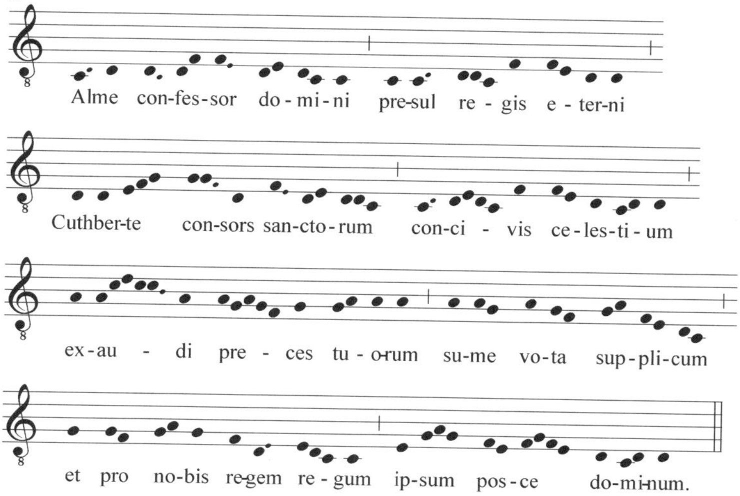
Alme con-fes-sor do-mi-ni pre-sul re-gis e-ter-ni
Cuthber-te con-sors san-cto-rum con-ci-vis ce-les-ti-um
ex-au-di pre-ces tu-o-rum su-me vo-ta sup-pli-cum
et pro no-bis re-gem re-gum ip-sum pos-ce do-mi-num.

5

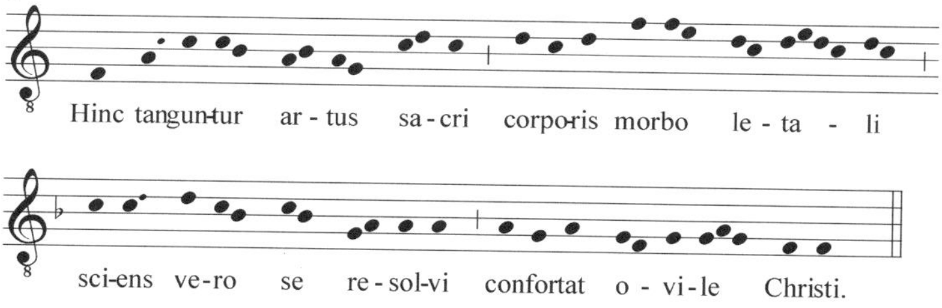
Hinc tangun-tur ar-tus sa-cri corpo-ris morbo le-ta-li
sci-ens ve-ro se re-sol-vi confortat o-vi-le Christi.

7

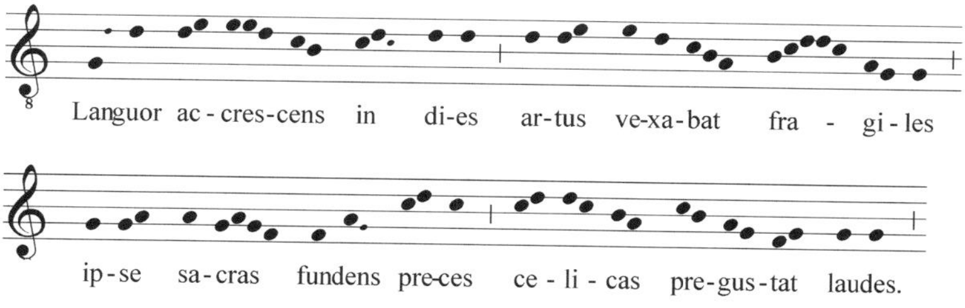
Languor ac-cres-cens in di-es ar-tus ve-xa-bat fra-gi-les
ip-se sa-cras fundens pre-ces ce-li-cas pre-gus-tat laudes.

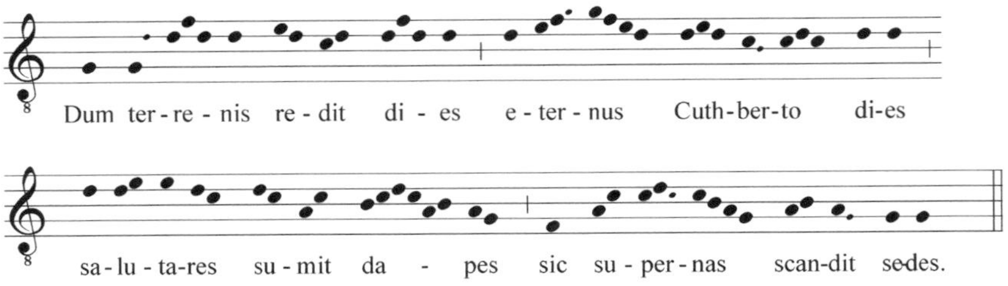

8

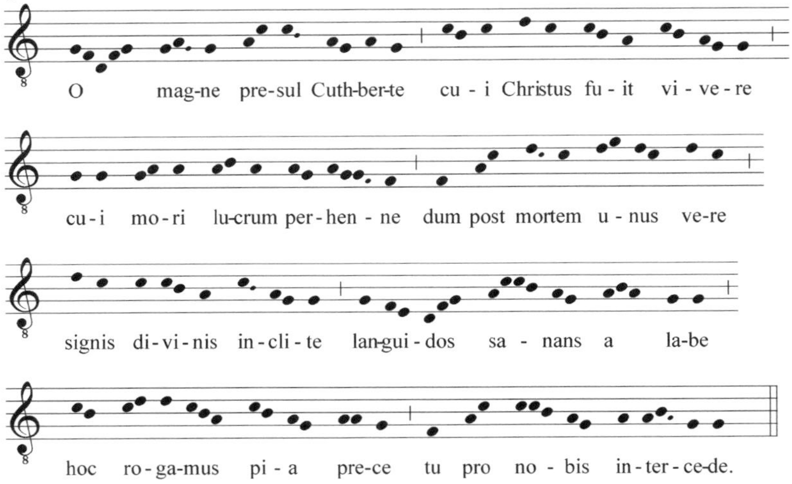

search appears to end in the North French/Lotharingian area at the beginning of the tenth century.

What of responsories? As far as stylistic features are concerned the way to proceed seems fairly simple. One looks for the verses that use the old standard tones, those where the second half of the tone is altered in order to end on the finalis, and those where the traditional tone is more or less abandoned. Since different sources often assign different verses to responsories, the task of sorting all this out may be rather laborious. The search for standard formulas in the main part of the responsory also takes time and patience. On the other hand, a simple glance through a chant can give one a first impression of its tonal behavior. Example 6.5 gives one of the responsories of the Cuthbert office. (One should note that the verse uses the traditional tone for mode 1 responsories, which points up the necessity for treating responsories and their verses as two different categories.) In fact there are almost no series from the

Ex. 6.5 Responsory *Cuthbertus puer* from the Office of St. Cuthbert, early ninth century (Worcester, Cathedral Chapter Library, F 160)

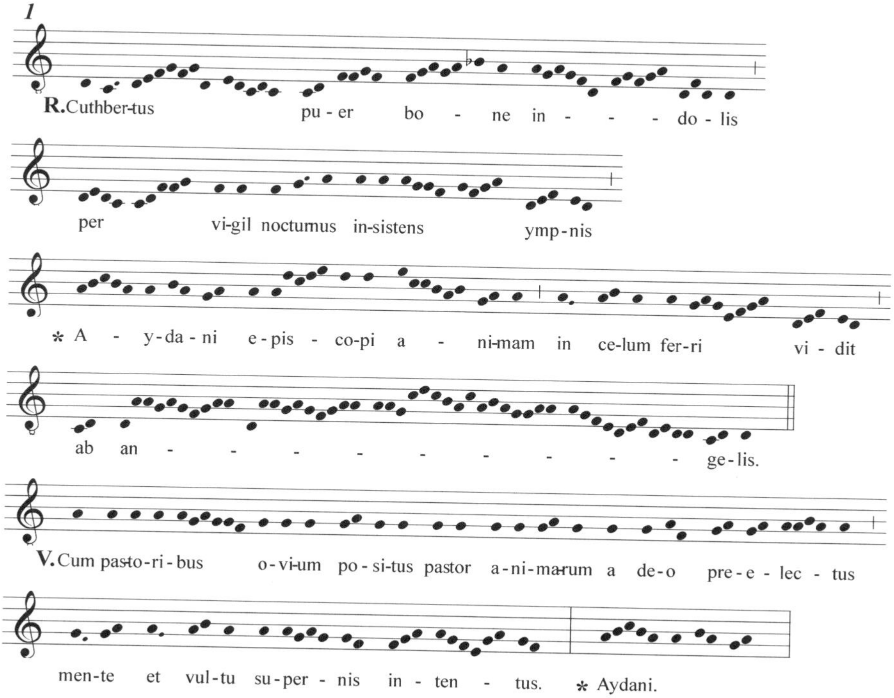

tenth century with progressive stylistic features. The three offices attributed to Stephen of Liège have them, and so does the Cuthbert office. But Stephen, John the Evangelist, Holy Innocents and Peter do not. As far as the more widely distributed offices of the eleventh century are concerned, there are numerical responsory series for Gregory and Nicholas, but not for Vincent, the Annunciation or Mary Magdalene. But from the eleventh century there are, as is well known, plenty of local offices that are fully numerical.

Only those three cycles of the Christmas season, with the possible addition of Peter, hint at a numerical or otherwise modernizing 'project' involving more than one feast, and the transmission of those series is not uniform. It was left largely to musicians of the eleventh century to initiate their own local projects, only a few of which achieved wide distribution. But the new melodic style gradually gained the upper hand all over Europe. As is well known, it was not restricted to chants of the office, and tracing its origins and progress through the chant repertory as a whole is a task of some importance for future scholarship.

Notes

1 These features have often been discussed in the specialist literature. My own work is especially indebted to the work of Richard Crocker, Ruth Steiner and László Dobszay. See in particular Crocker's essay 'Matins Antiphons at St. Denis', *JAMS* 39 (1986), 441–90.

2 Utto Kornmüller, 'Der heilige Wolfgang als Beförderer des Kirchengesanges', in *Der heilige Wolfgang – Bischof von Regensburg – Jubiläumsschrift 994–1894* (Regensburg: F. Pustet, 1894), 140–62; Franz A. Stein, 'Das ältere Offizium des hl. Wolfgang in der Handschrift Clm 14872 aus St. Emmeram zu Regensburg in der Bayerischen Staatsbibliothek München', in id. (ed.), *Sacerdos et cantus Gregoriani magister: Festschrift Ferdinand Haberl zum 70. Geburtstag* (Regensburg: Bosse, 1977), 279–302. My own edition of the office appeared just as the present volume was going to press: *Hermannus Contractus (1013–1054): Historia Sancti Wolfgangi Episcopi Ratisbonensis*. Wissenschaftliche Abhandlungen/Musicological Studies 65/7 (Ottawa: Institute of Medieval Music, 2002).

3 Wilhelm Brambach, *Die verloren geglaubte Historia de sancta Afra und das Salve regina des Hermannus Contractus* (Karlsruhe: C. T. Groos, 1892); Peter Wagner, *Einführung in die gregorianischen Melodien*, iii: *Gregorianische Formenlehre* (Leipzig: Breitkopf & Härtel, 1921), 316; Karlheinz Schlager and Theodor Wohnhaas, 'Zeugnisse der Afra-Verehrung im mittelalterlichen Choral', *Jahrbuch des Vereins für Augsburger Bistumsgeschichte*, 18 (1984), 199–226.

4 Hans Oesch, *Berno und Hermann von Reichenau als Musiktheoretiker* (Bern: P. Haupt, 1961), 153. The reference is to Bomm's review in *AfMw* 1 (1950), 403, of J. Maier's monograph *Studien zur Geschichte der Marienantiphone 'Salve regina'* (1939).

5 *Antiphonen*, ed. László Dobszay and Janka Szendrei, 3 vols (MMMA 5; Kassel: Bärenreiter, 1999), 25*, 30*.

6 David Hiley, 'The Regensburg Offices for St Emmeram, St Wolfgang and St Denis', in *Musica Antiqua X* (Bydgoszcz: Filharmonia Pomorska im I. Paderewskiego, 1997), 299–312, was a first attempt to summarize the achievements in office composition at Regensburg and their relation to contemporary theory. I offer a more detailed exploration of some chants from the Wolfgang office in 'Das Wolfgang-Offizium des Hermannus Contractus – Zum Wechselspiel von Modustheorie und Gesangspraxis in der Mitte des XI. Jahrhunderts', in Walter Berschin and David Hiley (eds), *Die Offizien des Mittelalters: Dichtung und Musik* (Tutzing: H. Schneider, 1999), 129–42.

7 The diagram is reproduced in the editions of Wilhelm's treatise by Müller and Harbinson. See Hans Müller, *Die Musik Wilhelms von Hirschau: Wiederherstellung, Übersetzung und Erklärung seines musik-theoretischen Werkes* (Frankfurt: [n.pub.], 1883); Wilhelm of Hirsau, *Musica*, ed. Denis Harbinson (Rome: American Institute of Musicology, 1975). See also the reproduction with commentary in my article 'Das Wolfgang-Offizium des Hermannus Contractus'.

8 Crocker, 'Matins Antiphons at St. Denis'.

9 I do not know what is being continued here, since neither R nor D has a numerical series of Matins antiphons.

10 *Antiphonen*, ed. Dobszay and Szendrei.

11 Keith Falconer has recently drawn attention to items in the office for St. Medard, represented in C: 'Zum Offizium des hl. Medardus', in Berschin and Hiley (eds), *Die Offizien des Mittelalters*, 69–85. Whether of 'Gallican' origin or not, of the chants he reproduces only one might belong in the 'progressive' category outlined above.

12 See the edition by Rembert Weakland in 'The Compositions of Hucbald', *Etudes grégoriennes*, 3 (1959), 155–62.

13 Cf. the observations by Hartmut Möller on the early tenth-century Otmar office composed at St. Gall, in Walter Berschin, Peter Ochsenbein and Hartmut Möller, 'Das Otmaroffizium – Vier Phasen seiner Entwicklung', in Berschin and Hiley (eds), *Die Offizien des Mittelalters*, 25–57, esp. 55–7. Möller rightly leaves open the question of the date of the Otmar office, which has antiphons in numerical modal order.

14 See Christopher Hohler, 'The Durham Services in Honour of St. Cuthbert', in C. F. Battiscombe (ed.), *The Relics of St. Cuthbert* (Oxford: Oxford University Press for the Dean and Chapter of Durham Cathedral, 1956), 157–91. The attribution of authorship to a foreign clerk is a probability, based on an estimate of the sophistication of the composition, though not ultimately provable. David Rollason has recently challenged the belief that the earliest source, Cambridge, Corpus Christi College 183 (without musical notation), was actually presented by Athelstan together with Bede's two lives of the saint to the shrine of St. Cuthbert in Durham in the 930s. See his 'St Cuthbert and Wessex: The Evidence of Cambridge, Corpus Christi College MS 183', in Gerald Bonner, David W. Rollason and Clare Stancliffe (eds), *St Cuthbert, his Cult and his Community to AD 1200* (Woodbridge, Suffolk: Boydell Press, 1989), 413–24, esp. 421–4. But I find the recent arguments presented by Laura Sole persuasive: Laura M. Sole, 'Some Anglo-Saxon Cuthbert *Liturgica*: The Manuscript Evidence', *Révue bénédictine*, 108 (1998), 104–44.

Chapter 7

From the Advent Project to the Late Middle Ages: Some Issues of Transmission

David G. Hughes

For the last decade, my work has been largely with Mass books of the later Middle Ages – from the twelfth, thirteenth and fourteenth centuries, specifically those from northern France, Flanders and Aquitaine, and hence only remotely related to the earliest periods of chant history. My purpose here is to examine some of the processes that got the musical text of the chant from somewhere in the seventh century – when much of it, at least, originated, as we know from James McKinnon's superb *Advent Project*[1] – to my own period five or six centuries later.

It is obviously possible to divide this long period of transmission into three segments: first, the purely oral phase, then that in which only unheighted neumes were used, and finally that in which accurately heighted or staff notation replaced the neumes. But the second of these periods, at least, must be subdivided, for – as we shall see – the period of the earliest surviving manuscripts differs qualitatively (and quantitatively) from, say, the eleventh century.

The first segment, when the chant was sung without the aid of notated books – the oral phase – will not be considered here. That period lasted from the first fixing of the melodies in the seventh century until the invention of notation, whenever that may have occurred,[2] and it is enormously important.[3] But this essay is concerned only with written documents and what they do and do not tell us. Still, one must always bear in mind that period without documents, since it may have lasted in some places much longer than we might suppose. Thus it is useful to think about musical transmission with the aid of the diagram presented in Fig. 7.1; the local singing tradition – not a static, unchanging collection of melodies, but something that develops, however slightly, over the years – is a continuous vertical time line.

The manuscripts – whether they are unheighted or heighted – are precipitations of the tradition at any given moment, and can be shown in the diagram in their correct chronological places. Whether in any given case they are related as exemplars and copies is another matter. If it can be proved that they are, well and good, and something resembling a stemma may result. My belief is that in general they are not; rather they express independently the local *modus canendi* of their time. But as we shall see, the word 'local'

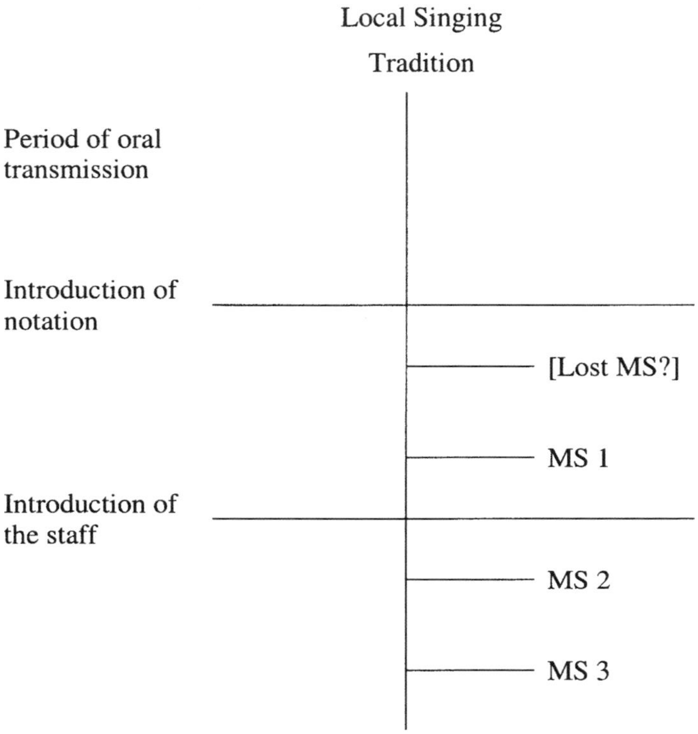

Fig. 7.1 Model of musical transmission

generally implies a date relatively late in the second of my two basic segments, and we must turn back a little.

In my own work there is a temptation to look at the earliest manuscripts as being 'authentic' much in the way the author of the little pseudo-Alcuin treatise on modes looked on his authorities: 'Unde et libros antiquissimos atque firmissimos autenticos vocamus, utpote qui pro sui firmitate aliis possint auctoritatem magisteriumque prebere.'[4] To put it another way, I find myself inclined to respect one of my late manuscripts that much the more as it agrees the more frequently with its remote ancestors. Surely, however, this is a hypothesis that needs testing.

To deal with this issue of the hypothetically old, pure manuscripts versus the turbulent and doubtless degenerate crowd of late ones, it has seemed to me for some years that a quantification of the relations among the musical texts of manuscripts might prove a useful tool. Hence for some time I have used a computer program that produces such information. Like most mechanical approaches to textual criticism, it yields somewhat crude results, and ultimately requires refinement by other methods; but it at least shows the areas that need looking at. The program was worked out by Paul Merkley of the University of Ottawa, who wrote its original form in Turbo Pascal from my algorithm. Since most of what follows is based on that program, it will be necessary to describe roughly how it works.

The collection of data on which it operates was done in much the same way as described in my 'Evidence for the Traditional View', of 1987,[5] but the repertoire here is larger: from two to four complete Mass Propers, depending on the sample. Each chant is divided into numbered 'columns' corresponding to a syllable, or, in the case of melismas, a group of four to six notes. There are in both of my samples about 550 columns,[6] but often some are unusable because of illegibility, lacunae and so on. I have collated close to 200 manuscripts, quite a few of them in both samples, thus generating about 100,000 items of data. These range from the simplest (when all or almost all manuscripts are the same) to quite complex (where there are multiple readings each with a number of witnesses). For each of the manuscripts collated, the musical text of every column is given a reading number: '1' if the reading is the same at that point as that of the Dijon Mass-tonary (which I used as a base reading), '2' if it differs, or some higher number if it differs from any reading thus far recorded (the music corresponding to these numbers is recorded separately). For unheighted manuscripts, neumes are given the number of the first compatible pitch version,[7] or, if none exists, numbered in a different series, '2a' and so on. (All performing instructions – all 'nuances' – are left out of consideration. It would be a major problem to factor them in.) Where there are illegible or lacunary places, this is noted so that no comparison will be based on such points. Thus the musical readings of each manuscript (or rather of the sample studied) can be represented by a data file of about 550 lines, consisting of the column identification plus the reading number.

The program examines the data files of all possible pairs of my nearly two hundred manuscripts in turn (200 manuscripts generate nearly 20,000 pairs). For each column it returns a value of 'same' or 'different', and calculates for each pair the percentage of difference, and the number of comparisons on which the percentage is based. Here I must make an important reservation. Naturally the program gives its output in decimals, carried out to as many places as one wishes. But I shall only rarely use precise figures in this essay; there will be all too many phrases including the word 'about'. A great deal of checking remains to be done in the data files on which the program feeds; it would be improper to give here apparently exact percentages, knowing that they could well be off by an appreciable amount. Nevertheless, the *relative* figures are, I am quite sure, reliable enough, and phrases like 'closer to', or 'much more distant from' may be taken without any reservations.

The program was devised primarily to deal with staff manuscripts; but it works also for unheighted manuscripts,[8] and I ran it for a small group of very early French sources that I had been using in connection with later ones. In this run, the celebrated manuscripts of Laon, Chartres and the Mont-Renaud manuscript showed very close affinities to each other: Laon and

Mont-Renaud showed about 7 percent deviation from each other,[9] Laon and Chartres in the neighborhood of 11 percent, Chartres and Mont-Renaud about 9 percent. These numbers are, as we shall see later, very low; even though the manuscripts are from different centers, the figures are close to the amount of deviation found between later manuscripts from the same place.[10] Almost all of the other unheighted ones in this first run had significantly greater deviations than the three earliest. In other words, at this early time, the local element is rather small.

Now while Corbie or Noyon (or wherever Mont-Renaud may have come from) and the area of Laon are close enough, neither is close to Redon or anywhere else in Brittany where the Chartres manuscript originated. All three manuscripts are similar, however, in that they are very early (Mont-Renaud the least so), and this encouraged me in my innocent belief. All these sources also stand quite close to the famous Dijon Mass-tonary, itself not so early, but not so late either, and of course from yet a different region. The tenth-century gradual from the library at Angers[11] is a bit more distant from the other members of this group, but scarcely enough to invalidate the general sense of close relationship among the earliest sources.

Still, Laon, Corbie, Redon, Angers and Dijon are after all local in the sense of being French; does this hypothesis work on a larger scale? To answer this question I ran the program again with a larger complement of manuscripts from a larger variety of places, including the East and Italy. Here the results were also striking. Even the Eastern sources, while closest to each other, were surprisingly close to Laon and Chartres. The St. Gall sources especially (four were available for that run) were closer to Laon and Chartres than to any but a couple of other early Eastern sources. But the St. Gall sources were even closer to one another – almost identical. Thus this run produced a fairly tight cluster of manuscripts that included one much tighter, local subgroup.

There were also other closely related sources, but they were related *only* because they are from the same place. Thus the three manuscripts from Vercelli (again, not very early) are tightly related, but they are definitely not close to any others. It is close relations reaching beyond locality that we find only in the earliest period. Even then, an incipient division into an Eastern and a Western tradition seems to be visible, but within these large areas the agreement is strong, and the separation between them still weak. As we shall see, local agreement was about the only sort of close relation that seems to have survived in later times.

Now it must be conceded that there are far too few manuscripts from the earliest periods to lift all of this above the level of what one might call informed speculation. But the consistency of the figures suggests that the speculation is not merely idle; it reposes on a reasonably solid statistical basis.

If in the period of the earliest manuscripts the tradition was very unified, then it became less so – became more local – as notation became more common thereafter. This is surely a bit odd; a useful technology is developed to help make the preservation of musical texts easier and more accurate, and it seems to have the opposite effect. This is not the place to say much as to why this may have happened, but one unorthodox thought may be mentioned: notation may have become (among other things) a kind of defensive weapon, by means of which a cantor could say, 'Our way is the right way, *and we have this notated gradual to prove it.*' But that of course evades the issue of how the differences got there to begin with (this latter a difficult question that will be only briefly addressed later in this paper).

Unfortunately, there are few manuscripts that can be used to demonstrate the next phase – the still unheighted traditions that are more truly local, in the sense that they agree well enough with others from the same place, but poorly with those from other centers. Since my work has been in the West, from this point on my concern will be exclusively with French sources; and it is only rarely that two or more unheighted manuscripts survive from one place in France. Among these, an obvious choice is Saint-Denis, from which two unheighted manuscripts and several staff ones remain.

The two early Saint-Denis sources, both from the eleventh century, agree just about exactly with each other; so far I have not found a single indisputable variant in the samples I have studied. In this they resemble the manuscripts from St. Gall (and indeed some other sources from the East); whether there ever were any other Western examples like them is something we may never know. But Saint-Denis differs in one crucial aspect from St. Gall: the rate at which it varies from the earliest nucleus of sources is about one and a half times that found within the nucleus. Thus while it is spectacularly successful in reproducing its own tradition, that tradition is already more strongly local than that of the early manuscripts. As a consequence, the diagram in Fig. 7.1 might better be replaced by one identical to it in its upper part, but showing branches off the main vertical line (representing local traditions) beginning in, perhaps, the early eleventh century.

What makes the Saint-Denis agreement particularly impressive is that one of the two manuscripts was almost certainly written at Saint-Vaast, not Saint-Denis.[12] While in general, a manuscript written at one place for the use of another uses the musical text of the place where it is executed, in this case the Saint-Vaast scribe must have had a Saint-Denis book, or conceivably a Saint-Denis singer, at his disposal, for his music is unmistakably Sandionysian. (I am grateful to Anne Walters Robertson for confirmation of this notion.) Despite the difference in notational style, one has the impression that one manuscript has been directly copied from the other, or that both were very carefully copied from an exemplar no longer extant. Saint-Denis has its closest connection to the preceding generation in the Mont-Renaud manuscript – which would be particularly natural if in fact Mont-Renaud originated at Corbie, as David Hiley (and others) suspect.[13] 'Close' in this case means there are differences in about 14 percent of the columns. Neither the Chartres manuscript nor that of Laon is even that close, both falling in the 17–20 percent area. It is not surprising that the early Eastern sources stand at about the same distance; this is a quasi-Euclidean corollary of the tightness of the early nucleus.

Now if two manuscripts differ in nearly 20 percent of the columns, that means there are about 100 variants between them (here and in similar expressions later, a number of variants means of course 'within the sample studied'). One might well ask how so many differences are possible. The following paragraphs try to answer that question now, not only for Saint-Denis but in advance for the rest of the manuscripts that will be discussed.

Verbal text resists tinkering. If more than one or two letters are changed, the result is almost certain to be nonsense – with the result that even stupid scribes rarely make errors of that sort (and when they do, later scribes or readers can often correct them). The sense of the text acts as a powerful elastic that pulls the details into correct shape even when carelessness might cause changes. But for the same reason an alteration that still makes approximately the same sense may not even be noticed – just as musical changes seem not to have been noticed – and will be recopied until (or if) conflation or deliberate revision restores the original. One often sees in missals a gospel that begins 'Dixit Jesus discipulis suis', when the correct text at that point is really 'Dixit Jesus turbis Judeorum'. That makes no real difference, and hence is not worth correcting, or at least is often not corrected.

Such neutral but literally incorrect gospel beginnings are a little like musical text, which is relatively 'soft'. Minor musical changes do not in general alter the sense of a passage, and hence they may be introduced and perpetuated without causing remark. The elastic that help preserve the integrity of a verbal text is much weaker in music.[14] Example 7.1 shows three different points chosen more or less at random from the offertory *Angelus Domini*. All of the versions shown in the example may be found, although some are rare or unique. (As is evident, the example generalizes a bit, mixing readings whose difference could be seen even in unheighted sources with others detectable only in staff manuscripts.) These are only three of hundreds of similar cases that may be found in the samples studied. Now such minor differences are of many different kinds, but they are reducible to a fairly small number of categories.[15] There is, as is well known, a general tendency for the notes *E* and *b* to be replaced in later sources by *F* and *c*,[16] and this tendency is almost universal in the manuscripts under consideration here.[17] The matter is by no means a simple one, and one's expectation that late manuscripts will have *F* and *c* while early ones will have *E* and *b*, while essentially correct, is very often frustrated. In any event, the semitonal divergences seem not to be variants so much as they are expressions of a stylistic or even aesthetic attitude. Yet they really do change the musical text, and it would be odd not to include them.

There are beyond this only two basic types of variant.[18] By far the commoner involves the addition or omission of one note, or less frequently more than one (Ex. 7.2, A). The most frequent form of this type is the filling in of a third (or the 'emptying' of a third: no chronology is implied). Variants of the add–omit type may account for as many as two-thirds of those found between certain pairs of sources. The other principal type involves a change in melodic direction with or without changing the number of notes (Ex. 7.2, B and C). While this sounds more serious than the mere addition of a (usually ornamental) note, it is scarcely more obtrusive. Not surprisingly, variants of this sort are usually less frequent than those of the add–omit type. But one must be careful not to overgeneralize, as different sources have different

Ex. 7.1 Variant readings in the Offertory *Angelus Domini*

Ex. 7.2 Basic types of variants

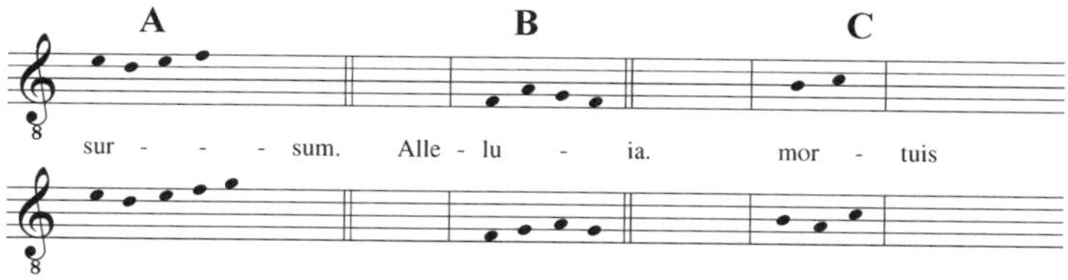

proportions of the variant types: in some places, variants involving direction are less frequent, in others more, while those of the *E*/*F* type may be more numerous (as they seem to be at Saint-Denis, for example), or relatively rare.

Another problem is far more difficult than it looks, and only a brief glance at it is possible here. Every time a musical text is changed – and there are thousands and thousands of changes in the chant repertoire – there has to have been a point in time at which the earlier version still prevailed, and then a subsequent one at which the later one had replaced it; there may also have intervened a time of uncertainty – of vacillation – between the two readings. How could this be? Did no one notice? Were they such really 'pravi cantores' that they would make changes and remain happily unaware that they were doing so? I should hope not, at least on a regular basis. Yet the issue is indeed difficult. Deviations arose somehow,[19] were perhaps only tolerated at first, but became fixed parts of the local traditions in the course of time. There is some evidence suggesting that in Paris sometime before 1200 there was a conscious effort to see that all the churches sang things the same way – to eliminate random variation at least within the city itself.[20] Yet the Parisian manuscripts never agree exactly – not even the two that Michel Huglo believes are related as exemplar and copy.[21] So also, as we shall see, in other places: a local way of singing is evident, but there is always a good deal of sub-local variation.

This sub-local stratum – a kind of irreducible minimum of variance – seems to me overwhelmingly likely to be no more than 'noise' in the transmission: a cumulation of random changes that reflect no relationships – indeed no causes of any kind except for the inevitable tendency of people to reproduce a text in a form slightly different from that in which they received it. It is only fair to add that some of the variants certainly are artificial ones that I myself have introduced – errors in reading manuscripts, errors in copying and errors later in manipulating the data. But this contribution has not, I believe, been large, and in any event it has doubtless been spread fairly evenly over the entire mass of data. In any case it is of those variants created by the entropy of noise – and of those alone – that one may fairly use the term 'errors'. Whether the error is of medieval or modern origin is in a certain sense irrelevant.

My experience suggests that the level of 'noise' from all sources is around 8 percent – that is between forty and fifty variants in the samples I have been using. But this is only an extremely rough approximation. Some manuscripts have a much lower level, as we have seen in the case of the Saint-Denis sources. Others have a significantly higher level; of them we may, I think, correctly say that they were carelessly copied. But throughout the transmission, at least from the eleventh century on, some quantity of noise is almost invariably present, and any attempt to reckon without it will lead, in my opinion, to a fruitless search for nonexistent causes.

After this long digression we may return to our unheighted manuscripts. Other than Saint-Denis, the only pair of unheighted sources I have had available for collation is from Cambrai. These two manuscripts show a vivid contrast with the unanimity of those from Saint-Denis: they differ in about

12 percent of the columns. They are, however, certainly from the same place, as their Paschal Alleluia cycles agree down to the least detail. The best one can say is that their relation to each other is much closer than that of either to anything else. It is, I think, important to note that these two manuscripts are significantly later than those from Saint-Denis – they come from the end of the eleventh or even the early part of the twelfth century.

Of course with such a small base to argue from, no serious conclusions are possible, but there is surely a hint here that the later one gets the more numerous the variants become – that the earliest manuscripts are *autentici* in the Alcuinian sense. Here we have local sources, but they are relatively late, and perhaps for that reason extremely various.

Now we might suspect the beginning of a process in which the degree of variation from the early central tradition increases as the date of a manuscript gets later. But while it is doubtless true that late manuscripts by and large deviate more than early ones, the situation cannot be described by a formula as simple as that. The primary complication lies in the nature of the manuscripts themselves. Some are very quirky – 'extravagant', to use Dom Hesbert's term;[22] others are more sociable. The number of unique readings presented by a source is a suggestive if not entirely accurate measure of this quality: it varies from zero in some manuscripts to over thirty (in one of the two samples) for others. As a result of this and doubtless other factors not as yet isolated, no linear function relating date to quantity of variance is possible.

To sum up the first phases: the earliest manuscripts from different places vary from each other on the order of 11 percent or so; the two Saint-Denis sources, from the eleventh century, are virtually identical to each other, but vary from the earlier ones in the range of 16 percent or more – a significant increase. Clearly the identity of the two Saint-Denis manuscripts to each other is testimony to extreme care, and this becomes evident when we consider the Cambrai manuscripts, which differ from one another at about 12 percent, and from the early sources at around twice that. Thus despite the absence of a linear function, the passage of time seems to have increased both localization and random variation.

The next step is of course the change from unheighted to staff notation. If the end of the tenth century or the first half of the eleventh may be seen as marking a shift from a central tradition to a number of local ones – if, that is, the increase in number of notated books first permitted and then perpetuated local deviations, then the radical change that ensued about a century later – the change from unheighted or inexactly heighted to precisely heighted notation – might be expected to have had equally profound effects. The scribe now had to make a staff version of melodies that up to that time had existed only as sounds and as unheighted (or imperfectly heighted) neumes. Naturally it was his memory (aided perhaps by that of other singers) that determined the pitches chosen.

Now from the statistical point of view comparing unheighted with heighted manuscripts is like comparing eggs with apples: the heighted ones show specific pitches that may or may not be those intended by the unheighted ones. The only way to deal with this is to ignore, in such comparisons, all variants that involve pitch only – to pretend, in fact, that both manuscripts in the comparison are unheighted. No doubt this approach will let slip some variants, but it will at least give relative figures that are basically correct. If this step is not taken – if heighted and unheighted manuscripts are compared with respect to all variants, one emerges, not surprisingly, with figures showing that all unheighted manuscripts are fairly closely related to each other (for example, a manuscript from Saint-Maur-des-Fossés is 'close' to one from Verona, only because both are unheighted). In fact there is no other way to proceed.

For this step there are rather more examples available. There is Saint-Vanne of Verdun, with one inexactly heighted and one staff manuscript, valuable since the two manuscripts are quite close in time. Saint-Maur-des-Fossés also has one unheighted and one much later staff manuscript. There are also Saint-Vaast, with one unheighted manuscript and two staff sources, Noyon, with one of each, and Saint-Bénigne of Dijon, from which there survives a heighted source from the thirteenth century, as well as the early Mass-tonary with its neumes and letter notation. Finally, I have collated two late sources from Saint-Denis to compare with the unheighted ones we just considered.[23] In fact it is only at Saint-Denis that each of the steps in the transmission process can be observed – unheighted manuscripts compared to each other, unheighted compared to staff manuscripts, and staff manuscripts compared to each other.

Let us first consider the two manuscripts from Saint-Bénigne of Dijon. The chronological spread is considerable here, from some time in the eleventh century (probably before 1050), to the middle of the thirteenth. And the two manuscripts are remarkably close given that time span, differing significantly in fewer than 8 percent of the columns – barely if at all above the predicted noise level. (Since all divergences that depend only on pitch have been excluded from consideration at this point, the antiquity of Dijon's pitch-specific tradition does not count one way or the other.)[24]

After the Dijon manuscripts, the next pair in order of similarity is that of the two manuscripts from Noyon, differing in about 11 percent of the columns. Then Saint-Vanne and Saint-Maur come in virtually tied at about 12 percent,[25] followed by Saint-Denis at an average of 14.5 percent and Saint-Vaast at around 16 percent. Now while these numbers are nowhere near identical, they are perhaps close enough for us to estimate the probable difference between an unheighted source and its staff descendent as somewhere in the neighborhood of 12 percent. The circumstances that put some sources above that and some below are doubtless out of reach, although mere care in copying is doubtless one of them.

Now 12 percent, representing nearly seventy variants, is a fairly large number of differences. Thus, just as the generalized introduction of notation seems to have come at the same time that the central melodic tradition of the chant began to split into local traditions, so the introduction of the staff, designed to make possible a more efficient recording of the melodies, seems to have coincided with an increase in the variants even within the local ways of singing. Again, the question 'why' is difficult to handle. No doubt this was at least in part the result of difficulties in shifting from one type of notation to another – of different demands made on the scribe's memory. It may also be that a change in the rank of the person who copied the music – from the relatively exalted cantor of the early period to some petty functionary later on, as argued by Margot Fassler[26] – is in part responsible. In addition, by the twelfth century the chant was perhaps held more in formal honor than in real respect, and the care needed to preserve it accurately was no longer found at any level of the hierarchy. But it may be no more than an accumulation of local preferences, each one believed in good faith to be 'correct'.

The last step is of course to examine the way staff manuscripts behave in relation to one another. From this point on variants of pitch along with those of other sorts will of course be included.[27] The generalization of the staff caused one change even more radical than the introduction of notation in general. From the mid-twelfth century on, the role of the scribe (whatever his rank) could be fundamentally different: he *might* be merely a copyist, reproducing the content of an exemplar. He had no need to have memorized the melodies, since the exemplar would provide him with every pitch. And since all of the nuances of performance had become extinct before staff notation appeared, it was only the pitches that needed to be copied.[28] Thus it was not necessary to know much or understand much; copying music could be as mechanical as copying verbal text could be. Yet the almost complete absence of really absurd mistakes convinces me that the new scribes were paying attention – that they were musical, at the very least.

In comparing staff manuscripts with one another, we have several local traditions to choose from, and often more than two manuscripts from one locality. As before, while the results are not the same from one place to another, they are comparable. I shall restrict myself here to four places – Saint-Denis, Saint-Vaast, Rouen and Paris – but the results from Sens or Reims or Châlons-sur-Marne would not be greatly different.

The two staff manuscripts from Saint-Denis that have been available to me, one from the thirteenth and the other from the fourteenth century, agree about as closely as staff manuscripts ever do: at about 6 percent. This means there are about thirty-five variants altogether, almost evenly divided between those that are only pitch differences and those that involve a difference in the number of notes. Of the pitch differences half a dozen involve the semitones – perhaps a relic of the times when there was significant difference among manuscripts in the treatment of the *E*/*F* and *b*/*c* pairs. It is curious that Saint-Denis seems to have had a problem in getting from the unheighted to the heighted phase, but was remarkably consistent both before and after. For Saint-Vaast we cannot determine the strength of the pre-staff tradition, but between the two staff sources the differences run at about 12 percent – a notably higher rate than that of Saint-Denis.

From Rouen there survive three manuscripts from the cathedral, all of them from the thirteenth century. They are very closely related, with the rate of variation running between 9 percent and 11 percent (thus neatly filling the gap between the figures from Saint-Denis and from Saint-Vaast) – or about fifty to sixty variants.[29]

Now one more digression. The words 'closely related' have appeared once again, and the reader might want to know what would constitute 'distantly related', or some such. Let us take the first of the Rouen sources, Paris, BNF lat. 904, recalling that it has at most sixty variants with other Rouen sources, and compare it with a few sources from other places (see Table 7.1; the example shows numbers of variants rather than percentages). In these comparisons I have avoided eccentric manuscripts – there is one from Auxerre that would show about 180 variants with Rouen, for example. Thus 'distantly related' means having between one and a half and twice the number of variants that occur between related sources. This is not an enormous difference, to be sure, but it is outside of the range of mere statistical error. The figures for other places are roughly comparable to these, and I need not present them here.

Consultation of the many hundreds of such numbers at my disposal shows, not surprisingly, that the resemblances between musical texts are a function of propinquity. Wherever manuscripts believed to be from the same place have musical texts that do not resemble each other closely, one is justified in looking for other evidence that would invalidate the traditional provenance. Thus, for example, even if we did not know that one of the manuscripts given an Evreux siglum in *Les Sources* was in fact a product of Paris, its indices – around 15 percent with other Evreux sources, and 10 percent or less with sources from Paris – would show that its musical tradition was Parisian.[30]

The information available from Dijon, Noyon, Saint-Vaast and Rouen provides a background that helps give a context to the manuscripts for Paris. There are many notated sources from Paris, and they offer a glimpse of what one might call the group dynamics of local manuscripts. By and large the manuscripts form a closely related group. But the group is not homogeneous; the closest Parisian sources have a percentage of variation of about 8 percent, and the mean hovers around 10 percent. We do not know – or at least I do not know – the institutions from which all of these manuscripts come, and hence we cannot easily find reasons for their observed behavior; but it is not difficult to show what that behavior is.

Table 7.2 represents the *mean* value of the index of relation of each of the Parisian manuscripts (these correspond to figures from about forty-five divergences for the first to nearly eighty for the last). With the exception of the last entry (or perhaps the last two), this is a very smooth picture: each item differs from the adjacent one by only a few tenths of a percent. But the last one (Paris, BNF lat. 9441) certainly does not fit very well.[31] There is no doubt

Table 7.1 Distant relationships

Rouen and Saint-Maur	100 variants
Rouen and Saint-Denis	110 variants
Rouen and Saint-Vaast	90 variants
Rouen and Sens	105 variants
Rouen and Tours	115 variants
Rouen and Paris	105 variants

that it is Parisian like all the rest,[32] but it does not reproduce the Parisian musical idiom very accurately. We cannot merely say 'carelessly copied' and let it go at that; for if we take *all* of the figures for this manuscript – not just its relation to other Parisian manuscripts – its mean is not inordinately high. This sort of eccentricity resists easy explanation, and it turns up in other ways as well. There are one or two Parisian manuscripts with quite eccentric calendars, and there are different ones that have somewhat eccentric Alleluia cycles – both of them areas in which inadvertent alterations are less likely than in the musical text. And there are one or two possible analogies from other places. Once again, this merely illustrates that manuscripts may have (for reasons we usually do not know) individualities of their own, though taken in sufficient numbers, they behave in statistically normal fashion.

The period of manuscripts written in square notation has lasted from the late twelfth century to well beyond the end of the Middle Ages, but the latest witnesses I have consulted date from the fifteenth century. Thus this is as far as the present essay will attempt to go. About the next link in the chain of transmission, the shift to printed books in the fifteenth and sixteenth centuries, I have no information whatever; and the step after that – the restoration of chant in the nineteenth and twentieth centuries – is qualitatively different from all of the others. I have attempted to show that the early tradition of the chant was stable universally; that the introduction of notation seems to reflect that state of affairs, but that the wider dissemination of notated books is contemporaneous with a sharp increase in the number of local variants. The replacement of unheighted or inexactly heighted notation

Table 7.2 Means of relation between each Parisian manuscript and all other Parisian sources

MS	*Century*		*Mean relationship*
BNF lat. 861	14		0.083
BNF lat. 830	13		0.086
Arsenal 197	13		0.089
Arsenal 110	14		0.091
Arsenal 608	14		0.097
BNF lat. 15615	13		0.099
BNF lat. 8885	14		0.101
BNF lat. 1337	13–14		0.101
Mazarine 411	14		0.104
BNF lat. 1112	13		0.107
BNF lat. 14452	13		0.108
Walters W. 302	15		0.108
Ste-Geneviève 1259	13		0.111
BNF n. a. lat. 2649	14		0.123
BNF lat. 9441	13		0.142
		Mean:	*0.103*
		SD:	*0.014*

by staff writing coincides with a further multiplication of variants, even among manuscripts from the same locality; and the long period during which staff notation was universal for the most part increased the amount of variety, although at a decreasing rate. In virtually no cases do the variants have an appreciable effect on the substance of the chant melodies; indeed most changes are so trivial that one would hear them only if one were looking for them. Yet the singers, or at least the cantors, were probably aware that their own traditions differed from those of other places.

Most scholars would probably agree that the period of square notation was in many senses one of decline in the chant. What was sung in the time of the Gothic cathedrals and churches of the later Middle Ages would doubtless have sounded both lifeless and perfunctory to a singer of Carolingian times; all of the subtlety and refinement of execution had vanished, to be replaced by a uniformity that would surely have seemed mechanical to one accustomed to the old ways. So might Mozart played by an untalented child sound to us now. In those later centuries, the chant was in fact for most purposes lifeless. Newer musics had arisen, and it was those that interested most progressive musicians. All the more amazing then, the relative fidelity with which at least the substance of the melodies had been preserved over so many difficult centuries.

Appendix

List of manuscripts referred to, in alphabetical order of presumed place of origin

Brittany (?), Gradual, 10th c.	Angers, BM 93
Cambrai, Gradual, 11th–12th c.	Cambrai, BM 60
Cambrai, missal, 12th c.	Cambrai, BM 234
Dijon, Gradual, 13th c.	Brussels, Bibl. Royale II.3824
Dijon, Mass-tonary, 11th c.	Montpellier, Fac. Méd. H. 159
Laon, region of, Gradual, 10th c.	Laon, BM 239
Noyon (?), Gradual/antiphonal, 10th–11th c.	Private Collection ('MS of Mont-Renaud')
Noyon, Gradual, 11th c.	London, BL Egerton 857
Noyon, missal, 13th–14th c.	Abbeville, BM 7
Paris, missal, 12th c.	Paris, Bibl. Ste-Geneviève 93
Paris, missal, 13th c.	Paris, Bibl. Ste-Geneviève 1259
Paris, missal, 13th c.	BNF lat. 830
Paris, missal, 13th c.	BNF lat. 1112
Paris, missal, 13th c.	BNF lat. 9441
Paris, missal, 13th c.	BNF lat. 15615
Paris, missal, 13th c.	London, BL Add. 38723
Paris, missal, 13th c.	Rome, Bib. Casanatense 1695
Paris, missal, 13th c.	London, BL Add. 38723
Paris, missal, 14th c.	Bibl. de l'Arsenal 608
Paris, Gradual, 14th c.	Bibl. de l'Arsenal 110
Paris, missal, 14th c.	BNF n. a. lat. 2649
Paris, missal, 14th c.	Bibl. Mazarine 411
Paris, missal, 14th c.	BNF lat. 861

Paris, missal, 14th c.	BNF lat. 1337
Paris, missal, 14th c.	BNF lat. 8885
Paris, missal, 15th c.	Baltimore, Walters Art Gal. W. 302
Paris (Saint-Victor), Gradual, 13th c.	Bibl. de l'Arsenal 197
Paris (Saint-Victor), Gradual, 13th c.	BNF lat. 14452
Redon (?), Gradual, 10th c.	Chartres, BM 47
Rouen, Gradual, 13th c.	BNF lat. 904
Rouen, Gradual, 13th c.	Rouen, BM Y 50
Rouen, missal, 13th c.	BNF n. a. lat. 541
Rouen, missal, 12th c.	Naples, BN VI.G.11
Saint-Denis, Gradual, 11th c.	Paris, Bibl. Mazarine 384
Saint-Denis, missal, 11th c.	BNF lat. 9436
Saint-Denis, missal, 13th c.	BNF lat. 1107
Saint-Denis, missal, 14th c.	BNF lat. 10505
St. Gall, Gradual, 11th c.	St. Gall, SB 339
St. Gall, Gradual, 11th c.	St. Gall, SB 376
St. Gall, Gradual, 11th c.	St. Gall, SB 340
St. Gall, Gradual, 12th c.	St. Gall, SB 375
Saint-Maur-des-Fossés, Gradual, 11th c.	BNF lat. 12584
Saint-Maur-des-Fossés, Gradual, 13th c.	BNF lat. 13253
Saint-Vaast, Gradual, 11th c.	Cambrai, BM 75
Saint-Vaast, Gradual, 13th c.	Arras, BM 437
Saint-Vaast, missal, 13th c.	Arras, BM 44
Vercelli, Gradual, 11th c.	Vercelli, BC 161
Vercelli, Gradual, 12th c.	Vercelli, BC 146
Vercelli, Gradual, 12th c.	Vercelli, BC 162
Verdun, Saint-Vanne, missal, 12th c.	Verdun, BM 758
Verdun, Saint-Vanne, missal, 13th c.	Verdun, BM 759

Notes

I owe thanks to many libraries and librarians. I should mention the staffs of the Département des Manuscrits of the Bibliothèque Nationale de France, and the Institut de Recherche et d'Histoire des Textes, both of Paris, as well as the British Library Reproductions Service, the Bibliothèque Royale of Brussels, Isham Memorial Library of Harvard, Dom Jean Claire of the Abbaye Saint-Pierre de Solesmes, and many other individual librarians and staff members in Paris and other cities throughout France and in other countries as well. Without their assistance and cordial cooperation, my work would have been impossible.

1 James McKinnon, 'The Eighth-Century Frankish-Roman Communion Cycle', *JAMS* 45 (1992), 179–227, *passim*, and, more importantly, his *The Advent Project: The Later-Seventh-Century Creation of the Roman Mass Proper* (Berkeley: University of California Press, 2000).

2 Kenneth Levy has written eloquently in opposition to the usual dating of the origin of notation. See, for example, his 'Charlemagne's Archetype of Gregorian Chant', *JAMS* 40 (1987), 1–30. Still, the question cannot yet be said to be entirely settled.

3 See Peter Jeffery, *Re-envisioning Past Musical Cultures: Ethnomusicology in the Study of Gregorian Chant* (Chicago: University of Chicago Press, 1992) for a recent and stimulating survey of the issues involved in the oral period.

4 Quoted after *Aureliani Reomensis Musica disciplina*, ed. Lawrence Gushee (n.p.: American Institute of Musicology, 1979), 79, since the 'Alcuinian' paragraphs appear in Aurelian's treatise also.

5 David G. Hughes, 'Evidence for the Traditional View of the Transmission of Gregorian Chant', *JAMS* 40 (1987), 377–404.

6 The two samples, one comprising the third Mass of Christmas and the Epiphany Mass, the other the Easter Mass and the Masses of the three ferias following, were used so that manuscripts wholly lacunary in one or the other of those two places could still be included. In almost all of what follows, the second of these samples is used. It should be noted that the results from the two samples (in those cases where I have data for both) differ somewhat more than one might expect. This is probably in part the result of a higher proportion of responsorial chants in the Christmastide sample. But the matter is by no means a simple one, and I shall return to it on another occasion.

7 This is obviously an area in which methodological dispute is possible, to say the least. One might well wish to say 'the closest compatible pitch version', but that raises obvious problems of definition: 'close in what respect?' is merely the simplest of these. In the end, the method I have chosen will produce errors, but they will probably be evenly distributed through the sample, which is a good deal better than systematic errors that might significantly influence the final results.

8 I should like to observe something that seems to me underemphasized in the literature: in 'unheighted' notation the lack of heighting is indeed total between neumes regardless of the pitches intended; but within almost all of the individual neumes there is heighting of at least a consistently relative kind. There can be no doubt of the melodic direction signified by a climacus, to take the most obvious case, but even for the rest of the symbols, the directions are clear enough, only the purely ornamental effects being height-indifferent. (One may compare this with Byzantine neumes, most of which show little graphical trace of their meaning.) It is at least curious that a principle deeply embedded within all forms of the symbol system was so long in being extended to the relation among the symbols.

9 Or in other words, in the 550 columns, the two manuscripts agreed in their musical readings in 93 percent and disagreed in 7 percent (thus disagreeing about forty-nine times).

10 These figures must be regarded with some caution, as Laon and Chartres can be compared in two different samples, and Mont-Renaud in only one. Still, the relative positions are accurate enough. An idea of just how low these numbers are may be conveyed by noting that Chartres compared to an unheighted twelfth-century source from Verdun shows deviation of about 17 percent.

11 Angers, BM 93.

12 See Anne Walters Robertson, *The Service Books of the Royal Abbey of Saint-Denis* (Oxford: Clarendon Press, 1991), 388–9.

13 David Hiley, *Western Plainchant: A Handbook* (Oxford: Clarendon Press, 1993), 338. As is observed there, Mont-Renaud might come from Saint-Denis itself. I am inclined to doubt that, however, simply because the melodic tradition of Mont-Renaud is not close enough to that of the unheighted manuscripts from Saint-Denis.

14 Two points need to be added. First, and more simply, the music to which I am referring is of course medieval monophony. Lacking meter, it permits the addition or omission of notes without causing grammatical violations. And lacking the control of consonance and dissonance found in polyphony, it allows pitches to be changed as well, again without necessarily causing offensive or impossible

results. The second point concerns the relative roles of writing and singing in transmission: do both media permit minor variation to about the same extent? In the absence of much-needed study of this point I am inclined to suppose that they do – that a change may be as easily introduced into a singing tradition without having recourse to written music as in a situation where one document is being copied from another.

15 Here also I shall anticipate, including pitch variants as well as those deducible from unheighted manuscripts.

16 A fundamental study on this issue remains that of Dom Joseph Gajard, 'Les Récitations modales des 3e et 4e modes dans les manuscrits bénéventains et aquitains', *Etudes grégoriennes*, 1 (1954), 9–45.

17 This is often described in the literature as an Eastern or Germanic phenomenon, but it occurs also in the West. Now of course it may be asked: how can we ascertain the presence of a pitch variation like *F* for *E* in sources that do not show pitch? In fact it is only possible at times, and even then often without perfect certainty. Still, if we find an unheighted source that has, say, a *pes subpunctis*, and if that is rendered *FFED* in some or all staff sources, and if there are no other surviving readings that might represent the unheighted version, then we may, I think, safely conclude that the unheighted source intended *EFED*. There may of course be many other variants of the *E/F* type that we cannot discover now, but we have no choice but to ignore what we cannot control.

18 With some misgivings I have largely abandoned considering 'redistribution' – minor changes in the way that notes are assigned to syllables of the text – as a musical variant. (It was given considerable importance in my 'Evidence for the Traditional View'.) It does occur very often, to be sure, but almost as frequent are passages where the assignment of notes to syllables is not at all clear. In the end, it seems preferable to ignore the phenomenon except in those cases where it clearly alters (however slightly) the sense of the phrase, or in the much rarer case in which one manuscript seems to have copied the idiosyncrasy of another.

19 In a small minority of cases the reason may be evident. In the Offertory *Tui sunt celi*, the melisma on 'est terra' contains, in the Dijon Mass-tonary, the figure *GFE* repeated three times. It is not difficult to imagine a later scribe deciding that this was faulty, and in fact the passage is rarely reproduced in the Dijon version. There are also cases where it would appear that theoretical thinking has caused alterations. But for most changes the reasons are not at all evident.

20 For the evidence of the calendars, see my 'Parisian Sanctorals of the Late Middle Ages', in Bryan Gillingham and Paul Merkley (eds), *Chant and its Peripheries: Essays in Honour of Terence Bailey* (Ottawa: Institute of Mediaeval Music, 1998), 277–309.

21 Michel Huglo, 'Notated Performance Practices in Parisian Chant Manuscripts of the Thirteenth Century', in Thomas Forrest Kelly (ed.), *Plainsong in the Age of Polyphony* (Cambridge: Cambridge University Press, 1992), 35.

22 Hesbert employs it virtually as a technical term throughout the later volumes of the *CAO* (1963–5).

23 I have so far been unable to consult the fourteenth-century Saint-Denis missal at the Victoria and Albert Museum.

24 In this special case we can also find variants involving pitch only; there are twenty-eight of these. We have a total of about seventy variants altogether between the two Dijon manuscripts, of which about half are pitch variants that only the letter notation of the earlier source has preserved. Thus the transmission probably does include noise after all.

25 Based on the Easter sample. For reasons not immediately apparent, the Saint-Vanne manuscripts are a great deal closer in the Christmastide sample.

26 Margot Fassler, 'The Office of the Cantor in Early Western Monastic Rules and Customaries', *EMH* 5 (1985), 29–52.

27 There might seem to be a problem of method here, since the later unheighted manuscripts are usually nuance-poor; they tell the singer the number of notes to be sung to each syllable, and the direction from one note to another (within the neumes). The staff manuscripts convey in addition the actual pitches to be sung. Do not they, then, transmit significantly more information? And for that reason should we not expect them to vary rather more? While this issue deserves a hearing, I believe that the question itself carries within it a mistaken assumption about the nature of the copyist's work; he is not doing piecework measured by the bits of information he transcribes, but rather reproducing (whether by eye or ear) what is regarded in his day as the essential elements of a melody. Thus his job is neither harder nor easier than that of the scribe copying from an unheighted source.

28 Michel Huglo made a fundamentally similar observation several years ago, in his 'Tradition orale et tradition écrite dans la transmission des mélodies grégoriennes', in Hans Heinrich Eggebrecht and Max Lütolff (eds), *Studien zur Tradition in der Musik: Kurt von Fischer zum 60. Geburtstag* (Munich: Musikverlag Katzbichler, 1973), 31–42.

29 There is one other Rouen missal with notation: Naples, Bibl. Naz. VI.G.11. While I have only recently had access to this source, and that briefly, my initial inclination is to consider its provenance doubtful. Neither its Alleluias nor its musical text are characteristic of Rouen, or at least of the cathedral group. See, however, *Le Graduel romain*, ii: *Les Sources* (Solesmes: Abbaye St-Pierre, 1957), 85, and Raffaele Arnese, *I codici notati della Biblioteca Nazionale di Napoli* (Florence: Olschki, 1967), 132. Arnese in fact says merely, 'Notazione normanna con caratteristiche calligrafiche della scuola di Rouen'. Unfortunately, I have not had access to any Rouen manuscripts of that early a date, and hence cannot either confirm or refute that statement. Since the manuscript is considerably earlier than the rest of the Rouen sources, it is of some consequence, and I hope to return to it on another occasion. The St. Petersburg manuscript O.v.I.6, tentatively ascribed to Rouen by *Les Sources*, 58–9, is not from there but from Meulan, with strong relations to Bec. See David Hiley, 'The Norman Chant Traditions–Normandy, Britain, Sicily', *PRMA* 107 (1980–81), 1–33 at 18.

30 To be fair, *Les Sources*, 107, makes exactly the same point. The manuscript is described as 'Missel de Paris, . . . le Calendrier (remanié) est celui d'Evreux . . .'.

31 Since this essay was written, I have also seen photographs of two other authentically Parisian missals. Rome, Bibl. Casanatense 1695 has a musical text still more remote from the norm than that of BNF lat. 9441. On the other hand, London, BL Add. 38723 is clearly a faithful witness to the Parisian tradition, even though not near the top of the list in terms of fidelity. Both of these deserve fuller treatment than is possible here.

32 This may be shown by the content of the calendar and by the series of Alleluia verses. Solesmes assigns it to Notre Dame, which makes its non-compliance even more awkward.

Chapter 8

Glosses on Music and Grammar and the Advent of Music Writing in the West

Charles M. Atkinson

This study is the complement to one published in a volume honoring David Hughes.[1] There I advanced the idea that prosodic accents, as presented in ancient treatises on grammar, had formed the basis for the corpus of early notational signs known as the Paleofrankish script, with the acute accent becoming the *podatus*, the grave the *clivis*, and the circumflex the *torculus*.[2] These findings seemed to contradict those of Leo Treitler and Kenneth Levy, both of whom had recently dismissed the notion that prosodic accents could have played a role in the development of Western musical notation.[3] What my article actually did, however, was to make a distinction between the accents themselves, as described in Classical sources, and the nineteenth-century 'accent theory' of musical notation, which held that the acute accent of Classical prosody became the neume known as a *virga*, the circumflex accent a *clivis* and the grave accent a *punctum*.[4] In my view, this 'accent theory' had been wrong from the outset; hence, Treitler and Levy were correct in dismissing it. What cannot be dismissed, I think, is the newly reforged link between prosodic accents and the rise of practical musical notation in the West.

The present essay will not attempt to explore the implications of this link for the development of neumatic notation per se. What it proposes to do instead is to explore further the relationship between ancient treatises on grammar, specifically those of Donatus and Martianus Capella, and the intellectual and artistic ferment of the Carolingian era that gave rise to the system of musical notation we know as neumes. We shall find that the glosses entered by Carolingian commentators into the ancient texts treating prosodic accents explain and illustrate various grammatical terms with terminology and descriptions drawn from both the theory and practice of music.[5] Included in these glosses is rather compelling evidence that the prosodic accents and early signs for musical notation were seen as directly analogous to each other.

Let me begin by stating *expressis verbis* a principle I took as given in my earlier study because it is one upon which historians of Latin are in nearly unanimous agreement as far as I can tell: by the end of the fourth century, if not earlier, the accent in Latin was one of stress, rather than pitch.[6] The evidence for this comes primarily from the behavior of the language itself, in which one finds many examples of reduction or suppression of vowels following accented syllables, indicating 'unmistakably' the presence of a stress accent (this according to Lindsay).[7] Corroborating evidence comes from a few later grammarians, such as Servius and Pompeius (both fifth century), who state that 'Accentus in ea syllaba est quae plus sonat.'[8] As perusal of Keil's *Grammatici Latini* reveals, however, most of the Latin grammarians, from Varro and Quintilian through Donatus and Priscian, describe accents in terms of pitch inflection, translating them from the Greek προσῳδία, with its ὀξεία, βαρεία and περισπωμένη.[9] These become in Latin the prosodic accents acute, grave and circumflex. These accents are treated by the grammarians in the same way that their Greek counterparts were, despite fundamental differences between the two languages.[10] Indeed, it is in the slavish application of Greek terms and principles to the Latin language that a scholar such as W. S. Allen sees proof that Latin accent was not characterized by pitch inflection. In Allen's view, 'The very similarity of the Latin statements to those which apply to Greek is . . . an embarrassment rather than a support to the idea of a pitch accent for Latin.'[11] Supporting this view even further is the fact that apart from treatises on grammar, graphic evidence of prosodic accents is almost completely absent from written Latin texts either in Antiquity or in the Middle Ages.[12]

We shall discover below that the treatises on grammar by Donatus and Martianus Capella are among those describing accents characterized by inflection of pitch, that is, as prosodic. Yet as we encounter these treatises being taught and commented upon in the ninth and tenth centuries, the Latin language itself had been characterized for almost half a millennium by the use of stress – and not prosodic – accent.

Let us turn our attention now to the milieu in which these treatises were being copied and glossed – namely, the various monastic and cathedral schools that were home to the Carolingian educational reform. As all of us know, that reform was chiefly the design of Charlemagne's 'minister of education', Alcuin of York.[13] Its structure can be seen most easily in the educational program that Alcuin established at St. Martin of Tours. The school at Tours had one division for Bible study, a second one for the liberal arts and a third devoted specifically to grammar.[14] From this design and from the preface to Alcuin's treatise on grammar, one can deduce that the ultimate and highest goal of instruction was study of the Bible, but one would progress to that through study of the liberal arts.[15] And the first of these – in both a literal and a figurative sense – was grammar. Beyond the most fundamental types of elementary instruction, such as the learning of reading and writing and the memorization of certain liturgical texts,[16] the discipline of grammar was the one liberal art whose study we can reasonably assume to have been expected of everyone.[17] And as we know from the testimony of Alcuin's own treatise on grammar, along with ninth-century library catalog and editions and commentaries by many Carolingian authors, the chief authority for grammar was Donatus.[18] The saying that 'Every schoolboy had his Donatus' was no less true in the Carolingian period than it was in late Antiquity. In our quest to learn what the Carolingians would have learned about prosodic accents, we must therefore turn our attention to the *Ars grammatica* of Donatus, along with the section on grammar in one of the other 'standardized textbooks' for the Carolingians – namely, Martianus Capella's *De nuptiis Philologiae et Mercurii*.[19]

TEXT I

Donatus, Ars maior, I.5

DE TONIS: Tonos alii accentus, alii tenores nominant. Toni igitur tres sunt, acutus, gravis, circumflexus. Acutus cum in Graecis dictionibus tria loca teneat, ultimum, paenultimum et antepaenultimum, apud Latinos paenultimum et antepaenultimum tenet, ultimum numquam. Circumflexus autem, quotlibet syllabarum sit dictio, non tenebit nisi paenultimum locum. Gravis poni in eadem dictione vel cum acuto vel cum circumflexo potest, et hoc illi non est comune cum ceteris . . . In trisyllabis et tetrasyllabis et deinceps, si paenultima correpta fuerit, acuemus antepaenultimam, ut Tullius Hostilius; si paenultima positione longa fuerit, ipsa acuetur et antepaenultima graui accentu pronuntiabitur, ut Catullus, Metellus.

Acutus accentus est nota per obliquum ascendens in dexteram partem ´, gravis nota a summo in dexteram partem descendens `, circumflexus nota de acuto et gravi facta ^.

Text I is drawn from chapter 5 of book I of Donatus' *Ars maior*.[20] As one can see there, a close connection with music is established by the heading, *De tonis*, and the first sentence: *Tonos alii accentus, alii tenores nominant* ('Some call tones "accents", others "tenors"').[21] Although it echoes a passage in Quintilian, this definition goes back ultimately to the Greek grammarians, for whom τόνος (from the verb τείνω) is the standard term for vocal inflection and the most important element of prosody.[22] Its direct lineage from the Greek may be seen in the fact that two of its terms, *tonus* and *tenor*, have Greek roots, and that the term *accentus* is a translation of the Greek προσῳδία.[23]

After listing the three types of accents – acute, grave and circumflex – Donatus contrasts Greek usage with Latin, stating, for example, that the acute can appear in any of three syllabic positions within a word in Greek, but in only two positions in Latin.[24] He also mentions that the grave accent can be placed in the same word with either an acute or circumflex, but says that this trait is peculiar to it – that is, an acute and a circumflex may not appear together in the same word.[25] In the examples demonstrating the placement of accents in words of varying numbers of syllables and quantities of vowel sounds, he points out that in words of three, four or more syllables, the antepenult will receive an acute accent if the penultimate is short, and a grave accent if it is long.[26] In the sentence that concludes the example, Donatus finally tells us what the accents actually are: 'An acute accent is a *nota* ascending toward the right in oblique motion ´ ; a grave accent is a *nota* descending toward the right from above ` ; a circumflex accent is a *nota* made from acute and grave ^ .'[27]

A good sense of the flavor of Carolingian commentaries on the opening sentence of this passage is provided by Donatus Gloss texts I and II below. (In these and in all subsequent examples I have given the base text in normal type, interlinear glosses in italics within angle brackets, and marginal glosses in italics within square brackets.)

DONATUS GLOSS I. Paris, BNF lat. 7490, fol. 44v

DE TONIS: Tonos alii accentus, alii tenores nominant.
[(Tonus) *id est sonus; unde tonitruum dicitur. quod sonus eius terreat*]
toni igitur tres sunt; acutus, gravis <*deprimens tonus gravans*>, circumflexus.

DONATUS GLOSS II. Paris, BNF n. a. lat. 1620, fol. 28

DE TONIS. Tonos <*a tonando. quasi ad cantus*> alii accentus alii tenores nominant <*tenores a tenendo eoquod teneant sonum in una syllaba*>. Toni <*soni*> tres sunt, acutus, gravis, circumflexus.

In Donatus Gloss I, from Paris, BNF lat. 7490 (ninth century),[28] the commentator expands the meaning of *tonus* with the phrase 'id est sonus. Whence thunder is called "tonitruum", because its *sound* can create fear.' In the next sentence he specifies that the grave accent is a tone that 'lowers and makes more weighty'.

Gloss II, from Paris, BNF n. a. lat. 1620 (tenth century),[29] takes Donatus' words directly into the realm of music. Its author says that *tonos* comes from *tonando*, 'thundering', then adds the phrase *quasi ad cantus*, 'as if in singing' or 'for the purpose of song, so to speak'.[30] Sound likewise plays a role in his explanation of the term *tenores*, which are so called from *tenendo* because they *hold the sound* in one syllable.[31] Indeed, for him, the accents can be called either 'tones' or 'sounds', as the last sentence in the example makes clear.

Whereas the emphasis in these first two glosses is upon the meanings of words, and upon sound and the inflection of the voice, the next example, Donatus Gloss III, from Paris, BNF lat. 13025 (ninth century),[32] draws attention to the graphic signs conveying those inflections.

DONATUS GLOSS III. Paris, BNF lat. 13025, fol. 27v

si paenultima positione longa fuerit, ipsa acuetur et antepaenultima gravi accentu pronuntiabitur, ut càtéllus, mètéllus.

Although the signs themselves, the *notae,* have not yet been introduced in the running text of the treatise, the glossator places them over the syllables of *catellus* [*sic*] and *metellus*. I have included them here because one finds them in many manuscripts of the *Ars maior*, even ones that have few glosses. As these sources suggest, the commentators were apparently intrigued by the idea that every syllable could carry an accent, but that only one syllable would typically receive an acute or circumflex.

DONATUS GLOSS IV. Paris, BNF lat. 13025, fol. 58v (after 'De posituris')

[INTEREST DE ACCENTU. *Accentus quid est? Accentus est, qui grece prosodia dicitur. accentus quasi acantus. accentus habet acutum ´ et gravem ` seu circumflexum* ^.]

The fourth gloss reinforces the connection with song noted in Gloss II, but also establishes a further link with yet another glossing tradition, that for the treatise of Martianus Capella (in this case, perhaps by way of Isidore of Seville).[33] As we shall see in a moment, the phrase 'qui grece prosodia dicitur' is drawn almost verbatim from Martianus, as indeed is the phrase 'accentus quasi ad cantus'.[34]

But before turning our attention to Martianus, I must say something about what might at first glance appear to be the Rosetta Stone of accents and neumes. I am referring to Donatus Gloss V, drawn from the manuscript Munich, BSB clm 14737 (tenth century).[35]

DONATUS GLOSS V. Munich, Bayerische Staatsbibl. clm 14737, fol. 33ᵛ

Tonos alii accentus, alii tenores nominant

[ (tonos) *A tonando, eoquod tonare, id est resonare facit syllabas.*]

[ (accentus) *Quasi ad cantus, eoquod ad cantilenam vocis facit agnoscere syllabas.*]

[ (tenores) *A tenendo dicuntur quia tenent syllabas*]

Toni igitur tres sunt. Acutus <*qui acuit vocem*>, Gravis <*qui gravat*>, Circumflexus <*qui acuit et gravat*> cum in grecis dictionibus tria loca teneat, ultimum, penultimum & antepenultimum <*quod est primum*>. Apud latinos penultimum & antepenultimum tenet, ultimum numquam.

As the reader will probably already have noticed, three different neumes – a clivis, a podatus, and a pressus – appear over the words *tonos, accentus*, and *tenores*. Inasmuch as they represent three different melodic gestures, and are all either two- or three-note neumes, they could well claim their ancestry in the prosodic accents of Donatus. As further scrutiny of this and the surrounding passages reveals, however, these neumes were not intended to illustrate the accents, but rather to serve as cues to the marginal glosses that explicate the terms in the treatise. With phrases such as *ad cantilenam vocis facit agnoscere syllabas* ('allowing one to recognize the syllables of the voice in song'), the glosses themselves do underscore the connection of the accents with music, but they do not themselves embody that connection directly.

Let us now turn our attention to two passages on accent in Book III of *De nuptiis Philologiae et Mercurii* by Martianus Capella. Perhaps because it was a more comprehensive treatise than that of Donatus, encompassing all the liberal arts, Martianus' work received some of the most interesting and illuminating glosses of all. The quality and character of its glosses may also be due to its making a direct connection between prosodic accents and music. We can see this in Text II, the introduction to Martianus' treatment of prosodic accents, *de fastigio*.[36]

TEXT II

Martianus Capella, De nuptiis Philologiae et Mercurii, Bk. III

> Hactenus de iuncturis; nunc de fastigio videamus. qui locus apud Graecos πεϱὶ πϱοσῳδιῶν appellatur. hic in tria discernitur: unaquaeque enim syllaba aut gravis est aut acuta aut circumflexa; et ut nulla vox sine vocali est, ita sine accentu nulla. et est accentus, ut quidam putaverunt, anima vocis et seminarium musices, quod omnis modulatio ex fastigiis vocum gravitateque componitur, ideoque accentus quasi adcantus dictus est. omnis igitur vox Latina simplex sive composita habet unum sonum aut acutum aut circumflexum; duos autem acutos aut inflexos habere numquam potest, graves vero saepe.

Upon introducing this topic, Martianus says that it is called in Greek πεϱὶ πϱοσῳδιῶν and that it is divided into three aspects. He continues, saying:

> Every single syllable is either grave, acute or circumflex; and just as there is no utterance without a vowel, so too there is none without an accent. As some assert, accent is the soul of utterance and the seed-bed of music (*seminarium musices*), because every melody is composed of elevation or depression of the voice. Thus *accentus* is named, as it were, 'for the purpose of song' (*ad cantus*).[37]

He concludes this introduction by making the point that every word has either an acute or a circumflex accent, but that two of them cannot appear in the same word; graves, on the other hand, can occur frequently.

As one might expect of a passage that has at least one phrase of Greek, along with several Latin words and phrases whose meanings were not entirely obvious, this passage inspired a lively response on the part of medieval commentators. A typical example is that given in Martianus Gloss I, from Leiden, Bibl. Rijksuniv., BPL 88 (ninth century).[38]

MARTIANUS GLOSS I. Leiden, Bibl. Rijksuniv., BPL 88, fol. 41

> Hactenus de iuncturis; nunc de fastigio <*id est accentu*> videamus. qui locus apud grecos .πεϱὶ πϱοσῳδιῶν. <*de accentibus*> appellatur . . . et est accentus ut quidam putaverunt anima <*id est vivificatio*> vocis et seminarium <*origo vel exordium*> musices <*genetivus grecus, id est modulationis. eo*> quod omnis modulatio ex fastigiis <*elevatione*> vocum gravitateque componitur. Ideoque accentus quasi ad cantus dictus est. Omnis igitur vox latina simplex sive composita habet unum sonum <*accentum*> aut acutum aut circumflexum. Duos autem acutos aut inflexos habere nunquam potest, graves <*scilicet plures*> vero saepe <*scilicet potest habere*>.

Its author explains virtually every problematic term, starting with *de fastigio* and πεϱὶ πϱοσῳδιῶν – *accentu* and *de accentibus* respectively – and concluding with two glosses devoted to the idea that several grave accents can occur in a single word. Particularly important are his glosses on the phrase *seminarium musices*: *seminarium* is 'origin' or 'beginning'; *musices* is explained as a Greek genitive, meaning 'of modulation'.[39]

MARTIANUS GLOSS II. Leiden, Bibl. Rijksuniv., BPL 36, fol. 27v

Hactenus de iuncturis; nunc de fastigio videamus. qui locus apud Graecos peri prosodion <*de accentibus*> appellatur.
[*Pros. grece ad. Ode. cantus. Inde accentus. ad prosodion grece dicitur. Hinc et exo(r)dion initium cantilene dicitur & praecentor exo(r)diarius appellatur.*]
et est accentus <*diffinitio vocis*>, ut quidam putaverunt, anima vocis <*origo*> et seminarium musices, quod <*eoquod*> omnis modulatio ex fastigiis <*elevationis*> vocum gravitateque componitur.

A later glossator, whose work is seen in Martianus Gloss II, from Leiden, Bibl. Rijksuniv., BPL 36 (tenth century),[40] goes even further in relating the phrase περὶ προσῳδιῶν to music. In a rather extensive marginal gloss he explains that 'pros' in Greek is 'ad' in Latin, and that 'Ode' is 'cantus', whence 'accentus' is called 'prosodion' in Greek. He then tries to demonstrate his erudition by providing a parallel example: 'From this it follows that the beginning of a chant is called the "exordium", and the precentor an "exordiarius".' The only problem here is that instead of *exordium* and *exordiarius*, the anonymous commentator actually wrote *exodion* (i.e., *exodium*) and *exodiarius* – *exodium* being a staged piece of comic description, and an *exodiarius* a player in the *exodium*! Assuming that the commentator's Latin was better than his Greek, his references to the *initium cantilene* and to the *praecentor* certainly make clear the musical referent of this gloss.

The musical implications of this section of Martianus are underscored even further by a passage from Leiden F. 48 (mid-ninth century),[41] a commentary attributed to Martin of Laon[42] (Martianus Gloss III).

MARTIANUS GLOSS III. Leiden, Bibl. Rijksuniv., Voss. lat. F. 48, fol. 22v

Hactenus de iuncturis; nunc de fastigio videamus. qui locus apud Graecos peri prosodion <*id est de accentibus*> appellatur. hic <*locus*> in tria discernitur: unaquaeque enim syllaba aut gravis est aut acuta aut circumflexa; et ut nulla vox sine vocali est, ita sine accentu nulla. et est accentus, ut quidam putaverunt, anima <*pulcritudo*> vocis et seminarium <*matheries*> musices <*id est, musicae artis*>.
[*Tonus id est cantus id est emissio vocis. accentus autem exaltatio vel depositio eius unde accentus quasi ad cantus dicitur.*]

In the sentence beginning *et est accentus*, Martin (?) glosses the word *anima* (soul) with *pulcritudo* (pulchritude or beauty); *seminarium musices* becomes for him the *matheries musices, id est, musicae artis* – 'the very stuff or substance of music, that is, of the musical art'. He concludes with a marginal commentary on the theory of accent introduced by Donatus' term *tonus*. I translate: '*Tonus*, that is *cantus*, which is the projection of the voice. Accent is its elevation or deposition; whence accent is named, as it were, "for the purpose of song" (*ad cantus*).' In this passage it is hard to tell whether music or grammar is the primary referent, so complete is the interweaving of elements from the two disciplines.

TEXT III

Martianus Capella, De nuptiis Philologiae et Mercurii, Bk. III

> acutus accentus notatur virgula a sinistra parte in dexteram ascendente, gravis autem a sinistra parte ad dexteram descendens, inflexi signum est sigma super ipsas litteras devexum. accentus partim fastigia vocamus, quod litterarum capitibus apponantur, partim cacumina, tonos vel sonos, Graeci prosodias. sciendum etiam uni vocabulo accidere omnes tres accentus posse, ut est Argiletum.

Our final excerpt from Martianus, Text III,[43] begins by describing the graphic signs for notating prosodic accents, signs that Donatus calls *notae* (as we saw in Text I).

> An acute accent is notated as a virgula ascending from left to right; a grave [is notated as a virgula] descending from left to right; the sign of the circumflex (*inflexus*) is a sigma facing downwards over its respective syllable.

Unlike the sources for Donatus, however, those for Martianus do not present the *notae* themselves in the running text. Indeed, in a number of the best manuscripts they do not appear at all.[44] This is the case, for example, in Bamberg, Staatsbibl., Class. Hs. 39, the B source for the editions of both Dick and Willis (see Pl. 8.1). It is also the case for the manuscript that was the A source for Dick's edition, Bern, Burgerbibl. B 56 (see Pl. 8.2).[45] As one can see here, a later hand has added the *notae* for the accents in the margins.

Apart from the presence or absence of the accent signs, however, there is a more substantive feature that distinguishes Martianus' text from that of Donatus. The latter author had stated that the grave accent could be placed in a single word together with one of the other accents, but that it could not appear with both of the others. But after describing the *notae* for the acute,

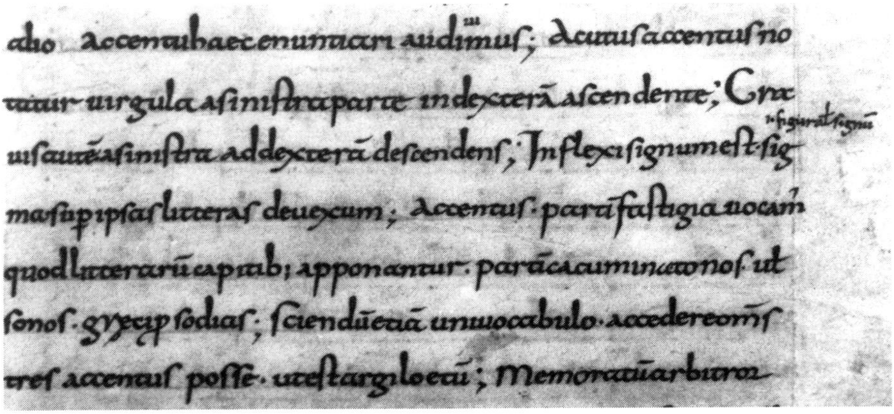

Pl. 8.1 Description of graphic signs for notating prosodic accents in Martianus Capella (Bamberg, Staatsbibl. Classische Hs. 39, fol. 47)

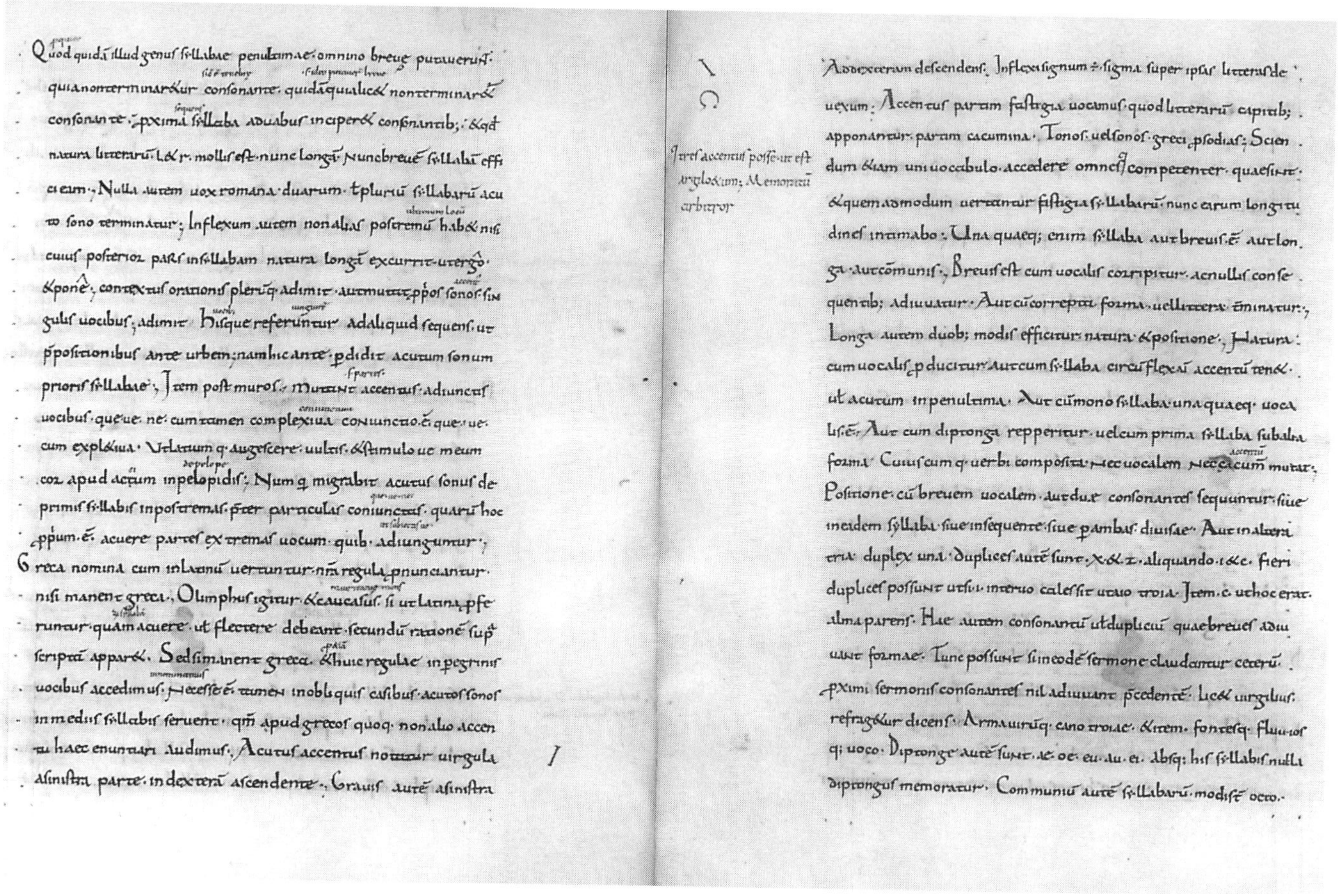

Pl. 8.2 Description of graphic signs for notating prosodic accents in Martianus Capella (Bern, Burgerbibl. B 56)

grave, and 'inflexus' accents as noted above, Martianus states: 'It should be known that all three accents can occur together in one word, as is the case in *Argiletum.*'[46] Thus, according to Martianus at least, the syllabic inflections of a single word could be represented through the use of all three accent signs – acute, grave and circumflex. With all three accents over its syllables, the word *Argiletum* thus encapsulates a significant change in the theory of prosodic accents.

Unfortunately, Martianus did not say which accents should go over which syllables in *Argiletum*. Perhaps because the scribes were not comfortable enough with the rules of prosody to place them correctly, most texts contain no accents at all over the word – either in the original hand or in that of a glossator.

MARTIANUS GLOSS IV. Leiden, Bibl. Rijksuniv., BPL 36, fol. 29

acutus accentus [´] notatur virgula a sinistra parte in dexteram ascendente, gravis [`] autem a sinistra parte ad dexteram descendens, inflexi signum est sigma super ipsas litteras devexum. [∩] accentus partim fastigia vocamus
[*Tunc vocantur fastigia cum apponuntur litteris. Cum vero elevantur cacumina.*]
quod litterarum capitibus apponantur, partim cacumina, tonos vel sonos, Graeci <*vocant*> prosodias. sciendum etiam uni vocabulo accidere omnes tres accentus posse, ut est Argiletum <*ubi argila est vel mors argi*>.

Rather than commenting on the position of the accents in *Argiletum*, several commentators explain the meaning of the word itself. My favorite is a line that appears at the end of Martianus Gloss IV: Argiletum <*ubi argila est vel mors argi*>, 'where the argila is ["argila" is "clay"], or *mors argi* – death of Argos'. Remigius of Auxerre would later gloss *Argiloetum* as 'locus ubi sepultus est Argus occisus ab Evandro', 'the place where Argus was buried upon being killed by Evander'.[47]

The lexical and prosodic difficulties of *Argiletum* notwithstanding, a few glossators deal directly with the main point of Martianus' text, namely the proper inflection of *Argiletum* and the placement of all three accent signs to convey it. The text of one such gloss appears as Martianus Gloss V, taken from Paris, BNF lat. 8669.[48]

MARTIANUS GLOSS V. Paris, BNF lat. 8669, fol. 25v

Sciendum etiam uni vocabulo accidere omnes tres accentus posse, ut est àrgílœ̂tum.

Its author has added the accent signs over *Argiloetum* – incorrectly, as it turns out. Since the penultimate is long, with a circumflex accent, the antepenultimate should receive a grave; the first syllable, long by position, should then receive an acute. As one can see, that is not the case here. But at least he tried!

Yet another glossator takes a different route in order to show that each of the syllables in *Argiletum* can carry an accent. Plate 8.3 shows the manuscript Paris, BNF lat. 14754, a late eleventh- or early twelfth-century source from northern France.[49] At the beginning of section 273 the glossator adds

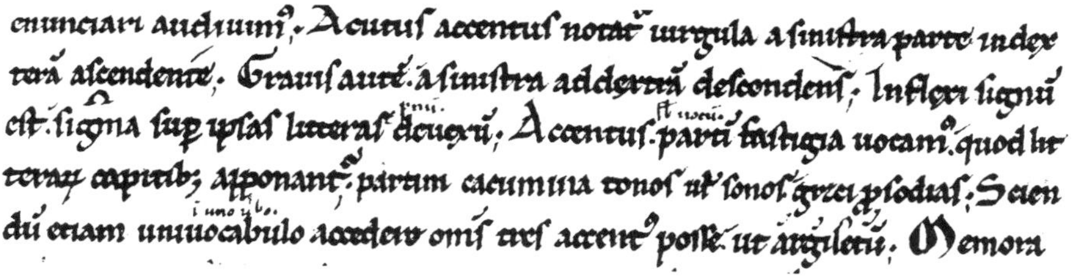

Pl. 8.3 Description of graphic signs for notating prosodic accents in Martianus Capella (Paris, BNF lat. 14754, fol. 121)

the graphic signs for the accents – the *notae* – just as we have seen them in several other sources. Rather than placing these accent signs over *Argiletum*, however, he illustrates the inflection of the word by writing neumes over the syllables that do not already carry an accent! (The circumflex seems to be in the original hand.) Granted, all the neumes are *pedes*, and thus represent acute accents, but the glossator seems to have been interested in showing that there can be an accent on every syllable, a reasonably logical illustration of Martianus' statement.

Whatever his motivation, and regardless of his knowledge of the rules of prosody, the important fact for us is that this glossator clearly saw the *notae* for prosodic accents and the '*notae* that are called neumes' as directly analogous to each other. We should not be surprised that neither he nor the person responsible for Gloss V could place the accents correctly. After all, graphic signs for prosodic accents as a component of actual linguistic usage had long since disappeared in Latin – if indeed they had ever been used at all. That meant that those very signs, and a fully developed theory to explain their use, were available to the Carolingians as a basis for the graphic representation of the inflected speech they knew as plainchant.[50] In the words of the Vatican anonymous: 'De accentibus toni oritur nota quae dicitur neuma.' By the late eleventh or twelfth century, the date of Paris 14754, the place of the graphic signs for the prosodic accents could be taken by the graphic signs from the notational system that they had helped to spawn – the neumes. In this case, music and its sister discipline of grammar were not only mutually influential, but mutually beneficial. And all of us have reaped the reward.

Notes

1 Charles Atkinson, '*De accentibus toni oritur nota quae dicitur neuma:* Prosodic Accents, the Accent Theory, and the Paleofrankish Script', in Graeme M. Boone (ed.), *Essays on Medieval Music in Honor of David G. Hughes* (Cambridge, Mass.: Harvard University Press, 1995), 17–42.

2 Ibid., esp. 35–42. I should mention that similar conclusions had been reached and expounded by Mathias Bielitz in his book *Die Neumen in Otfrids Evangelien-Harmonie* (Heidelberg: Universitätsbibliothek Heidelberg, 1989), a work not available to me in the period 1988–90 when I was conducting research for '*De*

accentibus toni'. In *Die Neumen*, as well as in his earlier *Musik und Grammatik* (Munich: Musikverlag Katzbichler, 1977), Bielitz calls for fundamental and thorough study of the manuscript sources themselves. The present article is, I hope, at least a modest answer to this call. See also Bielitz, *Zum Bezeichneten der Neumen, insbesondere der Liqueszenz* (Neckargemünd, Germany: Männeles Verlag, 1998).

3 For example, Leo Treitler has stated unequivocally that 'Carolingian notation could not possibly have been derived from the accents'; Leo Treitler, 'Reading and Singing: On the Genesis of Occidental Music-Writing', *EMH* 4 (1984), 135–208 at 184. Kenneth Levy listed prosodic accents as but one of several earlier explanations that he then dismissed in favor of his 'positional-graphic' theory of neumatic origins; Kenneth Levy, 'On the Origin of Neumes', *EMH* 7 (1987), 59–90; repr. in Levy, *Gregorian Chant and the Carolingians* (Princeton: Princeton University Press, 1998), 109–40.

4 One of the clearest descriptions is that given by Peter Bohn, 'Das liturgische Rezitativ und dessen Bezeichnung in den liturgischen Büchern des Mittelalters', *Monatshefte für Musikgeschichte*, 19 (1887), 29–36, translated and discussed in Treitler, 'Reading and Singing', 181 ff.

5 The principal sources for this article are ninth- and tenth-century glossed manuscripts for the *Ars maior* of Donatus and *De nuptiis Philologiae et Mercurii* of Martianus Capella. The manuscript sources for Donatus are listed and described in Louis Holtz, *Donat et la tradition de l'enseignement grammatical* (Paris: Centre National de la Recherche Scientifique, 1981), 354–423. Those for Martianus Capella can be found in Claudio Leonardi, 'I codici di Marziano Capella', *Aevum*, 33 (1959), 443–89; 34 (1960), 1–99, 411–524. I have also consulted a number of early manuscripts of the *Etymologiae* of Isidore of Seville (St. Gall, Stiftsbibl. 231, 237; Bern, Burgerbibl. 36 and 101; Munich, BSB clm 6250 and 6275; Leiden, Bibl. Rijksuniv., F.74, F.82 and F.122; Paris, BNF lat. 7583–85, 7670 and 7671; Reims, BM 426), but found these manuscripts to be much less rich in glosses than those for Donatus and Martianus. I should hereby like to express my deepest appreciation to the librarians in the holding institutions of the above-named sources, as well as those in the Bodleian Library, Oxford, the Badische Landesbibliothek, Karlsruhe, and the Bibliothèques municipales of the cities of Besançon and Orléans, for their generous assistance.

6 This view is presented most succinctly by W. Sidney Allen in his *Vox Latina: A Guide to the Pronunciation of Classical Latin* (2nd edn, Cambridge: Cambridge University Press, 1978), 83: 'There is little disagreement that the prehistoric accent of Latin was a stress accent, and that this fell on the first syllable of the word.' See also Allen's *Accent and Rhythm: Prosodic Features of Latin and Greek. A Study in Theory and Reconstruction* (Cambridge: Cambridge University Press, 1973), 151 ff. According to Guy Serbat, *Les Structures du latin: le système de la langue classique* (Paris: A. & J. Picard, 1975), 41: 'Ce qui est sûr, c'est qu'au IVe siècle p.C. l'accent latin était (ou était devenu) un accent d'intensité, comme le prouvent plusieurs témoignages concordants.' For an account of earlier scholarship on this topic see Wallace Martin Lindsay, *The Latin Language: An Historical Account of Latin Sounds, Stems, and Flexions* (Oxford: Clarendon Press, 1894), 148–217.

7 Lindsay, *The Latin Language*, 150. Lindsay's example of reduction of the unaccented vowel is *ábigo*, as compared with the Greek ἀπάγω; examples of syncope or suppression of syllables following the accent are, e.g., *objúrgo* from *objúrigo*, *cáldus* from *cálidus*.

8 Cf. Marius Servius Honoratus, *Commentarius in Artem Donati*, ed. H. Keil, *Grammatici Latini* (Leipzig: Teubner, 1868; repr. 1961), iv, 426; and Pompeius,

Commentum Artis Donati, ibid., v, 127. The collected statements of the Roman grammarians on accent may be found in Fritz Schoell, 'De accentu linguae Latinae', *Acta Societatis Philologiae Lipsiensis,* 6 (Leipzig: Teubner, 1876).

9 Cf. Allen, *Vox Latina*, 84.

10 Cf. Bielitz, *Die Neumen*, 83–99. In discussing differences between the treatment of the prosodic accents in the Latin West and in Byzantium following the Theodosian reform (fifth century), Bielitz states: 'Im Gegensatz dazu [i.e., to the Byzantine usage], übernahm der Westen das geschlossene, und vom praktisch-grammatischem Gebrauch kaum berührte System der antiken grammatischen Akzente. Im Westen war keine Reform der Akzente notwendig, da man sie für die lateinische Sprache sowieso nicht brauchte; d. h. sie wurden als System tradiert aber nicht als angewendetes, notwendiges Zeichensystem' (p. 83).

11 Allen, *Vox Latina*, 84.

12 I cannot pretend to have examined carefully each of the plates of the 1,811 manuscripts described in E. A. Lowe's *Codices Latini antiquiores: A Palaeographical Guide to Latin Manuscripts Prior to the Ninth Century*, 12 vols (Oxford: Clarendon Press, 1934–66), but the negative results of my cursory search would serve to confirm Sir Edward Maunde Thompson's statement that 'Accents were seldom used by Latin scribes' (*An Introduction to Greek and Latin Paleography* [Oxford: Clarendon Press, 1912], 64). There is an abundance of evidence for stress accents in written Latin texts, as Leonard Boyle pointed out in a plenary address for the Kalamazoo Congress on Medieval Studies in 1998. Father Boyle talked about the 'scoring' of manuscripts for reading aloud, that is, the indication of the accented syllables in words in which the accent might not fall naturally. He said that the graphic indication of accent is usually a small apostrophe or tick, and never a sign that could be construed as an acute, grave or circumflex accent. For a treatment of stress accent in a work from the eleventh century, see Magister Siguinis, *Ars lectoria*, ed. C. H. Kneepkens and H. F. Reijnders (Leiden: E. J. Brill, 1979).

13 On this see Franz Brunhölzl, 'Der Bildungsauftrag der Hofschule', in *Karl der Große: Lebenswerk und Nachleben*, ii: *Das geistige Leben*, ed. Bernhard Bischoff (Düsseldorf: Schwann, 1965), 28–41; and M. L. W. Laistner, *Thought and Letters in Western Europe, A.D. 500 to 900* (Ithaca: Cornell University Press, 1931; repr. 1966), 192–9.

14 Brunhölzl, 'Der Bildungsauftrag', 30. In a letter to Charlemagne from late 796 or early 797 (Alc. epist. 121 in *MGH,* Epist. Kar. Aevi , iv, 176–7, ll. 32 ff.), Alcuin states: 'Ego vero Flaccus vester secundum exhortationem et bonam voluntatem vestram aliis per tecta sancti Martini sanctarum mella scripturarum ministrare satago; alios vetere antiquarum disciplinarum mero inaebriare studeo; alios grammaticae subtilitatis enutrire pomis incipiam; . . .'. In another letter an unknown bishop (Arno?) tells Alcuin that he should oversee instruction, and names grammar, reading and study of the Bible as subjects (Alc. epist. 161; ibid., 260, ll. 13 ff.). In Brunhölzl's view, such witnesses tell us that Alcuin's poem 26 also depicts the court school itself.

15 Brunhölzl, 'Der Bildungsauftrag', 33–44. The preface to Alcuin's treatise on grammar is the *Disputatio de vera philosophia.* For its text, see *PL* 101, cols. 849–54. In the *Disputatio*, Alcuin is asked by his students to explain the stages leading up to philosophy. Alcuin responds by quoting the Bible: 'Wisdom hath builded her house, she hath hewn out her seven pillars' (Prov. 9: 1). The seven pillars are to be understood not just as the seven Gifts of the Holy Spirit, but also as the seven liberal arts. Cf. *PL* 101, cols. 853–4. On Alcuin as a teacher, see Eleanor Duckett, *Alcuin, Friend of Charlemagne: His World and his Work* (Hamden, Conn.: Archon Books, (1965), 109–17.

16 The texts in question here are the Pater noster, the Credo, and the Psalms. Cf. Bernhard Bischoff, 'Elementarunterricht und Probationes Pennae in der ersten Hälfte des Mittelalters', in Leslie Weber Jones (ed.), *Classical and Medieval Studies in Honor of Edward Kennard Rand* (New York: L. W. Jones, 1938), 9–20, the expanded form of this article in Bischoff, *Mittelalterliche Studien*, i (Stuttgart: Hiersemann, 1966), 74–87, and Brunhölzl, 'Der Bildungsauftrag', 39.

17 Cf. Pierre Riché, *Ecoles et enseignement dans le Haut Moyen Age: fin du ve siècle–milieu du XIe siècle* (Paris: Picard, 1989), 111–12; Franz Brunhölzl, *Geschichte der lateinischen Literatur des Mittelalters*, i: *Von Cassiodorus zum Ausklang der karolingischen Erneuerung* (Munich: Fink, 1975), 246–7. Brunhölzl characterizes grammar as the 'Grundlage aller Wissenschaften', and continues (247): 'Es ist dabei von sekundärer Bedeutung, daß man in der Praxis von den artes liberales zunächst fast nur die Fächer des Triviums – Grammatik, Dialektik, Rhetorik – pflegte, unter denen wiederum die Grammatik den weitaus größten Raum einnahm, während die Einbeziehung der rechnenden Disziplinen des Quadriviums – Arithmetik, Geometrie, Musik und Astronomie – in nennenswertem Umfang erst etwa seit der Mitte des 9. Jahrhunderts und auch da allmählich und an den verschieden Schulen in sehr verschiedenem Maße erfolgte.'

18 Cf. Alcuin, *Grammatica*, *PL* 101, cols. 854–902. Donatus is cited early in the treatise (855C: 'Ut reor, in Donato legimus . . .') and several times subsequently. Cf. Brunhölzl, 'Der Bildungsauftrag', 39. For listings of Donatus in ninth-century library catalogues, see Paul Lehmann, *Mittelalterliche Bibliothekskataloge Deutschlands und der Schweiz*, i (Munich: Beck, 1918), in particular the catalogs from St. Gall and Reichenau. For a listing of the most important extant manuscripts, as well as a discussion of medieval editions of and commentaries upon Donatus, see Holtz, *Donat*, 354–421 (manuscripts) and 438–41 (Carolingian editions and commentaries).

19 On this point as it pertains to instruction in music, see Michel Huglo, 'Le Développement du vocabulaire de l'*Ars musica* à l'époque carolingienne', *Latomus*, 34 (1975), 131–51.

20 Donatus, *Ars maior*, I.5, in Holtz, *Donat*, 609.

21 This connection is established most directly via the word *tonos*, in Latin the accusative plural of *tonus* (Gr. τόνος). As Scott Fisher has shown in '*Tonos* and its Relatives: A Word Study' (Ph.D. diss., Ohio State University, 1989), the term *tonus* in its early history has multiple meanings, not only in the field of music, but also in the fields of hunting, mechanics and furniture-building, to name only a few. By about 300 BC, however, it is firmly in place as a technical term in the vocabularies of both music and philosophy (p. 1). Fisher goes on to point out that 'while τόνος takes on a variety of meanings over time, the word early on finds its way into contexts having to do with music and never loses that musical connection' (p. 2). As we shall see below, the terms *accentus* and *tenores* in the first sentence of Donatus, I.5, also have strong musical connections. Cf. 'Accentus', *Lexicon musicum Latinum medii aevi*, ed. Michael Bernhard (Munich: Verlag der Bayerischen Akademie der Wissenschaften, 1992–), ii, cols. 20–23; and Dagmar Hoffmann-Axthelm, 'Tenor', *Handwörterbuch der musikalischen Terminologie*, ed. H. H. Eggebrecht (Stuttgart: Franz Steiner Verlag, 1973).

22 M. Fabius Quintilianus, *Institutionis oratoriae libri XII*, ed. L. Radermacher (Leipzig: Teubner, 1965), 1. 5. 31. On the Greek usage, see, for example, Dionysius Thrax, *Ars grammatica*, ch. 3: Περὶ τόνου. Τόνος ἐστὶν ἀπήχησις φωνῆς ἐναρμονίου, ἢ κατὰ ἀνάτασιν ἐν τῇ ὀξείᾳ, ἢ κατὰ ὁμαλισμὸν ἐν τῇ βαρείᾳ, ἢ κατὰ περίκλασιν ἐν τῇ περισπωμένῃ ('On *tonos*. *Tonos* is the sounding of the harmonious voice, via ascent in the *oxeia*, via leveling in the *bareia*, and via arching

['twisting around'] in the *perispomene*'). Dionysius Thrax, *Ars grammatica*, ed. Gustav Uhlig (Leipzig: Teubner, 1883), 6–7.

23 Allen, *Vox Latina*, 84. See below, n. 33.

24 'Acutus cum in Graecis dictionibus tria loca teneat, ultimum, paenultimum et antepaenultimum, apud Latinos paenultimum et antepaenultimum tenet, ultimum numquam' (The acute, although it may hold three positions in Greek words – ultimate, penultimate, and antepenultimate – among the Latins holds the penultimate and antepenultimate, never the ultimate).

25 'Gravis poni in eadem dictione vel cum acuto vel cum circumflexo potest, et hoc illi non est comune cum ceteris' (A grave accent can be placed in the same word with either an acute or a circumflex, and this is [a trait] not shared between it and the others).

26 'In trisyllabis et tetrasyllabis . . . ut Catullus, Metellus'.

27 Note that Donatus does not describe accents in terms of pitch inflection, restricting himself instead to the graphic signs representing such inflection. As we shall see below (Texts II and III), one of the authors who does describe accents in terms of both vocal inflection and graphic representation is Martianus Capella.

28 Description in Holtz, *Donat*, 380–82.

29 Description ibid., 395–6.

30 Murethach (ca. 825–30) likewise glosses *tonus* with *tonando*, but then relates this to stress accent: 'Toni igitur dicuntur a tonando, id est sonando, eo quod illa syllaba, quae accentu regitur, plus sonet in dictione'; *Murethach [Muridac]: In Donati Artem maiorem*, ed. Louis Holtz (Turnhout: Brepols, 1977), 37. Virtually the same gloss appears in Sedulius Scottus, *In Donati Artem maiorem*, ed. Bengt Löfstedt (Turnhout: Brepols, 1977), 40, and in the Lorsch commentary on Donatus (*Ars Laureshamensis: Expositio in Donatum maiorem*, ed. Bengt Löfstedt [Turnhout: Brepols, 1977], 177].

31 Cf. the earlier commentary by Murethach (*In Donati Artem maiorem*, 37) and that from Lorsch (*Ars Laureshamensis,* 178), both of which have the same phrase: 'Tenores denique dicuntur, eo quod naturalem sonum in syllabis seruent.'

32 Description in Holtz, *Donat,* 371–4.

33 Donatus Gloss IV derives the word *accentus* itself from the Greek προσῳδία (*Accentus est, qui grece prosodia dicitur. accentus quasi acantus*). A similar connection is made by Sedulius Scottus (*In Donati Artem maiorem,* 40: 'Dictus autem accentus quasi adcantus, quod sit "iuxta cantum"; est enim compositum ex ad et cantus, quod Grece sonat prosodia: πρός "ad", ᾠδή "cantus"') and the Lorsch commentator (*Ars Laureshamensis,* 177: 'Accentus autem qui Grece prosodias dicitur quasi adcantus, eo quod ex Greco nomen accepit. Nam Grece πρός Latine ad, oden Grece Latine cantus dicitur'). The connection of accent with *prosodia* is made in Martianus Capella (*De nuptiis Philologiae et Mercurii*, III, ed. Adolph Dick [1925; repr. Leipzig: Teubner, 1978], 98: 'nunc de fastigio uideamus, qui locus apud Graecos περὶ προσῳδιῶν appellatur'), and also in Servius (*Commentarius in Artem Donati*, ed. Keil, *Grammatici Latini*, iv, 426: 'Accentus dictus est quasi adcantus secundum Graecos, qui prosodian vocant. nam apud Graecos πρός dicitur ad, cantus vero ᾠδή vocatur'), and also Sergius (*Explanationes Artis Donati*, ed. Keil, *Grammatici Latini*, iv, 482: 'dictus autem accentus est quasi adcantus iuxta Graeci nominis interpretationem, quod prosodia dicitur Latine adcantus'). The wording in Donatus Gloss IV, however, is much closer to that in Isidore of Seville's *Etymologiae*: 'Accentus, qui Graece prosodia dicitur [ex Graeco nomen accepit]. Nam Graece πρός Latine "ad", ᾠδή Graece, Latine

"cantus" est' (*Etymologiarum sive Originum Libri XX*, ed. Wallace Martin Lindsay [Oxford: Clarendon Press, 1911], 1. 18. 1).

34 The phrase 'quasi ad cantus' also appears in Donatus Gloss II, discussed above, there not as a gloss on *accentus*, but on *tonus*.

35 Description in Holtz, *Donat,* 404–5.

36 Martianus Capella, *De nuptiis Philologiae et Mercurii*, Bk. III, sec. 268–9, ed. James Willis (Leipzig: Teubner, 1983), 71, 4 ff.

37 On this passage see Bielitz, *Die Neumen,* 100–103.

38 Description in Leonardi, 'I Codici di Marziano Capella', *Aevum*, 34 (1960), 62–3.

39 I should like to thank Leofranc Holford-Strevens for sharing with me his reading of this passage.

40 Description in Leonardi, 'I Codici', 61–2.

41 Description ibid., 67–8.

42 On Martin of Laon, see Jean G. Préaux, 'Le Commentaire de Martin de Laon sur l'œuvre de Martianus Capella', *Latomus*, 12 (1953), 437–59; Cora Lutz, 'Martianus Capella: 1. Martinus Laudunensis', in *CTC*, ii, 370–71; and J. Contreni, in Addenda to the *CTC*, iii, 451–2. Contreni expresses strong reservations as to the putative authorship of Martin, hence the question mark following Martin's name in the text here.

43 Martianus Capella, *De nuptiis Philologiae et Mercurii*, Bk. III, sec. 273, ed. Willis, 74, 9–13.

44 Given the clarity of the description, inserting the *notae* themselves may have been considered superfluous. It is interesting that Martianus does provide descriptions of the vocal inflections represented by the *notae*, descriptions that Donatus had not provided – presumably because the inflections and the signs representing them were considered to be inextricably linked together. On these relationships and their implications for the rise of musical notation see Marie-Elisabeth Duchez, 'Description grammaticale et description arithmétique des phénomènes musicaux: le tournant du IXe siècle', in *Sprache und Erkenntnis im Mittelalter: Akten des VI. Internationalen Kongresses für mittelalterliche Philosophie (Bonn, 1977)* (Berlin and New York: Walter De Gruyter, 1981), 561–79, esp. 563–76; ead., 'Des neumes à la portée: élaboration et organisation rationnelles de la discontinuité musicale et de sa représentation graphique, de la formule mélodique à l'échelle monocordale', *Revue de musique des universités canadiennes*, 4 (1983), 22–65, esp. 25–30; and Bielitz, *Die Neumen*, *passim*.

45 On these manuscripts see *Martianus Capella*, ed. Dick and ed. Willis.

46 From Text III: 'sciendum etiam uni vocabulo accidere omnes tres accentus posse, ut est Argiletum'.

47 Paris, BNF lat. 8674, fol. 37^{v}: 'Argiloetum, id est locus ubi sepultus est Argus occisus ab Evandro, volens abstrahere regnum eius.' This is from Lutz's 'B' family of manuscripts containing Remigius' commentary; hence it does not appear in her edition, *Remigii Autissiodorensis Commentum in Martianum Capellam* (Leiden: E. J. Brill, 1962). The word 'Argiletum' and the source of Remigius' gloss is Virgil's *Aeneid*, viii, ll. 345–6: 'nec non et sacri monstrat nemus Argileti // testaturque locum et letum docet hospitis Argi' ('he [Evander] shows the wood of sacred Argiletum, and calls the place to witness and tells of the death of Argus, his guest'). According to P. J. Fordyce, *P. Vergili Maronis Aeneidos libri VI–VIII with a Commentary* (Oxford: Oxford University Press for the University of Glasgow, 1977), 243, 'the Argiletum lay in the low ground south of the Quirinal: in historical times it was a trading quarter, where Cicero owned shops (Att. xii. 32. 3) and Martial's bookseller had his premises (i. 3. I). The name clearly meant "clay-pits" (from *argilla*: a parallel formation to *arboretum*, *quercetum*, *dumetum*,

but popular etymology interpreted it as *Argi-letum* and invented an *aition* for it in the story of an Argus who was Evander's guest and was killed by Evander's people for seeking to dethrone his host. Varro, *De lingua Latina*, v. 157, impartially offers both the true explanation and the invention.' The line in Varro is: 'Argiletum sunt qui scripserunt ab Argo La(ri)saeo, quod is huc venerit ibique sit sepultus, alii ab argilla, quod ibi id genus terrae sit' ('The Argiletum, according to some writers, was named from Argus of Larisa, because he came to this place and was buried there; according to others, from the argilla 'clay', because this kind of earth is found at this place'). Varro, *On the Latin Language*, trans. Roland G. Kent (Cambridge, Mass.: Harvard University Press, 1938), 148–9.

48 Description in Leonardi, 'I Codici', 436–7.

49 Description ibid., 444–5.

50 Cf. Bielitz, *Die Neumen*, p. xiv, and 211 n. 8; and the following: 'Die neue, "musikalische" Verwendung der Prosodie- bzw. Akzent-Zeichen, die ja aus der antiken-griechischen Tradition stammten, im Westen, zu einer Zeit, in der Griechisch-Kenntnisse etwa so verbreitet waren wie heute, war möglich, weil die lateinischen Grammatiker das System in seiner Gesamtheit weitergegeben haben, auch wenn es für die eigene Sprache nicht ganz passen konnte und auch in seiner Subtilität unnötig war' (79–80). See also the articles by Duchez cited in n. 44 above. That the *notae* for prosodic accents were not in themselves sufficient for the needs of notating the subtleties of plainchant is suggested by the fact that even the earliest notated musical sources contain signs for liquescence that are not among the *notae* for the prosodic accents. On this see A. Haug, 'Zur Interpretation der Liqueszenzneumen', *AfMw* 50 (1993), 85–100, esp. 99–100 (cf. Bielitz, *Zum Bezeichneten der Neumen*). As Haug points out, however, the system of musical liquescence is based on the *litterae semivocales*, whose treatment is part of virtually every work on grammar, including those by Donatus and Martianus Capella.

Chapter 9

Concerning a Chronology for Chant

László Dobszay

The final category of evidence is the music itself.

(James McKinnon)

About a hundred years ago half-legendary notions prevailed concerning the age and development of Gregorian chant, based on historical and ecclesiastical presuppositions no longer considered tenable. In recent decades, as a reaction to the earlier approach, a kind of agnosticism has become dominant with regard to the unwritten period of chant history. It is as if, at the point of emergence of musical notation, a veil had been lowered, one no mortal eye is able to see behind, obscuring the historical process and preventing insight into earlier times. There is no continuity between 'before' and 'after' this point or, if there is, there are no means at our disposal to explore this continuity.

The question was made the focus of attention again by Leo Treitler and Helmut Hucke,[1] whose theses met with controversy.[2] Though excellent scholars like James McKinnon have achieved much in the field of early chant history and chronology,[3] Gregorian chant is still frequently considered as something born *with* (the arrival of) and *in* (the form of) notation, while the period before notation is, at least from a heuristic point of view, like a prehistoric era.

However, this grapholatria itself seems illogical. As is well known, early music notation was capable of recording the gestures of music and the number of notes, but not specific pitches. In spite of this convention, a decisive role is attributed to the invention of notation in the emergence of Gregorian music. But how could notation produce, stabilize and preserve this vast repertory if it did not indicate pitch, that most essential element of music, with exactness? Furthermore, if the essence of music (the notes themselves) were retained in memory so perfectly in the period of adiastematic notation, if the melodies written in neumes and later on the staff 'are essentially the same' and, consequently, if the melodies 'existed in their mature form by about 900 at the latest', as McKinnon claims,[4] why then should we be distrustful of the power of memory during the centuries *before* notation? Agnosticism combined with grapholatria would be consistent only if people had sung *different* melodies from the *same* signs of mechanically copied codices, and if the chant repertory had been born at the moment of the introduction of the staff.

* * *

Ethnomusicological experience gained in the course of producing or studying thousands of transcriptions contributes to a better understanding of the relationship between oral and written forms of music and of the historical meaning of the material transcribed.

The first thing that strikes us on examining folk song transcriptions is the conflict between perfect musical action and imperfect musical notation. Some scholars were satisfied with recording the essential features of the melodies by means of the ordinary, or at best slightly refined, notational devices in use at the time they made their transcriptions. Others have created sophisticated sets of signs almost akin to photographic reproductions of the tiniest details of performance. By doing so they meant to immortalize the vanishing perfection of a field performance. Musicians like Bartók,[5] Rajeczky or Lajtha[6] made complex transcriptions that appear analogous to the nuance-rich Laon or St. Gall manuscripts, while Kodály's recordings, which focused on the essence of the music,[7] seem in contrast more like sources containing the notational style of central France.[8]

It would be foolish to suppose that shades of melody or performance represented by Bartók's transcriptions were repeated in exactly the same manner in subsequent performances by the same singer, by other singers or by singers of other villages.[9] The *essence* of a melody may be the same in different transcriptions; the manner of performance, however, shows greater similarity in specimens originating from a closely limited area and proves to be less similar in more widely separated regions. Within the repertory one can observe a wide range of stability and variability. There are tunes that are identical almost note-for-note in communities living 300–400 miles apart; other tunes are stable only in their essential notes.[10] Other tune families allow the performer great freedom but preserve the identity of the music through generative rules.[11] The style, genre, function and social role of a given music determine the place it occupies on this scale of musical stability.

The variability of oral transmission raises doubts concerning the *historical meaning* of written tunes. Can such material have a 'history'? Is there anything permanent in the sequence of individual performances? Can we draw a conclusion from these records and suppose the existence of an absolute or relative chronology? At any rate, upon comparing sixteenth- or seventeenth-century documents with twentieth-century field recordings,[12] an amazing reliability of memory has been proved not only in instances when the written documents supported living memory but also when the old notation cannot have had any influence on later musical practice. Similarly, in the folk music material of ethnic groups living together at some time in history but separated centuries ago, essentially identical tunes and types have been found.[13] These and other experiences led Kodály to declare that variation helps rather than hinders memory and that the common features – the virtual structure behind the variants – represent what is historically permanent in music.[14] This means that memory is capable of preserving the remnants of past historical periods and layers, not as does a magnetic tape, yet revealing, in some sense, more exactly all the potentials of a type of music.

One aim – or, at least, outcome – of the twentieth-century transcriptions was to canonize individual variants: to isolate one single form from the colorful variety of performances and disseminate it among schools, teachers and composers. As a result, one representative item of a type became generally known as the type itself – both to the detriment and the benefit of musical practice. The same happened to chant: a style that had existed earlier in many variants was reduced[15] to a set of more or less fixed melodies, which implied once again a loss of wealth but laid the common basis for the development of European music.

Naturally there are great differences between the living conditions of folk music and liturgical chant.[16] The repertory of liturgical chant is much larger and more complex. Its performance required regulated practice; it was cultivated by institutions and permanent bodies. Its sacred character and canonical texts created a special environment for the music as well. Nevertheless, without the experiences accumulated in the study of living oral cultures one cannot fully understand the living conditions and historical dimensions of a repertory where notation was of secondary character in relation to sound production.[17]

* * *

Not only the nature of early notation but the material itself gives rise to a train of thought. The early manuscripts listed by Dom Hesbert in the *Corpus antiphonalium officii* recorded a repertory that is not rudimentary but complex, elaborated and stylistically articulated. If Gregorian chant had emerged in notation, or shortly before being notated, one could expect early manuscripts to contain much more homogeneous musical material. The composition of *historiae* represents the style of the age in which the first notations originated. Even if we disregard this most 'modern' layer of the early codices, the rest remains heterogeneous. The same people cannot have produced pieces of such different styles, at the same age, simultaneously. Let us add that the musically varying items frequently belong to different liturgical groups as well. Naturally, the differences may sometimes stem from geographical circumstances or matters of genre, but the essential differences must in all probability be attributed to *chronological* factors.[18] Gregorian chant as notated in the early manuscripts shows the same image as a profile of archeological excavations that illustrates the vestiges of different ages.

In oral cultures music material inherited from the past forms not only part of everyday practice but inspires adaptations as well.[19] Subtle changes of taste or outside data can help distinguish models from copies. This chronological approach is valid in one direction only. The image of excavation implies that while motifs of Roman antiquity were imitated in the Middle Ages, the possibility of imitating Gothic motifs in Roman antiquity is excluded. Antiquity does not exist *less* because it was imitated later. Chronological uncertainty may affect our perception of the age of *individual* pieces; the *type* itself may have originated in earlier times, while admitting later changes in its elements.

The case of Office antiphons is a good example of chronological layers. We tried to classify the full antiphon repertory of the Hungarian manuscripts[20] based on the achievements of Gevaert,[21] Frere[22] and Nowacki,[23] and supported by our own ethnomusicological experiences. The 8th-mode antiphons, the largest and most articulated unit, are suitable for representing the entire corpus. Table 9.1 compares types and stylistic groups with their liturgical functions. The assignments cannot be quite exact, but the basic tendencies are manifest. The meaning of the abbreviations in the table is as follows:

( )	unclear musical forms
*	antiphons to the Great Canticles (distinguished if necessary)
Adv	Advent
Ann	per annum
BMV	(officium, festum) Beatae Mariae Virginis
ConsEccl	Consecratio Ecclesiae
Corp	Corpus Christi
CS	Commune Sanctorum
D	Sunday
D70, etc.	Dominica Septuagesima
DedEccl	Dedicatio Ecclesiae
Fer	feriae
Fest	Office of the (old) great feasts: Nat (Nativitas), Ep (Epiphania), Pasc (Pascha), Pent (Pentecostes)
HMaj	Hebdomada major
InvSteph	Inventio Stephani
MMagd	Maria Magdalena
Oct, iOct	Octava, infra Octavam
OffDef	Officium Defunctorum
OS	Festum Omnium Sanctorum
psalmodic	short antiphons with text taken from the Psalms (from per annum Psalter or for feasts)
Qu	Quadragesima
Sanct	Sanctorale. The Sanctorale is divided in two chronological groups (I–II); pieces of the same day are sometimes assigned differently if they belong to different liturgical and musical layers. The abbreviation of the saints' names can be easily solved.
TP	Tempus Paschale
Trin	Dominica Trinitatis
VTcantica	Old Testament canticles of Lauds

As can be seen, there is a certain kind of parallelism, even if no full concordance, between the two parameters. No safe chronological conclusions can be drawn; however, what we know about the development of the Roman liturgy does not exclude the possibility of a chronological hypothesis referring to blocks rather than individual pieces. For dating individual items historical data (mostly missing) would be needed.

Table 9.1 Mode 8 antiphons by type and stylistic group

MMMA 5 Type/Subtype Numbers	*Number of cases and % in common with the Old Roman repertory*	*Liturgical function*
A/1 8001–9	9 (55%)	9 psalmodic (100%) (8 Ann, 1 QuD)
A/2 8010–19	10 (70%)	10 psalmodic (100%) (6 Ann, 1 D60, 1 QuD, 1 HMaj, 1 CS)
A/3 8020–39	20 (75%)	14 psalmodic (65%) (1 Ann, 6 HMaj, 3 Fest, 3 CS, 1 Laurent) +2 AdvFer (+ Innoc, Paul, Martin, OS: ad psalmos)
A/4 8040–55	16 (63%)	13 psalmodic (81%) (4 Ann, 4 Qu, 4 HMaj, 1 DedEccl) +1 Adv, 1 QuFer, 1 Asc
A/5 8056–79	24 (40%)	13 psalmodic (44%) (7 OffDef, 1 HMaj, 3 Adv, 1 contrafactum, 1 QuVT cantica) +1 QuFer + 2 OctNat, 2 OctPasc, 3 CS (+ Cecilia, Nicol, OS)
A/6 8080–104	25 (55%)	2 psalmodic (Ann, HMaj) 7 Qu, HMaj, +2 Adv 4 CS, JohBapt 7 ev 1 OctEp + OS, NatBMV
A Total **8001–104**	104 (59%)	61 psalmodic (59%) 14 Adv, QuFer 6 Fest (Nat, Asc, Ep) 7 ev 7 CS, JohBapt 9 alia
B Total **8105–32**	28 (63%)	13 psalmodic (46%) (3 Ann, 1 OffDef, 2 HMaj, 2 CS, 5 Fest) 2 QuFer +11 Fest (3 Nat, 7 Pasc, 1 Asc) (+2 MichAng)
C/1–2 8133–54	21 (62%)	19 psalmodic (90%) + QuFer, CS, Clemens
C/3–4 8155–81	27 (79%)	8 psalmodic (30%) (5 HMaj, 2 QuD, 1 CS) 7 Temp (4 AdvFer, 2 QuFer) 6 Temp (OctEp, Pasc)

Table 9.1 (continued)

MMMA 5 Type/Subtype Numbers	*Number of cases and % in common with the Old Roman repertory*	*Liturgical function*
C/5–6 8182–213	32 (56%)	1 HistSap 3 JohBapt, Sebast, Agatha +2 Martin, 1ExCrucis 2 psalmodic (Nat, HMaj) 5 Adv, QuFer 5 CS +1 Laurent 1 DedEccl, 1 Pasc, 2 iOctNat 6 ev (TP, D70–60) (3 QuFer, 3 CS, 2 ev, 2 Innoc)
D/1 8214–46	33 (32%)	8 Pasc 1 psalm* 1 Adv (ev), 2 Hist 12 Sanct I (Laurent, Sebast, Andr, Agnes, Cecilia, Paul, Lucia) 6 Sanct II (Martin, Brict, Innoc, MMagd) 3 CS
D/2 8247–92	46 (49%)	23 Sanct I (50%) (Agnes, Agatha, Paul, Sebast, Petr, Joh. et Paul, Cosmas, Cecilia, Andr, JohBapt, Laurent) 3 Sanct II (MichAng, OS) 7 CS 8 ev (4 Ann, 2 Hist, 2 TP) 5 Adv, QuFer
D/1–2 (Total, 8214–92)	79 (40%)	8 Pasc 11 ev, Hist 35 Sanct I (44%) 9 Sanct II 10 CS (12.5%) 5 Adv, QuFer, 1 psalm
D/3–4 8293–352	60 (32%)	13 ev (Ann, Hist) 15 ev (Adv, Qu, Pasc) 17 Sanct I 9 Sanct II 4 CS (3 psalm)
E/1 8353–85	33 (29%)	3 ev, Hist 6 ev (QuD, Pasca, Pent) 1 QuD psalm 4 AdvFer 6 iOctNat et Ep

Table 9.1 (continued)

MMMA 5 Type/Subtype Numbers	*Number of cases and % in common with the Old Roman repertory*	*Liturgical function*
		1 CS 7 Sanct I (JohBapt, Paul, JohAp, Cecilia, Agatha, Lucia) 4 Sanct II (Nicol., August., Lucas, Annunt. BMV) 1 Pent* 1
E/2 8386–420	35 (25%)	6 ev, Hist 5 ev, TP 3 psalm (QuD, DedEccl) 2 Adv, QuFer 3 Fest (AdvD, Nat, Pent) 4 iOctNat et Ep 2 CS (5 Sanct I), (5 Sanct II)
F 8421–70	50 (24%)	4 psalm 9 TP 5 ev, Hist 5 Qu, Adv 5 TempNat, Ep 6 CS 18 Sanct I (JohBapt, Laurent, Clemens, Andr) 8 Sanct II
G 8471–514	44 (15%)	19 ev (43%) (Trin, Hist) 11 ev (25%) (TP, Adv, DedEccl) 4 iOctNat, et Ep 3 QuFer 4 Sanct I (Agnes*, Laurent*, Sebast*, BMV*) 1 Sanct II (Paul*) 2 CS*
H 8515–60	46 (0%)	Sanct II (56.5%) 6 psalm (D-laudes) 7 Temp (Trin, Corp) 2 Sanct I 2 CS 3 BMV (Nat)
I 8561–90	30 (0%)	30 Sanct II (100%)

* * *

The above hypothesis is supported by a comparison of the Gregorian, Old Roman and Ambrosian repertories.[24] The Carolingian, post-Carolingian, Ottonian and post-millennial styles of Gregorian chant are completely missing from the Old Roman and Ambrosian repertories. On the other hand, the basic Gregorian types are also available in these other two collections – apart from some interesting exceptions, and the number of correspondences is far greater in the case of *types* than of individual *pieces*. In my opinion, this relationship cannot be attributed to Gregorian influence on the other repertories; Gregorian imports are rather easy to recognize. As in linguistics, too close a similarity is the result of recent contacts rather than genetic relations.

The place of an item in the liturgy is of course not the *ultima ratio* in argumentation – all the less so, as the material may have been repeatedly reordered in the course of centuries, items may have been added to the Proper of a day, and others transferred to a different function. Moreover, it may well be that the chants (or, at least, some of them) existed originally in some neutral (e.g., numerical) order and only later received their precise place in the liturgical year. Let me remark in parenthesis that Jean Claire also used liturgical arguments for drawing chronological conclusions. They do not hold up, in my opinion, for the simple reason that they were linked to the introduction of the theory of the Octoechos, something that in reality happened much later than the supposed development of the liturgical year.[25] But this does not lessen the relevance of liturgical arguments.

Do literary documents confirm this analysis? In spite of my full acknowledgment of recent scholarship in this field, I must confess that I am rather disappointed about the citations of early writers contained in them. Their meaning is in most cases so obscure (or limited to the *argumenta ex silentio*) that the actual practice can hardly be reconstructed. The problem is well exemplified by the antiphon. One would expect the early authors to use the word 'antiphon' to mean: (1) the refrain of a psalm, (2) something performed by alternating choirs, (3) a piece the textual, musical and liturgical function of which should be the same as in the medieval antiphoners. Since their citations are not of this kind, one is tempted to deny straightaway the existence of the antiphon at an early age, or to suppose that behind the word lies something quite different from what we know later as an antiphon.

But should the existence of the refrains always be linked to psalmody performed by alternating choirs? Is it certain that the musical material of some antiphons did not exist earlier in *other* liturgical functions? Is it not possible that the word 'antiphon' was used without a precise and consistent meaning, in the same way as were the later terms 'sonata' and 'symphony'? The only informative witness to the early Roman Office is the Rule of Benedict, which adapted fifth-century urban usage to the living conditions of Benedictine monasticism. The Rule lists precisely the same genres that can be seen in the liturgical books of the later ninth century, and distinguishes clearly the two kinds of responsories from each other and from the antiphon. Furthermore, it testifies to the existence of the core repertory of the *proprium*, including as a matter of course the weekly psalmody, parts of the Temporale existing at the time, and the feasts of the old Roman saints – in other words, the parts that dominate certain groups in Table 9.1. One may doubt, of course, whether the antiphons used by St. Benedict's monks were identical with the pieces recorded in the early medieval antiphoners. Moreover, one may suppose that the term 'antiphon' in the Rule meant something different from medieval practice. What does 'antiphon' mean if Benedict's monks recited the psalms in solo performance?[26] While traditional scholarship saw the meaning of the early documents in light of the medieval state of affairs, we are now inclined to reject these presuppositions relentlessly and to make up for the missing points of the old narrative with hypotheses no better documented than the traditional ones. When the Rule uses the expression 'imponere' for the monks' rendering of a psalm or an antiphon in succession, it can imply either singing the psalm and antiphon solo or in chorus (only intoned by the soloist). The latter explanation is no more supported by evidence from the text itself than is the idea of a mere solo performance. But today all interpretations are acceptable except the traditional ones. There *were* undoubtedly changes in the course of time, yet when it comes to accepting equally possible or equally questionable interpretations, hypothesis should rather take the side of tradition, since early liturgies are characterized by mostly steady, continuous – hence traditional – practice.

The examination of antiphons raises another question. One wonders what the reason for the different behavior of the Office and Mass genres may be. The only exceptions are the inter-lectionary chants of the Mass. The Office items (together with the Gradual, the Tract and the Old-Latin Alleluia) show modal preferences while the rest of the Mass extends equally to all modes. The Office items (as well as the Gradual, the Tract and the Alleluia) emerged in extensive tune-families while the Introits, Offertories, and Communions are more or less individual works. As a result, the genres of the first group adopt relatively few melodic models, whereas those of the second group include many different melodies. Is there any plausible reason why the antiphons should exist in *types* while the Introits should not? Is there any explanation for such differences other than that the core repertories were produced under different living conditions at different historical periods?[27]

* * *

As a last example let me refer to the Alleluia. Alleluias are characterized, already in the earliest Gregorian manuscripts, by an abundance of text variants and heterogeneous musical features. When compared with the Old Roman Mass, a clear distinction within the genre can be seen.[28] On one side stand the descendants of the four Old Roman basic melodies; on the other are all the rest, that is, the stylistically very different items. In addition, the first group has musical correspondences in the Ambrosian[29] and in part in the Beneventan[30] repertories. Among the Gregorian–Old Roman parallels it is easy to isolate the small portion of Old Roman growth under Gregorian influence (e.g., *Dum complerentur*, *Gaudete justi*, *Beatus vir*, *Angelus Domini*,

Multipharie olim).[31] The two groups of the Gregorian repertory cannot possibly have originated in the same age. The earliest sources already contain *different* chronological layers; in other words, oral transmission was responsible for preserving a certain part of the old repertory for a new era. The old models could undoubtedly be adapted to new texts as well, and so the classifications 'old' and 'new' refer to the type and not to individual pieces, still less to the actual, note-to-note shape of the pieces.

* * *

From the foregoing I offer the following methodological considerations:

1. One should not resign oneself to the position that historical events before the age of notation are hidden from our view through impenetrable darkness. Even partial results are results.
2. Quotations from the patristic literature cannot be dispensed with,[32] but their evidence is less conclusive than one would expect. The actual practice behind the text can rarely be reconstructed and arguments from silence are often misleading.
3. These early literary documents are not enough for an absolute or relative chronology; we need to consider the testimony of the liturgy, morphology, the distribution of the material and the stylistic quality of the music. As James McKinnon stated: 'The final category of evidence is the music itself.'[33]
4. The best starting point for the interpretation of early data is the practice of later times. I suppose that this statement will provoke conflict, and as a basis for interpretation it could be refuted by weighty reasons and objections. But preferring twentieth-century interpretation to medieval practice need not make the former true.
5. The analysis of the *anni circulus* carried out so brilliantly in McKinnon's works provides important arguments. But it cannot be excluded that a certain part of the chant repertory existed at an early stage without a strict liturgical assignment.[34]
6. The analysis of the Mass Proper is not enough to support broad historical conclusions, all the less so since the cycles of the Mass and the Office probably originated in different chronological periods.
7. Chronological hypotheses should be adapted cautiously in considering individual items. On the other hand, individual pieces should be treated with utmost care when it comes to drawing general conclusions.
8. We may be tempted to say that music conceived in types corresponds better to the living conditions of oral transmission (particularly if the music is handed down in everyday practice). By contrast, the individual creation can better be understood in the context of institutionalized practice, conscious memorization and written record. The practice of the Eastern Churches corroborates McKinnon's statement, according to which memory was relied on much more in the early Middle Ages than in this century. It is difficult to understand why the force of oral trans-

mission could not extend to a period earlier than fifty or a hundred years before the recorded use of notation. If this power was strong enough to preserve something from Christmas in 720 to Christmas in 721, why should it have been insufficient (at least in principle) to retain something from Christmas in 420 to Christmas in 820?[35]

9. If we deny the force of long-term memory, there is only one consistent argument built exclusively on notation. Such an argument, given the shortcomings of the early neumatic notation, would compel one to place the starting date of Gregorian chant not in 830, but 1030, the time of Guido's innovation.
10. I do think that historical studies that strive to attain the exactness of the natural sciences should necessarily stop with factual limitations, or else they will prove to be a fiasco. Positivism and agnosticism are twin brothers. To be fruitful, chronological conjectures must be satisfied with indices, plausible views and approaches to be revised by colleagues and posterity. In short, in words taken from scholastic philosophy: with *intelligentia* instead of *ratio*.

Notes

1 Helmut Hucke, 'Toward a New Historical View of Gregorian Chant', *JAMS* 33 (1980), 437–67; id., 'Gregorianische Fragen', *Musikforschung*, 41 (1988), 304–30. Leo Treitler, 'Homer and Gregory: The Transmission of Epic Poetry and Plainchant', *MQ* 60 (1974), 333–72; id., 'Centonate Chant: Übles Flickwerk or E pluribus unus?', *JAMS* 28 (1975), 1–23; id., 'Oral, Written and Literate Process in the Transmission of Medieval Music', *Speculum*, 56 (1981), 202–11.

2 David G. Hughes, 'Evidence for the Traditional View of the Transmission of Gregorian Chant', *JAMS* 40 (1987), 377–404. Cf. Communications in *JAMS* 41 (1988), 566–75; Kenneth Levy, 'On Gregorian Orality', *JAMS* 44 (1990), 185–227. Cf. Communications in *JAMS* 41 (1988), 575–8 and 44 (1991), 524–5. Hendrik van der Werf, *The Emergence of Gregorian Chant. I–II* (Rochester, NY: [the author], 1983). Cf. Communications in *JAMS* 42 (1989), 432–4 and 44 (1991), 517–24.

3 See the following publications of James McKinnon: 'The Fourth-Century Origin of the Gradual', *EMH* 7 (1987), 91–106; 'The Patristic Jubilus and the Alleluia of the Roman Mass', in *Cantus Planus: Papers Read at the Third Meeting of the International Musicological Society Study Group, Tihany, Hungary, 1988*, ed. László Dobszay (Budapest: Hungarian Academy of Sciences Institute for Musicology, 1990), 61–70; idem, 'The Emergence of Gregorian Chant in the Carolingian Era', in id., ed. *Antiquity and the Middle Ages from Ancient Greece to the Fifteenth Century* (London: Macmillan, 1990), 88–119; 'The Roman Post-Pentecostal Communion Series', in *Cantus Planus: Papers Read at the Fourth Meeting of the International Musicological Society Study Group, Pécs, Hungary, 1990*, ed. László Dobszay (Budapest: Hungarian Academy of Sciences Institute for Musicology, 1992), 175–86; 'The Eighth-Century Frankish-Roman Cycle', *JAMS* 45 (1992), 179–227; 'Antoine Chavasse and the Dating of Early Chant', *PMM* 2 (1992), 123–47; 'Desert Monasticism and the Psalmodic Movement of the Fourth Century', *M&L* 75 (1994), 505–19; 'Properization: The Roman Mass', in *Cantus Planus: Papers Read at the Sixth Meeting of the International Musicological Society Study Group, Eger, Hungary, 1993*, ed. László Dobszay (Budapest:

Hungarian Academy of Sciences Institute for Musicology, 1994), 15–22. The summarizing masterwork of McKinnon, *The Advent Project: The Later-Seventh-Century Creation of the Roman Mass Proper* (Berkeley: University of California Press, 2000), was not yet accessible when I prepared this essay.

4 'The Emergence of Gregorian Chant', 94.

5 Cf. Béla Bartók, *Magyar Népdalok, Egyetemes Gyűjtemény* [Hungarian Folk Songs, a Comprehensive Collection], i, ed. Sándor Kovács and Ferenc Sebő (Budapest: Akadémiai Kiadó, 1991); cf. Benjamin Rajeczky and G. Kerényi, 'Über Bartóks Volksliedaufzeichnungen', *Studia musicologica*, 5 (1963), 441–8.

6 For example, P. Domokos Pál and Benjamin Rajeczky, *Csángó népzene* [The Folk Songs of the Csángó-Magyars], i–iii (Budapest: Editio Musica, 1956, 1961, 1991); L. Lajtha, *Szépkenyerüszentmártoni gyűjtés* [Collection from Szépkenyerüszentmárton] (1954); id., *Széki gyűjtés* [Collection from Szék] (Budapest, 1954); id., *Körispataki gyűjtés* [Collection from Körispatak] (1955).

7 Compare the recordings in *Hungarian Folk Music Collected by Kodály, Phonograph Cylinders* (ed. Tari, Budapest, Hungaroton LPX 18075–78) with the transcriptions included there.

8 Bartók himself prepared double transcriptions, a nuance-rich one parallel with another representing the 'essence'. See e.g., *Hungarian Folk Music–Gramophone Records with Bartók's Tranascriptions*, Hungaroton LPX 18058–60; Transcriptions on pp. 6, 7, etc.

9 See e.g. Domokos Pál and Rajeczky, *Csángó népzene*, ii, nos 16, 16a, 16b, 16c.

10 See e.g. László Dobszay and Janka Szendrei, *Catalogue of Hungarian Folksong Types Arranged According to Styles* (Budapest: Institute for Musicology of the Hungarian Academy of Sciences, 1992), 71–81.

11 L. Kiss and Benjamin Rajeczky, *A Magyar Népzene Tára*, v: *Siratók* [The Corpus of the Hungarian Folk Music, v: Laments] (Budapest: Akadémiai Kiadó, 1966), 115–25 and the transcriptions. Cf. Dobszay and Szendrei, *Catalogue*, 220–30; László Dobszay, *A siratóstílus dallamköre zenetörténetünkben és népzenénkben* [The Melodic Sphere of the Lament Style in Hungarian Music History and Folk Music] (Budapest: Akadémiai Kiadó, 1983).

12 Janka Szendrei, László Dobszay and Benjamin Rajeczky, *XVI–XVII. századi dallamaink a népi emlékezetben* [Tunes in Folk Memory of the 16th and 17th Centuries], i–ii (Budapest: Akadémiai Kiadó, 1979).

13 Zoltan Kodály, 'Sajátságos dallamszerkeszet a cseremisz népzenében' [A Peculiar Melodic Structure in Cheremis Folk Music], repr. in *Visszatekintés* [Retrospection] (Budapest: Editio Musica, 1974), i, 141–54. L. Vargyas, 'Ugorszkoj szloj v vengerszkoj narodnoj muzüke', *Acta ethnographica*, 1 (1950), 161–96.

14 Zoltan Kodály, 'Néprajz és Zenetörténet' [Ethnography and Music History], repr. in *Visszatekintés*, i, 231.

15 This occurred several times during the history of chant, e.g., in the ninth–tenth, twelfth, sixteenth and twentieth centuries.

16 Theodore Karp, *Aspects of Orality and Formularity in Gregorian Chant* (Evanston, Ill.: Northwestern University Press, 1998), 16–28.

17 Benjamin Rajeczky, 'Gregorianik und Volksgesang', in *Handbuch des Volksliedes*, ed. Rolf Wilhelm Brednich, Lutz Röhrich and Wolfgang Suppan (Munich: Wilhelm Fink Verlag, 1975), ii, 393–405. Peter Jeffery, *Re-envisioning Past Music Cultures: Ethnomusicology in the Study of Gregorian Chant* (Chicago: University of Chicago Press, 1992).

18 'The singers of the late tenth and eleventh centuries were apparently quite conscious of the relative antiquity of the various chants', according to Karp, *Aspects*, 31.

19 For example, nos. 8038, 8099–100, 8130–313 of *Antiphonen*, ed. László Dobszay and Janka Szendrei, 3 vols. (MMMA 5; Kassel: Bärenreiter, 1999) are clearly adaptations of the the preceding pieces.

20 Ibid.; cf. László Dobszay, 'Experiences in the Musical Classification of Antiphons', in *Cantus Planus: Papers Read at the Third Meeting of the International Musicological Society Study Group, Tihany, Hungary, 19–24 September 1988*, ed. László Dobszay (Budapest: Hungarian Academy of Sciences Institute for Musicology, 1990), 143–56.

21 François Auguste Gevaert, *La Melopée antique dans le chant de l'église latine* (Ghent: A. Hoste, 1895–6; repr. 1967).

22 *Antiphonale Sarisburiense: A Reproduction in Facsimile from Early Manuscripts*, ed. Walter Howard Frere, 3 vols. (London: PMM Society, 1901–24; repr. ed., 6 vols. Farnborough, Hants, England: Gregg Press, 1966).

23 Edward Nowacki, 'Studies on the Office Antiphons of the Old Roman Manuscripts' (Ph.D. diss., Brandeis University, 1980); id., 'The Gregorian Office Antiphons and the Comparative Method', *JM* 4 (1985), 243–75.

24 László Dobszay, 'The Types of Antiphons in Ambrosian and Gregorian Chant', in Bryan Gillingham and Paul Merkley (eds), *Chant and its Peripheries: Essays in Honour of Terence Bailey* (Ottawa: Institute of Mediaeval Music, 1998), 50–61.

25 Jean Claire, 'Les Répertoires liturgiques latins avant l'octoéchos. I. L'Office férial romano-franc', *Etudes grégoriennes*, 15 (1975), 5–192. Cf. László Dobszay, 'Some Remarks on Jean Clair's *Octoechos*', in *Cantus Planus: Papers Read at the Seventh Meeting of the International Musicological Society Study Group, Sopron, Hungary, 1995*, ed. László Dobszay (Budapest: Hungarian Academy of Sciences Institute for Musicology, 1998), 179–94.

26 Joseph Dyer, 'The Singing of Psalms in the Early Medieval Office', *Speculum*, 64 (1989), 535–78.

27 Cf. James McKinnon, 'Lector Chant versus Schola Chant', in Janka Szendrei and David Hiley (eds), *Laborare fratres in unum: Festschrift László Dobszay zum 60. Geburtstag* (Hildesheim: Weidmann, (1995), 201–11; cf. id., 'The Emergence of Gregorian Chant', 112.

28 Bruno Stäblein, s.v. 'Alleluja', in *MGG*, i (1949–51), cols. 338–50.

29 Terence Bailey, *The Ambrosian Alleluias* (Englefield Green: PMM Society, 1983), 46–61.

30 Thomas Forrest Kelly, *The Beneventan Chant* (Cambridge: Cambridge University Press, 1989), 76–7 and 119–24.

31 *Die Gesänge das altrömischen Graduale Vat. lat. 5319*, ed. Bruno Stäblein and Margareta Landwehr-Melnicki (MMMA 2; Kassel: Bärenreiter, 1970).

32 Such as, for example, Terence Bailey, *Antiphon and Psalm in the Ambrosian Office* (Ottawa: Institute of Mediaeval Music, 1994), 55–124.

33 McKinnon, 'The Emergence of Gregorian Chant', 98.

34 Ibid., 102. McKinnon explained, however, his doubts in his *Advent Project*. Cf. McKinnon, 'Festival, Text and Melody: Chronological Stages in the Life of a Chant', in Gillingham and Merkley (eds), *Chant and its Peripheries*, 1–11.

35 McKinnon, 'The Emergence of Gregorian Chant', 99: '. . . one must conclude that the chants existed in substantially the same form for a considerable period before the manuscripts were written'. Cf. ibid., 80–81.

Chapter 10
Tollite portas: An Ante-Evangelium Reclaimed?

Kenneth Levy

Our focus is on the first millennium. That is James McKinnon's millennium, his intellectual pond, the Lake Erie of his musicological boatings. Of those thousand years, only the last hundred and fifty have left music. So the waters are murky. We want to see to the bottom, but Jim is the one who has seen it best. He knows the history, theology, liturgy, music; and he is judicious with his knowledge. He honors Montaigne's injunction to historians, that they leave traces so those who come afterward can see where they went and how they got around.[1] It is easy to muddy prehistoric waters. Jim hasn't done that. He's cleaned up after others.

My first-millennial excursion here runs considerable risks of muddying. Its title, '. . . An Ante-Evangelium Reclaimed', needs the question mark at its end. The Antiphons before the Gospel are a diverse lot of nearly four dozen chants, dispersed mainly among north Italian sources. Alejandro Planchart devoted significant energies to these, leading to a splendid paper in 1982.[2] James Borders picked up in 1988 with a detailed catalog and illuminating commentary that emphasizes the possibilities of Gallican background.[3] In what follows I focus on a single chant, one that has so far been considered an unicum. I will propose some fresh witnesses and explore its potential roots in Gaul.

The Twenty-Third Psalm is one of the Psalter's shorter items, with just ten verses. It ends on a forceful note. Line 7 is an exhortation, *Tollite portas. . .* 'Lift up your heads o ye gates, and be ye raised ye ancient doors, so that the King of glory may enter.' Line 8 is a mini-dialog, *Quis est iste rex. . .* 'Who is this King of glory?'; the answer: 'The Lord, strong and mighty'. All this is essentially repeated in lines 9 and 10. Gregorianists know these lines in three familiar settings: a verse of the Advent responsory *Adspiciens a longe*, prominent at the beginnings of antiphoners; an Advent Gradual with music of the '*Justus ut palma* type'; and a Christmas Eve Offertory, sometimes assigned to church dedications.[4]

Tollite also has some less familiar uses, though none so obscure as the Ante-Evangelium for Thursday in Easter Week, shown in Pl. 10.1. This appears only in Verona, Biblioteca Capitolare 107 (fol. 92), a troper-proser compiled at Mantua in the early eleventh century, containing twenty-four of the forty-two chants in Borders's list.[5] The text uses only line 7 of the psalm. From the staffless neumes we learn nothing about modal-melodic substance;

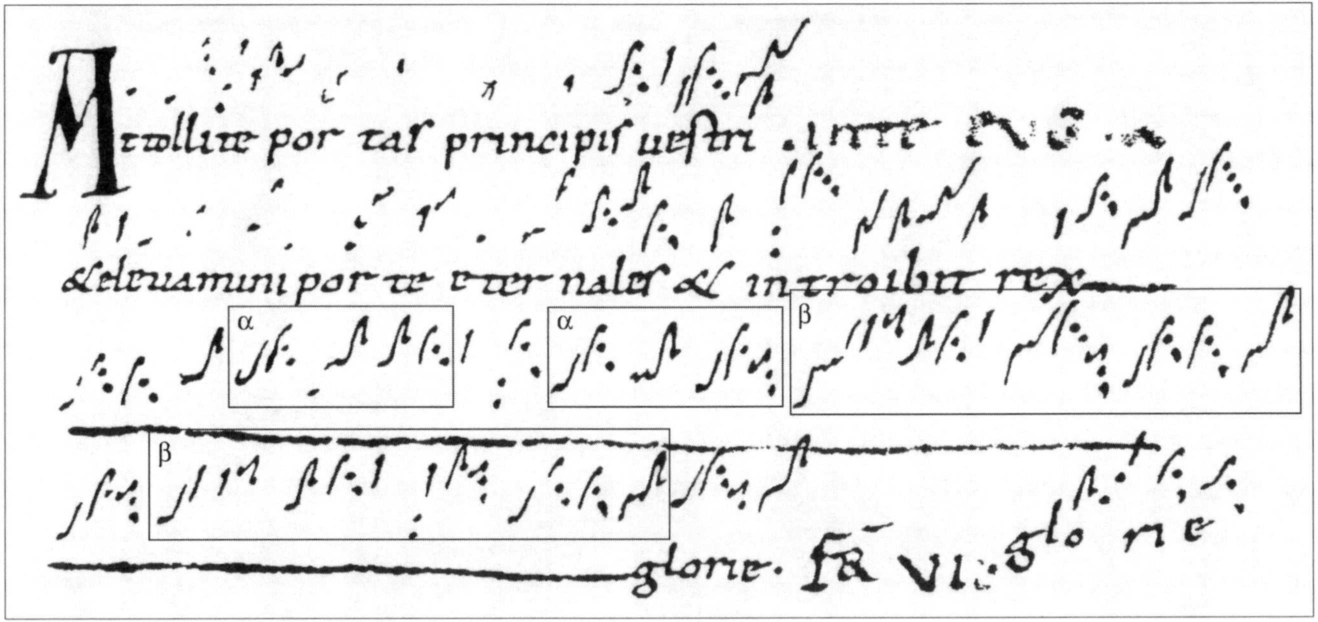

Pl. 10.1 'Mantua *Tollite*' (Verona, BC 107, fol. 92), eleventh century

but they show a moderately florid musical style. And at the end there is a structured melisma on 'Rex', with the repetition scheme: . . . alpha . . . alpha, beta . . . beta. Borders remarks that such melismas are not common in this repertory;[6] he also emphasizes the possible Gallican ancestry.[7]

The *Tollite portas* of Mantua has been seen as an unicum, but it has some potential relatives. One is a *responsorium cum infantibus* that is sung at neighboring Milan on the Sixth Sunday of Advent (Ex. 10.1).[8] The music is not the same. Milan concludes with a structured melisma on 'Rex', but it is more elaborate; the Milanese scribe has analyzed the repetition pattern, which is I, II, II repeated, III and IV; then I, II, III, IV again. Elements I, II and III are all launched by ascending fourths (marked by deltas in Ex. 10.1); and there is an impulse to intensify, as elements I and II lead to a climactic III; we will see more of fourths and intensification.

Ex. 10.1 'Milan *Tollite*' (London, BL Add. 34209)

The third of these lesser-known *Tollite*s has so far remained obscure. It is noted in staffed/cleffed Tuscan neumes of around 1100 on an introductory leaf of a music-theory manuscript at Florence. I will call it the Florence *Tollite* (Ex. 10.2).[9] Michel Huglo identified its notation, but he seems not to have dealt with the music.[10] There is no rubric visible; legibility is sometimes poor; the use of clefs is eccentric; it amounts to a stray entry whose transcription is unsure. Yet the music needs to be considered in light of the pieces at Mantua and Milan. Florence has something of a rhetorical plan. Line 1 is introductory; lines 2 through 5 are in rough parallel; there is a musical gesture that returns: melodic arcs of the type ([*b*]–*c*–*d*–*c*–*b*–*a*), marked by alphas in Ex. 10.2. At the end is another structured melisma on 'Rex', longer than at Mantua, and in its way as ample as the melisma at Milan.

Now what relationship might these three northern Italian *Tollite*s have? In recent work I have been using the term 'multiples' to describe situations where chants with similar functions in sibling liturgies have musical similarities that are attributable not to notational copyings, but to independent aural descent from a common aural source.[11] With these *Tollite*s, some link may be suspected, at the start, between Mantua's pitchless neumes (Pl. 10.1) and the melody at Florence (Ex. 10.2), but this diminishes later on. Between Milan's and Florence's pitched versions (Exs. 10.1 and 10.2), there may be a modal-melodic relationship, perhaps clearest at 'aeternales . . .' in line 4. These slender indications suggest that the chants shared a common mode and even some melodic substance. And that might reinforce the notion of 'Gallican' antecedents raised by Borders.

In Italy, there were 'Gallican' chants north of the river Po, in Cisalpine Gaul, of which some may survive in idiomatic remodelings in the Milanese rite; the responsory in Ex. 10.1 might be one of these. In seventh/eighth-century Spain, there were 'Gallican' chants that survive in the tenth/eleventh-century 'Mozarabic' repertories, noted in staffless neumes; in the earlier times there was ecclesiastical community between Visigothic Spain and Narbonnais Gaul, so that the Old-Hispanic ancestors of the Mozarabic chants can be seen as Hispano-Gallican. In 1950 Dom Louis Brou made an important point about this repertory, establishing that its texts were already fixed by the early eighth century; some were entered in the Orationale of Verona, which was taken from Spain to a refuge in northern Italy in the wake of the Muslim invasions of 711.[12] In a 1984 article dealing with 'Toledo, Rome, and the Legacy of Gaul', I extended this into the realm of melody, arguing that some notational-musical linkages among Mozarabic, Gregorian and Milanese offertories were traceable to a Gallican musical source before ca. 700;[13] and since Gregorian chants were involved, the likely source was Frankish-Gallican rather than Hispano-Gallican.[14]

There is a fourth, potentially related, *Tollite* in the Gregorian repertory itself. Ex. 10.3[15] compares the familiar Christmas Eve Offertory with the *Tollite* of Florence. The musical linkage is far from certain, yet the chants may be said to share a high G mode, and even some melodic contour. Beyond such particulars there is a larger issue, which is to explain a musical linkage between an Offertory of the central Gregorian corpus, whose antecedents

Ex. 10.2 'Florence *Tollite*' (Florence, BNC, Conv. sopp. F III 565, fol. 2)

are ostensibly Roman, and a peripheral north Italian chant whose antecedents may be Gallican. My explanation bears significantly on the early developments of Gregorian, Old Roman and Ambrosian musical repertories. Some points require a full-dress presentation, but because of the *Tollites*' potential involvement I will set out the main lines briefly.

In my article of 1984 my purpose was to show that certain Offertory melodies had attained musical fixity in a Franco-Gallican rite ca. 700, and

Ex. 10.3 'Florence *Tollite*' / Gregorian Offertory

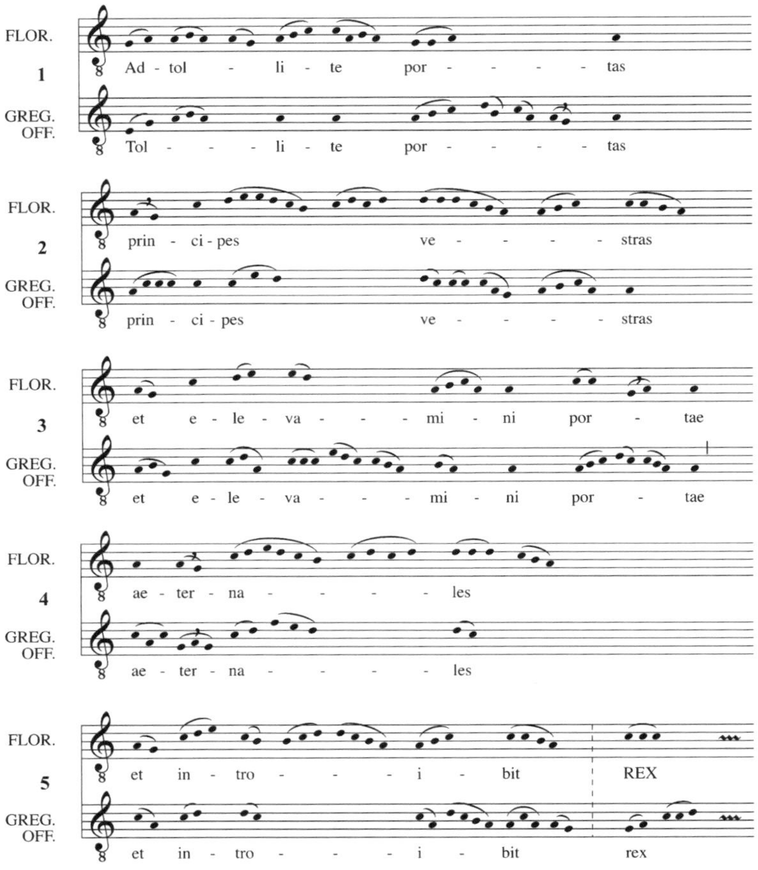

then were taken into the Gregorian Offertory cycle during the later eighth century. These melodies, using non-psalmic texts such as *Sanctificavit Moyses*, *Erit vobis* and *Vir erat in terra*, formed a small and liturgically peripheral minority within the Gregorian repertory. There was also something else to that proposal, but as I was already going well beyond accepted wisdom, it seemed better not to emphasize the rest. The point is that there are no substantial differences in musical style between the minority of Gregorian Offertories that are built on non-psalmic texts and the majority, built on psalmic texts. With all the Gregorian Offertories sharing in essentially the same style, it follows that if the non-psalmic Offertories are traceable to Gallican melodic antecedents, then those with psalmic texts (including the Christmas Eve *Tollite portas* in Ex. 10.3) should be traceable there as well. Quite large amounts of Gregorian music would be involved: about a third of the musical content of the Carolingian Mass antiphoner, taken over more or less intact from melodic entities that were crystallized in Frankish Gaul.

That music-based conjecture must also fit into some credible historical background. As I see it, the Gregorian editors, themselves mainly Franks, received from Rome during the later eighth century an authorized repertory of Offertories using mainly psalmic texts; they took the Roman texts, but ignored the Roman music and applied their own Gallican Offertory music to the texts.[16] The Roman music, judged from its surviving eleventh-century state, was too prolix and repetitious; its constant melodic twistings, which were scarcely distinguishable from one another, suited it poorly for the task of memorization faced by each of the empire's choirmasters when the new Gregorian edition circulated. The Gallican chants, on the other hand, with melodies that were already crystallized in the Gallo-Hispanic rite by ca. 700, were more distinctive, more memorable; and they were already familiar to many northern choirmasters. There are further considerations involved,[17] but the end result is that nearly all the Gregorian Offertories would represent Gallican music applied to Roman texts, with little if any Roman musical input. That in turn would bear significantly on the prehistory of the Old Roman Offertory music, which shares amounts of melodic substance with its Gregorian counterparts. The general understanding until now has been that Roman musical matter was reworked in producing the Gregorian melodies. My proposal is that the historical flow went just the other way: first Gallican melodic matter went into the Gregorian repertory during the later eighth century, and then Gregorian melos was accommodated by and reworked into Roman, that likely occurring by the early ninth century.[18]

The present occasion is not one for dealing with these large and almost inevitably controversial issues. For the moment, I would return to the Gregorian Offertory melos in Ex. 10.3 and observe only that it may now perhaps be seen as traceable to a Gallican melos, which might link it more closely with the Gallo-Italic *Tollite*s in Pl. 10.1 and Exs. 10.2–3. All these chants then may descend from a sometime Gallican modal-melodic formulation that by ca. 700 was well enough attached to Psalm 23: 7 for it to retain something of its musical profile even when given a variety of liturgical assignments and subjected to a variety of local idiomatic remodelings.

Let me say just a word about the structured melismas with which the three Italian *Tollite*s end. No two of them are alike, which is not surprising in view of their ornamental function and perhaps improvisational origin, which left them susceptible to being moved and changed. A broad-based study of structured melismas would doubtless throw light on the origins of the Carolingian sequence. Here I would look only at the newly emerged Florence melisma (Ex. 10.2). There are two main materials: melodic arcs (alphas) and rising fourths (deltas). The fourths occupy key points in the structure and serve as generators of melodic continuity. We have seen fourths with similar functions in the 'Rex' melisma of the Milanese responsory (Ex. 10.1). Beyond such details, what is striking about the Florence melisma is its rhetorical, even emotional dimension. Line 6 is introductory, an A–B–A form, alpha–delta–alpha, whose delta prefigures others to come. Line 7 soars upward, powered by deltas that rise progressively from *g* to *c* to *d*; the peak is on a delta variant, a unique ascending fifth, *c* to *g*, whose thrust carries to an astonishing high *c*. Line 8 seems to be catching breath, with deltas on *g* and *a*, and it marks further time with *g* and *a* again. Line 9 has the final flight; it parallels line 7 with deltas on *g* then *c* then *d*, but its energies fall short, reaching only to a high *a*. All this has emotional qualities that would seem as much at home in the era of Pius IX as that of Stephen II.

Two other uses of *Tollite portas* deserve mention.[19] Both the Latin West and Orthodox East sing the text in the ceremonial of opening doors at the dedication of a church.[20] Among known melodies for this function there are no multiples for our four *Tollite*s,[21] but a systematic search of Latin Pontificals may be fruitful. The final use of *Tollite* is the most universal. It is sung in the Divine Liturgy of Eastern rites at the ceremony of Great Entrance with which the Mass of the Faithful begins.[22] Byzantine sources from the time of Empire have just a single melody, which is clothed in the authoritative musical stylization of the Asmatikon, the book of Hagia Sophia's choristers. Its music reaches back only to the thirteenth century, but its mode is documented as far back as the ninth-century Typikon of the Great Church,[23] where the modal assignment is Fourth Authentic, a high G mode; perhaps coincidentally, that is also the mode of the Latin *Tollite*s in Exs. 10.1–3. No specific melodic relationships can be seen. The Latin settings have little use for the direct fifth skip *g–d*, which is given prominence by the Byzantines; among our Western settings it appears just once, in the climactic seventh line of the Florence *Tollite*.

In closing, I would emphasize again that with such matters there can be no pretensions to certainty. It comes down to two maybes.

One: maybe the musical parallels between Milan and Florence (Exs. 10.1 and 2) tell us something about the music of the Ante-Evangelium noted in staffless neumes at Mantua (Pl. 10.1). That is, two or three of the north Italian *Tollite*s may reflect an archaic 'Gallo-Italian' musical formulation whose shape was well enough tied to the text of Psalm 23: 7 for it to keep something of its modal-melodic integrity even when taken to different places, assigned different liturgical functions, and remodeled to suit local musical tastes.

And a second: maybe the Gregorian Christmas Eve Offertory, now perhaps able to claim Gallican musical antecedents, was related in that way to the north Italian *Tollite*s. This reaches far back in Gallican chant history, and also has major consequences for our notions of how the Gregorian, Old Roman and Milanese melodic repertories developed. All that needs airing on another occasion.[24]

Notes

1 'Qu'ils estalent hardiment leur eloquence et leurs discours, qu'ils jugent à leur poste; mais qu'ils nous laissent aussi dequoy juger apres eux, et qu'ils n'alterent ny dispensent, par leurs racourciments et par leur chois, rien sur le corps de la matiere . . .'; *Essais*, Bk. II, ch. 10 (Paris: Pléiade, Gallimard, 1950), 460.

2 Read at the annual meeting of the American Musicological Society; never published.

3 James Borders, 'The Northern Italian Antiphons *Ante evangelium* and the Gallican Connection', *JMR* 8 (1988), 1–53; also Anne Walters Robertson, on antiphons *ante Evangelium* at St. Denis, 'The Reconstruction of the Abbey Church at St-Denis (1231–81)', *EMH* 5 (1985), 205–31.

4 As in the tenth-century Abruzzese manuscript, Vatican, BAV Vat. lat. 4770, fol. 223v.

5 See Heinrich Husmann, *Tropen- und Sequenzenhandschriften* (RISM B V/1; Munich-Duisberg: Henle Verlag, 1964), 187.

6 Borders, 'The Northern Italian Antiphons', 37, 'a departure from the neumatic treatment typical of evangelical antiphons . . .'.

7 Ibid., 36 ff., citing the mention of *Tollite portas* in the description of the Gallican rite sometimes attributed to St. Germanus of Paris (d. 576); Johannes Quasten, *Expositio antiquae liturgiae gallicanae* (Munster: Aschendorff, 1934); *Ordo antiquus gallicanus: Der gallikanische Messritus des 6. Jahrhunderts*, ed. Klaus Gamber (Regensburg: F. Pustet, 1965), 18; Robertson, 'The Reconstruction', 208.

8 London, BL Add. 34209; see PM 5 (facs.), 6 (transcriptions) (1899–1900), MS 36–37 = Transcription, 41 ('cum pueris'). The music is shown here a fifth higher than in its twelfth-century soft-hexachord reading, hence with the F♮ s in line four replacing the manuscript's B♭ s). This class of responsories is studied by E. Moneta Caglio, 'I responsori "cum infantibus" nella liturgia ambrosiana', in *Studi in onore di Carlo Castiglioni* (Milan: A. Giuffre, 1957), 481–578, esp. 493, 514.

9 Florence, Bibl. Naz. Centr., Conv. soppr., F.III.565, fol. 2. See Pieter Fischer, *The Theory of Music from the Carolingian Era up to 1400*, ii: *Italy* (RISM B III/2; Henle Verlag: Munich-Duisburg, 1968), 25–32.

10 Michel Huglo, *Les Tonaires: inventaire, analyse, comparison* (Paris: Société française de musicologie, 1971), 188–9.

11 Kenneth Levy, 'On Gregorian Orality', *JAMS* 43 (1990), 185–227; repr. in Levy, *Gregorian Chant and the Carolingians* (Princeton: Princeton University Press, 1998), 141–77.

12 Louis Brou, 'L'Antiphonaire wisigothique et l'antiphonaire grégorien au début du viii siècle', *Anuario musical*, 5 (1950), 3–10.

13 'Toledo, Rome, and the Legacy of Gaul', *EMH* 4 (1984), 49–99; repr. in Levy, *Gregorian Chant*, 31–81.

14 The tenth-century Mozarabic repertory supplies a point of comparison with our three Italian *Tollite*s. It is a Sono of the Office, a liturgical class related to the

Hispanic Sacrificia or Mass Offertories. Soni are sung at Matins and Vespers in an elaborate style close to that of the Sacrificia or Offertories; at least one chant *(Alleluia elegerunt apostoli)* serves as both a Sono and Sacrificium; cf. Don Michael Randel, *An Index to the Chant of the Mozarabic Rite* (Princeton: Princeton University Press, 1973), 309, 458; id., 'Mozarabic rite', in *NG* xii, 672 ff. In the description of a Gallican rite sometimes attributed to St. Germanus of Paris, the Offertory is called a Sono; see Gamber, *Ordo antiquus gallicanus*, 19; Kenneth Levy, 'Latin Chant Outside the Roman Tradition', in *NOHM* II*: The Early Middle Ages to 1300*, ed. Richard Crocker and David Hiley (Oxford: Oxford University Press, 1990), 93–101. The Sono on Ps. 23 appears in the *Antifonario visigótico mozárabe de la catedral de León, edición facsimil*, ed. Louis Brou and José Vives (Barcelona: Centro de estudios e investigación S. Isidoro, 1953), fol. 282. It starts with verse 1 of the Psalm, and goes on to verse 7, hence like the Milanese Responsory (Ex. 10.2) with the order reversed. Near the end there is a structured melisma on 'aeternales', with a pattern: doubled alpha, doubled beta and gamma. The staffless neumes suggest no musical link to any of the three Italian chants. But this Hispano-Gallican piece can perhaps be seen as an example of what Offertories were like in the Frankish-Gallican liturgies that flourished in the Carolingian heartland region where Gregorian chant was given its definitive form in the later eighth century.

15 *GT*, 40; *Offertoriale sive versus offertoriorum*, ed. Carolus Ott (Paris: Desclée, 1935), 14; both have the readings of the Dijon Tonary, seen in PM 7 (1901), 275; variant readings and transpositions are detailed by Hubert Sidler, *Studien zu den alten Offertorien mit ihren Versen* (Fribourg: Verlag des Musikwissenschaftlichen Instituts der Universität, 1939), 43–7.

16 They might take music that was already set to the same psalm texts received from Rome (a hint of such in the Mozarabic Sono; see n. 14); or they might salvage Gallican music that went with about-to-be-suppressed non-psalmic texts by accommodating it to Roman psalmic texts. Such operations seem to have taken place with the Offertories *Angelus Domini* and *Posuisti*; see *Offertoriale*, ed. Ott, 57 and 136.

17 A fuller presentation of this hypothesis appears in my 'A New Look at Old Roman Chant', *EMH* 19 (2000), 81–104, and 'A New Look at Old Roman Chant – II', *EMH* 20 (2001), 173–97.

18 That is not without parallel: the situation of the *Veterem hominem* antiphons would be similar. See Oliver Strunk, 'The Latin Antiphons for the Octave of the Epiphany', in *Essays on Music in the Byzantine World* (New York: Norton, 1977), 208–19; Edward Nowacki, 'Constantinople–Aachen–Rome: The Transmission *of Veterem hominem*', in Peter Cahn and Ann-Katrin Heimer (eds), *De musica et cantu: Studien zur Geschichte der Kirchenmusik und der Oper - Helmut Hucke zum 60. Geburtstag* (Hildesheim: Olms, 1993), 95–115.

19 Liturgical applications of the 23rd Psalm are surveyed by André Rose, '"Attollite portas, principes, vestras": aperçus sur la lecture chrétienne du Ps. 24 (23)', in *Miscellanea liturgica in onore di Sua Eminenza il Cardinale Giacomo Lercaro, arcivescovo di Bologna*, 2 vols. (Rome: Desclée, 1966), 453–78.

20 Michel Andrieu, *Les Ordines Romani du haut moyen âge* (Louvain: Spicilegium Sacrum Lovaniense Administration, 1956–65), iv, 316 ff.

21 Thomas Davies Kozachek, 'The Repertory of Chant for Dedicating Churches in the Middle Ages' (Ph.D. diss., Harvard University, 1995).

22 Textual and liturgical aspects are dealt with by Robert F. Taft, *The Great Entrance: A History of the Transfer of Gifts and other Pre-Anaphoral Rites* (Rome: Pontificium Institutum Studiorum Orientalium, 1978).

23 *Le Typicon de la Grande Eglise: Ms. Saint-Croix no 40, Xe siècle*, ed. Juan Mateos, 2 vols. (Rome: Pontificium Institutum Studiorum Orientalium, 1962–3), i, 146.
24 See the articles cited in n. 17.

Chapter 11

The Diagrams Interpolated into the *Musica Isidori* and the Scale of Old Hispanic Chant

Michel Huglo

After the Edict of Constantine the Great in 313, the Latin liturgy was developed and then transmitted to all regions of the Roman Empire. Nevertheless, the liturgy was not the same in the different parts of Europe, as is the case today in the modern Roman Catholic Church. On the contrary, each archdiocese used its own rites, its own Psalter and its own repertory of liturgical chant.

The Christian Latin texts from the fourth century, carefully assembled and translated by James McKinnon, are witnesses to this variety, evident first in Jerusalem with the pilgrim Egeria;[1] second in Milan with Augustine, the disciple of Ambrose;[2] third with the deacon Paulinus telling us about the creation of Western hymnody by Ambrose and the introduction of antiphonal psalmody to Milan in 366;[3] and fourth in the liturgy of the African church known from the writings of Augustine.[4]

According to Louis Duchesne and Edmund Bishop, the most important branches of the Latin liturgies during the seventh and eighth centuries were the Italian and Gallican families.[5] The two liturgical families are very distinct, as much in the style of their prayers as in the musical settings of their liturgical chants.

I. The Italian and Gallican Liturgical Families

The Italian family represents the south and the north of the peninsula. The south is comprised of the dioceses of Naples, Benevento, Bari, Montecassino and Canosa, near Monte Gargano. The well-known repertory of chants from the 'Beneventan zone' is very primitive and uniform, progressing by stepwise motion without the larger intervals of fourths and fifths.[6]

In Rome and in the suburban dioceses of Latium, the style of the liturgical prayers is characterized by sobriety of expression and concise choice of vocabulary. Old Roman chant,[7] as preserved in only five surviving notated manuscripts from the twelfth and thirteenth centuries,[8] was greatly influenced by the so-called 'Gregorian chant' introduced in Rome in the tenth century, first in St. John Lateran.[9] Nevertheless, Old Roman chant presents the same characteristics of sobriety as the prayers of the Sacramentary, particularly in the verses of the Offertories and in the melismas of the Alleluia.

In another way, the musical repertory of Old Roman chant is typified by a lack of responsories for the nocturnal office, because so few chants were composed for the Nocturns. Indeed, forty 'responsories' were actually borrowed Offertories or Communions from the Mass repertory; in Old Roman chant there is no distinction of 'genres' for the Mass and for the Office, because until the tenth century both Mass and Office antiphons were contained in only one book of chant, the Antiphoner.

Another flaw of Old Roman chant is its musical style,[10] which is less expressive and rather repetitive. Instead of the leap of a fifth to define the tonic–dominant relationship, Old Roman chant often prefers the monotonous repetition of podatus or torculus (see Ex. 11.1).

It is impossible to characterize the musical repertories of Florence and Aquileia before the Carolingian era since the sources consist merely of a few antiphons scattered in the Italian books of Gregorian chant.[11] On the other hand, the musical repertory of Milan is currently well known because this repertory is retained in many antiphoners, including the antiphons and responsories for the diverse offices and the chants of the Mass.[12] The sources of the ten sung elements of the Mass are of diverse origin: Roman, Syrian and Gallican.[13] The schema of the night and day 'hours' of the Ambrosian office is far more variable than that of the Roman liturgy, because many kinds of antiphons and responsories were used in differing order according to the calendar of the liturgical year.[14] Nevertheless, the multiple forms of Ambrosian antiphonal psalmody can be reduced to four classes according to the final notes of the antiphon (see Table 11.1).

Ambrosian psalmody did not use melodic formulas at the mediant of the verse but only a short pause, as in Old Hispanic psalmody. The Milanese cantor could improvise any psalm tone using the melodic structure of the antiphon as a point of departure, and then combine an intonation, the psalmodic dominant and the appropriate final formula (see Table 11.1). In spite of so many possibilities, only eight patterns are very similar to the eight tones of 'Gregorian' psalmody. Other tones are so much simpler that – according to Augustine in his *Confessiones* – 'the reader of the psalm [was required] to perform it with so little inflection of voice that it was closer to speaking than to singing'.[15]

In Milan, this very old psalmodic antiphony was accompanied by the Ambrosian hymnody composed in large part by Ambrose (d. 397). Augustine once more bore witness to the aesthetic qualities of these hymns, of which some are pentatonic in structure. By the fifth century, Ambrosian hymnody was widespread in Gaul and in Spain, but it did not reach Rome before the twelfth century.

Milan is at the crossing of the Italian and Gallican families. The Gallican families comprise the different repertories of Gaul (Cambrai, Tournai, Reims, Paris, Autun, Lyon, Toulouse, etc.) and those of the different kingdoms of the Iberian Peninsula: Aragón, León, Toledo, Andalusia, etc. The style of the prayers and especially of the *Contestatio*, the Preface, is very different

Ex. 11.1 Comparison of Old Roman, Gregorian and Old Hispanic chant

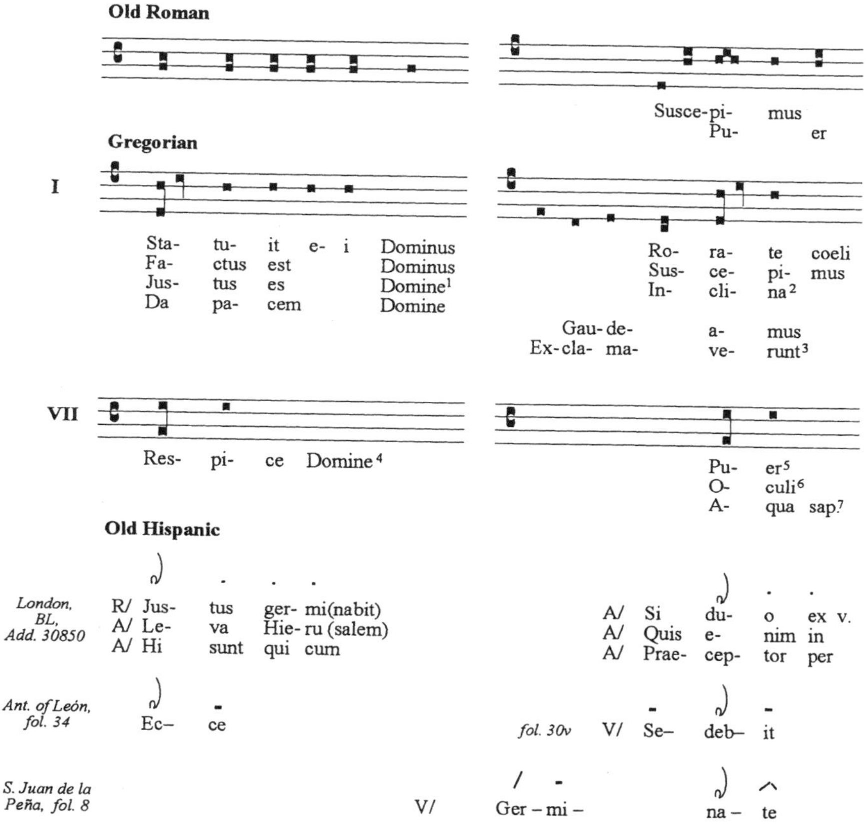

1) Justus es ends on F in the Old Roman chant (*MMMAE*, II, 59).
2) The intonation of Inclina is different in the Old Roman chant (*MMMAE*, II, 8).
3) The melody of Exclamaverunt (ending on G) is very different in the Old Roman chant (*MMMAE*, II, 70).
4) Melody ends on F in the Old Roman chant (*MMMAE*, II, 57).
5) Melody ends on D in the Old Roman chant (*MMMAE*, II, 9).
6-7) Different melodies in the Old Roman chant (*MMMAE*, II, 34 and 70).

from the Roman style; Gallican Prefaces include a wealth of rhetoric, symbols and quotations from the Bible. The melismas of the Alleluia and of the *Sacrificium*, the Offertory, are very extensive, sometimes consisting of more than 200 or even 300 notes.[16] Moreover, in Gallican and Spanish churches, cantors often sang at the Mass diverse *Preces*, litany-like prayers recited by the deacon, with a short refrain from the assembly, to implore God's forgiveness (for example, *Domine miserere, Miserere Pater juste et omnibus indulgentiam dona, Rogamus te rex saeculorum* and so on).[17]

Table 11.1 The tones of Ambrosian psalmody

	1	2	3	4	5
Finals	*Intonation*	*Reciting tones*	*Number of cadential formulas*	*Possible final notes of cadences*	*Related Greg. tone*
1st psalm series: antiphons with final on **D**	F G a C (D) E G C D F C D E	a G F E	14 14 14 4 46	a G F D G F E D G F E D C E D C	I II
2nd psalm series: antiphons with final on **E**	G a c G a b E G a E F G C D F C D E	c b a G F E	3 4 14 16 8 6 51	a a G E a G F E D G F E D C E D C E D C	III IV
3rd psalm series: antiphons with final on **F**	F a c F G a F G C D F	c b a G F	12 3 11 1 27	d c b a G G F G F E D C D	V VI
4th psalm series: antiphons with final on **G**	G b d G a c G a b G a	d c b a ***General Total***	16 10 3 5 34 ***158***	d c b G c b a G b G b a G F	VII VIII

The Ambrosian antiphonal system, using only four final tones, determines the four important groups of psalmody: D, E, F, G (col. 1). The end of any antiphon, by means of one of the many different intonations (col. 2), can be connected with the following psalmody, which conforms to the respective height of the reciting tone (col. 3). In Ambrosian chant, as in Old Hispanic, there is no melodic cadence at the mediant of the verse. For its termination the singer is able to choose a formula (col. 4) freely in such a way that the repetition of the antiphon follows the psalmody comfortably. From Michel Huglo et al., *Geschichte der Musiktheorie*, ed. Zaminer and Ertelt, iv: *Das Mittelalter* (2000), 61.

The different genres of the liturgical chants were explained in Gaul in two letters attributed to Germanus of Paris[18] and in Spain by Isidore of Seville in his *De ecclesiasticis officiis*, intended for newly ordained priests.[19] In the Third Book of his encyclopedic *Etymologiae*, Isidore deals with music – not the liturgical music of his time but rather music as a liberal art. Subsequently, during the middle of the eighth century, the nine chapters of *De musica* were completed and applied to chant by an anonymous theorist from southern Spain.

II. The Manuscript Tradition of Isidore of Seville's *Etymologiae*

The tradition of the Etymologiarum libri XX by Isidore of Seville is represented by a considerable number of manuscripts – more than 1,100. According to Wallace M. Lindsay, that tradition can be divided into three large families:[20]

1 The Franco-Germanic family (Lindsay's α family) is the most widely disseminated in Europe.[21] It transmits the text of the *Ars musica* in Book III and locates it between *Geometria* and *Astronomia.*
2 The Italo-Germanic family (Lindsay's β family), represented by many pre-Carolingian manuscripts, modifies the order of the books and chapters, thus displacing *Musica* to the beginning of Book IV.
3 Finally, the Hispanic family (Lindsay's γ family) – my main focus here – is represented by eleven manuscripts in Visigothic script, of which three date from before the year 800.[22] This accounts for only one percent of the manuscript tradition of the 'Isidorean Encyclopedia'.

The third branch is divided in two groups: first, the manuscripts from southern Spain with Arabic annotations – the earliest ones,[23] and second, the manuscripts from the north of the peninsula, mostly from the eleventh century and thus completed before the Reconquista of Toledo in 1095.[24]

The Hispanic family is characterized by four criteria, which are always found together in these eleven manuscripts:

1 The eight letters (and not six, as elsewhere in the families α and β) of the correspondence between Isidore and Braulio, archdeacon of Saragossa, and collaborator of Isidore;
2 A special title written in red, added in the Book III, ch. 22, before the listing of the different qualities of voice: *Vocis species multae*;
3 A brief interpolation in Book XV, ch. 1, *De civitatibus*, intended as an encomium of the city of Saragossa and of its relics of martyrs.[25] Of course, the author of the interpolation is Braulio, the archdeacon, later (in 631) bishop of Saragossa. This brief interpolation, known as the 'praise of Saragossa', is also found in a rather large number of manuscripts from outside Spain, even in southern Germany;[26]
4 A long interpolation of geometric figures and diagrams of music theory interspersed with brief explanatory passages that appear between *Geometria* and *Musica* in the middle of Book III on the Quadrivium.

These large-scale geometric figures should not be confused with the much smaller figures of the original text, which come from the Second Book of the *Institutiones* of Cassiodorus, as transmitted in the *Breviarium Pauli*. This last is Paul the Deacon's abbreviated version of the *Institutiones* written at Montecassino.

After a brief presentation of these interpolated figures, I will proceed to an analysis of the diagrams which, according to the definition of the *Introductio harmonica* attributed to Euclid, 'are figures of plane geometry which, with the help of numbers, are intended to represent the notes of song'.[27]

The geometric figures and the interpolated harmonic diagrams in the 'Musica Isidori' were reproduced by Rudolf Beer in 1909 in his facsimile edition of Toledo MS 15.8, since 1868 preserved in Madrid.[28] In 1798, Arevalo had them redrawn for his edition of the *Etymologies* and Migne reproduced them in volume 82 of the *Patrologia Latina* (see Pl. 11.1).

Finally, in 1911, Lindsay's edition of the *Etymologiae* again reproduced the small plane geometry figures of Isidore's original text (nos. 1–12 in Pl. 11.1) and the figures of solid geometry: sphere, cube and so on (nos. 13–17), then the interpolated figures applied to the study of constellations, but also (no. 24) to cosmic music or the music of the spheres. It should be noted that number 22 as given in Escorial, Monasterio, Real Bibl., T II 24 (ninth century) has the Arabic names of the twelve signs of the Zodiac written in Arabic in each of its twelve sections.

At the bottom of Pl. 11.1 are the small interpolated harmonic diagrams (nos. 25–30: cf. my corrected versions in Fig. 11.1). They are followed by either a full-page or a half-page illustration of the large diagram that Arevalo and Lindsay reproduced from the *Toletanus* in their editions (no. 31).

I must admit that I had never paid attention to these interpolated diagrams until one day in May 1983, when I was examining the manuscript facsimiles in the Bobst Library of New York University. I cannot describe my amazement at the sight of these diagrams of the *Toletanus* of the eighth century in the large facsimile edition of Rudolf Beer! At that moment I decided to extend my investigation to all the early manuscripts of the *Etymologiae* – not on microfilm, but the original manuscripts themselves.[29]

III. The Interpolated Diagrams of the *Musica Isidori*

The source of the interpolated diagrams (nos. 25–31) and of the explanatory passages that accompany them is indicated by the author of the interpolation: *Secundum Porphyrium et Platonem ita haec formula exponitur*, that is: 'This diagram is explained according to Porphyry and Plato.' Here of course the anonymous author refers to the commentary of Porphyry on Plato's *Timaeus*. In this commentary, unfortunately lost but partially reconstructed by Angelo Sodano,[30] Porphyry indicated on a line segment the series of numbers that constitute the 'Soul of the [physical] World', namely: 1 2 3 4 / 9 8 27, which Plato had enumerated in the *Timaeus*; if in fact this series of

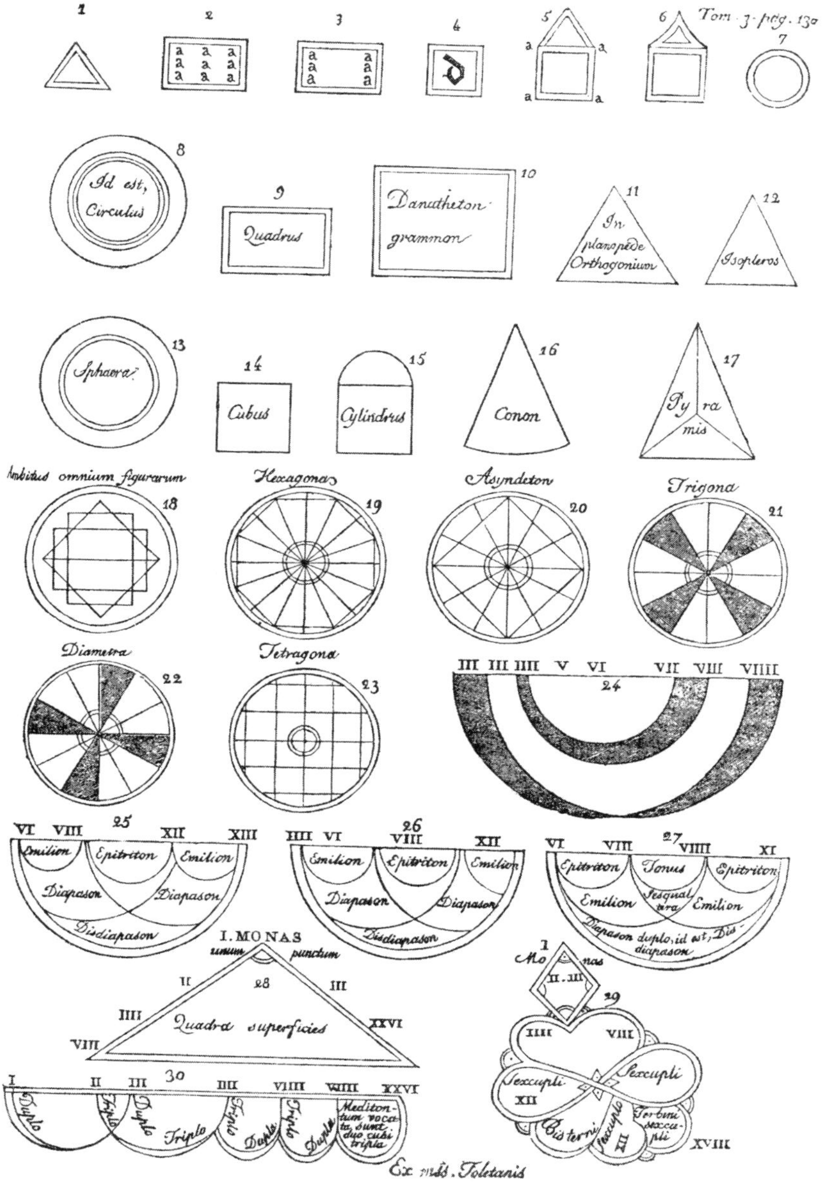

Pl. 11.1 The interpolated diagrams in Isidore of Seville's *Etymologiae*; geometric figures and harmonic diagrams reproduced from J. P. Migne, *Patrologia Latina*, 82 (1850)

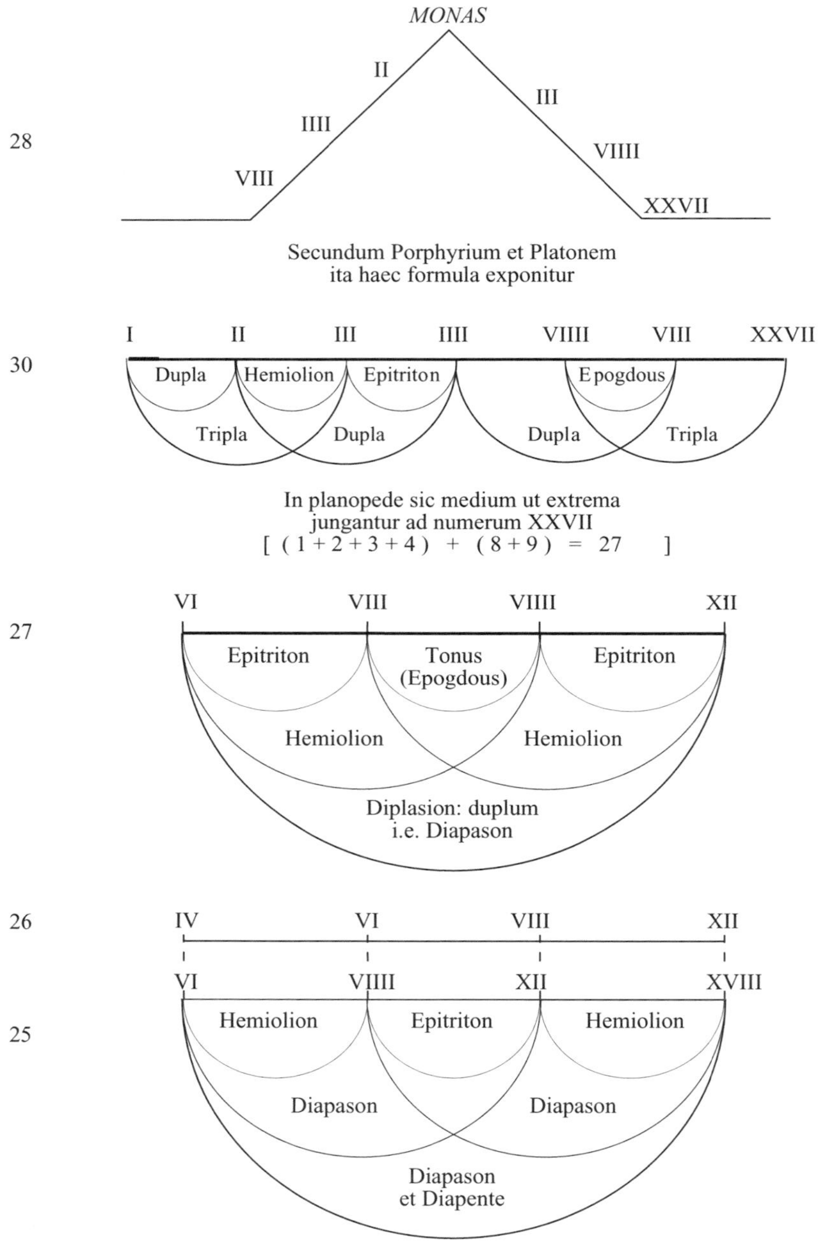

Fig. 11.1 The interpolated diagrams in the *Musica Isidori*, corrected and reorganized

numbers is distributed alternately on the left and on the right of the two sides of a lambda, 9 comes before 8 (see diagram 28 in Fig. 11.1).

On the linear diagram 30, the author uses semicircles to indicate all the proportions that create the perfect consonances: octave, double octave, fifth and fourth. As is shown clearly by diagram 28, the lambdoid diagram places on the left the two numbers resulting from 2 raised to the second and third power (namely 4 and 8), and on the right the two numbers resulting from 3 raised to the second and third power (namely 9 and 27). The numerical proportions, the foundation of the consonances, are always constructed by an even number and an odd number: that is 2 to 1, 3 to 2, 4 to 3, and 9 to 8.

This lambdoid diagram was known in the West through manuscripts with the commentary on the *Timaeus* by Calcidius[31] and also through the Commentary of Macrobius on the 'Dream of Scipio', after the *De republica* of Cicero.[32] But here, in the Hispanic manuscript tradition, the term *Monas* is written near the number 1, drawn at the top of the lambda in Calcidius and Macrobius. The occurrence of this term, which designates simultaneously the first principle of numbers (unity), the smallest geometrical figure (the point) and the smallest quantity of matter (the atom), is very rare in the dialogs of Plato (five instances), but much more frequent (200 instances) in his Greek commentators, among them Theon of Smyrna and Porphyry.[33]

In the two diagrams 26 and 25, following 27 (Fig. 11.1), the numbers are manipulated so that they always highlight the same proportions, creating both simple consonances and combined ones, such as the octave plus the fifth.

In diagram 27, we can see the succession of the numbers 6, 8, 9 and 12, whose proportional relationships create the tone, the fourth, the fifth and the octave. According to his biographer Iamblicus, we owe to Pythagoras this synthesis created from the arithmetic mean (6, 9, 12) and the harmonic mean (6, 8, 12).[34]

At the end of Pl. 11.1, Arevalo and Lindsay reproduced as number 29 an odd diagram that cannot be understood without returning to the manuscripts, because the lower part was unfortunately left out by the engravers working for the two editors. In fact, this is the diagram representing the four elements that constitute the matter of physics: solid matter (*terra*), liquid matter (*aqua*), gas (*aer*) and one of these three elements in combustion (*ignis*). Moreover, curves or lines connect these elements in pairs according to the resemblance of their physical properties (humidity, heat, etc.) or instead the repellents between them owing to these same properties.

This figure of the four elements was already included in the Visigothic manuscript of the *De natura rerum* by Isidore preserved in the Library of the Escorial, where it is attributed to Eulogius of Córdoba, archbishop of Toledo.[35]

IV. The Lambdoid diagram of the 'Musica Isidori'

Let us turn now to the large lambdoid diagram (no. 31), which establishes the musical scale of the old Spanish chant (Fig. 11.2). The diagram, which closes the major interpolation in the *Musica Isidori,* sometimes occupies a full page, as in the large manuscripts of the *Etymologiae* such as the *Toletanus* of the eighth century. In other cases, for example in the Escorial MSS P I 6 and T II 24 from the eleventh century, it is squeezed into one column so that the small diagram just discussed can be added in the other column.

This diagram, designated here under the name *lambda* – a reference to the commentaries on the *Timaeus*[36] – has been reproduced not with the *lambda* but with the trilobe arch characteristic of Hispanic architecture under Arabic influence since the eighth century. The diagram includes five levels, indicated by Roman numerals on Fig. 11.2 in the margin of my transcription in order to facilitate the commentary. In all Visigothic manuscripts the numbers on the first four levels are written in red, as in some Greek manuscripts with

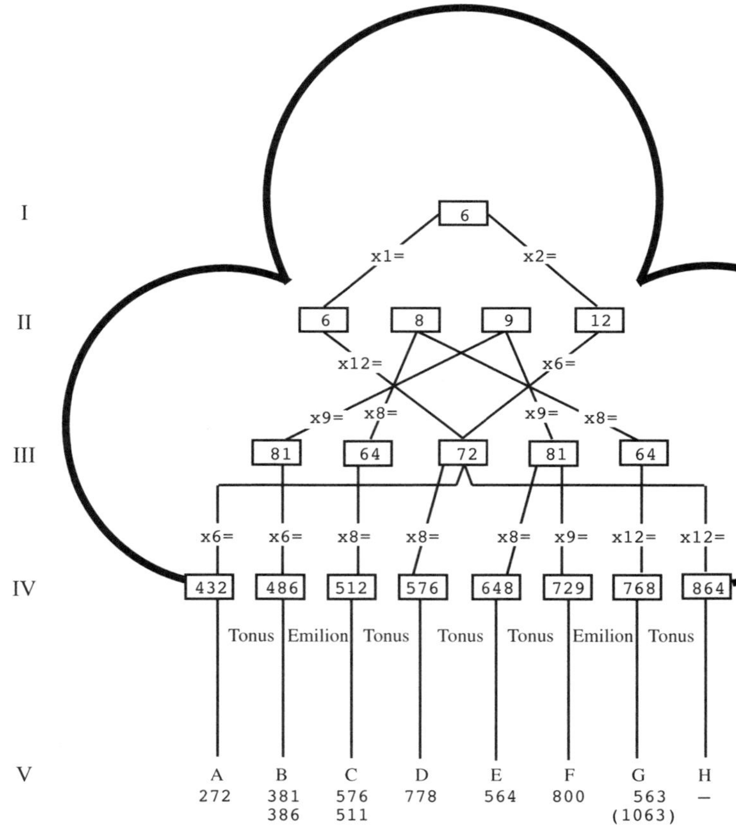

Fig. 11.2 Simplified transcription of Diagram 31 interpolated in the Old Spanish manuscripts of the *Musica Isidori*

Theon of Smyrna's diagram, and on the fifth in black. Between each level, connecting lines link the multiplicands of each upper level to the products obtained on the lower level by the multiplication written all in letters – not in numbers! – inside the connector.

On the first level, the number 6 is written at the top of the diagram, as in diagram VIII of Calcidius,[37] because the number 6 is the *senarius perfectus*, being the product of 2 (the first of the even numbers) and 3 (the first of the odd numbers). We may recall that the 1 at the top of the *lambda* was replaced by the term 'Monas' (Fig. 11.1, diagram 28). On the second level, we find the Pythagorean series (6 8 9 12) determining the four consonances of octave, fifth, fourth and whole tone. This series, borrowed from diagram 27 (see Fig. 11.1), is formed by the numbers 6, 6+2, 6+3 and finally 6+6. The third level consists of five numbers that are the product of the multiplication of the numbers of level 2 by themselves or by one of the three other numbers of this level.

Finally, level 4 consists of eight numbers obtained by multiplying the numbers of level 3 by one of the four 'harmonic numbers' from level 2. The resulting system consists of eight degrees, each separated by one tone (*tonus*) or one half-tone. Note that the author of the diagram has confused *(h)emi(o)lion*, which is the proportion of 3 to 2, with *hemitonon*, the half step. This error, perhaps due to similarly sounding foreign terms, is easily corrected by use of the Pythagorean half-step 256 to 243, indicated explicitly in the *Timaeus*.[38] As Plutarch has demonstrated in his treatise *The Generation of the Soul in the Timaeus*, the number 512 over the letter C is indeed obtained by dividing the product of 486 × 256 (which is 124,416) by 243.[39] This number, 512, corresponds of course to the half-step higher than the preceding note.

On the fifth and last level, there is a series of eight letters that resemble alphabet notation, but which are instead, as in Boethius, letters indicating points on a line. Under the eight letters in question appears a new series of numbers, not written in red ink as the preceding ones, but in black. In this part of the diagram, there are many variants among the Visigothic manuscripts, but despite numerous attempts at correction, I have never been able to deduce a coherent system from this puzzling series of numbers.[40]

Now, before drawing any conclusions, it is necessary to compare the scale given by the Visigothic manuscripts of Isidorus with the scales of the Timaeus from Locri[41] and of Proclus.[42] The comparison makes clear that while the three Greek authors were constructing an instrumental scale, the anonymous interpolator intentionally gave a vocal scale divided into two disjunct tetrachords.

The identity of this scholar must be sought in the south of Spain, where he worked in contact with Arab circles, the latter informed by the work of Ptolemy, Porphyry and of the Timaeus Locri. This medieval Platonist, rather than inserting philosophical reflections on music in general into the Third Book of the *Etymologiae*, sought to show that the scale of the liturgical chant of Spain existed in a universe where, according to Pythagoras, 'All is number' (πᾶν ἀριθμός). This anonymous author shows by his diagrams (Pl. 11.1) that cosmic music (diagram 24), like the material universe composed of four elements (diagram 29), is ruled by the same laws as the 'Harmony, Soul of World' (diagram 27 and 28), that is, by the same simple proportional relationships.

V. Conclusions

In sum, the most important benefit to the study of the old liturgical repertories lies in this large diagram from the Visigothic manuscripts, with the scale of the chant used in Spain before the Carolingian reform.

From the philological point of view:

- This diagram, which mentions both Plato and Porphyry, offers a valuable complement to the restoration of the lost *Commentary on the Timaeus* published by Angelo Raffaele Sodano in 1964.
- We can note for the first time in the history of music theory how scribes and illustrators were confronted with the problems of 'mise en page' as they introduced large diagrams into the text. The same problems would be posed later, during the ninth century, with the treatises of Boethius and in the *Musica* and *Scolica enchiriadis*.

From the musicological point of view:

- The large diagram with the two disjunct tetrachords interpolated in the *Musica Isidori* was widespread only in the Iberian peninsula and never traveled beyond the Pyrenees.
- The two central tetrachords of the scale depicted in the *Musica enchiriadis* are very similar to those of the large diagram interpolated in the 'Isidorian encyclopedia' (see Fig. 11.2). This similarity is not by chance, because the construction of the two scales is based on the same principle, which is – according to the *Musica enchiriadis* – that each tetrachord is formed by four steps with the semitone in the middle: T S T. The author of the *Musica enchiriadis* continues: 'By a continuous multiplication of these tones, an unlimited series is made as they proceed in similarly constituted groups of four until they run out ascending or descending . . . This . . . shows that you may extend the tones up or down in a series until the voice gives out . . .'.[43]
- Among the literary sources of the *Musica* and *Scolica enchiriadis*, we note Calcidius' translation and commentary on the *Timaeus*, but no reference to the *Musica Isidori*. This lack of citation is surprising, since the excerpt in nine chapters from the Third Book of the *Etymologiae*, known as *Musica Isidori*, was widespread in the north of France.[44]
- Just as in the *Musica enchiriadis*, the Old Hispanic diagram consisting of two disjunct tetrachords T S T could be extended up and down according to the range of the human voice. But at the bottom of the

Ex. 11.2 The Scale of Old Spanish Chant

		T	T	S	T	T	T	S	T	T
Calcidius	192	216	243	256	288	324	364s	384	432	
Timaeus Locr.	384	432	486	512	576	648	729	768	864	972 . . .
Proclus Diad.	384	432	486	512	576	648	729	768		
Ps. Isidore		432	486	512	576	648	729	768	864	
	A	B	C	D	E	F	G	H		

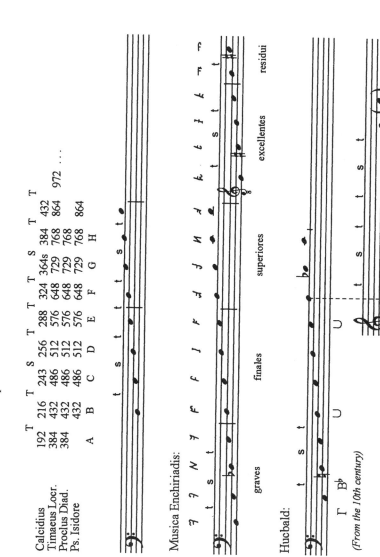

Musica Enchiriadis:

Hucbald:

(From the 10th century)

scale, as at the top, there is no longer a concordance between the scale of the chant and the Greater Perfect System constructed of five tetrachords, including the *synemmenon*.

- Given the close connection between the two distinct branches of the Gallican repertories, we must admit that their common source is a scale of the Byzantine chant, probably the *trochos* or cycle of fifths, attested only by Johannes Koukouzelis in the fourteenth century.
- Now we can understand how the first collaborators of Charlemagne, educated in Spain or in Septimania – Theodulf, Helisachar, Witiza (Benedict of Aniane), Agobard and others – could easily change from Old Hispanic chant to the new Gregorian chant, and why they could criticize it by comparison with their own repertory.
- Later, after 820/830, with the introduction of the *De institutione musica* of Boethius, the urgent problem was to find a correct adaptation of the Greater Perfect System of Greco-Roman music that corresponded to the scale of the chant. Hucbald of St-Amand, who changed the division of the Greater Perfect System into tetrachords T S T, was the first to propose such an adaptation.[45] Nevertheless, it was necessary to introduce Gamma under *proslambanomenos* at the bottom of the scale. This was done – with much disputation – during the tenth century (see Ex. 11.2).

Taken together, the Platonic diagrams that are interpolated into the *Musica Isidori* show the importance that these intervals of fourth, fifth and octave must have had in the melodic composition of the Old Hispanic repertory, as in Gregorian chant – the heir to Gallican chant. Their importance applied not only in psalmody, but also in the melodic texture of the antiphons and responsories. Nevertheless, I believe that there are at least two small differences between the two Gallican repertories (the Old Hispanic and the Gallican from Gaul preserved in the Aquitanian processionals): first, the psalmody; second, the style of the final cadences:

1. Old Hispanic psalmody contains only four modes, with a large variety of final cadences. At the mediant of the verse there is only a short rest without melodic formula, exactly as in Ambrosian psalmody.
2. Another difference between the two Gallican repertories rises from the treatment of the final cadences of each antiphon and responsory. In Old Hispanic chant, as in Ambrosian chant, several final cadences fall abruptly; in Gregorian chant, on the contrary, the cadence is embellished by a slow, progressive, and very conclusive preparation.

During the reign of Charles the Bald, in the ninth century, priests and clerics from Toledo received invitations to sing the Mass in the royal chapel at Compiègne. The Gallican rite had been abolished for at least sixty years, but Old Hispanic chant was surely perceived as a close partner of the 'recent' Gregorian chant.

Notes

1 *MECL*, pp. 111–17. Ezio Franceschini and R. Weber, 'Itinerarium Egeriae', in *Itineraria et alia geographica* (Turnhout: Brepols, 1965), 27–103.
2 *MECL*, pp. 155 ff. On psalmody, see James McKinnon, 'Liturgical Psalmody in the Sermons of St. Augustine', in Peter Jeffery (ed.), *The Study of Medieval Chant, Paths and Bridges, East and West: In Honor of Kenneth Levy* (Rochester, NY: Boydell & Brewer, 2001), 7–24.
3 'Hoc in tempore primum antiphonae, hymni ac vigiliae in ecclesia Mediolanensi celebrari coeperunt. Cujus celebritatis devotio usque in hodiernum diem non solum in eadem ecclesia, verum per omnes pene Occidentis provincias manet.' Paulinus, *De vita sancti Ambrosii*, no. 13, in *PL* 14: 31D. Cf. *Bibliotheca hagiographica latina* (repr. Brussels: Société des Bollandistes, 1992), no. 377.
4 Wunibald Roezter, *Des heiligen Augustinus Schriften als liturgie-geschichtliche Quellen* (Munich: M. Hueber, 1930).
5 Louis Duchesne, *Origines du culte chrétien: étude sur la liturgie latine avant Charlemagne* (5th edn, Paris: De Boccard, 1925), 100–109, 158–63, 167–70, 200–40; Edmund Bishop, *The Genius of the Roman Rite* (Liturgica Historica; Papers on the Liturgy and Religious Life of the Western Church; Oxford: Clarendon Press, 1918), 1–20.
6 Thomas Forrest Kelly, *The Beneventan Chant* (Cambridge: Cambridge University Press, 1989).
7 Philippe Bernard, *Du chant romain au chant grégorien* (Paris: Cerf, 1996).
8 Michel Huglo, 'Le Chant "vieux-romain": liste des manuscrits', *Sacris erudiri*, 6 (1954), 96–124; Paul F. Cutter, *Musical Sources of the Old Roman Mass: An Inventory of MS Rome, St. Cecilia Gradual 1071, MS Rome, Vaticanum latinum 5319, MSS Rome, San Pietro F 22 and F 11* ([Rome]: American Institute of Musicology, 1979).
9 *Bernhardi cardinalis et Lateranensis ecclesiae prioris Ordo officiorum ecclesiae Lateranensis*, ed. Ludwig Fischer (Munich and Freising: Dr. F. P. Datterer, 1916). This *Ordo* was written ca. 1139–45.
10 Bernard, *Du chant romain*, 381, 416, 636.
11 Michel Huglo, 'Antifone antiche per la "fractio panis"', *Ambrosius*, 31 (1955), 85–95.
12 Giacomo Baroffio, '*Iter liturgicum ambrosianum*. Inventario sommario di libri liturgici ambrosiani', *Aevum*, 74 (2000), 583–601 (handlist of 192 antiphoners, twelve processionals and many othr books of chant).
13 Michel Huglo et al. (eds), *Fonti e paleografia del canto ambrosiano* (Archivio ambrosiano, 7; Milan: Pontificio Istituto di Musica Sacra, 1956), 117–37.
14 PM 6 (1900), 9–12.
15 'Tam modico flexu faciebat sonare lectorem psalmi ut pronuncianti vicinior esset quam canenti'; *Confessiones*, X.33.50; *PL* 32; trans. McKinnon, *MECL*, p. 155.
16 Louis Brou, 'L'Alleluia dans la liturgie mozarabe', *Anuario musical*, 6 (1951), 3–90.
17 Michel Huglo, 'Les *Preces* des graduels aquitains empruntées à la liturgie hispanique', *Hispania sacra*, 8 (1955), 361–83.
18 For letters on the Gallican liturgy by Pseudo-Germanus, bishop of Paris (fifth century), see K. Gamber, ed. *Ordo antiquus gallicanus* (Regensburg: F. Pustet, 1965); see also *Expositio antiquae liturgiae gallicanae*, ed. E. C. Ratcliff (Henry Bradshaw Society Publication, 98; London: Henry Bradshaw Society, 1971); and see the supplement to the introduction by Michel Huglo, *Scriptorium: Bulletin codicologique*, 26 (1972), 411, no. 903.

19 *De ecclesiasticis officiis, c.V–c.X* (*PL* 83: 742–4); ed. C. Lawson (CCSL 113 (Turnhout: Brepols, 1989), 7–10.

20 *Isidori Hispalensis episcopi Etymologiarum*, ed. Wallace Martin Lindsay, 2 vols (Oxford: Clarendon Press, 1911).

21 Bernhard Bischoff, 'Die europäische Verbreitung der Werken Isidors von Sevilla', *Mittelalterliche Studien* (Stuttgart: Anton Hiersemann, 1966), i, 174–94; Marc Reydellet, 'La Diffusion des "Origines" d'Isidore de Séville au haut Moyen Age', *Mélanges de l'Ecole française de Rome*, 78 (1966), 383–437; Michel Huglo, 'Die *Musica Isidori* nach den Handschriften des deutschen Sprachgebietes', in Walter Pass and Alexander Rausch (eds), *Mittelalterliche Musiktheorie in Zentral Europa* (Tutzing: Hans Schneider, 1998), 79–86.

22 Michel Huglo, 'Les Diagrammes d'hamonique interpolés dans les manuscrits hispaniques de la *Musica Isidori*', *Scriptorium*, 75 (1994), 171–86 at 181.

23 Escorial, Monasterio, Real Bibl. & I 14 (8th–9th c.), P I 6 (9th c.) and T II 24 (10th c.); Madrid, BN Vitr. 14.3, *olim* Toletanus 15.8 (end of 8th c.); cf. Manuel C. Díaz y Díaz, *Manuscritos visigóticos del sur de la Peninsula* (Seville: University of Seville, 1995); Agustín Millares-Carlo, *Corpus de códices visigóticos*, ed. Díaz y Díaz et al., i: *Estudio*, ii: *Album* (Las Palmas de Gran Canaria: Universidad Nacional de Educación a Distancia, Centro Asociado de Las Palmas de Gran Canaria, Gobierno de Canarias, 1999), 221 ff. (Topographic Index).

24 Escorial & I 3, P I 7, P I 8; Madrid, RAH 25, RAH 76; Madrid, BN 10008; Paris, BNF n. a. lat. 2169. On this last manuscript, see Michel Huglo, 'Le *De musica* des Etymologies de saint Isidore de Séville d'après le manuscrit de Silos', *Revista de Musicología*, 15 (1992), 565–78; Millares-Carlo, *Corpus*, ii, 221.

25 Original text: 'Terraconam in Hispania Scipiones construxerunt: ideo caput est Terraconensis provinciae.' [Interpolated text: 'Caesaraugusta Terraconensis Hispaniae oppidum a Caesare Augusto et situm et nominatum, loci amoenitate et deliciis praestantius civitatibus Hispaniae cunctis atque inlustrius florens sanctorum martyrum sepulturis.'] *Etymologiae* 15. 1. 65–6.

26 Huglo, 'Die *Musica Isidori*', 81.

27 *Euclidis phaenomena et scripta musica. Fragmenta*, ed. J. L. Heiberg (Leipzig: B.G. Teubner, 1916), 68.

28 *Isidori Etymologiae. Codex Toletanus*, ed. Rudolf Beer (Leiden: A. W. Sijthoff, 1909).

29 See the list of manuscripts in *Scriptorium*, 48 (1994), 183. I discuss here the prefatory letters of the *Etymologiae* and the 'praise of Saragossa'.

30 *Porphyrii in Platonis Timaeum commentariorum fragmenta*, ed. Angelo Raffaele Sodano (Naples: [n. pub.], 1964). In his commentary on Ptolemy's *Harmonics*, Porphyry alluded to his own commentary on the *Timaios*; see *Porphyrios Kommentar zur Harmonielehre des Ptolemaios*, ed. Ingemar Düring (Göteborg: Elanders boktryckeri aktiebolag, 1932), 115, l. 30.

31 *Timaeus a Calcidio translatus commentarioque instructus*, ed. Jan Hendrik Waszink (London: Warburg Institute, 1962; 2nd edn, London: E. J. Brill, 1975), 82, diagram VII.

32 Michel Huglo, 'La Réception de Calcidius et des *Commentarii* de Macrobe à l'époque carolingienne', *Scriptorium*, 44 (1990), 15–17.

33 After the Program PANDORA 2.1 (search program for the Thesaurus linguae Graecae) that I used during my research at the Institute of Advanced Study in Princeton, 1990–91.

34 *Jamblichi de vita pythagorica liber*, ed. Ludovicus Deubner, rev. Uldaricus Klein (Leipzig: B.G. Teubner, 1975), 68. Commentary by Frieder Zaminer, 'Pythagoras und die Anfänge des musiktheoretischen Denkens bei den Griechen', *Jahrbuch*

des Staatlichen Instituts für Musikforschung Preussischer Kulturbesitz, 1979–80, 203–11.

35 Escorial, R II 18 (8th c.), fol. 6v; E. A. Lowe, *Codices Latini antiquiores*, Part II: *Spain* (Oxford: Clarendon Press, 1966), no. 1632.

36 *Theonis Smyrnaei philosophi Platonici expositio rerum mathematicarum ad legendum Platonem utilium*, ed. Eduard Hiller (Leipzig: B. G. Teubner, 1878).

37 *Timaeus*, ed. Waszink, 90.

38 Plato, *Œuvres complètes*, x: *Timée, Critias*, ed. Albert Rivaud, 4th rev. edn (Paris: Société d'édition Les Belles Lettres, 1963), 148, 36b.

39 Plutarch, *Moralia*, xiii, pt. 1: *De animae procreatione in Timaeo*, ed. Harold Cherniss (Cambridge, Mass.: Harvard University Press, 1976), 301.

40 I am grateful to my father-in-law, Dr. Raymond Haggh, professor emeritus at the University of Nebraska at Lincoln, for his help in verifying the numbers of this diagram.

41 *De natura mundi et animae*, ed. Walter Marg (Leiden: E. J. Brill, 1972), 125–7, 72.

42 *Procli Diadochi in Platonis Timaeum commentaria*, ed. Ernst Diehl, 3 vols. (B. G. Teubner, 1903–6), iii, 170 ff.; Proclus, *Commentaire sur le Timée*, André Marie Jean Festugière (Paris: Les Belles Lettres, 1967), vol. 3, bk. 3, 215–57.

43 *Musica enchiriadis and Scolica enchiriadis*, trans. Raymond Erickson, ed. Claude V. Palisca (New Haven: Yale University Press, 1995), 2.

44 See 'Isidorus' in Michael Bernhard, 'Überlieferung und Fortleben der antiken lateinischen Musiktheorie im Mittelalter', in *Rezeption des antiken Fachs im Mittelalter* (Geschichte der Musiktheorie, 3; Darmstadt: Wissenschaftliche Buchgesellschaft, 1990), 33–5.

45 Yves Chartier, *L'Œuvre musicale d'Hucbald de Saint-Amand: les compositions et le traité de musique* (Saint-Laurent Québec: Bellarmin, 1995).

Chapter 12

Old Roman Votive-Mass Chants in Florence, Biblioteca Riccardiana, MSS 299 and 300 and Vatican City, Biblioteca Apostolica Vaticana, Archivio San Pietro F 11: A Source Study

John Boe

Besides the five well-known and more or less complete manuscript sources for Old Roman chant – three for the Mass and two for the Office[1] – which remain of the 'fifty antiphoners, graduals, missals, and other service books' destroyed by order of the Orsini pope Nicholas III between 1277 and 1280,[2] there survive three lesser sources having notation for a limited number of Old Roman chants: manuscripts 299 and 300 in the Biblioteca Riccardiana at Florence and one manuscript in the Archivio San Pietro, F 11, at the Vatican. These lesser sources have also been known for some time. I shall revise the conventional descriptions, taking into account more recent paleographical studies by Paola Supino Martini and J. F. Ramacker's proposals in regard to Riccardiana 299,[3] and summarizing my comparisons of the Proper chants from one of the votive Masses they contain, namely the *Missa pro congregatione*, and providing a transcription of another, the *Missa sponsalicia*. When possible, my comparisons will include notational and melodic variants from pieces in the complete Old Roman sources, but I shall try to avoid comparing the Roman melodies to their Frankish counterparts. I shall also examine the kalendar implied by the rubrics and collects of San Pietro F 11. Although I can show that the descriptions given for these three manuscripts in older studies were often mistaken in regard to provenance, I cannot as of now point to specific basilicas, monasteries or other Roman churches as the sure source for any of these three manuscripts, though I shall tentatively propose where San Pietro F 11 might have originated. A similar inspection of the chants and the Mass for the greater litanies on 25 April and of the votive Masses for the dead in some of these manuscripts – and especially the notated Roman Office for the dead in San Pietro F 11 – might help locate them, but limitations of space and time foreclose their consideration here.

Florence, Biblioteca Riccardiana 299

The two manuscripts now at the Biblioteca Riccardiana in Florence bearing the shelf marks 299 and 300 were thought to have come from the 'Vallombrosa Abbey of the Camuldulese monks, an abbey dedicated to SS. Philip and James in the diocese of Siena'.[4] Johannes Ramackers's 1965 study has shown that this ascription is erroneous,[5] and with it the proposition that Old Roman chants were being copied and sung in the diocese of Siena in the eleventh or early twelfth centuries. He demonstrated that the added entry on the last folio of Riccardiana 299 must refer to the cathedral of Sorrento, the only cathedral dedicated to SS. Philip and James among hundreds of Italian cathedrals:

> Anno domini millesimo centesimo XIII^mo^, indictione sexta, consecrata est hec ęcclesia anno XV^mo^ presulatus domni Pascalis secundi pape a domno Ricardo Albanensi episcopo, XVII^mo^ kal. april., feria I, ad honorem domini nostri Iesu Christi et beatę Marię semper virginis et sanctę Crucis omniumque angelorum atque ad honorem beatissimorum apostolorum Philippi et Iacobi omniumque apostolorum mar[tirum] confessorum, virginum et omnium sanctorum. In qua posite sunt ex reliquiis sanctorum Stephani confessoris, Felicis papę, Felicis mar[tiris], Cyriaci, Savini, carbonibus sancti Laurentii mar[tiris], Helene, Emerentiane, Martinę, Quirillę, Quiriacę. Precepitque etiam supranominatus episcopus, ut, quicumque ad istam ecclesiam apostolorum Philippi et Iacobi venerit in die kalendarum maii, pro maxima pietate duodecim dierum suorum peccatorum habeat indulgentiam. Amen. (Riccardiana 299, fol. 230^v^).

The year, the day of the month, the indiction, and the day of the week – all coincide with the fourth Sunday in Lent, *Laetare* Sunday, 16 March 1113. (But it was the fourteenth year of Pope Paschal II's *praesulatus*, not the fifteenth, at least as we reckon years today.)

Richard, cardinal-bishop of Albano and one of the suffragan bishops who assisted at the consecration of the pope, was often sent as papal legate to England and France. He was one of Paschal II's closest advisers and accompanied him during his stay in south Italy during the difficult years 1111–12.[6] The pope briefly returned to Rome in October 1111 for a council at the Lateran. After holding a synod in Benevento in February 1113, Paschal left for Rome on 15 March. He had returned to the Lateran palace by 9 April or a few days earlier, probably in time for Easter, 6 April. Presumably Richard of Albano had rejoined him.

Richard is known to have witnessed papal documents in Benevento between 2 January and 15 February 1113. He then traveled to Sorrento, it is thought by way of Salerno, where he would have seen the widow of Roger I of Apulia. Clearly either the pope or the cardinal had been invited by Archbishop Barbatus of Sorrento to consecrate his recently rebuilt cathedral. If the invitation had been extended to the pope, Paschal would have sent the cardinal to Sorrento to act in his stead.[7] The entry on the last folio of the manuscript, given above, leaves little doubt that it was Cardinal Richard who presented the sacramentary, now Florence, Riccardiana 299, to Sorrento

Cathedral or to the archbishop. A collection of relics also presented to the cathedral and named in the entry on fol. 230^{v} was probably more highly regarded than the sacramentary itself. The exclusively Roman nature of the relic collection suggests that the consecration of Sorrento Cathedral was planned well in advance of Richard's departure from Benevento, since the gathering of these relics from all over Rome would have taken some time. Every saint whose relics are listed was either buried in one of the Roman cemeteries, or had been translated to and was honored at a Roman basilica or other church or chapel, or else was included in the twelfth-century Roman kalendars. None of the saints whose relics are included in the list was native to or otherwise associated with Sorrento or its diocese. Moreover, in Riccardiana 299, the Mass for the feast of SS. Philip and James on 1 May is treated in an altogether normal manner: there is no indication – such as larger rubrics or special illumination – of its being the patronal festival. Even if the clear evidence of Roman notation, Roman chant and Roman script were disregarded, an origin at Sorrento for the manuscript would have to be ruled out. Paola Supino Martini nicely summarizes Ramackers's account:

> Si deve a Ramackers tale localizzazione del *Sacramentario* e l'identificazione con il Duomo di Sorrento della chiesa del SS. Giacomo e Filippo (230^{v}), dice consacrata il 16 marzo 1113 dal cardinale Riccardo di Albano: prodotto fra la seconda metà e il penultimo quarto del secolo XI, il *Sacramentario*, della curia pontificia, sarebbe pervenuto con Pasquale II a Benevento – dove nel febbraio 1113 si celebrò uno sinodo – e, successivamente, sarebbe stato offerto in dono alla cattedrale di Sorrento dal cardinale Riccardo, venuto al seguito del pontefice. Poiché la scrittura del *Sacramentario*, il testo e la decorazione riconducono a Roma e alla regione romana e d'altra parte il manoscritto è un libro di lusso sotto ogni aspetto. . . . La scrittura, tuttavia, è a mio avviso più tarda di quanto non abbia ritenuto Ramackers, della fine del secolo XI, e dovuta a due mani principali anziché ad una.[8]

When I saw the manuscript many years ago, not then realizing its Roman origin and of course unaware of its presentation to Sorrento Cathedral, I indicated in my notes that the colors of the initial letters – red, green and yellow – and the beautiful script were 'reminiscent of Vat. 5319'; that the Roman stations were usually given and also collects *ad ues[peras]* with 'lots of extra collects here and there'; that there was a rich kalendar of saints, temporale and sanctorale being combined; that *Dom*[*inica*] *uacat* rubrics were entered for the fourth Sunday in Advent (but followed nonetheless by the Mass *Memento nostri*), for the second Sunday in Lent (station *ad S. Mar*[*iam*] *in dominic*[*am*] (recte *in domnica*), with the Mass *Dominus illuminatio mea*), and for the Saturday before Palm Sunday (*q*[*ua*]*n*[*do*] – *or* q[*uo*]*n*[*iam*] – *dominus pontifex elemos*[*inam*] *dat*, but with the Mass *Domine exaudi*); that Good Friday had only the Tract *Qui habitat* after the second collect; and, notably for Rome, that the text *Exultent* [sic] *iam angelica turba* was sung on Holy Saturday. The *ordo missae*, which supplies private prayers to occupy the celebrant fully throughout Mass, is placed after the octave of Pentecost. All Sundays after Pentecost are given consecutively. (There is of course no *Omnes gentes* Mass for the seventh – or eighth – Sunday.) The sanctorale and the votive Masses are entered following the Masses for the Sundays after Pentecost. The manuscript, then, is correctly referred to as a sacramentary, but a sacramentary including the singers' Propers integrated with the celebrant's prayers. (Though written much smaller, these Propers seem not to have been intended for notation.) But the Masses usually lack the readings, which, however, are exceptionally supplied for the wedding Mass. The only notation original to the manuscript is for the singers' Propers of the *Missa sponsalicia* on fols. 182^{r}–185^{v}, where more room than elsewhere was left so as to accommodate *c* and *F* clefs and lines. The delicate Roman notation they bear dates from the early twelfth century.[9]

Why was the *Missa sponsalicia* singled out for notation? The short answer is the one given by Huglo – although, following Ebner, as we have seen, Huglo then thought that the manuscript was destined for a Sienese monastery:

> La présence d'un formulaire vieux-romain dans ce ms. et le suivant [i.e., Riccardiana 300] s'explique sans peine: comme le répertoire grégorien n'a prévu aucune pièce de chant spéciale pour la messe de mariage, on a puisé dans le chant de Rome qui comportait le répertoire propre suivant: Intr. *Deus Israel*; Gr. *Uxor tua*; All. *Mittat tibi* [recte: All. *Diffusa est gratia* – the verse *Mittat tibi* is found in Rome, Bibl. Angelica 123]; Off. *In te speravi* (emprunté au Temporal); Comm. *Ecce sic*.[10]

The question 'Why was the *Missa sponsalicia* singled out for notation?' needs to be rephrased: 'In a Roman sacramentary combined with a Mass antiphoner mostly lacking neumes, why were the wedding Mass Propers singled out for notation?' It is at least possible that the sacramentary Riccardiana 299 was prepared for a papal legate's personal use while traveling. If a papal legate was to sing Mass or otherwise preside at a noble, royal or imperial wedding, it may have been thought useful for the legate to have available not only the text of the Roman wedding Propers but also their melodies, so that they could be copied and sung – seeing that the chants of the wedding Propers did not exist in most Gregorian books.[11] Our sacramentary might indeed have been prepared for Richard of Albano, but more probably it would have been prepared earlier, perhaps for the Rainerius whom Gregory VII, soon after 1078, made abbot of St. Lawrence *fuori le mura* and cardinal-priest of San Clemente.[12] Pope Urban II sent him as his legate to Spain and southern France in 1089 and 1091. When he was elected pope under difficult circumstances at his own titular church of San Clemente on 13 August 1099, Cardinal Rainerius took the name of Paschal II. If our sacramentary was indeed prepared for Rainerius – or at least used by him before his election – then, as pontiff with the Lateran archives at his disposal, he might have handed the now superfluous sacramentary over to Richard of Albano to present to Sorrento Cathedral or its bishop in 1113. A date for the manuscript when Rainerius was still cardinal-priest of San Clemente would suit the liturgical circumstances Kelly described as surrounding the Exultet text in the manuscript.[13] In fact we do not know and may never know exactly when and where Riccardiana 299 was written, except that it was in Rome toward the end of the eleventh century.[14]

Florence, Biblioteca Riccardiana 300

In its present state, the manuscript Riccardiana 300 is best described as an incomplete votive missal. Both the beginning and the end of the manuscript have disappeared. Most of the now-missing first part of the manuscript might have been a rituale. Or, in its complete state, the manuscript may have indeed been a votive missal, beginning with Masses for the greatest feasts and having more votive Masses for special intentions than it contains at present. Lessons are supplied for most of the Masses. The texts of some Proper chants are also supplied, but only the chants for the *Missa pro congregatione* (fols. 7^v–9^r, beginning with the Introit *Salus populi*) and for the *Missa ad sponsas benedicendas* (fols. 9^v–11^v , beginning with the Introit *Deus israhel*) are notated.[15] In the wedding Mass, there are slight but significant differences between the versions of the Proper chants in Riccardiana 300 and 299, not only in title but in the melodies and their notation. Furthermore, differences from Riccardiana 299 in the wording and even the content of the special wedding prayers in the present manuscript argue even more clearly for a Roman provenance for 300 distinct from that of 299. (Its Roman origin is confirmed by script, illumination and chant.)[16] But because of the contiguous shelf mark, Riccardiana 300 has always been assigned the same provenance as Riccardiana 299.[17] It is indeed likely that the two manuscripts entered the Biblioteca Riccardiana in Florence at the same time in the sixteenth century from the collection of the Riccardi family. Alas, there is no entry in this votive missal linking it to Sorrento or to Richard of Albano. In addition to the differences in chant versions, the later style of Roman notation – at least fifty years later than the style employed in Riccardiana 299 – make it certain that 300 is a considerably later manuscript. In fact, all we know of its history, apart from its origin at Rome, is that it has reposed next to MS 299 on the shelves of the Biblioteca Riccardiana at least since 1756, when Lami published his catalog.[18]

Vatican City, Archivio San Pietro, Codex F 11

The manuscript San Pietro F 11, since 1940 held at the Biblioteca Apostolica Vaticana, consists of a rituale combined with a collectar. It is sometimes called a rituale-orationale.[19] The rituale and most of the collectar were written by the same scribe – a point worth noting. The rituale concludes in the middle of the recto of fol. 101, and the collectar begins with a full title page on the verso, continuing in the same hand as the rituale. Beginning at fol. 133^v, another hand completed the collectar, still others occasionally intervening. The opening folios have been torn away; the first leaves remaining – part of an *ordo* for the making of a catechumen – are moldy and often illegible. The rest of the baptismal order is followed by an order for the visitation and communion of the sick and the dying. The entire Office for the dead, beginning with first Vespers, follows. The antiphons and responds of the Offices are notated with *c* and *F* clefs, a red line for *F*, and a partly faded yellow line for *c*. The lessons for Nocturns are included. A notated Mass for the dead begins at fol. 52^{v};[20] the absolution of the body, with chants, begins on fol. 57^{r}, and the committal at the grave, with chants, on fol. 59^{r}. Masses for the third, seventh and thirtieth days *post mortem* follow, beginning on fol. 66^{v}. Only the first of these Masses is notated.[21] The *Missa sponsalicia* begins on fol. 81^{v}; the chants *In letania maiores* and the notated Mass *Exaudiuit* for 25 April begin on fol. 86^{r}; and an *Ordo misse* without chant follows on fol. 90^{v}. In the blank space toward the bottom of fol. 101^{r}, an unknown sixteenth- or possibly early seventeenth-century hand has entered the ex libris: *Bibliothecae Basilicae S. Petri.*

The title page for the collectar, on fol. 101^{v}, reads as follows:

IN $\overline{\text{N}}$ D$\overline{\text{NI}}$ N$\overline{\text{RI}}$ I$\overline{\text{HV}}$ X$\overline{\text{PI}}$
INCIPIT ORATIONALES T$\overline{\text{OTIVS}}$ ANNI C$\overline{\text{irc}}$.
EXPOSITO A S$\overline{\text{CO}}$ $\overline{\text{GG}}$
PaPa VRBIS ROME
DOMINICA PRIMA DE ADVENTVM

'In nomine Domini nostri Ihesu Christi: incipit orationales totius anni circulo, exposito a sancto Gregorio, Papa Urbis Rome': an impressive if ungrammatical title, written in a mixture of *capitalis* and uncial letters reminiscent of twelfth-century Roman inscriptions. Stations are entered for many of the prayers. The temporale, including consecutively numbered Sundays after Pentecost, thus entitled, is intermingled with saints' days. When I examined the collectar, I jotted the comment, 'This will yield a kalendar.' In an influential study, Pierre Jounel extracted just such a kalendar from the collectar.[22] Jounel assumed that the manuscript was originally written for and probably at St. Peter's.[23] It is true that the manuscript has been in the Archivio San Pietro at least from the sixteenth century (or possibly the early seventeenth). Jounel himself takes occasional notice of incongruities in the collectar of F 11 when compared with usage at St. Peter's.[24] Yet Jounel entitles the kalendar he extracted from the F 11 collectar 'Sanctoral du Collectaire de Saint-Pierre' without qualification and cites it repeatedly to establish late eleventh-century practice at St. Peter's.[25]

Unfortunately, we have at present no firm evidence covering the entire year for the liturgical kalendar used at St. Peter's during the eleventh and twelfth centuries (at least, so far as I know) before the double witness of the Roman Office antiphoner San Pietro B 79: namely (1) its separate extensive kalendar (fols. 1^{r}–3^{v}) and (2) its more restricted series of feasts that can be extracted from the Offices and commemorations in the notated antiphoner itself and from its highly and idiosyncratically abbreviated rubrics. San Pietro B 79 cannot have been written before 1173, when Thomas Becket was canonized; more probably it was written between 1181 and 1187.[26] The evidence from its two lists of feasts, reprinted by Jounel (pp. 416–24) from Vezzosi's seventeenth-century edition of Tommasi and now fortunately available from the facsimile edition, is reinforced by a more selective list of feasts I have extracted from the Mass Propers and rubrics of the early thirteenth-century Roman Gradual from St. Peter's, Archivio San Pietro F 22. Their content proves – not too strong a word – that these two manuscripts were written to be used at St. Peter's.[27]

Moreover, many of the rubrics in these two manuscripts employ first-person plural declarative verbs: 'We sing (this piece)', 'We go to the baptistry'. This self-confident mode of rubrication ('What we have been doing, we will continue to do') without implied reference to authority or any external tradition seems to have been peculiar to the chapter of St. Peter's. These first-person declarative verbs contrast with the jussive subjunctives ('Let there be', 'Let them rise', 'Let it be sung'), direct imperatives or even second- and third-person indicatives ('[Now] you are silent – *taces*)[28] generally or occasionally found elsewhere. I have not come across rubrics voiced in the Petrine manner in manuscripts from any other Roman institution – certainly not in manuscripts other than those from St. Peter's. If rubrics like these were to turn up in manuscripts from northern institutions eager to imitate the details of Roman use, like Metz, it would not be surprising.[29]

For example, the abbreviated rubrics for the commemoration of the consecration of the new high altar over the confession by Pope Callistus II on 25 March 1123, and for the feast of the Annunciation falling on the same date – with priority given to the altar-consecration commemoration – are expanded by Jounel (p. 230) to read as follows:

> In Annuntiatione beatae Mariae est Consecratio maioris Altaris beati Petri, de qua Consecratione Vesperas et Matutinum facimus. Tertium vero Nocturnum de beata Maria facimus.

The rubrics in San Pietro F 22, fol. 53^{v}, for the procession to and from the font on Holy Saturday are similarly phrased (my expansions of the abbreviations):

> Cantato tracto, processionaliter imus ad fontes. finitis xii lectionı́bus et scrutinio, tractus: [*Sicut ceruus*]
>
> Celebrato baptismo redimus ad altare cum breui letania. nam [or tum?] letania cantauimus, viij [viiij?] *Kyrie leyson*, sollempniter cum *Gloria in excelsis deo*. Lecta uero epistula, domnus episcopus annuntiet tribus uicibus: *Alleluia*.

Of course, not every rubric in San Pietro B 79 and San Pietro F 22 is phrased in the first-person plural. The rubrics in F 22 just after those given above for the Holy Saturday vigil and the following Easter Mass revert to the third-person passive:

> Eodem die non cantatur *Credo* . . . et pacis osculum non datur. Sed communicato episcopo, absolute incipitur *Laudate dominum omnes gentes*.

Nevertheless, when other indications are appropriate to an origin at Rome from the late eleventh century to the early thirteenth, I suggest that the occurrence of 'we' rubrics indicates provenance from St. Peter's Basilica or, at least, intended use there.[30] Certainly the rubrics throughout B 79 and F 22 support a Petrine origin for these manuscripts, whose attribution to St. Peter's has in any case never been questioned.

The rituale-collectar San Pietro F 11 has no 'we' rubrics. If one is thereby led to question the traditional assignment of F 11 to St. Peter's – especially in view of its many other anomalies if regarded as Petrine (some of which were noted by Jounel himself) – one ought to begin by comparing the kalendar extracted from its collectar with the kalendars from the Petrine manuscripts B 79 and F 22. The comparisons will be lengthy and I am afraid tiresome; I shall endeavor to reduce them to essentials.

Besides the kalendars he assigned to the Vatican or the Lateran, Jounel printed three others dating from the second half of the eleventh century through the second half of the twelfth. One of these, now Rome, Bibl. Vallicelliana MS E 15, was written for and perhaps at the ancient titular basilica of St. Lawrence *in Damaso*;[31] the second, Archivio San Pietro F 14, was written for a new or newly rebuilt twelfth-century urban church, which Jounel calls 'St. Trypho'.[32] (Jounel's third kalendar, drawn from Vallicelliana C 62, is not in fact Roman.)[33] I have transferred Jounel's kalendars from Vallicelliana E 15 (St. Lawrence *in Damaso*)[34] and San Pietro F 14 ('St. Trypho') to a list of my own, which also includes the kalendars from the collectar of San Pietro F 11 and the three authentic kalendars from St. Peter's Basilica.[35] Tables 12.1 and 12.2 are intended to bring into relief the salient differences between the authentic Vatican kalendars and the kalendar from F 11. I have reproduced the orthography and punctuation of the Vatican kalendar entries and and rubrics and the rubrics of F 11 as exactly as possible – except that I have spelled out the abbreviation for *et*.

First we need to see how the kalendar from F 11 relates to the non-Petrine kalendars from the Damasian sacramentary, Vallicelliana E 15, and San Pietro F 14, the sacramentary of St. Trypho (or its neighbor and *Doppelgänger*, St. Savior *in Primicerio*). There are approximately seventeen feasts in F 11 not found in E 15.[36] Most of them commemorate Italian but non-Roman saints, such as Ambrose, Sabinus, Eustratius, Quiricus and Julitta, Nazarius and Celsus, the Maccabees and Giles – saints who had gained an early if limited cult at individual Roman churches, shrines and monasteries.[37] Thence they seeped into the older Roman and even the papal kalendar. Most of the seventeen instances are not surprising, in light of the seventy-five years or more that must separate the Damasian sacramentary from the copying of the later rituale-collectar F 11. But two feasts included in F 11 that are absent in E 15 deserve special attention. In F 11 the rubrics of these two feasts are written entirely in capital letters, an exceptional treatment for saints' days entered by the first hand of the collectar (fols. 102^r–133^r). Many occasions in the temporale were, however, rubricated by the same hand in *capitalis* or in uncial capitals. (In E 15, the Damasian sacramentary, almost all the rubrics heading feasts have varicolored capitals.) But – as is by no means evident from Jounel's transcription of F 11 – most of the saints' rubrics entered by the *second* main hand of F 11, beginning at folio 133^v, are regularly distinguished from the text of the collects by uncial capitals for some at least of their letters. (At least one of the intervening hands reverts to ordinary Roman minuscule for rubrication.) In most liturgical manuscripts, isolated capital entries like those in the first half of the F 11 sanctorale call attention to the greatest feasts or to the patronal festivals of the churches the manuscripts were intended for. Yet, in view of the above, it remains unclear whether the two saints' rubrics entered by the first hand of the manuscript entirely in capital letters should be reckoned as significant and (if so) what it is that they might signify.

Let us briefly consider the second entry in F 11. It is for the feast of the Annunciation, 25 March: 'ANNVNTIATIO GLO[RIO]SE D[E]I GENITRICIS ET VIRGINIS MARIE'. It is remarkable that this universal feast of the incarnation of our Lord – regarded here chiefly in its Marian aspect – was omitted in E 15, the Damasian kalendar (as Jounel has extracted and printed it). If the Mass for the Annunciation was indeed omitted, its absence must have been due to scribal oversight. And *if* the Damasian sacramentary served as one of the models for F 11, then the first scribe of F 11 may have wished to emphasize – by using the ubiquitous capitals of the E 15 rubrics for his Annunciation rubric – that he had corrected his model in his collectar.[38]

The other of the two perhaps significant entries in the collectar of F 11 not contained in the Damasian E 15 is for the *natale*, the martyrdom or heavenly birthday, of SS. Cyrus and John in Alexandria during the Diocletian persecution:[39]

> Nat[ale] S[AN]C[T]OR[VM] CYRI ET IOH[ANN]IS. OR[ATIO]. INTERCESSIO O[MNIPOTEN]S D[EV]S D[OMI]NE BEATOR[VM] MARTIRV[M] CYRI ET IOH[ANN]IS BEATA NOS FOVEAT. [fol. 112v] ut eor[um] sacra natalicia. et temporaliter frequentemus et conspiciamus eterna. P[er].

If these capital letters, uniquely extending to the beginning of the collect itself, do indeed indicate the patron saints of the church for which the manuscript was intended (and if they were not merely copied from an exemplar), then the only Roman church that can be considered as having commissioned and used the manuscript would be SS. Cyrus and John *de Militiis* in the Via Biberatica.[40] Although its exact whereabouts in the vicinity of the Torre delle Milizie and the Foro Traiano is disputed, by 1130 or earlier the church was a *chiesa filiale* of SS. Philip and James (now Santi Apostoli), as confirmed in a bull of (Anti)pope Anaclete II in that year. By the thirteenth century, however, *S. Abbacyri de Militiis* had become a *cappella papale* paying an annual tribute to the Lateran. An *archipresbyter ecclesiae SS. Cyri et Iohannis de Urbe* is recorded as having been entrusted with papal commissions, and Nicholas IV in 1289 granted indulgences 'dilectis filiis archipresbytero et capitulo ecclesiae nostrae Sanctorum Cyri et Iohannis in Militiis de Urbe'.

On the other hand, there are approximately thirty-one feasts in the rich kalendar of the Damasian sacramentary that are *not* found in F 11. Twelve of these could be considered feasts that were omitted from F 11 because they were in some sense peculiar to St. Lawrence *in Damaso*. Thus – supposing for the moment that F 11 was modeled chiefly upon E 15 – the omission of the NAT. SCE BARBARE (4 December, St. Barbara's being a chapel at St. Lawrence *in Damaso*) and of the octave day of St. Lawrence (although often found in Roman books) would belong to this category. The feast SCI SABE MONACHI ET HEREMITE (5 December) and the VIG[ILIA] SCI BENEDICTI

(20 March) seem to reflect a certain interest at St. Lawrence *in Damaso* in monastic kalendars and local monasteries not shared by F 11. (The *transitus* of Benedict on 21 March and the feast of his sister St. Scholastica on 10 February are regularly found in twelfth-century Roman books, monastic or not.) The double commemoration in E 15 of the apostle Matthias on 30 April as well as on the standard date of 24 February, and of Bartholomew on 13 June (the south Italian feast of his translation to Lipari and Benevento from India) as well as on the standard date of 24 (or 25) August are understandably discarded in F 11 in favor of the standard dates. The APPARITIO SCI MICHAELIS ARCHANGELI (at the Gargano peninsula, 8 May) and the TRANSFIGURATIO D[OMI]NI N[OSTR]I IH[ES]V XR[IST]I (6 August), both universally kept in southern Italy, were for a time adopted in many Roman kalendars in the early twelfth century but not in F 11.[41] The 13 May date of the DEDIC[ATIO] SCA[E] MARIA[E] AD MAR[TYRES] (that is, the dedication of the Pantheon as a Christian church in 609 – a day used in southern Italy for the dedication feast of local churches) was already being dropped from Roman books during the twelfth century in favor of specific dedication dates, often in October or November, in imitation of the dedication feast of the Lateran on 9 November. The Beneventan feast XII FR[ATRV]M (1 September) is linked in E 15 with the *natale* SCI PRISCI (a martyr at Capua), but Priscus is omitted from F 11. The suspiciously named virgins SVPHIE PISTIS ELPIS AGAPIS were entered on 30 September. They are omitted in F 11. A strange conjunction on 13 November, NAT. SCORVM IOH[ANN]IS CHRISOSTOMI ET BRICCII, disappears in F 11. (The feast of John Chrysostom, the Antiochene patriarch of Constantinople, seems to have reached Rome in the tenth century. Brittius was a disciple and successor of St. Martin of Tours.)

It would be harder to account for the omission in F 11 of an additional fourteen or so feasts found in E 15 that were widely kept in twelfth-century Rome – most of them at the Vatican as well (as we shall see) and many of them old. Thus F 11 omits the feasts SCE AGNES SECVNDE (28 January); SCARVM PERPETVE ET FELICITATIS (7 March); SCI NICOMEDIS (in E 15 on 1 June, the dedication of his basilica; but Nicomedes is also omitted in F 11 on his more generally kept *natale* of 15 September); MODESTI ET CRESCENTIANA[E] (15 June, but their companion, St. Vitus, was included in F 11); SCI IACOBI ALPHEI (22 June – not a common date); SCI LEONIS PAPE (28 June – perhaps dropped because of the vigil of SS. Peter and Paul on that day?); SCI EVPLI LEVITE ET LEVCII MAR. (12 August); SCORVM EVSEBII ET PARMENI PRESBYTER [I] (14 August – this Eusebius was the founder of the ancient *titulus Eusebii* on the Esquiline and according to a general pattern was transformed into a martyr-saint some time before 595, but Parmenius, perhaps martyred in Persia, seems not otherwise to have been venerated at Rome); SCE SAVINE [Sabinae] (29 August – foundress of the ancient *titulus Sabinae* on the Aventine and likewise promoted to sainthood before 595); SCORV[M] PROTI ET IACYNTHI (11 September – authentic Roman martyrs; Hyacinth's tomb and relics were discovered intact near the old Via Salaria in 1849); the DEDIC[ATIO] BASILICE SALVATORIS

(9 November – the Lateran Basilica); SCE [*sic*; recte SCI] MENNE (11 November – Menas, a Libyan martyr whose famous tomb-basilica attracted crowds from Alexandria, achieved an early but limited cult at Rome and was included in the Hadrianum); and SCI SATVRNINI (29 November – a Roman martyr buried on the Via Salaria; Pope Felix IV [526–30] reconstructed his cemetery basilica. Saturninus is found in both the old Gelasian and Gregorian sacramentaries.)

The considerable number of differences between the kalendar of the mid-eleventh century Damasian sacramentary E 15 and the kalendar underlying the collectar of F 11 – specifically the contrasts between feasts that are not found in E 15 but do appear in F 11 and in particular the number of feasts present in E 15 but not found in F 11 (whether of exotic saints and of feasts peculiar to St. Lawrence *in Damaso* or, more tellingly, of authentically Roman feasts) – render unlikely the supposition, momentarily entertained above, that F 11 could have been derived from or was closely related to the Damasian kalendar. The so-called St. Trypho sacramentary, F 14, on the other hand, is patently related to that of its mother church, St. Lawrence *in Damaso*.

The relationship, or lack of it, between the kalendars of the F 11 collectar and the kalendar of the Damasian sacramentary and between the kalendar of F 11 and the three later Petrine kalendars is made harder to grasp by the widely differing dates that have been assigned to F 11. The substance of the F 11 kalendar, it is true, seems in the main to belong rather to the later eleventh century than to the twelfth. But such an early date cannot be reconciled with Supino Martini's reliable dating of the script to the mid-twelfth century and with my dating of its notation in the rituale to the same period. Perhaps the scribe was copying an older collectar or, more likely, he extracted his set of feasts to be supplied with collects for the officiant from older Office books that lay at hand. A mid-twelfth century date for the copying of the rituale-collectar F 11 would suit the known status in the later twelfth and early thirteenth centuries of the church of St. Abbacyr *de Militiis* (or SS. Cyri et Iohannis de Urbe), as discussed above. But we have no real proof for this proposed connection – only the hint given by the capital letters of the rubric and beginning of the collect for SS. Cyrus and John (see above)

I have stated that San Pietro F 11 could not have been copied for St. Peter's Basilica. The conclusion is inescapable if we trouble to assemble the cumulative evidence and set the F 11 collectar as copied in the mid-twelfth century alongside the slightly later San Pietro B 79 kalendars and the early thirteenth-century San Pietro F 11, subtracting feasts later than around 1150 from the comparison. Table 12.1 isolates features peculiar to St. Peter's Basilica, whether of omission or inclusion. These Vatican features are then compared with the kalendar underlying the collectar of F 11. Table 12.2 instead begins with the omissions peculiar to the F 11 collectar and compares these omissions with the Petrine kalendars. (The compendious introductory kalendar of B 79 probably contains feasts not actually celebrated liturgically at St. Peter's that were garnered from martyrologies or other kalendars for completeness' sake. Consequently, feasts found only in the introductory kalendar of B 79 are left out of the comparison, unless – as is rarely the case – they also appear in F 22.) Annotations for the tables are given below, rather than in the tables themselves. For ease of reference, hagiographic details given earlier are sometimes repeated.

Annotations for Table 12.1

Features in Vatican Kalendars Compared with San Pietro F 11

11 December. *Damasus*. Pope (366–11 Dec. 384), buried at the family cemetery church on the Via Ardeatina; his remains were later transferred to St. Lawrence *in Damaso*, which he built, presumably on family property. E 15: MEN. DECEMBER DIE XI DEPOSITO S[AN]C[T]ISSIMI DAMASI PAPAE. F 14: *Nat S. Damasi pp. III id. Dec.* Included in F 11, but entered out of place between 13 and 21 December: *In nat. Sci damassi PP. cff.* His feast was introduced in eighth-century Gelasian sacramentaries under the influence of returning pilgrims who had read his verse epitaphs in Roman basilicas and catacombs for the martyrs and popes. The feast was ignored by the kalendars from St. Peter's now extant and by the earlier Gregorian sacramentaries, such as the Hadrianum and the related Padua, Bibl. Capitolare D 47. Was it because of the mob violence and bloodshed Damasus employed to seize the papacy after a divided election, or was it because his relics had been transferred to St. Lawrence *in Damaso* instead of to St. Peter's? (See Jounel, *Le Culte*, 323, and *The Oxford Dictionary of Popes*, 32–4.)

25 January. *Conversion of St. Paul.* A feast of Gallican origin, presumably transmitted to E 15 and F 14 via eighth-century Gelasian sacramentaries and kalendars. Not in the Hadrianum nor other pure Gregorian sacramentaries nor in the old Gelasian sacramentary. A proper preface for the feast, however, was inserted in the Aniane supplement to the Hadrianum.[42] The feast was entered in the B 79 kalendar but excluded from the antiphoner and the F 22 Gradual, where instead the ancient Roman *natale* of the martyrs Peter and Paul, 29 June, was naturally given the greatest possible prominence. The feast of the Conversion of St. Paul was included in F 11.

25 March. *Consecration of the New High Altar of St. Peter's.* The commemoration is found in both kalendar and antiphoner of B 79, along with the Annunciation of the Blessed Virgin Mary. F 11 provides a collect for the Annunciation only. Jounel (*Le Culte*, 230, with additions from 192) writes:

> Le 25 mars 1123, le pape Callixte II consecra l'autel de la Confession [qu'il avait construit au-dessus de la tombe de saint Pierre] en présence des trois cents evêques réunis pour le Ier Concile général du Latran. [Cet autel, qui enveloppait celui de saint Grégoire le Grand, devait demeurer en usage jusq'à l'érection de celui de Clément VIII in 1594.] Pierre de Mallio compte cette fête parmi les principales de l'année dans sa *Descriptio basilicae vaticanae* (p. 432). L'office de la dédicace avait la préséance sur celui de l'Annonciation. L'antiphonaire [B 79] donne, en effet, les précisions suivantes: In *Annuntiatione beatae Mariae est Consecratio*

Table 12.1 Special features in twelfth- and thirteenth-century Vatican kalendars

Unusual feasts included or feasts usually omitted in San Pietro B 79 and San Pietro F 22, compared with their inclusion or omission in the collectar San Pietro F 11, copied mid-twelfth century.

	Feast or saint	*B 79: kalendar*	*B 79: antiphoner*	*F 22: gradual*	*F 11: collectar*
11 Dec.	Damasus	—	—	[pre-Christmas December saints missing]	In nat̄ Sc̄i damassi P̄P̄. c̄ff
25 Jan.	Conversion of St. Paul	Conu'sio sc̄i pauli.	—	—	Conuersio. S. Pauli.
25 Mar.	Consecration of new high altar at St. Peter's by Callistus II in 1123	[ānūtiatōe b'ate Marie.] et Consec̄tio altāis sc̄i Pet.	[In ānūtiatōe b'e maie] ē (Con)sec̄tio maioris altāis b'i Pet.	[In annuntiatio s̄ marie.] —	[ANNUNTIATIO GL'OSE DĪ GENITRICIS ET VIRGINIS MARIE.]
31 May	Petronilla	Petronille uginis.	Resp. and Ant. 'Surge petronilla' [no rubric]	—	—
9 June	Primus and Felicianus	Primi et feliciani mr̄.	—	—	SC̄OR$_x$ PMI ET FELICIANI.
11 June	Barnabas	Barnabe apl'i.	—	—	IN. S. BARNABE.
12 June	Basilides, Cyrinus, Nabor [and Nazarius]	Basilidis. cyrini. Nabōis. et Nazāi. m.	—	—	IN SC̄OR$_x$ BASILIDIS. CIRINI NABORI. [et nazarii]
22 June	The 1,480 martyrs of Samaria (massacred by the Persians in 625)	—	—	—	IN SCĪ MVLTI.
1 Sept.	The Twelve Brothers	—	—	—	[IN .S. EGIDII CONFESSORI.] Eod̄ die. xii. fr̄m.
18 Nov.	Dedication Feast of St. Peter's Basilica	D'dicatō basilicār apl'or$_x$ Pet et S'. Pauli	In dedicatiōe basilice bī pet pncipis apl'or$_x$.	In dicatione ecclesie. [last item in original hand]	—
23 Nov.	Felicity	—	—	—	[In Sc̄i. Clem̄tis.] Eodem die. S̄. felicitatis.

Note: In the B 79 antiphoner, no feasts are entered between 31 May and 29 June. In the kalendar, the entries for 9, 11 and 12 June were left out by Jounel in his edition of Vezzosi's edition of Tommasi – see Jounel, *Le Culte*, 413 and 418.

> *maioris Altaris beati Petri, de qua Consecratione Vesperas et Matutinum facimus. Tertium vero Nocturnum de beata Maria facimus.* Les Laudes sont pareillement de la Dédicace.

If F 11 had been copied for St. Peter's after 1123, it would be impossible to imagine that it would not have included a collect for the commemoration of the altar consecration. As mentioned, a mid-twelfth-century date for the copying of F 11 now seems secure.

31 May. *Petronilla.* The feast is absent in E 15 and F 14. An authentic Roman martyr, Petronilla was buried in the cemetery of Domitilla, where a mid-fourth century fresco bears the legend PETRONELLA MART. and her sarcophagus the inscription AVRELIAE PETRONILLAE FIL[IAE] DVLCISSIMAE – that is, she was 'of the *gens* Aurelia' related to the Flavian *gens*, whose ancestor was Titus Flavius Petro. However,

> la légende fit de Pétronille la fille de saint Pierre en raison de la ressemblance de leurs noms. C'est à ce titre qu'elle fut l'object d'un culte spécial de la part de Pépin le Bref. Pour être agréable au roi franc, le pape Paul Ier transféra en 757 le corps de sa protectrice (*auxiliatricis vestrae* [as he wrote the king]) au Vatican, dans le mausolée funéraire de la famille de Théodose, près du transept sud de Saint-Pierre.[43]

The mausoleum rotunda was already standing when Constantine erected the basilica. Eventually two rotundas, one called St. Petronilla's and the other St. Andrew's, both with multiple altars, were connected to the south transept of St. Peter's. Hers was the central altar of the rotunda named after her. In Rome her cult seems not to have spread beyond the Vatican until the twelfth century. Apart from her ancient cemetery chapel, neglected after her translation to the Vatican, only one other Roman church was dedicated to her, attached to an obscure hospital on the Esquiline. Her feast is absent in F 11.

9 June. *Primus and Felicianus.* In E 15, F 14 and eighth-century Gelasian sacramentaries, but not in the old Gelasian, the Hadrianum and other pure Gregorian sacramentaries. Pope Theodore (643–9) translated the remains of the two martyrs from the cemetery on the Via Nomentana to St. Stephen the Round on the Coelian hill. As Jounel himself remarks (*Le Culte*, 244), 'on explique donc difficilement l'absence de la fête . . . au Vatican'. But it is present in F 11.

11 June. *Barnabas.* In E 15, F 14, and the kalendar of B 79. This is the Byzantine date of the supposed *inuentio corporis* on Cyprus in 458, adopted by Bede in his martyrology and so found in the West. The feast of the apostle and companion of St. Paul spread slowly in the north and at last to Rome in the eleventh century. Jounel (*Le Culte*, 244–5) remarks: 'On ne saurait dire pourquoi le calendrier et l'antiphonaire de Saint-Pierre le passent sous silence. Il est vrai que l'antiphonaire présent un vide inexplicable dans le sanctoral de juin. On n'y trouve aucun nom de saint entre le 31 mai et le 24

[*recte* 23] juin.' But eight feasts of saints are found in the kalendar of B 79 during this period, and Barnabas is indeed among them. (See the note at the bottom of Table 12.1 and Baroffio and Kim, *Archivio S. Pietro B 79*, i, color facs. of fol. 2r after p. 16.) The gradual F 22 omits Barnabas. The feast is present in F 11.

12 June. *Basilides, Cyrinus, Nabor and Nazarius*. In E 15 and in F 14, where the rubric reads *Nat. scor basilidis et sociorum eius II id. iunii*, and the kalendar of B 79. 'Le passion de [ces saints] est un parfait exemple des légendes romaines qui jonglent avec la chronologie et la géographie pour bâtir un roman d'édification' (Jounel, *Le Culte*, 245, with details). The feast is not in the Hadrianum Paduensis D 47 but is in the old Gelasian sacramentary but without Basilides. All four saints were added to the eighth-century Gelasians and even to the 'corrected Gregorian' sacramentaries north of the Alps. The feast also appeared at Modena, and finally arrived at Rome, where it entered the B 79 kalendar but not the antiphoner or the gradual F 22. It is present in F 11.

22 June. *The 1,480 Martyrs of Samaria*. Massacred by the Persians in 625. In E 15, the rubric reads *Natale* SCOR MAR[TYRUM] *mille* CCCCLXXX *quorum uigilia cum silentio ieiunium est celebranda et confessionem eis pro illo uno die anno uno dimittere in penitentia*[44]; in F 14, *Nat. scor. multor[um] X kl. iulii*. The scribe of F 11 reduced the rubric to the equally ungrammatical if more succinct IN SANCTI MULTI. No trace of the commemoration is found in San Pietro B 79 or San Pietro F 22. Its presence in F 11 implies clearly that the manuscript was not copied for use in the divine Office at St. Peter's.

1 September. *The Twelve Brothers*. In E 15 the rubric reads KAL. SEPT SCI PRISCI ET SCORV[M] MAR. XII FR[ATRV]M and in F 14, *Kl. sept. Nat. scor. Duodecim fr[atru]m Prisci mr. egidii abb[at]is*. In 760, the Beneventan prince Arichis II assembled the relics of twelve martyrs – in their legend reputed to be brothers – at his palace church and monastery of Santa Sofia. The feast, one of the most important in the old Beneventan sanctorale, was introduced to Rome around the time when Benevento became a papal fief and was adopted by the Lateran kalendars of the twelfth and thirteenth centuries, but not by St. Peter's. Of the saints named in the rubrics above, only St. Giles, founder of the abbey named for him on the pilgrimage route to Rome, was admitted to the B 79 kalendar, although not to the antiphoner itself. Thus the presence of the feast of the Twelve Brothers in F 11 argues against a Vatican origin for the book.

18 November. *Dedication of St. Peter's Basilica*. Absent in E 15 and F 14, which instead have the 13 May dedication of St. Mary *ad Martyres* (the Pantheon) not found in B 79 and F 22. The exact date of the dedication of St. Peter's is unknown. (The event was reported though not dated by the church historian Eusebius.) The choice of the November date may have been influenced by the 9 November date for the Lateran dedication, *Dedicatio*

basilicae Saluatoris, attested as early as the late tenth century (Jounel, *Le Culte*, 305–7). The antiphoner B 79, fols. 169v–170r, provides a complete Office for the dedication of St. Peter's, with three nocturns at the Night Office. Moreover, the dedication feast was observed with an octave. As Baroffio and Kim mention (*Archivio S. Pietro B 79*, i, 18), 'Il 22 novembre, festa di s. Cecilia, "Totum tertium nocturnum cantatur de festo dedicationis" si legge nell'antifonario in referimento alla dedicazione della basilica di San Pietro.' After the Cecilian antiphon *In euāg. Dum aurora finem* . . ., the antiphon *Hec est domus* is cued to commemorate the dedication: *Seqt d' dedicatiōe*. The rubrics that follow on fol. 171v are even more explicit (here I expand the abbreviations):

> cotidie facimus uesperas de dedicatione usque in octauum cum commemoratione sanctorum.
>
> In festo sancti clementis pape et martyris. *Orante sancto clemente apparuit ei agnus dei* . . .
>
> Totum tertium nocturnum de dedicatione facimus.

At the end, the commemorative antiphon is introduced and cued: 'Sequitur de dedicatione. *Hedificauit moyses*'. The feast of S. Grisogonus [Chrisogonus] has its commemorative antiphon and versicle of the dedication: '*Locus iste* V *Hec est domus*'. If F 11 had been copied for St. Peter's, the collectar would assuredly have provided a collect for the feast and its commemorations throughout the octave.

23 November. *Felicity*. In E 15 the rubric for her feast, on the same day as St. Clement's, reads M. NOV XXIII SCI CLEMENTIS ET SCE FELICITATIS CVM VII FILIIS SVIS; and in F 14, *Nat. s. clem[en]tis* VIIII *kl dec. de sca felicitate et filiis ei[us]*. The Hadrianum has NATALE SANCTAE FELICITATIS and the old Gelasian sacramentary IN N. SANCTAE FELICITATIS. (See Jounel, *Le Culte*, 314, and *DACL* s.v. 'Felicité', esp. 1282–6.) The sanctorale of the San Saba lectionary, Rome, Bibl. Angelica 1383, places her feast on 10 July. San Pietro B 79 and San Pietro F 22 inexplicably ignore this authentically Roman saint on both the uncommon July date (when the B 79 kalendar alone gives the Seven Brothers but without Felicity) and the more usual 23 November. But the feast is present in F 11.

Annotations for Table 12.2

Feasts Absent in San Pietro F 11

28 January. *The 'Second Agnes'*. Perhaps originally the octave of Agnes's feast on 21 January? The old Gelasian and the eighth-century Gelasian sacramentaries call the feast of the 21st *Agnetis de passione* and the feast of the 28th *Agnetis de natiuitate*. The Hadrianum calls the first NATALE SANCTAE AGNAE and the second NATALE SANCTAE AGNE SECUNDO. However designated, the second feast is almost always included – except in F 11.

Table 12.2 Feasts absent in San Pietro F 11

Feasts notably absent in the collectar of Archivio San Pietro F 11 though usually found in other eleventh- and twelfth-century Roman city kalendars and notably present in the Vatican kalendars of San Pietro B 79 and San Pietro F 22.

	Feast or saint	*B 79: kalendar*	*B 79: antiphoner*	*F 22: Gradual*	*F 11: collectar*
28 Jan.	'The Second' Agnes	Agnetis sed'o. [secundo]	— [feast of 21 Jan. present]	Sᵉ agnetis secūnde	— [21 Jan: In festiuīt. S̄ agnes.]
8 May	Apparition of the Archangel Michael (Gargano massif)	Michaelis archangl'i.	[Apparitio Michaelis: no rubric but with full Office]	—	—
1 June	Nicomedes (Dedication of cemetery-basilica, Via Nomentana, 619–25 – see 15 Sept.)	Nicomedis m̄r.	—	—	—
28 June	Leo the Great (d. 461, buried in atrium of St. Peter's); translated into the Basilica of St. Peter's itself by Sergius I, 28 June 688	Leonis p̄p.	[Commemorated on Vigil of SS. Peter and Paul; see rubrics, fol. 131ᵛ]	—	—
12 Aug.	Euplus and Leucius	Eupli et Leucii.	Ī festo s̄. Eupli et Eleuci.	—	—
13 Aug.	Hippolytus (and ____)	Ypoliti et Concordie	Ī festo s̄ ypoliti et socior$_\chi$ ei'.	Sc̄i ypoliti et cassi	—
29 Aug.	Sabina	[Decollatō sc̄i Ioh's bapt̄.] et sc̄e Sauine.	[In decollatōe b'i ioh'is bapt̄.] Eod' die festū S̄ Sauine.	[Decollatio S̄ iōhis Baptiste] —	[REVELATIO CAPITI IOANNIS BAPTISTE.]
8 Sept.	Hadrian	[Nāt sc̄e marie.] et sc'i Adàni	[In natiuīt d'i genitcis Marie.] Īt d' s̄. ad'ano.	[Nat̄ S̄ Marie] —	[IN NATIVITATE SC̄E MARIE.] —
11 Sept.	Protus and Hyacinth	Proti et Iacinthi.	—	Scor̄$_\chi$ pti et. Ia.	—
15 Sept.	Nicomedes (*natale* – see 1 June)	Nicomedis m̄r.	—	Sc̄i Nic[?]	—
29 Nov.	Saturninus	Saturnini m̄r.	[In uig̃ b'i Andree apl'i . . .] et festum sc̄i Saturnini.	[Vig̃. S̄ andree] —	[VIG̃. S̄ andree.] —

Note: In the B 79 kalendar, the entry for 29 August, 'et sc̄e Sauine', was added later. The following, 'Nāt sc̄e marie. et sc̄i Adani', was first entered a day too early, then erased and re-entered on the correct date by a later hand.

8 May. *Apparition of Michael the Archangel.* In E 15, APPARITIO SCI MICHAELIS ARCHANGELI; and in F 14 (but in the margin), *Apparitio S. Michaelis.* The 8 May date commemorates St. Michael's descent to the Gargano massif in northern Puglia in the fifth century, where in a grotto – now the *sacro specchio* in Monte Sant'Angelo – he left behind his red cape. The south Italian and Lombard feast of 8 May spread to Rome in the late eleventh and early twelfth centuries (a time when the papal court traveled widely in the south and the pope often resided in Benevento). This feast gradually gave way before the authentically Roman date of 29 September, commemorating the dedication of a basilica on the seventh mile of the Via Salaria under the archangel's name. The 8 May feast had all but disappeared at Rome by the thirteenth century. It is absent in F 22. If F 11 was copied in the mid-twelfth century, as held by Supino Martini and myself, and if it had been intended for St. Peter's, one might nevertheless have expected to find a collect for the 8 May feast in the collectar, since it is present in the kalendar and antiphoner of B 79.

1 June. *Nicomedes.* In E 15, NAT. SCI NICOMEDIS, and in F 14, *Kl. iunii sci nicomedis mar.* The Hadrianum correctly lists KALENDIS IVNIIS DEDICATIO SANCTI NICOMEDIS (i.e., the dedication of a cemetery-basilica at the martyr's tomb on the Via Nomentana, built under Boniface V, 619–25) as well as XVII KALENDAS OCTOBRES ID EST XV DIE MENSIS SEPTEMBRIS NATALE SANCTI NICOMEDIS. The 1 June dedication also appears in eighth-century Gelasians but not in the old Gelasian sacramentary. Both dates are entered in the B 79 kalendar but neither appears in the B 79 antiphoner. The 15 September *natale* is entered in F 22; neither feast is found in F 11.

28 June. *Leo the Great.* In E 15, SCI LEONIS PAPE, and in F 14, *Nat. S. Leonis pp.* Also in the Hadrianum, NATALE SANCTI LEONIS PAPAE. The prevalent date of 28 June commemorates the translation by Sergius I on 28 June 688 of Leo's body from the atrium of St. Peter's – where he was originally interred, the first pope to be buried at St. Peter's – into the basilica itself, near the altar of the confession. Sergius constructed an oratory dedicated to Leo in the south wall of the basilica over his new tomb, which Leo IV (847–55) embellished further. But F 14 has yet another feast, on 11 April, *S. Leonis PP.* – which is the date given in the *Liber Pontificalis* for his *natale*. (Leo in fact died on 10 November 461. See Jounel's valuable discussion, in *Le Culte*, 231, 249 and 393–4.) But Jounel, following the printed editions of Tommasi and Vezzosi (413 and 421–4 in Jounel) fails to note the significant commemoration of St. Leo in the B 79 antiphoner within the very Office of the vigil of SS. Peter and Paul on 28 June. The rubric on fol. 131^{v} (if I expand the abbreviations correctly) reads as follows:

> Si uigilia beati Petri in dominica ueniret. Sabbato preuenimus omnia officia celebrare. Dominica uero omnia de sancto Leone papa facimus.
>
> Ad matutinum uigilie apostolorum Petri et Paul. Super *uenite. Regem apostolorum* . . . a. *Significauit dominus.*

Sed si ueniret in dominica officia uigilie. Sabbato celebramus ad uesperum.
a. *Petrus et Iohannes*. cum suis antiphonis et psalmis festiuis. Super canticum.
a. *Significauit*. Sequitur de sancto Leone. *Dum esset summus pontifex*.

A collect for the commemoration of St. Leo would certainly have been included in F 11, as well as for the vigil of the apostles Peter and Paul, if the manuscript had been intended for St. Peter's Basilica. In F 11 there is no commemoration whatever of Leo the Great.

12 August. *Euplus and Leucius*. The two saints appear together both in E 15, SCI EVPLI LEVITE ET LEVCII MAR., and in F 14, *Nat. sci Eupli et leuci. II id. aug*. The deacon Euplus was martyred at Catania, Sicily; Pope Theodore (642–9) built an oratory under Euplus' patronage just outside the Porta San Paolo (see Hülsen, *Le chiese*, 250), and his name appears in evangeliaries and capitularies from the seventh and eighth centuries but not in the old Gelasian nor in pure Gregorian sacramentaries like the Hadrianum. Leucius was bishop of Brindisi; his *natale* was 11 January. The date 12 August is peculiar to Rome and is perhaps connected with a monastery under his name that is said to have existed 'at the sixth mile of the Via Flaminia' in the time of Gregory the Great (see Jounel, *Le Culte*, 273). It is uncertain when the two saints began to be commemorated at St. Peter's. They are absent from F 11.

13 August. *Hippolytus and* . . . .. The rubric for the feast in E 15 reads NAT. SCI YPPOLITI, and in F 14, *Nat. scor yppoliti et socior[um] eius idib. aug*. The Hadrianum has NATALE SANCTI YPPOLITI and the old Gelasian sacramentary *ypoliti*. The *Depositio Martyrum* of 354 correctly gives *Ypoliti in Tiburtina* (i.e., the cemetery where St. Lawrence had been buried, now Campo Verano) *et Pontiani in Calisti* (the catacombs of Callistus). Hippolytus, the learned and contentious Roman priest and would-be antipope, together with his rival, the legitimate Bishop Pontianus, were deported with imperial impartiality to the fatal mines of Sardinia by the persecuting emperor Maximinus Thrax. Reputedly reconciled before their common deaths in the mines, the contenders' remains were brought back to Rome under more tolerant emperors and reinterred on 13 August by Pope Fabian in 236 or 237. Pontianus, the legitimate bishop, was unfairly dropped from liturgical observance (though recently restored) and replaced by saints whose association with Hippolytus is purely legendary. Of these companions, Cassianus, a martyr at Imola on 13 August, was given an altar in the rotunda of St. Andrew at the Vatican: hence his name appears in San Pietro F 22, *Sc̄i ypoliti et cassi[ani]*. A statue of Hippolytus in third-century style, which was unearthed near the Via Tiburtina in 1551 inscribed with a list of his (Greek) writings, was installed at the entrance to the Vatican Library by John XXIII in 1959. (See Jounel, *Le Culte*, 274–5, who fails to mention Hippolytus' schismatic role and the writing generally attributed to him. Also see the biographies of the popes Victor I, Zephyrinus, Callistus I, Urban I and Pontianus – all contemporary with Hippolytus, e.g., in *The Oxford Dictionary of Popes*, 12–17.)

29 August. *Sabina*. In E 15, EODE[M] DIE (i.e., *Decollatio Iohannis Baptistae*) SCE SAVINE; in F 14 *Nat. sce Sauine eodem die*; and in the Hadrianum, NATALE SANCTAE SABINAE. The *titulus Sabinae* on the Aventine was rebuilt in the time of Pope Celestine I (422–32). In the course of the sixth century, the foundress was transformed into a martyr-saint and supplied with an imaginary passion giving the supposed date of her *natale* as 29 August. It is true that the words *et sc̄e Sauine* were added in a later hand to the B 79 kalendar entry for 29 August; but the rubrics in the antiphoner itself (fol. 152[r–v]) are original to the manuscript and explicit in their wording. I expand the abbreviations:

> In decollatione beati iohannis baptiste. omnia facimus de communi unius martyris usque ad uersum [or uersiculum] tertii nocturni.
>
> Eodem die festum Sancte Sauine Versiculum. *Elegit eam deus*. Septimum responsorium. *Elegit eam deus* viii Responsorium *Ego sauina gratias ago domino* . . .

Lauds and Vespers of the Beheading of John Baptist follow, but after the Magnificat on fol. 152[v] the commemoration of Sabina is inserted: 'De Sancta Sauina sequitur antiphona. *Adesto domine cum ancilla tua . . . magnitudine*'. The antiphon is followed by the versicle and response beginning *Veni sponsa accipe*. If the F 11 collectar had been copied for use at St. Peter's, a prayer for the commemoration of St. Sabina would have had to be included, to be sung at the end of Vespers of the Beheading of John Baptist.

8 September. *Hadrian*. In F 14, *Eodem die* (i.e., *Natiuitate S. Mariae*) *sci Adriani*; and in Padua D 47, EODEM DIE NATALIS SANCTI ADRIANI MARTYRIS. (The core of the *Paduense* derives from an early non-papal edition of the Gregorian sacramentary – of which the Hadrianum is the later and purely papal instance.) Under Pope Honorius I (625–8), the former senatorial Curia in the Forum was dedicated to Christian worship under the patronage of St. Hadrian, who was martyred at Nicomedia, presumably in the Diocletian persecution. His *natale* of 8 September appears in a 645 Roman evangeliary, well before the feast of the Nativity of Mary was introduced to Rome. It is not known why his name was chosen for the new church in the former Curia. (See Hülsen, *Le chiese*, 260–61, and Jounel, *Le Culte*, 285–6. Also see Armellini, *Le chiese*, i, 202–3, with a picture of the building and a description written before the 1930s, when the church was removed while the senatorial Curia was being restored. Also see *Le chiese*, ii, 1227.) An entry for Hadrian is found in the B 79 kalendar, and he is commemorated by rubric in the antiphoner (fol. 156[v]): 'Item de sancto Adriano. *Qui uult uenire post me* . . .'. The feast is absent in F 11.

11 September. *Protus and Hyacinth*. In E 15, SCORV[M] PROTI ET IACYNTHI; in F 14, *Nat. martyru[m] P[ro]ti et Iacinthi*; and in the Hadrianum, NATALE SANCTORUM PROTI ET IACYNTHI. Jounel, *Le Culte*, 287, describes the discovery in 1845 of the intact tomb of Hyacinth on the old Via Salaria, bearing the inscription D[E]P[OSITUS] III IDVS SEPE[M]BR[ES] YACINTUS

MARTYR. Though present in the kalendar of B 79 and in the gradual F 22, the feast is absent in F 11.

15 September. *Nicomedes*. In F 14, *Nat. S. Nicomedis mar.*, and in the Hadrianum, NATALE SANCTI NICOMEDIS. The Hadrianum also has the dedication of the cemetery-basilica on 1 June, q.v. Both dates are entered in the B 79 kalendar but neither appears in the B 79 antiphoner. The 15 September *natale* is entered in F 22. Neither feast is found in F 11.

29 November. *Saturninus*. In E 15 the rubric reads VIGILIA SCI ANDREE AP[OSTO]LI EODE[M] DIE SCI SATVRNINI, and in F 14, *Nat. S. Saturnini et Sisinii*. The Hadrianum has the rubric NATALE SANCTI SATVRNINI and the old Gelasian sacramentary *Saturnini, Cresanti, Mauri, Dariae, et aliorum*. See Jounel, *Le Culte*, 317, for details of the burial of Saturninus and the rebuilding of his cemetery chapel by Pope Felix IV (526–30). The feast is in the kalendar and antiphoner of B 79, but not in F 11.

Although any single discrepancy between San Pietro F 11 and the Vatican kalendars of San Pietro B 79 and San Pietro F 22 (or even several discrepancies) evident in Tables 12.1 and 12.2 might be explained as the product of scribal inadvertence or of faulty exemplars, the massive discrepancy of these differences when taken together renders a Vatican origin or intended destination at St. Peter's Basilica for San Pietro F 11 impossible. The conclusion holds even if F 11 should have been copied as early as 1125 (rather than the more likely mid-century date proposed by Supino Martini) and is further strengthened by the complete absence of 'we' rubrics in F 11. The differences in chant versions between the Mass chants of the rituale section of F 11 and those chants also found in F 22, and between the chants for the Office of the dead in F 11 and those in B 79, corroborate this conclusion – even when allowance is made for the *Zersungenheit* of Old Roman chant in San Pietro F 22.[45]

I wish I could point out a likely place of origin at Rome for the manuscript Archivio San Pietro F 11. I can only propose the case for SS. Abbacyr and John *de Militiis* in the Via Biberatica, solely on the flimsy basis of the capitalized rubric for the collect of their feast. Perhaps more careful scrutiny of the texts and chants of the F 11 rituale and of the Office for the dead will help determine a definite source for the manuscript.

The *Missa pro Congregatione*

The votive *Missa pro congregatione*[46] does not appear in Riccardiana 299 or in San Pietro F 11; it appears under this title only in Riccardiana 300. Three of its Proper chants are also found in the Old Roman Mass for the eighteenth Sunday after Pentecost (in Vat. lat. 5319, *Dominica III post S. angeli*) – namely, the non-scriptural Introit *Salus populi*, the Offertory *Si ambulauero* (without verses in Riccardiana 300) and the Communion *Tu mandasti* (without psalm verse or differentia in 300). The Gradual *Oculi omnium* with the verse *Aperis tu manum tuam* of the *Missa pro congregatione* is found in the Old Roman Mass for the nineteenth Sunday after Pentecost (*Dominica IIII post S. angeli*), however. All these pieces appear in the Mass for Thursday in the third full week of Lent,[47] the station chosen being the diaconal basilica of SS. Cosmas and Damian in the Forum.[48] As is well known, the Masses for Thursdays in Lent, previously aliturgical, were added to the series of Lenten ferial Masses under Pope Gregory II (715–31). The pieces for several Thursdays in Lent seem to have been borrowed from the Sundays after Pentecost. But the fourth Thursday in Lent (III.5) is exceptional in several respects.[49] In the collect and postcommunion of the Hadrianum (the papal sacramentary), the patron saints of the stational church for Lent III.5 are commemorated by name. They are the Syrian martyrs Cosmas and Damian.[50] In their legend the saints are described as physicians, but physicians who took no money for their services – hence the appellation ἀνάργυροι (the 'no-money' doctors).[51] No other collect for a Lenten ferial Mass names the saints of the stational church. Lenten collects are usually penitential in character, whereas the opening collect of this Lenten Mass glows with jubilation: 'Magnificet te domine sanctorum tuorum cosmae et damiani beata sollemnitas, quia et illis gloriam sempiternam, et opem nobis ineffabiliter prouidentiae contulisti. Per . . .'.[52] The collect for the actual feast day of Cosmas and Damian on 27 September is an undistinguished prayer used for four other saints' days in the Hadrianum by inserting appropriate names: 'Praesta quaesumus omnipotens deus, ut qui sanctorum tuorum cosmae et damiani natalicia colimus a cunctis malis imminentibus eorum intercessionibus liberemur. Per dominum . . .'.[53] The rest of the Hadrianum Propers for the *natale* of 27 September are also common to other feasts. But for the Lenten Thursday Mass, the first three Hadrianum collects appear in the old Gelasian sacramentary for the feast day itself on 27 September,[54] where the collect *Ad completa* (the Postcommunion) reads just as in the Lenten stational Mass of the Hadrianum: 'Sit nobis domine sacramenti tui *certa saluatio*, quae cum beatorum tuorum cosmae et damiani meritis imploratur. Per . . .'.[55] The nominative *certa saluatio*, which is emphasized by being displaced, echoes the third line of the distichs inscribed beneath the remarkable apse mosaic in SS. Cosmas and Damian's, erected by Pope Felix IV (526–30):

AVLA DEI CLARIS RADIAT SPECIOSA METALLIS
IN QVA PLVS FIDEI LVX PRETIOSA MICAT
MARTYRIBVS MEDICIS *POPVLO SPES CERTA SALVTIS*
FECIT ET EX SACRO CREVIT HONORE LOCVS
OPTVLIT HOC DOMINO FELIX ANTISTITE DIGNVM
MVNVS VT AETHERIA VIVAT IN ARCE POLI[56]

The resemblance between the beginning of the Introit for the Lenten stational Mass at SS. Cosmas and Damian, *Salus populi ego sum*, and the third line of the distichs inscribed in the apse of the stational church is striking, to say the least. In view of the similar connection (mentioned above) between the phrase *spes certa salutis* of the apse mosaic with the phrase *certa saluatio* of the postcommunion prayer (beyond doubt composed for 27 September, for which date it appears in the Gelasian sacramentary), we may reasonably regard the distichs as having inspired the Introit, and the Introit as original to the patronal festival of SS. Cosmas and Damian on 27 September. The text is the only non-scriptural Introit in the entire eighth-century Roman Introit repertory.[57]

Salus populi ego sum dicit dominus
de quacumque tribulatione clamauerint ad me
exaudiam eos et ero illorum dominus in perpetuum

The Introit is nevertheless reminiscent of the Old Testament, but its exact wording cannot be traced to any specific passage in Scripture.[58] The phrase *de quacumque tribulatione clamauerint ad me* reminds one of 1 Kings 8: 38–40, Solomon's prayer at the dedication of the temple: 'Whatever plague, whatever sickness there is; whatever prayer, whatever supplication is made by any man or by all thy people Israel . . . then hear thou in heaven thy dwelling place, and forgive and act . . .'. Indeed this phrase of the Introit (and Solomon's prayer) appear to be echoed by the first verse *In quacumque die inuocauero te exaudi me*, of the Offertory *Si ambulauero* for the *Missa de congregatione* and for Lent III.5.

The relationship between the other Proper-chant texts in the Mass for Lent III.5 and the patronal festival of the physician-martyrs Cosmas and Damian is less clear. As just mentioned above, the Offertory *Si ambulauero* and the Communion *Tu mandasti* are also sung in the Mass for the eighteenth Sunday after Pentecost like the Introit, while the Gradual *Oculi omnium* with its verse *Aperis tu manum tuam* comes from the Mass for the nineteenth Sunday after Pentecost. Now the Gradual for the eighteenth Sunday is *Letare Hierusalem* – which (if it had been chosen for Lent III.5) would have recurred just three days later on *Laetare* Sunday, Lent IV. Was it to avoid anticipating the *Laetare* text that *Oculi omnium* from the next Sunday after Pentecost was chosen instead?

Of the three Proper chants after the Introit in the Lenten Mass – Gradual, Offertory and Communion – I can imagine a connection with the feast of SS. Cosmas and Damian only for the Offertory. I have just noted the similarity between the first verse of the Offertory and the second line of the Introit, and of course the respond of the Offertory is well suited to the feast of the physician saints. But then, the entire Offertory is equally suitable for any day in Lent or, for that matter, for a Sunday after Pentecost.

Si ambulauero in medio tribulationis uiuificabis me domine
et super iram inimicorum meorum extendis manum tuam
[R_x] ET SALVVM ME FACIT DEXTERA TUA.
  V. *In quacumque die inuocauero te exaudi me* domine
  multiplicabis in anima mea uirtutem tuam
[R_x] ET SALVVM ME FACIT DEXTERA TUA.
  V. Adorabo ad templum sanctum tuum
  et confitebor nomini tuo domine
  super misericordiam tuam et ueritatem tuam
[R_x] ET SALVVM ME FACIT DEXTERA TUA.

The Communion chant *Tu mandasti* chosen for Lent III.5 and hence included in the *Missa pro congregatione* reads:

Tu mandasti domine mandata tua custodiri nimis
utinam dirigantur uie mee ad custodiendas iustificationes tuas
[In Bodmer 74 only:] Ps̄ Beati inmaculati in uia

The italicized phrase above – probably serendipitously – anticipates the italicized ending of the collect *super populum* (an extra prayer that concludes Lenten ferial Masses):

Subiectum tibi populum quaesumus domine
propitiatio caelestis amplificet,
et his faciat seruire mandatis. Per . . .

But this prayer *super populum* for Lent III.5 is not unique; it also appears as one of the supernumerary collects *pro peccatis* in the Hadrianum,[59] and the resemblance with the Communion may be fortuitous. In any event, the prayer obviously belongs to the Lenten feria and not to the festival of the physician-saints. It is unlikely that the inappropriate Communion *Tu mandasti* would have been sung on 27 September.

The old Gelasian sacramentary, BAV, Reg. lat. 316, leaves no doubt that except for the *super populum* collect, the celebrant's prayers that are found in the Lenten Thursday stational Mass in the Hadrianum were borrowed from the earlier patronal festival of the physician-saints on 27 September. Two of these prayers invoke Cosmas and Damian by name, and one of them refers to the inscription beneath the apse mosaic of SS. Cosmas and Damian in the Forum. The atypical text of the Introit *Salus populi* very likely derives from the same patronal festival, which probably commemorated the dedication of the remodeled basilica. It may well have been composed expressly for the feast, but it need not have been composed at the same time as the celebrant's collects; indeed, I should think it later. But not so late as the start of the eighth century, when Lenten Thursdays were assigned their stations and their Masses furnished with borrowed items.

It might be objected that *Salus populi* was selected from among an existing pool of Introits because it already began with two words that appeared on the apse inscription of the patronal or the stational church. It seems to me that the chance of a text so well suited turning up among a group of six or perhaps a dozen Introits is minuscule. Moreover, the argument leaves the question unanswered as to why a single non-scriptural Introit should have been included among texts all others of which were taken directly from Scripture or adapted from Scripture.[60] Thus I prefer to think that the Introit *Salus populi* was originally intended for the patronal feast of the basilica of SS. Cosmas and Damian.

In the Riccardiana 300 *Missa pro congregatione*, the discursive prayers for the celebrant have no connection with SS. Cosmas and Damian or with the stational Mass of Lent III.5.[61] Perhaps the compiler of the *Missa pro congregatione* joined the Proper chants from the Lenten Thursday with the celebrant's discursive votive prayers simply because the start of the Introit, *Salus populi*, seemed a suitable and emblematic way to begin a Mass for the people. Although one can see why the *Missa ad sponsas benedicendas* was notated, it is not at all clear why the *Missa pro congregatione* was selected to receive notation from among the many votive Masses in Riccardiana 300.

I turn now to the chants of the *Missa pro congregatione* and summarize the conclusions – such as they are – drawn from my tables comparing the versions in neumes from Riccardiana 300 with the same chants in the Masses for Lent III.5 from Bodmer 74, Vat. lat. 5319 and San Pietro F 22. In Riccardiana 300, we find a style of notation later by fifty years or more than that used in Riccardiana 299 but earlier than the notation of San Pietro F 22. The notations of Bodmer 74 (dating from just before 1071) and of Vat. lat. 5319 (around 1100?) are richer in nuance, especially in their use of liquescents and oriscus neumes. The oriscus, often used in Bodmer 74 and Vat. lat. 5319 to begin a descending group of three or more notes, is consistently replaced in Riccardiana 300 by an ordinary slanted punctum just like the following lower notes of the group, as in F 22. But most of the alterations in pitches found in F 22 – evidence for Hucke's theory of melodic *Zersungenheit* – are absent in Riccardiana 300.

INTROIT: *Salus populi* Ps̄ *Adtendite populus* V̄ *Narrantes laudes*
(The psalm and *versus ad repetendum* are from Ps. 77: 1, 4b.)
Mode: Deuterus authenticus
Sources: Ricc 300, fol. 7^{v}; F 22, fols. 31^{v}–32^{r} (cued at fol. 72^{v}); Bod 74, fol. 55^{r}; 5319, fol. 57^{r} (cued at fol. 131^{v}), MMMA 2: 18[62]

My transcription of the version of Riccardiana 300 appears in Ex. 12.1. In this piece, significant sets of variants link Riccardiana 300 and F 22 together against the older readings of Vat. lat. 5319 and Bodmer 74. (It would be gratifying to report the same natural linkage in other pieces. Unfortunately, this is seldom the case.) A group of several notes, first at *dicit* and then again at *ad me* (the group marked 'X' in Ex. 12.2 below) introduces interior cadences, whether *ouvert* (*EF*) or *clos* (*FE*). This group rises to the note *b* in Riccardiana 300 and F 22 but only to *a* in Bodmer 74 and Vat. lat. 5319. The figure 'X' is found throughout the deuterus Introit repertory in similar positions. The same variants are found in the Introit *Deus israhel* of the wedding Mass at *coniugat te* (see below), except that their position in the manuscripts is reversed: the version rising to *b* appears in Riccardiana 299, F 11 and Vat. lat. 5319, while the version rising only to *a* is found in Riccardiana 300! The two versions are not mere scribal variants; they are notational witnesses to different ways of singing the same formula but always with the same function. The two ways must have been maintained in oral tradition for a long time before they were notated. I cannot explain their erratic application in Riccardiana 300.

Another ubiquitous deuterus formula occurs in *Salus populi* as well as in *Deus israhel* – the interior cadence to *G* at *eos*, figure 'Z' in Ex. 12.2. At *eos*,

Ex. 12.1 Introit *Salus populi* of the *Missa pro congregatione* (Florence, Riccardiana 300, fol. 7v)

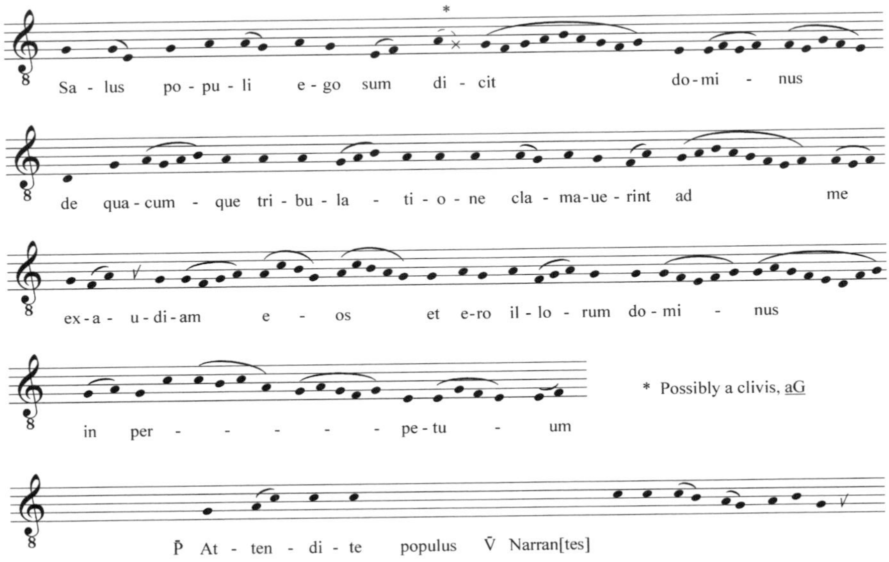

all the versions (except 5319, which inserts the passing *b* between *a* and *c* of the first rising third) are in accord with the second appearance of the figure in *Deus israhel* at the word *unicis*, Ex. 12.3b. But when the figure first appears at *uobiscum* (in *Deus israhel*), its opening neume is expanded as shown in Ex. 12.3a, except in Vat. lat. 5319. (The version of Riccardiana 300 adds a note to fill in the descending third, *b* to *G*.)

Variants of a more substantive sort for the figure introducing the last long phrase of the *Salus populi* melody – marked 'Y' in Ex. 12.2 – are similarly paired at the word *exaudiam*. The Riccardiana 300 and F 22 versions alternately fill in or gap the interval of the rising third, while the version of the earlier manuscripts Vat. lat. 5319 and Bodmer 74 instead employs the interval of the rising fifth for the accented syllable. They both lead at once to the ubiquitous G-cadence formula on *eos* ('Z' in Ex. 12.2). These alternative patterns in their position introducing a new phrase are virtually unique in the entire deuterus Introit repertory. The form with the rising fifth, *Da*, for the accented syllable appears to have a loose counterpart only in the Introit for Lent V.2, *Miserere michi domine*, at the words *tota die* (Vat. lat. 5319, fol. 67v, MMMA 2: 25). I have found the latter form with the rising third, *F*(*G*)*a*, in this introductory position only once, at *et mane* of the Christmas vigil Introit *Hodie scietis* (Vat. lat. 5319, fol. 10r, MMMA 2: 29). On the other hand, the introductory formula for interior phrases in the Introit *Deus israhel*, leading to a recitation on *a* at *qui misertus* (see below) is

Ex. 12.2 Variants in the Introit *Salus populi* (Vat. lat. 5319, Bodmer 74, Riccardiana 300 and San Pietro F 22)*11

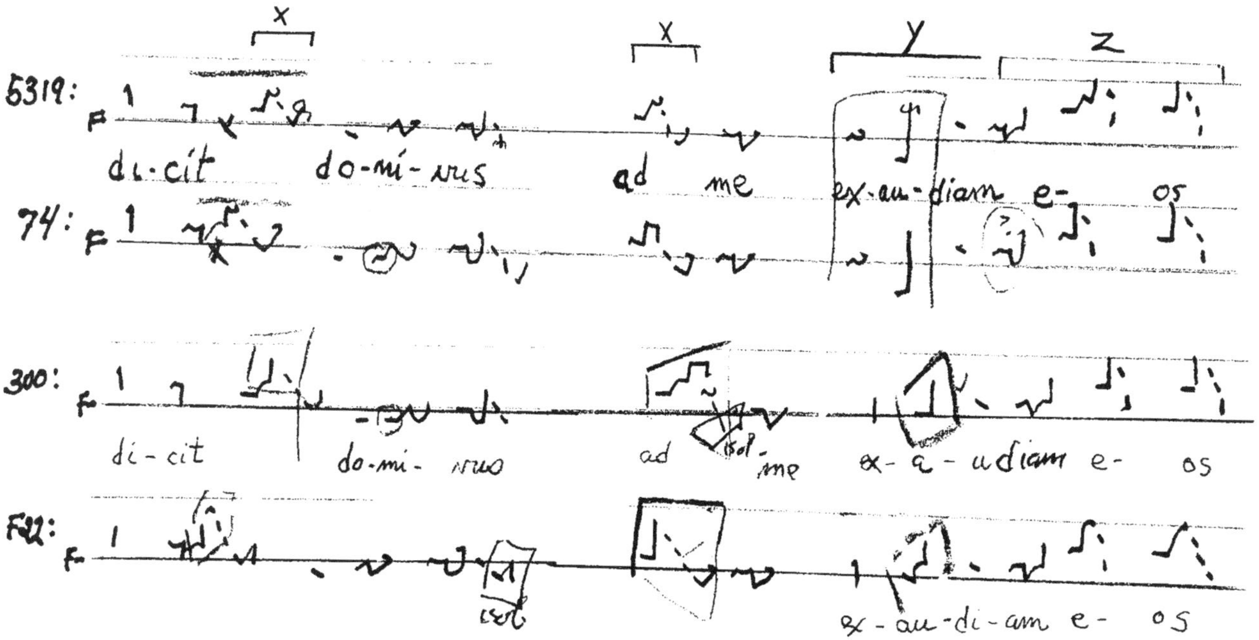

* The neumed examples in this article are reproduced faithfully from handwritten exemplars furnished by the author.

Ex. 12.3 Variants in medial cadences of the Introit *Deus israhel* (Vat. lat. 5319, San Pietro F 11, Riccardiana 299 and 300)

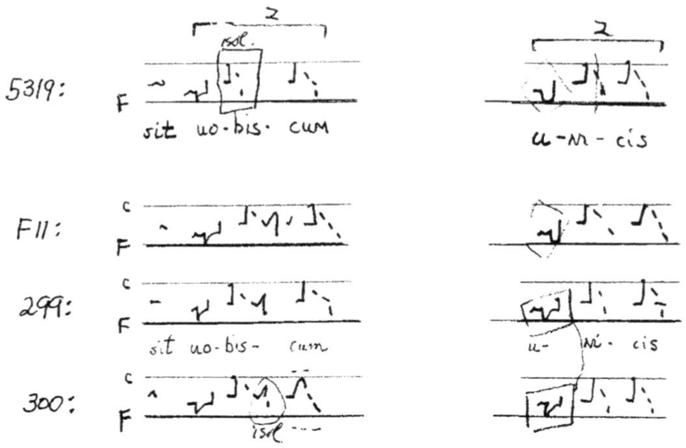

extremely common among deuterus Introits and is even sometimes found twice in one piece.

Two other figures found in *Salus populi* appear elsewhere but not very often. The notes *D G aGáb a* for *de quacúmque* – which introduces a recitation on *a* after an interior cadence on *E* – function similarly in two other deuterus Introits: *Nunc scio uere* for the octave of SS. Peter and Paul at the phrase *et de omni* (Vat. lat. 5319, fol. 117^{r}, MMMA 2: 21–2) and *Nos autem gloriari* for feasts of the Holy Cross and for Tuesday and Thursday in Holy Week, at the phrase *in cruce domini* (Vat. lat. 5319, fol. 76^{v}, MMMA 2: 42). See Ex. 12.4. The second figure is a special neumatic flourish immediately preceding a final accent, which shows how formulas were used in oral composition and how they assisted aural memory. In all cases, the flourish is placed on the weak syllable preceding the final accented syllable of a piece, phrase, or word – as at *perpétuum* in *Salus populi* (see Ex. 12.1). (In the first three Introits listed in Table 12.3, the flourish is sung to the same syllable, *per*.) These concordances belong to the festal category of deuterus Introits to which I believe *Salus populi* originally belonged, or else to Sundays. Four are for saints' days, one is for the Sunday after the Ascension, and two are for Sundays after Pentecost. The flourish never appears in the properly Lenten Introits. (See Table 12.3 and Ex. 12.5.)

Most Lenten deuterus Introits begin with one of several formulas. (One of these formulas is used for the wedding Introit, *Deus israhel*.) *Salus populi*, however, begins with its own unique figure (see Ex. 12.6).[63] The versions of Riccardiana 300 and Vat. lat. 5319 are alike[64] in having a single punctum on *G* for the second syllable of *ego*; the versions of Bodmer 74 and F 22 assign that syllable a clivis, *GF* – an insignificant difference.

Ex. 12.4 Introduction to interior recitation on *a*: the version of *Salus populi* (5319, 74, 300 and F 22) compared with the same introduction in the Introits *Nunc scio uere* and *Nos autem gloriari* (5319, fols. 117r and 76v)

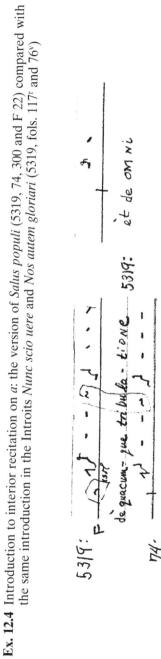

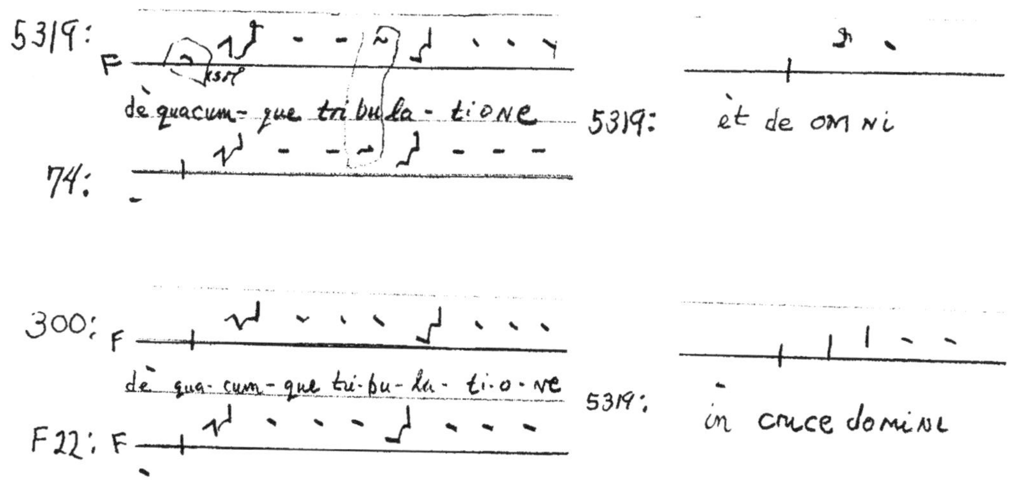

Table 12.3 Deuterus concordances for the *Perpetuum* flourish

Introit [*mode*]	*Vat. lat. 5319*	*MMMA II*	*Phrase or word*
Salus populi [A][a] Cosmas & Damian (?)	57^{r}	18	*per*-pétuum
Iudicant sancti [A] Processus & Martinianus Protus & Hyacinthus	116^{v}, 126^{v}	29	*per*-pétuum
Protector noster [A] 13th Sun. p. Pent.	125^{r}	17	[su-]*per* mília
Timete dominum [A] Cyriacus	120^{v}	26–7	[om-]*ni* bóno
Dum clamarem [Plag.] 9th Sun. p. Pent.	40^{r}	41	[ipse] *te* nútriet
Clamauerunt iusti [Plag.] Alexander & Theodulus Marcellinus & Peter	104^{r}	40	[Al-]*le*-lúia (next to last)
Exaudi dne . . . Alleluia [Plag.] Sun. p. Ascens.	106^{r}	43	[Al-]*le*-lúia (next to last)[b]

[a] Deuterus authenticus = A; Deuterus plagalis = Plag.
[b] The last half of the flourish differs.

The melody of *Salus populi*, in spite of its deuterus modality – a modal region where formulas abound, especially during Lent – is nevertheless carefully wrought, using common patterns with restraint. In a general way, it thus resembles many individually crafted Introits in deuterus modality sung during Holy Week and Eastertide. It stands apart from the formula-laden deuterus melodies sung with most of the twenty-six Lenten ferial Introit texts.

GRADUAL: R_x *Oculi omnium* V̄ *Aperis tu manum tuam*
(Ps. 144: 15, 16)
Mode: Tritus
Sources: Ricc 300 (fol. 8^{v}); 5319 (fol. 57^{r}, cued at fol. 132^{r}; MMMA 2: 154); Bod 74, fol. 55^{r-v}; F 22 (fol. 32^{r}, cued at fol. 72^{v})

The F-mode Gradual *Oculi omnium* with the verse *Aperis tu manum tuam* in the *Missa pro congregatione* is also found in the Thursday stational Mass (Lent III.5) at SS. Cosmas and Damian in the Forum – but not in the Mass for the eighteenth Sunday after Pentecost, which contains the rest of the Lenten Thursday Proper chants (see above). Instead, *Oculi omnium* serves as the Gradual for the nineteenth Sunday after Pentecost.[65] Only a brief discussion of the piece is possible here.[66] My transcription of the version of Riccardiana 300 appears in Ex. 12.7.

Ex. 12.5 Flourish in final cadence: the version of *Salus populi* (5319, 74, 300 and F 22) compared with that of the Introit *Dum clamarem* (Bodmer 74, fol. 38v)

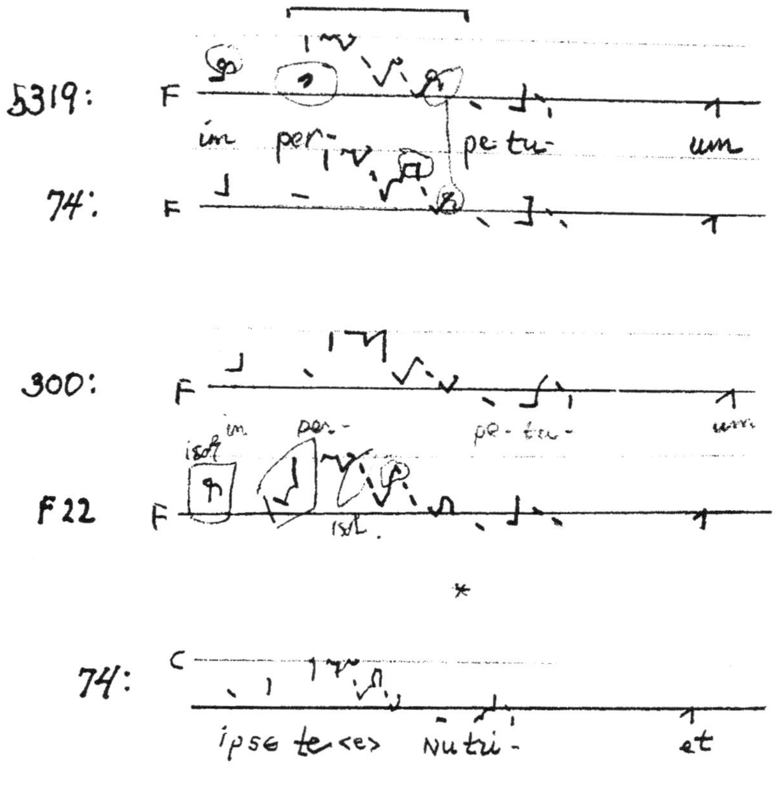

The similar features between the versions of Riccardiana 300 and F 22 observed in the Introit *Salus populi* are contradicted by the Gradual, where the resemblance of Riccardiana 300 and Vat. lat. 5319 on the one hand and of Bodmer 74 and F 22 on the other is at once established by the cleffing and the unusual B♭s notated for the opening phrase in Riccardiana 300 and Vat. lat. 5319 (see Ex. 12.8).[67] The versions of Riccardiana 300 and Vat. lat. 5319 are very close throughout, as are those of Bodmer 74 and F 22. A typical

Ex. 12.6 Unique opening figure of *Salus populi*

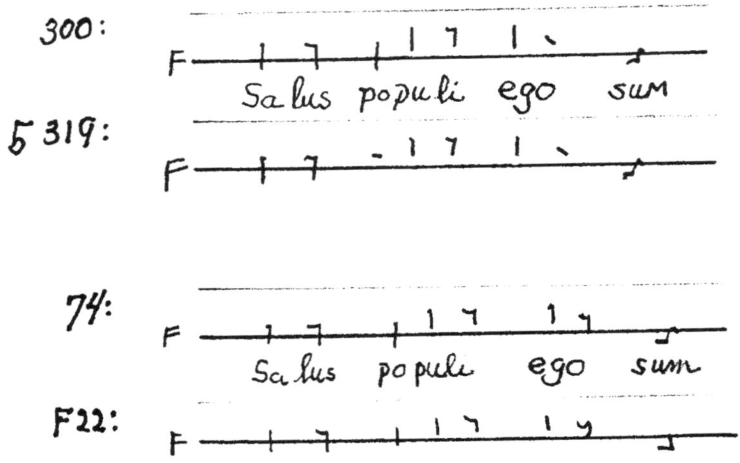

instance occurs in the final melisma of the respond, on the last syllable of *oportuno* (see Ex. 12.7). In Riccardiana 300 and Vat. lat. 5319 a rising third is filled in, *FGa*, but not in Bodmer 74 and F 22, which have *Fa*. In the final melisma of the verse, on the last syllable of *benedictione*, a small but substantive difference again joins Bodmer 74 and F 22 against Vat. lat. 5319 (see Ex. 12.9; in Riccardiana 300, the end of the well-known cadence formula was omitted).

OFFERTORY: *Si ambulauero in medio tribulationis* (Ps. 137: 7)
V. 1. *In quacumque die inuocauero te* (Ps. 137: 3)
V. 2. *Adorabo ad templum sanctum tuum* (Ps. 137: 2a+)
(The verses are omitted in Riccardiana 300 and F 22.)
Mode: Tetrardus
Sources: Ricc 300 (fol. 9r); 5319 (fol. 57, cued at fol. 131v; MMMA 2: 393–5); Bod 74 (fol. 55v); F 22 (fol. 32r, cued at fol. 72v)

Ex. 12.10 gives my transcription of the version of Riccardiana 300. The several versions of the Offertory show little evidence of derivation or of any other relationship.[68] The *Zersungenheit* of F 22 sets that version apart from the rest. The version of Vat. lat. 5319 shows minor idiosyncrasies besides the purely notational way that the neumes were written and sequenced – but these idiosyncrasies are of little importance. A few purely neumatic similarities seem to pair Bodmer 74 and F 22, but these apparent similarities might be regarded as resulting from the peculiar features of Vat. lat. 5319. I cannot establish any significant linkage between manuscripts on the basis of this Offertory.

Ex. 12.7 Gradual *Oculi omnium* of the *Missa pro congregatione* (Florence, Riccardiana 300, fol. 8v)

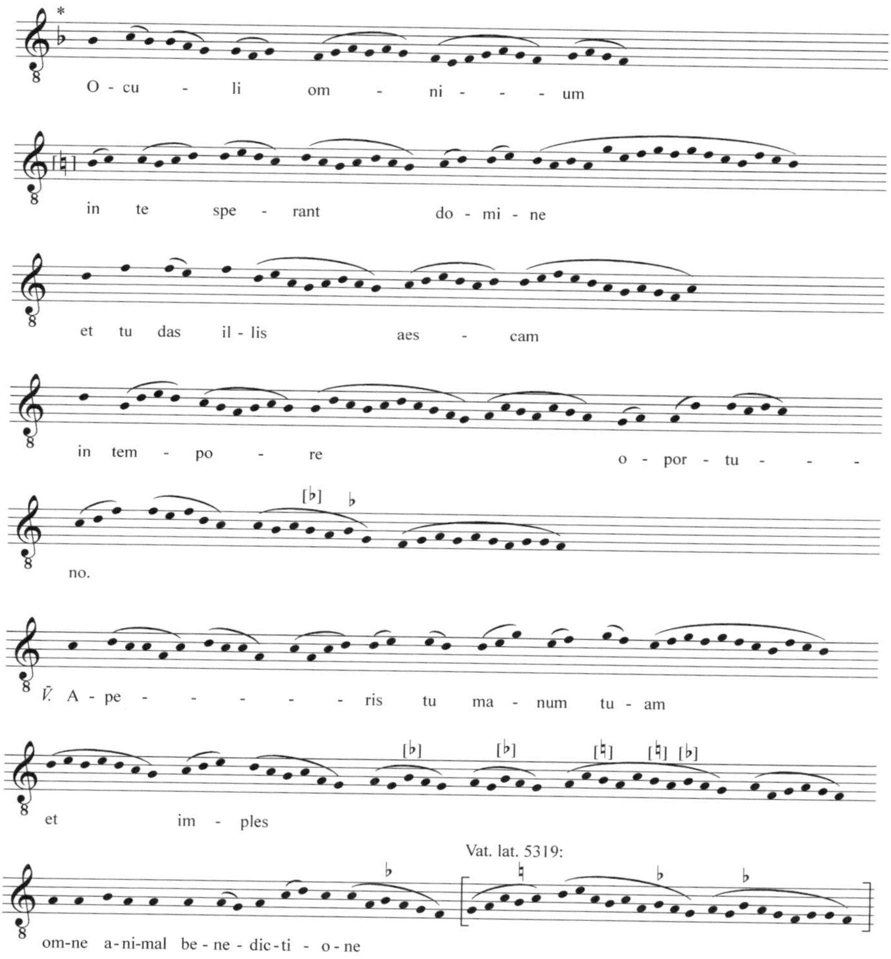

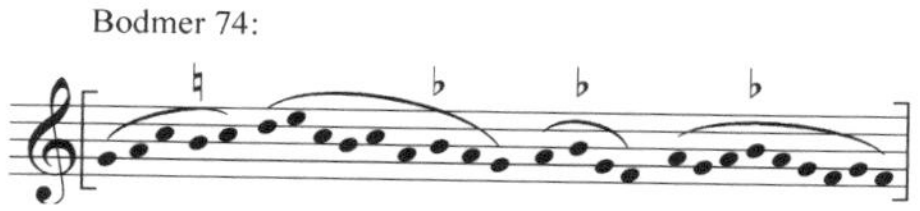

* A green line after the *b-flat* extends through *omnium*.

Ex. 12.8 Variants in the Gradual *Oculi omnium* (Riccardiana 300, Vat. lat. 5319, Bodmer 74 and San Pietro F 22: in 300, the initial ♭ clef is followed by a green line, and in 5319, mid-line, a custos on ♭ replaces an erased custos on *c*)

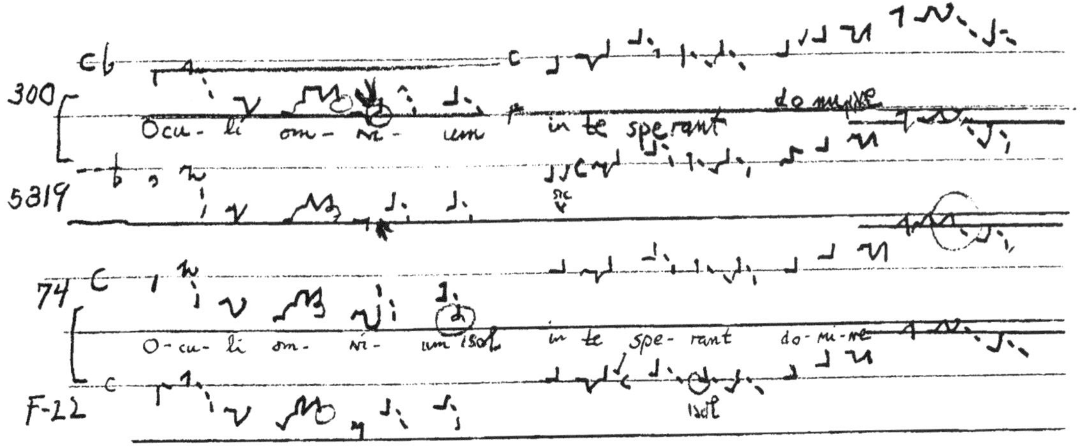

Ex. 12.9 Variants in the final cadential melisma in the verse *Aperis tu manum tuam* of the Gradual *Oculi omnium* (5319, 74 and F 22 – in 300 only the beginning of the melisma is notated)

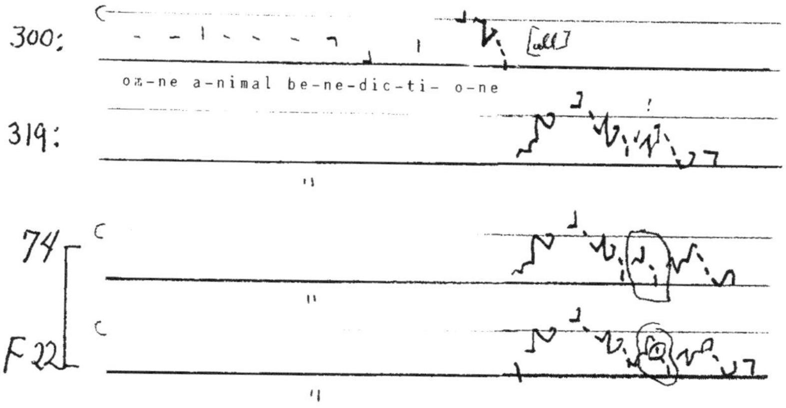

Did *Si ambulauero* with its verses originate as the Offertory for the eighteenth Sunday after Pentecost (*Dominica III post S. Angeli* in Vat. lat. 5319) or conceivably as the Offertory for the patronal feast of SS. Cosmas and Damian, as seems likely in the case of the Introit *Salus populi*? The question remains open. If it was indeed composed for or at least sung at the patronal festival, it would then have been transferred along with the sacramentary prayers to the stational Mass for Lent III.5 early in the eighth century. If it was not part of the patronal festival Mass, *Si ambulauero* might have been borrowed for the new Lenten Thursday Mass either directly from the eighteenth Sunday after Pentecost or else from a pool of Offertories *quale uolueris*.[69]

COMMUNION: *Tu mandasti domine mandata tua* (Ps. 118: 4, 5)
Psalm. *Beati inma(culati in uia)* (Ps. 118: 1)
(The psalm verse is found only in Bodmer 74. A differentia – not the same as in Bodmer 74 – is given in Vat. lat. 5319 without text.)
Mode: Deuterus authenticus
Sources: Ricc 300 (fol. 9ʳ); 5319 (fol. 58ʳ, cued at 131ᵛ, MMMA 2: 441); Bod 74 (fols. 55ᵛ–56ʳ); F 22 (fol. 32ᵛ, cued at fol. 72ᵛ)[70]

The version of Riccardiana 300 is transcribed in Ex. 12.11. At the start, Riccardiana 300 and Vat. lat. 5319 show like variants for the phrase *custodiri nimis* when compared with the similarity of Bodmer 74 and F 22. But toward the end, in the neume that precedes the last word *tuas*, Riccardiana 300 and

Ex. 12.10 Offertory *Si ambulauero* of the *Missa pro congregatione* (Riccardiana 300, fol. 9r)

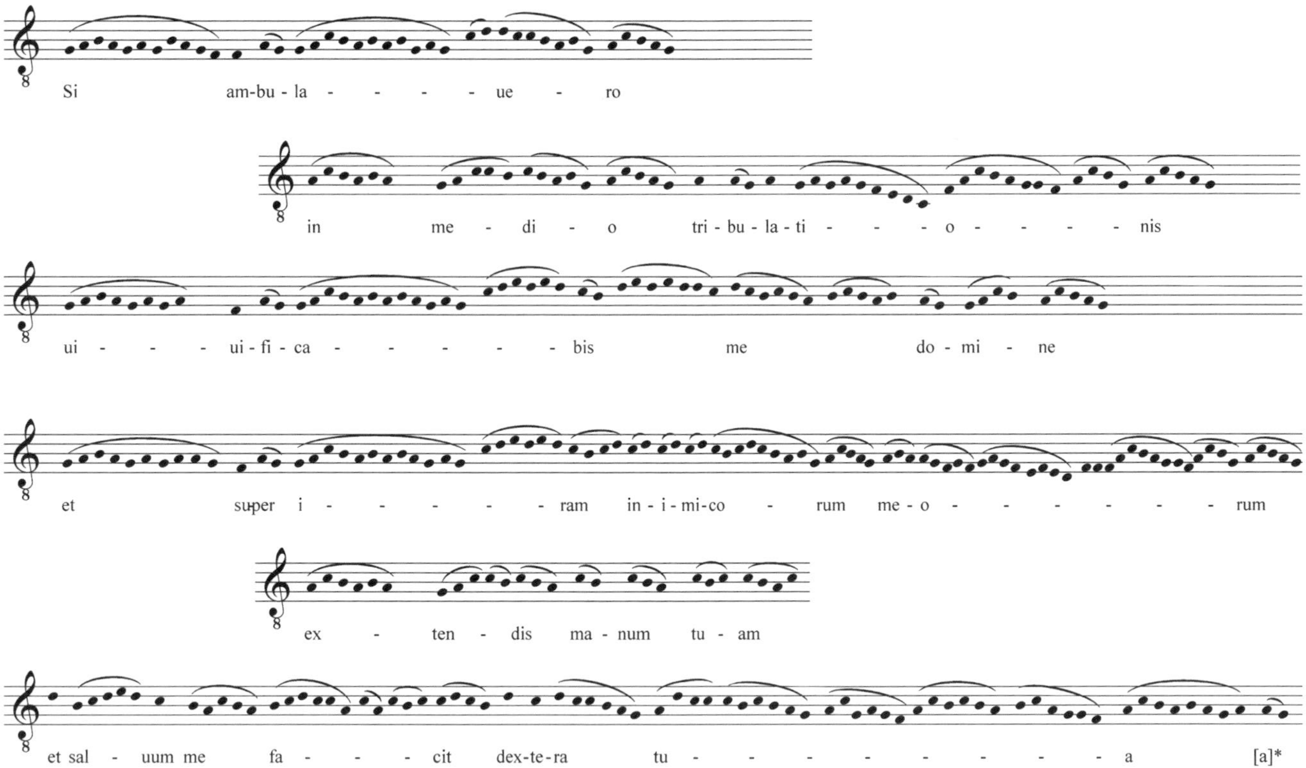

* The versions of Bodmer 74, Vat. lat. 5319, and San Pietro F 22 place the final syllable of *tua* under the last two notes.

Ex. 12.11 Communion *Tu mandasti* of the *Missa pro congregatione* (Riccardiana 300, fol. 9r)

Tu man - das - ti do - mi - ne man - da - ta tu - a
cus - to - di - ri ni - mis
u - ti-nam di - ri - gan - - tur ui - e me - ae
ad cus - to - di - en - das ius - ti - fi - ca - ti - o - nes
?
[♭]
tu - as
[Vat. lat. 5319]
Be - a - ti inma[culati]
[Bodmer 74]

Ex. 12.12 Three passages in the Communion *Tu mandasti* with variants (Vat. lat. 5319, Bodmer 74, San Pietro F 22 and Riccardiana 300)

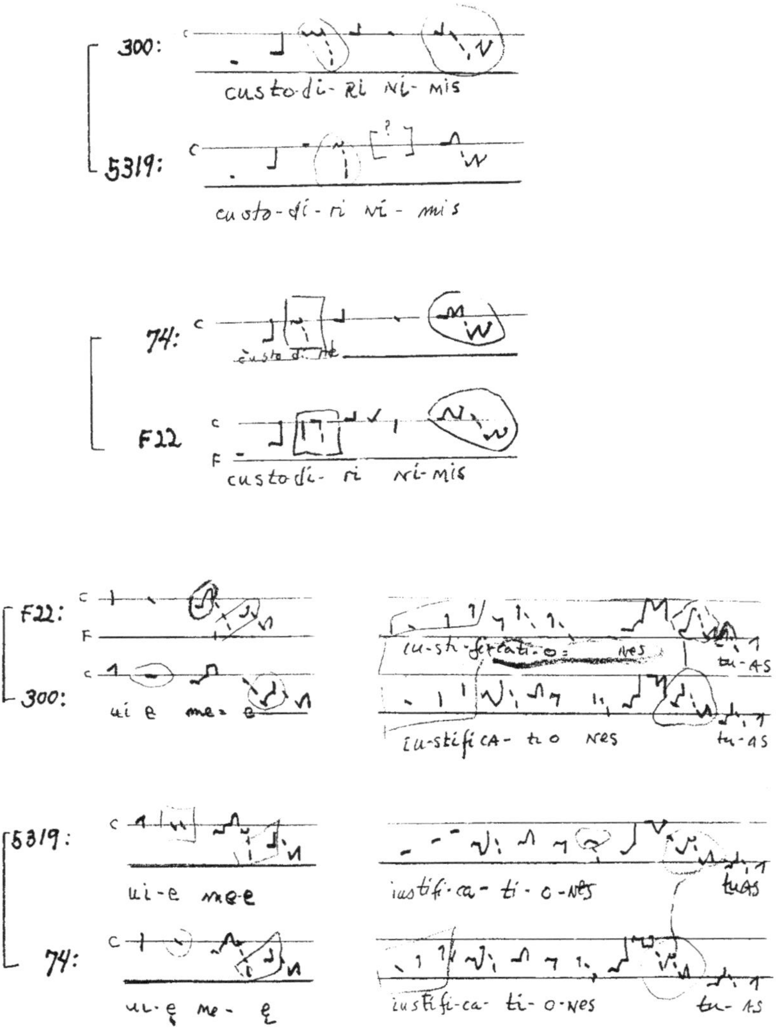

F 22 are paired against Vat. lat. 5319 and Bodmer 74 (see Ex. 12.12). As often, F 22 has its own isolated readings – in this case, involving the omission of the middle note of rising thirds at *mee* and *tuas*. The displaced word underlay at *iustificationes* must be intentional.

Comparisons of the chants in the Riccardiana 300 *Missa pro congregatione* with those from other Old Roman sources fail to disclose consistent relationships. The notation of the Introit *Salus populi* and that of the Gradual *Oculi omnium* in Riccardiana 300 show definite but conflicting affinities: the Introit in Riccardiana 300 is similar to F 22 but the Gradual to Vat. lat. 5319.[71] The variants in the Offertory *Si ambulauero* fall into no clear pattern, and the paired variants in the Communion *Tu mandasti* – even within so brief a chant – are contradictory.

Although examination of the *Missa pro congregatione* reveals little about Riccardiana 300 except that it comes from Rome, we have learned a bit more about the tantalizingly inaccessible immediate sources of its notation, doubtless among the fifty-odd destroyed Roman service books, and about the venerable if nebulous oral tradition standing behind them. Our investigation has turned up a likely destination for the non-scriptural Introit *Salus populi*: namely, the patronal festival of SS. Cosmas and Damian *in Foro* on 27 September. If indeed it was intended for the *natale* of the physician-martyrs (or more probably, the dedication feast of their basilica), the Introit might have been composed any time between the last half of the sixth century and the late seventh century; it need not have been introduced along with the Mass prayers for 27 September that are found in the old Gelasian sacramentary, which, in the Gregorian sacramentary, were transferred to a Lenten Thursday. At the very least, we have determined why *Salus populi* was chosen for the Thursday Mass during the third full week of Lent.

The *Missa Sponsalicia*

The Roman *Missa sponsalicia*[72] appears with notation in all of our three sources and also in Vat. lat. 5319. It does not appear in the St. Cecilia Gradual, Bodmer 74, nor in San Pietro F 22. In our sources, the wedding Mass is made up of three layers: (1) the prayers of the celebrant, which ultimately go back to the marriage-Mass set and nuptial blessing in the so-called Leonine sacramentary (XXXI) – but derived through their rearrangement as seen in the Hadrianum;[73] (2) the readings at the wedding Mass, nearly identical in all three sources, and all drawn from the Vulgate text of the Bible; and (3) the chants of the wedding-Mass Propers, of which the Introit, the Gradual and the Communion are unique to the Roman wedding Mass and the other two (the Alleluia with its verse and the Offertory) taken from elsewhere in the Old Roman repertory. Evidently the unique chant Propers were the last layer of the Mass to be composed, since their texts are not found in the earliest neumeless Frankish collections of Roman chant texts.[74]

Ex. 12.13 Introit *Deus israhel* of the *Missa ad sponsas benedicendas* (Riccardiana 300, fol. 9v)

*Here 300 has ccc instead of ccb, while 299, 5319, and 74 (the last in other introits using this differentia) all have the b, as in the reconstruction of Roman psalmody given above.

Ex. 12.14 Gradual *Uxor tua* of the *Missa ad sponsas benedicendas* (Riccardiana 300, fol. 10r)

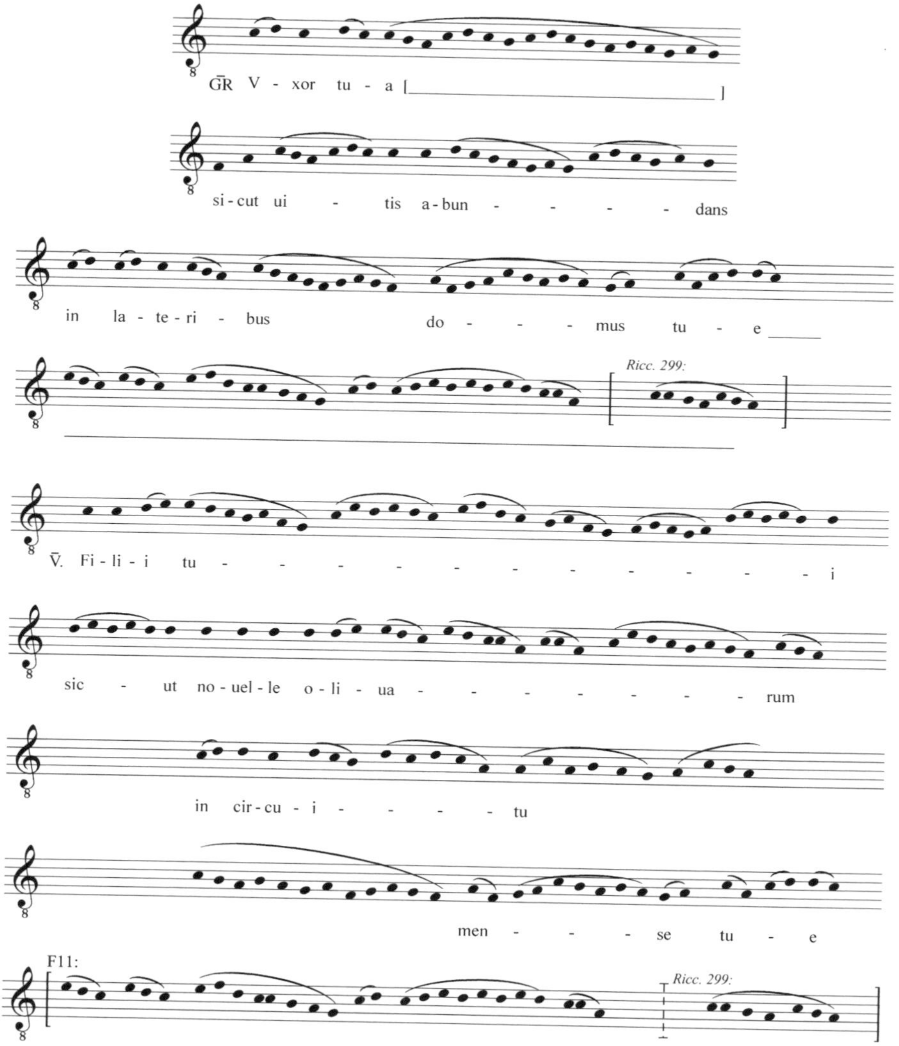

Ex. 12.15 Alleluia *Diffusa est gratia* of the *Missa ad sponsas benedicendas* (Riccardiana 300, fol. 10r)

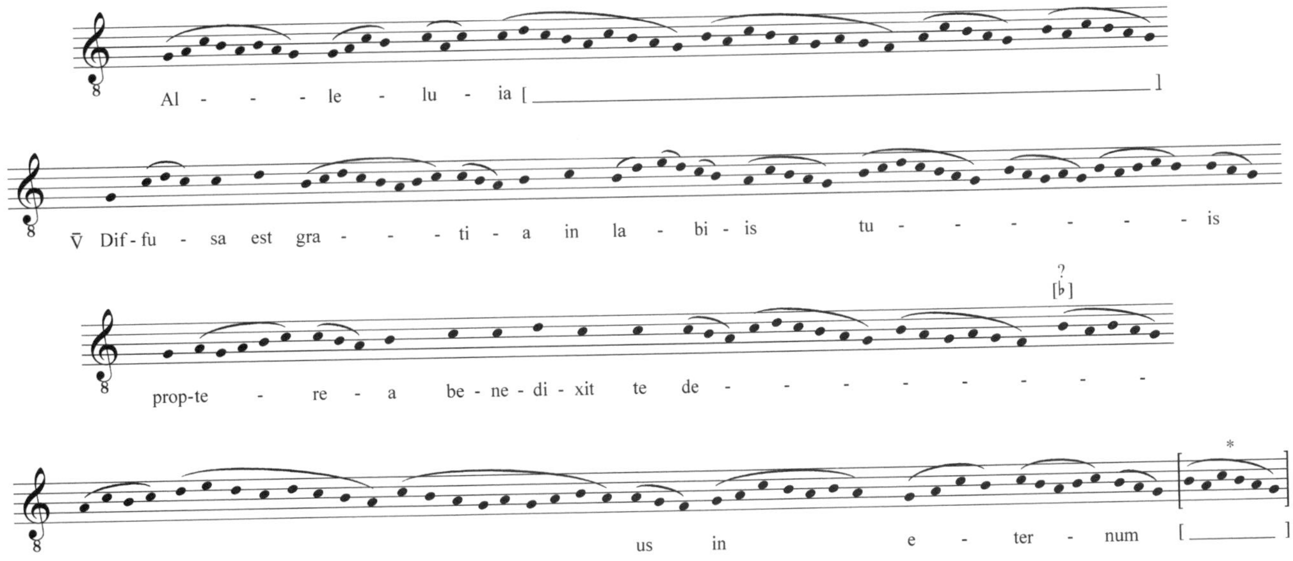
Al - - - le - lu - ia [ ]
V̄ Dif - fu - sa est gra - - - ti - a in la - bi - is tu - - - - - - is
?
[♭]
prop-te - re - a be - ne - di - xit te de - - - - - - - -
*
us in e - ter - num [ ]

* Ending thus in 299, 5319, and 74

Ex. 12.16 Offertory *In te speraui* of the *Missa ad sponsas benedicendas* (Riccardiana 300, fol. 10v)

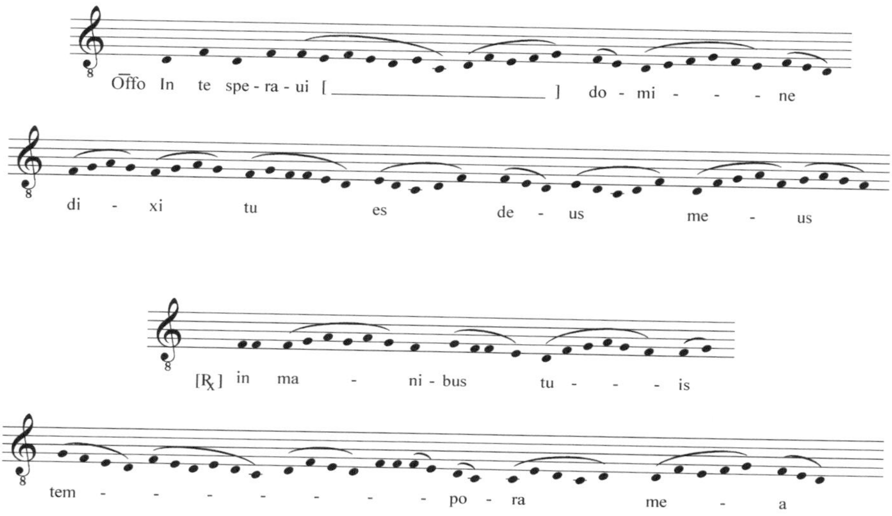

Space does not allow an examination of the Roman wedding Mass in a thorough way that might relate these chants to the larger and earlier Roman repertory. I therefore postpone full treatment of the *Missa sponsalicia*,[75] giving here only the transcription of the wedding chants from Riccardiana 300, expertly sung by Professor Richard Crocker on the compact disc accompanying this volume, to which CD I shall fortunately be able later to refer (see Exs. 12.13–17).[76]

Notes

1 The earliest major source for Old Roman chant is the Gradual written for and at the basilica of Santa Cecilia in Trastevere, now Cologny-Geneva, Bibl. Bodmeriana, Codex 74 (hereafter 'Bodmer 74') and published in a facsimile edition, *Das Graduale von Santa Cecilia in Trastevere, Cod. Bodmer 74*, ed. Max Lütolf, 2 vols. (Cologny-Geneva: Fondation Martin Bodmer, 1987). The second Gradual to survive, Vatican City, BAV Vat. lat. 5319 (hereafter 'Vat. lat. 5319'), was published in a transcription by Margareta Landwehr-Melnicki with an introduction by Bruno Stäblein, *Die Gesänge des altrömischen Graduale, Vat. lat. 5319* (Kassel: Bärenreiter, 1970). The latest of the three Graduals (from the early thirteenth century), Vatican City, Arch. San Pietro, F 22 (hereafter 'F 22') has not been published with its music. An Office antiphoner of uncertain provenance (but not St. Peter's), London, BL Add. 29988, is thought to date from around the middle of the twelfth century. The Office antiphoner from St. Peter's Basilica (late twelfth century, after 1173) has recently appeared in facsimile, *Biblioteca*

Ex. 12.17 Communion *Ecce sic benedicetur* of the *Missa ad sponsas benedicendas* (Riccardiana 300, fol. 11v)

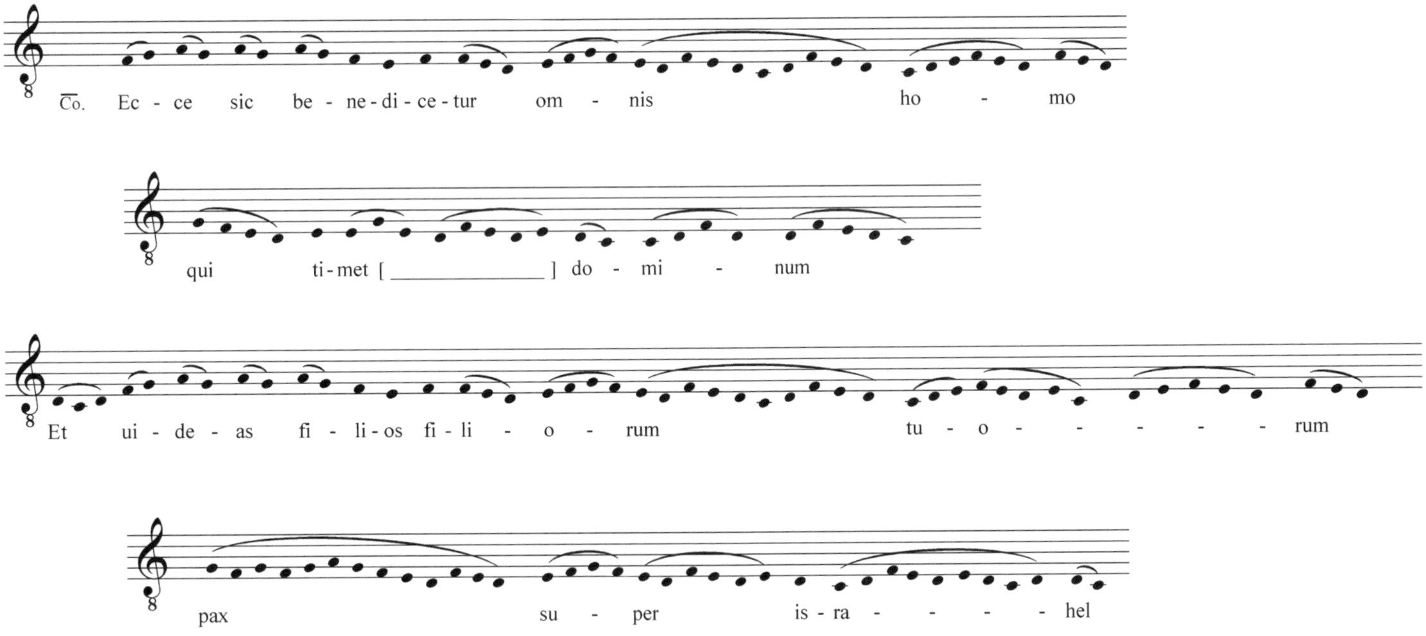

Apostolica Vaticana Archivio San Pietro B 79, Antifonario della Basilica di S. Pietro (Sec. XII), ed. Bonifacio Giacomo Baroffio and Soo Jung Kim, 2 vols. (Rome: Torre d'Orfeo, 1995).

2 The Brabantian observer and liturgist Radulph de Rivo (ca. 1345–1403), who spent 1381 and 1396–7 in Rome, is the authority for this event. There seems to be no reason to doubt his careful testimony, though he wrote more than one hundred years after the event he describes. He was curious about the Roman liturgy and made careful inquiries on the spot. In his *De canonum observantia liber* (1397) he writes: 'Sciendum tamen, quod Nicolaus papa tertius, natione Romanus de genere Ursinorum, qui coepit anno Domini millesimo ducentesimo septuagesimo septimo et palatium apud sanctum Petrum construxit, fecit in ecclesiis Urbis amoveri antiphonarios, gradualia, missalia, et alios libros officii antiquos quinquaginta et mandavit, ut de cetero ecclesiae Urbis uterentur libris et breviariis Fratrum Minorum, quorum regulam etiam confirmavit. Unde hodie in Roma omnes libri sunt novi et Franciscani, et forma notularum in cantu antiqua, qua tum Ambrosiani quam Alemaniae nationes utuntur, cum pluribus aliis observationibus ecclesiasticis ab Urbe relegata.' I take this passsage from the convenient quotation in *Die Gesänge des altrömischen Graduale*, 141, where further references are given. I have not found a specific decree of Nicholas III (Giovanni Gaetano Orsini, a native noble Roman) touching this matter. Before his election, Nicholas III had been cardinal deacon of St. Nicholas in Carcere for thirty years and, for little over a year before his election as pope in 1277, archpriest of St. Peter's in the Vatican. (The conclave that elected him had been deadlocked for six months in Viterbo.) His predecessor Urban IV had named Nicholas protector of the Franciscans, and Nicholas did much for the friars throughout his pontificate. He 'carried out a radical restoration of St. Peter's and . . . made the Vatican palace his residence, enlarging and remodeling it, and purchasing plots for its gardens'. He must thus have been well acquainted with the Old Roman chant at St. Peter's which he suppressed.

His immediate predecessor John XXI (1276–7), a notable scholar also called 'Peter of Spain', was elected, briefly reigned, and died in Viterbo shortly after his 'hastily built study collapsed on him'. His predecessor, Hadrian V (July to August 1276) was elected in Rome but died a month later in Viterbo 'without being ordained priest, consecrated, or crowned'. Before Hadrian V, Innocent V (January to June 1276), a Dominican born in the Savoy and active in Paris, was elected in Arezzo but died five months later in Rome. Earlier, the cardinals at Viterbo had taken three years to elect Gregory X (1271–6) while this former archdeacon of Liège was crusading in the Holy Land. 'He reached Viterbo [from Acre] . . . then went to Rome, in which neither of his two predecessors [between 1261 and 1268] had set foot, and was consecrated in St. Peter's in March 1272.' He traveled constantly, especially north of the Alps, and died in Arezzo. I have reviewed the roster to show how feeble was the papal presence in Rome during the period before Nicholas III, when exclusively non-Italian popes reigned, mostly from their palace in Viterbo. An Orsini pope resident at the Vatican must have come as an unwelcome shock to the independently minded canons of St. Peter's. (The quotations in the above paragraph are drawn from J. N. D. Kelly, *The Oxford Dictionary of Popes* [Oxford: Oxford University Press, 1986]).

3 See below, esp. nn. 5 and 8.

4 Thus in Michel Huglo, 'Le Chant "vieux-romain": liste des manuscrits et témoins indirects', *Sacris erudiri*, 6 (1954), 96–124. The attribution was based on Adalbert Ebner, *Quellen und Forschungen zur Geschichte und Kunstgeschichte des Missale Romanum im Mittelalter: Iter Italicum* (Freiburg im Breisgau: Herder, 1896), 47–51.

5 Johannes Ramackers, 'Die Weihe des Domes von Sorrent am 16 März 1113 durch Kardinal-bischof Richard von Albano', in Clemens Bauer, Laetitia Boehm and Max Muller (eds), *Speculum Historiale: Geschichte von Geschichtsschreibung und Geschichtsdeutung* (Freiburg and Munich: Alber, 1965), 578–89.

6 After the fiasco when Paschal's coronation of Emperor Henry IV on 12 February 1111 was interrupted by the riot in St. Peter's that ended in Henry's arrest of the pope and the cardinals, Paschal was forced to yield to the emperor the right to invest his bishops and abbots with ring and staff – the so-called 'pravilegium' of 12 April 1111. (Cardinal Richard was absent from Rome during these events.) The reform party severely criticized the pope for yielding, and Paschal considered abdication. Instead he retired from Rome to his fief in Benevento in the south.

7 Ramackers has calculated distances and traveling times between Benevento, Salerno, Sorrento and Rome and finds the journeys of pope and cardinal could easily have been accomplished in the periods known to have been available to them. He has also noted that Paschal's predecessor, Urban II (1088–99), on his trip to south Italy in 1089, consecrated Elias bishop of Bari and also consecrated the crypt of St. Nicholas in Bari as well as Brindisi Cathedral. He points out that these consecrations were no small source of income for the papal treasury: 'Wenn der Papst selber oder einer seiner engsten Mitarbeiter eine Kirchweihe vornahmen, konnten sie gewiss sein, dafür eine ansehnliche, in den meisten Fällen sogar eine fürstliche Entschädigung als Geschenk zu erhalten.'

8 Paola Supino Martini, *Roma e l'area grafica romanesca* (Alessandria: Edizioni dell'Orso, 1987), 54. For Richard of Albano, see Rudolf Hüls, *Kardinäle, Klerus und Kirchen Roms, 1049–1130* (Tübingen: Niemeyer, 1977), 93–4, and Hans-Walter Klewitz, *Reformpapsttum und Kardinalkolleg: Die Entstehung des Kardinalkollegiums* (Darmstadt: H. Gentner, 1957), 105 and 120. Cardinal Richard had been dean of the chapter of canons at St. Stephen's Cathedral, Metz, before he came to Rome a little after 1080. He had been expelled from Metz, along with his bishop, as an ardent supporter of Hildebrand and was therefore warmly welcomed by the now Pope Gregory VII, who made him a cardinal. Also see Carlo Servatius, *Paschalis II (1099–1118)* (Stuttgart: Hiersemann, 1979), 44–5, 150, 164, 189–91, and 234.

9 Partial notation was added for the blessing of the font at the Easter vigil in a very light later script.

10 Huglo, 'Le Chant "vieux-romain"', 101. In n. 3 on the same page Huglo adds: 'Rien de prévu pour la messe de mariage dans les graduels grégoriens les plus anciens. Dans les missels, la messe de mariage comporte oraisons et lectures propres mais pas de pièces de chant spéciales: ainsi par exemple, dans Lyon 537, fol. 107; Cambrai 234 (224), fol. 408v. D'autres missels donnent parfois comme pièces de chant celles de la messe de la S. Trinité: voir les témoins citées dans *Surtees Society* vol. 63 (1875), p. 157–69. C'est en Italie que le formulaire vieux-romain des messes de mariage est passée dans les mss. grégoriens: la messe *Deus Israhel* figure, sans neumes dans le Graduel Rome Angelica 123, fol. 152v, copié en 1039. [The text in Angelica 123 has been severely edited: the Introit begins: *Dominus deus israel*; the Gradual is *R Ecce sic benedicetur omni homo qui timet dominum* with *V Benedicat uos dominus ex syon et uideatis filios filiorum uestrorum*; the Alleluia verse (as mentioned) is *Mittat uobis dominus auxilium de sancto et de syon tueatur uos.* The Offertory and the Communion texts are the same as in the Roman books.] Ce n'est qu'au xiie siècle qu'on rencontre pour la première fois une mélodie de type "grégorien" pour ces textes (Modène O. I. 20 . . .).' The last sentence is not quite accurate: Paris, BNF lat. 903, the eleventh-

century Gradual from St-Yrieix (PM 13), has the notated Mass *Ad nuptias* (but not with the Roman melodies) beginning *Dominus Deus israhel* and having other variants from the Roman texts, some of them like those in Angelica 123.

11 For instance, there is no wedding Mass in any of the surviving missals and graduals from Benevento; see Jean Mallet and André Thibaut, *Les Manuscrits en écriture bénéventaine de la Bibliothèque Capitulaire de Bénévent*, 2 vols. (Paris: Editions du Centre national de la recherche scientifique, 1984–97), ii, 656–60. Benevento, a papal fief definitively from 1053, was the site of many papal synods and councils.

12 Rainerius came from the minor nobility, probably from a family in the Romagna. See the extensive discussion of his origins in Servatius, *Paschalis II*, 1–6.

13 Thomas Forrest Kelly, 'Texts Related to the Exultet at Rome' (accompanying a lecture, 'The Exultet at Rome', at Royaumont, 20 September 1993), cautiously assigned Riccardiana 299 to 'a late eleventh-century Roman church'. 'The manuscript', he wrote, 'is attributed by some to the Papal chapel (Supino Martini, 54–5 and n. 35 [*recte* 'Papal curia' – she cites the opinion as Ramackers']), but the persistence of so many non-papal elements (the litany, the prayer before the lesson) makes much more likely its origin in another of the city's churches. The rubrics here seem to be an amalgam.'

14 By associating Riccardiana 299 with Vat. lat. 5319, Supino Martini seems to imply that an origin for Riccardiana 299 at the Lateran is possible. Apart from the question of whether Vat. lat. 5319 comes from the Lateran, a close comparison of the versions of the wedding Mass chants in these two manuscripts suggests instead that they did not originate in the same institution or scriptorium, Roman though both of them are.

15 A brief notated passage in Riccardiana 300 (fol. 21v) supplies an exception to this statement. Within the *ordo missae*, the celebrant's versicles of the Sursum Corda (which introduces the preface chant and thus the canon of the Mass) are notated *in campo aperto* with true Beneventan neumes, accurately heighted. The text of the bystanders' responses is left unnotated. In *Ordinary Chants and Tropes for the Mass from Southern Italy, A.D. 1000–1250*, pt. 3, *Preface Chants and Sanctus* (Beneventanum troporum corpus, 2 [hereafter BTC 2]; Madison, Wis.: A-R Editions, 1996), p. li, I wrote: 'No instances from Rome of notation for the Mass preface seem to be known before the latter part of the thirteenth century, when northern and Franciscan forms began to appear in Roman altar books. That the preface was sung at Rome is certain: exactly how it was sung in the eleventh century or earlier is not known. So far as we can tell, at Rome the preface chant still remained the unchallenged domain of oral tradition.' Although for years my transcription of these versicles had lain in my files, I did not yet realize that Riccardiana 300 was a Roman manuscript. Ought we to see in these fragments of notation a hint of how Sursum Corda and the preface were sung in Rome? Possibly; but it is more likely that these neumes were added by a celebrant using the manuscript somewhere in the south – or by a priest from the south celebrating in Rome. The notation is pure Beneventan, not Roman (the neumes from the notated Propers in Riccardiana 300 are purely Roman). Besides, the notes for the celebrant's versicles resemble versions used in the south during the eleventh century. Cf. the northern version called *Francisca* (Frankish) in Montecassino 127 (a missal from the Cassinese dependency of Albaneta) for the celebrant's phrases *Per omnia secula seculorum* and *Dominus uobiscum* and the same version intermingled in part with that of Montecassino 426 (an earlier votive missal), for the celebrant's *Sursum corda* – as given in BTC 2, pt. 3, pp. xlvi and lvii. The version in Riccardiana 300 of *Gratias agamus domino deo nostro* is *sui*

generis. The preface beginning *Vere et iustum est* [sic] is notated as a monotone, probably on the note *fa* within the tetrachord *ut, re, mi, fa* used in most preface chants.

16 Cf. Supino Martini, *Roma e l'area grafica romanesca*, 54–5 and nn. 37 and 38.

17 Thus Huglo, 'Le Chant "vieux-romain"', 102: 'Fragment de Missel noté de la fin du xie siècle (Ebner, p. 51) à l'usage du même monastere que le manuscrit précédent [. . . des Camaldules de S. Philippe et S. Jacques, au diocèse de Sienne]'. Supino Martini avoids committing herself to naming an exact provenance; see n. 16 above.

18 Giovanni Lami, *Catalogus codicum manuscriptorum qui in Bibliotheca Riccardiana adservantur* (Livorno: Antonii Sanctinii & sociorum, 1746).

19 The manuscript is designated 'F 11A' in the *schede* of the Vatican Library. But 'F 11B' consists only of a single *carta di guardia* that was found with the manuscript, of an earlier date than F 11A. I shall simply call the manuscript 'F 11', the usual designation.

20 Introit *Rogamus te*, Gradual *Qui lazarum resuscitasti*, Tract *De profundis* with the verses *Si iniquitates* and *Quia aput te*, Offertory *Domine conuertere*, and Communion *Lux aeterna*.

21 Introit *Requiem aeternam*, Gradual *Conuertere animam meam* with the verse *In memoriam eternam*, Tract *De profundis* (cued only), Offertory *Domine conuertere* (cued only) and *Alia Domine hiesu christe, rex gloriae* (without verse), Communion *Lux eterna* (cued only) and *Pro quorum memoria*.

22 Pierre Jounel, *Le Culte des saints dans les basiliques du Latran et du Vatican au douzième siècle* (Rome: Ecole Française de Rome, 1977), 67–70. Jounel dates the manuscript to the end of the eleventh century or the beginning of the twelfth. I think that his date – if it refers to the *copying* of the manuscript – is too early, and that the script and notation date from around the middle of the twelfth century or possibly even slightly later. Jounel extracted his kalendar of feasts from the sanctorale, omitting the great feasts of the temporale, the Sundays after Epiphany and Pentecost, the Septuagesima to Pentecost cycle and the Ember Days. The reader will perceive how greatly I am indebted to Jounel's study and especially to his transcriptions of the the kalendars drawn from Rome, Bibl. Vallicelliana E 15 and San Pietro F 14 – which I reproduce exactly (save for *u* and *v* of the manuscripts) in the text below and the tables – and to his 'Commentaire historique et liturgique' (pp. 207–331) on the saints venerated in twelfth-century Rome, arranged according to the order of their liturgical commemoration throughout the year. Nevertheless, Jounel was mistaken to accept the Vatican provenance traditionally assigned to San Pietro F 11, albeit with misgivings.

23 See Supino Martini, *Roma e l'area grafica romanesca*, 82–3 and nn. 99, 102 and 103. The authors she cites mostly assign F 11 to St. Peter's, usually without considering chant versions. Supino Martini says: 'Sembrerebbe invece romana [as opposed to San Pietro F 12 she has been discussing] l'ornamentazione del Vat. Arch. S. Pietro F 11A, che può pertanto essere trattato in questa sede quale testimonianza, nell'Urbe o nei suoi dintorni, dell'incipiente stilizzazione gotica della minuscola, pur nella sopravivenza di alcuni elementi della precedente tipizzazione.' In n. 102 she adds: 'La prima testimonianza certa dell'appartenenza del Vat. Arch. S. Pietro F 11A a S. Pietro sembra costituita dalla nota di possesso apposta da mano del secolo XVI a f. 101v: "Bibliothecae basilicae S. Petri".'

24 For example, in Jounel's description (p. 44) of the dedication feast of St. Peter's Basilica on 18 November, missing in F 11.

25 Jounel also assigned the evangeliary-sacramentary San Pietro F 12 to St. Peter's (relying on Ebner – see Jounel 34, n. 47) and entitled this extracted kalendar 'Sanctoral du sacramentaire de Saint-Pierre' (pp. 34–5 and 54). Here he is certainly mistaken; see John Boe, 'Music Notation in Archivio San Pietro C 105 and in the Farfa Breviary, Chigi C.VI.177', *EMH* 18 (1999), 1–45, at 7–15 and 24–5 (n. 38). Supino Martini says flatly of San Pietro F 12, 'né scrittura, né ornamentazione consentono di accettare una localizzazione romana o "romanesca"'. However, San Pietro F 12 must have entered the basilican library by 1363, when the earliest inventory of its manuscripts lists an 'evangeliary' under the signature 'GGG' – which signature occurs on fol. 1r of San Pietro F 12.

26 My dating of B 79 as 'early 13th c.' in BTC 2, pt. 3, p. lxxxiii, was based solely on the appendixed Mass Ordinary chants on fol. 196r–v, the only portion of this manuscript employed in that volume. With the facsimile edition now in hand, I realize that the script and neumes of fol. 196 – moldy and faded as they are – are nonetheless contemporary with the body of the manuscript, as opposed to the carelessly added clefs and lines. See the description of these Mass Ordinary chants in *Archivio San Pietro B 79*, ed. Baroffio and Kim, i, 36–7, with references to BTC 2, pts. 1 and 2.

27 Baroffio and Kim convincingly demonstrate the origin and destined use of B 79 at St. Peter's in the facsimile edition (vol. i, 18): 'La presenza dell'antifonario B 79 nel fondo dell'Archivio San Pietro orienta subito circa la sua provenienza: si tratta di un codice che è stato verosimilmente in uso presso la basilica vaticana . . . Un'analisi interna del ms B 79 mostra . . . chiaramente che sia il calendario sia l'antifonario sono stati scritti in vista delle celebrazioni liturgiche della basilica vaticana.' The editors present examples of rubrics that can only apply to St. Peter's, some of which will be discussed later here.

28 Thus in the old Gelasian sacramentary, *Liber sacramentorum Romanae aeclesiae, ordinis anni circuli (Cod. Vat. Reg. lat. 316 . . .), Sacramentarium Gelasianum*, ed. Leo Cunibert Mohlberg, Leo Eizenhöfer and Petrus Siffrin (Rome: Herder, 1960), 62–3: 'Iterum dicis [to the celebrating pontiff] *Dominus uobiscum*. Respondetur *Et cum spiritu tuo. Sursum corda* . . . [The Maundy Thursday consecration of the chrism follows, concluded by the rubric:] Hoc autem expleto uenies ante altare, ponis in ore calicis de ipsa hostia; non dicis *Pax Domini* nec faciunt pacem; sed communicant, et reseruant de ipso sacrificio in crastinum unde communicent.' Evidence for the gradual amalgamation of the four ancient monasteries serving St. Peter's into a single chapter of canons is presented in Boe, 'Music Notation in Archivio San Pietro C 105', 9–14, where the *de facto* change effected by 1053 is documented.

29 Such rubrics do in fact turn up in a codex from the leading abbey of Benevento, Santa Sofia, in the Maundy or monastic foot-washing service: 'It[em] quando non canimus ipse a[ntiphone] secund[u]m romano quo modo supra scripte sunt canimus sec[un]d[u]m ambro[siano] hoc modo' (Likewise, when we do not sing these antiphons according to Roman use, as are written above, we sing according to the Ambrosian this way; BAV, Ottoboni lat. 145, fol. 124r).

30 The reverse situation – where no rubrics employ the 'we' idiom – cannot be taken as absolutely ruling out *use* at the Vatican Basilica. Liturgical manuscripts known to have originated elsewhere certainly entered the Archivio San Pietro and may indeed have been used at St. Peter's, at least on occasion. Furthermore, a Vatican scribe (if there were scribes who worked regularly at the Vatican) might have copied rubrics of a non-Petrine exemplar, nevertheless intending it for use at St. Peter's. In this case, script, notation and illumination would all have to conform

to those known to have been used in authentically Vatican manuscripts of the period in question for it to be considered Petrine.

31 The sacramentary Vallicelliana E 15, from which he extracted the kalendar, was dated by Jounel to the second half of the eleventh century (see Jounel, *Le Culte des saints*, 35 and 61–5). The medieval basilica, which was completely rebuilt in 1496 within the palace that shortly came to house the papal Cancelleria, was founded by Pope Damasus (366–84), as the distich composed by him states:

HAEC DAMASVS TIBI CHRISTE DEVS NOVA TECTA DICAVI
LAVRENTII SAEPTVS MARTYRIS AUXILIO

Damasus' remains were translated to the basilica from the family cemetery on the Via Ardeatina, as the collect for his feast on 11 December in Vallicelliana E 15 (fol. 7v, as quoted by Jounel, 323, and Supino Martini, 119) implies: 'Propitiare, quaesumus Domine, nobis famulis tuis per huius sci Damasi Confessoris tui atque pontificis, qui in presenti requiescit aeclesia, merita gloriosa, ut eius pia intercessione ab omnibus protegamur adversis . . .'. Supino Martini (119–21 and n. 41) thinks the manuscript is from the first half of the eleventh century: 'Il *Sacramentario* è vergato da più mani abbastanza simili fra loro in miniscula romanesca della prima metà del secolo XI . . .'. See Christian C. F. Hülsen, *Le chiese di Roma nel Medio Evo* (Florence: L. S. Olschki, 1927; repr. Hildesheim: G. Olms, 1927), 284, and Mariano Armellini, *Le chiese di Roma dal secolo IV al XIX*, 2 vols. (2nd edn, Rome: Tipografia Vaticana, 1891; 3rd edn, corrected and augmented by C. Cecchelli, Rome: Edizioni R. O. R. E. di N. Ruffolo, 1942), i, 457–63, with pictures, a 1474 map, and various inscriptions.

32 Jounel, *Le Culte des saints*, 36–7, 70–74 and 308, assigns the sacramentary F 14, from which the kalendar was extracted, either to a basilica *S. Triphonis* that was built (or rebuilt) in 1106 or else to the church *S. Salvatoris de Primicerio*, later called San Trifone in Piazza Fiammetta, which was consecrated by Cardinal Leo of Ostia in 1113. (This was the year when Cardinal Richard of Albano consecrated Sorrento Cathedral and when Paschal II left Benevento to return to Rome.) In the St. Cecilia gradual, Bodmer 74, completed in 1071, the station for Saturday after Ash Wednesday – still aliturgical in the Hadrianum – was assigned *ad s. triphonem*. In Vat. lat. 5319, the corresponding rubric *Sabb. ad s. triphonem* was added in the margin. This station must surely refer to the first of the two churches, for the second was a small building, which still stood until it was converted into a house in the 1930s. The relics of the Roman martyr Eugenia, along with those of the perhaps historical St. Nympha, perhaps martyred at Porto (very close to Ostia), were deposited in this second building. Trypho and his legendary companion Respicius are commemorated together in F 14 – and in the introductory kalendar of B 79 on 10 November. Quite exceptionally, Trypho and Respicius plus Nympha are named in F 14 in the *Libera nos* that expands the *Pater noster*. Furthermore, the feast day of the martyr Eugenia (whose relics, it will be remembered, were deposited along with Nympha's in the smaller church *S. Salvatoris de Primicerio*) is here uniquely assigned to 20 December. (Although Eugenia had a long-lasting and widespread cult, she was unfortunately martyred on 25 December and therefore came to be commemorated on different days in different places. See Jounel's fascinating account, *Le Culte*, 327.) She was translated from her cemetery-basilica on the Via Latina to the basilica of SS. Philip and James (later Santi Apostoli) before her relics were moved to the church in the present Piazza Fiammetta. The first-named basilica of St. Trypho was eventually acquired by Augustinian hermits, who brought to it a relic of St. Monica – Augustine's mother, who died in Ostia; and in 1495 the immense new church

of S. Agostino and the associated buildings of which the Bibliotheca Angelica was a part came to overshadow the older adjacent basilica of St. Trypho, which lost St. Monica's relics to its giant neighbor and some of its privileges to the tiny church *S. Salvatoris* in the nearby Piazza Fiammetta – to which the Confraternity of the Blessed Sacrament, under the patronage of S. Trifone and S. Camillo, had moved. (It was about this time that the smaller church began to be called 'San Trifone in Piazza Fiammetta'.) Their sites were only three short blocks apart, just north of the present Via dei Coronari and its eastward extension, the Via di San Agostino. I hazard the guess that our sacramentary, San Pietro F 14, was prepared for the smaller church (*S. Salvatoris*) at the time of its consecration in 1113 by Cardinal Leo himself. But the case for the slightly older basilica *S. Triphonis* can also be made. (See Hülsen, *Le chiese di Roma*, 450–51, 491–5, and Armellini, *Le chiese*, ii, 1432, referring to i, 426.)

33 Supino Martini, *Roma e l'area grafica*, 335. To Supino Martini's objections to a Roman origin for Rome, Bibl. Vallicelliana C 62, I can add another. In C 62, the feast of SS. Cosmas and Damian, in Rome always celebrated on 27 September, is assigned the October date current in Spain – presumably the 22nd, from its position in the manuscript – which date is never found in Roman manuscripts.

34 The sixty-five *chiese filiali, soggette a S. Lorenzo in Damaso*, which are listed in Urban III's bull of 14 February 1186 quoted by Hülsen, exceed greatly in number those placed under any other basilica. (Parishioners of the *chiese filiali* had to have their children baptized at the mother church, for example.) These sixty-five churches include S. Salvatoris de Primicerio (the church in Piazza Fiammetta, consecrated by Cardinal Leo in 1113) but not the basilica S. Triphonis, rebuilt in 1106. Many of the churches named in the 1186 bull may have come under the influence of St. Lawrence *in Damaso* much earlier. That the Damasian sacramentary and its kalendar should have served as a model for churches in this region of Rome is therefore not surprising (see Hülsen, *Le chiese di Roma*, pp. lxxix and 132–3).

35 Jounel, *Le Culte des saintes*, 416–24, reprints J. M. Tommasi's accurate but orthographically sanitized edition in *Responsoria et Antiphonalia Romanae Ecclesiae* of 1686, which in turn was reproduced in A. F. Vezzosi's edition of Tommasi's *Opera omnia* (1728–54), iv, 1–169.

36 The count depends on how a martyr's 'companions' (often legendary) are regarded. In one manuscript, a companion may receive a Mass or Office of his own but elsewhere might be commemorated together with the historical martyr or with another 'companion'. And how should vigils and octaves of feasts be counted, as separate feasts, or not?

37 The omission from E 15 of the foundress of the *titulus Praxedis*, tranformed into the venerated martyr St. Praxedes, must be an oversight. The presence of her feast in F 11 when it is absent in E 15 is therefore not significant for our purposes.

38 The commemoration of Callistus II's consecration of a new high altar at St. Peter's Basilica on 25 March 1123, in the presence of three hundred bishops at the first Lateran Council, actually took precedence at St. Peter's over the feast of the Annunciation. Only the third nocturn at the Night Office was of the Annunciation; the rest of the hours and the chief Mass instead commemorate the consecration of the altar (see Jounel, *Le Culte*, 230, and above). But the Damasian sacramentary is certainly earlier than the 1123 altar consecration at St. Peter's. Supino Martini places this sacramentary in the first half of the eleventh century (*Roma e l'area grafica*, 120–21 and n. 30 above). And if the rituale-collectar F 11, having the Annunciation rubrics in capital letters, was written after 1123

(Supino Martini, 32, thinks it is from about the middle of the twelfth century: 'della metà circa del xii [secolo]'), then its capital letters could instead (or also) be interpreted as a criticism of the usage of St. Peter's Basilica.

39 The feast of Abbacyr – 'Father Cyr' – and John is also present in F 14, the 'St. Trypho' sacramentary, and in the kalendar and antiphoner of San Pietro B 79 (fol. 61^r^), but not in San Pietro F 22. The feast is entered in a now fragmentary Office lectionary attributed to the monastery of St. Andrew and Gregory *ad cliuum Scauri*, Vat. lat. 1189, which Jounel dates as '10th–11th c.' There the names of SS. Cyrus and John are entered, again in capital letters, also on 31 January. The manuscript breaks off after the feast of St. Gregory on 12 March, the rubrics of which are decorated with even greater solemnity. Supino Martini, *Roma e l'area grafica*, 100–102, dates the manuscript to 'X o XI secolo' but with reservations as to its place of origin.

Jounel, *Le Culte*, 220, pursues his description of the Alexandrian saints: 'Pour détruire à Ménouthi le culte d'*Isis medica*, Cyrille d'Alexandrie y fit transporter les reliques des deux saints. La renomée de leur basilique, qui attira les foules jusq'à l'invasion arabe, fut telle que le lieu prit le nom d'Aboukir (Abba Cyr). A une date qu'on ne peut déterminer (6e ou 7e siècle), la colonie alexandrine de Rome édifia une petite basilique en leur honneur via Portuense, sur la rive droite du Tibre, non loin de Saint-Paul, à peu près de la basilique de saint Ménas, un autre alexandrin . . . Puis le culte des deux thaumaturges pénétra au Transtévère et dans la cité. Saint Cyr fut adopté par les Romains, qui en firent saint Abbacyr, et même sainte Passera. Au 12e siècle, quatre églises étaient placées sous son patronage *intra muros*, mais dès le 8e siècle il figurait à Sainte-Marie-Antique sous les traits d'un majestueux viellard.' See Hülsen, *Le chiese di Roma*, 154–63 and 246–57, and Armellini, *Le chiese*, ii, 1226–7 (Cecchelli's 'Aggiunti').

40 A church dedicated to both St. Mary and the Alexandrine martyrs would admirably satisfy the two rubrics in capital letters in F 11, but no such Roman church is known to have existed.

41 The latter part of an Office for the Transfiguration occupies most of the recto of the last folio (179) of San Pietro B 79. Some of the text – in a different hand than the rest of the manuscript – is illegible in the facsimile. The fragment ends with antiphons rubricked *Ad laudes et Vesperas*, concluding with the antiphon *Ad Benedictus Celi aperti sunt super eum et uox patris intonuit Hic est filius meus dilectus in quo* [*michi?*] *bene complacui*. The feast of the Transfiguration of Christ is absent in the introductory kalendar and in the body of the B 79 antiphoner.

42 Jean Deshusses, *Le Sacramentaire grégorien, ses principales formes d'après les plus anciens manuscrits* (2nd edn, 3 vols., Fribourg: Editions Universitaires, 1971–88). The cited preface is in vol. i at no. 1535.

43 See Jounel, *Le Culte*, 242, and Richard Krautheimer et al., *Corpus Basilicarum Christianarum Romae*, v (Vatican City: Pontificio Istituto di Archeologia Cristiana, 1977), s.v. 'San Pietro'.

44 The latter part of the rubric must be read as if it were Romance. Jounel, *Le Culte* (63 n. 9) gives a correct Latin version from the thirteenth-century Lateran missal, Vatican, BAV, Archivio Lateranense Cod. 65: 'Quorum vigilia cum silentio et ieiunio est celebranda, et concessum est pro illo uno die annum dimittere in poenitentia.'

45 Hucke's term *Zersungenheit* (literally, the state of having been 'sung to pieces' or 'sung to death') is translated and glossed by Edward Nowacki in his article 'Chant Research at the Turn of the Century', *PMM* 7 (1998), 47–71, as follows:

'*Zersingen*, to change over the course of time through constant inaccurate singing, . . . may connote a range of viewpoints from descriptive neutrality to disapprobation, stopping short, however, of "corrupt". . . . I have translated *zersingen* as "(cause or allow) to deteriorate, lapse, or mutate", depending on the implied judgment' (p. 50).

46 The word *congregatio* often means a 'religious congregation' – that is, a monastic community. Sometimes the word is directly opposed to *populus* – the laity. But little in Riccardiana 300 supports a monastic destination for this votive missal, and a great deal of its contents seems to belie such a destination, including the prominence given to the wedding Mass.

47 Hereafter abbreviated 'Lent III.5', that is, feria V after the third Sunday of Lent.

48 The Mass is found in Bodmer 74, fols. 55^r–56^r (*Feria V, Ad S. Cosmam et Damianum*). See *Das Graduale von Santa Cecilia in Trastevere*, ed. Lütolf, i, 83. In San Pietro F 22, the Mass is on fols. 31^v–32^v, and in Vat. lat. 5319 on fols. 57^r–58^r (MMMA 2: 18, 154, 393, 441 and 642).

49 A similar exception occurs for the Thursday in the first full week of Lent (Lent I.5). The Introit *Confessio et pulchritudo* was taken over from the chief Mass of the Roman deacon and martyr St. Lawrence on 10 August, since the station assigned to Lent I.5 was *S. Laur. in formosum* (in Bodmer 74, *ad S. Laurentium in formoso*, later also called *S. Laurentii Panispernae*) on the Viminal hill – one of several Roman churches dedicated to St. Lawrence.

50 Deshusses, i, 151, nos. 244 and 246.

51 *The Greek-English Lexicon, Revised Supplement*, ed. P. G. W. Glare and A. A. Thompson (Oxford: Clarendon Press, 1996), 30, gives the definition for ἀνάργυρος, 'of a physician who practises without asking money', and quotes from the tenth-century *Suda, s.v. Χριστόδωρος Θηβαῖος: θαύματα τῶν ἁγίων ἀναργύρων Κοσμᾶ καὶ Δαμιανοῦ.*

52 *Corpus Orationum*, ed. Eugenio Moeller, Ioanne Maria Clément and Bertrand Coppieters t'Wallant (Turnhout: Brepols, 1994), 123, no. 3276. It also appears in San Pietro F 11, fol. 159^r, as the second of two collects for 27 September. (The first, beginning 'Omnipotens sempiterne Deus, qui ad immortales triumphos martires tuos cosmam et damianum . . . extulisti', is also proper to the feast.)

53 Deshusses, i, 279, no. 723. The collect is also used in the Hadrianum for Valentine; for Alexander, Eventius and Theodulus; for Pancratius; and for Mark and Marcellianus. In *Corpus Orationum*, vii, 120–4, the collect is no. 4520b – 'C'.

54 *Liber sacramentorum Romanae aeclesiae* (*Sacramentarium Gelasianum*), ed. Mohlberg et al., nos. 1029, 1030 and 1031. The set of prayers for Cosmas and Damian is not found in the so-called Leonine Sacramentary (an earlier collection of Mass prayers).

55 Deshusses, i, 151, no. 246; also *Corpus Orationum*, viii, 263, no. 5496.

56 The distichs are also recorded in early collections of epigraphs from the Christian basilicas and cemeteries of Rome. Jounel, *Le Culte*, 293, writes: 'Le pape Félix plaça en effet sous leur vocable [Cosmae et Damiani] un édifice antique qu'il voulait dédier au culte chrétien. La mosaïque absidiale du 6e siècle est conservée jusqu'à nos jours; elle exprime la confiance du Peuple romain: *Martyribus medicis populo spes certa salutis fecit.* Mais, avant même le pape Félix IV, Symmaque (498–514) avait érigé un oratoire en l'honneur des Anagyres sur l'Esquilin. Le culte des saints Côme et Damien est attesté au 7e siècle tant par les sacramentaires grégoriens . . . et gélasien . . . que par l'évangéliaire de 645.' In *The Oxford Dictionary of Popes*, 56, Kelly adds: 'With Queen Amalasuntha's permission [she was the Goth Theodoric's widow and the regent for her young son], Felix

converted several temples and public buildings in the Forum to Christian worship. The splendid mosaics in one of them, the church of SS. Cosma e Damiano, which features a portrait of Felix himself (the earliest surviving papal likeness), are due to him.' The portrait of Felix IV in its present state appears to be a restoration made around 1500. See Giovanni Battista de Rossi, *Mosaici cristiani: saggi dei pavimenti delle chiese di Roma anteriori al secolo XV*. (Rome: [n.pub.], 1899), pl. XV and text; *DACL*, s.v. 'Côme et Damien', iii, cols. 2350–67, fig. 3186; vii, col. 2417, fig. 6205; s.v. 'Mosaique', xii, cols. 290–91, fig. 8539. Also see Krautheimer, *Corpus Basilicarum*, i, s.v. 'SS. Cosme et Damiani', 137–43.

57 The earliest known and most famous use of the term *salus populi* is Cicero's 'ollis [scil. consulibus] salus populi suprema lex esto' (*De legibus* 3. 3. 8). Two or three centuries later, the phrase was incised on a block used as a cornerstone for what was presumed to be the original *tropaion* or cemetery shrine of St. Paul, buried under the medieval high altar and confession of San Paolo fuori le mura but temporarily excavated and brought to light in 1838 (after the disastrous fire of 1823) before the basilica was rebuilt. Krautheimer, *Corpus Basilicarum*, v (1977), 112–16, writes: 'The shrine [of St. Paul] . . . was located in the midst of a large necropolis extending along the [Via] Ostiense and its *diverticulum* was in constant use at least from the 2nd through the 4th century. . . . The mausoleum, at the time of its construction venerated as the shrine of St. Paul, rose below the High Altar. . . . It was uncovered early in 1838 and sketched . . . by Vespignani. (See Palazzo Venezia, Racc. Lanciani, Sketchbook, f. 11.) Given its later history, its site and appearance, the monument can hardly be anything but the *tropaion* . . . the shrine of St. Paul.'

Constantine built a small basilica that seems to have incorporated the shrine. The Emperor Valentinian II (375–92) paid for the enormous building which endured (with medieval alterations) until the fire of 1823. It was consecrated by Pope Siricius (375–92, Damasus' successor) in 390, but construction was not actually completed until 402–3. Prudentius described the building in glowing terms in the *Peristephanon*, xii, vs. 49. Thus it is uncertain whether the corner block of the shrine bearing the SALVS POPVLI inscription belonged to the shrine and was incised to refer to St. Paul and his works, or whether it came from some other and presumably pagan source in the necropolis and was incorporated in the shrine. Whatever its origin, the inscription served to keep the term alive in a Christian context during the third and fourth centuries. Other than that, there can hardly be a question of influence on our Introit text.

The use of the *Salus populi Romani* as a title for the antique icon of the Virgin at S. Maria Maggiore might appear to be a parallel instance but in fact dates only from 1870: 'Der Titel [*Salus Populi Romani*] lässt sich aufgrund von Archivalien aus dem Archivio Capitolare di Santa Maria Maggiore einem archäologisch versierten Canonicus zuschreiben (der später Kardinal geworden ist) und hat zunächst die Funktion, die liberalen Staatswohlkonzeptionen etwa der Anhänger Cavours (deren Wahlspruch das . . . Cicero-Zitat ist) zu konterkarieren. Später wird er allgemein verbreitet, in den zwanziger Jahren auch einmal von einem Papst verwendet, aber erst 1960 von Johannes XXIII. offiziell anerkannt.' I owe this quotation – from Gerhard Wolf, *Salus Populi Romani: Die Geschichte römischer Kultbilder im Mittelalter* (Weinheim: VCH, Acta humaniora, 1990), 354 n. 83, and also pp. xi and 19 – to the kindness of Professor Julian Gardner.

58 The following parallels have been suggested: Jer. 3: 23, 'In Domino Deo nostro salus Israel'; Ps. 38: 39, 'Salus autem iustorum a Domino est et protector eorum est in tempore tribulationis'; and Ps. 28: 11, 'Dominus uirtutem populo suo dabit et benedicet populum suum in pace.' IPs. 34: 36, 'Salus tua ego sum.'

59 Deshusses, i, nos. 247 and 854. Also see *Corpus Orationum*, viii, 279, no. 552.

60 Attempts to date the six Introits assigned to the seventeenth Sunday after Pentecost through the twenty-second Sunday, whether singly or as a group, have mostly been inconclusive. One of the Introits is psalmic, one is the non-scriptural *Salus populi*, and the other four were drawn from or edited from Scripture other than the Psalms. The non-psalmic *Omnia que fecisti* for the nineteenth Sunday after Pentecost was also borrowed for a Thursday in Lent (Lent V.5), with the station *ad s. Apollinarem*.

61 The opening prayer of the *Missa pro congregatione – Maiestatem tuam domine clementissime pater* – and the secret *Preces nostras clementissime deus clementer exaudi* are found in widely scattered votive supplements to the Gregorian sacramentary drawn mostly from Gallican sources. Deshusses, ii: *Textes complémentaires*, prints them at nos. 3093 and 3094 in versions very close to those of Riccardiana 300 under the title *Missa pro uiuorum et mortuorum*. His sources are the Bobbio Missal and the Rheinau Sacramentary. The text for the opening prayer, with variant wordings, appears in *Corpus Orationum*, x, 125, at no. 3280, with a longer list of sources, some of which are from the eighth or ninth century and include the late tenth-century Canosa Missal, Baltimore, Walters Art Gall. W. 6, and Benevento, Bib. Cap. 33. I do not know how the text of these prayers – which can hardly be described as collects – reached Rome.

62 Melnicki made a rare mistake in her transcription of this Introit in MMMA 2. A carelessly drawn, slanting red line for *F* in the manuscript causes the notes for the word *sum* to read one step too high – *FG* – instead of *EF* according to the diastematy, as in all other versions. The double *custodes* following the word *sum* reflect singers' uncertainty between the diastematy (correct) and the slanted red line (incorrect). Melnicki transcribed according to the slanting line. (She also converted the manuscript reading *P̄s Adtendite popl̄s* into the vocative *poplē*. The Roman psalter has *populus*, as do all the other chant versions of this piece. And she regularized the differentia – see below.

63 The only phrase similar to the start of *Salus populi* I have found in the deuterus Introit repertory of Vat. lat. 5319 is an introduction for an interior phrase (to the words *quia mirabilia*) in the Introit *Cantate domino canticum nouum* for the fifth Sunday after Easter (fol. 99ᵛ). The piece is in deuterus plagalis but transposed, with a final of *b*. Transposition apart, the pitch of the phrase differs: *c ca c de e d cd*. (The transposed pitch corresponding to the phrase *Salus populi* would be *d db d ef♯ f♯ e de*.) In *Cantate domino* the phrase really consists of the standard initial phrase *F G–a a* (untransposed) – a common introductory beginning in deuterus plagalis – prefaced by two introductory neumes for the weak conjunction *quia*. The notes for *quia mirabilia* are not comparable with the initial figure of *Salus populi*, which remains unique.

64 That is, according to the original clear diastematy of Vat. lat. 5319, before the carelessly slanting red *F*-line was drawn.

65 As mentioned above, in Vat. lat. 5319 the two Sundays are rubricked *Dominica III post S. angeli* and *Dominica IIII post S. angeli*, respectively.

66 The Gregorian version of this Gradual is especially interesting. The Frankish notations use the actual pitch level seen in the beginning of the Bodmer 74 version but transfer the whole piece to G mode. Many phrases are retained intact from the Roman model.

67 In Vat. lat. 5319, *B♭*s are notated in the following F-mode Graduals: *Discerne*, in the verse *Emitte lucem tuam*, MMMA 2: 125; *Iustorum anime*, MMMA 2: 127; *Propitius esto*, MMMA 2: 129; *Qui operatus est Petro*, MMMA 2: 137; and *Ex Sion*, in the verse *Congregate*, MMMA 2: 148.

68 See Joseph Dyer's definitive study, '*Tropis semper variantibus*: Compositional Strategies in the Offertories of Old Roman Chant', *EMH* 17 (1998), 1–60, esp. 59–60 (app. 3), where he places *Si ambulauero* among the Roman Offertories having 'large-scale repetition and return structures', but not among those employing 'Formula A' or 'Formula B'. Also see Dyer, 'Offertorium', *MGG*[2], Sachteil, vii, cols. 532–88. (The verses *In quacumque die* and *Adorabo ad templum sanctum tuum* are absent in San Pietro F 22 and of course in the votive missal Riccardiana 300, although I included them in my own comparative tables.)

69 See n. 60 above. The texts for the Offertories of the first sixteen Sundays after Pentecost are arranged for the most part in the rising but not consecutive order of their psalm numbers, like the Introits and Communions for those Sundays. Only the non-psalmic *Precatus est Moyses* for the eleventh Sunday after Pentecost – borrowed for Lent II.5 (Exod. 32: 11a, 12b, 13, 14; verse 1 being an amalgam and verse 2 deriving from Exod. 34: [9], 8) – and *Oraui deum* for the sixteenth Sunday after Pentecost (Dan. 9: 4, 17a, 17b, 19) interrupt the psalmic series of the first sixteen Offertories. But *Si ambulauero*, though drawn from a psalm, belongs to a miscellaneous group of three non-psalmic and three psalmic texts (the psalms that supply the texts occurring in reverse numerical order) that furnished Offertories for the last six Sundays of the post-Pentecost season. Some of these are virtuoso pieces, involving extensive text repetition – although not *Si ambulauero*. Almost certainly the pieces in such a pool, though perhaps not yet assigned to specific Sundays, would be earlier than Gregory II's institution of stational Masses on Thursdays in Lent. See Dyer's references in '*Tropis semper variantibus*' and Kenneth Levy, 'Toledo, Rome, and the Legacy of Gaul', *EMH* 4 (1984), 49–99, esp. 55–67 and 87–92.

70 See Joseph M. Murphy, 'The Communions of the Old Roman Chant' (Ph.D. diss., University of Pennsylvania, 1977), ii, 1018–23.

71 The tentative attribution of Vat. lat. 5319 to the Lateran in MMMA 2 and elsewhere, often treated as an established fact, needs to be regarded with reserve. We really do not know to which Roman basilica Vat. lat. 5319 should be assigned. The tendency on the part of musicologists to accept the Lateran assignment led Supino Martini to suggest a Lateran provenance for Riccardiana 300 as well. Unfortunately we do not know, even tentatively, where in Rome or its environs Riccardiana 300 originated nor how it reached the Biblioteca Riccardiana – except perhaps for the hint left in the added notation of the celebrant's *Sursum corda* chant (see nn. 14 and 15 above).

72 So entitled in Riccardiana 299 (fol. 182[r]), San Pietro F 11 (fol. 81[r]) and Vat. lat. 5319 (fol. 182[r]). In Riccardiana 300 (fol. 9[v]), the title reads *Missa ad sponsas benedicendas*.

73 Deshusses, i, 308–11, nos. 200, 833–9.

74 *AMS* (1935).

75 See 'The Roman *Missa Sponsalicia PMM* 11 (2002), 127–66, and its sequel, 'The Wedding Introit *Deus Israel* and the Roman Deuterus Introits', in a later issue of the same journal (where the above Exs. 12: 13–17 have been corrected).

76 The transcription of the Communion *Ecce sic benedicetur* in Ex. 12.17 assumes that the red line in 300 has its normal meaning, *F*, and that the yellow line a fourth below it (from *et uideas* to the end) means *C* – the most likely interpretation. But the red line might mean *f* and the yellow line *c*. Moreover, the custos after *dominum* and before *et uideas* is clearly placed one step higher than the opening red line and is clearly incompatible with it. So if the opening red line should in fact be a mistake for an opening *c* line (as found in 299 and 5319), the

custos would then force the following red line to be read as indicating top *f* and the bottom yellow line *c*, so that the repetition of the opening melody (beginning at *uideas*) would be sung a fourth higher than at the beginning – again as in 299 and 5319. See the discussion of variant pitch levels in the notation of this melody in my article 'The Roman *Missa sponsalicia*'.

Chapter 13
Reading the Melodies of the Old Roman Mass Proper: A Hypothesis Defended

Edward Nowacki

Before beginning with the main topic of my article, I would like to address the issue of insider and outsider research perspectives, what anthropologists have termed the etic/emic dichotomy. My research perspective is etic, that of an outsider, and I make no apology for it. The questions I ask are essentially similar to those posed by James McKinnon in the last chapter of *The Advent Project*.[1] Which of the two branches of Gregorian chant more closely resembles the eighth-century Roman prototype? Which exhibits structures influenced by contact with the Byzantine modal system, and which exhibits native structures that precede or follow that contact? Are the pre- and post-Byzantine structures signs of an alternative native modal system that was never formally described? Are the qualities of the Gregorian style – what McKinnon calls a timeless miracle – ones that were added by the Franks or that were lost by the Romans? These are questions that medieval thinkers never dreamed of. If we are to answer them, we have no choice but to adopt outsider research strategies.

Nevertheless, as a humanist, I am not satisfied with formal proofs. I would like the satisfaction that comes from harmonizing my discourse with that of medieval thinkers. Harold Powers has observed that the empirical investigation of medieval music, undertaken to discover the distinguishing features of the modes, often has little to do with anything medieval theorists would have recognized as modal. What they called modal analysis, in Powers's view, had more to do with the formation of the background scale, emphasizing the finals and the notes surrounding them in a distinctive intervallic environment.[2] I am prepared to concede Powers's point and to call what I do structural analysis rather than modal analysis. I doubt, however, that a genuinely medieval outlook requires this distinction.[3] Various medieval writers propose methods of modal analysis that emphasize melodic design and derive the terms of the analysis from empirical observation. *Alia musica*'s measurement of the Phrygian octave by the ratios 24, 18, 15 and 12, representing the notes *E*, *a*, *c* and *e*, is a stunning example of such empiricism. In truth, medieval writers are often not fastidious in separating the investigation of mode from the analysis of melodic design, considering both to be aspects of the same discourse. I willingly, and out of necessity, follow this less fastidious approach, but I also acknowledge that what I do may aptly be called *structural* analysis. Whether the structures are modal is not an assumption but something to be proved.

There is one issue of analytical procedure that may be disposed of immediately. The tetrachord enjoys no privilege as a unit of melodic analysis. The ancient Greeks considered the tetrachord a small system, or scale, and a constituent of the complete, or perfect, system spanning two octaves. Theorists in the Middle Ages continued to limit the use of the term tetrachord to discourse about systems. It is chiefly relevant in discussions of the synemmenon and diezeugmenon tetrachords, whose alternation entails a change of system. In discussions of melodic structure, especially the cursus of individual melodic phrases, the term used for the interval of the fourth is diatessaron, an interval that may span any four notes comprising two tones and a semitone in any order. The term tetrachord, on the other hand, refers to the particular fourths used to build the basic scale and to no others.

It is true that medieval theorists increasingly limited the terms of melodic analysis to the intervals of the fourth and fifth. This is evident, for example, in the theories of Hermannus Contractus (eleventh century). Such theories reflect the empirical facts of the post-Gregorian, post-millennial repertory, in which the fourth and fifth are vividly and unmistakably the controlling intervals of melodic design. However, when the subject of analysis is pre-millennial chant, it should come as no surprise that Hermannus' vocabulary of analytic units turns out to be too rigid. My decision to bypass the tetrachord as a predominant unit of analysis is based on my reading of the theoretical tradition, which reserves this concept for a different domain – the structure of scales rather than the cursus of melodies – and my observation that the interval of the fourth, however named, plays a minor role in the melodic design of the repertory that I am analyzing.

Before proceeding, I need to review briefly some key points that I made in an earlier study on mode in Old Roman chant.[4] The first is that the melodic language of the Old Roman Mass Proper can be understood in terms of a structure of conjunct and overlapping thirds, or trichords. Second, the ecclesiastical modes distinguish themselves by the particular selection of trichords that they habitually emphasize, usually two or three. These are shown in Ex. 13.1. Third, in selecting certain trichords for emphasis, the modes overlap one another to a remarkable degree, often sharing one or two of their structural trichords with other modes. Finally, because these structures are embodied in distinctive stereotyped figures, or clichés, there is a remarkably high level of figural affinity from one mode to the next. Roman singers had to work hard at distinguishing among the modes, since so much of their physiognomy is shared – distinctive, but not distinguishing.

In the discussion following the paper I gave on 'The Modes of the Old Roman Mass Proper', the reservations most troubling to me, and ultimately most helpful, were those of László Dobszay. Drawing on his rich experience of rehearsing and performing the Old Roman Mass Propers, he doubted that similar figures placed at different points on the background scale could be taken as evidence of underlying intervallic identity. Given the quasi-

Ex. 13.1 The principal trichords sorted by mode

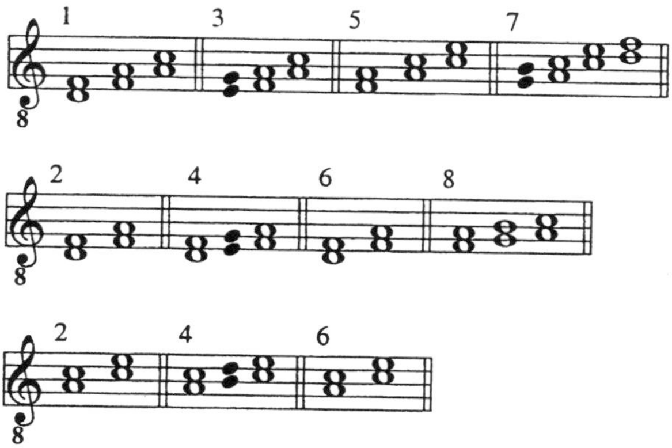

minimalist style of the Old Roman ductus, it seemed to him that these figures could occur in several intervallic environments in what appears as a kind of thoughtless profusion. I have concluded that this was not the case, at least not for the less prolix genres of the Introit and Communion. Here most of the distinctive figures are tied to single intervallic environments in ways that leave little room for controversy. Some are shown in Ex. 13.2. All the figures in the example except the last (13.2c) entail distinctive intervallic structures. They may be transposed – and often are – but only to positions on the scale whose intervallic structure is the same.

Examples 13.2b and 2c require special comment. 13.2c appears so often in undeniable *re–fa* and *ut–mi* environments[5] that I must conclude its presence not to be decisive as a token of underlying structure. This is truly a case of the minimalist style, where certain figural habits are exercised without regard to the intervallic context. The figure in Ex. 13.2b, I have argued, embodies interlocking *re–fa* and *ut–mi* trichords and should be solmized as *re–fa–mi–re–ut* wherever it occurs and especially when it ends on *F*, where the topmost note, *b*, must be solmized as *b-fa*. Singers familiar with the Old Roman style may argue that in G-mode chants, melodic figures emphasizing the notes *b* and *F* must retain *b-mi* in order to maintain the structural integrity of the G-mode. Shifting back and forth between *b-fa* and *b-mi* in the seventh and eighth modes in response to melodic figures whose meaning and weight are purely transitory would seem unmusical, since it loses sight of the larger sweep of the phrase. I agree with this view. The problem, however, does not occur, as far as I can tell, in the seventh and eighth modes, but in the first and third, where trichordal structures on *F*, *G* and *a* intermingle with disconcerting frequency. The occurrence of the figure on *F* in these contexts compels us to decide whether to solmize it as *re–fa–mi–re–ut*, with *b-fa*, or *ut–mi–re–sol–fa*, with *b-mi*. I have argued that the figure itself is the decisive criterion, embodying the same underlying structure regardless of position on the scale.

Ex. 13.2 Transposable figural clichés

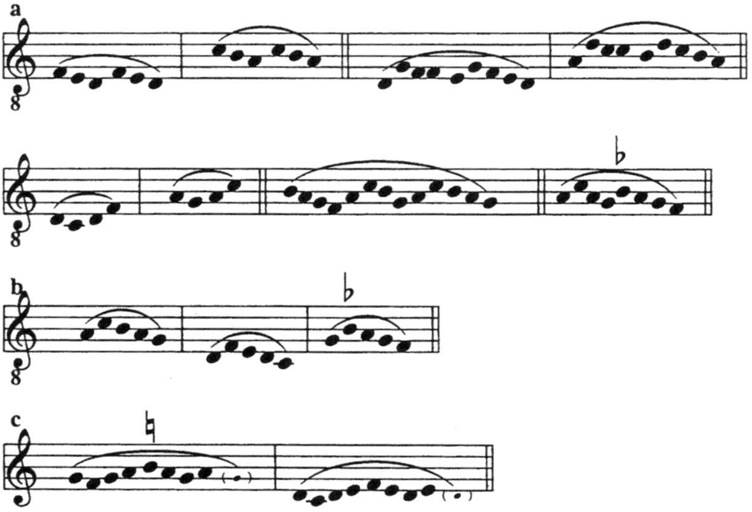

For those unpersuaded by this argument, I wish to add the following. The figure in question is ubiquitous in the fifth and sixth modes, where it occurs on *F* in concluding phrases preparatory to a full stop on that note (see the passages marked 'x' in Ex. 13.3). There is no doubt in these cases that the *b* must be sung *fa*. Having established its transposability in the fifth and sixth modes, should we nevertheless insist that when the figure occurs on *F* in the first and third modes, it might sometimes be sung with *b-mi*? In the light of the deep trichordal affinity of the first and third modes with modes 5 and 6, particularly in their projection of the *F–a* trichord, I believe that we are compelled to read this figure with the same intervallic structure in all its modes and transpositions.

McKinnon, in the Epilogue of *The Advent Project,* has cited Brad Maiani on the difficulty of memorizing Old Roman chant, mentioning in particular its repetitious figuration.[6] Surely anything that would promote distinctiveness, such as the identification of certain figures with certain intervallic structures, would make this task more feasible. To this argument I would add the following. Those of us who have learned Old Roman chant as readers rather than as listeners find it hard to ignore the distinctive neumes that are habitually used by the copyists to record certain melodic figures. In the case cited above, the figure of five notes is always notated as a *pes* conjoined to three descending *puncti* – never, say, as a *torculus* conjoined to a *clivis*. Perhaps this notational consistency can be taken as a sign that the scribes regarded all melodic figures so notated as equivalent.

The problem of the figure in Ex. 13.2b and others like it is not yet solved, for in addition to the cases cited above, it also occurs in its familiar position

Ex. 13.3 Introit *Deus in loco sancto suo*, mode 5 (Vat. lat. 5319, fol. 124)

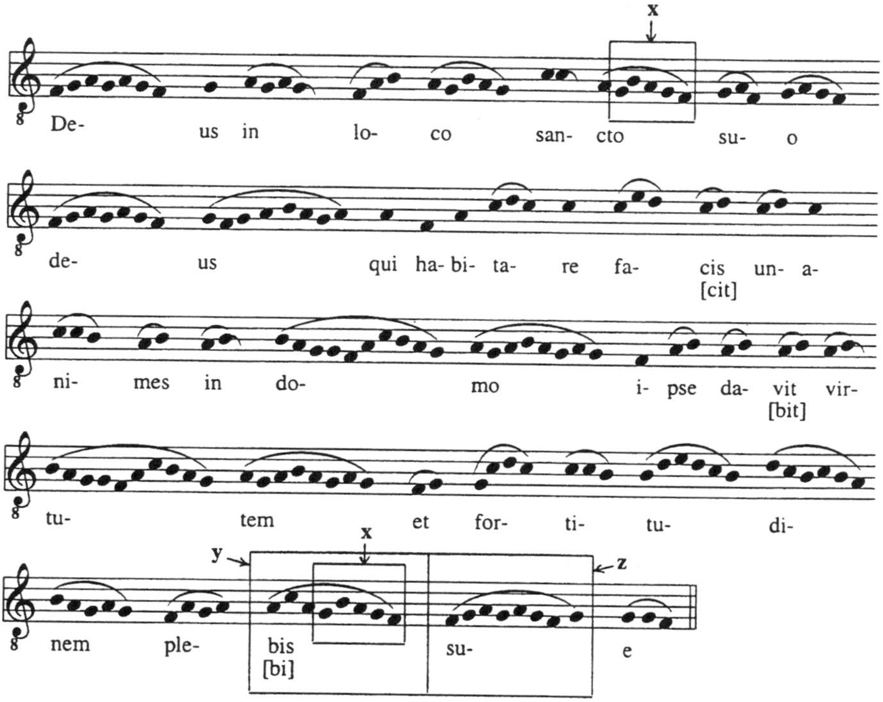

on *G* (*a–c–b–a–G*) in chants of the fifth mode, where we would expect *b-fa* to be in force throughout. If that were the case, the figure would have to be solmized *mi–sol–fa–mi–re*, with an intervallic structure entirely different from the usual one. I reject this hypothesis for all the reasons cited above and for one additional, more powerful reason. The theory of structure that I have proposed presents the modes as labile, establishing their sure footing only at key points in the structure, and often only at the very end. In the interior they project trichordal structures that are equally apt in several modes. This has long been recognized in the E-modes, which project a distinct Dorian physiognomy, emphasizing the *D–F* and *F–a* thirds throughout, settling on *E* only at the end. My trichordal analyses show that this labile quality pervades the whole musical language. In the first mode, for example, long interior passages embody the *F–a*, *G–b* and *a–c* trichords with a melodic ductus identical to that of the F- and G-modes. Such chants assert their D-mode identity only intermittently by returning to the *D–F* trichord and eventually terminating on *D*. When I read the figure *a–c–b–a–G* in the fifth mode as *re–fa–mi–re–ut*, suggesting a temporary Mixolydian emphasis, I am merely being consistent, recognizing that chants in the F-modes are no less labile than the chants of other modes.

Analysis of such chants in terms of their trichordal content provides the formal and consistent terms with which to understand this labile quality. As the melodies move into the *a–c* trichord, they adopt that trichord's normal intervallic structure *re–fa*. When they pause on *G*, they imply either the lower neighbor-tone to the *a–c* trichord, or an overlapping *G–b* trichord. Only when the melody firmly enters the *F–a* trichord does it obtain access to *b-fa* as the upper neighbor to *a*, the *fa* above *la*. This holds true without regard to the ultimate final of the particular chant, and hence the nominal determinant of its mode. The task of those who differ with me on this point is to present an alternative theory that maintains a tonality not of figures and phrases, but of whole chants, a tonality in which the final of each particular chant establishes that chant's whole system, or scale, and enforces that system throughout. Such a theory would also have to disregard the numerous figural affinities that I have proposed. I see the impediments to such a theory as overwhelming.

Specimen Readings

Now consider Ex. 13.4, *Suscepimus deus*. This is an Introit of the first mode. The first phrase immediately presents the problem of whether to read the *a* as the lower note of the *a–c* trichord or as the upper note of the *F–a* trichord. If the first reading is chosen, the *b*s will be read natural, if the second, they will be read flat. Here the repeated upward motions to *c* favor the first reading. The figure on *-us* of *deus* is not decisive, because this turning figure is not intervallically distinctive, but the figure on the first syllable of *deus* is. It can be read as *re–mi–fa–mi–re–ut* in all of its transpositions, and in some of them in only that way. On *miseri-* the melody dips into the *F–a* trichord briefly before returning to the *a–c* trichord on *-cordiam tuam in medio tem-*. Embedded within this phrase are subordinate allusions to the *G–b* trichord, solmized as *ut–mi*. Such allusions are typical of phrases sung in the *re–fa* trichord on *a*. The figure on *-pli* compels the melody into the *F–a* trichord, solmized *fa–la* with the necessary *b-fa* as its upper neighbor. To retain the reading of *b-mi* would force us into an inconsistency, since the figure is a typical one in F-mode chants, where the use of *b-fa* seems beyond question (see the passage marked 'y' in Ex. 13.3). I then read the remainder of the phrase on *tui* with *b-fa*s. The phrase *secundum nomen tuum deus* returns to the *a–c* trichord, forcing a return to *b-mi*, but only temporarily, for at *et laus tua* the melody returns to the *F–a* trichord with upper neighbor *b-fa*. If one takes the long view and resists changing back and forth between the two forms of *b* – an eminently musical response to the given context – one only postpones the inevitable, because the figures on *fines terre* are indisputable *fa–la* figures which entail *b-fa* necessarily (cf. the passages marked 'y' and 'z' in Ex. 13.3). The concluding phrase of the chant exhibits the typical arch, beginning in the *D–F* trichord, hovering for a while in the *F–a* trichord, and then returning to *D–F*, where it concludes on *D*, the final of the mode.

Next consider Ex. 13.5. This is another Introit of the first mode. The first phrase, *Inclina domine aurem tuam ad me*, travels in the *a–c* trichord, that

Ex. 13.4 Introit *Suscepimus deus*, mode 1 (Vat. lat. 5319, fol. 30v)

is, *re–fa*, with allusions to the *G–b*, or *ut–mi*, trichord in the interior of the phrase. Phrase 2, *exaudi me*, begins in the *fa–la* trichord on *F*, moving eventually to the *mi–sol* trichord on *E*. I read the pause on *F* and the whole figure on the last two syllables of *exaudi me* as a semi-cadence in the *E–G* trichord – that is, a cadence that fails to satisfy the tendency of the trichord to end on *E*, pausing instead on its middle note, *F*. Some might argue that this analysis is too clever by half. Why not read the passage simply as a full stop in the *F–a* trichord, where *E* functions as a lower neighbor? I have two reasons for not doing so. The turning figure *F–E–F* would be an extraordinary way of making a cadence on *F*. In chants of the F mode, terminal *F*s are normally approached from above, and we are well aware of the suspicion with which medieval theorists regarded the *subsemitonium modi*. The second, more compelling, reason for my proposed reading is that it is an instance of a familiar paradigm. Numerous instances of this cadence or ones nearly

Ex. 13.5 Introit *Inclina domine*, mode 1 (Vat. lat. 5319, fol. 125^v)

In-cli- na do- mi- ne au- rem tu- am ad
me et ex- au- di me sal- vum fac ser- vum
tu- um de- us me- us spe- ran- tem
in te mi- se- re- re mi- chi do- mi-
ne quo-ni-am ad te cla- ma- vi to- ta di- e

identical to it occur in the first, third and seventh modes, and nearly all of them are followed by a balancing or follow-up phrase that concludes on *E*, the note it was prevented from reaching in the earlier phrase (see Ex. 13.6). The pairing of two phrases of similar design, each aiming at the same goal, where the first is interrupted and only the second reaches the desired tone of completion, is such a cogent and familiar syntactical maneuver that I see no reason not to recognize it in this particular instance.

Now refer once again to Ex. 13.3. This is an example of a fifth-mode Introit. I read the entire first phrase of this chant, *Deus in loco sancto suo*, in the *F–a* trichord with *b-fa*s. Note especially the figure on the second syllable of *sancto*, which clearly marks the note *b* as *fa* and the *F–a* third as a *fa–la* trichord. I am not troubled by the *c* and liquescent *b* on *sancto*, which pass quickly. The second phrase, *deus qui habitare facit unanimes in domo*, quickly rises to the *a–c* trichord, which compels *b-mi*, since the normal solmization of *a–c* is *re–fa*. The figure on *domo* presents a problem. It may begin on *b-fa*, but must change eventually to *b-mi*. The reason for doing so is that the whole figure on the first syllable of *domo* is a familiar cliché for making or preparing internal cadences on *G*. (See Ex. 13.7, an eighth-mode Communion, where this figure occurs repeatedly.) It strains credulity to claim that this sharply profiled figure should be sung with *b-mi* when it occurs in the G

Ex. 13.6 Introit *Hodie scietis*, mode 3 (Vat. lat. 5319, fol. 10)

Ex. 13.7 Communion *Hoc corpus quod pro vobis*, mode 8 (Vat. lat. 5319, fol. 67[v])

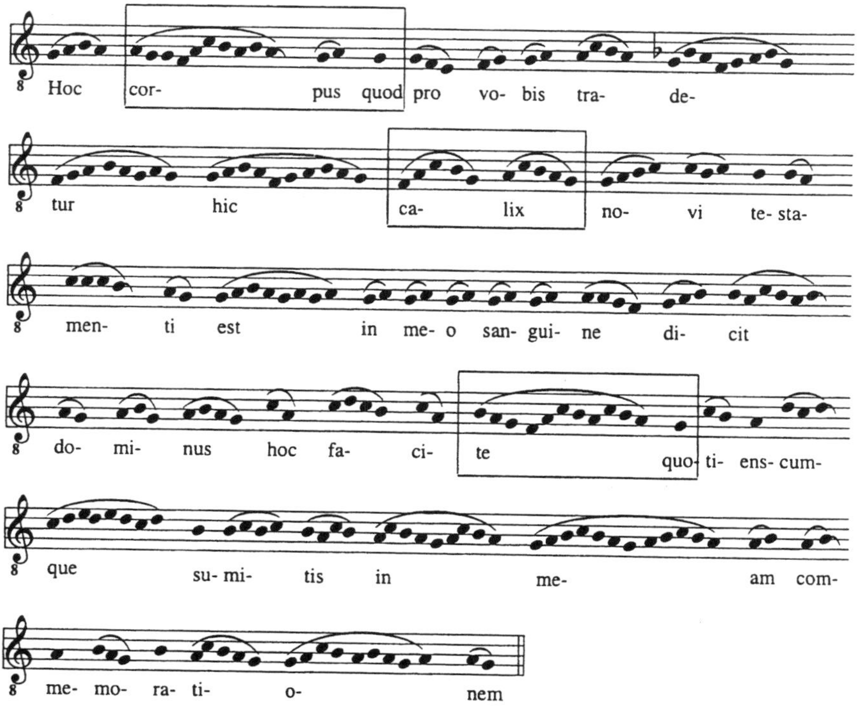

modes, but with *b-fa* when the mode is F. The melody continues on *ipse dabit virtutem* in the *F–a* trichord, clearly implying *b-fa*, yet returns on *-tutem* to the cliché for internal cadences on *G*. Again, I read the first *b* as *fa* and the subsequent ones as *mi*. The penultimate semi-phrase, *et fortitudinem*, because of its clear focus on *c*, implies *b-mi*. Only on *plebi sue* does the melody enter unequivocally into the *F–a* trichord with its attendant *b-fa*.

Conclusion

By adhering to the empirical evidence, I hope to have generated readings of the Old Roman Mass Proper that are analogs of the readings accepted by those who sang them in the Middle Ages. In addition to proposing abstract units of tonal syntax, the trichords, I have also proposed principles governing their organization. These principles include a notion of hierarchy, where some units of syntax are more prominent or determining than others. Connected to hierarchy is the notion of embedding, where some units of syntax can be embedded – or nested – in others, providing temporary contrast, but not disturbing the larger structure. Finally, I have proposed a notion of interruption or incompletion, where a clearly defined syntactical unit is not rounded off or concluded in the expected way. An example is the case where the *E–G* trichord is not permitted to conclude on *E*, but instead breaks off on *F*, creating an imbalance that must be redressed by a later phrase that concludes properly on the tone of completion. Whether a stop on *F* is a full stop in the *F–a* trichord, or a half-stop in the *E–G* trichord is, of course, not a matter of dogma, but of interpretation. The reader must consider the *F* in its context. Sometimes the context will be clear, sometimes ambiguous. That is as it should be in any complex musical system. The theories constructed to explain such systems need to provide alternative analyses for all such contingencies. Choosing which explanation fits a particular case will always depend on the idiosyncratic features of that case. And when the theory cannot help one decide between two intelligent readings, say, a full stop in *F–a* and a half stop in *E–G*, that may be more a reflection of the subtlety of the music than a failure of the theory. It seems to me that all the topics that I have just enumerated – hierarchy, embedding, interruption and provision for alternative interpretations – should be viewed as positives. They are not defects but the minimal flexibility any theory must have in order to deal with a complex musical system.

What I have tried to defend in this paper is a theory for reading the melodies of the Old Roman Mass Proper based on a structure of conjunct and interlocking trichords. I have also tried to show that this structure pervades the whole genus before it is differentiated into modal species. I have claimed, in other words, that the trichords are pre-modal in a conceptual sense – i.e., more general and more persistent within the tradition than the prescriptive structures of formal modal theory. It remains a matter of speculation whether this pre-modal nature can be understood in chronological terms. Roman chant on the eve of its Frankish reception must have possessed, fortuitously, a basic compatibility with Byzantine modal principles in order then to have assimilated them so thoroughly, at least in Frankish transmission. Did the Romans resist these principles, adopting them only as a superficial veneer while the Franks allowed them to fully determine the shape of their redaction? Or did trichordal organization in Rome infiltrate the tradition after it had been organized along doctrinaire modal lines, crowding out older modal distinctions and reducing them to secondary status? I believe that we should not hesitate to ask such questions, however speculative they may seem. While no substitute for the cautious examination of data, the pondering of great questions may prompt the imagination to form bold hypotheses that cause previously intractable data to make sense as never before. James McKinnon's *Advent Project* provides a model for such catalytic thought. I hope that in attempting to follow its example, I have retained the balance of discipline and boldness that it so finely embodies.

Notes

1 James McKinnon, *The Advent Project* (Berkeley: University of California Press, 2000), Epilogue: The Central Question of Gregorian Chant.

2 Harold S. Powers, s.v. 'Mode', in *NG*.

3 I have addressed this issue in an unpublished paper, 'The Pretheoretical Modes of Gregorian Chant', presented at the annual conference of the American Musicological Society in New Orleans in 1987. See also the article referred to in n. 4.

4 Edward Nowacki, 'The Modes of the Old Roman Mass Proper: What Kind of Glue?', in *Papers Read at Cantus Planus, Visegrád, 1998* (Budapest: Hungarian Academy of Sciences, 2001), 431–48.

5 Throughout this article I make use of solmization syllables to indicate intervallic structures. The interval *re–fa*, for example, implies *re–mi–fa*, an aggregate spanning a minor third with a tone between the lower two elements and a semitone between the upper two. There is no intent to imply that the singers of this music actually solmized or that the solmization syllables first proposed by Guido (ca. 1025) were common currency at the time of the Old Roman manuscripts (the earliest dated 1071). By the same token, my reference to the '*fa* above *la*' is not an allusion to the sixteenth-century schoolboy's jingle, 'Una nota super la', but to the simple fact that the note above *la* usually entails a mutation of *fa–la* to *ut–mi*, that is, to the soft hexachord.

6 McKinnon, *The Advent Project*, 400–401.

Chapter 14
'Epulari autem et gaudere oportebat'

Ruth Steiner

In chapter 15 of his Gospel, Luke describes what happened when Jesus found himself under criticism from the scribes and Pharisees for spending time with sinners. What Jesus did was to tell three stories, each of them featuring a man or woman who had lost something. He began with a shepherd who lost one sheep out of a flock of a hundred, went searching for it in the wilderness, and, when it was found, called his friends to rejoice with him. Next came a woman who had lost a coin. She went to work cleaning her house, found the coin, told all her friends and neighbors, and shared her happiness with them. Finally came the story of a far greater loss, that of a man whose younger son had left home with the intention of never returning. As we know, the young man did return, and the father's joy was boundless. He ordered a banquet to be prepared, one that would include meat – which was unusual in this culture – and feature not roast young goat but an even more succulent dish, veal. Yet there was a sour note in the proceedings, for the older brother of the once lost son could not help protesting when he learned of the festivities, and spoke these words to his father: 'Behold, for so many years do I serve thee, and I have never transgressed thy commandment, and yet thou hast never given me a kid to make merry with my friends: But as soon as this thy son is come, who hath devoured his substance with harlots, thou hast killed for him the fatted calf.'[1] The father begins his reply with the reassurance 'Son, thou art always with me, and all I have is thine', and then goes on to explain the celebration by saying that it was the right thing to do: 'epulari autem et gaudere oportebat' – 'but it was fit that we should make merry and be glad, for this thy brother was dead and is come to life again; he was lost, and is found'.

According to a modern commentary on this parable, it 'presents the loving father as a symbol of God himself. His ready, unconditioned, and unstinted love and mercy are manifested not only toward the repentant sinner (the younger son) but toward the uncomprehending critic of such a human being.'[2]

In the translation of the father's reply quoted above, a pronoun has been supplied that was not present in the Latin – 'we'. It does not appear in the Vulgate. Four of the sources cited in the critical notes for the edition of the Vulgate by Wordsworth and White supply *nos* – 'epulari autem nos et gaudere', one has *te* – 'you' – in place of *nos*, and four put *te* later in the phrase: 'epulari autem et gaudere te'.[3] The addition of this word – 'you' – seems a small change, but it transforms the thrust of the phrase, changing it from a general observation to a rebuke addressed to an individual: 'but *you* should have rejoiced and been glad'.[4]

The present study concerns both an antiphon and a Communion that are settings of a text based on this verse, one that begins 'Oportet te fili gaudere'. Evidently the initial phrase has been reworked: *epulari* has been dropped, the verb is in the present tense and not only the pronoun *te* but also a vocative, *fili*, directs the father's rebuke pointedly to the older brother: 'oportet te fili gaudere' – 'Son, you ought to rejoice.'

The chant *Oportet te* is one of those five Communions assigned to weekdays in Lent that have texts based on the Gospel of the day, and which appear to have been introduced in place of chants based on texts from the Psalms.[5] The remarks that follow draw on work by two of my former students at the Catholic University of America, Keith Fleming and Charles Downey, that is planned for publication in the near future.[6]

A comment in an essay by René-Jean Hesbert provided the starting point for Fleming's work. In the course of his study of the Beneventan liturgical tradition, Hesbert remarked that it would be interesting to see the result of a systematic investigation of the multiple melodies for those five Communions sung on weekdays in Lent for which the texts are taken not, as expected, from a psalm, but from the Gospel for the day,[7] and to demonstrate the extent to which a criterion of this type could be of use in the grouping of manuscripts.[8] That idea had evidently occurred to at least one other scholar. In 1952 Solutor Marosszéki reported that G. M. Beyssac, archivist of the Archbishopric of Paris, had shared with him the results of some forty years' investigation of this matter, data collected from the examination of 710 manuscripts.[9]

Fleming began work on this project by examining the manuscript tradition for the five Lenten Communions.[10] Many sources contain melodies for them that are quite simple in style. The explanation offered by Ferretti and others has been that they must have been office antiphons borrowed for use as Communion chants;[11] as confirming evidence, Ferretti provided parallel transcriptions of the Gregorian Communion *Videns Dominus* and the Old Roman antiphon with the same text, for which the melodies are virtually the same.

Marosszéki's explanation went a little further. He suggested that the Gospel Communion texts might have been introduced into the different churches without melodies. At some churches, melodies for these texts could be found in the antiphoner; at other churches where this was not the case, melodies had to be composed for the newly introduced texts.[12] To Marosszéki, as to Beyssac, the relatively large number of variants in the literary texts of these Communions provided confirmation for the hypothesis; if the texts had been circulated with melodies, fewer variant readings would appear in them.[13] Marosszéki cites the appearance of *Nemo te*, *Videns Dominus*, and *Qui biberit* as antiphons in certain sources.

Marosszéki's hypothesis found few adherents.[14] The generally accepted explanation for the multiple melodies is the one presented, for example, in the article 'Communion' in *The New Catholic Encyclopedia*: because the 'primitive' melodies resembled Office antiphons in their syllabic setting of the text, 'in various churches it was thought desirable to replace this simple melody by a more elaborate one that would conform to the style of the other communions'.[15] A notable feature of this explanation is that it postulates the deliberate replacement of the original melody for a chant of the Proper of the Mass with a new one – a practice of which other instances do not come readily to mind, except perhaps among the Alleluias.

Further confirmation that the simple melodies for these texts are those to which they are sung (or were once sung in certain places) as Office antiphons has been furnished by James McKinnon, who found all of them written as antiphons. Among the sources he cited are Toledo, BC 44.1, of the eleventh century, and Toledo 44.2, of the late eleventh or early twelfth century. Because there is a lacuna in the part of Toledo 44.2 that contains Lent, only two of the antiphons are present in that source; but all five are in Toledo 44.1, only one of them lacking musical notation.[16] McKinnon refers to the antiphon melodies as the 'original' melodies for these texts.

When scholars have specified the number of different melodies they have found for these Communions, the numbers have varied. One reason for this is that some of the melodies are quite rare and appear in sources to which it is difficult to gain access. Another reason is that among the melodies for a single text there are often strong similarities: it is often difficult to decide whether what one has found is a new melody or a variant of one already collected.

In his work on the melodies, Keith Fleming did not get far enough to take into account any similarities among them. Charles Downey went over Fleming's drafts and sketches and examined the melodies, searching for similarities among them and organizing them into groups. He then went on to establish an order in which the transcriptions in each group would be presented, one that would call attention to these similarities. He also prepared charts in which some melodies are laid out one above another in such a way as to facilitate comparison. In doing this he was guided by the concept of 'close multiples' set forth by Kenneth Levy in his study of the various readings of the Offertory *Elegerunt* preserved in sources from different regions.[17] Downey intends to incorporate all of this into an edition of the Communions with multiple melodies that he will publish as a joint author with Fleming. (This advance report on his findings is published with his full approval; as a matter of fact, he knew of Professor McKinnon's interest in this topic, and suggested it as a topic for consideration at the conference.)

The concordances given for each of the melodies in this study are those assembled by Fleming. All of his work was carried out in the Dom Mocquereau Foundation collection of microfilms of medieval liturgical sources containing musical notation at the Catholic University of America, and sources not represented in that collection were not included in his survey.

This report focuses on a single Communion, *Oportet te*. It is the one for which the largest number of different melodies have been reported. The number given in the *New Catholic Encyclopedia* is eleven; at one point, Keith Fleming believed he had found thirteen. Working with Fleming's transcriptions, Charles Downey identified seven variants of a single melody and five less closely related melodies, two of which occur in two versions, bringing the total to fourteen. The seven variants of the main melody are shown in the Appendix; they are labeled A.1 through A.7 (Audio CD, Track 17). The five other melodies also appear there, B.2, C.2, D, E and F (Track 18).

The syllabic melody for the chant is the one marked A.4 (Track 17, item 4). This is the melody associated with the antiphon in the three sources of the Divine Office that provide musical notation for it: Rome, Bibl. Vallicelliana C 5, from the monastery of Sant Eutizio di Norcia; Toledo 44.1, from Aquitaine; and Monza, Basilica S. Giovanni Battista C.12/79, from Monza. (There are other sources of the Divine Office in which the text appears as an antiphon, but without notation – Paris, BNF lat. 17436 and Durham, Cathedral Chapter Lib. B.III.11, among them.[18]) The melody shares the distinguishing features of a group of antiphons identified as mode 8, class *D* by László Dobszay and Janka Szendrei,[19] and it is the melody that is given for the Communion in the majority of the Mass manuscripts that Fleming investigated. It is also the one that appears in the *Graduale Romanum*. Two of the other melodies are regional: A.6 (Track 17, item 6) is the melody that appears in Beneventan sources, A.7 (Track 17, item 7) appears in most of the Aquitanian sources, but not all. (The list of sources is shown in Table 14.1.) A.1 (Track 17, item 1) appears only in some sources from Monza. (One of those sources, Monza C.13/76, has two layers of neumes written in the same hand above the text, the lower series indicating melody A.4, the upper, A.1. Also of interest is the fact that one thirteenth-century Monza source has melody A.4, another A.1.) A.2, A.3 and A.5 may be unica: A.2 has been found only in Limoges, BM 2, a fourteenth-century source from Fontevrault; A.3 only in Paris, BNF lat. 17312, thirteenth century, from Auxerre; and A.5 only in Paris, BNF lat. 1132, which comes from Saint-Martial, Limoges, after the reform of that monastery by Cluny in 1063 (Track 17, items 2, 3 and 5).

The relationship among the different versions of the melody may be observed in the phrase, 'quia frater tuus mortuus fuerat', shown in Ex. 14.1. At first glance one might be tempted to regard the variations in the melody as the result of progressive elaboration, changes that were made gradually over a period of time, but it is important to note that the sources containing the variant readings come from different places. Thus this comparison may simply confirm the view expressed in the *New Catholic Encyclopedia* article: that once a decision had been made to ornament the melody, the ornamentation took different forms in different churches.

The antiphon melody (A.4), generic though it may be, fits the text well. It even goes so far as to underline the pivotal function of one word in the text, 'fuerat', which is connected to what precedes it through its meaning, 'frater tuus mortuus fuerat', even as it serves as the beginning of a series of words for which a parallel is immediately provided: 'fuerat et revixit, perierat et inventus est'. The musical setting for the two phrases is virtually the same, differing only where the number of syllables requires it (see Ex. 14.2).

Having noted this feature in the archaic melody, one may search for it in the other settings. It is most evident in the Aquitanian melody, A.7 (Track

Table 14.1 Sources for different readings of *Oportet te* collected by Keith A. Fleming

Mel.	*Manuscript*	*Date*	*Provenance*
A.1	Monza, Basilica S. Giov. 12/75	early 11th	Monza
A.1	Monza, Basilica S. Giov. 13/76	11th	Monza
A.1	Monza, Basilica S. Giov. 14/77	13th	Monza
A.2	Limoges, BM 2	14th	Fontevrault
A.3	Paris, BNF lat. 17312	13th	Auxerre (diocese)
A.4	Monza, Basilica S. Giov. 13/76	11th	Monza
A.4	Monza, Basilica S. Giov. K. 11	13th	Monza
A.4	Berlin, Staatsbibl. Mus. ms. 40078	12th	Quedlinburg
A.4	Berlin, Staatsbibl. th. lat. qu. 664	12th	Trier (region)
A.4	Brussels, Bibl. Royale II.3823	early 12th	Clermont diocese (Cluniac)
A.4	Cambrai, BM B. 61	early 12th	Saint-Pierre, Lille
A.4	Chartres, BM 47	10th	Rennes
A.4	Chartres, BM 520	early 13th	Chartres
A.4	Cortona, Bibl. communale 12	12th	central Italy
A.4	Douai, BM 114	early 14th	Marchiennes
A.4	Einsiedeln, SB 121	early 11th	Einsiedeln (St. Gall?)
A.4	Florence, Bibl. Medicea-Laurenziana, Ashb. 61	11th–12th	Tuscany
A.4	Graz, UB 807	12th	Klosterneuburg
A.4	Harburg, I.2.4o.13	13th	Blaubeuern
A.4	Laon, BM 239	ca. 930	Laon
A.4	Leipzig, St. Thomas 391	end 13th	Leipzig
A.4	London, BL Add. 12194	ca. 1275	Salisbury
A.4	London, BL Egerton 857	11th–12th	Noyon
A.4	Madrid, BN Vitrina 20-4	1130s	Palermo
A.4	Manchester, Rylands lat. 24	13th	Exeter (Sarum use)
A.4	Le Mans, BM 437	14th	Le Mans
A.4	Milan, Bibl. Ambrosiana S. 74 Sup.	13th	northern Italy
A.4	Modena, BC O.I.7	11th–12th	Forlimpopoli
A.4	Munich, BSB clm 7919	13th	Kaisheim (but not Cistercian)
A.4	Naples, BN VI.G.11	13th	Acre
A.4	New York, Pierpont Morgan Lib. 797	13th	Padua
A.4	New York, Pierpont Morgan Lib. 107	14th	East Anglia (Sarum use)
A.4	Oxford, Bodl. Lib. Canon. lit. 340	ca. 1216	Moggio (near Udine)
A.4	Oxford, Bodl. Lib. Rawl. C. 892	12th	Downpatrick, Ireland
A.4	Padua, BC A. 47	early 12th	Ravenna
A.4	Paris, Bibl. de l'Arsenal 595	13th–14th	Châlons-sur-Marne
A.4	Paris, Bibl. Mazarine 384	11th	Saint-Denis
A.4	Paris, BNF lat. 1087	late 11th	Cluny
A.4	Paris, BNF lat. 1107	later 13th	Saint-Denis
A.4	Paris, BNF lat. 9436	11th	Saint-Denis
A.4	Paris, BNF lat. 9441	13th	Notre-Dame, Paris

Table 14.1 (continued)

Mel.	*Manuscript*	*Date*	*Provenance*
A.4	Paris, BNF lat. 12584	late 11th	Saint-Maur-des-Fossés
A.4	Paris, BNF lat. 13253	13th	Saint-Maur-des-Fossés
A.4	Paris, BNF lat. 13254	late 12th	Saint-Maur-des-Fossés
A.4	Paris, BNF lat. 15615	early 13th	Paris
A.4	Paris, BNF lat. 17307	late 12th	Compiègne
A.4	Paris, BNF lat. 18010	late 11th	Corbie
A.4	Paris, Priv. coll. (Mont-Renaud Grad.)	10th	Saint-Denis? Corbie?
A.4	Piacenza, BC 65	early 13th	Piacenza
A.4	Rome, Bibl. Angelica 123	early 11th	Bologna?
A.4	Rome, Bibl. Casanatense 1695	early 13th	Paris
A.4	Rouen, BM 249 (A 280)	12th	Saint-Victor, Paris
A.4	St. Gall, SB 339	early 11th	St. Gall
A.4	Trier, Stadtbibl. 2254	13th	Trier
A.4	Turin, Bibl. Naz. Univ. F.IV.18	12th	Bobbio
A.4	Turin, Bibl. Naz. Univ. G.V.20	11th	Bobbio
A.4	Udine, Bibl. Archivescovile, fol. 16	ca. 1200	Moggio
A.4	Udine, Bibl. Archivescovile, fol. 17	12th	Aquileia
A.4	Udine, Bibl. Archivescovile, oct. 2	13th	Aquileia
A.4	Vatican City, BAV Barb. lat. 559	ca. 1200	Saint-Michel de Lyon
A.4	Vatican City, BAV Patetta 10	13th–14th	Randazzo, Sicily
A.4	Vatican City, BAV Rossiani 76	13th	Aquileia
A.4	Vercelli, BC 186	11th–12th	Balerna (diocese of Como)
A.4	Verona, BC 105	11th–12th	Verona
A.4	Vienna, ÖNB 1845	11th	Seeon (upper Bavaria)
A.5	Paris, BNF lat. 1132	11th–12th	Saint-Martial (post-Cluny)
A.6	Benevento, BC 19–20	12th	Benevento
A.6	Benevento, BC 33	ca. 1000	southern Italy
A.6	Benevento, BC 34	12th	Benevento
A.6	Benevento, BC 35	early 12th	Benevento
A.6	Benevento, BC 38	early 11th	Benevento
A.6	Paris, BNF n. a. lat. 1669	12th–13th	Gubbio
A.6	Vatican City, BAV Barb. lat. 603	12th	Caiazzo
A.6	Vatican City, BAV Barb. lat. 699	12th	Veroli
A.6	Vatican City, BAV Ottob. lat. 576	12th–13th	southern Italy
A.6	Vatican City, BAV Vat. lat. 6082	early 12th	Montecassino
A.7	London, BL Harley 4951	11th	Toulouse
A.7	Madrid, RAH Aemil. 18	early 12th	San-Millan de la Cogolla
A.7	Madrid, Acad. Hist. 51	11th–12th	San-Millan de la Cogolla
A.7	Paris, BNF lat. 776	11th	Gaillac
A.7	Paris, BNF lat. 903	11th	Saint-Yrieix

Table 14.1 (continued)

Mel.	*Manuscript*	*Date*	*Provenance*
B.1	Vercelli, BC 146	early 12th	Vercelli
B.1	Vercelli, BC 161	late 11th	Vercelli
B.1	Vercelli, BC 162	12th	Vercelli
B.2	Rouen, BM 305 (A 166)	early 13th	Montaure (Evreux diocese)
C.1	Vatican City, BAV Borgia lat. 359	11th	Besançon
C.2	Brussels, Bibl. Royale 19389	13th	Quesnat (Brabant)
C.2	London, BL Add. 18031–18032	early 13th	Stavelot
C.2	Munich, BSB clm. 10075	12th–13th	near Düsseldorf
C.2	Namur, Mus. dioc. 1	12th–13th	Andenne
C.2	Namur, Mus. dioc. 2	13th	Liège
C.2	Namur, Mus. dioc. 3	14th	Andenne
D	Brussels, Bibl. Royale II.3824	13th	Saint-Bénigne, Dijon
D	Montpellier, Fac. de Méd. H.159	11th	Saint-Bénigne, Dijon
D	Paris, BNF lat. 904	13th	Rouen
D	Paris, BNF n. a. lat. 541	13th	Rouen
D	Rouen, BM 277 (Y 50)	13th	Rouen
E	Arras, BM 444	late 13th	Saint-Vaast d'Arras
E	St. Petersburg, lat. O.v.I.6	12th	Meulan (Le Bec)
E	Paris, BNF lat. 1105	late 13th	Le Bec
F	Paris, BNF lat. 780	11th–12th	Narbonne

17, item 7), though in a more elaborate form; and it also appears in the melody Downey has labeled D (Track 18, item 3, shown in the Appendix), which comes from regions where the influence of Blessed William of Dijon was felt – Saint-Bénigne in Dijon, and Normandy.[20] But in D the parallelism has lost force, being obscured by excessive elaboration.

The list of sources for the different melodies for *Oportet te* can be compared with other lists, first of all those for the four other Gospel Communions sung on weekdays in Lent. That work of comparison is in progress; the findings to date are not clear-cut and they are resistant to explanation. Yet another list that has been used for comparison is one showing sources for verses for the Offertory *Elegerunt* that was prepared several years ago.[21] In that list, Limoges 2 stood apart in giving the Aquitanian melody (rather than the common melody) for the Offertory *Elegerunt* without verses. The Aquitanian sources formed a close-knit group except for one, Paris 1132, that gives the Cluny Offertory for St. Stephen. In the list for *Oportet te* there are two Aquitanian manuscripts that differ from the others: not only Paris 1132 but also Paris, BNF lat. 780.

A more detailed analysis of the different melodies for *Oportet te* is beyond the scope of this study, and in any case it would overlap with material that

Ex. 14.1 *Oportet te*, melodies A.1–A.7

A.1
qui - a fra - ter tu - us mor - tu - us fu - e - rat, et re - vix - it.
A.2
qui - a fra - ter tu - us mor - tu - us fu - e - rat, et re - vix - it.
A.3
qui - a fra - ter tu - us mor - tu - us fu - e - rat, et re - vix - it.
A.4
qui - a fra - ter tu - us mor - tu - us fu - e - rat, et re - vix - it.
A.5
qui - a fra - ter tu - us mor - tu - us fu - e - rat, et re - vix - it.
A.6
qui - a fra - ter tu - us mor - tu - us fu - e - rat, et re - vix - it.
A.7
qui - a fra - ter tu - us mor - tu - us fu - e - rat, et re - vix - it.

Ex. 14.2 *Oportet te*, melody A.4

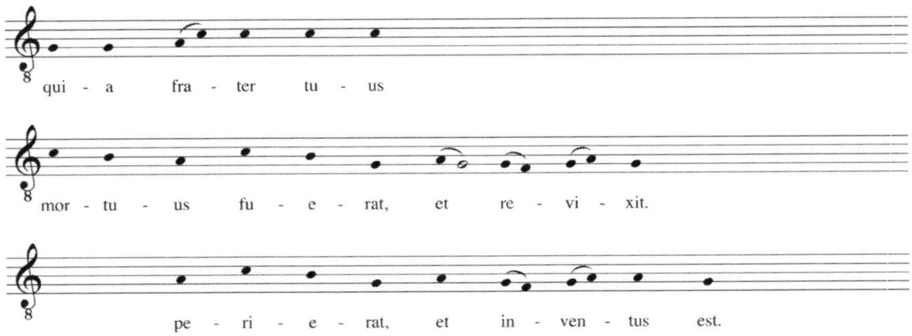
qui - a fra - ter tu - us
mor - tu - us fu - e - rat, et re - vi - xit.
pe - ri - e - rat, et in - ven - tus est.

Charles Downey is now preparing for publication. There is, however, yet another matter that needs to be considered: the position of *Oportet te* in the cluster of antiphons 'in evangelio', that is, on the Parable of the Prodigal Son, for the Saturday before the Third Sunday of Lent.

In clusters of this kind, antiphons are generally arranged in order according to the sources of their texts, and so one would expect to find *Oportet te* at the end. However, the Compiègne antiphoner, a carefully planned and meticulously laid-out source, places it first, at the bottom of fol. 48^{v}. There are five additional antiphons at the top of the next folio, and four of them appear in the same order in two north Italian sources, Monza C.12/75 and Piacenza, BC 65:[22]

> Vadam ad patrem meum et dicam ei: Pater, fac me sicut unum ex mercenariis tuis. (5299)
>
> Pater peccavi in caelum et coram te; jam non sum dignus vocari filius tuus. (4238)
>
> Dixit autem pater ad servos suos: Cito proferte stolam primam et induite illum, et date annulum in manu ejus, et calceamenta in pedibus suis. (2280)
>
> Fili, tu semper mecum fuisti, et omnia mea tua sunt. (2875)[23]

Toledo 44.1, which has half a dozen antiphons on this parable, puts *Oportet te* at the end of the series, where it belongs; it does not specify the liturgical contexts in which the antiphons are to be sung. (See Table 14.2, which shows lists prepared from index files in the CANTUS database.) Vallicelliana C 5, a twelfth-century monastic source from Norcia, clearly specifies the liturgical role for each of its six antiphons; they are not given in the order of Luke's narrative, and *Oportet te* is assigned to Sext, where it will accompany psalms rather than a canticle. This may seem to suggest that the two antiphons that are indeed assigned to canticles in this source, *Vadam ad patrem* and *Pater peccavi* are more important, more central to the tradition, than the others. However, the most widely known antiphon of this entire group, *Dixit autem pater*, the only one to appear in all the sources of *CAO*, is in Vallicelliana C 5 relegated to Prime. Thus what comes to light in a brief survey of a few sources that include *Oportet te* as an antiphon is that the repertories of antiphons 'in evangelio' based on the Parable of the Prodigal Son are unstable, not at all what we are accustomed to find when studying chants that belong to the bedrock of the repertory.

In the parable as a whole, and antiphons based on the first part of it, the emphasis is on the repentance of the Prodigal Son and the rejoicing and generosity expressed by his father on his return. In modern sermons based on this parable, the same emphases are often present.[24] If there is a lesson to be learned from this parable, it seems, it is the endless love of the Father for his children, no matter how far they have strayed, if their repentance is genuine and deeply felt. To be sure, the last verse of the parable may be heard as an admonition to those who consider themselves righteous: when the time comes, they should be prepared to rejoice over not only their own rewards for loyal service but also over the return to the fold of sinners who are truly repentant.

Table 14.2 CANTUS data for *Oportet te*

Fol.	*Office*[a]	*Pos.*[b]	*Incipit*	*Concordances*[c]		*Source*[d]
59^{r}	E	1	Surgam et ibo ad patrem meum			E-Tc 44.1
59^{r}	E	2	Pater peccavi in caelum et	C E		E-Tc 44.1
59^{r}	E	3	Dixit autem pater ad servos	CGBEMV	HRDFSL	E-Tc 44.1
59^{r}	E	4	Dedit pater paenitenti filio	C EM		E-Tc 44.1
59^{r}	E	5	Fili tu semper mecum fuisti	C E V	HR	E-Tc 44.1
59^{r}	E	6	Oportet te fili gaudere quia	CG M		E-Tc 44.1
121^{v}	L	B	Vadam ad patrem meum et dicam	C E V	HRDF	I-Rv C.5
122^{r}	P		Dixit autem pater ad servos	CGBEMV	HRDFSL	I-Rv C.5
122^{r}	T		Fili tu semper	C E V	HR	I-Rv C.5
122^{r}	S		Oportet te fili gaudere quia	CG M		I-Rv C.5
122^{r}	N		Dedit pater paenitenti filio	C EM		I-Rv C.5
122^{r}	V2	M	Pater peccavi in caelum et		D SL	I-Rv C.5
313^{v}	L	B	Vadam ad patrem meum et dicam	C E V	HRDF	I-PCsa 65
314^{r}	E	1	Pater peccavi in caelum et	C E		I-PCsa 65
314^{r}	E	2	Dixit autem pater ad servos	CGBEMV	HRDFSL	I-PCsa 65
314^{r}	E	3	Fili tu semper mecum fuisti	C E V	HR	I-PCsa 65
72^{v}	E	1	Vado ad patrem meum et dicam	C E V	HRDF	D-KA Aug. LX
72^{v}	E	2	Dixit autem pater ad servos	CGBEMV	HRDFSL	D-KA Aug. LX
72^{v}	N		Fili tu semper mecum fuisti	C E V	HR	D-KA Aug. LX
47^{v}	L	B	Vadam ad patrem meum et dicam	C E V	HRDF	GB-WO F.160
47^{v}	X	1	Pater peccavi in caelum et	C E		GB-WO F.160
47^{v}	X	2	Dixit autem pater ad servos	CGBEMV	HRDFSL	GB-WO F.160
240^{r}	L	B	Vadam ad patrem meum et dicam	C E V	HRDF	F-Pn lat. 15181
240^{r}	V2		Dixit autem pater ad servos	CGBEMV	HRDFSL	F-Pn lat. 15181
240^{r}	V2	M	Dedit pater paenitenti filio	C EM		F-Pn lat. 15181

Table 14.2 (continued)

Fol.	*Office*[a]	*Pos.*[b]	*Incipit*	*Concordances*[c]		*Source*[d]
66^{r}	L	B	Vado ad patrem meum et dicam	C E V	HRDF	A-VOR 287 (29)
66^{r}	V2	M	Dixit autem pater ad servos	CGBEMV	HRDFSL	A-VOR 287 (29)
324^{r}	N		Fili tu semper mecum es et	C E V	HR	A-VOR 287 (29)
84^{r}	L	B	Vadam ad patrem meum et dicam	C E V	HRDF	I-Far
84^{r}	V2	M	Dixit autem pater ad servos	CGBEMV	HRDFSL	I-Far
75^{v}	L	B	Vadam ad patrem meum et dicam	C E V	HRDF	NL-Uu 406 (3 J 7)
75^{v}	E		Dixit autem pater ad servos	CGBEMV	HRDFSL	NL-Uu 406 (3 J 7)

[a] Abbreviations include the initial letters of the services Lauds, Prime, Terce, Sext and None. 'V2' refers to Second Vespers. 'E' indicates that an antiphon is marked 'in evangelio', 'X' that the liturgical role is unspecified.

[b] 'B' is used for an antiphon that is intended for the Benedictus of Lauds, 'M' refers to the Magnificat. Numbers indicate the place in a series of antiphons 'in evangelio' that is occupied by a particular chant.

[c] Sigla as in *CAO*.

[d] The abbreviations stand for:

A-VOR: Vorau, SB 287
D-KA: Karlsruhe, Badische Landesbibl., Aug. LX
E-Tc: Toledo, BC 44.1
F-Pn: Paris, BNF lat. 15181
GB-WO: Worcester, Cathedral Lib. F. 160
I-Far: Florence, Arcivescovado, antiphoner without call number
I-PCsa: Piacenza, BC 65
I-Rv: Rome, Bibl. Vallicelliana C 5
NL-Uu: Utrecht, Universiteitsbibl. 406

For detailed information concerning these sources, consult the descriptions of them at the CANTUS Website, http://publish.uwo.ca/cantus.

Yet the rewording of *Oportet te* has introduced yet another note, that of rebuke for the sin of envy. As a Communion in the Mass, *Oportet te* would have been sung after the Gospel; and in missals the wording of the last verse in the Gospel is that of the Vulgate. Were the shift in wording and the resultant shift in meaning between the Gospel and the Communion noticed by those who attended or took part in the Mass? If so, what did they make of it? One writer has made the following observation:

> This parable plays upon the hearers' knowledge of 'two-brothers' stories, in which the younger brother triumphs over the older brother(s). See, e.g., Esau and Jacob (Gen 25:27–34; 27:1–36); Joseph and his brothers (Gen 37:1–4). Jesus doubly reverses expectations: the prodigal son is a parody of the successful younger brother; the elder son is not vanquished, but invited to the feast.[25]

The story of Joseph and his brothers features a father, Jacob, who does not love all of his sons equally: Genesis reports that he loved Joseph 'more than all his children'[26] and that 'when his brethren saw that their father loved him more than all his brethren, they hated him'.[27] What the change in the wording of *Oportet te* has done to the hearer's perception of the Parable of the Prodigal Son is to make it more like that of the story of Joseph and his brothers. Skipping over the rest of the parable to the final verse, in a version that is reworked in such a way as to focus attention on the envy of the older brother, and using that as the sole chant based on the parable that is sung in Mass has the effect of skewing the impact of the Gospel on the ensemble of texts heard on one particular day.

It seems unlikely that this was accidental; but what could the reason for it have been? It may lie in the 'Lectio continua' of the Old Testament that took place in Matins beginning in Lent. As it happens, on the day when *Oportet te* is sung, Joseph and his brothers are close at hand. The lessons in Matins on the very next day, the third Sunday of Lent, come from Genesis 37, and the responsories are about the deadly envy on the part of the brothers that led them first to throw Joseph into a dry well, and then sell him into slavery. The first responsory presents the situation in horrifying clarity:

> Videntes Joseph a longe, loquebantur mutuo fratres, dicentes: Ecce somniator venit; venite, occidamus eum, et videamus si prosint illi somnia sua.
> V. Cumque vidissent Joseph fratres sui quod a patre cunctis fratribus plus amaretur, oderant eum, nec poterant ei quicquam pacifice loqui; unde et dicebant – Venite.
>
> When they saw him afar off, his brothers spoke to each other saying, behold, the dreamer cometh. Come, let us kill him, and then it shall appear what his dreams avail him.
> V. When the brothers saw that Joseph was loved by the father more than all his brothers, they hated him, and they could not speak peaceably to him.

In sources where a chant for Sunday is anticipated in Vespers of the Saturday that precedes it, a responsory from the Joseph series is heard before the final chant of the Prodigal Son. One example is to be found in Vallicelliana C 5, where *Dixit Judas*, which details the plan of the brother named Judas not to kill Joseph but to sell him into slavery, precedes *Pater peccavi in caelum et coram te*, the antiphon for the Magnificat: 'Dixit Judas fratribus suis: Ecce Ismaelitae transeunt; venite, venumdetur, et manus nostrae non polluantur; caro enim et frater noster est.' There is no question that the juxtaposition of these two narratives in the liturgy magnifies their impact. It demonstrates that an understanding of the interplay of texts in the Mass may often be enhanced by a familiarity with the texts of the Office.

The Latin of the Bible, of scholars and of worship served as a lingua franca for Western Europe during the Middle Ages; the literature of the Bible provided a background for the development of a unified culture. The public reading and singing of words chosen from the Bible for use in the liturgy made characters like the lost sheep and the Prodigal Son into familiar figures. We all know who they are; we recognize their modern counterparts; some of us even have them in our families. The timeliness and the relevance of these old, old stories is nothing short of astonishing.

Appendix

Variants of the melody *Oportet te*

A.1 Monza, Bas. S. Giov. 14/77

O-por - tet te fi - li gau - de - re,
qui - a fra - ter tu - us mor - tu - us fu - e - rat et re - vi - xit,
pe - ri - e - rat, et in - - - ven-tus est.

A.2 Limoges, Bibl. mun. 2

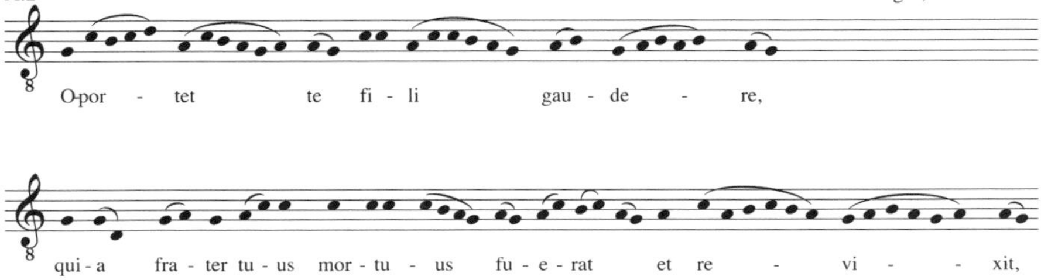
O-por - tet te fi - li gau - de - re,
qui - a fra - ter tu - us mor - tu - us fu - e - rat et re - vi - - xit,

pe - ri - e - - rat, et in - ven - tus est, di - cit Do-mi - nus.

A.3 Paris, BN lat. 17312

O - por - tet te fi - li gau - de - re,
qui - a fra - ter tu - us mor - tu - us fu - e - rat et re - vi - xit,
pe - ri - e - rat, et in - ven - tus est.

A.4 Paris, BN lat. 1107

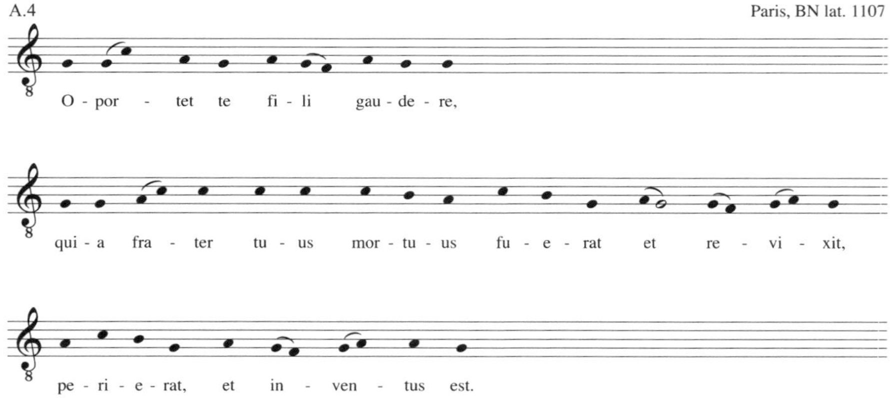
O - por - tet te fi - li gau - de - re,
qui - a fra - ter tu - us mor - tu - us fu - e - rat et re - vi - xit,
pe - ri - e - rat, et in - ven - tus est.

A.5 Paris, BN lat. 1132

O - por - tet te fi - li gau - de - re,
qui - a fra - ter tu - us mor - tu - us fu - e - rat et re - vi - xit,

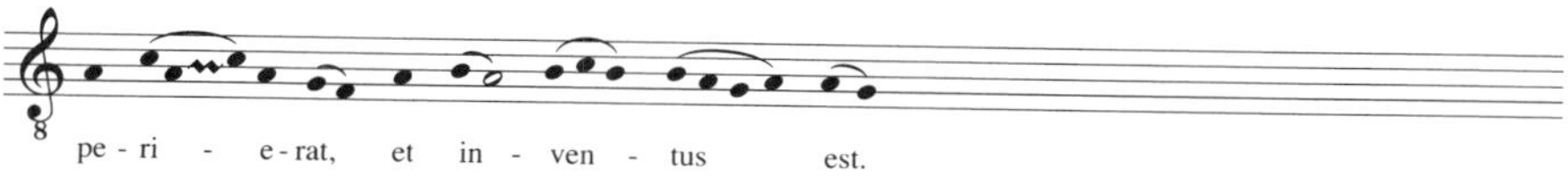
pe - ri - e - rat, et in - ven - tus est.

A.6

Benevento, Bibl. cap. 34

O - por - tet te fi - li gau - de - re,
qui - a fra - ter tu - us mor - tu - us fu - e - rat et re - vi - xit,
pe - ri - e - rat, et in - ven - tus est.

A.7

Paris, BN lat. 903

O - por - tet te fi - li gau - de - re,
qui - a fra - ter tu - us mor - tu - us fu - e - rat et re - vi - xit,
pe - ri - e - rat, et in - ven - tus est.

B.1

Vercelli, Bibl. cap. 162

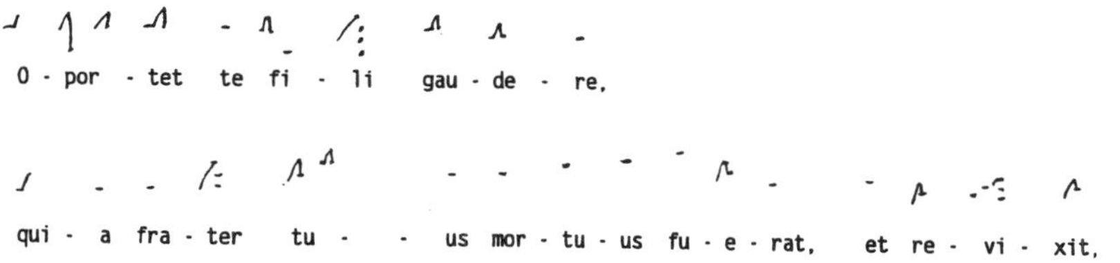
O - por - tet te fi - li gau - de - re,
qui - a fra - ter tu - - us mor - tu - us fu - e - rat, et re - vi - xit,

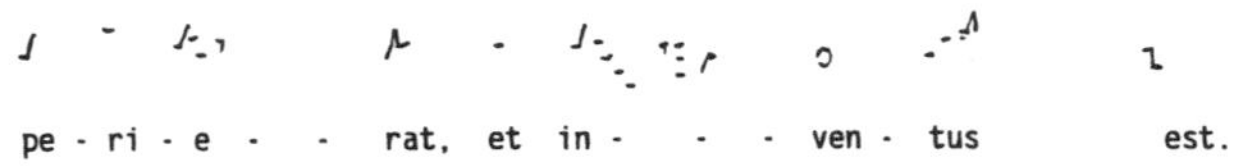
pe - ri - e - - rat, et in - - - ven - tus est.

B.2 Rouen, Bibl. mun. 305 (A 166)

O - por - tet te fi - li gau - de - re,
qui - a fra-ter tu - - - - us mor - tu - us fu - e - rat, et re - vi - xit,
pe - ri - e - rat, et in - - - - ven - tus est.

C.1 Rome, Bibl. Apost. Vat., Borgia lat. 359

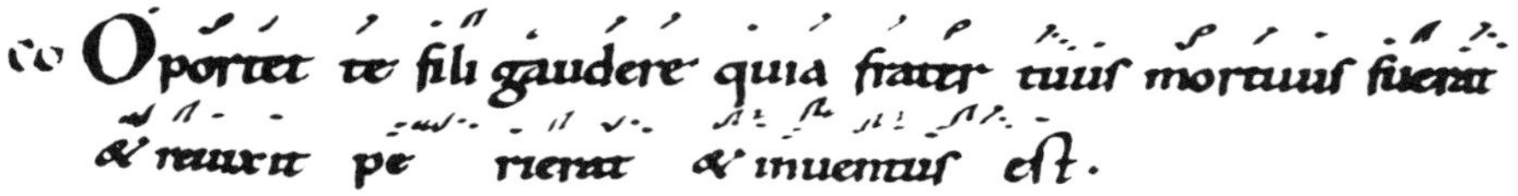

C.2 Brussels, Bibl. Royale 19389

O - por - tet te fi - li gau - de - re,
qui - a fra - ter tu - us mor - tu - us fu - e - rat, et re - vi - xit,
pe - ri - e - rat, et in - ven - tus est.

D

Montpellier, Fac. de Méd., H159

O - por - tet te fi - li gau - de - re,
qui - a fra - ter tu - us mor - tu - us fu - e - rat et re - vi - xit,
pe - ri - e - rat, et in - ven - tus est.

E

St. Petersburg, lat. O.v.I.6

O - por - tet te fi - li gau - de - re,
qui - a fra - ter tu - us mor - tu - us fu - e - rat et re - vi - xit,
pe - ri - e - rat, et in - ven - - - - tus est.

F

Paris, BN lat. 780

O - por - tet te fi - li gau - de - re,
qui - a fra - ter tu - us mor - tu - us fu - e - rat et re - vi - xit,

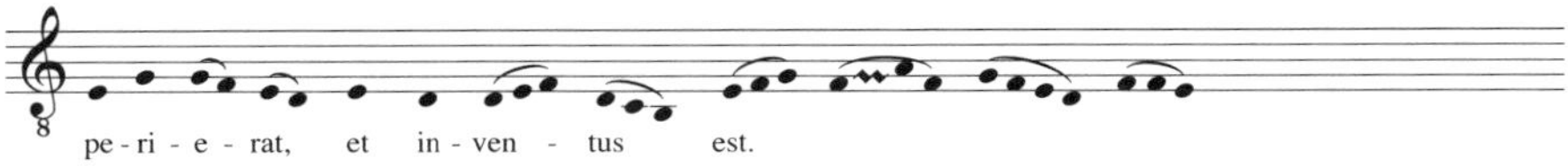
pe - ri - e - rat, et in - ven - tus est.

Notes

1 The translation is that of the Douay Version.
2 Joseph A. Fitzmyer, *The Gospel According to Luke* (The Anchor Bible 28–28A; Garden City, NY, 1981–5), ii, 1085.
3 *Novum Testamentum Domini Nostri Iesu Christi Latine*, ed. John Wordsworth and Henry White (Oxford: Clarendon Press, 1889–98), i, 420. Adolf Jülicher, *Itala: Das neue Testament in altlateinischer Überlieferung* (Berlin: Walter de Gruyter, 1954), iii, 183, cites the same variants.
4 In the old-Latin version preferred by Jülicher, the verb is in the present tense, 'oportet'.
5 These chants are more fully described below. The Communion that *Oportet te* replaced is perhaps *Cantabo*, which is assigned to the second Sunday after Pentecost in the sources surveyed by R.-J. Hesbert in *AM*, LXXV, 174–75. Dominique Delalande, *Le Graduel des Prêcheurs: recherches sur les sources et la valeur de son texte musical* (Paris: Editions du Cerf, 1949), 256–57, presents a 'restored' version of *Cantabo* that contains both B♭ and B♮ and E♭ and E♮. It may be assumed that the two variable degrees in the melody of this chant are the cause of the variant readings found in the sources, rather than attempts to transform its style or character. *Cantabo* is the first of three Communions for Sundays after Pentecost that may be identified loosely as 'fugitives' from Lent. The others are *Ego clamavi*, which is based on Psalm 16, on the third Sunday, which was displaced from its Lenten weekday by *Qui biberit*, and *Dominus firmamentum*, on a text from Psalm 17, on the fourth Sunday, which was displaced by *Nemo te*. It should be noted that on these three Sundays only the Introit and the Communion are new; the other Proper chants have been sung earlier in the year and are being reused. May one conclude that the date of the displacement coincided with the creation of series of Proper chants for the first few Sundays after Pentecost? If so, then are the Introits for those days 'late' chants? And if they are, why are there so few variants in the readings for them in the sources? If the date of displacement did not coincide with the creation of this series of Propers, then are we to believe that in the period before musical notation came into use it was possible to retain in memory chants that had no role in the liturgy?
6 Keith Fleming died in 1993. Charles Downey has examined his transcriptions and arranged them into groups on the basis of thematic similarities. He intends to include commentaries on the melodies in his edition.
7 Concerning these see James McKinnon, 'The Eighth-Century Frankish-Roman Communion Cycle', *JAMS* 45 (1992), 179–227, esp. 201–04; and McKinnon, *The Advent Project* (Berkeley: University of California Press, 2000), ch. 13.
8 R.-J. Hesbert, 'La Tradition bénéventaine dans la tradition manuscrite', in PM 14 (Solesmes: Abbaye Saint-Pierre, 1931), 60–465, at 225. In Hesbert's words, 'Il serait sans doute fort intéressant de donner, dans un travail d'ensemble, le résultat du dépouillement de la tradition manuscrite sur ce point particulier, et de montrer de quel secours peut être un critère de cette nature pour le groupement des manuscrits en familles.' In *Les Tonaires: inventaire, analyse, comparaison* (Paris:

Société française de musicologie, 1971), 152–4, Michel Huglo showed how effective this could be even when the number of sources under investigation was relatively small.

9 Solutor Rodolphe Marosszéki, *Les Origines du chant cistercien: recherches sur les réformes du plain-chant cistercien au XIIe siècle* (Vatican City: Tip. poliglotta vaticana, 1952), 104. Marosszéki observes that any investigation of this type ought to be extended so that it covers 'la totalité des manuscrits', and asks 'Y arriverons-nous jamais?' (p. 103 n. 4). Beyssac's *Nachlass* is preserved in Sion-en-Valais under the care of Dom François Huot, Foyer St. Benoît, Le Bouveret, Lac Léman, Switzerland. Charts showing transcriptions made of the chants in question from several hundred different sources were prepared long ago at Solesmes. They are still in existence, and Kees Pouderoijen makes reference to them in 'Die melodische Gestalt der Communio "Videns Dominus"', in *Cantando praedicare: Godehard Joppich zum 60. Geburtstag* (Regensburg: G. Bosse, 1992), 129–55.

10 Unaware of the charts at Solesmes, and in any case intensely committed to approaching the material in his own way, he spent about a year and a half going through microfilms of manuscripts and making prints and transcriptions, from February 1990 until August 1991.

11 Paolo Ferretti, *Estetica gregoriana: trattato delle forme musicali del canto gregoriano*, i (Rome: Pontificio Istituto di Musica Sacra, 1934), 296: 'Noi pertanto pensiamo che si tratti di Antifone dell'Ufficio trasportate alla Messa come Antifone del *Communio*.'

12 Marosszéki, *Les Origines*, 102. In a note, he observes, 'Nous répétons que ce n'est qu'une hypothèse; nous avons vu, en effet, un bon nombre de paléographes et d'historiens respectables pour qui l'idée même d'une pareille supposition est "monstrueuse". Selon eux, un texte liturgique ne se peut concevoir sans l'accompagnement obligé de sa mélodie. Ce que nous avançons ici ne doit être, par conséquent, considéré que comme une hypothèse pure et simple, et rien d'autre.'

13 In Fleming's transcriptions one variant is cited for the text of *Oportet te*, a 'dicit Dominus' added at the end of melody A.2. Paris, BNF lat. 17436 adds 'in aeternum' at the end of both the antiphon and the Communion.

14 After the conference at which I read this paper, Michel Huglo wrote to me saying that it 'm'a rappelé l'époque où je travaillais dans l'équipe de l'édition critique à la "Paléo" dans les années 50. . . . On ne peut donc dire avec Marosszéki . . . que le "répertoire originel", transporté par voie orale, "ne comportait pas de mélodies pour ces cinq antiennes". – C'est "monstreux", comme je lui avais dit à cette époque! (je souris en lisant votre ftn., . . . qui me rappelle mon "explosion" de stupeur, lorsqu'il avançait son hypothèse devant nous trois, Cardine, Hourlier et moi!)" (letter to the author dated 1 February 1998 [*recte* 1999].)

15 Michel Huglo, 'Communion', in *The New Catholic Encyclopedia*, iv (1967), 40. Pouderoijen gives essentially the same explanation ('Die melodische Gestalt', 140), but in more detailed form and with additional observations to support it.

16 McKinnon, 'The Eighth-Century Frankish-Roman Communion Cycle', 211. The antiphon *Qui biberit* lacks notation in Toledo 44.1, but Marosszéki (p. 102) mentions having found it fully neumed in the Brescia gradual-breviary Oxford, Bodl. Canonici, set to a melody different from that given for the Communion with the same text elsewhere in the source. He does not fully identify his source, but it is Canon. lit. 366; the Communion appears on fol. 14^{v}, the antiphon on fol. 131^{r}.

17 Kenneth Levy, 'On Gregorian Orality', *JAMS* 43 (1990), 185–227.

18 These are referred to as manuscripts C and G in *CAO*.

19 For a general description of this class of antiphons see *Antiphonen*, ed. László Dobszay and Janka Szendrei, 3 vols (MMMA 5; Kassel: Bärenreiter, 1999), pt. 1: 98*, 106*; for the melodies themselves, pt. 3: 1123–1201, melodies numbered 8214–8352.

20 For an assessment of the work of William as a reformer of liturgy, see David Chadd, *The Ordinal of the Abbey of the Holy Trinity Fécamp* (Rochester, NY: Boydell Press for the Henry Bradshaw Society, 2000), i, 19–24; and John Boe, 'Music Notation in Archivio San Pietro C 105 and the Farfa Breviary, Chigi C.VI.177', *EMH* 18 (1999), 21–26.

21 For this list of sources, see Ruth Steiner, 'On the Verses for the Offertory *Elegerunt*', in *The Study of Medieval Chant: Paths and Bridges, East and West*, ed. Peter Jeffery (Rochester, NY: Boydell & Brewer, 2001), 283–301.

22 The number that follows each text is the one assigned to it in *CAO*, vol. iii.

23 The additional antiphon in Paris, BNF lat. 17436 is *Dedit pater* (2136). It follows *Dixit autem pater*, and it is unusual in that it summarizes the action without quoting the biblical account directly.

24 It is now possible to search electronically a very large number of sermons and biblical commentaries dating from the patristic and medieval periods for references in them to specific texts, including quotations from the Gospels. Unfortunately, time did not permit the carrying out of such a search for the present article. A study of allusions to the Parable of the Prodigal Son would undoubtedly be enlightening. (The tools in question include the Patrologia Latina Database, a searchable full-text presentation of all of Migne's *Patrologia Latina*, and the Cetedoc Library of Christian Latin Texts, which includes works edited in the Series Latina and Continuatio Medievalis of Corpus Christianorum. For further information concerning them, see Frank Anthony Carl Mantello and A. G. Rigg, *Medieval Latin: An Introduction and Bibliographical Guide* [Washington, DC: Catholic University of America Press, 1996], 52–3.)

25 *The New Jerome Biblical Commentary*, ed. Raymond E. Brown, Joseph A. Fitzmyer and Roland E. Murphy (Englewood Cliffs, NJ: Prentice Hall, 1990), 707.

26 Gen. 37: 3. The translation is that of the King James Version.

27 Gen. 37: 4.

Chapter 15
From Alleluia to Sequence: Some Definitions of Relations

Calvin M. Bower

I. Fundamental Historical Hypothesis

Frankish cantors frequently combined Alleluia, Verse and Sequence on certain festivals during the late eighth, ninth and tenth centuries to form a particularly splendid, indeed ecstatic prelude to the reading of the Gospel. Particular Alleluia melodies – designated by the textual incipit of their Verse – were associated with particular Sequences, designated by a variety of names; and the Sequences were intended – indeed conceived – to be sung together with a given Alleluia melody. The Sequences were created as untexted melismas, and their aesthetic was based on the concept of praise unfettered by the limitations of verbal signification.[1] Only around the middle of the ninth and during the tenth century did it become customary to add words to Sequence melodies; and the words were added at least partly as a means of 'fastening' the melodies in the mind of the cantor.[2] The Council of Meaux (845) expressed disdain for singing these 'prosae' – the added words – when one sang the Sequence.[3] Nevertheless, in the later ninth and tenth centuries Sequences-with-text were sung together with related Alleluias, while the textless melodies were preserved in East Frankish margins and West Frankish sequentiaries; the textless melodies, however, continued to be sung at certain times and places, with related Alleluias, as untexted melismas. As the *melodiae longissimae*[4] became Sequence-with-text, particularly in the late tenth and eleventh centuries, an aesthetic metamorphosis began; the Sequence-with-text took on a more autonomous nature and could be used – indeed could be conceived – with no reference to the Alleluia, even if it remained irrevocably in close proximity with the latter. In some of the sequentiaries of the tenth and eleventh centuries, the original Sequences and the later melodies for Sequence-with-text are found side by side.

While I have arrived at the position articulated in this hypothesis largely through working with primary sources containing Sequences and with historical texts documenting the early history of the genre, my thought has been significantly influenced by the writings of Lori Kruckenberg[5] and David Hiley.[6] My position and much of what I develop in this study may seem at odds with the work of Richard Crocker;[7] some of it is. Yet one must keep in mind that, in the world of the ninth-century liturgy, particularly when dealing with the quixotic genres of the Alleluia and the Sequence, *x* and *y* may at times be compatible and at other times contradictory. My work is incalculably indebted to the lucid and persuasive writings of Richard Crocker; I could not have arrived at most of the present conclusions had I not wrestled with his positions on this subject for the past twenty years.

In this study I wish to reflect on my underlying position from the perspective of the Alleluia and its relation to the Sequence. To the best of my knowledge, the Sequence has not been approached from this perspective; scholars have rather always looked back at the Alleluia from the Sequence. Having read James McKinnon's discussion of the Alleluia in *The Advent Project*,[8] I am deeply impressed by the clarity with which he has explained the appearance of this liturgical genre in the Roman and Frankish liturgy during the later seventh, the eighth and ninth centuries. Essential to his view of the Alleluia is the appearance of a second psalm in the Latin Fore-Mass, modeled liturgically and musically on the Byzantine Alleluia-Alleluiarion, a psalm that formed a prelude to the Gospel.[9] Negatively stated, the Alleluia was not a response to a first (or second) reading, but an overture to the second lesson, namely the Gospel. Insofar as the development of the Alleluia occurred at a late stage in the development of the Roman Proper, the genre was extended through the liturgical year as a combination of individual melodies, on the one hand, and, on the other, of basic melodies adapted to a number of different verses and feast days. Moreover, the transmission of the repertory of Alleluias to the Franks seems to have occurred around the middle of the eighth century at a time when the basic repertory was not yet fixed by the Roman Schola Cantorum. Consequently much work toward fixing and filling out the repertory fell to the Frankish cantors.[10] In this study I shall examine manuscript evidence and liturgical circumstances that argue for a relation between the Alleluia as sung by these Frankish cantors and the coeval Sequence, sometimes cursorily discussing specific musical relations. A thorough examination of the musical relations implied in this study lies beyond the scope of the present essay, and will form a second chapter of this inquiry.

II. The Sources and Basic Data for Alleluia–Sequence Relation

The material that forms the basis of this study is found in the East (German) and West (French) Frankish Sequentiaries, the earliest of which date from the early tenth century. To confine this study to a manageable scope, I must omit consideration of the earliest sources containing the English repertory and the earliest non-Aquitanian West Frankish sources. Inclusion of these sources would not alter the basic argument of the study, indeed it would strengthen them; and these sources have been examined by David Hiley.[11]

East Frankish Repertory

An outline of the St. Gall tradition is found in Table 15.1 (all tables are at the end of the chapter). The basis of this Germanic tradition can be established with one manuscript, namely St. Gall, SB 484.[12] In this table I have assigned numbers to the melodies according to the order of their appearance in this source – all prefaced by the letter 'd'.[13] The strict order of the 'd-melodies' can be followed in the unindented boxes in the left-hand column of Table 15.1. I have further integrated the contents of the sequentiary of St. Gall, SB 381[14] into Table 15.1, likewise making note of the East Frankish 'versus ad sequentias'[15] recorded in this source. The order of Sequences in the two sources can be traced in the columns labeled '484' and '381', and the essential agreement of repertory and order between the two sources is consistently evident. I have added four Sequences under 'Other' at the end of Table 15.1; while these four melodies are not found in St. Gall 484 or St. Gall 381, they are found in sources only slightly later, and they seem appropriately associated with the early East Frankish repertoire.[16] The 'Liturgical' column of Table 15.1 documents the feasts associated with given melodies and texts of Sequences and their 'versus'. In the three columns on the right-hand side of Table 15.1, I have recorded the Alleluia Verses that identify Alleluias related to the *sequentiae*, and I have attempted to define the relations between Alleluia and Sequence. I shall subsequently discuss these columns in detail. Where no data are found in the three right-hand columns, one may assume that no clear relation to a given Alleluia melody exists.

Several aspects of the organization and character of this repertory should be noted:

1. The basic repertory unfolds according to the seasons of the liturgical year: the Christmas season begins with the Mass for Christmas day and progresses through the Purification to the Saturday before Septuagesima – after which no Sequences will be sung until Easter. The Paschal Season begins with Easter Sunday and progresses through the octave of Pentecost. Dominical Sequences for the weeks following Pentecost and an Advent cycle are notably absent in the East Frankish collections. A Common of Saints following the sanctoral cycle is almost as large as the sanctoral cycle itself.
2. The repertory of St. Gall 484, while it is organized according to liturgical principles, is efficiently ordered with no redundancy. Melodies of this repertory may occur two or more times in St. Gall 381 as the 'versus ad sequentias' reveal the specific feasts for which a Sequence is proper. For example, the melody IUSTUS UT PALMA MINOR falls as the first melody in the Proper of Saints in St. Gall 484, that is d29 – for St. John the Baptist; it is used nevertheless six times in St. Gall 381: for St. Stephen (no. 3 in St. Gall 381), for Holy Innocents (no. 10), with St. Gall 484 for John the Baptist (no. 44), for St. Eusebius (no. 48), for St. Gallus (no. 55), and for the Common of Martyrs (no. 71). In each case the Alleluia Verse 'Iustus ut palma' confirms that the Sequence is proper to the feast.
3. The early East Frankish repertory reveals certain archaic features. The octave of Christmas (d06 – CIGNEA) is dedicated to Mary, an ancient tradition that subsequently waned as the Marian feast in September gained in import.[17] The celebration of Trinity a week after Pentecost is not yet a part of the liturgy. The principal focus on the Trinity lies in

the feast of Epiphany (d07 – TRINITAS); one must recall that the first manifestation of the Trinity at Christ's baptism formed a central theme for the celebration of Epiphany.[18] Further Trinitarian themes are found in the octaves of both Epiphany and Pentecost,[19] themes that were traditional to those Sundays before the establishment of an independent feast of Trinity in subsequent centuries. Finally, Sequences for the season of Advent are absent from the Germanic tradition.

4 East Frankish sources assign names to all melodies. (I consistently print melody names as recorded in the sources with small capitals.) The Sequence melodies are sometimes identified by the incipit of an Alleluia Verse (these I have printed in small capitals in italics), and sometimes with names that may be somewhat fanciful – CONCORDIA, AMOENA, SYMPHONIA, etc. None of the early East Frankish melodies from St. Gall 484 and St. Gall 381 is designated with the incipit of a 'versus ad sequentias'. The first East Frankish Sequence – if it indeed is an East Frankish Sequence – named by the incipit of its text is BENEDICTA SEMPER, and even this melody is named TRINITAS in one later East Frankish source.[20]

West Frankish Repertory

While organization of the basic East Frankish repertory is relatively transparent and consistent – given the rather conservative nature of East Frankish liturgical custom – the organization of the West Frankish melodies presents almost insurmountable difficulties. Until now Crocker's dissertation has served as the principal – and invaluable – tool for making sense of the repertory.[21] In Table 15.2 I have tried to carry the organization a step further. No single West Frankish manuscript such as St. Gall 484 will serve to order this repertory. Nevertheless, by using the sequentiaries of Paris, BNF lat. 1118 and lat. 1084 much as I used the single East Frankish source, and by supplementing the repertory of these sources with that found in Paris, BNF lat. 909, lat. 1121, lat. 1137, and n. a. lat. 1871,[22] one can set out a repertory that unfolds in a strikingly similar manner to that found in St. Gall 484, yet vastly larger.

The following observations are central to grasping the import of Table 15.2:

1 The basic order of melodies conforms to Paris 1118 and Paris 1084, but for each souce I have given numbers that indicate the order of the melody in the individual sequentiary. Insofar as Paris 1084 actually offers two sequentiaries (or more), later numbers appear among the earlier numbers in the column recording its repertory.[23] Similarly, insofar as Paris 1121 contains a section of melodies 'no longer in use',[24] the numbering in the column for that source offers some odd series as the later series is integrated into the earlier. Yet given these anomalies, the progression of basic repertory among these seven sources is strikingly similar. In certain unstable periods of the liturgical calendar, for example the ending of the Paschal Season with the celebration of Trinity, I have followed the more consistent order of the later sources.

2 Like the East Frankish tradition, the melodies of Table 15.2 are ordered according to liturgical principles: a section of Advent melodies begins the

collections from the Eastern realm, followed by melodies for the Nativity and the Paschal Seasons. A rather extended Sanctorale ensues, with considerable weight given to St. Martial, particularly in the two codices copied by Adémar de Chabannes.[25] The Common is rather diminutive in the Western sources, while the collection of melodies for the Dedication is somewhat larger than its Eastern counterpart. The West Frankish sequentiaries all conclude with a collection of Sequences for the Sundays after Pentecost. I have assigned numbers to this repertory according to its liturgical order. An 'f' identifies the melodies as West Frankish or 'French', while 'a' signifies advent, 'c' nativity, 'p' Easter, 's' Sanctorale, 'sc' Common of Saints, 'dd' dedication and 'dm' dominical. The numbering of sanctoral melodies is according to the sanctoral calendar: fs0630, for example, signifies June 30, the feast day of St. Martial.

3 Like the East Frankish tradition, certain archaic traits are evident in the earlier sources (Paris 1084 and Paris 1118), but they seem to disappear in the second generation of manuscripts. A melody for Mary (fc45 – BEATA TU) – a Sequence related to the corresponding melody in the Germanic sources (d06 – CIGNEA) – is offered for the Octave of Christmas in Paris 1118 and Paris 1084, but the melody is not found in Paris 909, Paris 1121, Paris 887 or Paris 1137. In Paris n. a. lat. 1871 it has been moved to the Paschal season, where it fits liturgically because of its melodic incipit. Similarly, the celebration of Trinity on the Octave of Pentecost is not evident in Paris 1118 or Paris 1084, while the feast of Trinity follows Pentecost consistently in most of the later sources. Unlike the Eastern sources, no specific emphasis on the Trinity appears in the celebration of Epiphany or its octave.

4 Given the fact that no single manuscript serves as a stable record of West Frankish melodies, and given the variable and evolving nature of West Frankish sources, nine Sequence melodies emerge with two rather clearly defined liturgical positions in Table 15.2: fc45 or fp25; fc53 or fs0815b; fc73 or fp63; fc92 or fdd3; fc93 or fdd2; fp36 or fdm08; fp46 or fs1101a; fs0624c or fdm20; and fs0630f and fdm05. The melody BEATA TU (fc45) mentioned above, for example, is associated with the Nativity melodies in Paris 1118 and Paris 1084, but has been moved to the Paschal cycle in Paris n. a. lat. 1871 (fp25). Thus an identification number is assigned to both appearances of the melodies in the table, and each iteration is marked by 'cf.' with reference to the corresponding position.

5 The Sequences in the earlier West Frankish sources seem to have existed with no further designation than the 'alleluia' that served as 'text' for the opening of the melodies. The melodies found in Paris 1118 unfold with no names whatsoever. The cantor would simply have to know the musical or liturgical identity and usage of any given Sequence in this collection. The names of melodies in the first section of Paris 1084 were added in the margin by a later scribe. The frustratingly few names that occur in the vast repertory of Paris n. a. lat. 1871 were added by a later hand. When the melodies begin to be named in the later sections of Paris 1084 and in the second generation of manuscripts, the names are taken principally from

the incipits of Alleluia Verses *or* from the incipits of *prosae* that fit a given melody. A few names similar to those used in the Eastern sources are found, e.g., PLANCTUS BERTANAE and PASCHALIS ANTICA, but such appellations are exceptional.

The relationships between the East Frankish and West Frankish repertories are multivalent and complex, and become ever more difficult to reduce to simplistic parallels. Kruckenberg has defined a 'reception barrier' negating transmission of melodies and texts accross the Rhine during the period in which the sources in Tables 15.1 and 15.2 were compiled,[26] and no attempt has been made in the tables to reduce similar or related melodies to a single entity. While previous scholars have – with good cause – demonstrated the similarities between melodies such as CONCORDIA and EPIPHANIAM,[27] between CONCORDIA and ECCE VICIT,[28] between ROMANA and DIC NOBIS,[29] I have preserved the relative isolation of the two repertories in the above tables. I suggest that, given the reception barrier so convincingly demonstrated by Kruckenberg, relations between Sequence melodies and repertories was not lateral – that is, transmission across the Rhine during the tenth and eleventh centuries – but rather vertical, that is, transmission to both sides of the Rhine before the breakup of the Carolingian kingdom, and individuation of melodic tradition and repertory unfolded after erection of the barrier. While some of the differences in the melodies that occur in both repertories are subtle, many are substantial and even structural, and the basic melodies too often have to be bent – if not broken – when reduced to a single 'original version'.

Notker does indeed testify that a priest from west of the Rhine arrived in St. Gall with an antiphoner containing 'versus ad sequentias', but he considered the West Frankish 'versus' corrupt.[30] I suggest that the corruption of which Notker spoke may not have been in the Latinity of the West Frankish texts, but in the way the West Frankish texts fit his East Frankish versions of related melodies. The French texts 'notated' Notker's melodies incompetently, and thus he wrote new 'versus' to fasten his East Frankish melodies in his memory. Nevertheless, it is essential to recognize East and West Frankish iterations of particular melodies, for the related Sequence melodies often point to the same Alleluia melody. Table 15.3 records the related melodies that appear in Tables 15.1 and 15.2, and in the final tables of this essay the related melodies will be indicated by an approximate sign (≈).

III. Definitions of Alleluia–Sequence Relations

Three fundamental characteristics of the liturgical genre of Alleluia must be recognized before basic relations between Alleluia and Sequence can be defined: (1) a smaller number of melodies exists than the number of texts for Alleluia Verses, and any single Alleluia melody may be adapted to fit a plurality of texts; (2) a given text of an Alleluia Verse may be adapted to more than one Alleluia melody; (3) the liturgical assignment of both Alleluia Verse and Alleluia melody represents the most unstable aspect in the history of the Roman Gradual. The complex relation between texts and melodies of this genre has been thoroughly documented in Karl-Heinz Schlager's *Thematischer Katalog*; the 'S.' numbers offered in tables of this essay refer to the melodies as recorded in this catalog.[31] Schlager has established that about one hundred melodies were found in the manuscripts contemporaneous with the sources examined in this study, a set of melodies that belonged to the oldest standard repertory of the liturgical genre, or at least can be demonstrated to be trans-regional.[32] A cursory glance at Jean-René Hesbert's *Antiphonale missarum sextuplex* documents the instability of liturgical assignment of specific Alleluia Verse to feast – particularly in the later part of the liturgical year and in the sanctoral cycle. No other liturgical genre is designated with the words 'Quale volueris'.[33]

Three functional definitions of Alleluia–Sequence relation emerge in Tables 15.1 and 15.2:

1 Alleluia and Sequence share the same name or title, a designation derived from the incipit of the Alleluia Verse; an 'N' in the column entitled 'Definitions' designates this relation, and Sequences of this type may be easily recognized by the italics used in printing their names.

2 The melodic incipit of the Alleluia and Sequence is identical or strikingly similar; an 'M' under 'Definitions' designates this relation.[34]

3 When one Sequence is consistently assigned to a feast with a stable Alleluia melody and Verse (i.e., both melody and Verse are stable in a broad liturgical manuscript tradition), the liturgical position shared by Alleluia, Verse and Sequence on this feast at least *implies* a relation; this relation is indicated with a 'P'. But a definition of relation by liturgical position amounts to little more than a tautology, for Introits and Offertories, for example, are associated with the same feast by 'liturgical position'; nevertheless one claims no organic relation between Sequence and other liturgical genres, or between these genres with each other.[35] Thus merely a 'P' in the column noting definitions is insufficient to argue for a relation between a given Alleluia melody and a Sequence. Yet the Alleluia as liturgical musical genre is essentially different from other genres of Mass Propers, for Alleluia melodies are adapted to different texts and thus occur on different feasts, while each piece in other genres tends to represent an unicum and most appear only once during the liturgical cycle. Thus if the same Sequence and Alleluia melody – either, or both, sometimes with different texts – are sung together consistently on several feasts, the relation implied through liturgical position is strengthened; this consistency of association is indicated with a 'C'. I suggest that *consistent* association of an Alleluia melody – possible because of the unique character of Alleluia melodies in the liturgy – and Sequence through *liturgical position* creates a third definition of relation, a relation I name consistent liturgical association, and this category is marked with 'P+C' in Tables 15.1 and 15.2. Moreover, consistency of association between Alleluia and Sequence can strengthen and enlighten relations defined by name and melodic incipit.

Other aspects of Alleluia and Sequence might amplify or enlighten a relation between the two, for example, the text of the Sequence may be related exegetically to the text of the Alleluia Verse,[36] or the two may share some melodic fragment or function;[37] I indicate the presence of such aspects with an 'O'. No single definition excludes another definition; thus an Alleluia melody and a Sequence might be related by name, melodic incipit, liturgical position, consistent relation and some other relation. The more definitions of relations established in the column defining relations, the stronger the argument for a relation between Alleluia and Sequence.

The import and application of the three definitions become clearer if each is explicated in relation to Tables 15.1 and 15.2.

1. Name

The most obvious definition of relation between Alleluia and Sequence occurs when the Sequence is named after the Verse of an Alleluia. In such cases I do not question the relation if an obvious Alleluia Verse corresponds to the name of the Sequence. The first Sequence of Table 15.1 may serve as example, that is d01 or DIES SANCTIFICATUS. Richard Crocker questions the melodic relation between the melody DIES SANCTIFICATUS and the Alleluia with the same Verse.[38] While one could argue for a melodic relation, I have classified the melody with no 'M' in Table 15.1, yet this melody consistently occurs on feasts when Alleluia S. 27/28[39] occurs, thus the 'C' entered in Table 15.1. The melody is found again in the Sanctorale with the text *Christe sanctis unica* (*AH* 53: 150), a text that places the melody on the feast of St. Gall. In subsequent East Frankish sources DIES SANCTIFICATUS is used for feasts of particular saints, and on such occasions it would be paired with the same Alleluia melody, S. 27/28, but sung with the Verse 'Iustum deduxit' or 'Pretiosa est'.[40] The feast of Mary's nativity reveals DIES SANCTIFICATUS associated with the Virgin in the text *Summa stirpe genita* (*AH* 10: 17), in which iteration it would be sung with S. 27/28 and the Verse 'Beata est virgo'. Moreover, since I consider the structural alternation between *protus* and *tritus* pitches (for example, between D and F) a shared characteristic of both melodies, I have also placed an 'O' in the definition of relations.[41] I should point out that this Sequence represents the sole example of a melody named after an Alleluia Verse with no accompanying 'M'. The most consistent pattern in the repertory is found in the correspondence of Sequences named for an Alleluia and a melodic incipit of the Sequence with strong resemblance to the Alleluia melody.

2. Melodic Incipit

Identity of melodic incipit of a Sequence melody with an Alleluia incipit has been – up to the the present study – the principal, if not the sole criterion for defining a relation between the two genres. While this relation is empirical for a brief moment – sometimes very brief indeed – and it is musical, the application of this definition as the only criterion for relating Alleluia and Sequence remains an unproven assumption. When melodic relation is recorded along with other definitions, the relation itself is strengthened, on the one hand; but, on the other, the multiple nature of the Alleluia–Sequence relation is demonstrated through liturgical associations and other dimensions and should not be limited to melodic incipit.

An 'M' relation, for example, is easy to establish in a melody such as d38 (AUREA) in Table 15.1; the identity of incipit is clearly evident between Alleluia and Sequence, and a strongly related melody in the West Frankish repertory – fa12a (OSTENDE) – reconfirms the relation with a name for the Alleluia melody, although a different Verse would be sung with AUREA for the commemoration of an apostle. The relation between d36 (METENSIS MINOR) and Alleluia S. 26 offers a more challenging case. This Sequence is almost identical with the famous STANS A LONGE of the West Frankish tradition found in Table 15.2 as fp36 and fdm08, for the melody is used both in Paschaltide and in the Sundays after Pentecost. Example 15.1 offers Alleluia *Eripe me* with STANS A LONGE as recorded in Paris 1084 (fdm08). A series of five pitches that opens both pieces is identical (the *e* in brackets in the Sequence may be implied by the quilisma in Paris 1084, but most sources, both East and West, begin this melody with the pitches *C–D–D–F–D–E–D*). But melodic relation can be traced further than the opening pitches in this pair: the descending tetrachord – *G–F–E–D* – that opens the second distinction of the Sequence echoes a gesture from the Alleluia (see second system), and the ascending version of these same pitches that opens the third distinction of the Sequence likewise echoes a gesture from the Verse (fourth and third systems from the bottom).

In the Western repertory STANS A LONGE is found among both Easter and Dominical melodies.[42] Alleluia S. 26 is used in Paschaltide in Western sources with the Alleluia Verse 'Surrexit pastor bonus', thereby explaining the presence of the Sequence STANS A LONGE as a paschal melody (fp36). The same Alleluia melody is discovered in the dominical series with the Verse 'Eripe me', a text particularly appropriate to the lament of the Publican. In the Eastern tradition the melody METENSIS MINOR is associated with martyrs, a feast for which the assignment of Alleluia Verse is notably unstable. The Verse 'Eripe me' could function well in such a context, or one of the other Verses listed by Schlager for this melody may have been employed.[43] Thus the test of liturgical consistency strengthens and elucidates the relation of this particular pair, first associated because of similar melodic incipits.[44]

3. Consistent Liturgical Association

When discussing the liturgical placement of Alleluias and the use of basic melodies that were adapted to different texts, McKinnon highlights the extensive use of the melody 'Dies sanctificatus' – or S. 27/28 – during Christmastide.[45] This melody is used for the Mass of the day on Christmas with the Verse 'Dies sanctificatus', on the next day – Feast of St. Stephen – with the Verse 'Video caelos', on the following day – feast of St. John the Evangelist – with the Verse 'Hic est discipulus', and finally for Epiphany with the Verse 'Vidimus stellam'. These texts – with the 'Dies sanctificatus' melody – are among the most stable Alleluias for the entire liturgical year. Thus when a Sequence occurs on one of these days that exhibits neither the name of the

Ex. 15.1 Alleluia *Eripe me* compared with the Sequence melody STANS A LONGE (Paris, BNF lat. 1084, fols. 192v, 212v)

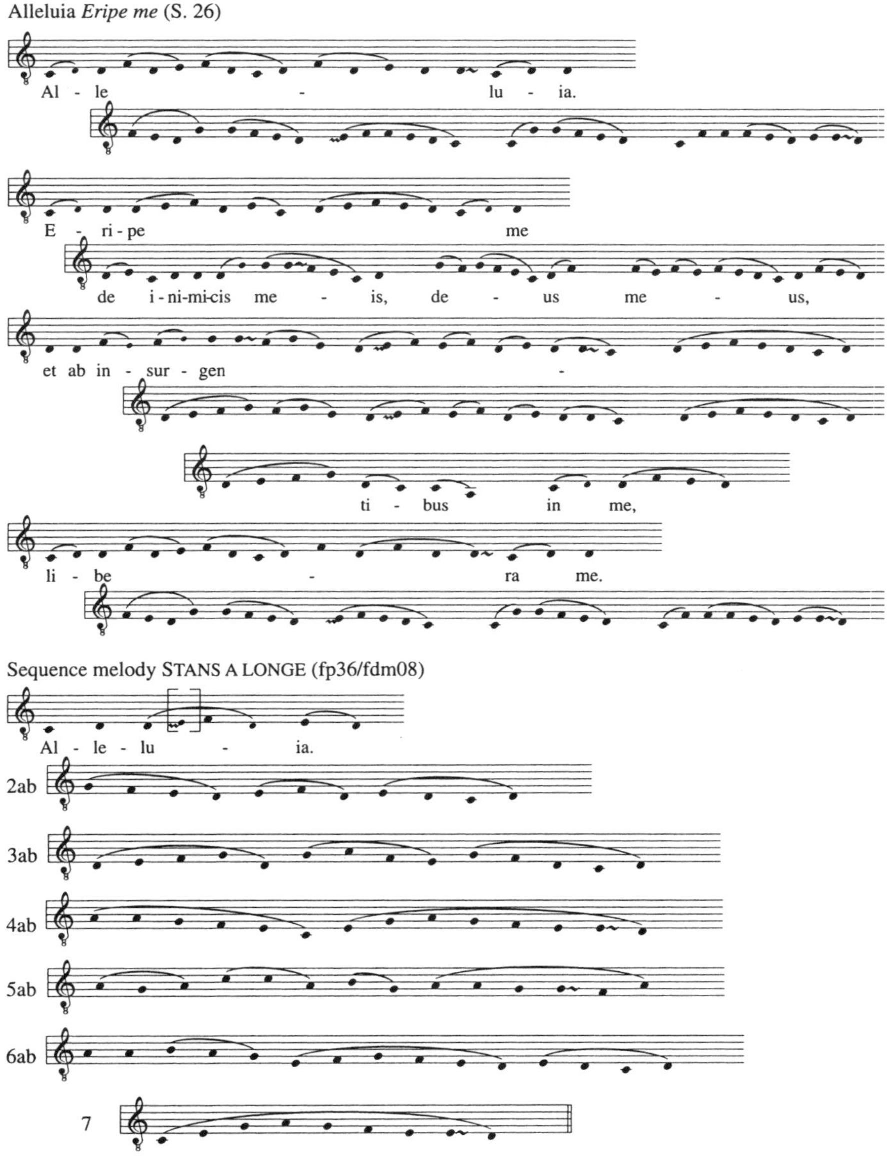

Alleluia Verse nor the exact melodic incipit, I suggest that we should nevertheless consider a possible relation and test that relation with the principle of liturgical consistency. In Table 15.1 I have suggested that the melody CONCORDIA may be associated with Alleluia S. 27/28, with the Verse 'Video caelos', and that ROMANA may be associated with S. 27/28, with the Verse 'Hic est discipulus'. The principle of liturgical consistency reinforces these associations, for in the repertory of Table 15.1 CONCORDIA is also associated with the feast of Peter and Paul, a feast for which the Verse 'Tu est Petrus' is sung to the same Alleluia melody (S. 27/28). Similarly, ROMANA is also associated with the feast of St. Lawrence, a feast for which the Verses 'Pretiosa est' or 'Iustum deduxit' are appropriate; both are sung to melody S. 27/28. The settings of these melodies in subsequent East Frankish sources continue convincingly to confirm the association of CONCORDIA and ROMANA with the melody McKinnon calls 'Dies sanctificatus'. Moreover, these associations can be extended into the Western Frankish repertory: ECCE VICIT (Table 15.2 – fp37) and EPIPHANIAM (Table 15.2 – fc81) exhibit strong kinship with CONCORDIA,[46] and they would be associated with Alleluia 'Dies sanctificatus' through the Verses 'Redemptionem missit dominus' for the Paschal season and 'Vidimus stellam' for Epiphany, both of which are sung to melody S. 27/28; the West Frankish Sequence named CLARA GAUDIA or DIC NOBIS (Table 15.2 – fp33) – texts associated with Paschaltide – shows clear kinship with the East Frankish ROMANA,[47] and it would be again associated with Alleluia 'Dies sanctificatus' through the Verse 'Redemptionem missit dominus'.

Moreover, basic musical features of these melodies resonate with each other when Alleluia and Sequence melodies are sung in association. I have already mentioned the strong impression made by the alternation of *protus* and *tritus* pitches in this Alleluia, and the same pitches assume crucial functions in these two Sequences. Moreover, these Sequence melodies (*and* NATUS ANTE SAECULA) exhibit a rather constricted musical character when compared with other Sequence melodies, a character wholly consistent with Alleluia 'Dies sanctificatus'. I offer the association of Alleluia S. 27/28 with ROMANA in Ex. 15.2. The opening distinction of the Sequence elaborates the basic pitches of the Alleluia – with particular emphasis on the *protus* and *tritus D* and *F* – before moving to *G* as a new final. But as the melody unfolds pitches related to *G*, the *protus–tritus* functions are transposed to *G* and *b*♭, a tonal quality that becomes particularly clear from the sixth distinction forward. The tonal realm of this melody is thus constructed around two conjunct tetrachords, *D–E–F–G* in the opening distinction, then *G–a–b*♭*–c* in the remainder of the melody. The gesture that opens the seventh and final distinction – *F–G–b*♭–G – hauntingly resonates with the same gesture in the middle of the Alleluia written on *C–D–F–D*. One should not be surprised that a new final is established in the Sequence, for tonal expansion and the establishment of a new tonic are musical principles employed repeatedly in this repertory.

McKinnon sees a pattern similar to the use of 'Dies sanctificatus' during Christmastide in the use of the melody 'Excita' for Ascension and Pentecost.[48] The Alleluia Verse 'Ascendit deus' is sung as the first Alleluia for Ascension

Ex. 15.2 Alleluia *Dies sanctificatus* (MMMA 7) with the Sequence melody ROMANA (d04; Graz, UB 17, fol. 272^v, adjusted from St. Gall, SB 484 and 381)

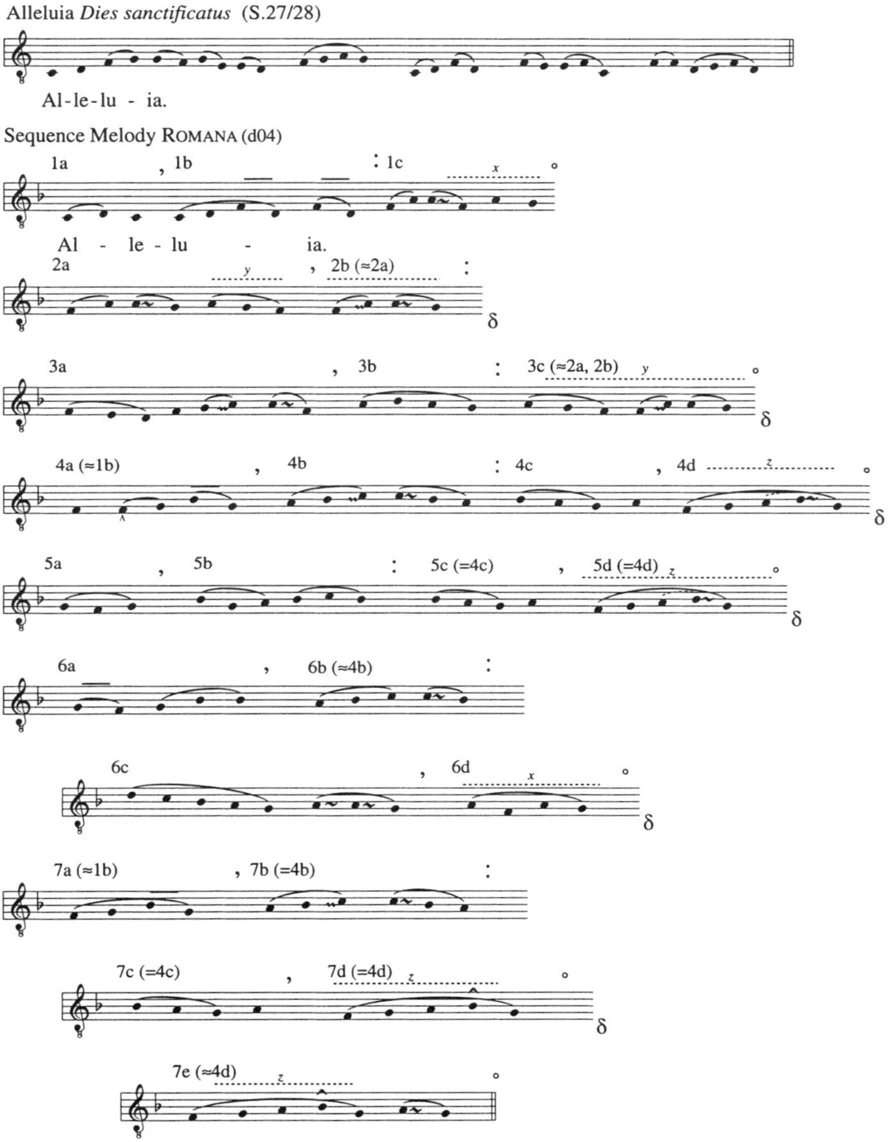

to 'Excita domine potentiam tuam' (Alleluia S. 205), and the same melody is sung as the first Alleluia for Pentecost with the Verse 'Emitte spiritum tuum'. An interesting pattern of association emerges if one compares the Alleluia melody with the Sequence repertory. REX OMNIPOTENS (Table 15.2 – fp51) is the Sequence consistently associated with Ascension in the West, while the related melody OCCIDENTANA (Table 15.1 – d28) is associated with the feast of Pentecost in the East. Thus these related Sequence melodies are in turn associated with Alleluia S. 205 by liturgical position, and the association proves consistent with the Alleluia melody on different feasts, but with different Verses. The pronounced effect of *protus* tonality in the middle of these Sequences – built on *G* but unfolding with a *b*♭ in the tetrachord above – forms a resonance with the *deuterus* Alleluia melody that is sung with a set of pitches exhibiting the same quality and function, and again with a *b*♭. A significant set of Sequence melodies associated with *deuterus* Alleluias are written on *G* with *b*♭s in numerous sources,[49] and the tonal functions within these Sequences and associated Alleluias should be further explored. These pairs include GRAECA (d16) with S. 205, AMOENA (d19) with S. 186,[50] CAPTIVA (d25) with S. 205, and OCCIDENTANA (d28) or REX OMNIPOTENS (fp51) with S. 205. The tonal space, pitch collections and structural aspects used in these Alleluias and Sequences merit a thorough study in themselves.

I have used three principal means of defining relations between Alleluia and Sequence: name, melodic incipit and consistent liturgical association. I have tested these criteria against each other, and I have tested them all with the criteria of liturgical consistency and with the category called 'other'. The first two definitions – name and melodic incipit – are clearly more empirical, the third, consistent liturgical association, more circumstantial. Nevertheless the quantity of evidence that accrues under the third definition makes it at least moderately persuasive in most cases, and wholly convincing in others.[51] I am hesitant to suggest a relation between Alleluia and Sequence that cannot be justified by name, melodic incipit or consistent liturgical association. Thus I omit, for example, the association of MATER with Alleluia S. 274 that I suggested in an earlier publication;[52] I have not changed my mind, but the underlying criteria for suggesting that relation are not as rigorous as those I have developed in this study.

The basic numbers that emerge from Tables 15.1 and 15.2 reveal quantitative evidence concerning the relation of Alleluia and Sequence. In the East Frankish repertory – a repertory of fifty Sequences – twenty-one Sequences are named according to one or more Alleluia Verses, while twenty-six Verses are cited in the naming of Sequences.[53] In this repertory seven further Sequences are associated with an Alleluia by melodic incipit, while relation of Alleluia and Sequence is suggested by consistent liturgical association in eleven instances. Thus thirty-three of fifty melodies of the East Frankish repertory – approximately two-thirds – are associated with Alleluias using the tougher principles of name and melodic incipit; forty-four of fifty – approximately four-fifths – are related if the criterion of consistent liturgical association is accepted. In the West Frankish repertory – a repertory of 142 melodies – sixty-four Sequences are named according to one or more Alleluia

Verses, while only fifty-three Verses are cited in the naming the Sequences.[54] In this repertory thirty-three melodies are associated with an Alleluia by melodic incipit, while association of Alleluia and Sequence is suggested by consistent liturgical association in six instances. Thus eighty-six of 141 melodies of the West Frankish repertory – slightly less than two-thirds – are associated with Alleluias using the tougher principles of name and melodic incipit; while almost exactly two-thirds are related if those related through liturgical placement are added. A fundamental conclusion seems obvious: a major portion – approximately two-thirds – of the Sequences found in Eastern and Western Frankish sources are related to Alleluias.

IV. From Alleluia to Sequence

Having examined the primary sources of Sequence melodies and explained criteria for defining relations between Sequence and Alleluia, I must return to one of the central objectives of this essay, namely to look at the Sequence from the perspective of the Alleluia. Tables 15.4 and 15.5 thus take the Alleluia Verses from Tables 15.1 and 15.2 and compile a list of Alleluias organized by Verse and melody number. Most Verses listed in Table 15.4 are associated with only one Sequence melody, and most of the Alleluia melodies listed in the table are sung with only one given Verse. In other words, most Alleluias listed in Table 15.4 are among those McKinnon would describe as being 'individual' melodies.[55] Nevertheless, many Verses listed in Table 15.4 are followed by a reference to Table 15.5, a table devoted to Alleluias, the melodies of which are adapted to a multiplicity of Verses or sung on a multiplicity of feasts; thus the order of Table 15.5 follows the order of Schlager's thematic catalogue. But what are the liturgical, historical, musical and aesthetic implications implicit in the list of Alleluias with reference to Sequences? Let us address these questions in order:

1. Liturgical Implications

A tenth- or eleventh-century cantor familiar with one of these repertories could sing a Sequence with any of the considerable number of Alleluias listed in Table 15.4. The eighty-three Verses sung to fifty-six melodies recorded in the table reveal a substantial repertory of Alleluias that could have been paired with specific Sequences in the tenth and eleventh centuries. Because the Sequence was sung during Advent in the Western realm, and because the repertory in the West was in itself more expansive, the Aquitanian cantor would have had more opportunity to sing the Alleluia–versus–Sequence triptych than his south German contemporary. Nevertheless even the Eastern cantor was by no means significantly limited in his opportunities to perform the extended three-part prelude to the Gospel that was unified in concept and liturgical function.

An important liturgical and musical principle emerges from Tables 15.4 and 15.5: *Those Alleluia melodies that are most often sung during the liturgical year tend to be associated with a plurality of Sequence melodies.* Thus the Sequence becomes a means of individuating the moment immediately prior to the reading of the Gospel when an often-used Alleluia melody is sung. 'Alleluia, Iustus ut palma', S. 38 in Table 15.5, for example, is sung often throughout the sanctoral cycle; two melodies serve to individuate these iterations in the East, while four melodies serve that function in the West. Yet it is in consideration of McKinnon's three basic Alleluia melodies – Dies sanctificatus (S. 27/28), Excita (S. 205) and Ostende (S. 271)[56] – that the use of the Sequence to individuate the Alleluia is most notable, for these three Alleluias are associated with more Sequences than any others in Tables 15.4 and 15.5. 'Alleluia, Dies sanctificatus' – S. 27/28 (Table 15.5) – would unfold at St. Gall as follows: on Christmas it would be sung with DIES SANCTIFICATUS (d01), on December 26 (St. Stephen) it could be sung with CONCORDIA (d02) or ΥΠΠΩΔΙΑΚΟΝΙCCA (d03), on December 27 (St. John Evangelist) it would be sung with ROMANA (d04), for Tuesday in Easter Week it would be sung with OBTULERUNT/PRETIOSA EST (d15), on June 29 (Sts. Peter and Paul) it would be sung again with CONCORDIA (d02), then on July 10 (St. Lawrence) it would be sung again with ROMANA (d04), and for various feasts of a martyr it would be sung again with OBTULERUNT/PRETIOSA EST (d15). The variety of Sequences associated with McKinnon's 'Dies sanctificatus' clearly make the Alleluia melody 'Dies sanctificatus' more 'proper' as it recurs on different feasts.

2. Historical Implications

A basic tenet of McKinnon's exposition of the Alleluia lies in his argument that the oldest repertory of Alleluias is that defined by the Verses recorded in Rome, BAV Vat. lat. 5319.[57] This repertory, although incomplete at the time, was transmitted to the Frankish cantors in the mid-eighth century, and the Northern cantors then expanded and completed the repertory. The early Frankish repertory can be discerned from the Verses listed in the earliest Frankish graduals, or in Hesbert's *Antiphonale sextuplex*. Thus in Tables 15.4 and 15.5 I have placed an 'RM' (for 'Rome') under annotations for those Alleluia Verses found in Vat. lat. 5319, and I have placed an 'SX' for those Verses found in *Antiphonale sextuplex*. I do not wish to use these annotations as a knife to carve an inflexible argument for chronology, but a consideration of chronological implications of Sequences *with* associated Alleluias may prove rather fruitful. The six Alleluias cited in the Mont-Blandin gradual as having *sequentiae*, for example, are all marked with both 'RM' and 'SX.' One can recognize these Alleluias easily in Tables 15.4 and 15.5, for they are marked 'c/s' after 'SX' in each case. As already argued by Crocker, these are in all likelihood among the earliest of Sequences.[58] Of these six, five are marked with 'Kohrs' plus a number, indicating that they are among those Sequences classified as 'asymmetrical' and edited by Klaus Heinrich Kohrs.[59]

At this point I must express a certain discomfort with the classification 'aparallel' as a species of Sequence, particularly when that classification is further described as 'jubilus-replacement'.[60] 'Aparallel' was obviously not a criterion for classifying melodies among the cantors who assembled the early East and West Frankish sequentiaries, for melodies now called 'aparallel' or 'asymmetrical' are found side by side 'parallel' and 'symmetrical' melodies. I find many symmetrical elements in those Sequences classified as 'asymmetrical', and I think the notion of 'asymmetry' led Dreves to some incompetent editions of four texts associated with the melody CONFITEMINI (fp11) – the melody sung at the Paschal vigil and also known through Kenneth Levy's study of 'Lux de luce'.[61] It seems to me that 'asymmetrical' elements in Sequences represent a stylistic continuum rather than a clearly defined subset, and it is often difficult to establish a boundary for this stylistic element that would define a species within the genre. Is AMOENA symmetrical? Is GRAECA symmetrical? In these melodies and many others one finds prominent asymmetrical elements, yet for some reason they have not been discussed as 'asymmetrical' or 'aparallel' and 'early' Sequences by Crocker and Kohrs.[62] Both, incidentally, are annotated with 'RM' and 'SX' in Table 15.5 (see S. 186 and S. 205). Moreover, repetition forming symmetry represents one of the most unstable elements in the transmission of Sequence melodies. I think the association of a Sequence melody with an Alleluia among the Roman and/or early Frankish repertory forms a considerably stronger criterion for posing questions of possible antiquity and chronology.

Many of the Alleluias associated with the dominical Sequences are among McKinnon's earliest layer of Alleluias (those marked with RM), as are the melodies McKinnon designated with the names 'Dies sanctificatus', 'Excita' and 'Ostende'. I suggest that we might venture the hypothesis that the earliest Sequences are found among those associated with these Alleluia melodies, and that some of these Sequence melodies *may* even have been brought to the Franks from Rome with their corresponding Alleluias. Amalarius, only a few decades after the six Alleluias of the Mont-Blandin Gradual were recorded as being sung 'cum sequentia', described the Alleluias of the Roman vespers as having been sung 'with the eminence of verses and sequences' – 'cum . . . excellentia versuum et sequentiarum'.[63] Then we might hypothesize that the Sequences based on the Alleluias of McKinnon's second layer, those annotated with 'SX' but not with 'RM', represent melodies composed by that first generation of Frankish cantors who received the Roman Proper and filled out the series of Alleluias. Finally, we might conjecture that those melodies associated with Alleluias that are found in neither the Roman source nor the earliest Frankish graduals represent later – perhaps ninth-century – compositions of the Franks. In short, the consideration of the Alleluia with which a Sequence is associated might yield very significant evidence concerning the temporal and chronological origins of the Sequence.

3. Musical Implications

A ninth-century gloss on Martianus Capella explains a form of music that is totally independent of words for its signification, a form in which pitches related with other pitches through a rational structure establish the basis of the concept *harmonica.* The gloss concludes with the phrase 'ut sequentiae apud cantores', *as Sequences are among cantors*.[64] While a Sequence might begin with a quotation of an Alleluia, and while it might individuate an Alleluia for a particular feast, the musical matter of the Sequence is not limited by the Alleluia. Much work remains to be done on the nature of the musical relation between Alleluia and Sequence, but based on the multiple *sequentiae* associated with single Alleluia melodies in Table 15.4, one can affirm that the Sequence is not a mere appendage to the Alleluia, that is it not a mere 'variation' on the Alleluia – above all, it is not a 'trope' on the Alleluia. Sometimes a Sequence might repeat a motive or phrase from an Alleluia other than the melodic incipit, as we witnessed in STANS A LONGE in Ex. 15.1, or as one finds so clearly in VOX EXULTATIONIS.[65] But the Alleluias associated with these two melodies are not from McKinnon's first two layers of Alleluias, and I suggest that such obvious 'quotation' might represent a later procedure. Such 'quotation' seems indeed rare among melodies from the first two layers. We have already noted that the Sequence often expands the tonal realm of that defined by the Alleluia, and that a new final is often established in the Sequence. The Sequence, as it iterates repetitions of distinctions and plays with motivic entities, sometimes even offering repetitions within repetitions, reveals tonal functions and qualities as does no other form of liturgical song. I find the tonal dimension of the Sequence to represent the most definitive musical quality of the genre, particularly when viewed from the perspective of the Alleluia. But we have not yet heard and examined many of the melodies listed in Tables 15.1 and 15.2; we will probably never be able to recover several of them. Yet by listening to and reconsidering Alleluias together with their associated Sequences, we may gain new insights into the purely musical elements not only of Alleluia and Sequence, but of the repertory of plainchant as a whole. The musical structures of these melodies, enlightened by the ninth-century gloss on Martianus Capella, might lead us to describe the Sequence as the closest manifestation of *absolute music* found in the Middle Ages.

4. Aesthetic Implications

Amalarius described the Sequence as a 'iubilatio' that leads us to a higher mental realm where words are no longer necessary, where intellect reveals the intellectual to itself in its own terms.

> Haec iubilatio, quam cantores sequentiam vocant, illum statum ad mentem nostram ducit, quando non erit necessaria locutio verborum, sed sola cogitatione mens menti monstrabit quod retinet in se.[66]

McKinnon – toward the end of his study 'The Patristic Jubilus and the Alleluia of the Mass' – demonstrates that this description is ultimately rooted in the thought of Augustine.[67] The most Platonic of patristic writers considered this state of mind a higher plane in the ascent to contemplating the Divine than thought or discourse limited by words. By placing the Sequence – pure musical structure unfettered by words – after the Verse of the Alleluia, the mind of the cantor and the listener rises to a higher level of contemplation, a level from which one can, ironically, return to words – but now to the words of the highest verbal signification, that is the Gospel. The ecstatic character of the Sequence is largely determined by its position in the Mass between Alleluia and Gospel, and by the fundamentally Platonic ontology forming a hierarchy of knowing and being. This essential character of the genre remains even after the Sequence becomes the Sequence-with-text, for the texts almost invariably conclude with an 'ascent' from the realm of time to that of eternity.[68]

Yet Amalarius' description cuts both ways: the 'iubilatio' is both a part of the Alleluia and a step away from it – or a step above it. One of Richard Crocker's greatest contributions to our dialog concerning the Sequence is his criticism of the tendency to reduce the Sequence to a trope on the Alleluia – a mere appendage – and thereby to diminish its artistic integrity and significance. In reaffirming the relation between many Sequences and the Alleluia, I would by no means reduce the Sequence to a 'trope', or, even worse, to a 'liturgical accretion'. I am even uncomfortable with the term 'neuer Ansatz' introduced by Andreas Haug as a more neutral description of liturgical developments in the ninth century.[69] While I find it difficult to consider any work of medieval art an autonomous entity, and while I am uneasy with the notion of a 'creative leap',[70] I would reaffirm that the genre of Sequence remains *sui generis*, even when considered from the perspective of the Alleluia, especially when one considers its esthetic function between Alleluia Verse and Gospel. Nevertheless, I find it essential to approach the genre with the relation between Alleluia and Sequence bearing significant import, particularly when that liturgical and musical relation can be established with a degree of certainty. Only then can we come to a fuller understanding of the liturgical, the historical, the musical and the aesthetic dimensions of this complex but sublime genre.

I was tempted to conclude this essay with the above sentence, but such a rhetorical *Schlußfigur* would be misleading. Many questions and problems remain. I, like Richard Crocker, am puzzled by the celebration of Mary on the octave of Christmas with the Alleluia melody for 'Pascha nostrum' (S. 346),[71] a tradition that we can trace on both sides of the reception barrier in the French melody BEATA TU (fc45) and the German melody CIGNEA (d06). I can find no Verse used with that Alleluia melody that would be appropriate to the Blessed Virgin or the feast of Circumcision. Similarly, while I can justify the presence of the theme of the Trinity on Epiphany, I am troubled that no Sequence for 'Vidimus stellam' (S. 27/28) is found in the East Frankish tradition. Liturgical and musical questions such as these persist where question marks are found in the four tables. There remain, furthermore, the numerous Sequences in Tables 15.1 and 15.2 for which I can suggest no Alleluia. Some of these may be subsequently discovered, but pieces like ALMA CHORUS (fdm24) in the West and VENI SPIRITUS AETERNORUM (dd03) in the East seem independent on both textual and musical grounds from any Alleluia.[72] How do these seemingly autonomous creations relate to the contemporaneous members of the genre that were created in relation to an extant Alleluia and Verse? What are the three pieces that seem to be taken from the repertory of Offertory verses doing at the end of the Sequence collection of St. Gall 381 written with 'alleluia' as the first word and given melody titles like the Sequences in the same collection?[73] Why does the melody CONFITEMINI (fp11) – more familiarly known as 'Lux de luce' – reappear in an Offertory verse, even with a prosula?[74] I can empathize with Crocker's treatment of the relation between Alleluia and Sequence with such skepticism, and I can understand why he ultimately considered the two liturgical genres rather distant and distinct. I offer this study not as a refutation, but rather as a counter-balance to his position. The evidence of name, melodic incipit and consistent liturgical association I have compiled, even in the face of persistent, unanswered questions, has convinced me that some significant relation existed between Alleluia and Sequence in the eighth and ninth centuries, and I consider that relation worthy of serious exploration.

Table 15.1 The East Frankish (St. Gall) tradition

Mel. ID	*Title*	*484*	*381*	*Versus ad sequentias*	*Liturgical*	*Definitions*	*All. ID*	*Verse*
Tempus Nativitatis								
d01	*DIES SANCTIFICATUS*	1	1	Natus ante saecula	In nat. dni. iii	N P C O	S. 27	Dies sanctificatus
d43	EIA TURMA		2	Eia recolamus	In nat. dni.	P + C O	S. 382	Adorabo
d29	*IUSTUS UT PALMA* MINOR		3	Festa Stephani	S. Stephanus	N M C	S. 38	Iustus ut palma
d02	CONCORDIA	2	4	Hanc concordi	S. Stephanus	P + C O	S. 27	Video caelos
d03	YΠΠΩΔYAKONNYCCA	3	5	Xpi dni militis	S. Stephanus	M P C	S. 27	Video caelos
d03	YΠΠΩΔYAKONNYCCA		6	Protomartyr dni	S. Stephanus	M P C	S. 27	Video caelos
d04	ROMANA	4	7	Iohannes Ihu Xpo	S. Johannes ev.	P + C O	S. 27	Hic est discipulus
d05	*IUSTUS UT PALMA* MAIOR	5	8	Laus . . . sapit	Ss. Innocentes	N M	S. 38	Iustus ut palma
d41	*TE MARTYRUM*		9	Laus . . . humilis	Ss. Innocentes	N M	S. 397	Te martyrum
d29	*IUSTUS UT PALMA* MINOR		10	Salvete agni	Ss. Innocentes	N M	S. 38	Iustus ut palma
d19	AMOENA		11	Blandis vocibus	Ss. Innocentes	P + C O	S. 186	Laudate pueri
d26	VIRGUNCULA CLARA		12	Laus . . . hodie	Ss. Innocentes	M	S. 271	Confitebuntur caeli
d42	*MIRABILIS DEUS*		13	Laus . . . ds omnip.	Ss. Innocentes	N M	S. 128	Mirabilis deus
d06	CIGNEA	6	14	Gaude Maria	In oct. dni.	M	S. 346	?
d07	TRINITAS	7	15	Festa Christi	Epiphania	M	S. 302	Benedictus es
d08	PLANCTUS STERILIS	8	16	Iste dies celebris	In oct. epiph.	M	S. 302	Benedictus es
d10	SYMPHONIA		17	Hunc diem cel.	In oct. epiph.	P + C O	S. 382	Adorabo
d09	FILIA MATRIS	9	18	Virginis venerandae	De una virgine [S. Agneta]	M C	S. 350	Quinque prudentes
d10	SYMPHONIA	10	19	Concentu parili	In purif. bMv	P + C O	S. 382	Adorabo ad templum
d37	*BEATUS VIR QUI SUFFERT*		20	O Blasi dilecte	S. Blasius	N M	S. 62	Beatus vir qui suffert
d11	NOSTRA TUBA	11	21	Nostra tuba	Sabb. ante lxx	M O	S. 34	Dominus regnavit

Table 15.1 (continued)

Mel. ID	*Title*	*484*	*381*	*Versus ad sequentias*	*Liturgical*	*Definitions*	*All.* ID	*Verse*
Tempus Paschale								
d13	MATER		22	Laudes Xpo red.	In resurr. dni	O	S. 274	
d12	FRIGDOLA	12	23	Laudes salvatori	Dom. paschae	P C	S. 346	Pascha nostrum
d13	MATER[a]	13	24	Pangamus creatoris	Dom. paschae	O	S. 274	
d14	*DNS REGNAVIT*	14	25	Is qui prius	Feria ii	N M	S. 34	Dominus regnavit
d15	*OBTULERUNT*	15	26	Christe domine	Feria iii	N M	S. 27	Obtulerunt
	PRETIOSA EST							
	REDEMPTIONEM MISIT							
d16	GRECA	16	27	Agni paschalis	Feria iiii	P C O	S. 205	Lauda Ierusalem
d17	DUO TRES	17	28	Grates salvatori	Feria v	P C O	S. 347	Dicite in gentibus
d18	ORGANA	18	29	Laudes deo	Feria vi	P O	S. 123	Eduxit dominus
d19	PASCHA	19	30	Carmen suo	Sabbato	P C O	S. 186	Laudate pueri
	AMOENA							
d20	VIRGO PLORANS	20	31	Haec est sancta	In oct. paschae	P C O	S. 271	Haec dies
d21	*DEUS IUDEX IUSTUS*	21	32	Iudicem nos	Dom i post oct.	N M	S. 288	Deus iudex iustus
d22	*IN TE DOMINE*	22	33	Laus tibi sit	Dom ii post oct.	N M	S. 211	In te domine
d23	*QUI TIMENT DNM*	23	34	En regnator	Dom iii post oct.	N M	S. 121	Qui timent dominum
	OMNES GENTES						S. 144	Omnes gentes
d24	*EXULTATE DEO*	24	35	Laeta mente	Dom iv post oct.	N M	S. 377	Exsultate deo
d20	VIRGO PLORANS		36	Haec est sancta	De crucis invent.	P C O	S. 271	
d25	CAPTIVA	25	37	Summi triumphum	In ascens. dni.	P O	S. 205	Ascendit deus
d26	*DNS IN SYNA*							
	NIMIS HONORATI SUNT							
	VIRGUNCULA CLARA	26	38	Christus hunc diem	In ascens. dni	N M	S. 271	Dominus in Sina
d27	*CONFITEMINI*	27	39	O quam mira sunt	Dom. post asc.	N M	S. 58	Confitemini . . . et invocate
d40	METENSIS MAIOR		40	Nos Gordiani	Ss. Gordianus, etc.	O	S. 26	(from MET. MINOR?)
d10	SYMPHONIA		41	Summis conatibus	S. Desiderius	P O	S. 382	Adorabo
d28	OCCIDENTANA	28	42	Sci sps adsit	Pentecost	P C O	S. 205	Emitte Spm tuum
d08	PLANCTUS STERILIS		43	Benedicto gratias deo	In oct. Pentecost	M ?	S. 302	Benedictus es

Table 15.1 (continued)

Mel. ID	*Title*	*484*	*381*	*Versus ad sequentias*	*Liturgical*	*Definitions*					*All.* ID	*Verse*
Sanctorale												
d29	*Iustus ut palma* minor	29	44	Sancti Baptistae	S. Johannes Bapt.	N	M				S. 38	Iustus ut palma
d02	Concordia		45	Petre summe	Ss. Petrus & Paulus			P	C	O	S. 27	Tu es Petrus
d19	Pascha		46	Laudes deo perenni	S. Afra			P	C	O	S. 186	Laudate pueri
d04	Romana		47	Laurenti David	S. Laurentius			P	C	O	S. 27	Pretiosa est? Iustum deduxit?
d29	*Iustus ut palma* minor		48	Rex regum deus	S. Eusebius	N	M				S. 38	Iustus ut palma
d13	Mater		49	Congaudent	In assump bMv					O	S. 274	
d30	*Adducentur Veni dne* Dulcedine paradisi	30	50	Stirpe Maria	In nat. bMv	N	M				S. 203	Adducentur regi
d39	Puella turbata		51	Ecce solemnis	In nat. bMv							
d16	Graeca		52	Magnum te	S. Michaelis			P	C	O	S. 205	Laudate deum omnes angeli
d31	*Laudate deum Excita*	31	53	Angelorum ordo sacer	S. Michaelis	N	M				S. 205	Laudate dominum
d36	Metensis minor		54	Sancti belli	S. Mauricius		M		C	O	S. 26	Eripe me?
d29	*Iustus ut palma* minor		55	Dilecto deo	S. Gallus	N	M				S. 38	Iustus ut palma
d01	*Dies sanctificatus*		56	Christe sanctis unica	S. Gallus	N		P	C	O	S. 27	Iustum deduxit or: Pretiosa est
d32	*Laetatus sum*	32	57	Psallat ecclesia	In ded. ecclesiae	N	M				S. 113	Laetatus sum
d33	*Adorabo*	33	58	Tu civium deus	In ded. ecclesiae	N	M				S. 382	Adorabo
d34	*Vox exsultationis*	34	59	Omnes sancti	Omni sancti	N	M				S. 223	Vox exsultationis
d36	Metensis minor		60	Pangat ymnum	S. Ianuarius		M		C	O	S. 26	Eripe me?
d35	*Beatus vir qui timet*	35	61	Sacerdotem Xpi	S. Martinus	N	M				S. 227	Beatus vir qui timet
d05	*Iustus ut palma* maior		62	Tuba nostrae	S. Martinus	N	M				S. 38	Iustus ut palma
d36	Metensis minor	36	63	Laude dignum	S. Otmarus		M		C	O	S. 26	Eripe me?
d37	*Beatus vir qui suffert*	37	64	A solis occasu	S. Columbanus	N	M				S. 62	Beatus vir qui suffert
d26	*Nimis honorati sunt*		65	Deus in tua	S. Andreas	N	M				S. 271	Nimis honorati sunt

Table 15.1 (continued)

Mel. ID	*Title*	*484*	*381*	*Versus ad sequentias*	*Liturgical*	*Definitions*	*All.* ID	*Verse*
Commune sanctorum								
d38	AUREA	38	66	Clare sanctorum	In nat apost.	M	S. 271	Nimis honorati sunt
d34	*VOX EXSULTATIONIS*		67	Agone triumphali	In nat. martyrum	N M	S. 223	Vox exsultationis
d17	DUO TRES		68	Tubam bellicosam	In nat. martyrum		S. 347	Gloria et honore
d20	VIRGO PLORANS		69	Quid tu virgo	De uno martyre	P C O	S. 271	Iustum deduxit?
d15	*PRETIOSA EST*		70	Miles inclite	De uno martyre		S. 27	Pretiosa est
d29	*IUSTUS UT PALMA* MINOR		71	Rex regum deus	De uno martyre	N M	S. 38	Iustus ut palma
d39	PUELLA TURBATA	39	72	Scalam ad caelos	De ss. virginibus			
d39	PUELLA TURBATA		73	Cantemus cuncti	Diebus dominicis			
d40	METENSIS MAIOR	40				O	S. 26	(from MET. MINOR?)
d41	*TE MARTYRUM*	41				N M	S. 397	Te martyrum
d42	*MIRABILIS*	42				N M	S. 128	Mirabilis deus
d43	EIA TURMA	43				O	S. 382	Adorabo
d45	IN LONGITUDINE DIERUM		74	Laetemur gaudiis	*Off. prosula*			
d46	ET VERITATE		75	Quem aethera	*Off. prosula*			
d47	SICUT CAEDRUS		76	Et sicut liliorum	*Off. prosula*			
d44	FIDICULA	44	77	Sollemnitatem huius devoti				
Other								
dd01	*IUSTUS GERMINABIT*	Einsieldeln 121: 51; Bamberg 5: 54			Confessor	N M	S. 119	Iustus germinabit
dd02	SUMMI REGIS ARCHANGELI	Einsiedeln 121: 70; Oxford Ss27: 49			S. Michaelis			
dd03	VENI SPIRITUS AETERNORUM	Bamberg 5: 41; Oxford Ss27: 36			Pentecostes			
dd04	BENEDICTA SEMPER	Einsiedeln 121: 53; Bamberg 5: 49			Trinitas	M P	S. 302	Benedictus es

[a] I have argued as elsewhere that Mater is related to S. 274; while I would continue to claim that relation, my arguments do not need the stricter requirements of the present study, so I cite no specific Alleluia verses for d13 or fc41 in these tables.

Table 15.2 The West Frankish (Aquitanian) tradition

Mel. ID	*Title*	*1118*	*1084*	*909*	*1121*	*887*	*1137*	*1871*	*Definitions*	*All. ID*	*Verse*
Tempus adventus											
fa11	PRECAMUR	1	1	1		1	1	1	M P	S. 271	Ostende
fa12a	*OSTENDE* SALUS		a3			2		2	N M P	S. 271	Ostende
fa12b	*OSTENDE* SALUS		a4	4			2		N M P	S. 271	Ostende
fa13	VENIET REX	2	2	3		3			M P	S. 271	Ostende
fa14	*OSTENDE* ORBIS VITAE		3	2					N M P	S. 271	Ostende
fa15	*OSTENDE*		a2		66				N M	S. 271	Ostende
fa16	*OSTENDE*		92		65				N M	S. 271	Ostende
fa21	REGNANTEM		4	6	2	4	3	3	M P	S. 113	Laetatus sum
fa22	PANGAT LAUDES	3	67						M P	S. 113	Laetatus sum
fa23	*LAETATUS SUM*		68	5	1				N M P	S. 113	Laetatus sum
fa24	*LAETATUS SUM*				67				N M P	S. 113	Laetatus sum
fa31	*EXCITA* QUI REGIS	4	5	7	3	5	4	4	N M P	S. 205	Excita domine
fa41	*VENI DOMINE* *PARATUM* IUBILEMUS	5	6	8	4		5	5	N M P	S. 203	Veni domine
fa42	[*PARATUM*] ALME CHRISTE			9	5				N M P	S. 203	Veni domine
Tempus nativitatis											
fc11	*OSTENDE*[a] (a,b,c) VENIET REX	6(a)				6(b)		6(c)	M P	S. 271	Dns dixit ad me
fc21	*DOMINUS REGNAVIT*	7	7	10	6	7		7	N M P	S. 34	Dns regnavit
fc22	NOSTRA TUBA			11	7	8	6		M	S. 34	Dns regnavit
fc31	VENERANDA	11 51	59		68	12		9	M P	S. 27	Dies sanctificatus
fc41	CHRISTI HODIERNA CAELICA RESONANT	8	10	13	9	11	8	11	O	S. 274	
fc42	*MULTIFARIE*	17	12	12	8	9	7	10	N M P	S. 389	Multifarie olim deus

Table 15.2 (continued)

Mel. ID	*Title*	*1118*	*1084*	*909*	*1121*	*887*	*1137*	*1871*	*Definitions*	*All.* ID	*Verse*
fc43	CELEBRANDA	9	9	14	10	10	9	8			
	ADEST UNA			20							
	EPITHALAMIA										
	<Ecce puerpera>										
fc44	*IUSTUS UT PALMA*[b]	10	8	34	29	17	27	12	N M C	S. 38	Fulgebit lux vera
	HAEC DIES EST SANCTA		91								
	PRAEFULGIDA										
	DA CAMENA										
fc45	BEATA TU	18	105						M	S. 346	?
cf. fp25	[*PASCHA NOSTRUM*]										
fc51	*BEATUS VIR*	14	11	15	11	14	10	14	N M	S. 227	Beatus vir qui timet
	GLORIOSA										
fc53	*VIDEO*		14						N M	S. 27	Video caelos apertos
cf. fs0815b											
fc54	CELSA POLORUM	15	15	69	12	13	11	13	M	S. 102	Cum autem esset S.
	<Via lux veritas paxque>										
fc55	PRECIOSA CANDIDATA	12	13		69	15		15			
	CAELICA CATERVA										
	<Adest dies sacra>										
fc61	*IUSTUS*	16	16	16	13	16	12	17	N M	S. 38	Iustus ut palma
	ORGANICIS										
fc62	SOLEMNITAS CUNCTIS							16	O	S. 271	Nimis honorati sunt?
											In omnem terram?
fc71	*MIRABILIS*	35	30	17	14	18	13	62	N M	S. 128	Mirabilis deus
fc72	REX MAGNE DEUS		a1	18	15	20	14	19	M	S. 377	Quoniam ds magnus
fc73	ALTISSIME		17					18			
cf. fp63	[PLANCTUS CIGNI]										
fc81	EPIPHANIAM	19	21	19	16	21	15	20	P + C O	S. 27	Vidimus stellam eius
fc91	CLARIS VOCIBUS	20	18	47	44	23		24	M	S. 382	Adorabo ad templum
	VIRGO ISRAEL										
fc92	*ADORABO*	23							N M	S. 382	Adorabo ad templum
cf. fdd3	[EXSULTET ELEGANTIS]										

Table 15.2 (continued)

Mel. ID	*Title*	*1118*	*1084*	*909*	*1121*	*887*	*1137*	*1871*	*Definitions*	*All. ID*	*Verse*
fc93	O BEATA					22			M P C	S. 382	Adorabo ad templum
cf. fdd2	*<Gloria victoria>*										
	[AD TEMPLI]										
fc94	SALVE PORTA	22	19	45	41	51		58	M	S. 164	Post partum
fc95	HAC CLARA DIE	21	83	44	40	52	39	23	M	S. 164	Post partum
fc96	EGREGIA PLEBS							22	M	S. 164	Post partum
Tempus Paschale											
fp11	*CONFITEMINI* IUBILATE	24	29		71			26	N M	S. 254	Confitemini dno quoniam bonus
fp21	FULGENS PRAECLARA <Rex in eternum>	25	25	21	17	24	16	27			
fp22	*PASCHA NOSTRUM* PASCHALIS ANTICA EXULTET NUNC HAEC EST VERA		75 107	22	18	58	17		N M P	S. 346	Pascha nostrum
fp23	ADEST ENIM FESTA	65	74		78	30		28	M P	S. 346	Pascha nostrum
fp24	CLARET RUTILANS (a,b)		73		72				M P	S. 346	Pascha nostrum
fp25	[*PASCHA NOSTRUM*]							36	M P	S. 346	Pascha nostrum
cf. fc45	[HAEC EST VERA RED.]										
fp33	CLARA GAUDIA DIC NOBIS	26	28	25	20	26	19	29	P + C O	S. 28	Redemptionem misit
fp34	*EDUXIT* PROME CASTA	30	39	26	21	25	20	33	M	S. 123	Eduxit dominus
fp35	LAUDES DEO	28	22		75			40	M P C	S. 123	Eduxit dominus
fp36	STANS A LONGE	29		24	19	27	18	38	C	S. 26	Surrexit pastor bonus
cf. fdm08	LAETABUNDA CUNCTA SIMUL										
fp37	ECCE VICIT	27	84		73			41	P + C O	S. 28	Redemptionem misit

Table 15.2 (continued)

Mel. ID	*Title*	*1118*	*1084*	*909*	*1121*	*887*	*1137*	*1871*	*Definitions*	*All. ID*	*Verse*
fp41	GAUDEAT TELLUS	34	24		74			34			
	CANAT OMNIS TURBA										
fp42	HAEC DIES	32	26		76			35	P + C O	S. 347	Dicite in gentibus
	QUAM EXCELSUS										
fp43	*CONFITEBOR*										
	FESTUS ADEST	31	82		77			32	N M	S. 353	Confitebor tibi dne
fp44	CREATOR POLI		72	55	49	28					
fp45	*QUI CONFIDUNT*		49	23	61	31		37	N M	S. 159	Qui confidunt
	O BEATA ET										
fp46	VEXILLA [REGIS]	33	27					31			
	QUONIAM VITA										
cf. fs1101a	[ECCE PULCHRA]		111								
fp47	HAEC EST FESTIVITAS	36	31					69			
fp48	[*SURREXIT PASTOR*]							46	M	S. 26	Surrexit pastor
fp51	REX OMNIPOTENS	37	32	27	22	32	21	47	P + C O	S. 205	Ascendit deus
fp61	*APPARUERUNT*		106	31	27	35	22	48	N M P	S. 15	Apparuerunt apostolis
	LAUDIFLUA		108								
fp62	AD TE SUMME		109	29	24	33	23	84			
	ADEST SANCTA										
fp63	ORBIS CONDITOR	39	33	56	50	36					
	PLANCTUS CIGNI										
	PLANGANT FILII										
cf. fc73	[ALTISSIME]	73+									
fp64	NUNC EXSULTET	38	23	30	23	34		30	P + C O	S. 346	Euntes in mundum or: Spiritus dni repl.
	CANTEMUS ORGANA										
fp65	*LOQUEBANTUR*		76		79				N M P	S. 149	Loquebantur
	SPIRITUS SANCTUS										
fp66	*SPIRITUS DOMINI*		87		80				N M P	S. 206	Spiritus dni replevit
fp67	*SPIRITUS DOMINI*		77						N M P	S. 206	Spiritus dni replevit
fp68	ALMIPHONA		110					79			

Table 15.2 (continued)

Mel. ID	*Title*	*1118*	*1084*	*909*	*1121*	*887*	*1137*	*1871*	*Definitions*	*All. ID*	*Verse*
fp71	BENEDICTA SIT	63	51	28	25	37	24	72 81	M P	S. 302	Benedictus es
fp72	O ALMA TRINITAS O ALMA MINOR		88	32	26	38	25				
fp73	O ALMA TRINITAS DEUS O ALMA MAIOR <Iam nunc intonant>	57	93	33	28	39	26	68			
Sanctorale											
fs0321a	LAUDUM CARMINA					48			M	S. 276	Ecce quam bonum
fs0624a	PRAECURSOR	44	34		86			52	M	S. 38	Iustus ut palma
fs0624b	HODIERNA	45	35		85						
fs0624c	HODIERNA[c]				70						
cf. fdm20	[MENTE PURA]										
fs0629a	*IN OMNEM TERRAM* LAUDE IOCUNDA	46	36	35	30	41	28	51	N M	S. 222	In omnem terram
fs0629b	ADONAI SANCTUS PETRUS ALME REX CHRISTE	58	44	36	31	40	29	49			
fs0629c	AD TE CUNCTI					42					
fs0630a	*LAETABITUR* CONCELEBREMUS	47	37	41	33	44	31	54	N M	S. 274	Laetabitur iustus In omnem terram
fs0630b	*IUSTUS GERMINABIT* *ADNUNCIAVERAT* VALDE	49	38	39	32	43	30	55	N M	S. 119	Iustus germinabit Adnunciaverat
fs0630c	*IUSTUM DEDUXIT* ALLE SUBLIME		100	50	35	45	35	78	N M	S. 383	Iustum deduxit
fs0630d	*TE GLORIOSUS* ALME DEUS		101 113	40	34	46	33		N M	S. 41	Te gloriosus

Table 15.2 (continued)

Mel. ID	*Title*	*1118*	*1084*	*909*	*1121*	*887*	*1137*	*1871*	*Definitions*	*All.* ID	*Verse*
fs0630e	*Os iusti*		99	51	36	47	36	80+	N M	S. 63	Os iusti
	Alle boans										
	Alma cohors										
fs0630f	Adest nempe				37		32		M	S. 7	Verba mea
cf. fdm05	[*Quoniam deus*]										
fs0630g	Arce polorum			37			34		M	S. 79	Non vos me elegistis
fs0630h	Apostolorum gloriosa			38					M	S. 41	Te gloriosus
fs0710a	[*Levita Laurentius*]										
	[Clara tibi]							56	M	S. 351	Levita Laurentius
fso801a	Pollet alma							89+	M	S. 117	Iustorum animae
fs0815a	Aureo	50	40	42	38	49	37	57	M	S. 246	Hodie Maria
fs0815b	Virgo dei			43	39	50	38	21	M	S. 27	Orietur sicut sol
cf. fc53											
fs0908a	Alle caeleste	52	41	46	42	53	40	59			
fs0914a	*Dulce lignum*		78						N M	S. 242	Dulce lignum
fs0922a	*Iusti epulentur*	55	42	48	47	57	41	25	N M	S. 77	Iusti epulentur
	Alludat laetus										
fs0929a	Ad celebres	53	48	49	43	54	42	60			
fs1101a	Ecce pulchra			52	45	19	43				
cf. fp46	[Vexilla (regis)]										
fs1101b	*Iustorum animae*	56	43	53	46	56	46	65	N M	S. 117	Iustorum animae
	Vexilla [martyrum]										
fs1101c	Oremus	60	46					64	M	S. 117	Iustorum animae
fs1101d	Hic est sonus	54	47		83						? (Kohrs 11)
fs1101e	Exsultet nostra		85	54	48	55					
fs1101f	Alme sanctorum	59	45		82			61			
fs1111a	O Martine	61	54					66			
fs1111b	Alma pangat					59		67			

Table 15.2 (continued)

Mel. ID	*Title*	*1118*	*1084*	*909*	*1121*	*887*	*1137*	*1871*	*Definitions*	*All. ID*	*Verse*
Commune sanctorum											
fsc1	*Beatus vir*	13	69						N M	S. 227	Beatus vir
fsc2	*Iustus ut palma*	48	70						N M	S. 38	Iustus ut palma
fsc3	*Laudate pueri*		71						N M	S. 186	Laudate pueri
fsc4	*Tu es sacerdos*		79						N M	S. 239	Tu es sacerdos
In dedicatione ecclesiae											
fdd1	*Adorabo* Laetetur	40	53	68	63	62	44	43	N M P C	S. 382	Adorabo ad templum
fdd2	Ad templi	41	52	70	64			44	M P C	S. 382	Adorabo ad templum
cf. fc93	[O beata theotocos]										
fdd3	*Adorabo*		20	67	62	61	45		N M P C	S. 382	Adorabo ad templum
cf. fc92	Exsultet elegantis Nova gratia										
fdd4	*Adorabo*	42	80						N M	S. 382	Adorabo ad templum
fdd5	*Adorabo*	43							N M	S. 382	Adorabo ad templum
Sequentiae dominicales											
fdm01	Omnipotens deus	62	89		81			71	N M	S. 302	Benedictus es
fdm02	*In te domine* Iam deprome	64		63	57				N M	S. 211	In te domine
fdm03	*Quoniam deus* Benedictus	66	50						N M	S. 377	Quoniam deus magnus
fdm04 ∂	*Quoniam deus* Coaequalis			66	60				N M	S. 377	Quoniam deus magnus
fdm05	*Verba mea*	67	55	57+		60		73	N M	S. 7	Verba mea
cf. fs0630f	Adest nempe										
fdm06	*Deus iudex* Fortis atque	68	56 97	60	54			76	N M	S. 288	Deus iudex
fdm07	[*Deus iudex*] Nostra tuba	69	57					74	N M	S. 288	Deus iudex

Table 15.2 (continued)

Mel. ID	*Title*	*1118*	*1084*	*909*	*1121*	*887*	*1137*	*1871*	*Definitions*	*All. ID*	*Verse*
fdm08 cf. fp36	STANS A LONGE	70	60 95						N M	S. 26	Eripe me
fdm09	*EXSULTATE*	71	58 96	64	58			75	N M	S. 337	Exsultate deo adiutori nostro
fdm10	*DILIGAM TE*		61						N M	S. 228	Diligam te
fdm11	*TE DECET* CORDE DEVOTE		62						N M	S. 360	Te decet
fdm12	*TE DECET* ARVAE POLIQUE			62	56			39	N M		
fdm13	*CANTATE* *QUI TIMENT* *OMNES GENTES* SANCTE REX		63	61	55				N M	S. 121 S. 144	Cantate dnm can. Qui timent dnm Omnes gentes
fdm14	*CONFITEMINI*		64						N M	S. 58	Confitemini domino et invocate
fdm15	*LAUDATE DOMINUM*		65						N M	S. 4	Laudate dnm
fdm16	PLANCTUS BERTANAE		66						M	S. 389	Miserere
fdm17	CHRISTE REX FESTUS	72	81			63		70			
fdm18	*VINDICA DOMINE*		86						N M	S. 182	Vindica domine
fdm19	*IN EXITU*		90							S. 27	In exitu
fdm20 cf. fs0624c	MENTE PURA [HODIERNA]			57	51						
fdm21	PER SAECULA			58	52						
fdm22	ALTE VOX CANAT		102	59	53				M	S. 242	Dulce lignum
fdm23	*DOMINE REFUGIUM*			65	59				N M	S. 283	Domine refugium
fdm24	ALMA CHORUS	74			84	64					
fdm25	*QUONIAM CONFIRMATA EST* MARGARITA		94						N M	S. 207	Quoniam confirmata est
fdm26	*VENITE*		98						N M	S. 375	Venite exsultemus v2: Praeoccupemus

Table 15.2 (continued)

Mel. ID	*Title*	*1118*	*1084*	*909*	*1121*	*887*	*1137*	*1871*	*Definitions*	*All.* ID	*Verse*
Aliae											
fp21	CELSA PERSONET <Carmen laudum>							42			
d28	SANCTI SPIRITUS					65		45			
	unidentified							50			
	unidentified							53			
	unidentified							56			
	unidentified							63			
	unidentified							77			
	unidentified							83			
	unidentified							85			
	unidentified		103						M	S. 27	?
	unidentified		104								

[a] A melody related to *Veniet rex*, yet unique by clear liturgical position for Nativity. All three melodies have minor, but significant variants.

[b] In Paris, BNF lat. 909, lat. 1121 and lat. 1137, this Sequence is in the position for John the Baptist, with text *Da camena*; in that context the Alleluia verse 'Iustus ut palma' would have been used. In other sources the liturgical context is clearly Nativity, and the verse 'Fulgebit lux' would have been sung.

[c] Named 'Hodierna', with rubric 'Ioh.' in Paris, BNF lat. 1121, but a melody related to 'Mente pura', yet clearly different in several phrases.

Table 15.3 Related melodies – East and West

Title in East		*Related melody in West*	
Adorabo	d33	Laetetur / *Adorabo* / *Adorabo* minor	fdd1
Aducenter / *Veni dne* / Dulcedine paradisi	d30	*Veni dne* / *Paratum* / *Iubilemus*	fa41
Aurea	d38	*Ostende* / Salus	fa12b
Beatus vir qui timet	d35	Gloriosa	fc51
Cignea	d06	*Beata tu* / [*Pascha nostrum*]	fc45/fp25
Concordia	d02	Ecce vicit	fp37
	d02	Epiphaniam	fc 81
Confitemini	d27	*Ostende* / Orbis vitae	fa14
Deus iudex iustus	d21	*Deus Iudex* / Fortis atque	fdm06
Dominus regnavit	d14	*Dominus regnavit*	fc21
Duo tres	d17	Haec dies quam excelsus	fp42
Eia turma	d43	*Adorabo* [minor] / Claris vocibus	fc91
Exultate deo	d24	*Exsultate*	fdm09
Frigdola	d12	Nunc exsultet / Cantemus organa	fp64
In te domine	d22	*In te domine* / Iam deprome	fdm02
Iustus ut palma maior	d05	Iustus ut palma / Haec dies est sancta / Praefulgida	fc44
Iustus ut palma minor	d29	Praecursor	fs0624a
Laetatus sum	d32	Pangat laudes	fa22
Laudate deum / *Excita*	d31	*Excita* / Qui regis	fa31
Mater	d13	Christi hodierna / Caelica resonant	fc41
Metensis minor	d36	Stans a longe	fdm08 /fp36
Nostra tuba / *Dominus regnavit*	d11	Nostra tuba	fc22
Obtulerunt / *Pretiosa est* / *Redemptionem missit*	d15	Veneranda	fc31
Occidentana	d28	Rex omnipotens	fp51
Organa	d18	Laudes deo	fp35
Qui timent dominum / *Omnes gentes*	d23	*Qui timent* / *Omnes gentes* / Sancte Rex	fdm13
Romana	d04	Clara gaudia / Dic nobis	fp33
Trinitas	d07	Omnipotens deus	fdm01
Virgo plorans	d20	Solemnitas cunctis	fc62

Table 15.3 Related melodies – East and West (continued)

Title in West	*Related melody in East*		
Adorabo [minor] / Claris vocibus	fc91	Eia turma	d43
Beata tu / [*Pascha nostrum*]	fc45/fp25	Cignea	d06
Christi hodierna / Caelica resonant	fc41	Mater	d13
Clara gaudia / Dic nobis	fp33	Romana	fp33
Deus Iudex / Fortis atque	fdm06	*Deus iudex iustus*	d21
Dominus regnavit	fc21	*Dominus regnavit*	d14
Ecce vicit	fp37	Concordia	d02
Epiphaniam	fc 81	Concordia	d02
Excita / Qui regis	fa31	*Laudate deum* / *Excita*	d31
Exsultate	fdm09	*Exultate deo*	d24
Gloriosa	fc51	*Beatus vir qui timet*	d35
Haec dies quam excelsus	fp42	Duo tres	d17
In te domine / Iam deprome	fdm02	*In te domine*	d22
Iustus ut palma / Haec dies est sancta / Praefulgida	fc44	*Iustus ut palma* maior	d05
Laetetur / *Adorabo* / *Adorabo* minor	fdd1	*Adorabo*	d33
Laudes deo	fp35	Organa	d18
Nostra tuba	fc21	Nostra tuba / *Dominus regnavit*	d11
Nunc exsultet / Cantemus organa	fp64	Frigdola	d12
Omnipotens deus	fdm01	Trinitas	d07
Ostende / Orbis vitae	fa14	*Confitemini*	d27
Ostende / Salus	fa12b	Aurea	d38
Pangat laudes	fa22	*Laetatus sum*	d32
Praecursor	fs0624a	*Iustus ut palma* minor	d29
Qui timent / *Omnes gentes* / Sancte Rex	fdm13	*Qui timent dominum* / *Omnes gentes*	d23
Rex omnipotens	fp51	Occidentana	d28
Solemnitas cunctis	fc62	Virgo plorans	d20
Stans a longe	fdm08 /fp36	Metensis minor	d36
Veneranda	fc31	*Obtulerunt* / *Pretiosa est* / *Redemptionem missit*	d15
Veni dne / *Paratum* / *Iubilemus*	fa41	*Aducenter* / *Veni dne* / Dulcedine paradisi	d30

Table 15.4 Alleluias with Sequences

RM	Presence of the text of the Alleluia verse in Vat. lat. 5319
SX	Presence of Alleluia verse in *Antiphonale Sextuplex*
– c/s	Annotation in the Mont-Blandin Antiphonale marking six Alleluias *cum sequentia*
Kohrs no.	Number of 'asymmetrical' Sequence cataloged in Kohrs, *Die aparallelen Sequenzen* (see fn. 59)

Alleluia verse	*All.* ID.	*Liturgical*	*Seq. id.*	*Prose*	*Annotations*
Adorabo	See Table 15.5 – S. 382				
Aducentur regi	See Table 15.5 – S. 203				
Adnunciaverat	See Iustus germinabit				
Apparuerunt	S. 15	Pentecost	fp61	Laudiflua cantica	
Ascendit deus	See Table 15.5 – S. 205				
Beatus vir qui timet	See Table 15.5 – S. 227				
Beatus vir qui suffert	S. 62	Martyr:	d37		
		Blaise		O Blasi dilecte	
		Columbanus		A solis occasu	
Benedictus es	See Table 15.5 – S. 302				
Cantate domino	See Qui timent				
Confitebuntur caeli	See Table 15.5 – S. 271				
Confitebor tibi	S. 353	Easter	fp43	Festus adest	RM
					SX
					Kohrs 10
Confitemini et invocate	S. 58	Dominical	d27 ≈	O quam mira sunt	SX – c/s
		Dominical	fdm14		Kohrs 4
Confitemini . . . quoniam	S. 254	Paschal Vigil	fp11	Iubilate deo omnis arva	
Cum autem esset Steph.	S. 102	Stephen	fc54	Celsa polorum	
Deus iudex iustus	S. 288	Dominical (Easter)	d21 ≈	Iudicem nos	
		Dominical	fdm06	Fortis atque amara	
—	S. 288	Dominical	fdm07	[Nostra tuba]	
Dicite in gentibus	See Table 15.5 – S. 347				
Dies sanctificatus	See Table 15.5 – S. 27/28				
Diligam te	S. 228	Dominical	fdm10		

Table 15.4 (continued)

Alleluia verse	*All. ID.*	*Liturgical*	*Seq. ID.*	*Prose*	*Annotations*
Domine refugium	S. 283	Dominical	fdm23	Eia simul	
Dominus dixit at me	See Table 15.5 – S. 271				
Dominus in Sina	See Table 15.5 – S. 271				
Dominus regnavit	S. 34	Easter	d14 ≈	Is qui prius	
		Nativity	fc21	Age nunc die	RM
					SX – c/s
—	S. 34	Sabb. ante lxx	d11 ≈	Nostra tuba regatur	Kohrs 7
		Nativity	fc22	Nostra tuba nunc tua	
Dulce lignum	S. 242	Inventio crucis	fs0914a		
—	S. 242	Dominical	fdm22	Alte vox canat	
Ecce quam bonum	S. 276	Benedict	fs0321a	Laudum carmina	
Eduxit dominus	S. 123	Easter	fp34	Prome casta	SX
—	S. 123	Easter	d18 ≈	Laudes deo concinat	
		Easter	fp35	Laudes deo omnis	
Emitte Spiritum tuum	See Table 15.5 – S. 205				
Eripe me	See Table 15.5 – S. 26				
Excita domine	See Table 15.5 – S. 205				
Exsultate deo	S. 337	Dominical (Easter)	d24 ≈	Laeta menta	SX
		Dominical	fdm09	In cithara Davidis	Kohrs 9
Fulgebit lux	See Table 15.5 – S. 38				
Gloria et honore	See Table 15.5 – S. 347				
Haec dies	See Table 15.5 – S. 271				
Hic est discipulus	See Table 15.5 – S. 27/28				
Hodie Maria	S. 246	Assumption BMV	fs0815a	Aureo flore primae matris	
In exitu	See Table 15.5 – S. 27/28				
In omnem terram	S. 222	Peter and Paul	fs0629a	Laude iocunda	SX
In omnem terram	See Table 15.5 – S. 271				
In omnem terram	See Laetabitur iustus				
In te domine	S. 211	Dominical	d22 ≈	Laus tibi sit	SX
		Dominical	fdm02	Iam deprome	Kohrs 12
Iusti epulentur	S. 77	Maurice	fs0922a	Alludat laetus	SX
Iustorum animae	S. 117	All saints	fs1101b	Vexilla martyrum	
—	S. 117	All saints	fs1101c	Oremus omnes	

Table 15.4 (continued)

Alleluia verse	*All. ID.*	*Liturgical*	*Seq. ID.*	*Prose*	*Annotations*
Iustum deduxit	See Table 15.5 – S. 27/28				
Iustum deduxit	See Table 15.5 – S. 271				
Iustum deduxit	S. 383	Martial	fs0630c	Alle sublime	
Iustus germinabit	S. 119	Benedict	d49	Qui benedicti cupitis	
Iustus germinabit	S. 119	fs0630b	fs0630b	Valde lumen	
or: Adnuntiaverat					
Iustus ut palma	See Table 15.5 – S. 38				
Laetabitur iustus	S. 274	Martial	fs0630a	Concelebremus	
or: In omnem terram					
Laetatus sum	See Table 15.5 – S. 113				
Lauda Ierusalem	See Table 15.5 – S. 205				
Laudate dm omnes angeli	See Table 15.5 – S. 205				
Laudate dominum	S. 4	Dominical	fdm15		sx
Laudate pueri	See Table 15.5 – S. 186				
Levita Laurentius	S. 351	Lawrence	fs0710a	Clara tibi nos Christe	
Loquebantur	S. 149	Pentecost	fp65	Spiritus sanctus	
Mirabilis deus	S. 128	Innocents	d42	Laus . . . ds omnipotentiae	sx
—	S. 128	Innocents	fc71	Mirabilis deus in sanctis	
Miserere	See Table 15.5 – S. 389				
Multifarie	See Table 15.5 – S. 389				
Nimis honorati sunt	See Table 15.5 – S. 271				
Non vos me elegitis	S. 79	Martial	fs0630g	Arce polorum	
Obtulerunt	See Table 15.5 – S. 27/28				
Omnes gentes	See Qui timent dominum				
Orietur sicut sol	See Table 15.5 – S. 27/28				
Os iusti	S. 63	Martial	fs0630e	Alle boans	
				Alma cohors	
Ostende domine	See Table 15.5 – S. 271				
Pascha nostrum	See Table 15.5 – S. 346				
Post partum	S. 164	Purification et al.	fc94	Salve porta	
—	S. 164	Purification et al.	fc95	Hac clara die	
—	S. 164	Purification	fc96	Egregia plebs	
Pretiosa est	See Table 15.5 – S. 27/28				

Table 15.4 (continued)

Alleluia verse	*All. ID.*	*Liturgical*	*Seq. ID.*	*Prose*	*Annotations*
Qui confidunt	S. 159	Easter	fc45 ≈ d06	O beata tu venerabilis	RM SX
Quinque prudentes	S. 350	Virgin	d09	Virginis venerandae	
Qui timent dominum (SX)	S. 121	Dominical	d23 ≈	En regnator	
Cantate domino (SX – c/s)		Dominical	fdm13	Sancte rex	SX – c/s
Omnes gentes (SX)	S. 144				Kohrs 19
Quoniam confirmata	S. 207	Dominical	fdm25		RM – SX!
Quoniam deus	See Table 15.5 – S. 377				
Redemptionem misit dns	See Table 15.5 – S. 27/28				
Spiritus domini	S. 206	Pentecost	fp66	Canat cuncta	SX
—	S. 206	Pentecost	fp67		
Spiritus domini	See Table 15.5 – S. 346				
Surrexit pastor bonus	See Table 15.5 – S. 26				
Te decet	S. 360	Dominical	fdm11	Corde devote	RM SX – c/s Kohrs 20
—	S. 360	Dominical	fdm12	Arvae polique	
Te gloriosus	S. 41	Martial	fs0630d	Alme deus	
	S. 41	Martial	fs0630h	Apostolorum gloriosa	
Te martyrum	S. 397	Martyrs	d41	Laus . . . humilis	SX
Tu es Petrus	See Table 15.5 – S. 27/28				
Tu es sacerdos	S. 239	Common	fsc4		
Veni domini	See Table 15.5–S. 203				
Venite exsultemus	S. 375	Dominical	fdm26		RM SX Kohrs 22
Verba mea	S. 7	Dominical Martial	fdm05 fs0630f	Adest nempe	
Vidimus stellam	See Table 15.5 – S. 27/28				
Video caelos	See Table 15.5 – S. 27/28				
Vindica domini	S. 182	Dominical	fdm18		SX Kohrs 23
Vox exsultationis	S. 223	All Saints Martyrs	d34	Omnes sancti seraphim Agone triumphale	

Table 15.5 Alleluia melodies with multiple texts and/or multiple liturgical usage, and thus with multiple Sequences

Alleluia verse	*Sequence*	*Liturgical*	*Prose*	*Annotations*
S. 26 – Eripe me				
Eripe me	fdm08	Dominical	Stans a longe	
Eripe me ?	d40	Martyrs/confes.		
or other text		Mauritius	Sancti belli	
		Ianuarius	Pangat ymnum	
		Otmarus	Laude dignum	
Surrexit pastor bonus	fp36	Easter	Laetabunda	
			Cuncta simul	
S. 27/28 – Dies sanctificatus				
Dies sanctificatus	d01	Nativity iii	Natus ante saecula	RM SX
—	fc31 ≈ d15	Nativity iii	Veneranda	Kohrs 21(&14)
Hic est discipulus	d04	John evan.	Iohannes Ihu Xpi	RM SX
In exitu	fdm19	Dominical		SX
Orietur sicut sol	fs0815b	BMV	Virgo dei	
Pretiosa est	d15 ≈	Martyr	Miles inclite	
Iustum deduxit	fc31			
or other text for martyr				
—	d01	Gallus	Christe sanctis unica	
—	d04 ≈	Lawrence	Laurenti David	
Redemptionem misit	fp33	Paschal	Clara gaudia	SX
			Dic nobis	
—	fp37	Paschal	Ecce vicit	
Obtulerunt	d15	Paschal	Christe domine laetifica	
Tu es Petrus	d02	Peter & Paul	Petre summe	RM SX
Video caelos	d02	Stephen	Hanc concordi	RM SX
—	d03	Stephen	Christi domini militis	
			Protomartyr domini	
	fp53	Stephen		
Vidimus stellam	fc81	Epiphany	Epiphaniam	RM SX
S. 38 – Iustus ut palma				
Fulgebit lux vera	fc44	Nativity	Haec dies est sancta	
Iustus ut palma	fc44 ≈	Andrew	Praefulgida	RM
		John bapt.	Da camena	SX
	d05	Innocents	Laus . . . cui sapit	
		John bapt.	Sancti Baptistae	
		Martin	Tuba nostrae vocis	

Table 15.5 (continued)

Alleluia verse	*Sequence*	*Liturgical*	*Prose*	*Annotations*
—	fs0624a≈ d29?	John bapt.	Praecursor	
—	d29	Stephen	Festa Stephani	
		Innocents	Salvete agni	
		Gallus	Dilecto deo Galle	
		Confessors	Rex regum deus	
		(Common)	Rex regum deus	
—	fc61	John evang.	Organicis	
—	fsc2	Common		
S. 113 – Laetatus sum				
Laetatus sum	fa22 ≈	Advent ii	Regnantem	RM (but Ostende)
	d32	Dedication	Psallat ecclesiae	SX
—	fa22	Advent ii	Pangat laudes	
—	fa23	Advent ii?		
—	fa24	Advent ii?		
S. 186 – Laudate pueri				
Laudate pueri	d19	Easter	Carmen suo dilecto	RM (but Ostende)
—	d19	Innocents	Laudes deo perenni	SX
—	fsc3	Common		Kohrs 13
S. 203 – Veni domini				
Adducentur regi	d30 ≈	BMV	Stirpe Maria	SX
Veni domine	fa41	Advent iv	Iubilemus omnes una	SX
or: Paratum cor meum (SX, and RM but Ostende)				
S. 198				
Iubilate deo omnis terra				RM
				SX – c/s
S. 205 – Excita domine				
Ascendit deus	d25	Ascension	Sumi triumphum	RM
	fp51 ≈	Ascension	Rex omnipotens	SX
Emitte spiritum tuum	d28	Pentecost	Sancte sps assit nobis	RM
				SX
Excita domine	fa31 ≈	Advent iii	Qui regis sceptra	RM
	d31			SX
				Kohrs 8
Lauda Ierusalem Qui posuit fines	d16	Paschal	Agni paschalis	RM (but Ostende)
				SX
Laudate deum omnes angeli	d16	Michael	Magnum te Michaelem	RM
				SX
	d31 ≈ fa31	Michael	Angelorum ordo sacer	Kohrs 8

Table 15.5 (continued)

Alleluia verse	*Sequence*	*Liturgical*	*Prose*	*Annotations*
S. 227 – Beatus vir qui timet				
Beatus vir qui timet	d35	Sanctoral: Martin	 Sacerdotem Xpi	RM SX – c/s
—	fc51	Stephen	Gloriosa	
—	fsc1	Common		Kohrs 2
S. 271 – Ostende nobis domine				
Confitebuntur caeli	d26	Innocents	Laus . . . cui hodie	SX
Dominus dixit ad me	d51 ≈ fa11	Nativity i	Grates nunc omnes	RM SX Kohrs 15
Dominus in Sina	d26	Ascension	Christus hunc diem	RM SX
Haec dies	d20 ≈ fc62	Easter	Haec est sancta	RM (but indiv.) SX
Iustum deduxit?	d20	Martyrs	Virgo plorans	
Nimis honorati sunt	d26	Andrew	Deus in tua virtute	
Nimis honorati sunt or: In omnem terram or: Confitebuntur caeli	d38 ≈ fa12b	Apostles	Clare sanctorum	SX
	fc62 ≈ d20	John evan.	Solemnitas cunctis	SX
Ostende nobis	fa11 ≈ d51	Advent i	Precamur	RM SX Kohrs 15
—	fa12a	Advent i	Salus eterna	
—	fa12b ≈ d38	Advent i	Salus eterna	
—	fa13	Advent i	Veniet rex	
—	fa14	Advent i	Orbis vitae	
—	fa15	Advent i		Kohrs 16
—	fa16	Advent i		Kohrs 17
S. 302 – Benedictus es				
Benedictus es	d07 ≈ fdm01	Epiphany Dominical	Festa Christi Omnipotens deus	SX
—	d49 ≈ fp71	Trinity	Benedicta semper sit Benedicta sit	
—	d08	Oct. Epiphany Oct. Pentecost	Iste dies celebris Benedicto gratias deo	

Table 15.5 (continued)

Alleluia verse	*Sequence*	*Liturgical*	*Prose*	*Annotations*
S. 346 – Pascha nostrum				
?	d06 ≈ fp22/fc45	Nat. BMV	Gaude Maria	
Pascha nostrum	d12 ≈ fp64	Easter	Laudes salvatori	RM
—	fp22 ≈	Easter	Exsultet nunc	
	d06		Haec est vera redemptio	SX
—	fp23	Easter	Adest enim festa	
—	fp24	Easter	Claret rutilans	Kohrs 18
Euntes in mundum	fp64 ≈	Pentecost	Nunc exsultet	SX
or: Spiritus dni replevit	d12		Cantemus organa pulchra	
S. 347 – Dicite in gentibus				
Dicite in gentibus	d17 ≈	Easter	Grates salvatori	
—	fp42	Easter	Haec dies quam excelsus	
Gloria et honore	d17	Martyrs	Tubam bellicosam	
S. 377 – Quoniam deus				
Quoniam deus	fdm03	Dominical	Benedictus es dne deus	SX
—	fdm04	Dominical	Coaequalis patri	
—	fc72	Innocents	Rex magne deus	
S. 382 – Adorabo				
Adorabo ad templum	fc91	Purification	Claris vocibus	SX
			Virgo Israel	
—	d43	Christmas	Eia recolamus	
—	d10	Oct of Epiph.	Hunc diem celebret	
		Purification	Concentu parili	
		Desiderius	Summis conatibus	
—	fdd3	Dedication	Exsultet elegantis	
	fc92	Purification		
—	fc93	Purification	O beata theotocos	
	fdd2		Ad templi huius limina	
—	d33	Dedication	Tu civium deus	Kohrs 1
—	fdd1	Dedication	Laetetur et concrepet	
—	fdd4	Dedication		
—	fdd5	Dedication		
S. 389 – Multifarie				
Miserere	fdm16	Dominical		
Multifarie olim deus	fc42	Nativity	Nato canunt omnia	

[a] Schlager, with good reason, considers the melodies for ‘Veni domine’ and ‘Iubilate deo’ as different melodies, although the melodic incipits of the two Alleluias are essentially the same. Here I consider the two melodies as essentially one.

Notes

1 See below, n. 64.

2 See Prooemium to *Liber ymnorum*: 'coepi tacitus mecum volvere, quoniam modo eas potuerim colligare', in Wolfram von den Steinen, *Notker der Dichter und seine Geistige Welt*, 2 vols (Bern: A. Francke, 1948; repr. 1978), Editions Band, 8, sen. 2. Even a poet as sublime as Notker conceived his *versus* as means of remembering the melodies, if we are to take him at his word. The texts were, to some extent, a form of musical notation.

3 MGH *Concilia* 3: 129: 'et in sequentiis, quae in Alleluia sollempniter decantari solent, quaslibet compositiones, quas prosas vocant, vel ullas fictiones addere, interponere, recitare, submurmurare aut decantare presummat. Quod si fecerit, deponatur.' Cf. Andreas Haug, 'Ein neues Textdokument zur Entstehungsgeschichte der Sequenz', in Rudolf Faber et al. (eds), *Festschrift Ulrich Siegele zum 60. Geburtstag* (Kassel: Bärenreiter, 1991), 9–19.

4 'Melodiae longissimae' represents Notker's 'terminus technicus' for *sequentiae* (see Prooemium, 8, sen. 2), while the word *prosa* tended to be used in the West Frankish kingdom (see n. 3 above).

5 Lori Ann Kruckenberg-Goldenstein, 'The Sequence from 1050–1150: Study of a Genre in Change' (Ph.D. diss., The University of Iowa, 1997); 'Sequenz', in *MGG*², Sachteil, 8 (1998), cols. 1254–86.

6 David Hiley, 'Rouen, Bibliothèque Municipale, MS 249 (A. 280) and the Early Paris Repertory of Ordinary Mass Chants and Sequences', *M&L* 70 (1989), 467–82; 'Cluny, Sequence and Tropes', in Claudio Leonardi and Enrico Menestro (eds), *La tradizione dei tropi liturgici* (Spoleto: Centro Italiano di Studi sull'Alto Medioevo, 1990), 99–113; 'Editing the Winchester Sequence Repertory of ca. 1000', in *Cantus Planus: Papers read at the Third Meeting, Tihany, Hungary, 19–24 September 1988,* ed. László Dobszay et al. (Budapest: Hungarian Academy of Sciences Institute for Musicology, 1990), 99–113; 'The Sequentiary of Chartres, Bibliothèque Municipale, Ms. 47', in *La Sequenza medievale: Atti del Convegno Internazionale Milano 7–8 aprile 1984*, ed. Agostino Ziino (Lucca: Libreria Musicale Italiana, 1992), 105–17; 'The Sequence Melodies Sung at Cluny and Elsewhere', in Peter Cahn and Ann-Katrin Heimer (eds), *De musica et cantu: Studien zur Geschichte der Kirchenmusik und der Oper — Helmut Hucke zum 60. Geburtstag* (Hildesheim: Olms, 1993), 131–55; 'Changes in English Chant Repertoires in the Eleventh Century as Reflected in the Winchester Sequences', in *Anglo-Norman Studies 16: Proceedings of the Battle Conference 1993* (Woodbridge, Suffolk: Boydell Press, 1994), 137–54; 'The Repertory of Sequences at Winchester', in Graeme M. Boone (ed.), *Essays on Medieval Music in Honor of David G. Hughes* (Cambridge, Mass.: Harvard University Press, 1995), 153–93.

7 See especially 'The Repertory of Proses at Saint Martial de Limoges in the 10th Century', *JAMS* 11 (1958), 149–64; 'The Troping Hypothesis', *MQ* 52 (1966), 183–203; 'Some Ninth-Century Sequences', *JAMS* 20 (1967), 367–402; 'The Sequence', in Wulf Arlt, Ernst Lichtenhahn and Hans Oesch (eds), *Gattungen der Musik in Einzeldarstellungen: Denkschrift Leo Schrade* (Bern: Francke, 1973), 269–322; *The Early Medieval Sequence* (Berkeley: University of California Press, 1977).

8 James McKinnon. *The Advent Project* (Berkeley: University of California Press, 2000), esp. ch. 10, 'The Alleluia', 249–79.

9 Ibid., 252–7.

10 Ibid., 260–70.

11 Concerning the English repertory, see Hiley, 'Editing the Winchester Sequence Repertory' and 'The Repertory of Sequences at Winchester'. Concerning non-Aquitanian, West Frankish repertories, see Hiley, 'Cluny, Sequence and Tropes', 'The Sequentiary of Chartres, Bibliothèque Municipale, Ms. 47' and 'The Sequence Melodies Sung at Cluny and Elsewhere'.

12 For a facsimile edition, see *Stiftsbibliothek Sankt Gallen Codices 484 & 381: Kommentiert und in Faksimile*, ed. Wulf Arlt, Susan Rankin and Cristina Hospenthal (Winterthur: Amadeus, 1996).

13 The numbers that identify melodies in this study are taken from *Clavis sequentiarum,* a relational database that collects comprehensive data concerning printed editions of sequences, melodies of sequences, texts of sequences, manuscripts containing sequences and detailed contents of the manuscripts. Letters identifying melodies follow general international standards: 'd' implies German (or *deutsch*), 'f' French, 'fa' French Aquitanian, etc. Our goal is to make *Clavis sequentiarum* available through the internet.

14 See *Stiftsbibliothek Sankt Gallen Codices 484 & 381.*

15 Concerning terminology for naming texts added to sequences, see above, nn. 3 and 4. When discussing the East Frankish repertory I shall use Notker's term 'versus' for the texts; when discussing the West Frankish repertory, I shall use the term 'prosa' as preserved in West Frankish sources.

16 The melodies named IUSTUS GERMINABIT, SUMMI REGIS ARCHANGELI, VENI SPIRITUS AETERNORUM and BENEDICTA SEMPER are found among the melodies recorded in Einsiedeln, SB 121; Bamberg, Staatsbibl. lit. 5; and Oxford, Bodl. Lib. Selden supra 27, three of the oldest and most authoritative sources for the East Frankish repertory. The letters 'dd' designate the second generation of East Frankish melodies.

17 Concerning the celebration of Mary on 1 January, particularly north of the Alps in the eighth century and thereafter, see Jacques-Marie Guilmard, 'Une antique fête mariale au 1er janvier dans la ville de Roma?', *Ecclesia orans*, 11 (1994), 25–67. The rich and complex interrelations of Marian feasts and their development are concisely traced in Margot Fassler, 'Mary's Nativity, Fulbert of Chartres, and the *Stirps Jesse*', *Speculum*, 75 (2000), 389–434, esp. 392–9. It must be noted that Notker's text devoted to Mary on the Octave of Christmas – *Gaude Maria virgo dei genetrix* – also commomorates Christ's naming and circumcision, themes that have subsequently become central to the celebration of the Octave of Christmas:

> Te nomen Iesu edocuit caelestis nuntius,
> Quod circumciso imponeres, intacta, filio,
> Qui scit solus nostra crimina
> Cum patre sanctoque spiritu
> Rite circumcidere' (*AH* 53: 27).

18 Concerning the origins of Epiphany, see Franz Nikolasch, 'Zur Ursprung des Epiphaniefestes', *EL* 83 (1968), 393–429, and K. Holl, 'Die Ursprung des Epiphaniefestes', in *Sitzungsberichte der Preussischen Akademie der Wissenschaften* (1971), 402–38; for the origins of the feast of Trinity, see Peter Browe, 'Zur Geschichte der Dreifaltigkeitsfestes', *AfLw* 1 (1950), 65–81. A central theme of Epiphany – particularly in the earlier Middle Ages – is the baptism of Christ by John, the event at which the Trinity is first manifested in the Gospels through the voice of the Father, the representation of the Spirit by the dove, and the physical presence of Christ.

19 Notker's text for the Octave of Pentecost, *Benedicto gratias deo* for the Sequence PLANCTUS STERILIS, offers distinctly trinitarian themes in citing each person of the Trinity, while the East Frankish text for the Octave of Epiphany, *Iste dies celebris constat* (also sung to PLANCTUS STERILIS) details the appearance of the three persons with specific reference to the Trinity:

Iste dies celebris constat
Ob trinitatis manifestam in terris notionem,
Cuius Iohannes mediastinus fuit semper felix.
Fit patris vox ad filium baptizantum
Et spiritus in specie corporali
Hunc invisit ut columba. (*AH* 53: 31)

20 *Benedicta semper sancta sit trinitas* is the Sequence in question, *AH* 53: 81; see Henry Marriott Bannister's brief but insightful discussion of the piece, *AH* 53: 141–3. The melody of this Sequence is titled TRINITAS in Einsiedeln, SB 366, fol. 28.

21 Richard Crocker. 'The Repertoire of Proses at Saint Martial de Limoges (Tenth and Eleventh Centuries)' (Ph.D. diss., Yale University, 1957).

22 For general background on the West Frankish tropers, see Jacques Chailley, 'Les Anciens tropaires et séquentiaires de l'école de Saint Martial de Limoges (X^e^–XIe siècles)', *Etudes grégoriennes*, 2 (1957), 163–88; Crocker, 'The Repertoire of Proses at Saint Martial de Limoges'; Jacques Chailley, *L'École de Saint Martial de Limoges jusqu'à la fin du XIe siècle* (Paris: Les Livres essentiels, 1960), 73–118; Heinrich Husmann, *Tropen- und Sequenzenhandschriften* (RISM B V/I; Munich-Duisberg: Henle Verlag, 1964); Paul Richer Evans, *The Early Trope Repertory of Saint Martial de Limoges* (Princeton: Princeton University Press, 1970), 29–53.

23 Fols. 197–212 contain the first two quires of the sequentiary, in which names were added later in the margin; fols. 213–20 contain two additional quires, forming a second sequentiary, in which the titles are written in a space within the writing area prepared for this purpose.

24 At fol. 70^r^, before beginning a new series of OSTENDE melodies, one reads: 'Aliae sequentiae quae non sunt valde in usu.' A new series of melodies begins at that point.

25 James Grier, 'Editing Adémar de Chabannes', *Plainsong and Medieval Music*, 6 (1997), 97–118.

26 Kruckenberg-Goldenstein, 'The Sequence from 1050–1150'; see esp. ch. 3, 86–139: 'An East-West Reception Barrier: Sequence Transmission – Sequence Repertoires'.

27 Henry Marriott Bannister, 'Una sequenza per l'Epifania', *Rassegna gregoriana*, 4 (1905), 5–14; cf. Jacques Handschin, 'Trope, Sequence, and Conductus', in *NOHM*, ii: *Early Music up to 1300*, ed. Anselm Hughes (London: Oxford University Press, 1954), 128–74, esp. 156–8.

28 Bruno Stäblein, 'Die Sequenzmelodie "Concordia" und ihr geschichtlicher Hintergrund', in Horst Heussner (ed.), *Festschrift Hans Engel zum siebzigsten Geburtstag* (Kassel: Bärenreiter, 1964), 364–92. Cf. Crocker, *The Early Medieval Sequence,* 75–93.

29 Crocker, *The Early Medieval Sequence*, 146–59.

30 See Prooemium to *Liber ymnorum*: '. . . in quo aliqui versus ad sequentias erant modulati, sed iam tunc nimium vitiati. Quorum ut visu delectatus, ita sum gustu amaricatus' (*Notker der Dichter*, Editions Band, 8, sen. 3–4).

31 Karlheinz Schlager, *Thematischer Katalog der ältesten Alleluia-Melodien aus Handschriften des 10. und 11. Jahrhunderts, ausgenommen das ambrosianische, alt-römische und alt-spanische Repertoire* (Munich: W. Ricke, 1965).
32 Karlheinz Schlager, 'Alleluia', in *MGG*[2], Sachteil, 1, cols. 445–62; see esp. col. 450.
33 See, e.g., *AMS* 102, no. 83; 104, no. 85; 114, no. 95; 126, nos. 107–110a.
34 'Demonstrable melodic relationship' represents the only definition of relation between Alleluia and Sequence recognized by Crocker (see *The Early Medieval Sequence,* 11 and 240); the clearest statement of Crocker's position on relation between Alleluia and Sequence is found on pp. 239–41, but cf. ch. 22, 'Sequence, Alleluia, and Liturgy', 392–409.
35 I am indebted to Thomas Forrest Kelly for this astute observation.
36 Notker's cycle for Easter Week serves as an example of this principle; cf. *Is que prius* (*AH* 53: 47) with Alleluia *Dominus regnavit*; *Christe domine laetifica* (*AH* 53: 48) with Alleluia *Obtulerunt*; *Agni paschalis esu* (*AH* 53: 50) with Alleluia *Laude Ierusalem/Qui posuit*; *Grates salvatori* (*AH* 53:52) with Alleluia *Dicite in gentibus*; *Laudes deo* (*AH* 53: 53) with Alleluia *Eduxit dominus*; *Carmen suo dilecto* (*AH* 53: 54) with Alleluia *Laudate pueri*; and *Haec est sancta* (*AH* 53: 56) with Alleluia *Haec dies*.
37 See discussion of DIES SANCTIFICATUS below.
38 *The Early Medieval Sequence*, 235.
39 McKinnon (*The Advent Project,* 277–8) has named this basic Alleluia melody 'Dies sanctificatus'. The 'alleluia' section of the melody appears identical in two iterations in Schlager's catalogue, melody nos. 27 and 28; differences at the end of the verse in five texts (S. 28) led Schlager to break the melody into two entries, although the two are fundamentally manifestations of one melody. Thus, following McKinnon, I will cite 'Dies sanctificatus' as S. 27/28.
40 See *Christum laude celebri* for St. Januarius (*AH* 34: 252) and *Laude condignissima* for St. Nicholas (*AH* 54: 252). Cf. *Summa stirpe genite* (*AH* 10: 17), a Marian text of possible Italian origin, which could have been sung with the verse 'Beata est virgo'.
41 Even Crocker acknowledges this rather striking character of DIES SANCTIFICATUS; see *The Early Medieval Sequence,* 236.
42 See Table 15.2, fdm08, and cf. fp26, also in Table 15.2.
43 *Thematischer Katalog*, 77: the Verses *Beate Petre clemens* and *Beatus vir Donatus* attest to the use of S. 26 on feasts of saints, although Donatus was not a martyr.
44 Compare Crocker's discussion of STANS A LONGE in *The Early Medieval Sequence,* 398.
45 *The Advent Project,* 277–8.
46 Cf. above, nn. 25–6. Note that these melodies are not considered identical in this study, and hence they are given East Frankish and West Frankish numbers.
47 See Crocker, *The Early Medieval Sequence,* 146–59.
48 *The Advent Project,* 275, 277.
49 Work remains to be done in sorting out the melodic traditions of d16, d19, d25, d28 and fp51; in many sources these melodies employ *G* as final and the melody unfolds above *G* with a *B*♭, yet in other sources the melodies are written on *D*.
50 While the *alleluia* sections of S. 186 (*Laudate pueri*) with S. 205 (*Excita/Lauda Hierusalem*) are different, melodic structures within the Verses of each of these melodies are strongly related (cf. *Alleluia-Melodien I, bis 1100*, ed. Karlheinz Schlager [MMMA 7; Kassel: Bärenreiter, 1968], 284 and 281–2), the relation is even clearer if these German and Italian traditions recorded by Schlager are

compared. I would thus suggest that *Laudate pueri* is a related manifestation of McKinnon's *Excita* type.

51 See, e.g., DUO TRES (d17); I suggested at the national meeting of the American Musicological Society in 1978, based primarily on the textual association of Notker's *Grates salvatori* and the consistent liturgical association of DUO TRES with Alleluia S. 347, that DUO TRES was related to Alleluia DICITE IN GENTIBUS. At the end of Hiley, 'The Sequence Melodies Sung at Cluny and Elsewhere', the author edited a sequence melody entitled DICITE IN GENTIBUS from Cambrai, BM 75. The melody from the early French tradition entitled DICITE IN GENTIBUS is almost identical with the East Frankish DUO TRES. The melodic incipits of Alleluia and Sequence are not identical.

52 Calvin M. Bower, 'An Alleluia for Mater', in Robert Lamar Weaver (ed.), *Essays on the Music of J. S. Bach and other Divers Subjects: A Tribute to Gerhard Herz* (Louisville, Ky.: University of Louisville, 1982), 98–116.

53 Given the nature of the Alleluia, several Verses may be used for the same melody, and thus the incipits of several Verses may be used to designate the same Sequence melody when used on different liturgical occasions.

54 The lesser number of Verses cited in the West Frankish repertory is largely because of the number of Sequences named OSTENDE.

55 *The Advent Project,* 254–7.

56 Ibid., 254–7, 274–9.

57 See Table 21, ibid., 255–6.

58 *The Early Medieval Sequence,* 383–95.

59 Klaus Heinrich Kohrs, *Die aparallelen Sequenzen: Repertoire, liturgische Ordnung, musikalischer Stil* (Munich: Musikverlag Katzbichler, 1978).

60 See Crocker's discussion of 'aparallel' Sequences, *The Early Medieval Sequence*, 11, and his discussion of this group as 'jubilus-replacements', 293–4. 'Aparallel' seems to have become a historical as well as a stylistic concept; see also Kohrs, *Die aparallelen Sequenzen.*

61 I refer to Dreves's editions of *Iubilate deo omnis arva* (*AH* 7: 41), *Iam turma caelica* (*AH* 7: 42), *Hoc pium recitat* (*AH* 7: 43); see Calvin M. Bower, 'Alleluia, Confitemini Domino, quoniam bonus – An *Alleluia*, *Versus*, *Sequentia*, and Five *Prosae* Recorded in Aquitanian Sources', in Susan Parisi (ed.), *Music in the Theater, Church, and Villa: Essays in Honor of Robert Lamar Weaver and Norma Wright Weaver* (Warren, Mich.: Harmonie Park Press, 2000), 3–32; Kenneth Levy, '*Lux de luce*: The Origin of an Italian Sequence', *MQ* 57 (1971), 40–61.

62 Concerning AMOENA and GRAECA, see the essay by Theodore Karp in this volume, Ch. 16.

63 Amalarius, *Liber de ordine antiphonarii* LII (*Amalarii Episcopi opera liturgica omnia*, ed. Jean Michel Hanssens [Vatican City: Biblioteca Apostolica Vaticana, 1948], iii, 84): 'Ideo in ea statione in qua apostolicus celebrat vespertinale officium, alleluia canitur cum omni supplemento et excellentia versuum et sequentiarum.'

64 See Mariken Teeuwen, *Harmony and the Music of the Spheres: The* Ars musica *in Ninth-Century Commenatries on Martianus Capella,* Mittellateinische Studien und Texte, Bd. 30 (Leiden: Brill 2002); 499–500, § 360.8: 'Illa prima [species] i. quae in sonis invenitur, ad armoniam pertinet. Non etenim in ea verba aliquid significantia, sed soni tantum sibimet ipsis aliqua ratione coniuncti queruntur, ut sunt sequentiae apud cantores.' Cf. Teeuwen's thorough commentary on the passage, 326–32.

65 The third distinction of VOX EXULTATIONIS (at 'Quos in dei laudibus firmavit caritas') represents a quote from the melisma of the Alleluia Verse on the word 'tabernaculis'.

66 *Liber officialis* III, 16 (*Amalarii Episcopi opera liturgica omnia*, 304).
67 James McKinnon, 'The Patristic Jubilus and the Alleluia of the Mass', in *Cantus Planus: Papers read at the Third Meeting of the International Musicological Society Study Group, Tihany, Hungary, 19–24 September 1988,* ed. László Dobszay et al. (Budapest: Hungarian Academy of Sciences Institute for Musicology, 1990), 61–70, see esp. 69–70; I would disagree, however, with McKinnon's suggestion that Amalarius is not referring to the genre of Sequence, but rather to the melismatic ending of the Alleluia.
68 See Nancy van Deusen, 'The Use and Significance of the Sequence', *Musica disciplina*, 40 (1986), 5–47; see esp. 18.
69 Andreas Haug, 'Neue Ansätze im 9. Jahrhundert', in *Die Musik des Mittelalters*, ed. Hartmut Möller and Rudolf Stephan (Laaber: Laaber-Verlag, 1991), 94–128.
70 See Crocker, *The Early Medieval Sequence,* 401.
71 Ibid., 240–41.
72 VENI SPIRITUS AETERNORUM actually seems to be a melody based on the incipit of another sequence: OCCIDENTANA (d28), or *Sancti spiritus adsit nobis gratia.*
73 St. Gall 381, 493: *Laetemur gaudiis quos redemit verbum* to the melody IN LONGITUDINE DIERUM; 495: *Quem aethera et terra* to the melody ET VERITATE; and 495: *Et sicut liliorum candor* to the melody SICUT CAEDRUS.
74 See Ruth Steiner, 'The Prosulae of the MS Paris BN lat. 1118', *JAMS* 22 (1969), 367–93; and Gunilla Björkvall and Andreas Haug, 'Texting Melismas: Criteria for and Problems in Analyzing Melogene Tropes', *Revista de musicología*, 16 (1993), 805–31.

Chapter 16

Some Notkerian Sequences in Germanic Print Culture of the Fifteenth and Sixteenth Centuries

Theodore Karp

This essay stems from a fortuitous encounter with an unusual chant source, the *Graduale Herbipolense iussu atque authoritate Reverendissimi in Christo Patris, Principis & Domini, D. Iulii Episcopi Herbipolensis & Franciæ Orientalis Ducis emendatum meliorique ordine quam hactenus digestum, auctum locupletatum, sumptuquam eiusdem excusum.*[1] The title page indicates that this print was issued in Würzburg in 1583, thus some twenty years after the Council of Trent had banned the use of all but four Sequences and all tropes both for the Proper and the Ordinary. The ruling notwithstanding, the print contains fifty-four sequences and eighteen trope sets for the Proper, comprising two-score elements. In this tribute to the memory of James McKinnon I shall focus on two works drawn from the former repertory; I intend to deal with the latter in a future study.

The Sequence repertory presented by the Herbipolense is as follows (the numbers given in the central column represent the volume and page assignments in *Analecta hymnica*):

29v	Grates nunc omnes	53: 15	Nativitatis Christi: in gallicantu
31v	Eia recolamus	53: 23	Nativitatis Christi: in secunda missa
35r	Natus ante saecula	53: 20	Nativitatis Christi: in summa missa
37v	Hanc concordi	53: 345	In die sancti Stephani
40v	Iohannes Iesu Christe	53: 276	De sancto Iohanne
42v	Laus tibi Christe patris optime nate Deus	53: 258	De innocentibus
47r	Eia recolamus (cue)		In Circumcisione Domini
49r	Festa Christi omnis Christianitas	53: 50	In festo Epiphaniae
53r	Festa Christi (cue)		Dominica infra octavas Epiphaniae
146v	Laudes salvatori	53: 65	In die sancto Paschae: summam missam
150v	Laudes Christo redempti voce modulemur	53: 82	Feria secunda
153r	Agni paschali	53: 89	Feria tertia

155^{r}	Grates salvatori ac regi Christo	53: 92	Feria quarta
161^{r}	Haec est sancta solennitas solennitatem	53: 98	In octava Paschae
163^{r}	Victimae paschali laudes	34: 27	Dominica secunda post Pascha
169^{v}	Summi triumphum	53: 114	In die sancto Ascensionis Domini
172^{r}	O quam mira	53: 118	Dominica infra octa. Ascensionis
175^{v}	Sancti Spiritus adsit nobis	53: 119	In die sancto Pentecostes
176^{v}	Veni Sancti Spiritus	54: 234	Feria secunda
180^{r}	Veni Sancti Spiritus (cue)		Feria quarta
183^{r}	Benedicta semper sancta sit Trinitas	53: 139	De sancta Trinitate
186^{r}	Lauda Sion	50: 584	In festo corporis Christi
215^{r}	Clare sanctorum	53: 367	Sancti Thomae Apostoli
225^{v}	Dixit Dominus, ex Basan convertam	50: 348	In conversione Sancti Pauli
230^{r}	Concentu parili	53: 171	In purificatione beatae Mariae virg.
235^{r}	Psallat concors symphonia	55: 135	Dorotheae virginis
243^{v}	Victimae paschali (cue)		Marci Evangelistae
244^{r}	Clare sanctorum (cue)		Phillipi & Jacobi Apostolorum
244^{v}	Carmen suo dilecto	53: 96	Inventione sanctae Crucis
248^{v}	Verbum Dei, Deo natum	55: 211	Ioannis ante portam Latinam
252^{v}	O beata beatorum martyrum	55: 20	Bonifacii & sociorum
256^{v}	Agone triumphali	53: 370	Decem milium martyrum
259^{v}	Sancti baptistae Christi preconis	53: 267	Ioannis Baptistae
264^{v}	Petre summe	53: 336	Petri & Pauli: In die
266^{v}	Ave Verbi Dei parens	48: 423	Visitatione beatae Mariae virginis
268^{r}	O beata beat[orum] (cue)		In Vigilia sancti Kiliani
270^{r}	Adoranda, veneranda	55: 239	In Fest. sanctorum martyrum Kiliani
272^{r}	Exultent filiae Sion	50: 351	Septem fratrum
273^{v}	Caeli enarrant	50: 344	In Divisione Apostolorum
276^{v}	Laus tibi Christe, qui est creator	50: 346	Mariae Magdalenae
279^{r}	Gaude mater Anna	55: 72	De sancta Anna
281^{v}	O beata beatorum (cue)		Afra, sicut in die Kiliani, Ciriaci & soc.
283^{v}	Laurenti, David magni martyr	53: 283	Laurentii: In die sancto
286^{r}	Congaudent angelorum	53: 179	In Assumptione beatae Mariae
288^{v}	Clare sanctorum (cue)		Bartholomaei
289^{r}	Ad laudes salvatoris	54: 126	De Confessoribus
290^{v}	Psallite regi nostro	50: 349	Decollatione sancti Ioannis
294^{r}	Stirpe Maria regia procreata	53: 162	In Nativitate Mariae virginis
295^{r}	Agone triumphali (cue)		Mauritii & sociorum
296^{v}	Magnum te Michaelem	53: 301	sancti Michaelis
299^{r}	Psallat laete orbis cetus	55: 118	De sancto Burchardo
301^{v}	Omnes sancti Seraphim	53: 196	Omnium sanctorum
303^{r}	Sacerdotem Christi Martinum	53: 294	In octava Martini
305^{r}	Gaude Sion, quod egressus a te	55: 140	Elizabeth viduae
306^{v}	Altissima providente	54: 291	Praesentationis Mariae
310^{r}	Sanctissimae virginis votiva festa	55: 229	Katharinae virginis
312^{r}	Deus in tua virtute sanctus Andreas gaudet	53: 210	Andreae: In die sancto
313^{r}	Exultent filiae Sion (cue)		Barbarae virginis

313ʳ	Laude Christo debita, celebremus	55: 296	De sancto Nicolao
315ʳ	Stirpe Maria (cue)		In conceptione beatae Mariae virginis
318r	Psallat ecclesia mater illibata	53: 398	In Dedicationis
322ʳ	Ave praeclara maris stella	50: 313	De Beata virgine
324ʳ	Verbum bonum et suave	54: 343	Alia Sequentia
325ʳ	Virginis Mariae laudes intonent Christiani	54: 27	Alia Sequentia: tempore paschali

This repertory is very closely similar to that of another Würzburg source printed nearly a century earlier by Georg Reyser in 1496. The two differ in that the earlier one presents *Laudes crucis attollamus* as an added alternative to *Carmen suo dilecto*, and *Astra caeli resplendeant* as an added alternative for the Feast of the Conception. On the other hand, the earlier print lacks *Ad laudes salvatoris* for the Mass of Confessors. Those readings that I have compared are either identical or extremely close. Nevertheless, the later print is unlikely to have been a direct descendant of the earlier, given the repertorial differences between the two. We must, for example, account not only for the additional Sequence, *Ad laudes salvatoris*, in the later print, but also for the six trope elements present in the later print that are lacking in the earlier.

A cursory survey indicates that approximately 40 percent of the repertory is devoted to works attributable to Notker, whose memory remained vivid in the minds of a number of persons active in sixteenth-century Germany (see, for example, the rubric that heads the sequentiary in the manuscript Stuttgart, Württembergische Landesbibl., Cod. mus. fol. I 65, a Benedictine Gradual attributable to the years 1511–12: 'Ad summam Missam Sequen. beati Notkeri monachi sancti Galli compositoris sequenciarum'). Much of the Herbipolense repertory is widely known from other sources, but some is not. The unevenness of the distribution of the Notkerian Sequences among late sources of the Germanic orbit is, in fact, quite marked, as shown in Table 16.1.

None of the concordant sources listed contains any Notkerian Sequence that is lacking in the 1583 print. The chart seems to indicate a subdivision of Notker's oeuvre into works that, if not entirely absent from the late sources, were extraordinarily rare, those that were employed infrequently, and those that were nearly ubiquitous. Among the first group – apart from *O quam mira* – are Notker's seven remaining brief, aparallel Sequences, *Angelorum ordo, Christe domine, En regnator, Is qui prius, Laeta mente, Laus tibi sit* and *Tu civium*. The more standard *Benedicto gratias, Christus hunc diem, Dilecte deo, Gaude Maria virgo, Judicem nos, Laudes deo concinat, Quid tu virgo, Rex regum, Scalam ad caelos* and *Tubam bellicosam* are also lacking. (Among this latter group, *Dilecte deo Galle perenni* turns up in two Benedictine sources of 1623/24, Würzburg, UB Ch. f. 282 and 283.) Even the much earlier Utrecht Prosarium (Utrecht, Rijksuniversiteitsbibl. 417), which contains nearly two dozen Sequences more than the Herbipolense, has only three Notkerian Sequences lacking in the Herbipolense, while it is missing two pieces found

Table 16.1 Notkerian Sequences in the *Graduale Herbipolense* and their concordances among Germanic prints

Asterisks indicate presence in Utrecht, Universiteitsbibl. 417.

		a	*b*	*c*	*d*	*e*	*f*	*g*	*h*	*i*
1.	Natus ante saecula	cix^{r}	a ii^{v}	iii^{v}	xii^{v}	135^{r}	xv^{r}	196	ccx^{v}	74 *
2.	Hanc concordi	110^{v}	a iiii^{r}	v^{r}	—	135^{v}	xvii^{r}	197	ccxii^{r}	75 *
3.	Iohannis Iesu Christe	111^{v}	[a v^{r}]	vi^{v}	—	136^{v}	xviii^{v}	197^{v}	ccxiii^{v}	75 *
4.	Festa Christi	112^{r}	[a vii^{r}]	ix^{v}	lxxxviii^{v}	138^{r}	cxlvi^{v}	199	ccxvi^{r}	76 *
5.	Laudes salvatori	115^{v}	b ii^{v}	xxv^{r}	xcii^{r}	142^{r}	lvii^{r}	203	ccxx^{r}	77 *
6.	Agni paschali	—	—	—	—	—	—	202^{v}	—	79 *
7.	Grates salvatori	—	—	—	—	—	—	203	—	— *
8.	Haec est sancta solennitas	—	—	—	—	—	—	204^{v}	—	—
9.	Summi triumphum	119^{v}	[b v^{v}]	xxxi^{r}	xliiii^{v}	148^{r}	lxvii^{r}	207	ccxxiii^{v}	79 *
10.	O quam mira	—	—	—	—	—	—	—	—	—
11.	Sancti Spiritus adsit nobis	121^{r}	[b vii^{v}]	xxxiii^{v}	xcvi^{r}	149^{r}	lxx^{v}	208	ccxxv^{v}	27 *
12.	Clare sanctorum	137^{r}	[e vi^{v}]	lxviii^{r}	cxi^{v}	172^{r}	cxxix^{v}	267^{v}	ccliii^{r}	90 *
13.	Concentu parili	—	[a viii^{v}]	xi^{v}	xc^{r}	141^{r}	xxix^{r}	222	ccxvii^{v}	77 *
14.	Carmen suo	—	—	—	—	—	—	—	—	— *
15.	Agone triumphali	137^{v}	—	lxxiii^{r}	—	172^{v}	cxxxiiii^{v}	270^{v}	—	90 *
16.	Sancti baptistae Christi	125^{r}	[c v^{r}]	xl^{v}	cii^{v}	153^{r}	lxxix^{v}	232^{v}	ccxxxiii^{r}	81 *
17.	Petre summe	126^{v}	[c vii^{r}]	xlii^{v}	ciiii^{r}	153^{v}	lxxxii^{v}	233	ccxxxiiii^{v}	81 *
18.	Laurenti, David	131^{r}	d iii^{r}	li^{r}	—	160^{r}	xcvi^{r}	245^{v}	ccxxxix^{v}	84 *
19.	Congaudent angelorum	132^{r}	d iiii^{r}	liii^{r}	cv^{r}	160^{v}	xcix^{r}	247	ccxl^{v}	84 *
20.	Stirpe Maria regia	133^{v}	—	lv^{v}	cvii^{r}	162^{v}	cvi^{v}	251^{v}	ccxlii^{v}	86 *
21.	Omnes sancti Seraphim	—	[d viii^{r}]	lviii^{v}	cviii^{v}	165^{v}	cxviii^{r}	261	ccxlv^{v}	87 *
22.	Psallat ecclesia mater	136^{r}	f iii^{r}	lxxxvi^{v}	lxxxii^{v}	171^{v}	cxlix^{r}	276	cclix^{r}	89 *

Sources:
a: [Graduale Romanum, Constance? 1475?] London, BL 15154 (olim 6883). **b**: *Graduale Romanum*, Basel: Wenssler & Kuchen, 1486? London, BL 31372. **c**: Graduale Romanum] Augsburg: Ratdolt, 1494–8. **d**: [Graduale Moguntinum] Speyer: Biber & Drach, 1500. **e**: *Graduale secundum laudabilem cantum gregorianum*, Strasbourg: Pruess, 1501. **f**: *Graduale iuxta ritu[m] ecclesie Augustense*, Basel: Pforzheim, 1511. **g**: *Grad[uale] patavien[se]*, Vienna: Winterburger, 1511. **h**: *Graduale Speciale*, Basel: Pforzheim, 1521. **i**: Aachen, Stiftsarchiv 13.

in our source. The two Sequences to be examined here are the ones that do not appear in known Germanic prints apart from those from Würzburg.

O quam mira (Track 19 on the accompanying compact disc) is undoubtedly the best-known of Notker's aparallel Sequences. This Sequence was first made available to scholars in a transcription by Anselm Schubiger, in a book published in 1858.[2] Approximately a half-century later, *Paléographie musicale* issued facsimile editions of Laon, BM 239 (Vol. 10, 1909) and Chartres, BM 47 (Vol. 11, 1912), which contain respectively adiastematic readings of the Alleluia with melismatic expansion and a fragmentary reading of the sequentia Notker utilized for his text. Also in 1912, Peter Wagner published a facsimile of fol. 37 of the Leipzig, Stadtbibl. 169 (now Musikbibl. Rep. I 93), which preserves another adiastematic account of the Alleluia with its melismatic expansion.[3] Many years later, a second facsimile of this folio was published by Ewald Jammers.[4] During the interim period, there appeared the facsimile edition by Giuseppe Vecchi, *Troparium, Sequentiarium Nonantulanum, Cod. Casanat. 1741*.[5] There followed Vol. 16 of *Paléographie musicale* (1955) presenting in facsimile *Le Manuscrit du Mont-Renaud*, and Vol. 18 (1969) providing a facsimile of Rome, Bibl. Angelica 123, an adiastematic Bolognese Gradual-Troper (first half of the eleventh century) that contains both the *Alleluia Confitemini* with the melismatic expansion and a version of the Sequence itself. Karl-Heinz Schlager provided a valuable transcription and information in his *Alleluia-Melodien I*.[6] In 1978 Klaus Heinrich Kohrs published his book, *Die aparallelen Sequenzen. Repertoire, liturgische Ordnung, musikalischer Stil*.[7] Lastly, a transcription of *O quam mira* by Lance Brunner was published in 1999.[8]

A preliminary glance at the reading of *O quam mira* preserved in the Herbipolense print reveals immediately the concern for textual structure, a concern apparent throughout the source. The tones setting the individual words are set aside by tiny vertical strokes placed variously on the staff. According to the critical text edition established by Wolfgang von den Steinen,[9] the tradition for the text itself was firm, and the Herbipolense remains faithful to the tradition. There is only a single change to be noted, the use of *Pharaone* rather than *Pharao* in the last segment of the final phrase. The melodic result is a repeated *c′* that was not part of the original musical conception according to our earliest adiastematic sources. Yet the change itself is centuries old inasmuch as it is to be found also in the reading of Angelica 123. Notker's text consists of six subdivisible phrases that slowly grow in length (12, 14, 17, 17, 21 and 21 syllables in the original state). The rhyme that links the third and fourth phrases seems incidental rather than part of a premeditated design.

The ultimate basis for Notker's Sequence is the second-mode Alleluia *Confitemini Domino et invocate*, which occurs in a wide variety of liturgical assignments. It appears in the second and fifth Sundays following Easter and the fourth and eleventh Sundays after Pentecost in the sources of the *Antiphonale Missarum Sextuplex* (*AMS*). Schlager's thematic catalog of Alleluia melodies[10] indicates that the chant is given in a score of early German sources, including the well-known sources from St. Gall, Bamberg and

Einsiedeln. Often these occurrences are in collections of Alleluias, without specific liturgical assignments. It is curious that the chant is absent from later Germanic sources that are available in facsimile, such as Graz, UB 807,[11] Munich, UB 2° 156 (the Moosburger Gradual),[12] Leipzig, UB 391[13] and the *Graduale Pataviense* printed in Vienna in 1511.[14] In the Solesmes Graduals of 1943 and 1957 it is given in conjunction with the nineteenth Sunday after Pentecost. The Alleluia is a symmetrical melody, with the opening and jubilus recurring at the end of the verse. It is clear that the opening of the Sequence derives ultimately from the opening of the Alleluia (= the setting of the final two words of the verse), while the close of the Sequence is derived from the jubilus (or the end of the verse). In the Würzburg sources, such as the *Graduale Herbipolense*, the Sequence is separated from its source melody and appears instead following the Alleluias *Ascendet Deus* and *Dominus in Sina* (noted in cue) on the Sunday within the octave of Ascension. This is in fact the assignment given in the earliest sources for the Sequence, as indicated by von den Steinen.[15]

Notker, however, was not working directly with the Alleluia itself but with an intermediate source, an early sequentia. Bruno Stäblein pointed out many years ago that the *Alleluia Confitemini . . . et invocate* is one of six provided with the annotation *Cum Sequentia* in an Alleluia list that follows the entries for the twenty-third Sunday after Pentecost in the *Antiphonale missarum of Mont-Blandin* (Brussels, Bibl. Royale 10127–10144).[16] This early annotation establishes the existence of the sequentia decades before Notker's lifetime and well within the first millennium that is the focus of the present volume. Stäblein noted further that this sequentia is preserved in the Aquitanian troper-sequentiary-tonary, Paris, BNF lat. 1084, fol. 213v. This source is most often assigned to the eleventh century (with later additions), but some envisage a tenth-century origin. In addition, the sequentia was contained in the still earlier Chartres 47. This astute observation by Klaus Heinrich Kohrs appeared without further comment and is verifiable in the facsimile edition of that source.[17] Because of the damage to the later folios of the Chartres manuscript (beginning on fol. 40 and becoming increasingly severe), only the latter part of the sequentia was still in existence at the time the source was photographed. The sequentia itself appears as part of a group on p. 116 of the facsimile (fol. 60v of the destroyed manuscript), on the seventh line from the bottom (the *Alleluia Confitemini*, on the other hand, appears on p. 103 [fol. 54]).

The sequentia is normally thought of as a replacement for the repeat of the Alleluia, and it probably was so in most instances. When, however, we study the *Alleluia Confitemini Domini et invocate*, we find, thanks to the researches of Schlager, that the sequentia is also equivalent to a highly elaborated version of the final melisma from the verse that appears in conjunction with the words *opera eius*. This melisma has been made available according to the atypical reading of Paris, BNF lat. 780 in Schlager's edition of Alleluia melodies.[18] In his notes, Schlager informs us that the melisma appears in seven non-Germanic adiastematic sources, including the Antiphoner of Mont-Renaud; Laon 239; Oxford, Bodleian Lib., Bodley 775; Cambrai, BM 75;

Angelica 123; Paris, BNF lat. 9436 (first half only); and Leipzig Rep. I 93. If we combine the information provided by Paris 780 with that of the sequentia version in Paris 1084, and use the seven diastematic readings of the texted Sequence as a control, we can arrive at interpretations of the adiastematic neumes that should not be too far from the mark. In this fashion we may gain a rough idea of the melody as it may have been known to Notker. Example 16.1 compares the two pitch-readable models and a series of reconstructions.

Examining the neumations given in Ex. 16.1, one will readily observe that the later history of the sequentia was unstable. The most unusual of the readings is that of Paris 780, a late eleventh- or twelfth-century source from Narbonne. This is perhaps to be expected in view of previous findings concerning this source. In Vol. 4 of *Le Graduel romain*, edited by the monks of Solesmes, Paris 780 is found to be the most individual of the Aquitanian chant sources. And we have strong corroborating evidence for this finding in the treatment of the *Alleluia Pulchra facie*,[19] which contains an extensive idiosyncratic passage in this source. The final phrases of the *Alleluia Confitemini . . . et invocate* in Paris 780 are only loosely related to those employed by its counterparts elsewhere; Notker did not use (and likely did not know) a melody form that ended as does this one.

The reading for the other of our diastematic versions of the sequentia, that of Paris 1084, is also idiosyncratic, but to a much lesser extent. This reading lacks the third and sixth neumes of the sequentia, found in all the other readings for this melody. And, in the sixth phrase (in the normative reading), there is a descent to *A* (cf. the third bracket in Ex. 16.1) that is unparalleled elsewhere. The result of this descent is an ensuing upward leap of a minor sixth, back to *f*, a leap that is uncharacteristic of the melodic vocabulary of chant. Other readings are unusual in still other ways. The version of Cambrai 75 is more elaborate in its center than are its counterparts, while the reading of Laon 239 has two small gaps.

Given that our diastematic sources come from areas other than those of their adiastematic counterparts, this relative lack of unanimity poses difficulties in three areas when one attempts to reconstruct the various unheightened readings. These difficulties are compounded when one finds that one of our most valuable diastematic readings, Einsiedeln, SB 366, is very difficult to use, as will be discussed later. When considering the sequentia, the first of the problems occurs in the area equivalent to Notker's third text phrase, associated with the word *terribilem* (cf. the first bracket in Ex. 16.1). Paris 1084 reads *F–G–E–D* at this point, while Paris 780 gives *F–G D–C*. This latter is corroborated by the three Nonantolese versions of the Sequence, while the Würzburg readings for the Sequence give *E–F–D–C*. The Einsiedeln reading of the Sequence is apparently *F–G–G–F–D*. Inasmuch as seven of the nine sources agree that the lowest point of this juncture is *C*, I generally give preference to the reading of Paris 780. Our two diastematic sources for the sequentia are both Aquitanian, and it is difficult to make a case that one or the other would either have been a direct reflection of more northerly or easterly sources, or, alternatively, would have had a direct influence on any

Ex. 16.1 Sequence *O quam mira*: (a) Paris, BNF lat. 1084; (b) Chartres, BM 47; (c) Oxford, Bodleian Lib., Bodley 775; (d) Laon, BM 239; (e) Paris, 'Mont-Renaud MS'; (f) Cambrai, BM 75; (g) Rome, Bibl. Angelica 123; (h) Leipzig, Musikbibl. I 93; (i) Paris, BNF lat. 9436; (j) Paris, BNF lat. 780; (k) proposed reconstruction of St. Gall, SB 484

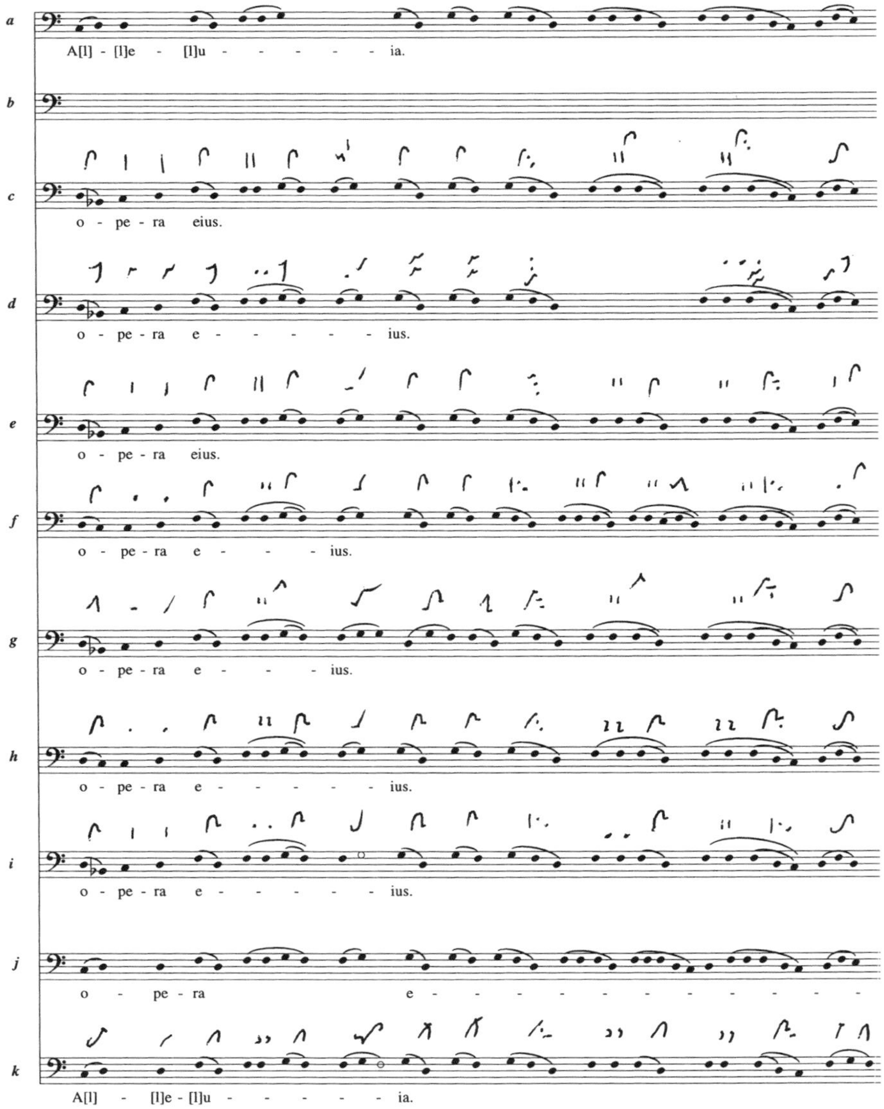

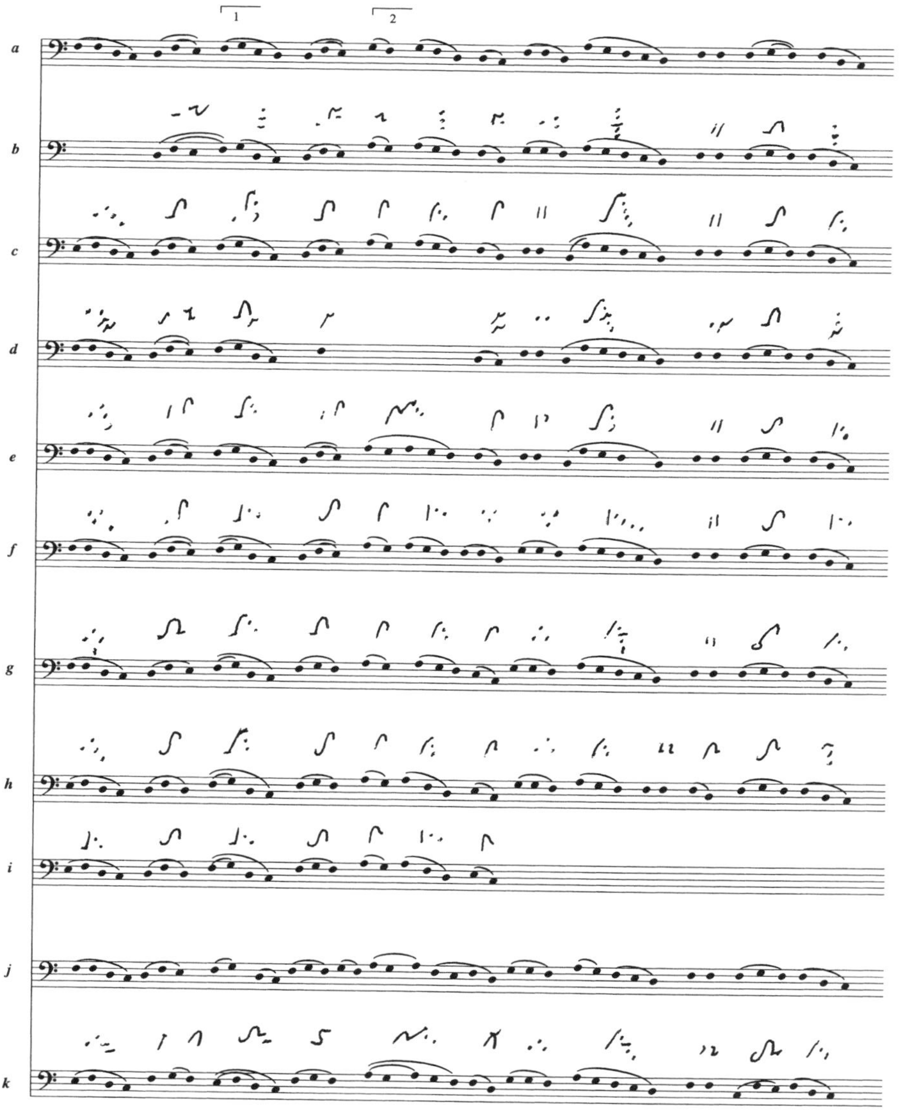
1
2
a
b
c
d
e
f
g
h
i
j
k

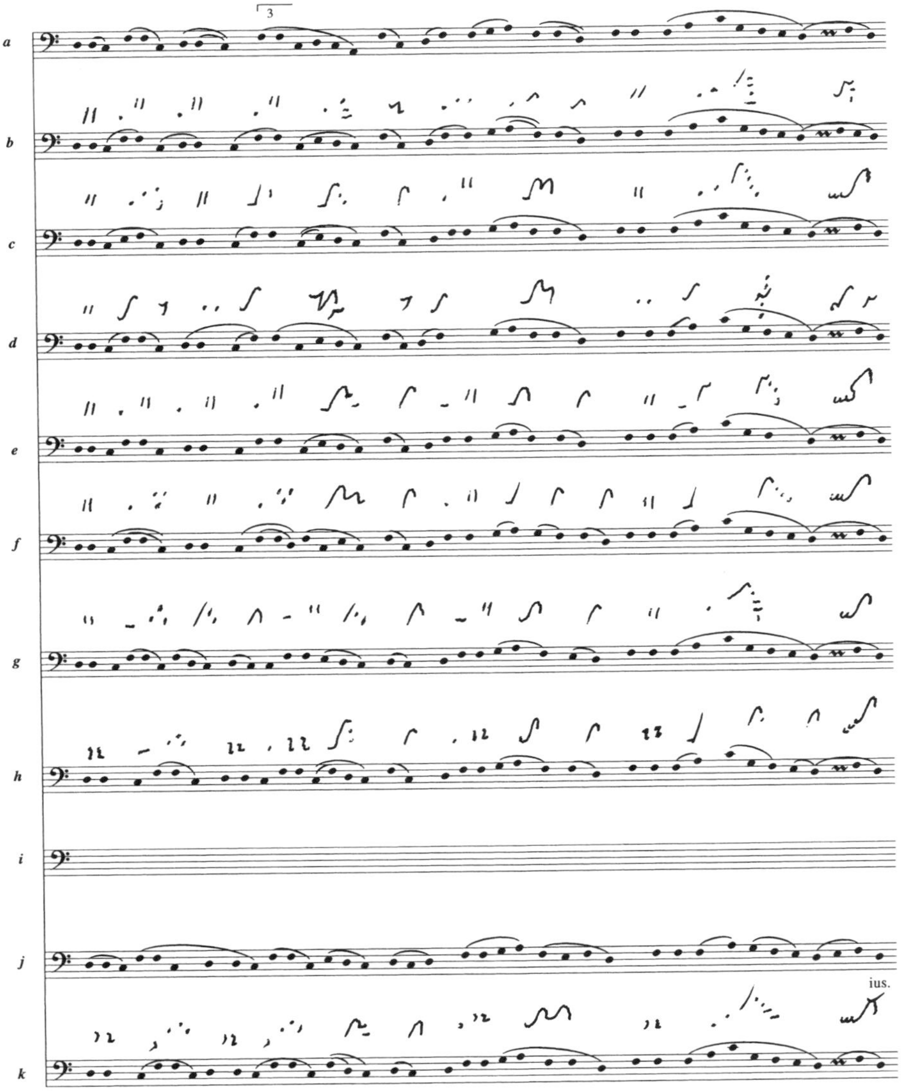
a
b
c
d
e
f
g
h
i
j
k
3
ius.

of them. I see no reason to belittle the testimony of the late sources. The Würzburg sources at least have the virtue of being in closer proximity to Notker's St. Gall than the remaining manuscripts.

The second area of difficulty begins at the outset of the fourth phrase of Notker's texted version (bracketed area 2 in Ex. 16.1). Here Paris 1084 reads *G–F, G–F–D, D–C, F–F–D*. Paris 780, on the other hand, gives *A–G–A, F–E F–D, G–G–F*. Einsiedeln 366 is quite close to this latter, reading *A G A G F F D G G F*. The Würzburg sources agree with this reading, while the Nonantolan sequentiary reads *A G A F D E C G G F*. Nonantola too begins on the *A* level and concludes *G G F*. The interior is slightly different (see above). I feel that in this instance we can accord a clear preference to the readings of MS 780, Einsiedeln and Würzburg. We cannot know whether Notker knew the first large descent as *A F E F D* or *A G F F D*, but the effect of this alternative on the larger picture is minimal.

The final area of difficulty begins with the section of Notker's text setting the syllables [*argen*]-*teum cogni*-[*tus*] (bracketed area 3 in Ex. 16.1). It is here that the reading of Paris 1084 descends to *A* in contradistinction to all other readings, which descend only to *C*. We need not label the variant in Paris 1084 as a mistake; it may simply represent a contrasting version that was known in one or a few locales. Nevertheless, I see no reason to take this reading as the basis for the interpretation of sources from other areas.

We may now focus our attention on the surviving sources for Notker's Sequence. Obviously, the adiastematic, untexted sources from St. Gall and related areas are most valuable in giving us our earliest accounts of the Sequence as it was created by Notker. Those who have not had occasion to work with films from St. Gall, Bamberg, Zurich or Munich, or with the recent facsimile edition of Einsiedeln, SB 121, may wish to consult the facsimile of fol. 16^{v} from London, BL Add. 19768 given by David Hiley in his book *Western Plainchant*.[20] The typical Germanic layout may be observed in which the text of the Sequence is given on the main body of the page toward the binding, with a largely syllabic notation entered above the relevant syllables. In a smaller column on the outer portion of the page a neumatic version of the same melody is given. Given this two-column format, there is insufficient space to complete a long verse on a single text line, and the verse must therefore be split between two lines, the beginning being differentiated by a small capital, and the continuation often being marked by some indentation. Both in Germanic areas and in other areas, there are alternatives to this side-by-side presentation. The earliest of the St. Gall sources, SB 484, presents only the neumatic version of the Sequence, with the opening letters of the syllables of Alleluia, and an identification by means of rubric. For this study I have collated the readings of St. Gall, SB 484, 376, 380 and 381; Bamberg, Staatsbibl. lit. 5 and lit. 6; Munich, BSB clm 14083; and Berlin, Staatsbibl. 4° 11. Readings for *O quam mira* are lacking from St. Gall 375, 378 and 382; London, Add. 19768; and Zurich, Zentralbibl. Rh. 132, while Paris, BNF lat. 9448 lacks notation.

Once the melody was firmly associated with a fixed text, the kinds of flexibility that were noted with regard to the melodies for the sequentia and the melismatic expansion of the verse were no longer possible. Relatively few significant variants are to be found. This does not mean that the neumations remain completely constant. With few exceptions, however, the variants do not affect the numbers of pitches or melodic shape. Nevertheless, our adiastematic readings can be brought to life only through comparative study of later diastematic sources.

Potentially the most valuable of these is Einsiedeln 366, ascribed variously to the late eleventh or early twelfth century. This source is relatively early and has the advantage of coming from an area not too distant from St. Gall. It is this source that provided the basis for the contributions of Schubiger and Jammers. Unfortunately, the manuscript is in very poor condition, many folios surviving only in part. While I am most grateful to have been given access to a reproduction, there are moments when I am simply unable to see what had been written and at these times I have sought help from the earlier transcriptions. By and large these corroborate one another. Like many other sources, this manuscript gives the texted form of the Sequence on the inner portion of each page, and an untexted form on the outer. Unfortunately, the verso folio on which *O quam mira* begins is lacking its outer portion. The neumatic version survives on the following recto for less than half the work. And while the syllabic and neumatic versions are fairly similar both for this work and for *Carmen suo*, they are not identical. Einsiedeln 366 was prepared using minimal vertical space for the neumes. This fact comes into play in two passages marked in the comparative transcription where the Einsiedeln version lies a second higher than all of its remaining companions, either through error or through knowledge of a divergent performance practice. It is particularly unfortunate that we are without the neumatic counterpart of the texted Sequence, because this might have clarified which of these alternatives is the more likely.

Of roughly comparable date are three sources from the region of Nonantola edited, as mentioned above, by Lance Brunner. The main source is the sequentiary Rome, Bibl. Casanatense 1741, dating from the end of the eleventh century. Rome, Bibl. Naz. Cen. 1343 is of similar date, while Bologna, Bibl. Univ. 2824 is later, stemming from either the twelfth or thirteenth century. As demonstrated in Brunner's critical notes,[21] the three readings are very close to one another, varying primarily in the doubling of certain notes and in the addition of a few liquescents.

The Würzburg tradition for *O quam mira*, also documented in three sources, is the latest. The earliest of the group is Würzburg, UB M p th f. 165, a fourteenth-century source mentioned in the literature by Andreas Haug[22] and by Volker Schier.[23] In 1496, there appeared the printed Gradual issued by Georg Reyser, and lastly we have the *Graduale Herbipolense* of 1583. In evaluating these, we ought to keep in mind the fact that the earliest of these three contains the fewest tropes, while the latest has the greatest number. Clearly the three cannot be regarded merely as direct descendants of one another. The variants between the three are quite rare; I shall discuss the only one of consequence.

On the whole, the readings represented on the top three staves of Ex. 16.2 are reasonably close to one another. Examining the first phrase of the

Ex. 16.2 Sequence *O quam mira*: (a) *Graduale Herbipolense*, 1583; (b) Rome, Bibl. Casanatense 1741 (repetition of first phrase with text Alleluia omitted); (c) Einsiedeln, SB 366; (d) proposed reconstruction of St. Gall, SB 484

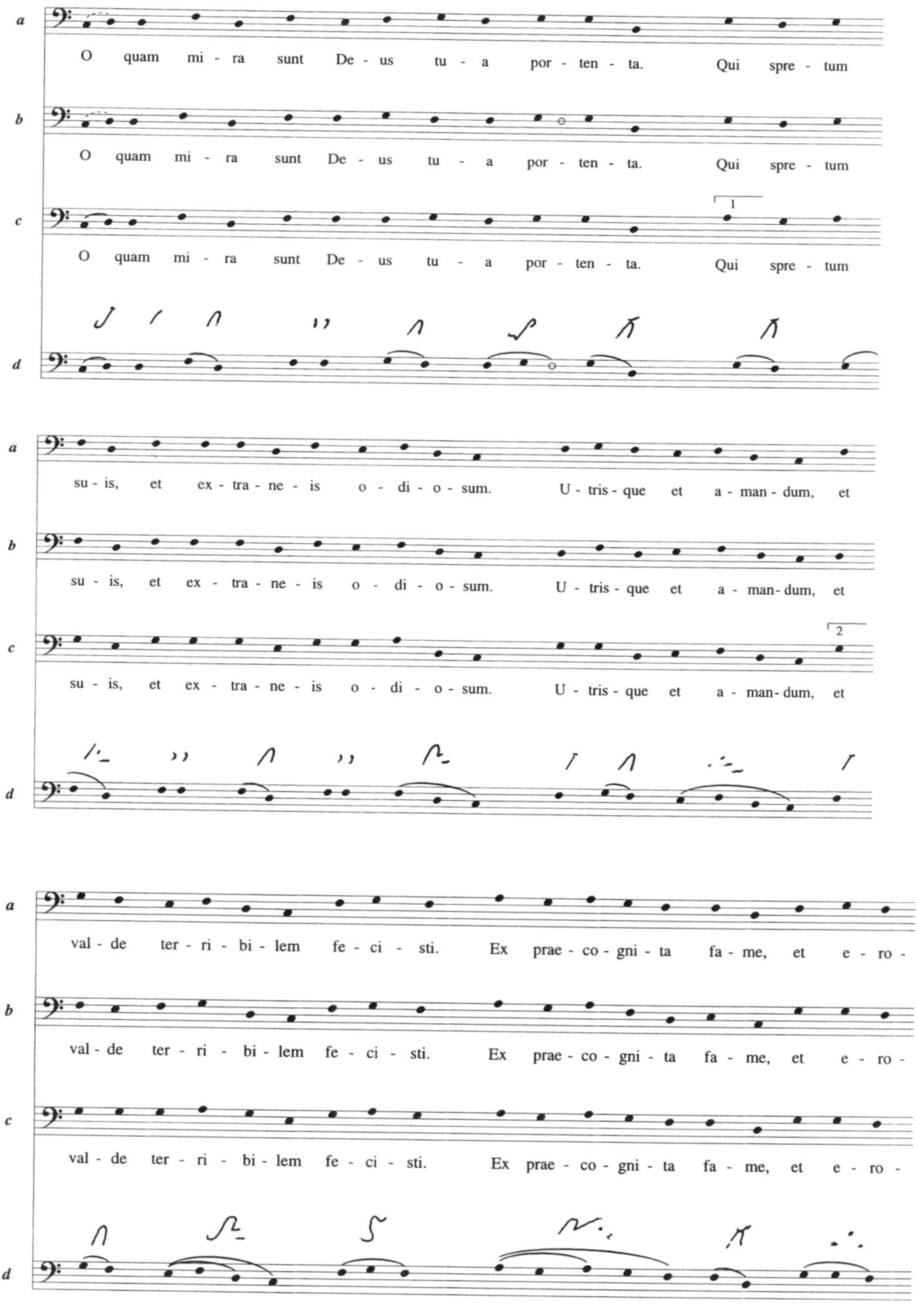

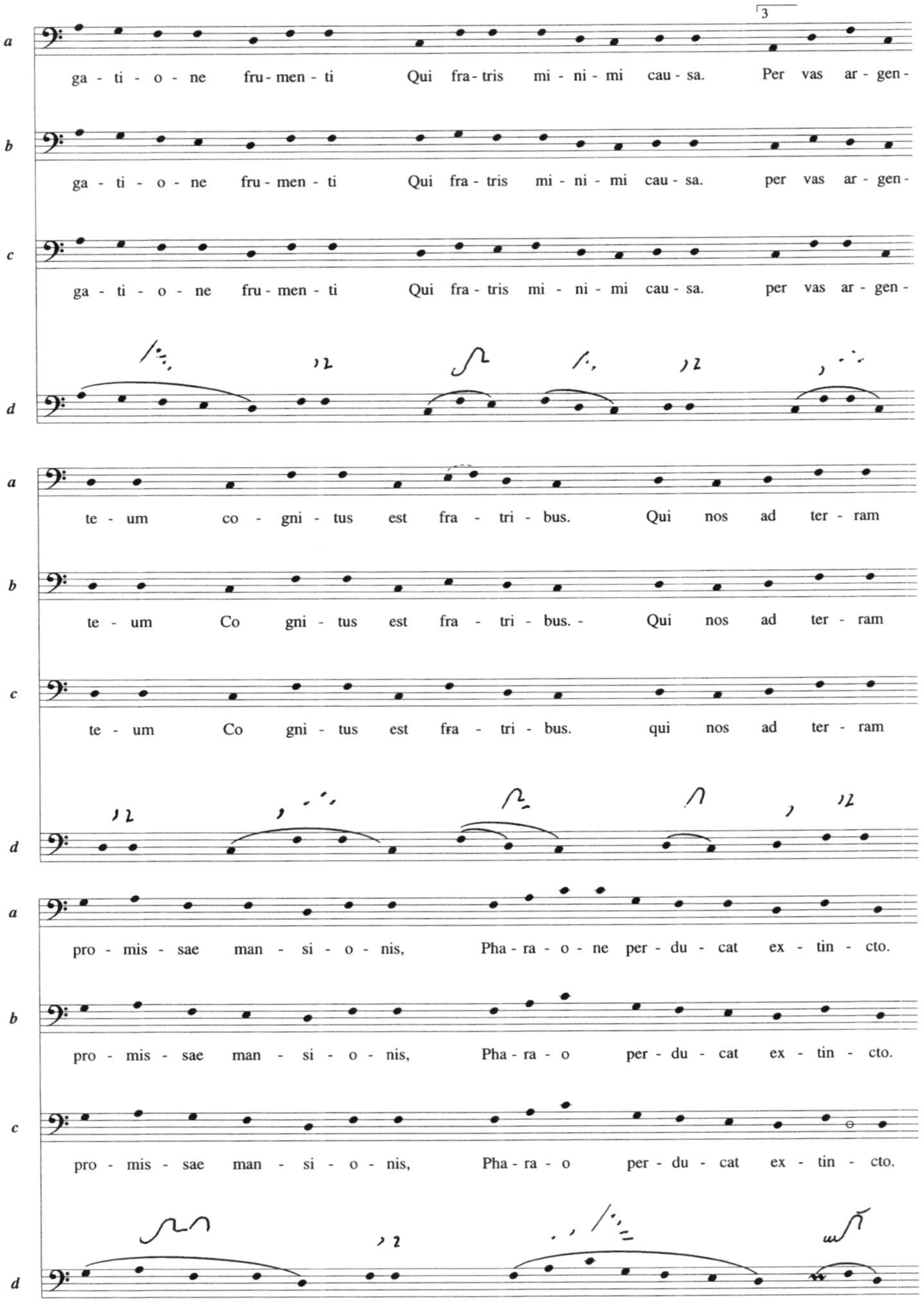
a
ga - ti - o - ne fru - men - ti Qui fra - tris mi - ni - mi cau - sa. Per vas ar - gen -
b
ga - ti - o - ne fru - men - ti Qui fra - tris mi - ni - mi cau - sa. per vas ar - gen -
c
ga - ti - o - ne fru - men - ti Qui fra - tris mi - ni - mi cau - sa. per vas ar - gen -
d
a
te - um co - gni - tus est fra - tri - bus. Qui nos ad ter - ram
b
te - um Co gni - tus est fra - tri - bus. - Qui nos ad ter - ram
c
te - um Co gni - tus est fra - tri - bus. qui nos ad ter - ram
d
a
pro - mis - sae man - si - o - nis, Pha - ra - o - ne per - du - cat ex - tin - cto.
b
pro - mis - sae man - si - o - nis, Pha - ra - o per - du - cat ex - tin - cto.
c
pro - mis - sae man - si - o - nis, Pha - ra - o per - du - cat ex - tin - cto.
d

Sequence, we may note that the reading of the Herbipolense corresponds quite well to the earlier readings available to us. We may note that the setting of the word *Deus* is distinctive, but this is not necessarily attributable to the lateness of the source and a deterioration of the tradition. The same reading is observable not only in the earlier readings of the 1496 Reyser print and Würzburg f. 165, but seems to be adumbrated in the adiastematic reading of Angelica 123, where the word in question is set by a punctum followed by a virga, apparently implying the upward motion specified in the three Würzburg sources. There is thus an early basis for the reading even though it is specifically denied by the succession of a bistropha and clivis found in all but one of the Germanic sources for the textless Sequence, as exemplified in the proposed reconstruction for St. Gall 484. (Berlin 4° 11 employs an idiosyncratic line break for this phrase; this seems to have caused a displacement in the remainder of the phrase, the last three neumes each moving one syllable to the right.) This small variant would scarcely be worth dwelling on were it not for the fact that it is symptomatic of a larger pattern that recurs frequently. We shall have occasion to note that disagreements among readings of various chants often affect the half-step clusters, *E–F* and *b–c*. The liquescent for the first syllable of *portenta*, present in the readings of St. Gall 484 and Casanatense 1741, is lacking in the two later Würzburg sources, and is given equally appropriately on the middle syllable of Würzburg f. 165. (In Angelica 123 we find an oriscus instead of a liquescent.)

In Einsiedeln 366, the second phrase is notated a second higher than normal (Ex. 16.2, bracket 1) with the exception of the two last notes. Given the agreement in pitch height among the two Aquitanian readings of the sequentia and the melismatic expansion, together with the unanimity of both the Nonantolese and Würzburg sources, we are justified in treating the Einsiedeln reading as inferior, regardless of the origin of the disparity. In the setting of the final word we again encounter variability affecting the half-step cluster. St. Gall 484, together with 376 and 380, Einsiedeln 121, Bamberg lit. 5 and Munich clm 14083, all employ a bistropha as the penultimate neume, thus indicating a tonal repetition on *F*. However, St. Gall 376, 381 and Berlin 4° 11 combine the tones in another fashion. The first element of the bistropha is incorporated into a preceding porrectus, while the second is assimilated into the final neume. This division allows a reading that corresponds to those of the Nonantolese and Würzburg sources, while the last neume recurs in the setting of the second and third words of the following phrase, allowing for motivic reinforcement.

In the third phrase, beginning with the words *et valde* (Ex. 16.2, bracket 2), Einsiedeln 366 again seems to be written a second higher than intended. All other readings cadence on *F*, and this tone serves as the goal for two later cadences, thus providing a subsidiary tonal center as a contrast to the eventual final, *D*. The cadence on *G* seems out of place in this framework and I again regard this reading as inferior.

The most striking variant in the Herbipolense reading of 1583 concerns the descent to *A* at the words *Per vas* (Ex. 16.2, bracket 3). This reading occurs also in the Reyser print of 1496, but Würzburg f. 165 has the normative *C–F*.

The lower alternative could very easily have resulted from a momentary clef-reading error. It is clearly an inferior reading. Nevertheless, I cannot help but recall that – at a later point in the melody – Paris 1084 also descends to the low *A*. This may be entirely coincidental, as is indeed likely. But I am not inclined to toss this passage from the Würzburg reading into the garbage bin for the time being. Perhaps prior to the turn of the millennium there was somewhat greater variety to the performance of this melody than we are able to document through our surviving sources.

The second of the Notkerian Sequences that is absent from late Germanic sources outside of the Würzburg orbit is *Carmen suo dilecto* (Ex. 16.3; Track 20 on the accompanying compact disc). This is a Sequence that presents a form closer to what is regarded as normative. Following a brief opening single of seven syllables, there are three double versicles of slightly varying lengths. The concluding section consists of another brief single of ten syllables, a double and a final single. The Sequence with its melody has been made available by Anselm Schubiger; by Nicolas de Goede in his edition of the Utrecht Prosarium (Utrecht 417); by Richard Crocker, in his book on the early medieval Sequence; and most recently in an article by Francesca Negro.[24]

Carmen suo may be judged unusual in at least two respects: (1) the frequent recurrence of certain melodic material; (2) the cadence structures. Crocker has dealt fully with the former aspect. Doubts concerning the latter may perhaps be allayed by consultation of a larger number of sources than was apparently available to previous editors. In addition to the appearance of this Sequence in numerous adiastematic sources, it is known now from the *Graduale Herbipolense* and its two Würzburg predecessors, as well as from Einsiedeln 366, Utrecht 417, Munich clm 4101, Klosterneuburg, SB 588 and Padua, BC B. 16.[25] The latter contains an unusual reading that I have been able to consult only through the aforementioned article by Negro. While most diastematic readings place the final on *D*, those in St. Gall 380 (a letter notation added for this one work) and Padua B. 16 lie a fourth higher. This pitch level may perhaps be more suitable for an accommodation to the liturgical position of the Sequence, which follows the *Alleluia Laudate pueri* on the Saturday of Easter Week. Nevertheless, in the Middle Ages the choice of pitch did not reflect any standard of absolute pitch, but was determined merely by the convenience of notating the constituent melodic gestures. The notated pitches did not necessarily imply any particular relationship to the notated pitches of chants that preceded or followed. Neither Padua B. 16 nor St. Gall 380 gives the melody in full, but the gaps can be remedied through consultation of counterparts in the other halves of the paired versicles. Among the adiastematic readings, I have collated those of St. Gall 484, 376, 380, 381, Einsiedeln 121, Bamberg lit. 5 and lit. 6, Berlin 4° 11, Munich clm 14083, and Zurich Rh. 132.

The normal notation for the phrases – other than the last – of *Carmen suo* has the cadences closing with an upward motion. The adiastematic sources preserved at St. Gall, Einsiedeln, Zurich, Bamberg and Berlin all give the final neume of the untexted versions as a salicus, normally implying the upward motion of a third.[26] The sole dissenting voice among the readings that I consulted is that of Munich clm 14083, which steadfastly ends the phrases with a pes stratus. The known surviving diastematic sources waver somewhat in their choices, but upward cadences spanning a minor third constitute the majority. It is of course possible that this was interpreted by the singers as *B♭–C–D*, but this hypothesis seems to entail in its wake more difficulties than it solves. At any rate, no source now known gives the cadence as a major third.

This cadence, *B–C–D* (or *E–F–G*), is decidedly atypical for the genre, all the more so since it is preceded by the descent of a diminished fifth, *F–D–B*. Sensitive to this fact, Richard Crocker proposed an editorial revision that had cadences on *C–D–E*, thus eliminating the troubling descent of a diminished fifth.[27] Whether the resultant rapprochement with the *Alleluia Laudate pueri* was a factor in his decision is not stated. Nevertheless, a cadence on *C–D–E* is at least equally atypical of those Sequences that I have had occasion to study; the interpretation does not succeed in producing an alternative that fits within stylistic norms. For the final cadence, Crocker proposes the reading *F–F–E*, which he presents as conforming with chant practice. I should like to suggest, however, that within the chant idiom cadences on *E* are lengthier than three notes. They normally involve two neumes, either *E–G–F–F, F–E* or *E–G–E–F, F–E*. The pattern of Notker's Sequence is not equivalent to either.

In reflecting on the nature of the cadence structures of *Carmen suo* we cannot afford to disregard the degree of unanimity among nine diastematic sources, including one from Notker's St. Gall. Moreover, we need note that terminations on *D* are unequivocally indicated by means of Romanian letters in at least one, if not two important adiastematic sources. The fourth versicle of this Sequence begins with an upward leap of a fifth, *D–a* (or its equivalent, *G–d*), in all diastematic sources. Occasionally an adiastematic source may hint at the size of the leap by employing the Romanian letter *s* at the opening of each member of the pair. St. Gall 381 has at each of these junctures the Romanian letter *e*, indicating that the leap begins at the same height as the previous cadential tone, which thus has to be *D*. It is possible – perhaps probable – that the same Romanian letter is to be found in the reading of Bamberg lit. 5, although this may be no more than wishful thinking on my part. If the letter is indeed to be read as *e*, one must remark that it is not formed in the same manner as other *e*s in this portion of the manuscript. Nevertheless, a comparable objection applies should one read the letter as *t*. I do not believe that other alternatives are possible, and the proposed reading as *e* at least has the virtue of existing within an understandable context and with corroboration from another source.

It remains to consider one further possibility, namely that the cadences for the main body of *Carmen suo* were intended to sound *B♭–C–D*. If we pursue this avenue, we attribute the lack of a signed *B♭* to the fact that this tone was not part of the Guidonian gamut and therefore was shunned in all but rare circumstances. We would be dealing with what became known in the late fourteenth century as the first *coniuncta*. This tone constituted a problem that arose from time to time in the associated realm of chant Propers and we may hope to learn something from the ways in which it is treated there. A simple instance occurs in the second-mode Introit *Multae tribulationes*, which has a final cadence area that includes a major third below the final. There are sources (including the *Graduale Herbipolense* of 1583) that notate the chant at the normal height and trust to the discretion of the singer to know that the *B*♭ is intended. In Graz 807, the flat is specified by means of a second *B* added to the letter clefs. More frequently, the chant is simply notated a fifth higher, and this is a standard solution for many other chants of this sort. The important point is that there are alternative notations and we are thus alerted to the existence of the problem in sources that seem to ignore it. Unfortunately, *Multae tribulationes* does not present a close parallel to the problems encountered in *Carmen suo*. The *coniuncta* occurs only once in the former work, not multiple times, and notation a fifth higher poses no difficulty. In *Carmen suo*, on the other hand, the problem degree is part of a regularly recurrent pattern. Furthermore, notation a fifth higher would require *F*♯ as part of the sixth versicle. Even so, this degree would occur only twice, and the necessity for the tone could be evaded, particularly in the Germanic dialect (the Introit *Adorate Deum* provides an example of such evasion). Notation at the upper fifth would be the lesser of the two evils. Those who were highly sensitive to this latter problem had still another solution open to them. They could notate the sensitive versicle a fourth rather than a fifth higher, momentarily adopting the notational practice of St. Gall 380 and Padua B. 16. These are only some of the devices that one finds in dealing with the various *coniunctae*. A host of solutions are to be found in investigating the notation of the Gradual *Salvum fac servum*. If, as in this chant, a scribe chose to notate *Carmen suo* at the original height and to use partial transposition, he could have followed the advice of Guido d'Arezzo and notated the segments involving the cadence a second higher; these segments would have been somewhat longer than three notes. Wherever one has theoretical evidence of the presence of a *coniuncta* in a Proper chant, one can find – when dealing with multiple sources – scribes experimenting with alternative notational solutions. This is not, however, true for *Carmen suo*. There was something about the cadence structures of the Sequence that caused scribes discomfort, as has been made clear in earlier discussion and as we shall see in Ex. 16.3, but the scribal alternatives never follow the routes that were employed with regard to the *coniunctae*.[28]

If we were dealing with no more than one to three sources for *Carmen suo*, we would have to take into account the possibility that our sources were atypical. In that event the hypothesis that we are dealing with a *coniuncta* would remain viable. Diastematic readings of *Carmen suo* that are lacking from Ex. 16.3 may yet be located among sources that were unavailable to me. Nevertheless I have searched a few dozen diastematic Germanic sequentiaries beyond those mentioned in this essay without locating this chant. The likelihood that further search will turn up more than two or three additional readings seems small. We do have sources coming from seven disparate locations, and I take it to be significant that none of them displays a reading consistent with known treatments of *coniunctae*. For this reason I am prepared reluctantly to allow the stylistically troubling readings of *B–C–D* to stand without emendation.

In its layout, Ex. 16.3 departs from the practice of the previous two examples. In order that the variants stand out as clearly as possible in a larger score format I have limited the entries on staves *b–f* to those pitches that diverge from the reading of the *Graduale Herbipolense*. The remaining staves, on the other hand, are given in full in order to distinguish between what is and is not present in the musical texts of St. Gall 380 and Padua B. 16. The proposed reconstruction of St. Gall 484 is of necessity given in full inasmuch as it is simply the product of my thinking.

An initial scanning of the variants will demonstrate quickly that many of these involve the half-step clusters, *B–C* and *E–F*. The contrast between the readings of Einsiedeln 366 (staff *e*) and Klosterneuburg 588 (staff *f*) on the one hand, and the Utrecht Prosarium (staff *d*) on the other, is especially striking. Note how frequently the Einsiedeln and Klosterneuburg sources employ *F* in instances where the Herbipolense and other readings utilize *E*. Even the customary triadic formation *C–E–C–E–G* becomes *C–F–C–F–G*. The Utrecht source, on the other hand, follows an opposite path. The reader will readily note how frequently this manuscript makes use of *E* when other sources prefer *F*. This is especially apparent with regard to the first two versicles.

The opening of the final double versicle (*Ecce* and *Tute*, respectively) is informative with regard to the history of transmission for this Sequence. In all of the adiastematic St. Gall sources, as well as those preserved at Bamberg, Einsiedeln and Zurich, the opening is notated as a virga followed by a higher bivirga. The latter should indicate a repeated pitch – in this instance, *c c* – as has already been made clear in Richard Crocker's transcription. Nevertheless, among the diastematic sources, this configuration is to be found only in the reading of the Utrecht Prosarium and, in a variant form, in the reading of Padua B. 16. The Würzburg sources give a diatonic ascent of a third, *a–b–c*. Einsiedeln 366, Munich clm 4101, Klosterneuburg 588 and St. Gall 380 have the upward leap of a minor third but then descend a half-step. One can only wonder about the possible inflection of the bivirga in the early performance tradition that might have produced such divergences in later diastematic notation.

Another area of change between the adiastematic and diastematic readings involves the latter half of the second versicle, where an elision must link the words *natura et* if symmetry in syllable count is to be maintained with the prior half. Indeed, the adiastematic readings consulted all demand this elision. On the other hand, the later diastematic sources, with the sole exception of Einsiedeln 366, all disregard the elision.

A similar disparity between adiastematic and diastematic readings affects the various phrase endings. The former present a consistent account of these, using the same neume for all. The latter, on the other hand, waver in their interpretations of the cadence, without, however, varying in its relative height or the surrounding interval constellation. Disregarding the very brief opening single, both the *Graduale Herbipolense* and the much earlier Einsiedeln 366

Ex. 16.3 Sequence *Carmen suo dilecto*: (a) *Graduale Herbipolense*, 1583; (b) Reyser, 1496 and Würzburg, UB 165; (c) Munich, BSB clm 4101; (d) Utrecht, Universiteitsbibl. 417; (e) Einsiedeln, SB 366; (f) Klosterneuburg, SB 588; (g) St. Gall, SB 380; (h) Padua, BC B. 16; (i) proposed reconstruction of St. Gall, SB 484

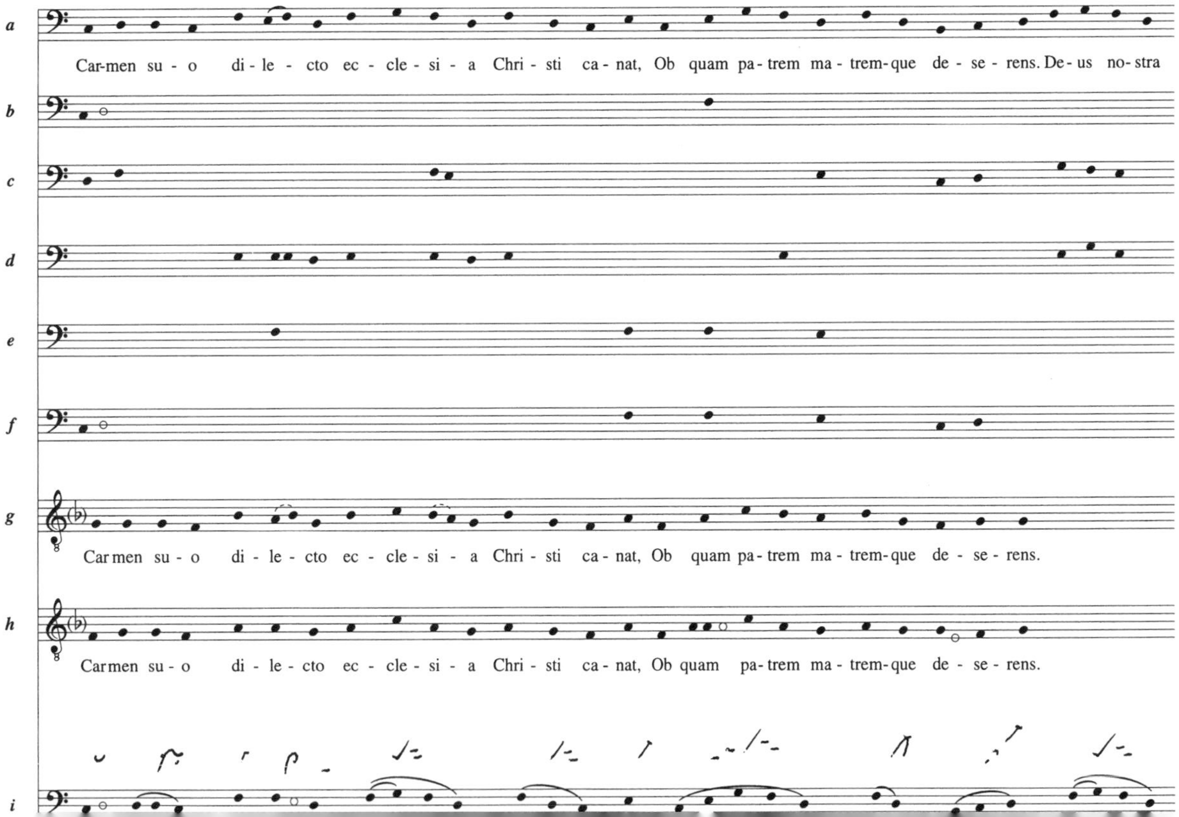

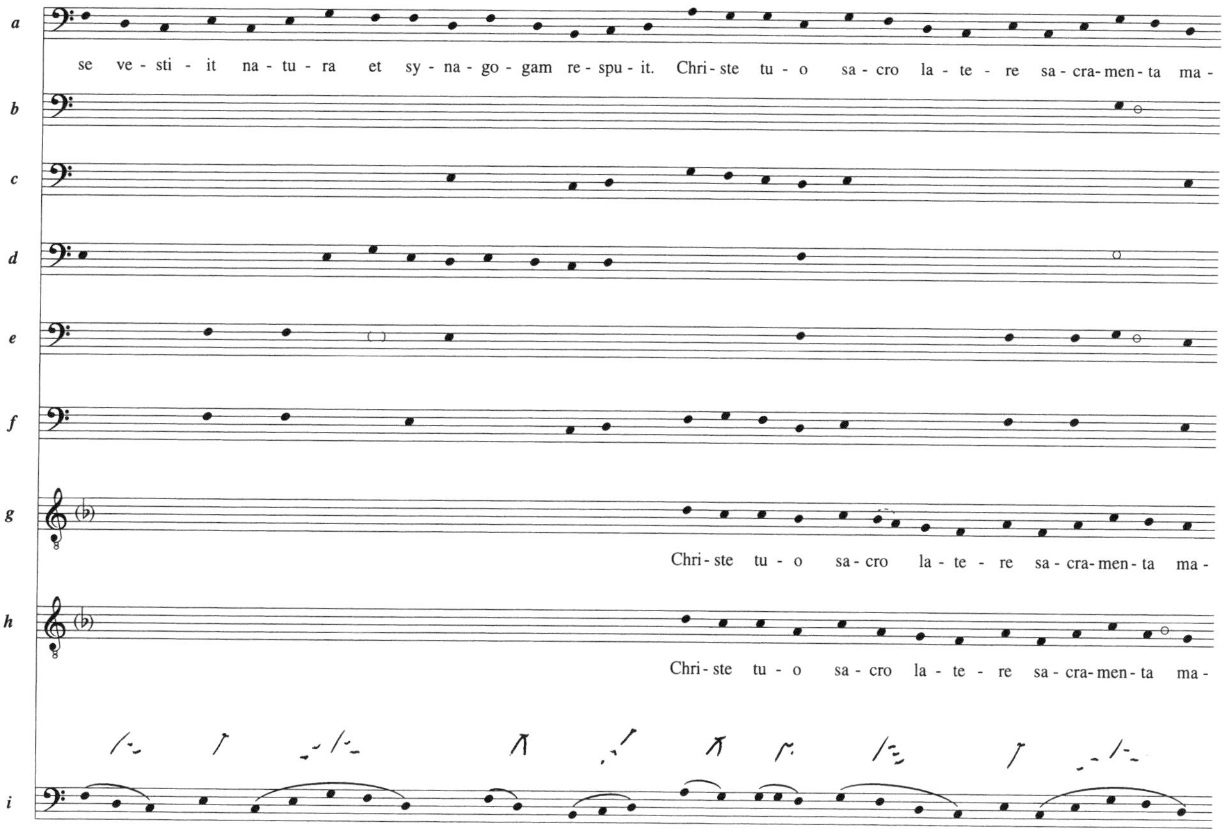
a
se ve - sti - it na - tu - ra et sy - na - go - gam re - spu - it. Chri - ste tu - o sa - cro la - te - re sa - cra - men - ta ma -
b
c
d
e
f
g
Chri - ste tu - o sa - cro la - te - re sa - cra - men - ta ma -
h
Chri - ste tu - o sa - cro la - te - re sa - cra - men - ta ma -
i

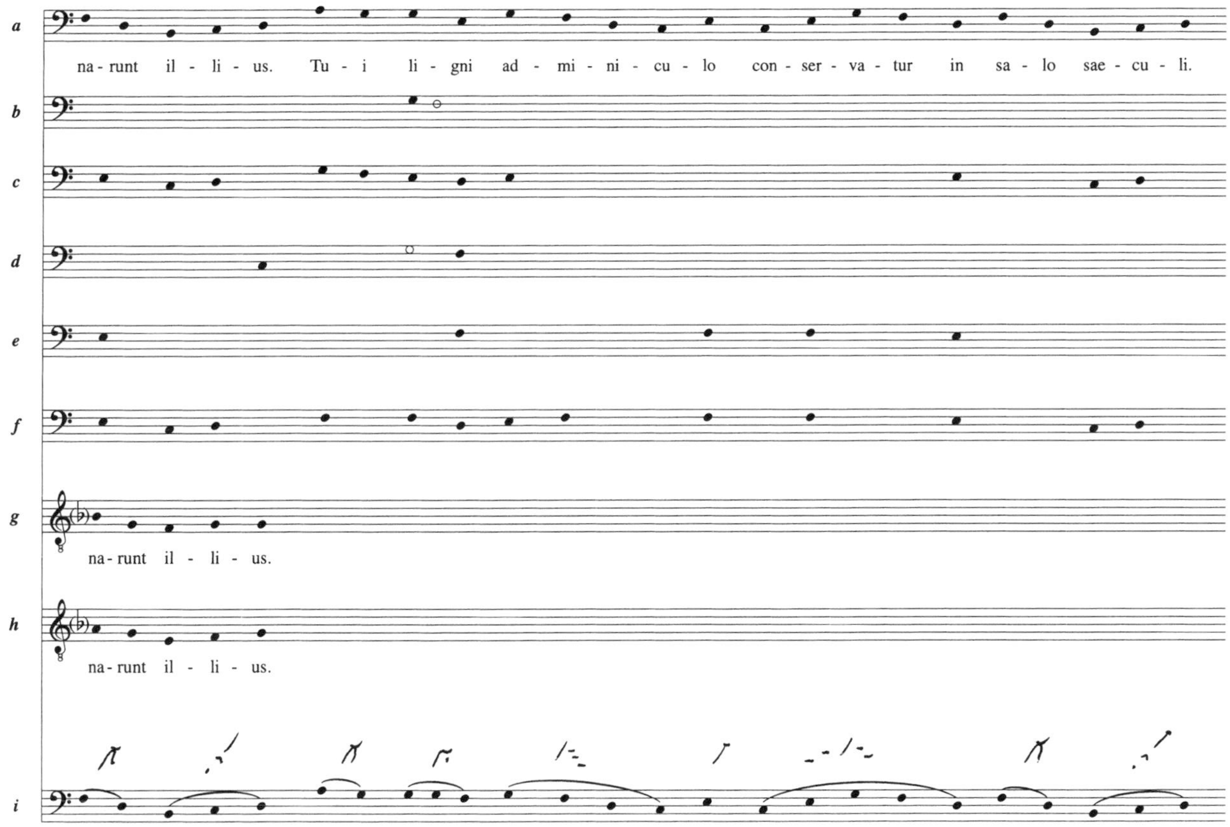
a
na - runt il - li - us. Tu - i li - gni ad - mi - ni - cu - lo con - ser - va - tur in sa - lo sae - cu - li.
b
c
d
e
f
g
na - runt il - li - us.
h
na - runt il - li - us.
i

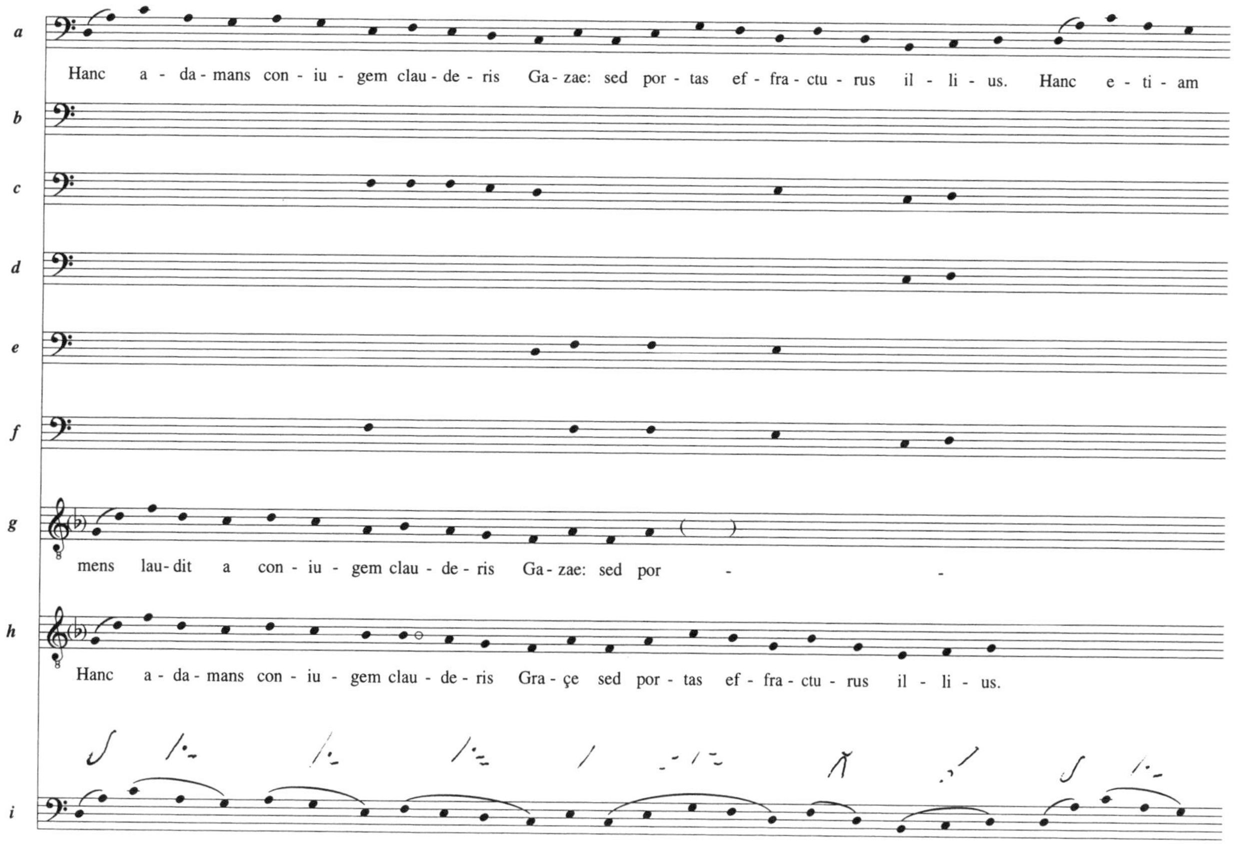
a
Hanc a - da - mans con - iu - gem clau - de - ris Ga - zae: sed por - tas ef - fra - ctu - rus il - li - us. Hanc e - ti - am
b
c
d
e
f
g
mens lau - dit a con - iu - gem clau - de - ris Ga - zae: sed por - -
h
Hanc a - da - mans con - iu - gem clau - de - ris Gra - çe sed por - tas ef - fra - ctu - rus il - li - us.
i

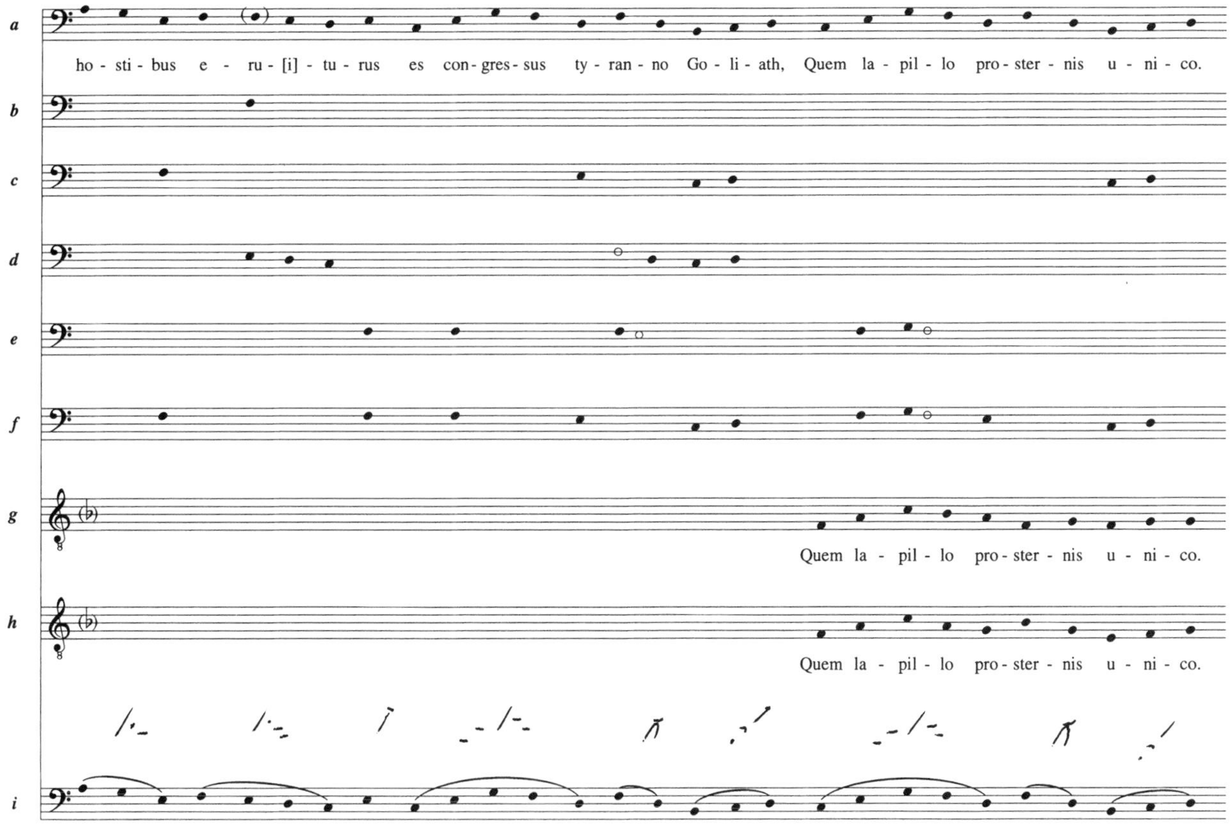
a
ho - sti - bus e - ru - [i] - tu - rus es con - gres - sus ty - ran - no Go - li - ath, Quem la - pil - lo pro - ster - nis u - ni - co.
b
c
d
e
f
g
Quem la - pil - lo pro - ster - nis u - ni - co.
h
Quem la - pil - lo pro - ster - nis u - ni - co.
i

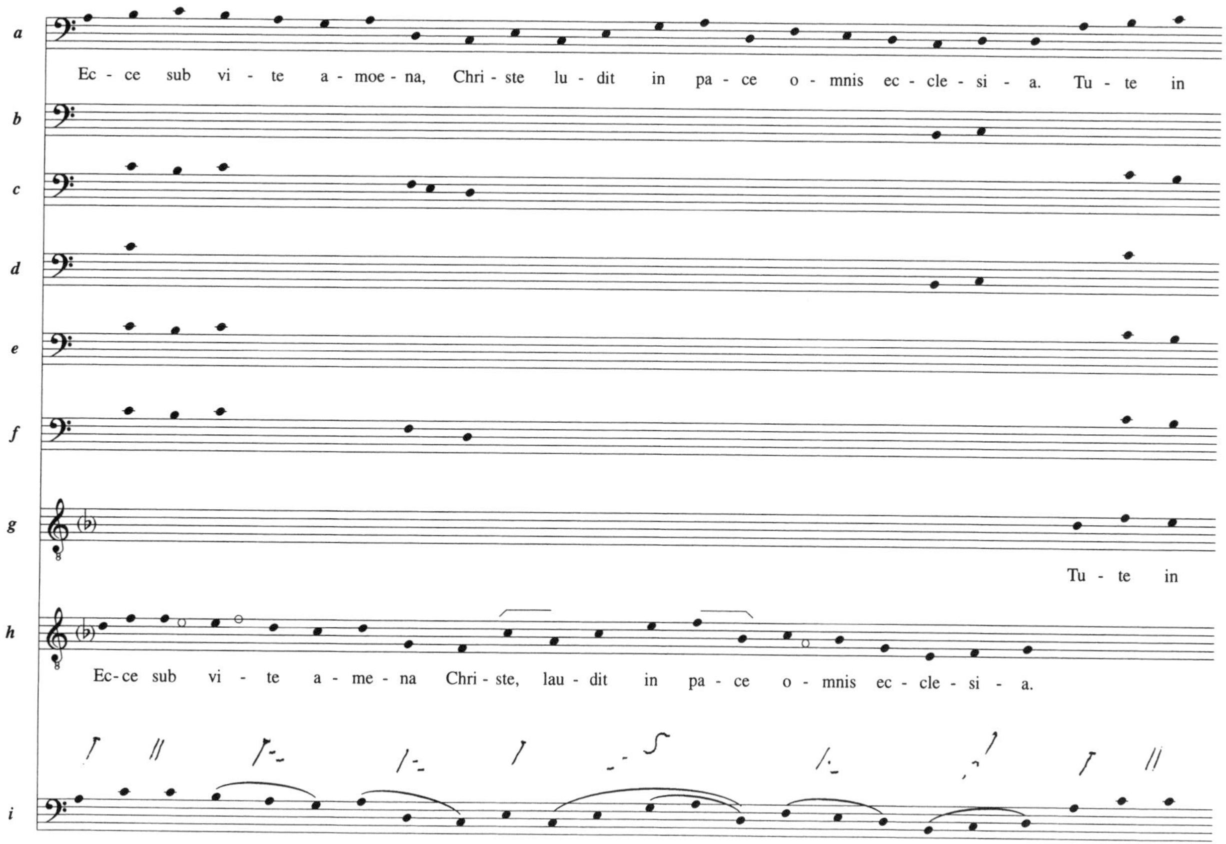
a
Ec - ce sub vi - te a - moe - na, Chri - ste lu - dit in pa - ce o - mnis ec - cle - si - a. Tu - te in
b
c
d
e
f
g
Tu - te in
h
Ec-ce sub vi - te a - me - na Chri - ste, lau - dit in pa - ce o - mnis ec - cle - si - a.
i

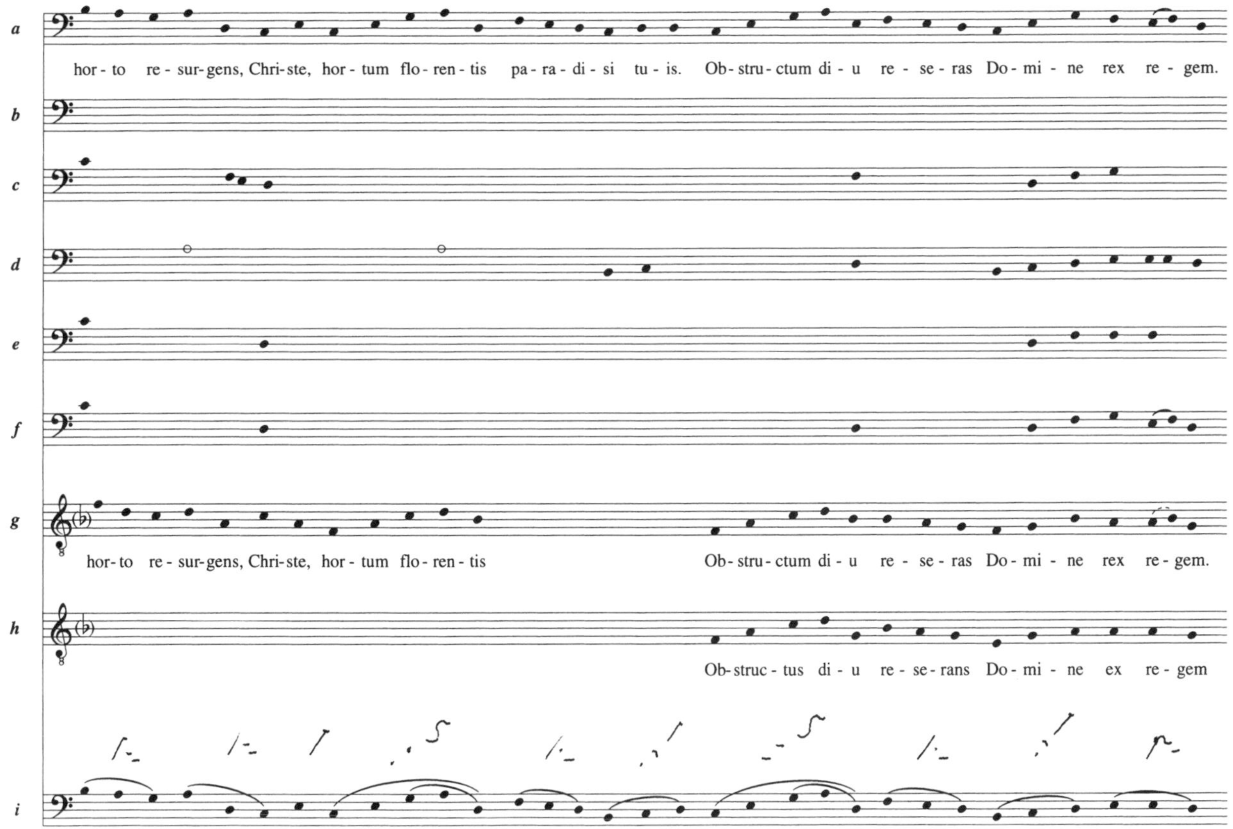
a
hor - to re - sur- gens, Chri- ste, hor - tum flo - ren - tis pa - ra - di - si tu - is. Ob - stru - ctum di - u re - se - ras Do - mi - ne rex re - gem.
b
c
d
e
f
g
hor - to re - sur- gens, Chri- ste, hor - tum flo - ren - tis
Ob - stru - ctum di - u re - se - ras Do - mi - ne rex re - gem.
h
Ob - struc - tus di - u re - se - rans Do - mi - ne ex re - gem
i

present a uniform account of the next seven cadences, *B–C–D*. The eighth and ninth, however, are given as *C–D–D*, while the preparation for the final cadence rises triadically, *C–E–G*. (Würzburg f. 165 gives the same cadence for eight lines, changing only for the ones following.) Munich clm 4101 and Klosterneuburg 588, on the other hand, employ the cadence *C–D–D* consistently, while St. Gall 380 does comparably (*F–G–G*) for those cadences that are provided with letters. Padua B. 16 basically maintains the diatonic ascending minor third. Again we are provided with an impulse to speculate about possible inflections of the cadence in performance, producing results that might be difficult to describe by means of the standard theoretical vocabulary.

I suggest that when viewed as an ensemble these various minutiae have broader lessons to offer, even if most take the form of questions. Close study of early Sequences inevitably leads us to wrestle with our precious adiastematic sources regardless of the difficulties that they pose, if only because these manuscripts may be between one and three generations earlier than the first available diastematic sources. The early sources bear on the origins of the genre, and their notation in Germanic manuscripts encourages continued thought on the functions of their double notations, texted and untexted. The latter form assuredly shows melodic shape with far greater clarity and specificity, while the former is superior in documenting the relationship between text and melody. But the two are not necessarily alternative forms of one and the same thing. The St. Gall and related manuscripts are replete with rhythmic indications for performance. If, to avoid controversy, one grants that these refer only to small nuances, one still needs consider whether these nuances are fully compatible with a completely texted performance. We may not be able to attain a definitive answer to this problem – and certainly not on the basis of only two melodies – but the matter should be kept in mind.

The study of diastematic variants provides a useful antidote to dogmatism in attempts to cope with sources that do not specify pitch. They warn that differences of dialect exist in the Sequence repertory in a manner similar to Proper chants of both Mass and Office. For those German Sequences that transcend regional boundaries, an early diastematic source of French provenance is not necessarily more accurate in detail than a much later source of German provenance. Earlier may well be better, but this can only be determined on a case-by-case basis. In seeking to reconstruct the readings of St. Gall 484 I have generally given preference to pitch constellations representative of the German dialect. The final cadence of *Carmen suo* poses a special problem when interpreting adiastematic sources. In interpreting this, I have posited that the penultimate salicus had the same meaning as those in earlier cadences, and I have relied on the presence of the Romanian letter *l* that appears in conjunction with the final neume in Bamberg lit 5. For this reason I rejected the various diastematic readings that approach the setting of the words *rex regem* either from above or from the same pitch height. A solution employing *F–F–D* for the final three pitches would have been equally appropriate and perhaps more in keeping with the Germanic dialect. I did not, however, feel that such a solution was mandatory and preferred the greater euphony of the version adopted.

While Sequences did of course each have an original form, the variants observed raise the question of whether this first form remained constant for any length of time, even within the milieu within which the particular Sequence was created. Can we reject the possibility that a small degree of flexibility in performance was accepted as a matter of course by the original creator? If we overemphasize the concept of an original form, do we not run the danger not only of exceeding the information contained in our surviving documents but also of positing a mindset that may not have existed during the ninth and tenth centuries? It is unfortunate that we know so little of the later *Rezeptionsgeschichte* of early Sequences, a topic indeed worthy of study.

The foregoing study of variants, although preliminary and sketchy, seems to indicate that the *Graduale Herbipolense*, while not flawless, is in general a fairly reliable source. This issue becomes of importance when we wish to deal with its trope repertory. In several instances the Herbipolense and – at times – its associated Würzburg sources furnish either the only diastematic accounts of certain early tropes or the only German diastematic readings for these works. Thus it is of some comfort to know that when the Würzburg group can be checked it is found to be reasonably trustworthy.

The information provided suggests that we need to strive for a fairly nuanced appreciation of the history of the Sequence. It should come as no surprise to learn that elements of conservatism and elements of change may exist side by side within the same time framework. Were the *Graduale Herbipolense* of 1583 an isolated source one might be tempted to attribute its repertorial idiosyncracies to the special antiquarian interests of a particular collector or patron. This thesis, however, is not consistent with the historical context for the source. Coming as the last of a group of three sources, it seems to indicate instead a remarkable degree of conservatism exhibited in the Würzburg area. Interest in the Sequence remained vigorous there, while it had declined significantly in other areas. The Sequences contained in sources such as the Graduals issued by Francisco de Brugis in Venice (1499–1500) and by Varisco in Venice (1565) are few in comparison with those of their northern counterparts. And even within the Germanic orbit, the ongoing use of Sequences was variable among late sources. However limited the scope of this essay honoring the memory of a valued colleague, it is capable of opening many avenues for further inquiry.[29]

Notes

1 This volume is preserved in the Musiksammlung of the Österreichische Nationalbibliothek (Vienna), under the shelf mark S.A.25.Aa.11. I am indebted to the kindness of the Library for a microfilm of the source.

2 Anselm Schubiger, *Die Sängerschule St. Gallens vom achten bis zwölften Jahrhundert: Ein Beitrag zur Gesanggeschichte des Mittelalters* (Einsiedeln: K. & N. Benziger, 1858), transcriptions, 22.

3 Peter Wagner, *Einführung in die gregorianische Melodien*, vol. 2 (2nd edn, Leipzig: Breitkopf & Härtel, 1912), 202.

4 Published in Ewald Jammers, 'Studien zu Neumenschriften, Neumenhandschriften und neumierter Musik', *Bibliothek und Wissenschaft*, 2 (1965), 85–161, opp. 96.

5 *Troparium, Sequentiarium, Nonantulanum, Cod. Casanat. 1741*, ed. Giuseppe Vecchi (Modena: Academia Scientiarum Litterarum Artium, 1955).

6 *Alleluia-Melodien I, bis 1100*, ed. Karlheinz Schlager (MMMA 7; Kassel: Bärenreiter, 1968).

7 Klaus Heinrich Kohrs, *Die aparallelen Sequenzen: Repertoire, liturgische Ordnung, musikalischer Stil* (Munich: Musikverlag Katzbichler, 1978).

8 *Early Medieval Chants from Nonantola*, ed. Lance W. Brunner and James Borders, 4 vols. (Recent Researches in the Music of the Middle Ages and Early Renaissance, 30–33; Madison, Wis.: A-R Editions, 1996–9), iv: *Sequences*, 76.

9 Wolfram von den Steinen, *Notker der Dichter und seine geistige Welt*, 2 vols. (Bern: A. Francke, 1948; repr. 1978), ii, 54.

10 Karlheinz Schlager, *Thematischer Katalog der ältesten Alleluia-Melodien aus Handschriften des 10. und 11. Jahrhunderts* (Munich: W. Ricke, 1965), 96.

11 *Le Manuscript 807, Universitätsbibliothek Graz (XIIe siècle): Graduel de Klosterneuburg*, ed. Jacques Froger (PM 19; Bern, 1974).

12 *Moosburger Graduale, München, Universitätsbibliothek, 2° Cod. ms. 156*, ed. David Hiley (Tutzing: Hans Schneider, 1996).

13 *Das Graduale der St. Thomaskirche zu Leipzig (14. Jh.) als Zeuge deutscher Choralüberlieferung*, ed. Peter Wagner (Publikationen älterer Musik, v [Leipzig, 1930], vii [Leipzig, 1932, repr. 1967]).

14 *Graduale Pataviense: Wien 1511*, ed. Christian Väterlein (Kassel: Bärenreiter, 1982).

15 von den Steinen, *Notker der Dichter*, 54, 168.

16 Bruno Stäblein, 'Zur Frühgeschichte der Sequenz', *AfMw* 28 (1961), 4–7. The full list had, of course, been published earlier in Hesbert, *AMS*, 198.

17 *Antiphonale missarum sancti Gregorii, Xe siècle: Codex 47 de la Bibliothèque de Chartres* (PM 11; Solesmes: Abbaye Saint-Pierre, 1912, repr. 1972).

18 *Alleluia-Melodien I*, 82 f.

19 See Karp, 'An Unknown Late Medieval Fragment', in *Cantus Planus, Papers Read at the 9th Meeting, Esztergom and Visegrád, 1998* (Budapest: Hungarian Academy of Sciences Institute for Musicology, 2001), 173–88.

20 David Hiley, *Western Plainchant: A Handbook* (Oxford: Clarendon Press, 1993), opp. 117.

21 *Early Medieval Chants*, ed. Brunner, lxix f.

22 Andreas Haug, *Troparia tardiva: Repertorium später Tropenquellen aus dem deutschsprachigen Raum* (Kassel: Bärenreiter, 1995).

23 Volker Schier, 'Propriumstropen in der Würzburger Domliturgie', *Kirchenmusikalisches Jahrbuch*, 76 (1992), 3–43.

24 Schubiger, *Die Sängerschule*; *The Utrecht Prosarium: liber sequentiarum ecclesiae capitularis Sanctae Mariae Ultraiectensis saeculi XIII, Codex Ultraiectensis, universitatis bibliotheca 417*, ed. N. de Goede (Amsterdam: Vereniging voor Nederlandse Muziekgeschiedenis, 1965); Richard Crocker, *The Early Medieval Sequence* (Berkeley: University of California Press, 1977); Francesca Negro, 'Le sequenze della tradizione liturgica Padovana', in Giulio Cattin and Antonio Lovato (eds), *Contributi per la Storia della musica sacra a Padova* (Padua: Istituto per la storia ecclesiastica padovana, 1993).

25 Professor Calvin Bower kindly notified me that this Sequence appeared also in Metz, BM 452 (now destroyed).

26 One ought, nevertheless, to acknowledge the possibility of the *salicus* at the unison, as mentioned by Dom Eugène Cardine.

27 Crocker, *The Early Medieval Sequence*, 210 f.

28 For further information concerning varied treatments of the *coniuncta* on *B*♭, see this author's *Aspects of Orality and Formularity in Gregorian Chant* (Evanston, Ill.: Northwestern University Press, 1998), 185–92.

29 I should like to express my gratitude to Professor Richard Crocker for his generosity in performing both *O quam mira* (together with the *Alleluia Confitemini . . . et invocate*) and *Carmen suo*, contained on the compact disc supplied with this book (Tracks 19–20). I believe that I speak for many who will welcome this rare opportunity to acquire a greater familiarity with the aural image of the early Sequence.

Chapter 17
Modal Neumes at Sens

Thomas Forrest Kelly

In his treatise on plainsong of 1745, entitled *Nouvelle méthode, ou Traité théorique et pratique du plain-chant*, Léonard Poisson writes: 'At Sens there are neumes, not only for Antiphons, but also for the Responsories; these are used only on solemn feasts. They have been retained from an ancient and uninterrupted usage.'[1] Indeed there were neumes for responsories at Sens in Poisson's day. Plate 17.1 shows the neumes for responsories, arranged by mode, as they are printed in the Sens processional of 1756. But what about the second part of Poisson's statement, about the ancient and uninterrupted use of them? That is the subject of this investigation: the relation of this list of neumes to the medieval tradition of the great primatial see of Sens.

What is a neume for a responsory? Substantial recent scholarship has investigated this phenomenon, and a word or two of background might be useful here.[2] The great responsories of Matins often end with some sort of melismatic flourish at the end of the main section before the verse begins. This is a perfectly normal musical event, and such melismas, even when they are quite long, are most often an integral part of the responsory.[3] It sometimes happens, however, that when the responsory is repeated in whole or in part after the verse, a longer melisma is substituted. This added melisma (or neume) is performed at the last singing of the repetenda. Some of these melismas were retained in the Solesmes *Processionale monasticum* of 1893.[4]

Melismas added to responsories have been known for a long time. Amalarius of Metz refers to the famous *neuma triplex* used for the office of St. John and which 'moderni cantores' sing with the responsory *Descendit de celis*;[5] versions of this *neuma triplex* are found in the Hartker antiphoner and the Mont-Renaud manuscript, and texted versions are found in Paris, BNF lat. 1118, of the late tenth or early eleventh century, so the phenomenon dates at least from the tenth century.[6]

Amalarius' triple neume is far from being the only melismatic addition to responsories. There are a variety of kinds of melisma which have been used at one place and time or another to embellish the end of a responsory.[7] Some melismas seem to be composed for use with a single responsory, and never appear anywhere else. Many responsories, as I have said, contain sizeable melismas at their ends, but when these are not varied in the repetition of the responsory – that is, when a different, or lengthened, melisma is not substituted – they are, so far as we can tell, an integral part of their parent chant.[8] It is the provision of a special neume for the end, different from what appears in the body of the responsory, that constitutes, in most cases, an addition to the responsory, a sort of melodic trope.

PROCESSIONAL
DE SENS
IMPRIMÉ PAR L'ORDRE
DE SON EMINENCE
MONSEIGNEUR
LE CARDINAL DE LUYNES,
ARCHEVÊQUE VICOMTE DE SENS,

Primat des Gaules & de Germanie, Premier Aumônier de Madame la Dauphine, &c. & du consentement des Doyen & Chapitre de ladite Eglise.

Processional

1760

1835

A SENS,
Chez André Jannot, Imprimeur de son Eminence, & du Clergé.

M. DCC. LVI.
AVEC PRIVILEGE DU ROI

Quand on fait la Nume, le ℣. du Répons ne se dit point, s'il n'est autrement marqué.

La Nume se chante sur une seule syllabe du dernier ou pénultiéme & méme antepenultiéme mot du Répons, & elle se commence à l'endroit du ℟. où se trouve cette marque ✻ suivant le mode du ℟. l'Orgue joue, & le Chœur chante alternativement.

La Nume étant finie, le Chœur acheve le Répons, en reprenant ce qui est après l'astérisque. ✻

POUR LES RÉPONS du 1. 2. & 4. & l'astérisque. ✻

MEL 1A

Le reste du Répons après l'astérisque.

[Si à l'astérisque ✻ on ajoute cette marque † on commence ainsi la Nume.

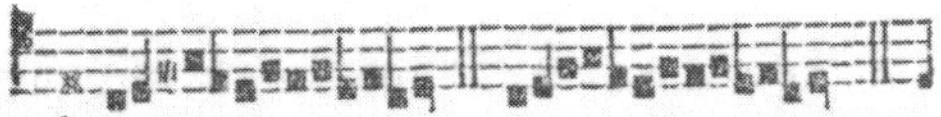

MEL 1B

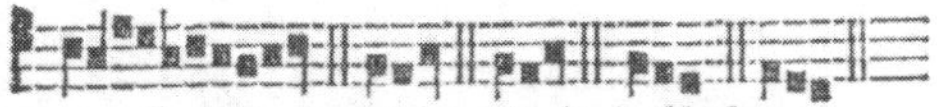

Le reste du Répons après l'astérisque.

POUR LE RÉPONS du 3.

MEL 3

Pl. 17.1 *Processional de Sens*, 1756: title page and neumes for responsories, pp. cciv–ccvj; the neumes numbered for reference

Melismas added to an original responsory can be recognized, in the first instance, by their presentation: they are given as alternatives, usually written after the verse or the Gloria and indicating their substitution for the earlier ending. This is a practice used widely, including in the earliest books of office music from Sens. Plate 17.2, from Paris, BNF n. a. lat. 1535 (a late twelfth-century antiphoner of Sens), shows a melisma added to the end of the responsory *Precursor* for St. John the Baptist. We will come to know it as Melisma 8.

An added melisma may also be detected when it appears only in some manuscripts, while others show a shorter melisma. A third way of identifying an addition is to recognize the melisma itself as being familiar from another context. The borrowing of melismas for use with responsories is a relatively common phenomenon, and closely related to the practice at Sens.[9]

A number of melismas used in responsories at Sens, at Laon and elsewhere have been borrowed from Offertories. I say borrowed from Offertories, rather than the other way around, because the melismas in question are almost always present in the Offertory, but used only sometimes with responsories.[10] These are generally melismas with the characteristic not quite clearly articulated repetitions that set Offertory melismas apart from many others.

Other melismas added to responsories are melodies in what seems to be a later style. Such melismas, with a regular AABBCC structure like little Sequences, serve as the melodic basis of many of the prosae that also are used to decorate the same place in responsories; and when a responsory presents the melody only of a very famous text, like *Sospitati dedit egros*, or *Inviolata integra et casta*, it is difficult not to imagine that the melisma in these cases is a wordless prosa. Indeed, texted additions have been used as long as melismas for the embellishment of responsories. Sometimes melismatic and texted versions appear together, which raises questions as to how they should be performed.[11] But here we want to concentrate on the use of added melismas like those of Sens.

Neumes for responsories may come from a variety of places: composed, transferred from another piece, or summarizing a texted piece. How does it happen that Sens has a set of melismas for use in each mode? Were they all composed together in a similar style? And when?

The Sens melismas are, so far as I know, the only practical evidence of passepartout responsory neumes for use in each mode. Modal melismas for antiphons, on the other hand, were long in use. They are mentioned by theorists, presented in tonaries, prescribed in ordinals, and evidently were in regular use from at least the tenth century. These neumes for antiphons are usually found attached to the echematic formulas, NOEANE etc., or to the modal formulas 'Primum querite regnum dei', etc., and are used as attachments to certain antiphons, usually the Gospel antiphons of major feasts.[12]

These modal neumes for antiphons are very widespread, and relatively uniform. It may be that their existence suggested a similar process for responsories. If so, the idea did not catch on very widely, since I know of no modal neumes for responsories except for those of Sens, with one exception: the list of 'caudae' or 'versiculi' provided by Jacques de Liège in his early fourteenth-century *Speculum musicae*. These are melodies to be sung to the

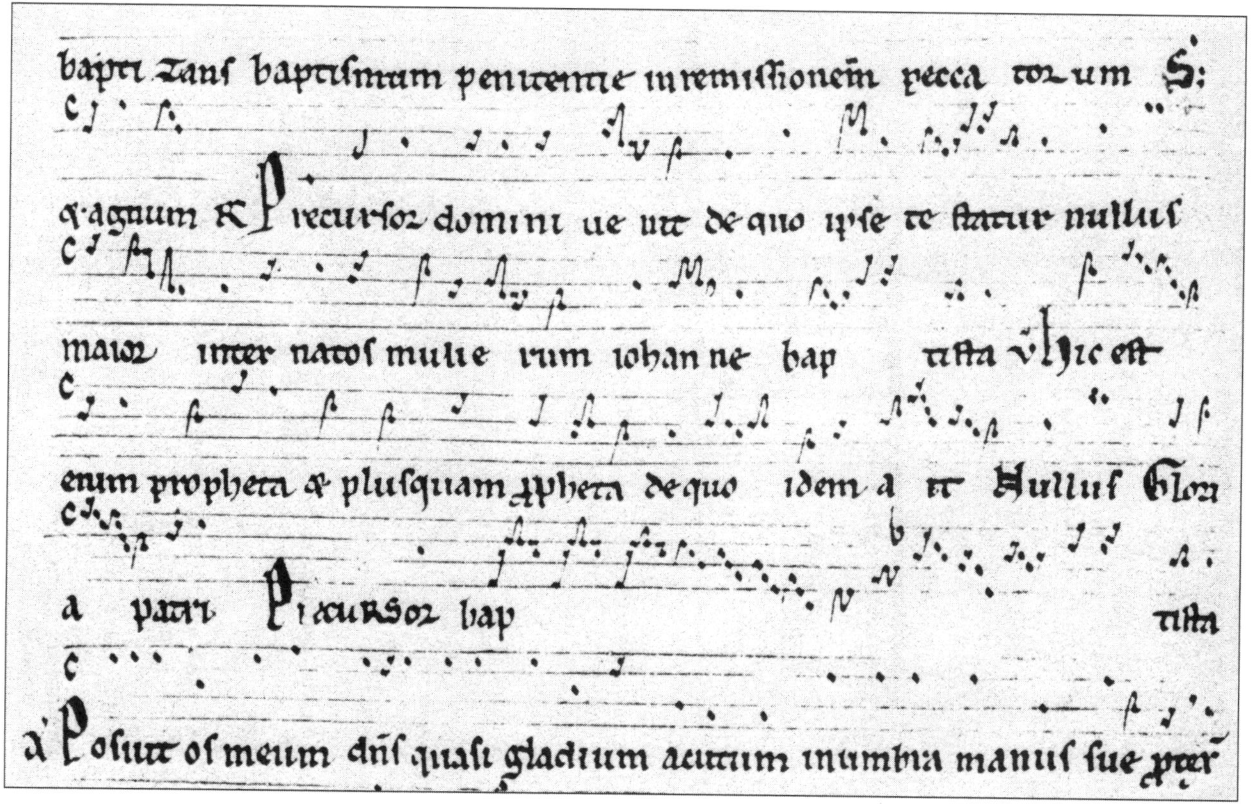

Pl. 17.2 The responsory *Inter natos* with added melisma, from Paris, BNF n. a. lat. 1535, fol. 87v

text 'Amen' at the ends of responsories, and there is a different versiculus for each mode. The melody for Mode 1 is reproduced here as Pl. 17.3 from Roger Bragard's edition of Jacques.[13]

These melodies are apparently unique to this treatise. Their style is not typical of the chant nor of its later additions; they resemble nothing so much as the charming two-voice pieces often called 'ductia' found in London, BL Harley 978.[14] Structured in puncta, AABBCC, like some reponsory prosae, Jacques's melodies have open and closed endings, which are not normally found in responsory melismas or indeed elsewhere in the chant. They also have some suggestion of rhythmic performance, and look in some cases as though they might be polyphonic. These are melodies to study on another occasion, for they are more nearly related to contemporaneous secular musical practice than to widely known ecclesiastical chant. They are wondeful melodies, but they appear nowhere else.

The Sens list of neumes, then, is the only one known from practical sources of the chant. But it dates from the eighteenth century. What about medieval Sens? We can show that from medieval times Sens regularly added melismas to responsories, and used the same melismas for a variety of responsories in the same mode. But it does not follow that an eight-mode system of neumes for responsories was in place at Sens from an early date. As we shall see, that systematization came much later.

The oldest source of office music from Sens is Paris n. a. lat. 1535, an antiphoner from the last quarter of the twelfth century.[15] Appendix §A summarizes the additions made to responsories in that manuscript. Neumes are not the only way to embellish responsories, and the use of melismas here is not systematic. In the course of the year, the clergy of Sens sang just about every known sort of responsory embellishment. They sang the most famous prosae (at least two of them): *Inviolata* and a set of 'Fabrices' (for some reason we do not have *Sospitati* for St. Nicholas).[16] They sang a variety of melismas, some of them borrowed from Offertories. They were already accustomed to using the same melisma for more than one responsory; note that the melisma marked MEL 7 is used twice, as is that marked MEL 1A. But they were not restricted to melismas. Some responsories were embellished with a prosa, not a melisma; and sometimes melisma and prosa were combined for the same responsory.

Essentially, then, the earliest evidence we have of embellishing responsories at Sens appears to be inclusive. There is a bit of everything, probably gathered from here and there as occasion offered and as taste dictated. There is no evidence that one particular way of decorating responsories is preferred or insisted on – using only prosae, for example, or only melismas, as is the case in some other places.[17] There does, however, appear to be a tendency to use melismas alone, and to repeat them in more than one responsory. Although there is no evidence of a system of modal neumes, three of the neumes that appear in the eighteenth-century list are already present in Paris 1535 (melismas 1A, 7 and 8).

A late twelfth-century ordinal of Sens matches the practice observed in the antiphoner, though not in every detail. This ordinal, summarized in Appendix

25 Item pro singulis tonis ponantur hic "amen" vel caudae quae dici possunt in solemnitatibus, vel quando chorialibus amplius cantare placet in fine alicuius antiphonae, responsorii vel sequentiae, seu prosae, et fit ad cantus primi <toni> finis talis:

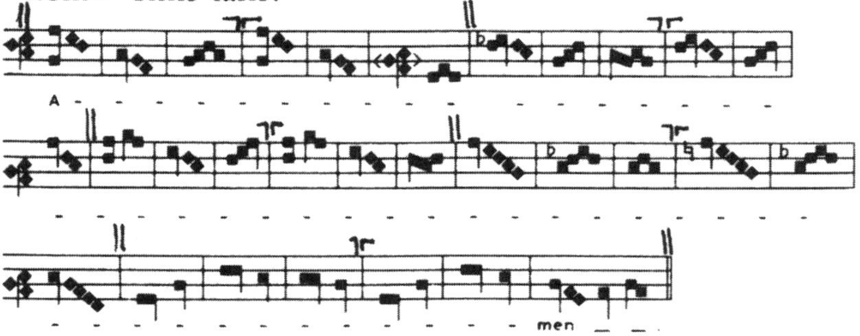

Pl. 17.3 Mode 1 melisma from Jacques de Liège, *Speculum musicae*, ed. Roger Bragard. Division marks have been added

§B, does not use notation. It indicates the presence of a melisma for a responsory, but does not tell us what melisma it is. The prosae, however, can be identified since their incipits are specified. We can see that most of the prosae are those of the antiphoner of Appendix §A; *Sospitati* for St. Nicholas has joined the group, while *Inviolata* is absent, owing to a rearrangement of the office of the Assumption. Some additional responsories have melismas: ones for Lent, the Assumption, John the Baptist, All Saints and St. Martin. We should note here that the ordinal specifies the repetitions of many responsories – with their melismas or prosae – at second Vespers on principal feasts.

A thirteenth-century notated breviary of Sens, Paris, BNF lat. 1028, has a similar repertory, detailed in Appendix §C. Notice the presence here of both versions of melisma 1 – that is, 1A and 1B – both of which appear among the modal neumes of the eighteenth century. This manuscript also adds a number of prosae imitated from older ones: versions of *Sospitati* for St. Katherine and for All Saints, and *Fabrice* imitations for the Assumption (these last were already present in the ordinal).

Later sources of Sens use do not add much to the picture. Manuscripts summarized in the Appendix (at §§ D–J) add no new melismas to the repertory used at Sens, though occasionally a new prosa appears.[18] In fact, to judge from Paris 1535 (Appendix §A), a wider variety of melismas was available in the twelfth century than was used later. Even so, and even though we might wish to detect a trend over time toward the increasing use of melismas instead of prosae, and toward a restricted number of increasingly mobile melismas, such trends are difficult to support with the evidence available. It might be worth noting that two sources of particularly local interest use melismas that will appear in the eighteenth-century modal list. These are the Office of Saints Savinianus and Potentianus, and the famous Circumcision office, both edited by Villetard.[19] In general it looks as though Sens used a variety of embellishments, adding new ones when they came along.

How then does the Sens modal list come into being? It is clearly not a medieval phenomenon. I should like to suggest a way in which it might have arisen that essentially has to do with typography. The answer, or an answer, lies in the Sens printed antiphoner of 1552, which announces the presence of neumes on its title page.[20] The neumes and prosae in this antiphoner are shown in Table 17.1. There are five different neumes here, most of them printed more than once. Although there are still some prosae, it does appear that neumes are a relatively regular feature of the solemnities at Sens in the sixteenth century. In this printed antiphoner, neumes for responsories are sung at Vespers, but not at Matins. Consequently, the neumes are printed at Vespers, while the responsories with which they are sung are printed at Matins. The result is that the neume appears as a separate element, and might seem to be separable from any specific chant. Any printer might wonder why he prints the same neume several times.

Plate 17.4 shows part of a folio from the 1552 antiphoner, with a portion of Vespers from the office of Saints Savinianus and Potentianus. The rubrics indicate that the antiphons at Vespers are those of Lauds, with psalms of one martyr. The capitulum *Sancti et iusti in domino* is followed by the responsory *Athletam domini*, with the rubric 'et reincipitur cum neumate sequente'. Only the intonation of the responsory is given, and the neume is provided with the text of the end of the responsory.

Printing neumes this way, separately and repeatedly, easily leads to the idea of printing each neume only once; if the printer had chosen to save space by making a table of neumes for this printed antiphoner, five neumes would have been needed: those listed in Table 17.1 as 'Cor', 'Fabrice C', the two versions of Melisma 1, and Melisma 7. It might seem a simple step to assign a melisma to each mode, and print them only once. This is of course what has happened in the eighteenth-century neume table (Pl. 17.1). But that table does not consist only of neumes known in medieval Sens, nor does it include all the neumes that were used in earlier sources. The omission of medieval neumes from the neume table seems to be done on the basis of style, since the three neumes not retained are two that are borrowed from Offertories and the long Fabrice C melisma. These have in common the absence of a reduplicated structure that would lend itself to antiphonal performance by the two sides of the choir or by choir and organ.

Three of the neumes in the neume table, however, do have a long history at Sens. These are neumes 1A/1B, 7 and 8. These accommodate responsories in five of the eight modes, and are used for these five modes in medieval manuscripts.

Neume 1 is the first neume in the eighteenth-century neume table, and it comes in two versions. The shorter version (1A) is of unknown origin, but its reduplicated form suggests that it may have come from a prosa. The longer version (1B) adds more music to the beginning of this melisma; this added

Table 17.1 Melismas and prosae in the printed antiphoner of Sens, 1552

The neumes are separated from their responsories to show their use at Vespers. The folio numbers here are those on which the responsory is found.

Fol.	*Feast*	*Mode/Text*	*Addition*
17v	De scss. sacr.	1 Unus panis	MEL 1A
73v	Dedicationis	1 Terribilis	MEL 1B
80v	Ioh. baptistae	1 Inter natos	MEL 1B
87v	Petri	4 Petre amas me	MEL ('cor'?, pasted over)
107v	M. Magd.	2 Felix Maria unxit	MEL 1B
121	Germani	8 Gloriosus domini	pr. *Pacis perpetue*
128v	Inv. Stephani	2 Igitur dissimulata	MEL 1B
131	Inv. Stephani	7 Lapides torrentes	MEL 7
132v	Inv. Stephani	1 Ecce iam coram te	MEL [Fabrice C]
147	Laurentii	2 Beatus Laurentius	MEL 1B
158	Assumptionis	1 Virginitas celum	pr. *Benedic/Benedicat/ Benedictus*
175	Decoll. J. Bapt.	4 Metuebat	MEL 1B
179	Lupi	1 O venerandum	pr. *Insignis de Christo*
179v	Lupi (Vespers)	1 O venerandum	MEL 1A
216	Sav. et Poten.	1 Athletam domini	MEL 1A
224	Omn. Scorum	1 Ecce iam coram te	MEL [Fabrice C]
225v	Omn. Scorum	1 Concede nobis	MEL 1A
233v	Martini	1 Martinus Abrahe	MEL 1A
249v	Katherine	1 Ex eius tumba	pr. *Sospitati*

music corresponds to the opening notes of the Alleluia *Posuisti*, and in this longer form the melody as a whole serves as the melodic basis of the prosa *Sedentem in superne*, which is used in the Sens Circumcision office and is widely known elsewhere, attached to one of several responsories.[21]

This melisma 1 in its two forms is often used at Sens. It may seem odd that a single melody should be used for three different modes in the later printed sources, but it was used for those same modes in medieval sources. The melisma's insistence on the note *a*, which is the tenor of fourth-mode psalmody, makes its use for responsories in the fourth mode plausible, especially when we remember that the melisma does not provide the final note of the performance, but is inserted shortly before the end of the original responsory, so that the responsory itself provides the final, whether *D* (for Modes 1 and 2) or *E* for Mode 4.

Neumes 7 and 8, both used in medieval Sens, are again two versions of the same melody. Melisma 7 is found also in the Offertory *Gressos meos*;[22] Melisma 8 is a transposed version of Melisma 7, without its first eleven notes. In this transposed form it is used in twelfth-century Sens for an eighth-mode responsory,[23] so the idea of transposition, and of using the same melisma for more than one mode, is not an eighteenth-century invention. The notion of

Pl. 17.4 Antiphoner of Sens, 1552, fol. 217 (detail): the melisma for the responsory *Athletam* for use at Vespers

using the same melisma for multiple modes does make one wonder, however, how Poisson in his treatise can say the following: 'The neumes for responsories, being much extended, make the properties of each mode easily understood.'[24]

With two medieval melismas the compiler of the Sens list manages to provide neumes for five modes. Only three more melismas are needed to provide melismas for every mode. One of these, the melisma for mode 6, was already known at Sens and elsewhere; it is found at the end of the processional antiphon *Ibo michi ad montem* (in Paris 1535 it is found at fol. 93ᵛ); with an added verse the antiphon with its melisma serves as a responsory in Paris, BNF n. a. lat. 12044, fol. 177 (St-Maur-des-Fossés, twelfth century). The same melisma is replaced by a prosa (*Alle resonemus omnes*) in the Circumcision offices of Sens and Beauvais.[25]

The Sens melismas for Modes 3 and 5 are as yet unidentified in medieval sources. Judging from the process involved in selecting the other melodies of the neume table, it would not be a surprise to find that these two neumes appear somewhere in the music books of Sens, but I have not succeeded in finding them. They both have the not quite exactly reduplicated structure that is characteristic of some Offertory melismas, but they do not seem to appear in any known Offertories. In any event, these last two neumes are used very little. In the 1756 processional (Table 17.2), the melismas for modes 3 and 5 are used once each.

When did this modal arrangement take place? Clearly the modal neumes were arranged at some time between the sixteenth-century printed antiphoners and the eighteenth-century printed versions. But between the two there is a great deal of political and ecclesiastical history.

Table 17.2 *Processional de Sens*, 1756: list of responsories sung with neumes

Page	*Feast*	*Responsory*	*Mode*
12	Natalis	Cantate Domino	6
16	Vespers of Christmas, at the cathedral	Stephanum virum	1
19	Stephani	Cum esset Stephanus	3
31	Epiphanie	Stella antecedebat	1
35	Reliquarum	Haec dicit Dominus	1
196	Purificationis	Benedixit illis Simeon	6
200	Annunc.	Virtus altissimi	6
228	Joh. Bapt.	Quid existis in desertam	1
231	Petri et Pauli	Quid sunt suae olivae	7
234	Petri et Pauli, in churches dedicated to St. Peter	Simon Joannis	?
252	Assumptionis	Apertum est templum	1
263	Lupi archiep.	Sapientia a peccatoribus	7
273	Sav. & Pot.	Laudemus viros	1
277	Omn. scorum	Laudebunt piae	5
xxij	Com. angel.	Audivi vocem angelorum	1
xxiv	Com. ang. gard.	Non accedet ad te malum	1
xxvj	Com. apost.	Non sunt loquelae	7
xxviij	Com. 1 mart.	In fraude circunvenientium	1
xxxij	Com. pl. mart.	Hi sunt qui veniunt	1
xxxvj	Com. 1 pont.	Ipse est directe	1
xl	Com. pl. pont.	Beati servi illi	2
xlij	Com. 1 doct.	Juxta manum Dei	1
xlvij	Com. Abb. & mon.	Perfectio tua et doctrina	1
l	Com. scorum laic.	Dispersit dedit pauperibus	4
lij	Com. virginum	Gaudeamus et exultemus	7
lvij	Com. non virg.	Erat in omnibus	1
lx	Poenitentiorum	Benedic anima mea	6
lxiij	Dedicationis	Si conversus populus	1

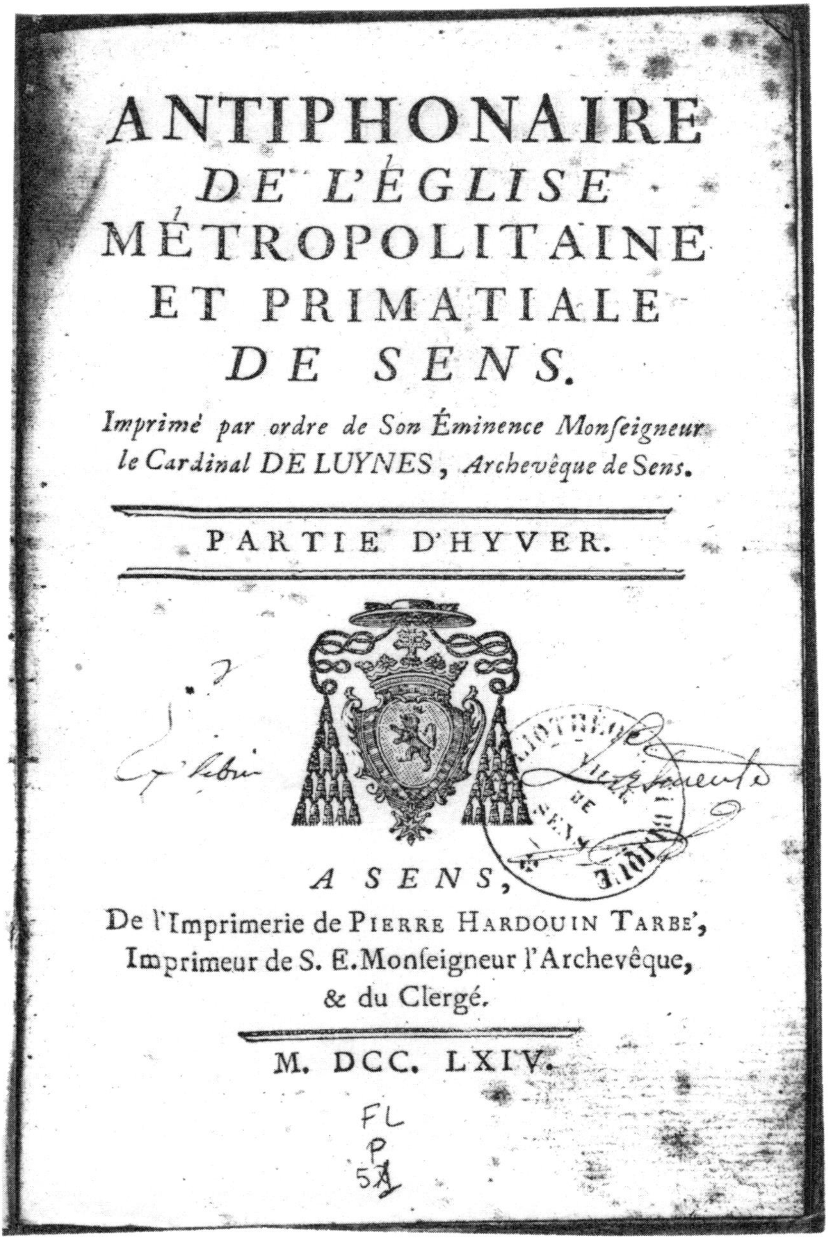

ANTIPHONAIRE
DE L'ÉGLISE
MÉTROPOLITAINE
ET PRIMATIALE
DE SENS.

Imprimé par ordre de Son Éminence Monseigneur le Cardinal DE LUYNES, Archevêque de Sens.

PARTIE D'HYVER.

A SENS,
De l'Imprimerie de PIERRE HARDOUIN TARBE',
Imprimeur de S. E. Monseigneur l'Archevêque,
& du Clergé.

M. DCC. LXIV.

Pl. 17.5 Antiphoner of Sens, 1764, title page

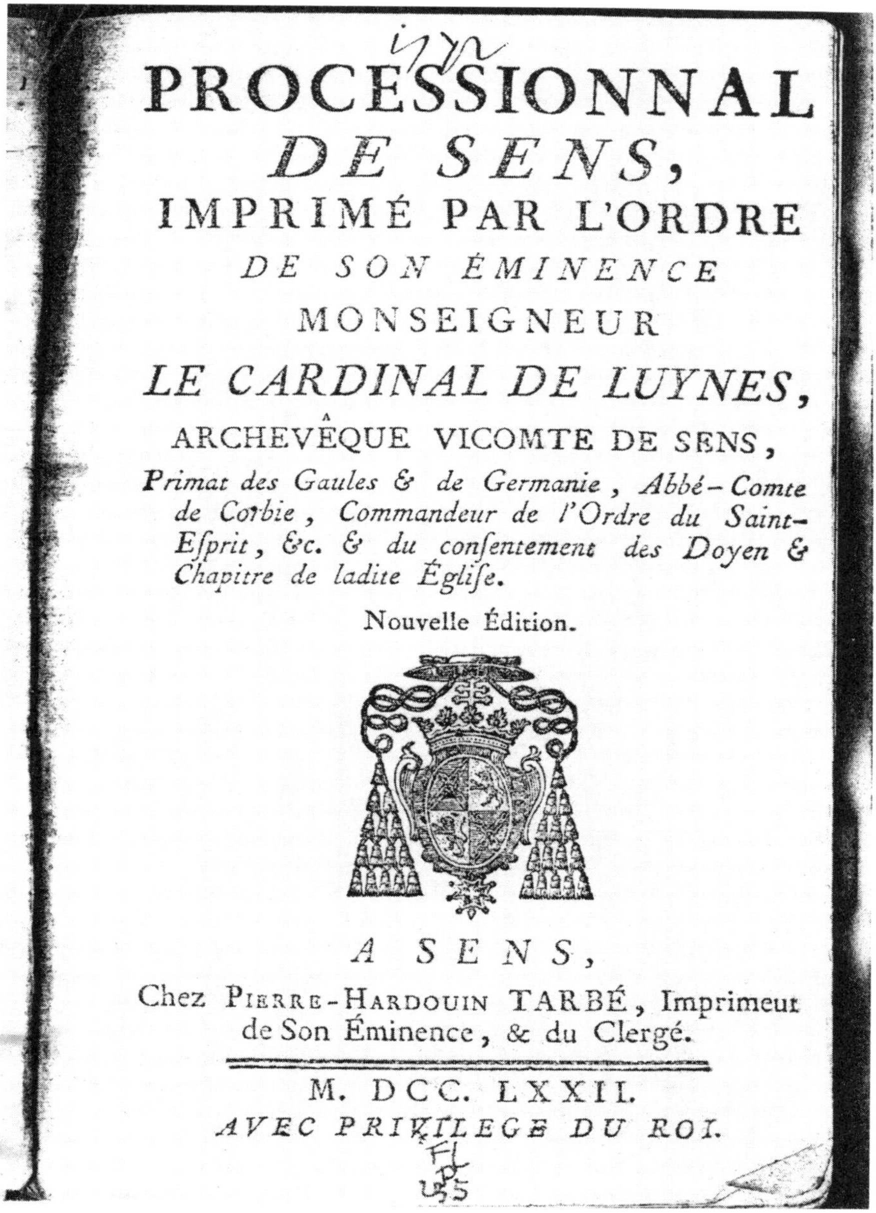

iyyr

PROCESSIONNAL

DE SENS,

IMPRIMÉ PAR L'ORDRE

DE SON ÉMINENCE

MONSEIGNEUR

LE CARDINAL DE LUYNES,

ARCHEVÊQUE VICOMTE DE SENS,

Primat des Gaules & de Germanie, Abbé-Comte de Corbie, Commandeur de l'Ordre du Saint-Esprit, &c. & du consentement des Doyen & Chapitre de ladite Église.

Nouvelle Édition.

A SENS,

Chez Pierre-Hardouin TARBÉ, Imprimeur de Son Éminence, & du Clergé.

M. DCC. LXXII.

AVEC PRIVILEGE DU ROI.

FL
135

Pl. 17.6 Processional of Sens, 1772, title page

Pl. 17.7 Neume table from *Processional, Graduel, Antiphonaire et Psautier à l'usage de l'église primatiale et métropolitaine de Sens* (Sens: Thomas-Malvin, 1844)

It seems probable that the neumes were introduced when the Gallicanized chant was adopted. The 1756 processional, which uses all the melismas, has responsories that are Neo-Gallican (see Table 17.2); these responsories are found also in the printed breviary of 1780,[26] where they proudly show their biblical sources. These are the responsories used also in the antiphoner of 1764–5 (Pl. 17.5), and the Processional of 1772 (Pl. 17.6). They are a regular feature of the newly revised Sens liturgy, perhaps a proudly archaizing one.[27]

The considerable revision of the liturgy was the likely moment of systematizing the melismas; the neume table purges the liturgy of all its prosae, with their non-biblical texts, but retains traditional, unobjectionable melodies from the Sens tradition. These melismas, in tabular form, still appear in the printed processional-Gradual-antiphoner of 1844 (Pl. 17.7),[28] where the description of neumes and their performance is reprinted from the eighteenth-century books. One wonders how long these neumes remained in use: perhaps until the reforms of the Second Vatican Council? I have asked senior clerics at Sens, but have yet to meet someone who remembers singing these neumes.

The moment of singing of the neume was an important event in the office of the great feasts. Its choreography, if we might call it that, is described in Poisson's treatise, and it involves movement, vestments and dignitaries that lend weight to what has become a musical high point of the office:

> The five leaders of the choir, vested in copes, standing before the lectern begin the responsory and sing the verse and the *Gloria patri*, after which the Precentor with the two Choristers in the middle of the choir re-intone the Responsory. While the choir sings the repetition, the five Dignitaries divide and return, each to his side, to stand with the Choristers in the middle of the choir. There they turn to face the side of the choir with which they sing. At the end of the Responsory, at the syllable or the note which precedes the one on which the neume is to begin, the whole choir stops, the right side begins the neume, which is alternated with the left side: at the end, the two sides of the choir unite their voices to finish the Responsory.[29]

This investigation, undertaken to discover an antique practice suitable for a collection of essays on chant in the first millennium, turns out to have as its subject a codification that appears to date from about a thousand years too late. But the result is interesting in itself, I think, for what it says about the invention of tradition, and about how readily elements of an ancient practice can be recombined and reinvented to produce something that has almost nothing to do with tradition.

Appendix

Prosulae and Neumes for Responsories in Medieval Manuscripts of Sens

pr.:	prosula whose incipit follows
MEL:	an added melisma, identified by one of the Sens modal melismas or otherwise
'Cor meum':	Offertory *Benedictus es*, verse 3, *Viam iniquitatis* (*Offertoriale*, ed. Ott, 30).
'meminero':	Offertory *Super flumina*, verse 2, *Si oblitus* (*Offertoriale*, ed. Ott, 121).
Fabrice C:	the third element of the *neuma triplex* added most often to the responsory *Descendit de celis* (see Kelly, 'Neuma triplex')

A. Paris, BNF n. a. lat. 1535; antiphoner (secular) of Sens, twelfth century (last quarter)

Fol.	*Feast*	*Mode/Text*	*Addition*
5	Nicolai	5 Qui cum audisset	pr. *Clementem*
19	Natalis	1 Descendit	pr. *Familiam/Fac/Facinora*
20	Natalis	7 In principio	MEL 7
20v	Natalis	2 Sancta et immaculata	pr. *Beata es virgo*
23v	Stephani	7 Lapides torrentes	MEL 7
24	Stephani	1 Ecce iam coram	MEL [Fabrice C]
24v	Stephani	4 S. Stephane sydus	MEL ['cor meum']
25	Stephani	2 O martyrum gemma	pr. *Qui scis infirma*
46	dom2inXL	6 Oravit Iacob	MEL [unknown: Offertory?]
80	Assumptionis	6 Gaude Maria	pr. *Inviolata*
85v	Ioan. bapt.	8 Precursor domini	MEL 8
89	Petri	4 Petre amas me	MEL ['cor meum'] + pr. *Psallat in isto die*
101	Lupi	1 O venerandum	MEL 1A + pr. *Insignis de Christo*
101v	Lupi	7 Dum beatus Lupus	MEL ['meminero']
126	Paule	1 O admirabilem	MEL 1A

B. Paris, BNF lat. 1206; ordinal of Sens, twelfth century (last quarter)

Fol.	*Feast*	*Mode/Text*	*Addition*
44	Natalis	1 Descendit	pr. *Fac deus/Facinora*
44	Natalis	1 In principio	cum neumate
44	Nat. (ad. proc.)	1 Descendit	cum prosis sicut est ad matut.
48	Stephani	7 Lapides	cum neumate (repeated at procession and Vespers)
48	Stephani	1 Ecce iam	cum neumate
47v	S. reliquarum	7 Lapides	cum neumate
	S. rel. (7 Feb)	1 Concede nobis	cum neumate sed sine versu (Sunday procession)

Fol.	*Feast*	*Mode/Text*	*Addition*
57[v]–	Pascha		(The Alleluias of the Mass with their sequences are sung at Vespers during Easter week)
66[v]	Nicolai	1 Ex eius tumba	cum prosa *Sospitati* (repeated at Vespers)
67	Inv. reliquarum	1 Concede	cum neumate (repeated at Vespers)
68	Purificationis	6 Gaude Maria	cum prosa *Inviolata* (repeated at Vespers)
70	Ioan. Bapt.	1 Inter natos	cum neumate
70[v]	Petri et Pauli	4 Petre amas	cum prosula sua *Psallat* (repeated at Vespers)
71[v]	Germani	8 Gloriosus	cum prosula sua *Pacem perpetue*
72	Inv. Stephani	7 Lapides[a]	cum neumate (repeated at Vespers)
		1 Ecce iam[a]	cum neumate
		4 Sancte Stephane[a]	cum neumate
72[v]	Assumptionis	1 Virginitas celum	pr. *Benedic/Benedicat/Benedictus* (repeated at Vespers)
73	Assumptionis	?Virgo thurifera	cum neumate
74	Lupi	1 O venerandum	cum prosula sua *Insignis* (repeated at Vespers)
76	Omn. scorum	1 Concede	cum neumate (repeated at Vespers)
76[v]	Martini	1 Martinus Abrahe	cum neumate (repeated at Vespers)

[a] These responsories are the next to last of each nocturn (nos. 3, 7, 11).

C. Paris, BNF lat. 1028; breviary (secular) of Sens, thirteenth century

Fol.	*Feast*	*Mode/Text*	*Addition*
50[v]	Natalis	1 Descendit	pr. *Familiam/Fac/Facinora*
51	Natalis	7 In principio	MEL 7
54	Stephani	7 Lapides torrentes	MEL 7
24	Stephani	1 Ecce iam coram	MEL [Fabrice C]
24[v]	Stephani	4 S. Stephane sydus	MEL 1B
79[v]	Epiphanie	1 Concede nobis	MEL 1A
120	Pascha	1 Et valde mane	pr. *Ortum predestinatio*
173	Dedicationis	1 Terribilis	MEL 1A
177	Nicolai	1 Ex eius tumba	pr. *Sospitati*
188[v]	Pauli	1 O admirabilem	MEL 1A
193	Annuntiatione	6 Gaude Maria	pr. *Inviolata*
204	Ioan. bapt.	1 Inter natos	MEL 1B
216[v]	Marie Magd.	2 Felix Maria	MEL 1B (internal)

Fol.	*Feast*	*Mode/Text*	*Addition*
221ᵛ	Germani	8 Gloriosus domini	pr. *Pacis perpetue*
233	Assumptionis	1 Virginitas celum	pr. *Benedic/Benedicat/ Benedictus*
243	Lupi	1 O venerandum	pr. *Insignis* (= MEL 1A)
263	Martini	1 Martinus Abrahe	MEL 1A
293ᵛ	Katherine	1 Ex eius tumba	pr. *Sospitati . . . Katherina*
309	Omn. scorum	1 Concede nobis	pr. *Sollemniter* (*Sospitati*) + MEL 1A

D. Auxerre, BM 60; breviary (secular) of Sens, late thirteenth century, pars aestivalis

Fol.	*Feast*	*Mode/Text*	*Addition*
175	Ioan. bapt.	8 Precursor	MEL 8
176ᵛ	Ioan. bapt.	1 Inter natos	MEL 1B
188ᵛ	Petri	4 Petre amas me	MEL ['cor'] + pr. *Psallat*
221ᵛ	Germani	8 Gloriosus domini	pr. *Pacis perpetue*
234ᵛ	Inv. Stephani	7 Lapides torrentes	MEL 7
37	Inv. Stephani	1 Ecce iam coram	MEL [Fabrice C]
240	Inv. Stephani	4 S. Stephane sydus	MEL ['cor']
266	Assumptionis	1 Virginitas celum	pr. *Benedic/Benedicat/ Benedictus*
308	Lupi	1 O venerandum	pr. *Insignis* (= MEL 1A)
370ᵛ	Omn. scorum	1 Ecce iam coram	MEL [Fabrice C]
372	Omn. scorum	1 Concede nobis	pr. *Sollemniter* (*Sospitati*) + MEL 1A
385ᵛ	Martini	1 Martinus Abrahe	MEL 1A
409	Katherine	1 O mater nostra	pr. *Sospitati . . . Katherina*
411	Kather. (ad vesp)	1 Ex eius tumba	pr. *Sospitati . . . Katherina*

E. Sens, BM 6; 'precentoris norma', thirteenth century

(This manuscript gives only incipits, the neumes being cited only in rubrics.)

Fol.	*Feast*	*Mode/Text*	*Addition*
32	Natalis	1 Descendit	pr. *Familiam/Fac deus/Facinora*
34ᵛ	Stephani	7 Lapides	cum suo neumate
48	Stephani	1 Ecce iam	cum pneumate
59	dom2inXL	6 Oravit Iacob (ad vesp.)	cum neupmate
71ᵛ	Pascha	1 Et valde mane	pr. *Ortum predestinatio*[a]
72–	Pascha		The Alleluias of the Mass with their sequences are sung at Vespers during Easter week
108ᵛ	Nicolai	1 Ex eius tumba	cum prosa *Sospitati* (at Vespers only)

Fol.	Feast	Mode/Text	Addition
111v	Inv. reliq.	1 Concede	cum neumate (at Vespers only)
117	Paule	1 O admirabilem	cum prosa *Ad sacrum* (at first Vespers)
(this list is provisional)			

[a] This prosula begins the Easter drama: the prosula is preceded by the rubric *Representatio Mariarum*.

F. Sens, BM 29; breviary (secular) of Sens, early fourteenth century

Fol.	Feast	Mode/Text	Addition
190	Natalis	1 Descendit	pr. *Familiam/Fac/Facinora*
193	Natalis	7 In principio	MEL 7
202v	Stephani	7 Lapides torrentes	MEL 7
204v	Stephani	1 Ecce iam coram	MEL [Fabrice C]
206	Stephani	4 S. Stephanus sydus	MEL ['cor meum']
234	8 Stephani	2 O martirum gemma	pr. *Qui scis infirma*
412	Pascha	1 Et valde mane	pr. *Ortum predestinatio*
507	Nicolai	1 Ex eius tumba	pr. *Sospitati*
552	Inv. Stephani	7 Lapides torrentes	MEL 7
554	Omn. scorum	1 Concede nobis	MEL 1A
579	Purificationis	6 Gaude Maria	pr. *Inviolata*
660	Com. non p.	1 Laudemus dominum	MEL 1A

G. Rome, BAV Vat. lat. 153; breviary (secular, no notation) of Sens adapted to Provins, fourteenth century

(In this manuscript without notation the neumes are not indicated.)

Fol.	Feast	Mode/Text	Addition
120	Natalis	1 Descendit	pr. *Familiam/Fac/Facinora* (repeated at Vespers)
197v	Pascha	1 Et valde	pr. *Ortum predestinatio*
198–	Pascha		(The Alleluias of the Mass with their sequences are sung at Vespers during Easter week)
299	Nicolai	1 Ex eius tumba	pr. *Sospitati*
301v	Conc. BMV	? O Maria clausa porta	pr. *Stella maris O Maria*
332	Purificationis	6 Gaude Maria	pr. *Inviolata*
354v	Cyriaci Martyr	? Christi pretiosus	pr. *Apposito salutis*
371v	Petri et Pauli	4 Petre amas me	pr. *Psallat in isto die*
398v	Germani	8 Gloriosus domini	pr. *Pacem perpetue*
417	Assumptionis	1 Virginitas	pr. *Benedic/Benedicat/Benedictus*
434	Lupi	1 O venerandum	pr. *Insignis de Christo*
492	Katherine	1 Ex eius (Vespers)	pr. *Sospitati*

H. Rome, BAV Vat. lat. 182; breviary (secular, no notation) of Sens, fourteenth century

(In this manuscript without notation the neumes are not indicated; only Vespers responsories are named, whence the absence, e.g., of R. *Et valde* of Easter.)

Fol.	*Feast*	*Mode/Text*	*Addition*
117v	Natalis	1 Descendit	pr. *Familiam/Fac/Facinora* (at Vespers)
145v–	Pascha		(The Alleluias of the Mass with their sequences are sung at Vespers during Easter week)
175v	Nicolai	1 Ex eius tumba	pr. *Sospitati*
188	Purificationis	6 Gaude Maria	pr. *Inviolata*
197	Cyriaci	? Martyr dei pretiosus	pr. *Apposito salutis*
202v	Petri et Pauli	4 Petre amas me	pr. *Psallat in isto die*
210	Germani	8 Gloriosus domini	pr. *Pacem perpetue*
221v	Assumptionis	1 Virginitas	pr. *Benedic/Benedicat/ Benedictus*
227	Lupi	1 O venerandum	pr. *Insignis de Christo*
245	Katherine	1 Ex eius	pr. *Sospitati*

I. Sens, BM 46A; office of the Circumcision, fourteenth century (ed. Villetard)

Fol.	*Text*	*Addition*
2	*Letemur gaudiis*, *Christus manens* [beginning of first Vespers]	MEL 1A
3	Descendit de celis	pr. *Fac/Familiam/Facinora*
9	In principio	MEL 7
10v	Te laudant angeli	MEL (similar to 1A)
12	Veni sancte (Alleluia verse, on *ignem*)	MEL 1B
14	[as Versiculus]	pr. *Sedentem* (similar to 1B)
23v	[as Versiculus]	pr. *Qui scis infirma*
24v	Gaude Maria	pr. *Inviolata*
25	[as Versiculus]	pr. *Sancta Dei genitrix*

J. Rome, BAV Vat. lat. 577 (Office of SS. Savinianus and Potentianus)

Fol.	*Text*	*Addition*
93	Athletam domini	MEL 1A

Notes

1 'À Sens on a des neumes, non-seulement pour les Antiennes, mais aussi pour les Répons, dont on ne fait usage qu'aux solemnités: on les a conservées d'un ancien usage non interrompu.' Léonard Poisson, *Nouvelle méthode, ou Traité théorique et pratique du plain-chant* (Paris: P. N. Lottin & J. H. Butard, 1745), 379. According to Henri Villetard (*Office de Saint Savinien et de Saint Potentien, premiers évèques de Sens* (Paris: Picard, [1956], 103, n. A), Poisson was curé of Marsangis in the diocese of Sens. Villetard's publication includes the most complete list of the liturgical manuscripts of Sens: 'Catalogue des livres liturgiques de l'ancien diocèse de Sens', 91–114.

2 Research on neumes and prosulae in the office include the following: Hans-Jörgen Holman, 'Melismatic Tropes in the Responsories for Matins', *JAMS* 16 (1963), 36–46; Helma Hofmann-Brandt, *Die Tropen zu den Responsorien des Officiums*, 2 vols. (diss., University of Erlangen, 1971); Ruth Steiner, 'The Responsories and Prosula for St. Stephen's Day at Salisbury', *MQ* 56 (1970), 162–82; ead., 'Some Melismas for Office Responsories', *JAMS* 26 (1973), 108–31; ead., 'The Gregorian Chant Melismas for Christmas Matins', in Jerald C. Graue (ed.), *Essays on Music for Charles Warren Fox* (Rochester, NY: Eastman School of Music, 1979), 241–53. All three of Steiner's articles have been reprinted in Steiner, *Studies in Gregorian Chant* (Aldershot: Ashgate Publishing, 1999). See also Thomas Forrest Kelly, 'Responsory Tropes' (Ph.D. diss., Harvard University, 1973); id., 'Melodic Elaboration in Responsory Melismas', *JAMS* 27 (1974), 461–74; id., 'New Music from Old: The Structuring of Responsory Prosas', *JAMS* 30 (1977), 366–90; id., 'Melisma and Prosula: The Performance of Responsory Tropes', *Liturgische Tropen: Referate zweier Colloquien des Corpus Troporum in München (1983) und Canterbury (1984)*, ed. Gabriel Silagi (1985), 163–80; id., 'Neuma Triplex', *Acta musicologica*, 60 (1988), 1–30.

3 This is not, however, the view of Holman, 'Melismatic Tropes', who sees almost any responsory melisma as a trope.

4 Solesmes: Abbaye Saint-Pierre, 1893. Neumes may be seen there for *Descendit de caelis* (27–8); *Ecce jam coram te* (31–2); *In medio* (227–8).

5 *Amalarii episcopi opera liturgica omnia*, ed. Jean Michael Hanssens, vol. 3 (Vatican City: Biblioteca Apostolica Vaticana, 1950), 54. See Kelly, 'Neuma Triplex'.

6 Hartker's antiphoner, St. Gall, SB 390–391 (ca. 1000), is published in facsimile in PM, ser. 2, vol. 1 (Solesmes: Abbaye Saint-Pierre, 1900; new edn, ed. Froger, 1970); the so-called manuscript of Mont-Renaud (tenth century), privately owned, is published in facsimile in PM 16 (1955–6). On the triple neume in these manuscripts, see Steiner, 'The Gregorian Chant Melismas', 241–4 and *passim*; Kelly, 'Neuma Triplex', 1–2 and *passim*.

7 For lists, see Hofmann-Brandt, *Die Tropen*; Kelly, 'Responsory Tropes'.

8 An example is the responsory *Illuminare*, which has a lengthy melisma from which it seems never to be separated; a modern edition is in *Liber responsorialis* (Solesmes: Abbaye Saint-Pierre, 1895), 75.

9 On melismas borrowed from other chants, see Steiner, 'Some Melismas'; Kelly, 'Responsory Tropes', 49–66; David G. Hughes, 'Music for St. Stephen at Laon', in Laurence Berman (ed.), *Words and Music: The Scholar's View. A Medley of Problems and Solutions Compiled in Honor of A. Tillman Merritt By Sundry Hands* (Cambridge, Mass.: Harvard University Press, 1972), 137–59.

10 Indeed, one of the melismas of the *neuma triplex* seems to have started life in the Offertory *Gloria et honore*. See Steiner, 'The Gregorian Chant Melismas', 251 and n. 3; Kelly, 'Responsory Tropes', 49–50.

11 On performance, see Kelly, 'Melisma and Prosula', and the literature cited there.

12 See Terence Bailey, *The Intonation Formulas of Western Chant* (Toronto: Pontifical Institute of Mediaeval Studies, 1974).

13 Jacques de Liège, *Speculum musicae*, ed. Roger Bragard, 7 vols. in 8 (Rome: American Institute of Musicology, 1955–73), iii, 256. Jacques's label for the first mode indicates that the melisma may be appended to antiphons, responsories, sequences or prosas; for the other seven modes only responsories are mentioned. The labels for the other modes read: 'Responsoria secundi [tertii, etc.] toni sic [for mode 5, 'sicut'] sunt terminanda versiculo sequente.'

14 On this manuscript, see Christopher Hohler, 'Reflections on Some Manuscripts Containing 13th-Century Polyphony', *Journal of the Plainsong and Mediaeval Music Society*, 1 (1978), 2–38; facsimiles of the polyphonic 'ductiae' are conveniently found in Willi Apel, *The Notation of Polyphonic Music 900–1600* (Cambridge, Mass.: The Mediaeval Society of America, 1942 and later edns), facsimile 49, 247 (the numbers vary with the edition); transcriptions in Timothy J. McGee, *Medieval Instrumental Dances* (Bloomington: Indiana University Press, 1989), 126–9.

15 On the manuscript see Steiner, 'Some Melismas', 108 n. 1; in the same article, 109, Steiner prints a facsimile of the responsory *Sancte stephane sydus* with its neume from this manuscript.

16 The prosa *Inviolata* can be seen in modern editions in *LU* (1961), 1861–2; *Variae preces* (Solesmes: Abbaye Saint-Pierre, 1888), 26; Peter Wagner, *Einführung in die gregorianische Melodien* (2nd edn, Leipzig: Breitkopf & Härtel, 1911–21; repr. 1962), ii, 192. Published facsimiles include *Antiphonale Sarisburiense*, ed. Walter Howard Frere (London: PMM Society, 1901–24; repr. edn, 6 vols Farnborough, Hants, England: Gregg Press, 1966), iv, 402–3; Henri Loriquet, *Le Graduel de l'église cathédrale de Rouen au XIIIe siècle* (Rouen: J. Lecerf, 1907), fol. 217^{r-v} (Paris, BNF lat. 904); PM 12: 271–2 (from Worcester F.160); PM 18 (Chartres, BM 260), fol. 64^{v}. See also Joseph Pothier, 'Inviolata', *RCG* 2 (1893–4), 19–22; Clemens Blume, 'Inviolata', *Die Kirchenmusik*, 9 (1908), 41–8. On the 'Fabrice' melismas, see above, n. 6. For some modern prints of *Sospitati dedit egros*, very widely disseminated and imitated, see *Antiphonale Sarisburiense*, ed. Frere, iv, 359–60; *MGG* 14 (1968), Tafel 89; Joseph Pothier, 'Ex ejus tumba', *RCG* 9 (1900–1), 49–52. On some later imitations of *Sospitati* see most recently Kay Brainerd Slocum, 'Prosas for Saint Thomas Becket', *PMM* 8 (1999), 39–54.

17 Some manuscripts that provide only melismas as additions to responsories include Rouen, BM A.164, an eleventh-century monastic breviary of Marmoutier, and Metz, BM 83, an early thirteenth-century monastic antiphoner (destroyed). Examples of manuscripts that provide only prosae as embellishments for responsories include three secular breviaries of Meaux (Paris, Bibl. de l'Arsenal 153, thirteenth century; Paris, BNF lat. 1266, ca. 1300; Paris, BNF lat. 12035, twelfth century), and the twelfth-century monastic antiphoner of St-Maur-des-Fossés, Paris, BNF n. a. lat. 12044 (see Kelly, 'New Music from Old'). On the repertories of these manuscripts see Kelly, 'Responsory Tropes', app. 2.

18 I have not been able to consult for this study the breviary of *c.*1300, perhaps from Sens, MS W. 108 in the Walters Art Gallery, Baltimore, cited in Steiner, 'Some Melismas', 108 and n. 1.

19 Villetard, *Office de Saint Savinien et de Saint Potentien*; id., *Office de Pierre de Corbeil (Office de la circoncision) improprement appelé 'Office des fous'* (Paris: A. Picard, 1907).

20 *Antiphonarius ad ritum et consuetudinem Metropolitis ac Primatialis Senon. ecclesie . . . ex integro officia cum tonis ac pneumatibus* (Sens: Franciscus Girault, 1552).

21 This melody and its prosula have been the subject of considerable discussion. See Steiner, 'Some Melismas', 120–22; Wulf Arlt, *Ein Festoffizium des Mittelalters aus Beauvais in seiner liturgischen und musikalischen Bedeutung*, 2 vols. (Cologne: Volk, 1970), Darstellungsband, 99–100, Editionsband, 55 (transcription of 'Sedentem' from London, BL Egerton 2614), 223; Kelly, 'Responsory Tropes', 74–7, 428–9.

22 The melisma appears on the words *iniustitia* at the end of the verse *Cognovi domine*. See *Offertoriale sive versus offertoriorum*, ed. Carolus Ott (Paris: Desclée, 1935), repr. with additions as *Offertoires neumés* (Solesmes: Abbaye Saint-Pierre,1978), 40. In addition to its appearances at Sens, the melisma is attached to the responsory *Lapides torrentes* in Paris, BNF n. a. lat. 1236 (a twelfth-century antiphoner of Nevers), fol. 46 in a later hand; Paris, BNF 17296 (twelfth-century antiphoner of Saint-Denis), fol. 30; and Metz, Bibl. de la Ville 461 (a breviary of the later thirteenth century), fol. 118. See Kelly, 'Responsory Tropes', 50–52. The melisma is attached to the reprise (on *collocaret*) at the end of the versus *Christus manens*, which in turn is attached to *Letemur gaudiis*, an Offertory prosula here used independently, in Sens, BM 46A (see Villetard, *Office de Pierre de Corbeil*, 133). On *Christus manens*, found also in the Beauvais Circumcision office, and its polyphonic settings, see Arlt, *Ein Festoffizium*, Darstellungsband 67–9, 231–3, 259–71; Editionsband, 6, 169–73, 196, 263–5; David G. Hughes, 'The Sources of *Christus manens*', in Jan LaRue et al. (eds), *Aspects of Medieval and Renaissance Music: A Birthday Offering to Gustave Reese* (New York: Norton, 1966), 423–34.

23 See Appendix §A, responsory *Precursor domini*.

24 'Les neumes des répons étant fort étendus, font aisément sentir les propriétés de chaque Mode.' Poisson, *Nouvelle méthode*, 379.

25 See Villetard, *Office de Pierre de Corbeil*, 131 n. B; Arlt, *Ein Festoffizium*, Editionsband, 19, 204–5 (citing further manuscript appearances).

26 *Breviarium senonense*, 4 vols. (Sens: Tarbé, 1780).

27 On the 'Neo-Gallican' reforms, see David Hiley, *Western Plainchant: A Handbook* (Oxford: Clarendon Press, 1993), 618–21.

28 *Processionnal, Graduel, Antiphonaire et Psautier à l'usage de l'église primatiale et métropolitaine de Sens* (Sens: Thomas-Malvin, 1844).

29 'Les cinq premiers du Choeur, revêtus de Chappes, debout devant l'aigle commencent le Répons, chantent le Verset et le *Gloria Patri*, après lequel le Préchantre avec les deux Choristes au milieu du Choeur recommencent le Répons. Pendant que le Choeur chante la répétition, les cinq Dignitaires se partagent et vont, chacun de leur côté, se joindre aux Choristes au milieu du Choeur; là, ils se tournent face à face de la partie du Choeur avec laquelle ils chantent. À la fin du Répons, à la syllabe ou à la note qui précède celle sur laquelle on doit commencer la Neume, tout le Choeur s'arrête, le côté droit commence la Neume, qui se chante alternativement avec le côté gauche: à la fin les deux parties du Choeur se réunissent leurs voix pour terminer le Répons.' Poisson, *Nouvelle méthode*, 379–80.

Chapter 18

Singing the *Nuance* in Communion Antiphons

Richard Crocker

The accompanying compact disc contains my performances of the Advent Communion antiphons that were the starting point of James McKinnon's *Advent Project*.[1] These antiphons are listed in Table 18.1, with references to the *Graduale triplex* (*GT*) and also to Dom Hesbert's *Antiphonale missarum sextuplex* (*AMS*).

I am singing from the *Graduale triplex*; but for the antiphon *Mirabantur omnes* I am using the reconstruction made by Theodore Karp.[2] For the first ten antiphons I have supplied psalm verses from the versarium included in St. Gall, SB 381, in the splendid facsimile edition of Wulf Arlt and Susan Rankin.[3] In singing these antiphons I have paid special attention to the so-called signs of *nuance*, following those in the manuscript Laon, BM 239 as closely as I could. Here I give a brief account of these signs and of the way in which I have tried to read them.

The 'square notation' used in twentieth-century chant books is apparently the result of a modern adaptation made by Dom Pothier of northern French notation of the twelfth century, as part of his program of revival of Gregorian chant. One of the results of his work was the implicit definition of a *normal* chant notation; this norm became the standard of the Vatican edition of the Graduale (1908). It was maintained in Solesmes publications down to the modifications proposed in the Solesmes *Hymnarium* of 1983. It seemed to be taken as definitive by many musical scholars.

Implicitly or explicitly, chant research in the Benedictine tradition of Solesmes seems to have analyzed all varieties of chant notation in terms of this standard. It was always apparent, however, that the earlier manuscript sources did not conform to this standard in various ways; and the marks in these earlier manuscripts that did not conform seem to have disappeared from the practice of chant notation during the later Middle Ages. It is usually assumed that their meanings – whatever those meanings might have been – also disappeared; but it may eventually be fruitful not to make that assumption.

More important here, however, is the general status of these non-conforming marks, for they can only be regarded as non-conforming if the 'standard' forms can be assumed to have been standard as early as the notational systems of the tenth century (or of the ninth, if indeed these systems go back that far). That assumption seems not likely to be agreed upon, either because of differing axioms used by researchers or because of lack of historical data. None

Table 18.1 Communion antiphons (Advent and Christmas cycles)

Antiphon	*Assignment*	*AMS formulary*	*Graduale triplex (page)*
Dominus dabit	Advent I	*AMS* 1	17
Ierusalem surge	Advent II	*AMS* 2	20
Dicite pusillanimes	Advent III	*AMS* 4	23
Ecce virgo	Ember iv	*AMS* 5	37
Ecce Dominus	Ember vi	*AMS* 6	26
Exultavit ut gigas	Ember vii	*AMS* 7	28
Revelabitur	Nativity Vigil	*AMS* 8	40
In splendoribus	Nativity I	*AMS* 9	44
Exulta filia	Nativity II	*AMS* 10	47
Viderunt omnes	Nativity III	*AMS* 11	50
Video caelos	St. Stephen	*AMS* 12	635
Exiit sermo	St. John	*AMS* 14	637
Vox in Rama	Holy Innocents	*AMS* 15	638
Beatus servus	St. Silvester	*AMS* 16	491
Tolle puerum	Sunday after Nat.	*AMS* 17	51
Vidimus stellam	Epiphany	*AMS* 18	59
Fili quid fecisti	Epiphany I	*AMS* 19	51
Dixit Dominus	Epiphany II	*AMS* 21	263
Mirabantur	Epiphany III	*AMS* 26	267

the less, the existence of the standard as a modern conception makes it expedient to refer to at least some of these non-conforming marks as 'adjunct' to those taken as standard. This should be considered merely a manner of speaking, however, since these marks might well be integral, rather than adjunct, to the kinds of notation in which they appear.

These adjunct marks, then, formed a principal part of Dom Cardine's program of research (he called it 'semiology')[4] into the meaning of all aspects of early notation, beginning with the two important forms found in the Graduale Laon, BM 239 and the Cantatorium St. Gall, SB 359, both of the early tenth century. These forms, supplemented for repertorial reasons by Einsiedeln, SB 121 from later in the tenth century, were entered into the *Graduale triplex* by Marie-Claire Billecocq and Rupert Fischer, above and below the square notation on the staff, which represented the Vatican Graduale. Singing daily from the *Graduale triplex* over the last ten years, I have made my way through the Gregorian repertory a number of times, with constant close attention to the tenth-century notations; it has been the most instructive experience in my musical education.

Dom Mocquereau was fully aware, of course, of these adjunct marks; indeed, he made abundant use of them – but as ingredients in his own rhythmic system, on a selective, perhaps arbitrary, basis. One of the primary elements of his system was the postulate of equal duration for successive pitches, unless they were to be lengthened for some special reason. The lengthenings were controlled by other aspects of his system that were not apparent in the notation. He seems to have intended the effect of the adjunct marks to be slight, so as not to disturb the overall impression of a gentle, serene flow of equally spaced pulses; hence, the marks were known as signs of *nuance*. I maintain the italic for that term in order to keep in mind that the term itself is the result of an aesthetic reading of the signs.

In renewing a program of research on early Gregorian notation, Dom Cardine disregarded Dom Mocquereau's rhythmic system (which he seems to have considered peculiar); nevertheless, Dom Cardine made no radical reinterpretation of the meaning of the signs of *nuance*. More important, he maintained the thrust of the Solesmes program, which was toward a single original version, a performance that could be considered authentic. I find Dom Cardine's emphasis on the adjunct signs as used in the earliest sources to be well placed; and I have learned much from the detailed comparisons of manuscript data carried out by the phalanx of semiologists, Johannes Göschl at the point.[5] I find less useful their application of the principles of traditional text criticism – the attempt to determine what a sign means in general; I want instead to understand the musical meaning of the notation as used in a particular piece by a particular scribe.

It has become clear to many observers working from the *Graduale triplex* that even though the staffless notations of Laon 239 and St. Gall 359 are nominally adiastematic, they are not without pitch content that indicates *direction*. And it is clear that this pitch content can be used to reconstruct tenth-century melodic versions that differ in slight but numerous details from the Vatican versions, which were based mostly on twelfth-century sources. Perhaps this will result eventually in a new edition; a start has been made by semiologists.[6] In the meantime, it is easy enough to make certain provisional restorations, and I have done so in my recordings. A simple instance is mentioned in the discussion further on concerning the antiphon *Dominus dabit*. Such changes are not very prominent, and may escape the notice of the casual listener; they may not substantially affect the melodies. Still, they seem to me to result in stylistic improvement.

More important here is that the way in which we can read the early notation so as to perceive the differing pitch content is the same way in which I can read the adjunct signs of *nuance*. When we read a melody in Laon 239 or St. Gall 359, we necessarily have in mind the melody as learned from a Vatican version or from a medieval staffed source; melodies without such sources, or without analogs in such sources, seem indeed to be inaccessible. It is relative to such a known melody that the small pitch discrepancies in Laon 239 or St. Gall 359 become apparent. Consider the case in which, for a given syllable, the version in my mind (from, say, the Vatican) has one pitch as a punctum, while Laon 239 has two pitches as a podatus; given the particularities of the melody at that point, there are not so many choices for a second pitch, and any one of them seems more likely than to sing only the Vatican pitch. With a little application anyone can determine for themselves how often such provisional restoration is called for. The need is demonstrable, and reasonable inferences for alternative readings in Laon 239 or St. Gall 359 can be offered case by case.

In like manner, I sing the melody with a certain rhythmic flow – never mind what kind of flow, or where I got it. Its differences relative to either Laon 239 or St. Gall 359 are immediately obvious, as when Laon 239 has a 't' for *tenete* (one of the most frequent signs of *nuance*), while I am singing a duration more or less equal to that of the surrounding pitches – either because I learned it that way from the Vatican edition, or because Dom Mocquereau shows neither an episema nor a dot for that pitch, or simply because that is the way I sing it. I immediately see that the scribe of Laon 239 wants that pitch longer, and I can sing it that way, too.

While such a reading proceeds from an inference, it may not qualify quite so readily as a reasoned inference, which reflects, perhaps, as much our limited understanding about rhythm in general as about tenth-century performance. My continuing experience, however, is that the readings I get in this way from the manuscripts are regularly better than the versions I had previously learned. To me such readings make apparent sense, and – given the nature of the historical data – I believe that apparent sense is the best I can hope for. Fortunately, the readings these sources present to me make such good sense that I feel the need of nothing more demonstrable.

In an earlier study[7] I presented a way of reading such signs in a very general – and, I fear, much too elaborate – context. A much better presentation, I believe, is to sing them, hence this recording. The best way you can judge them is to hear how you like them; and if you do not like one or the other reading, to imagine your own, then compare it to the manuscript sources.

The signs of *nuance* do not lend themselves to categorical description, primarily because their identification as 'adjunct' to standard forms is presumptive, as discussed. It is easy to see that some of the signs are alphabetic, hence could be called *adjunct letters*; verbal equivalents for these signs, not always clear, are provided in a well-known list made by Notker.[8] It is harder, however, to deal with these adjunct letters as a separate category. Some of them refer to length, some to pace, some to character, some to pitch. Then, too, the lengthening letters as used in, say, Laon 239 have analogs in St. Gall 359 in the forms of episema and tractulus, which are non-alphabetic. Another analogous notation in St. Gall 359 involves *la coupure neumatique,* or scribal interruption of the normal form of a group.[9] Identification of such interruption involves, of course, our agreement as to what constitutes a *normal* form. It is at this point that the problem of the modern standard becomes acute, and also where the use of the term *neume* becomes problematic. Midway between standard forms and adjunct signs are the special forms oriscus, quilisma, the 'stretched torculus' and varieties of liquescent (sometimes modified by letters used to indicate melodic direction but with implications for rhythm).

It seems to me that in these special forms, variant group-forms, and adjunct signs – however identified – there is something of great importance to Gregorian rhythm; but a systematic description (one that might be a 'semiology') seems doomed to misunderstanding, or misrepresentation, or simple lack of agreement. As an alternative approach, I find it necessary to make a reading of a melody as a hypothesis, in the form of a performance, then see if that can be matched with the notation. I have no conclusions in the form of general description or final determination; my determinations are purely *ad hoc*, contextual, pragmatic, and I present them only in the form of a performance.

While the conclusions of the semiologists seem to me much too concerned with finding readings that would be demonstrably valid in all contexts (and, concomitantly, with attempting a standard classification of contexts), I think that contrary objections, to the effect that the signs of *nuance* – if not the earlier notations in general – should be disregarded completely, suffer from the same misplaced confidence in scholarly ability to determine readings objectively. Doubts about the value of the signs of *nuance* seem to me to miss a unique entry into medieval musicality. If a scribe tells me to sing a particular pitch longer, I can match that against how I would have sung it, and thereby glimpse something of the scribe's sense of rhythm; if another scribe agrees about that particular pitch, then I can grasp their shared sense of rhythm that much better; if, on the other hand, the two scribes disagree, then my sense of the rhythm can be that much more discriminate.

I want to say in general only that *nuance* itself seems a very presumptive term, involving in addition to the idea of a notational standard the idea of a rhythmic one, namely, that modifications of a flow of equal durations should be slight. Hence, to balance *per contrarium* the objection that signs of *nuance* should not be observed at all, I myself bring the objection that it is the meaning 'slight' that should be ignored: it seems to me that lengthenings, for instance, could be as long as a performer cared to make them – spectacular, even.

Here I offer a very brief introduction to the use of signs of *nuance* with reference to a transcription of the first antiphon on the CD, *Dominus dabit*, which appears in Pl. 18.1 as in the *Graduale triplex* with notations from Laon 239 (= L) and Einsiedeln 121 (= E), since it is lacking in St. Gall 359 (= C). My comments are keyed to the syllables of the verbal text, in capitals; boldface shows adjunct letters.

DO- (L) The pair of uncini has an **a** (= *augete*); the pair could have been printed in the Vatican as a bivirga, as used in E, where each virga has an episema.

-MI- Cursive.

-NUS (L) Cursive torculus plus one more note preceded by **a**; hence, the last two of these four pitches are to be lengthened, just as in E, where the torculus ends with an episema and the fourth note is a tractulus.

The following four-note climacus is written in L with two separate uncini, then two concluding dots; hence, two longer pitches followed by two shorter ones. This corresponds to E, which has an episema on the virga, then a tractulus followed by two dots.

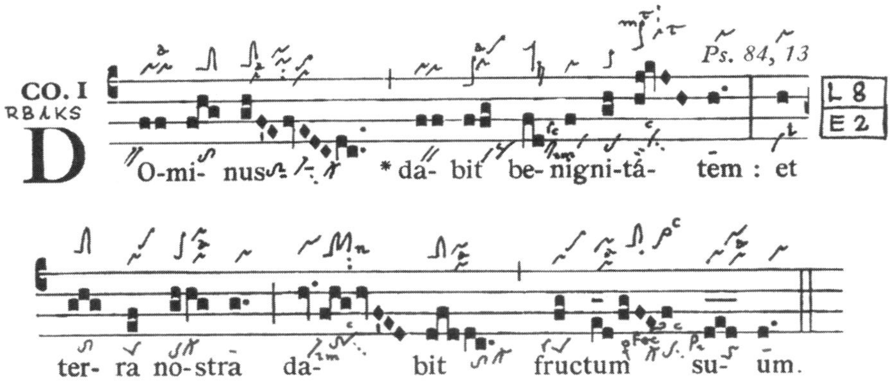

Pl. 18.1 Communion antiphon *Dominus dabit*, as printed in the *Graduale triplex* (notations from Laon, BM 239 [L] and Einsiedeln, SB 121 (E))

The clivis in L is written as two separate virga, corresponding to the clivis-with-episema in E; hence, both show the usual lengthening for the cadential appoggiatura clivis.

DA- L has again two uncini, but without **a**, apparently to vary a *redictum*, as so often in Gregorian style. Accordingly, the virgas in E lack episemas.

-BIT L has a pes followed by two separate notes and **a**; the square-note version needs another pitch, which I presume to be pitch *D*. MS E has only a virga.

For the other two notes, L has two separate notes, which is its usual way of showing a broadening. This appears in E as a pes quassus, and if the first half of that sign were taken to represent a reiteration *F–F*, then the first *F* would go with the preceding virga to form the equivalent of the pes in L.

BE- Cursive; L shows **h** (= *humiliter*), to produce pitch *D* not *E*, and MS E has **im** (= *iusum mediocriter*) for the same purpose.

-NI-GNI- Cursive.

-TA- L's pes has a **t** (= *tenete*) on the second note, with **m** so that we should not be carried away; then a rapid climacus, lengthened with **t** on the third note. E lengthens the first two notes with simple tractulus, then adds **c** (= *celeriter*), apparently to avoid the same extreme that concerned L. I myself do not find L's second **t** convincing, and I ignore it.

ET TER- Simple and cursive; the **l** (= *levate*) in E seems cautionary (it has been observed that E has abundant, sometimes redundant, markings).

-RA Lengthened in both versions.

NO- The first two pitches are cursive in both versions, the second two lengthened in both. This is a particularly clear example of what Guido seems to be talking about as 'groups like feet':[10] the whole passage *terra nostra* can be scanned analogically as three breves, two longs, two breves, two longs, long; or tribrach, spondee (epitrite?) minor ionic, catalectic spondee – or some more sophisticated analysis. That, of course, is metric metaphor; but this passage, like many others, does resemble a rhythm of logoaedic verse.

DA- L has an uncinus plus a cursive form in which lengthening is discouraged by **n** (= *non!*). E has the equivalent with virga-cum-episema and a cursive form hastened on its way with **c**. E's first virga has **lm** (= *levare mediocriter*), that is, pitch *a*, not *G*.

-BIT Cursive torculus plus lengthened clivis in both.

FRU-CTUM L has a lengthened pes, a lengthened clivis with **a** (hence a different amount of lengthening?), a cursive torculus plus dot, and a liquescent virga with **c**. E has the equivalent up to the end: lengthened pes, (some signs not clear to me), clivis-cum-episema, cursive pes plus two dots, with **c** (= *celeriter*) liquescent virga; but this liquescence is indicated as **i** (= *iusum*, lower), seeming to require an augmented liquescence that includes *D*; hence, the **c** (= *celeriter*) in L can be read as preempting that augmentation.

SU-UM Lengthened cadential torculus in both versions; but L maintains the form in which the lengthening is on the second pitch rather than the first – *pace* a traditional Solesmes manner of performing a concluding torculus.

I find the foregoing description virtually unreadable, and I do not intend to write any more of it. It seems as unsuited to literate expression or consumption as the equivalent kind of 'blow by blow' in commentary on symphony or opera; the proper ambient for all such discussion is *viva voce* in workshop, using mostly musical, not verbal, demonstration. That is what I had hoped to offer in person when I prepared this study, and I am deeply grateful to the editors of this volume for the opportunity to provide the demonstration on the accompanying CD.[11]

Notes

1 There are technical reasons for including all the Mass Propers through Epiphanytide in the Advent cycle. McKinnon listed the nineteen Communion antiphons for Advent, Christmastide and Epiphanytide in 'The Roman Post-Pentecostal Communion Series', in *Cantus Planus: Papers Read at the Fourth Meeting of the International Musicological Society Study Group, Pécs, Hungary, 1990*, ed. László Dobszay (Budapest: Hungarian Academy of Sciences Institute for Musicology, 1992), 175–86, esp. 177.

2 Theodore Karp, 'Performing from the Graduale triplex', in Bryan Gillingham and Paul Merkley (eds), *Chant and its Peripheries: Essays in Honour of Terence Bailey* (Ottawa: Institute of Mediaeval Music, 1998), 12–36, esp. 33.

3 *Stiftsbibliothek Sankt Gallen Codices 484 & 381: Kommentiert und in Faksimile*, ed. Wulf Arlt, Susan Rankin and Cristina Hospenthal (Winterthur: Amadeus, 1996), 50–141. See my review in *JAMS* 51 (1998), 625–30.

4 E. Cardine, 'Sémiologie grégorienne', *Etudes grégoriennes*, 11 (1970), 1–158; trans. Robert M. Fowels, *Gregorian Semiology* (Solesmes: Abbaye Saint-Pierre, 1982).

5 See *Beiträge zur Gregorianik*, 1 (1985).

6 See *Beiträge zur Gregorianik*, 21 (1996).

7 'Gregorian Studies in the Twenty-First Century', *PMM* 4 (1995), 33–86, esp. 75–6.

8 Jacques Froger, 'L'Epître de Notker sur les "lettres significatives"', *Etudes grégoriennes,* 5 (1962), 23–72.

9 Summary discussion in Cardine, 'Sémiologie grégorienne', 48–55.

10 Guido, *Micrologus*, cap. xv; see *Hucbald, Guido, and John on Music: Three Medieval Treatises*, trans. Warren Babb, ed. Claude V. Palisca (New Haven: Yale University Press, 1978), 72.

11 Ed. note: Professor Crocker was prevented by travel difficulties from attending the conference for which this paper was written.

Bibliography

Alleluia-Melodien I, bis 1100, ed. Karl-Heinz Schlager (MMMA 7; Kassel: Bärenreiter, 1968).

Allen, Pauline, 'Reconstructing Pre-paschal Liturgies in Constantinople: Some Sixth Century Homiletic Evidence', in A. Schoors and Peter Van Deun (eds), *Philohistôr: Miscellanea in honorem Caroli Laga Septuagenarii* (Orientalia Lovaniensia analecta, 60; Louvain: Peeters, 1994), 217–28.

Allen, W. Sidney, *Accent and Rhythm: Prosodic Features of Latin and Greek. A Study in Theory and Reconstruction* (Cambridge: Cambridge University Press, 1973).

—— *Vox Latina: A Guide to the Pronunciation of Classical Latin* (2nd edn, Cambridge: Cambridge University Press, 1978).

Allgeier, Arthur, *Die altlateinischen Psalterien: Prolegomena zu einer Textgeschichte der Hieronymianischen Psalmenübersetzungen* (Freiburg im Breisgau: Herder, 1928).

Das älteste Liturgiebuch der lateinischen Kirche: Ein altgallikanisches Lektionar des 5./6. Jhs. aus dem Wolfenbütteler Palimpsest-Codex Weissenburgensis 76, ed. Alban Dold (Texte und Arbeiten, 1; Beiträge zur Ergründung des älteren lateinischen christlichen Schrifttums und Gottesdienstes 26–8; Hohenzollern: Kunstverlag Beuron, 1936).

Amalarius, *Amalarii Episcopi opera liturgica omnia*, ed. Jean Michel Hanssens (Studi e testi, 138–40; Vatican City: Biblioteca Apostolica Vaticana, 1948–50).

Ambrose, *Ambroise de Milan: Hymnes: texte établi, traduit et annoté*, ed. Jacques Fontaine et al. (Paris: Editions du Cerf, 1992).

—— *Opera*, x: *Epistulae et Acta, Tomi 1–4*, ed. Otto Faller (vol. i, 1968) and Micaela Zelzer (vols. ii–iv, 1980–6) (CSEL 82/1–4; Vienna: Hoelder, Pichler, Tempsky [vols. i–iii]; Verlag der Österreichischen Akademie der Wissenschaften [vol. iv]).

Ancient Literary Criticism: The Principal Texts in New Translations, ed. D. A. Russell and Michael Winterbottom (Oxford: Clarendon Press, 1972).

Andrieu, Michel, *Les Ordines Romani du haut moyen âge*, 5 vols. (Spicilegium sacrum Lovaniense, Etudes et documents, fasc. 11, 23, 24, 28, 29; Louvain: Spicilegium Sacrum Lovaniense Administration, 1956–65).

The Ante-Nicene Fathers: Translations of the Writings of the Fathers down to A.D. 325, ed. Alexander Roberts and James Donaldson (American Reprint of the Edinburgh Edition, 8; Buffalo: The Christian Literature Company, 1886; many reprints).

Antifonario visigótico mozárabe de la Catedral de León: edición del texto, ed. Louis Brou and José Vives (Monumenta Hispaniae sacra, Serie litúrgica 5, no. 1; Barcelona: Centro de estudios e investigación S. Isidoro, 1959).

Antiphonaire de l'office monastique transcrit par Hartker: MSS. Saint-Gall 390–391 (980–1011) (PM II/1; Solesmes: Abbaye Saint-Pierre, 1900; new edn 1970, ed. Jacques Froger).

Antiphonale missarum sancti Gregorii, Xe siècle: Codex 47 de la Bibliothèque de Chartres (PM 11; Solesmes: Abbaye Saint-Pierre, 1912, repr. 1972).

Antiphonale Sarisburiense: A Reproduction in Facsimile from Early Manuscripts, ed. Walter Howard Frere, 3 vols (London: PMM Society, 1901–24; repr. edn, 6 vols. Farnborough, Hants, England: Gregg Press, 1966).

Antiphonarius ad ritum et consuetudinem Metropolitis ac Primatialis Senon. ecclesie . . . ex integro officia cum tonis ac pneumatibus (Sens: Franciscus Girault, 1552).

Antiphonen, ed. László Dobszay and Janka Szendrei, 3 vols (MMMA 5; Kassel: Bärenreiter, 1999).

Apel, Willi, *The Notation of Polyphonic Music 900–1600* (Cambridge, Mass.: The Mediaeval Academy of America, 1942 and later edns).

Apocalypse of Paul: A New Critical Edition of Three Long Latin Versions, ed. Theodore Silverstein and Anthony Hilhorst (Cahiers d'orientalisme, 21; Geneva: Patrick Cramer, 1997).

The Apocryphal New Testament: A Collection of Apocryphal Christian Literature in an English Translation, ed. J. K. Elliott (Oxford: Clarendon Press, 1993).

Les Apophtegmes des pères du désert: collection systematique, trans. Jean-Claude Guy (SC 387; Paris: Editions du Cerf, 1992).

Arlt, Wulf, *Ein Festoffizium des Mittelalters aus Beauvais in seiner liturgischen und musikalischen Bedeutung*, 2 vols. (Cologne: Volk, 1970).

Armellini, Mariano, *Le chiese di Roma dal secolo IV al XIX*, 2 vols. (2nd edn, Rome: Tipografia Vaticana, 1891; 3rd edn, corrected and augmented by C. Cecchelli, Rome: Edizioni R. O. R. E. di N. Ruffolo, 1942).

Arnese, Raffaele, *I codici notati della Biblioteca Nazionale di Napoli* (Florence: Olschki, 1967).

Arnobius Junior, *Opera omnia*, ii: *Opera minora*, ed. Klaus-O. Daur (CCSL 25A; Turnhout: Brepols, 1992).

Ars Laureshamensis: Expositio in Donatum maiorem, ed. Bengt Löfstedt (CCCM 40A; Turnhout: Brepols, 1977).

Athanasius of Alexandria, *The Life of Antony and the Letter to Marcellinus*, trans. and ed. Robert C. Gregg (Classics of Western Spirituality; New York: Paulist Press, 1980).

—— *Vie d'Antoine*, trans. Gerhard M. Bartelink (SC 400; Paris: Editions du Cerf, 1994).

Atkinson, Charles, '*De accentibus toni oritur nota quae dicitur neuma:* Prosodic Accents, the Accent Theory, and the Paleofrankish Script', in Boone (ed.), *Essays on Medieval Music in Honor of David G. Hughes*, 17–42.

Auf der Maur, Hans Jörg, *Das Psalmenverständnis des Ambrosius von Mailand: Ein Beitrag zum Deutungshintergrund der Psalmenverwendung im Gottesdienst der Alten Kirche* (Leiden: E. J. Brill, 1977).

Augustine, *The City of God*, trans. G. G. Walsh, SJ, D. B. Zema, SJ, G. Monahan, OSU, and D. J. Honan (1949, repr. New York: Doubleday, 1958).

—— *Confessions*, ed. James Joseph O'Donnell, 3 vols. (Oxford: Clarendon Press, 1992).
—— *Confessions*, trans. Henry Chadwick (Oxford: Oxford University Press, 1991).
—— *De doctrina christiana*, ed. and trans. R. P. H. Green (Oxford Early Christian Texts; Oxford: Clarendon Press, 1995).
—— *De moribus ecclesiae catholicae et de moribus Manichaeorum libri duo*, ed. Johannes Bauer (CSEL 90; Vienna: Hoelder-Pichler-Tempsky, 1992).
—— *Epistolae*, iii, ed. Alois Goldbacher (CSEL 44; Vienna: Tempsky, 1904).
—— *Enarrationes in Psalmos*, ed. Eligius Dekkers and Johannes Fraipont (CCSL 30–40; Turnhout: Brepols, 1956–65).
—— *Sermones de Vetere Testamento*, ed. Cyril Lambot (CCSL 41; Turnhout: Brepols, 1961).
Augustine through the Ages: An Encyclopedia, ed. Allan D. Fitzgerald et al. (Grand Rapids, Mich.: William B. Eerdmans, 1999).
Aurelian, *Aureliani Reomensis Musica disciplina*, ed. Lawrence Gushee (n.p.: American Institute of Musicology, 1975).
Bacht, Heinrich, *Das Vermächtnis des Ursprungs: Studien zum frühen Mönchtum* (Studien zur Theologie des geistlichen Lebens, 5, no. 8; Würzburg: Echter Verlag, 1972).
Bader, Günter, *Psalterium affectuum palaestra: Prolegomena zu einer Theologie des Psalters* (Tübingen: J. C. B. Mohr [Paul Siebeck], 1996).
Bagnall, Roger S., *Egypt in Late Antiquity* (Princeton: Princeton University Press, 1993).
Bailey, Terence, *The Ambrosian Alleluias* (Englefield Green: PMM Society, 1983).
—— *Antiphon and Psalm in the Ambrosian Office* (Musicological Studies, 50/3; Ottawa: Institute of Mediaeval Music, 1994).
—— *The Intonation Formulas of Western Chant* (Studies and Texts; Pontifical Institute of Mediaeval Studies, no. 28; Toronto: Pontifical Institute of Mediaeval Studies, 1974).
Bainton, Roland, 'The Origins of Epiphany', in *Early and Medieval Christianity: The Collected Papers in Church History*, 1 (Boston, 1962), 22–38.
Bannister, Henry Marriott, 'Una sequenza per l'Epifania', *Rassegna gregoriana*, 4 (1905), 5–14.
Basil, *Basili Regula a Rufino latine versa*, ed. Klaus Zelzer (CSEL 86; Vienna: Hoelder-Richler-Tempsky, 1986).
Bavel, Tarsicius van, 'The "Christus Totus" Idea: A Forgotten Aspect of Augustine's Spirituality', in *Studies in Patristic Christology: Proceedings of the Third Maynooth Patristic Conference, October 1996*, ed. Thomas Finan and Vincent Twomey (Dublin: Four Courts Press, 1998), 84–94.
Bede, the Venerable, *Opera historica*, with trans. by J. E. King, 2 vols. (Loeb Classical Library, 246; Cambridge, Mass.: Harvard University Press, 1930).
Benevento, Biblioteca Capitolare 40: Graduale, ed. Nino Albarosa and Alberto Turco (Codices Gregoriani; Padua: Linea editrice, 1991).
Bernard, Philippe, *Du chant romain au chant grégorien (IVe–XIIIe siècle)* (Paris: Editions du Cerf, 1996).

Bernhard, *Bernhardi cardinalis et Lateranensis ecclesiae prioris Ordo officiorum ecclesiae Lateranensis*, ed. Ludwig Fischer (Historische Forschungen und Quellen, 2–3; Munich and Freising: Dr. F. P. Datterer, 1916).

Bernhard, Michael, *Clavis Gerberti: Eine Revision von Martin Gerberts Scriptores ecclesiastici de musica sacra potissimum (St. Blasien, 1784)* (Veröffentlichungen der Musikhistorischen Kommission, 7; Munich: Verlag der Bayerischen Akademie der Wissenschaften, 1989).

—— 'Überlieferung und Fortleben der antiken lateinischen Musiktheorie im Mittelalter', in *Rezeption des antiken Fachs im Mittelalter* (Geschichte der Musiktheorie, 3; Darmstadt: Wissenschaftliche Buchgesellschaft, 1990), 33–5.

Berschin, Walter, and Hiley, David (eds), *Die Offizien des Mittelalters: Dichtung und Musik* (Regensburger Studien zur Musikgeschichte, 1; Tutzing: H. Schneider, 1999).

—— Ochsenbein, Peter, and Möller, Hartmut, 'Das Otmaroffizium – Vier Phasen seiner Entwicklung', in Berschin and Hiley (eds), *Die Offizien des Mittelalters*, 25–57.

Besnier, Niko, *Literacy, Emotion, and Authority: Reading and Writing on a Polynesian Atoll* (Studies in the Social and Cultural Foundations of Language; Cambridge: Cambridge University Press, 1995).

Biarne, Jacques, 'La Bible dans la vie monastique', in *Le Monde latin antique et la Bible*, ed. Jacques Fontaine and Charles Pietri (Bible de tous les temps, 2; Paris: Beauchesne, 1985), 409–29.

—— 'Le Temps du moine d'après les premières règles monastiques d'Occident (IVe–VIe siècles)', in *Le Temps chrétien de la fin de l'antiquité au moyen âge: IIIe–XIIIe siècles; Paris, 9–12 mars 1981* (Colloques internationaux du Centre national de la recherche scientifique, 604; Paris: Editions du Centre national de la recherche scientifique, 1984).

Biblioteca Apostolica Vaticana Archivio San Pietro B 79, Antifonario della Basilica di S. Pietro (Sec. XII), ed. Bonifacio Giacomo Baroffio and Soo Jung Kim, 2 vols. (Musica Italiae liturgica, 1; Rome: Torre d'Orfeo, 1995).

Bibliotheca hagiographica latina (repr. Brussels: Société des Bollandistes, 1992).

Bibliotheca sanctorum, 12 vols. (Rome: Istituto Giovanni XXIII nella Pontificia Università lateranense, 1961–70).

Bickerman, Elias Joseph, *The Chronology of the Ancient World* (2nd edn, London: Thames & Hudson, 1980).

Bielitz, Mathias, *Musik und Grammatik* (Munich: Musikverlag Katzbichler, 1977).

—— *Die Neumen in Otfrids Evangelien-Harmonie* (Heidelberg: Universitätsbibliothek Heidelberg, 1989).

—— *Zum Bezeichneten der Neumen, insbesondere der Liqueszenz* (Neckargemünd, Germany: Männeles Verlag, 1998).

Bischoff, Bernhard, 'Elementarunterricht und Probationes Pennae in der ersten Hälfte des Mittelalters', in Leslie Weber Jones (ed.), *Classical and Medieval Studies in Honor of Edward Kennard Rand* (New York: L. W. Jones, 1938), 9–20.

—— 'Die europäische Verbreitung der Werken Isidors von Sevilla', in *Mittelalterliche Studien: Ausgewählte Aufsätze zur Schriftkunde und Literaturgeschichte*, 3 vols. (Stuttgart: Anton Hiersemann, 1966).

—— *Mittelalterliche Studien: Ausgewählte Aufsätze zur Schriftkunde und Literaturgeschichte* (Stuttgart: Hiersemann, 1966).

Bishop, Edmund, *The Genius of the Roman Rite* (Liturgica Historica; Papers on the Liturgy and Religious Life of the Western Church; Oxford: Clarendon Press, 1918).

Björkvall, Gunilla, and Haug, Andreas, 'Texting Melismas: Criteria for and Problems in Analyzing Melogene Tropes', *Revista de musicología*, 16 (1993), 805–31.

Blaise, Albert, *Le Vocabulaire latin des principaux thèmes liturgiques*, rev. ed. by Antoine Dumas (Turnhout: Brepols, n.d. [ca. 1965]).

Blume, Clemens, 'Inviolata', *Die Kirchenmusik*, 9 (1908), 41–8.

Boe, John, 'Music Notation in Archivio San Pietro C 105 and in the Farfa Breviary, Chigi C.VI.177', *EMH* 18 (1999), 1–45.

—— 'The Roman *Missa Sponsalicia* in Florence, Riccardiana 299 and 300, Archivio San Pietro F 11 and Vaticanus lat. 5319', *PMM* (2002) (in press).

—— 'The Wedding Introit *Deus Israel* and Old Roman Introits for Lenten Ferias' (to be published in *PMM*).

Boese, Helmut, *Die alte 'Glosa Psalmorum ex Traditione Seniorum': Untersuchungen, Materialien, Texte* (Aus der Geschichte der lateinischen Bibel, 9; Vetus Latina: Die Reste der altlateinischen Bibel; Freiburg im Breisgau: Herder, 1982).

Boethius, Anicius Manlius Severinus, *De institutione musica*, in *Anicii Manlii Torquati Severini Boetii De institutione musica libri duo, De institutione musica libri quinque*, ed. Gottfried Friedlein (Bibliotheca scriptorum Graecorum et Romanorum Teubneriana; Leipzig: B. G. Teubner, 1867).

—— *The Fundamentals of Music*, trans. Calvin M. Bower (Music Theory Translation Series; New Haven: Yale University Press, 1989).

Bohn, Peter, 'Das liturgische Rezitativ und dessen Bezeichnung in den liturgischen Büchern des Mittelalters', *Monatshefte für Musikgeschichte*, 19 (1887), 29–36.

Bondi, Roberta C., *To Pray and to Love: Conversations on Prayer with the Early Church* (Minneapolis: Fortress Press, 1991).

Boone, Graeme M. (ed.), *Essays on Medieval Music in Honor of David G. Hughes* (Isham Library Papers, 4; Cambridge, Mass.: Harvard University Press, 1995).

Borders, James. 'The Northern Italian Antiphons *Ante evangelium* and the Gallican Connection', *JMR* 8 (1988), 1–53.

Bower, Calvin, 'Alleluia, Confitemini Domino, quoniam bonus – An *Alleluia, Versus, Sequentia*, and Five *Prosae* Recorded in Aquitanian Sources', in Susan Parisi (ed.), *Music in the Theater, Church, and Villa: Essays in Honor of Robert Lamar Weaver and Norma Wright Weaver* (Detroit Monographs in Musicology, Studies in Music, 28; Warren, Mich.: Harmonie Park Press, 2000), 3–32.

Bower, Calvin, 'An Alleluia for Mater', in Robert Lamar Weaver (ed.), *Essays on the Music of J. S. Bach and other Divers Subjects: A Tribute to Gerhard Herz* (Louisville, Ky.: University of Louisville, 1982), 98–116.

Bradshaw, Paul F., *Daily Prayer in the Early Church* (Alcuin Club Collections; New York: Oxford University Press, 1983).

—— *The Search for the Origins of Christian Worship: Sources and Methods for the Study of Early Liturgy* (Oxford: Oxford University Press, 1992).

Brambach, Wilhelm, *Die verloren geglaubte Historia de sancta Afra Martyre und das Salve Regina des Hermannus Contractus* (Karlsruhe: C. T. Groos, 1892).

Breviarium senonense, 4 vols. (Sens: Tarbé, 1780).

Brooks-Leonard, John K., 'Easter Vespers in Early Medieval Rome: A Critical Edition and Study' (Ph.D. diss., University of Notre Dame, 1988).

Brou, Louis, 'L'Alleluia dans la liturgie mozarabe', *Anuario musical*, 6 (1951), 3–90.

—— 'L'Antiphonaire wisigothique et l'antiphonaire grégorien au début du VIIIe siècle', *Anuario musical*, 5 (1950), 3–10.

—— 'Où en est la question des "Psalter Collects"?', in *Studia patristica*, ii: *Papers Presented to the Second International Conference on Patristic Studies Held at Christ Church, Oxford, 1955*, pt. 2, *Texte und Untersuchungen*, 64 (Berlin: Akademie-Verlag, 1957), 17–20.

Browe, Peter, 'Zur Geschichte der Dreifaltigkeitsfestes', *AfLw* 1 (1950), 65–81.

Brown, Howard Mayer, and Lascelle, Joan, *Musical Iconography: A Manual for Cataloguing Musical Subjects in Western Art before 1800* (Cambridge, Mass.: Harvard University Press, 1972; repr. 1998).

Brown, Peter, 'Asceticism: Pagan and Christian', in *The Cambridge Ancient History*, xiii: *The Late Empire, A.D. 337–425*, ed. Averil Cameron and Peter Garnsey (Cambridge: Cambridge University Press, 1998), 601–31.

—— *The Body and Society: Men, Women, and Sexual Renunciation in Early Christianity* (New York: Columbia University Press, 1988).

—— *The Making of Late Antiquity* (Cambridge, Mass.: Harvard University Press, 1978).

—— *Society and the Holy in Late Antiquity* (London: Faber & Faber, 1982).

Brunhölzl, Franz, 'Der Bildungsauftrag der Hofschule', in *Karl der Große: Lebenswerk und Nachleben*, ii: *Das geistige Leben*, ed. Bernhard Bischoff (Düsseldorf: Schwann, 1965), 28–41.

—— *Geschichte der lateinischen Literatur des Mittelalters*, i: *Von Cassiodorus zum Ausklang der karolingischen Erneuerung* (Munich: Fink, 1975).

Brunner, Gottfried, 'Arnobius eine Zeuge gegen das Weihnachtsfest?', *Jahrbuch für Liturgiewissenschaft*, 13 (1936), 178–81.

Bugnini, Annibale, *The Reform of the Liturgy 1948–1975*, trans. Matthew J. O'Connell (Collegeville, Minn.: Liturgical Press, 1990).

Bulst, Walther, *Hymni antiquissimi LXXV Psalmi III* (Heidelberg: F. H. Kerle, 1956).

Burkitt, F. C., 'The Early Syriac Lectionary System', *Proceedings of the British Academy* (1921–3), 301–8.

Cahn, Peter, and Heimer, Ann-Katrin (eds), *De musica et cantu: Studien zur Geschichte der Kirchenmusik und der Oper – Helmut Hucke zum 60. Geburtstag* (Musikwissenschaftliche Publikationen: Hochschule für Musik und Darstellende Kunst Frankfurt am Main, 2; Hildesheim: Olms, 1993).

Calati, B., 'La preghiera nella tradizione monastica dell'alto medioevo', in Vagaggini (ed.), *La preghiera*, 513–611.

The Cambridge Companion to Augustine, ed. Norman Kretzmann and Eleonore Stump (New York: Cambridge University Press, 2001).

Cardine, Eugène, 'Sémiologie grégorienne', *Etudes grégoriennes*, 11 (1970), 1–158; trans. Robert M. Fowels, *Gregorian Semiology* (Solesmes: Abbaye Saint-Pierre, 1982).

Cassian, John, *Conférences*, ed. Eugene Pichery, 3 vols. (SC 42, 54, 64; Paris: Editions du Cerf, 1953–9).

—— *Conlationes XXIIII*, ed. Michael Petschenig (CSEL 13; Vienna: C. Geroldi Filium, 1886).

—— *The Conferences*, trans. Boniface Ramsey (Ancient Christian Writers, 57; New York: Paulist Press, 1997).

—— *De institutis coenobiorum et de octo principalium vitiorum remediis libri XII*, ed. Michael Petschenig (CSEL 17; Vienna: F. Tempsky, 1888).

—— *The Institutes of John Cassian*, trans. Edgar Charles Sumner Gibson (Nicene and Post-Nicene Fathers of the Christian Church, Second series, 11; New York: The Christian Literature Company, 1894).

—— *Institutions cénobitiques Jean Cassien*, ed. Jean-Claude Guy (SC 109; Series de textes monastiques d'Occident, 17; Paris: Editions du Cerf, 1965).

—— *The Monastic Institutes, consisting of On the Training of a Monk and The Eight Deadly Sins*, trans. Jerome Bertram (London: Saint Austin Press, 1999).

Cassiodorus, *Explanation of the Psalms*, trans. P. G. Walsh, 3 vols. (Ancient Christian Writers, 51–3; New York: Paulist Press, 1990–91).

—— *Expositio psalmorum*, ed. M. Adriaen, 2 vols. (CCSL 97–8; Turnhout: Brepols, 1958).

Chadd, David, *The Ordinal of the Abbey of the Holy Trinity Fécamp: Fécamp, Musée de la Bénédictine, MS 186* (Henry Bradshaw Society, 111; Rochester, NY: Boydell Press for the Henry Bradshaw Society, 2000).

Chadwick, Owen, *John Cassian* (2nd edn, London: Cambridge University Press, 1968).

—— *Western Asceticism* (Library of Christian Classics, 12; Philadelphia: Westminster Press, 1958).

Chailley, Jacques, 'Les Anciens Tropaires et séquentiaires de l'école de Saint Martial de Limoges (Xe–XIe siècles)', *Etudes grégoriennes*, 2 (1957), 163–88.

—— *L'Ecole musicale de Saint Martial de Limoges jusqu'à la fin du XIe siècle* (Paris: Les Livres essentiels, 1960).

Chartier, Yves, *L'Œuvre musicale d'Hucbald de Saint-Amand: les compositions et le traité de musique* (Cahiers d'études médiévales, Cahier spécial, no. 5; Saint-Laurent Québec: Bellarmin, 1995).

Chitty, Derwas James, *The Desert a City: An Introduction to the Study of Egyptian and Palestinian Monasticism under the Christian Empire* (Oxford: Blackwell, 1966).

Chronographus anni CCCLIIII, ed. T. Mommsen (MGH *AA* 9/1; 1892).

Claire, Jean, 'Les Répertoires liturgiques latins avant l'octoéchos. I. L'Office férial romano-franc', *Etudes grégoriennes,* 15 (1975), 5–192.

Clark, F., 'Authorship of the Commentary *In 1 Regum*: Implications of A. de Vogüé's Discovery', *Révue bénédictine*, 108 (1998), 61–79.

Le Codex arménien Jérusalem 121, ed. Athanase Renoux, 2 vols. (PO 35, fasc. 1; 36, fasc. 2; Turnhout: Brepols, 1969, 1971).

Colish, Marcia L., *The Stoic Tradition from Antiquity to the Early Middle Ages*, ii: *Stoicism in Christian Latin Thought through the Sixth Century* (Studies in the History of Christian Thought, 35; Leiden: E. J. Brill, 1985).

Collectanea Pseudo-Bedae, ed. Martha Bayless and Michael Lapidge (Scriptores Latini Hiberniae, 14; Dublin: School of Celtic Studies, Dublin Institute for Advanced Studies, 1998).

Colombás, García M., *El monacato primitivo*, 2 vols. (Madrid: Biblioteca de autores cristianos, 1974–5).

Conomos, Dmitri, 'Change in Early Christian and Byzantine Liturgical Chant', *Studies in Music from the University of Western Ontario*, 5 (1980), 49–63.

Consultationes Zacchaei et Apollonii, ed. Germain Morin (Florilegium patristicum tam veteris quam medii aevi auctores complectens, 39; Bonn: P. Hanstein, 1935).

Copeland, Kirsti Barrett, 'Mapping the Apocalypse of Paul: Geography, Genre and History' (Ph.D. diss., Princeton University, 2001).

Coquin, René-Georges, Les Origines de l'Epiphanie en Egypte', in B. Botte, E. Mélia et al. (eds), *Noël, Epiphanie: Retour du Christ* (Lex Orandi, 40; Paris: Cerf, 1967).

—— 'Une Réforme liturgique du concile de Nicée (325)?', *Comptes rendus, Académie des Inscriptions et Belles-lettres* (1967), 178–92.

Corpus Orationum, ed. Eugenio Moeller, Ioanne Maria Clément and Bertrand Coppieters t'Wallant (CCSL 160A–K; Turnhout: Brepols, 1992–).

Corpus Praefationum, ed. Eugenio Moeller (CCSL 160F; Turnhout: Brepols, 1995).

Courcelle, Pierre, 'Date, source et genèse des Consultationes Zacchaei et Apollonii', *Revue d'histoire des religions*, 146 (1954), 174–93.

Coyle, John Kevin, *Augustine's 'De moribus ecclesiae catholicae': A Study of the Work, its Composition, and its Sources* (Paradosis, 25; Fribourg: University Press, 1978).

Crocker, Richard, *The Early Medieval Sequence* (Berkeley: University of California Press, 1977).

—— 'Gregorian Studies in the Twenty-First Century', *PMM* 4 (1995), 33–86.

—— 'Matins Antiphons at St Denis', *JAMS* 39 (1986), 441–90.

—— 'The Repertoire of Proses at Saint Martial de Limoges (Tenth and Eleventh Centuries)' (Ph.D. diss., Yale University, 1957).

—— 'The Repertory of Proses at Saint Martial de Limoges in the 10th Century', *JAMS* 11 (1958), 149–64.

—— 'The Sequence', in Wulf Arlt, Ernst Lichtenhahn and Hans Oesch (eds), *Gattungen der Musik in Einzeldarstellungen: Gedenkschrift Leo Schrade* (Bern: Francke, 1973), 269–322.

—— 'Some Ninth-Century Sequences', *JAMS* 20 (1967), 367–402.
—— 'The Troping Hypothesis', *MQ* 52 (1966), 183–203.
Cullmann, Oscar, *The Early Church* (Philadelphia: Westminster Press, 1956).
Cutter, Paul F., *Musical Sources of the Old-Roman Mass: An Inventory of MS Rome, St. Cecilia Gradual 1071, MS Rome, Vaticanum latinum 5319, MSS Rome, San Pietro F 22 and F 11* (Musicological Studies and Documents, 36; Neuhausen-Stuttgart: American Institute of Musicology, 1979).
Cyril of Jerusalem, *St. Cyril of Jerusalem's Lectures on the Christian Sacraments: The Procatechesis and the Five Mystagogical Catecheses*, ed. and trans. Frank L. Cross (Texts for Students, 51; London: S. P. C. K., 1951).
Cyril of Scythopolis, *Lives of the Monks of Palestine*, trans. Robert M. Price (Cistercian Studies Series, 114; Kalamazoo, Mich.: Cistercian Publications, 1991).
Daly, Robert J., *Christian Sacrifice: The Judaeo-Christian Background before Origen* (The Catholic University of America Studies in Christian Antiquity, 1; Washington: Catholic University of America Press, 1978).
Davril, Anselme, 'L'Origine de la fête de Noël', *Renaissance de Fleury: La revue des moines de Saint-Benoit*, 160 (1991), 9–14.
—— 'La Psalmodie chez les pères du désert', *Collectanea Cisterciensia*, 49 (1987), 132–9.
Dawson, David, *Allegorical Readers and Cultural Revision in Ancient Alexandria* (Berkeley: University of California Press, 1992).
De Bruyne, Donatien, *Préfaces de la bible latine* (Namur: Auguste Godenne, 1920).
De Bruyne, Lucien, 'La Décoration des baptistères paléochrétiens', in *Miscellanea liturgica in honorem L. Cuniberti Mohlberg*, i (Bibliotheca Ephemerides Liturgicae, 22; Rome: Edizioni liturgiche, 1948), 200–202.
Delalande, Dominique, *Le Graduel des Prêcheurs: recherches sur les sources et la valeur de son texte musical* (Bibliothèque d'histoire dominicaine, 2; Paris: Editions du Cerf, 1949).
De natura mundi et animae, ed. Walter Marg (Philosophia antiqua, 24; Leiden: E. J. Brill, 1972).
Deshusses, Jean, *Le Sacramentaire grégorien, ses principales formes d'après les plus anciens manuscrits* (2nd edn, 3 vols., Fribourg: Editions Universitaires, 1971–88).
Desprez, Vincent, *Le Monachisme primitif: des origines jusqu'au concile d'Ephèse* (Spiritualité orientale, 72; Bégrolles-en-Mauges: Abbaye de Bellefontaine, 1998).
—— *Règles monastiques d'Occident (IVe–VIe siècle), D'Augustin à Ferreol* (Bégrolles-en-Mauges: Abbaye de Bellefontaine, 1980).
Deusen, Nancy van, 'The *Cithara* as *Symbolum*: Augustine *vs* Cassiodorus on the Subject of Musical Instruments', in ead. (ed.), *The Harp and the Soul: Essays in Medieval Music* (Studies in the History and Interpretation of Music, 3; Lewiston, NY: E. Mellen Press, 1989).
—— *The Medieval Latin Sequence, 900–1600: A Catalogue of the Manuscript Sources*, 4 vols. (forthcoming).
—— 'Sequence Repertories: A Reappraisal', *Musica disciplina*, 48 (1994), 191–222.

Deusen, Nancy van, 'The Use and Significance of the Sequence', *Musica disciplina*, 40 (1986), 5–47.

—— (ed.), *The Place of the Psalms in the Intellectual Culture of the Middle Ages* (SUNY Series in Medieval Studies; Albany: State University of New York Press, 1999).

DeWald, Ernest Theodore, *The Stuttgart Psalter, Biblia folio 23* (Illuminated Manuscripts of the Middle Ages; Princeton: Pub. for the Department of Art and Archaeology of Princeton University, 1930).

Díaz y Díaz, Manuel C., *Manuscritos visigóticos del sur de la Peninsula: ensayo de distribucion regional* (Serie historia y geografia, 11; Seville: University of Seville, 1995).

Dinzelbacher, Peter, 'Die Verbreitung der apokryphen "Visio Pauli" im mittelalterlichen Europa', *Mittellateinisches Jahrbuch*, 27 (1992), 77–90.

Dionysius Thrax, *Ars grammatica*, ed. Gustav Uhlig (Leipzig: Teubner, 1883).

Dizionario degli istituti di perfezione, eds Guerrino Pelliccia and Giancarlo Rocca, 9 vols. to date (Rome: Edizione Paoline, 1974–).

Dobszay, László, 'Experiences in the Musical Classification of Antiphons', in *Cantus Planus: Papers read at the Third Meeting of the International Musicological Society Study Group, Tihany, Hungary, 19–24 September 1988*, ed. László Dobszay (Budapest: Hungarian Academy of Sciences Institute for Musicology, 1990), 143–56.

—— 'Some Remarks on Jean Claire's *Octoechos*', in *Cantus Planus: Papers Read at the Seventh Meeting of the International Musicological Society Study Group, Sopron, Hungary, 1995*, ed. László Dobszay (Budapest: Hungarian Academy of Sciences Institute for Musicology, 1998), 179–94.

—— 'The Types of Antiphons in Ambrosian and Gregorian Chant', in Gillingham and Merkley (eds), *Chant and its Peripheries*, 50–61.

—— and Szendri, Janka, *Catalogue of Hungarian Folksong Types Arranged According to Styles* (Budapest: Institute for Musicology of the Hungarian Academy of Sciences, 1992).

Duchesne, Louis, *Origines du culte chrétien: étude sur la liturgie latine avant Charlemagne* (5th edn, Paris: Du Boccard, 1925). Translated as *Christian Worship, its Origin and Evolution: A Study of the Latin Liturgy up to the Time of Charlemagne* (London: Macmillan, 1949).

Duchez, Marie-Elisabeth, 'Des neumes à la portée: élaboration et organisation rationnelles de la discontinuité musicale et de sa représentation graphique, de la formule mélodique à l'échelle monocordale', *Revue de musique des universités canadiennes*, 4 (1983), 22–65.

—— 'Description grammaticale et description arithmétique des phénomènes musicaux: le tournant du IXe siècle', in *Sprache und Erkenntnis im Mittelalter: Akten des VI. Internationalen Kongresses für Mittelalterliche Philosophie (Bonn, 1977)* (Miscellanea mediaevalia, 13/2; Berlin and New York: Walter De Gruyter, 1981), 561–79.

Duckett, Eleanor, *Alcuin, Friend of Charlemagne: His World and His Work* (Hamden, Conn.: Archon Books, 1965).

Dufrenne, Suzy, 'L'Illustration médiévale du psautier', in *Actes du colloque de l'Association des médiévistes anglicistes de l'enseignement supérieur publiés par les soins d'André Crépin sur les techniques narratives du Moyen Age* (Amiens: U.E.R. de langues et cultures étrangères, 1974), 59–72.

—— *Les Illustrations du Psautier d'Utrecht: sources et apport carolingien* (Association des publications près les universités de Strasbourg, fasc. 161; Paris: Ophrys, 1978).

Dyer, Joseph, 'Augustine and the *Hymni ante oblationem*: The Earliest Offertory Chants?', *Revue des études augustiniennes,* 27 (1981), 85–99.

—— 'Monastic Psalmody of the Middle Ages', *Revue bénédictine*, 99 (1989), 41–74.

—— 'The Offertory Chant of the Roman Liturgy and its Musical Form', *Studi musicali*, 11 (1982), 3–30.

—— 'The Psalms in Monastic Prayer', in Nancy van Deusen (ed.), *The Place of the Psalms in the Intellectual Culture of the Middle Ages* (SUNY Series in Medieval Studies; Albany: State University of New York Press, 1999), 49–89.

—— 'The Singing of Psalms in the Early Medieval Office', *Speculum*, 64 (1989), 535–78.

—— '*Tropis semper variantibus*: Compositional Strategies in the Offertories of Old Roman Chant', *EMH* 17 (1998), 1–60.

Dyggve, Ejnar, *History of Salonitan Christianity* (Instituttet for sammenlignende Kulturforskning, Serie A-Forelesninger, 21; Oslo: Aschehoug, and Cambridge, Mass.: Harvard University Press, 1951).

Early Medieval Chants from Nonantola, ed. Lance W. Brunner and James Borders, 4 vols. (Recent Researches in the Music of the Middle Ages and Early Renaissance, 30–33; Madison, Wis.: A-R Editions, 1996–9).

Early Monastic Rules: The Rules of the Fathers and the Regula Orientalis, ed. Carmela Vircillo Franklin et al. (Collegeville, Minn.: Liturgical Press, 1982).

Ebendorfer, Thomas, *Chronica pontificum Romanorum*, ed. Harald Zimmerman (MGH: Scriptores Rerum Germanicarum, Nova Series, 16; Munich: MGH, 1994).

Ebner, Adalbert, *Quellen und Forschungen zur Geschichte und Kunstgeschichte des Missale Romanum im Mittelalter: Iter Italicum* (Freiburg im Breisgau: Herder, 1896).

Echternacher Sakramentar und Antiphonar, ed. Kurt Staub, P. Ulveling and F. Unterkircher, 2 vols. (Graz: Akademische Druck- und Verlagsanstalt, 1982).

Ecrits apocryphes sur les apôtres: traduction de l'édition arménienne de Venise, i, ed. Louis Leloir (Corpus Christianorum, Series Apocryphorum, 3; Turnhout: Brepols, 1986).

Egeria: Diary of a Pilgrimage, trans. George E. Gingras (Ancient Christian Writers, 38; New York: Newman Press, 1968).

—— *Egeria's Travels*, ed. John Wilkinson (3rd edn, Warminster: Aris and Phillips, 1999).

—— *Egérie: Journal de Voyage (Itinéraire)*, ed. and trans. Pierre Maraval (SC 296; Paris: Editions du Cerf, 1982).

—— *Ethérie: Journal de voyage*, ed. and trans. Hélène Pétré (SC 21; Paris: Editions du Cerf, 1948).

Elm, Susanna, *Virgins of God: The Making of Asceticism in Late Antiquity* (Oxford: Oxford University Press, 1994).

el-Meskeen, Matta, *Coptic Monasticism and the Monastery of St. Macarius: A Short History* (Cairo: Monastery of St. Macarius Scetis, 1984).

Encyclopedia of the Early Church, ed. Angelo di Berardino, trans. Adrian Walford, 2 vols. (New York: Oxford University Press, 1992).

Engberg-Pedersen, Troels, *Paul and the Stoics* (Westminster: John Knox, 2000).

Epiphanius, *Panarion haer. 34–64*, ed. Karl Holl, rev. Jürgen Dummer (Berlin: Akademie-Verlag, 1980).

Etaix, Raymond, *Homéliaires patristiques latins: recueil d'études de manuscrits médiévaux* (Paris: Institut d'Etudes Augustiniennes, 1994).

—— 'Nouvelle Collection de sermons rassemblée par saint Césaire', *Revue bénédictine*, 87 (1977), 7–33.

Euclid, *Euclides Phaenomena et scripta musica*, ed. J. L. Heiberg (Euclid, Opera omnia, 8; Bibliotheca scriptorum Graecorum et Romanorum Teubneriana, 1314; Leipzig: B. G. Teubner, 1916).

Evagrius Ponticus: The Praktikos and Chapters on Prayer, trans. John Eudes Bamberger (Cistercian Studies, 4; Spencer, Mass.: Cistercian Publications, 1970).

Evans, Paul Richer, *The Early Trope Repertory of Saint Martial de Limoges* (Princeton Studies in Music, 2; Princeton: Princeton University Press, 1970).

Expositio antiquae liturgiae gallicanae, ed. E. C. Ratcliff (Henry Bradshaw Society Publication, 98; London: Henry Bradshaw Society, 1971).

Falconer, Keith, 'Zum Offizium des hl. Medardus', in Berschin and Hiley (eds), *Die Offizien des Mittelalters*, 69–85.

Farmer, David Hugh, 'St Gregory and St Augustine of Canterbury', in id. (ed.), *Benedict's Disciples* (Leominster: Gracewing, 1980; repr. 1995), 41–51.

Fassler, Margot, 'Mary's Nativity, Fulbert of Chartres, and the *Stirps Jesse*', *Speculum*, 75 (2000), 389–434.

—— 'The Office of the Cantor in Early Western Monastic Rules and Customaries', *EMH* 5 (1985), 29–52.

Férotin, Marius, *Liber ordinum mozarabicus: le Liber ordinum en usage dans l'église wisigothique et mozarabe d'Espagne du cinquième au onzième siècle* (Paris: Firmin-Didot, 1904; repr. Rome: Edizioni liturgiche, 1996).

Ferrari, Guy, *Early Roman Monasteries: Notes for the History of the Monasteries and Convents at Rome from the V through the X Century* (Studi di antichità cristiana, 23; Vatican City: Pontificio Istituto di archeologia cristiana, 1957).

Ferretti, Paolo Maria, *Estetica gregoriana: trattato delle forme musicali del canto gregoriano*, i (Rome: Pontificio Istituto di Musica Sacra, 1934).

Fickett, Martha van Zant, 'Chants for the Feast of St. Martin of Tours' (Ph.D. diss., Catholic University of America, 1983).

Fiedrowicz, Michael, *Psalmus vox totius Christi: Studien zu Augustins 'Enarrationes in Psalmos'* (Freiburg im Breisgau: Herder, 1997).

Fischer, Balthasar, *Die Psalmen als Stimme der Kirche: Gesammelte Studien zur christlichen Psalmenfrömmigkeit*, ed. Andreas Heinz (Trier: Paulinus-Verlag, 1982).

Fischer, Bonifatius, 'Bedae de titulis psalmorum liber', in Johannes Autenrieth and Franz Brunhölzl (eds), *Festschrift Bernhard Bischoff zu seinem 65.Geburtstag* (Stuttgart: A. Hiersemann, 1971), 90–110.

Fischer, Pieter, *The Theory of Music from the Carolingian Era up to 1400*, ii: *Italy* (RISM B III/2; Henle Verlag: Munich-Duisburg, 1968).

Fisher, Scott Alden, '*Tonos* and its Relatives: A Word Study' (Ph.D. diss., Ohio State University, 1989).

Fitzmyer, Joseph A., *The Gospel According to Luke* (The Anchor Bible 28–28A; Garden City, NY, 1981–5).

Foley, Edward, 'The Song of the Assembly in Medieval Eucharist', in Lizette Larson-Miller (ed.), *Medieval Liturgy: A Book of Essays* (Garland Medieval Casebooks; New York: Garland, 1997), 203–34.

Fordyce, P. J., *P. Vergili Maronis Aeneidos libri VII–VIII with a Commentary* (1977).

Forgas, Joseph P. (ed.), *Feeling and Thinking: The Role of Affect in Social Cognition* (Studies in Emotion and Social Interaction, 2nd ser.; Cambridge and Paris: Cambridge University Press and Editions de la Maison des Sciences de l'Homme, 2000).

Fossas, Ignasi M. 'L'epistola ad Marcellinum di Sant'Atanasio sull'uso del salterio: studio letterario, liturgico e teologico', *Studia monastica*, 39 (1997), 27–76.

Franceschini, Ezio, and Weber, R., 'Itinerarium Egeriae', in *Itineraria et alia geographica* (CCSL 175–6; Turnhout: Brepols, 1965), 27–103.

Frank, K. S., 'Johannes Cassian über Johannes Cassian', *Römische Quartalschrift für christliche Altertumskunde und Kirchengeschichte*, 91 (1996), 183–97.

Frank, Karl Suso, *ΑΓΓΕΛΙΚΟΣ ΒΙΟΣ: Begriffsanalytische und begriffsgeschichtliche Untersuchung zum 'engelgleichen Leben' im frühen Mönchtum* (Beiträge zur Geschichte des alten Mönchtums und des Benediktinerordens, 26; Münster in Westfalen: Aschendorff, 1964).

—— *Frühes Mönchtum im Abendland*, 2 vols (Die Bibliothek der alten Welt: Reihe Antike und Christentum; Zurich: Artemis-Verlag, 1975).

Froger, Jacques, 'Les Chants de la messe aux VIIIe et IXe siècles', *Revue grégorienne*, 26 (1947), 165–72, 218–28; 27 (1948), 56–62, 98–107; 28 (1949), 58–65, 94–102.

—— 'L'Epître de Notker sur les "lettres significatives",' *Etudes grégoriennes*, 5 (1962), 23–72.

Frøyshov, Stig Simeon, 'La Réticence à l'hymnographie chez des anachorètes de l'Egypte et du Sinaï du 6 au 8 siècles', in *L'Hymnographie: Conférences Saint-Serge, 46, Semaine d'études liturgiques, Paris, 29 juin–2 juillet 1999*, ed. A. M. Triacca et al. (Bibliotheca Ephemerides liturgicae, Subsidia 105; Rome: CLV, 2000), 229–45.

Gain, Benoît, *L'Eglise de Cappadoce au IVe siècle d'après la correspondance de Basile de Césarée (330–379)* (OCA 225; Rome: Pontificium Institutum Studiorum Orientalium, 1985).

Gajard, Joseph, 'Les Récitations modales des 3e et 4e modes dans les manuscrits bénéventains et aquitains', *Etudes grégoriennes*, 1 (1954), 9–45.

Gale, John, 'The Divine Office: Aid and Hindrance to Penthos', *Studia monastica*, 27 (1985), 13–15.
Gannon, Thomas M., and Traub, George W., *The Desert and the City: An Interpretation of the History of Christian Spirituality* (New York: Macmillan, 1969).
Garrigues, Jean-Miguel, and Legrez, Jean, *Moines dans l'assemblée des fidèles à l'époque des pères (IVe–VIIIe siécles)* (Théologie historique, 87; Paris: Beauchesne, 1992).
Die Gesänge des altrömischen Graduale Vat. lat. 5319, ed. Bruno Stäblein and Margareta Landwehr-Melnicki (MMMA 2; Kassel: Bärenreiter, 1970).
Gevaert, François Auguste, *La Melopée antique dans le chant de l'église latine* (Ghent: A. Hoste, 1895–6; repr. 1967).
Gillingham, Bryan, and Merkley, Paul (eds), *Chant and its Peripheries: Essays in Honour of Terence Bailey* (Musicological Studies, 72; Ottawa: Institute of Mediaeval Music, 1998).
Gors i Pujol, Miquel, 'Les Tropes d'introït du graduel de Saint-Félix de Gérone', in *Corpus troporum*, viii: *Recherches nouvelles sur les tropes liturgiques* ['Huglo Festschrift'], ed. Wulf Arlt (Acta universitatis stockholmiensis, Studia latina stockholmiensis, 36; Stockholm: Almqvist & Wiksell, 1993), 221–9.
Göschl, Johannes, et al., *Beiträge zur Gregorianik*, 1 (1985).
Gould, Graham, *The Desert Fathers on Monastic Community* (Oxford Early Christian Studies; Oxford: Clarendon Press, 1993).
Das Graduale der St. Thomaskirche zu Leipzig, ed. Peter Wagner (Publikationen älterer Musik, v [Leipzig, 1930], vii [Leipzig, 1932, repr. 1967].
Graduale Pataviense: Wien 1511, ed. Christian Väterlein (Das Erbe deutscher Musik, 87; Kassel: Bärenreiter, 1982).
Graduale Sarisburiense, ed. Walter Howard Frere (Plainsong and Mediaeval Music Society; London: Bernard Quaritch, 1894; repr. Farnborough: Gregg Press, 1966).
Das Graduale von Santa Cecilia in Trastevere, Cod. Bodmer 74, ed. Max Lütolf, 2 vols. (Cologny-Geneva: Fondation Martin Bodmer, 1987).
Le Graduel romain, ii: *Les Sources* (Solesmes: Abbaye Saint-Pierre, 1957).
Grammatici Latini, ed. H. Keil, 8 vols. (Leipzig: Teubner, 1857–80; repr. 1961).
Le Grand Lectionnaire de l'église de Jérusalem (V^e–VIIIe siècles), ed. Michel Tarchnischvili, 2 vols. in 4 (CSCO 188–9, 204–5; Louvain: Secrétariat de Corpus Scriptorum Christianorum Orientalium, 1959, 1960).
Grégoire, Réginald, *Homéliaires liturgiques médiévaux: analyse de manuscrits* (Biblioteca degli studi medievali, 12; Spoleto: Centro Italiano di Studi sull'Alto Medioevo, 1980).
Gregory of Nyssa, *The Easter Sermons of Gregory of Nyssa: Translation and Commentary*, ed. Andreas Spira and Christoph Klock (Patristic Monographs Series, 9; Cambridge, Mass.: The Philadelphia Patristic Foundation, 1981).
—— *Gregory of Nyssa's Treatise on the Inscriptions of the Psalms: Introduction, Translation, and Notes*, trans. Ronald E. Heine (Oxford Early Christian Studies; Oxford: Clarendon Press, 1995).

—— *In inscriptiones Psalmorum*, ed. J. McDonough (Gregorii Nysseni Opera, v; Leiden: E. J. Brill, 1962).

—— *Vie de Sainte Macrine*, ed. Pierre Maraval (SC 178; Paris: Editions du Cerf, 1971).

Gregory the Great, *Homiliae in Evangelia*, ed. Raymond Etaix (CCSL 141; Turnhout: Brepols, 1999).

Gribomont, Jean, 'Le Monachisme au IVe siècle en Asie Mineure de Gangres au Messalianisme', *Studia patristica*, 2 (1957), 400–15.

Grier, James, 'Editing Adémar de Chabannes' Liturgy for the Feast of Saint Martial', *PMM* 6 (1997), 97–118.

Griggs, C. Wilfred, *Early Egyptian Christianity from its Origins to 451 C.E.* (Coptic Studies, 2; Leiden: E. J. Brill, 1990).

Guigo II, *The Ladder of Monks: A Letter on the Contemplative Life and Twelve Meditations*, trans. Edmund Colledge and James Walsh (Garden City, NY: Doubleday Image Books, 1978; repr. as Cistercian Studies Series, 48; Kalamazoo: Cistercian Publications, 1981).

Guillaumont, Antoine, *Aux origines du monachisme chrétien: pour une phénoménologie du monachisme* (Spiritualité orientale, 30; Bégrolles-en-Mauges: Abbaye de Bellefontaine, 1979).

Guilmard, Jacques-Marie, 'Une antique fête mariale au 1er janvier dans la ville de Roma?', *Ecclesia orans*, 11 (1994), 25–67.

Guy, Jean-Claude, 'Les *Apothegmata Patrum*', in *Théologie de la vie monastique: études sur la tradition patristique* (Théologie, 49; Ligugé: Aubier, 1961).

—— 'Le Centre monastique de Scété dans la littérature du Ve siècle', *Orientalia Christiana periodica*, 30 (1974), 129–47.

—— *Jean Cassien: vie et doctrine spirituelle* (Paris: P. Lethielleux, 1961).

—— *Recherches sur la tradition grecque des Apophthegmata Patrum* (Subsidia hagiographica, 36; Brussels: Société des Bollandistes, 1962).

Handschin, Jacques, 'Trope, Sequence, and Conductus', in *NOHM*, ii: *Early Music up to 1300*, ed. Anselm Hughes (London: Oxford University Press, 1954), 128–74.

The Harper Collins Study Bible: New Revised Standard Version with the Apocryphal/Deuterocanonical Books, ed. Wayne A. Meeks et al. (New York: Harper Collins, 1993).

Harrison, Carol, *Beauty and Revelation in the Thought of Saint Augustine* (Oxford Theological Monographs; Oxford: Oxford University Press, 1992).

Haug, Andreas, 'Neue Ansätze im 9. Jahrhundert', in *Die Musik des Mittelalters*, ed. Hartmut Möller and Rudolf Stephan (Neues Handbuch der Musikwissenschaft, 2; Laaber: Laaber-Verlag, 1991), 94–128.

—— 'Ein neues Textdokument zur Entstehungsgeschichte der Sequenz', in Rudolf Faber et al. (eds), *Festschrift Ulrich Siegele zum 60. Geburtstag* (Kassel: Bärenreiter, 1991), 9–19.

—— *Troparia tardiva: Repertorium später Tropenquellen aus dem deutschsprachigen Raum* (MMMA, Subsidia, 1; Kassel: Bärenreiter, 1995).

—— 'Zur Interpretation der Liqueszenzneumen', *Archiv für Musikwissenschaft*, 50 (1993), 85–100.

Hausheer, Irénée, *Penthos: The Doctrine of Compunction in the Christian East*, trans. Anselm Hufstader (Cistercian Studies Series, 53; Kalamazoo, Mich.: Cistercian Publications, 1982).

Hawel, Peter, *Das Mönchtum im Abendland: Geschichte, Kultur, Lebensform* (Freiburg im Breisgau: Herder, 1993).

Heckenbach, Willibrord, 'Responsoriale Communio-Antiphonen', in Detlef Altenburg (ed.), *Ars Musica, Musica Scientia: Festschrift Heinrich Hüschen* (Beiträge zur Rheinischen Musikgeschichte, 126; Cologne: Gitarre und Laute, 1980), 224–32.

Hesbert, René-Jean, 'La Tradition bénéventaine dans la tradition manuscrite', in PM 14 (Solesmes: Abbaye Saint-Pierre, 1931), 60–465.

Heussi, Karl, *Der Ursprung des Mönchtums* (Tübingen: Mohr, 1936; repr. Aalen: Scientia, 1981).

Hilary of Poitiers, *Tractatus super Psalmos*, ed. J. Doignon (CCSL 61; Turnhout: Brepols, 1997).

Hiley, David, 'Changes in English Chant Repertoires in the Eleventh Century as Reflected in the Winchester Sequences', in *Anglo-Norman Studies, 16: Proceedings of the Battle Conference 1993* (Woodbridge, Suffolk: Boydell Press, 1994), 137–54.

—— 'Cluny, Sequence and Tropes', in Claudio Leonardi and Enrico Menestro (eds), *La tradizione dei tropi liturgici* (Spoleto: Centro Italiano di Studi sull'Alto Medioevo, 1990), 99–113.

—— 'Editing the Winchester Sequence Repertory of ca. 1000', in *Cantus Planus: Papers read at the Third Meeting, Tihany, Hungary, 19–24 September 1988,* ed. László Dobszay et al. (Budapest: Hungarian Academy of Sciences Institute for Musicology, 1990), 99–113.

—— 'The Norman Chant Traditions – Normandy, Britain, Sicily', *PRMA* 107 (1981), 1–33.

—— 'The Regensburg Offices for St Emmeram, St Wolfgang and St Denis', in *Musica Antiqua X. 10th International Musicological Congress 'Musica Antiqua Europae Orientalis', Bydgoszcz, September 7th–11th 1994* (Bydgoszcz: Filharmonia Pomorska im I. Paderewskiego, 1997), 299–312.

—— 'The Repertory of Sequences at Winchester', in Boone (ed.), *Essays on Medieval Music in Honor of David G. Hughes*, 153–93.

—— 'Rouen, Bibliothèque Municipale, MS 249 (A. 280) and the Early Paris Repertory of Ordinary Mass Chants and Sequences', *M&L* 70 (1989), 467–82.

—— 'The Sequence Melodies Sung at Cluny and Elsewhere', in Cahn and Heimer (eds), *De musica et cantu*, 131–55.

—— 'The Sequentiary of Chartres, Bibliothèque Municipale, Ms. 47', in *La sequenza medievale: Atti del Convegno Internazionale Milano 7–8 Aprile 1984*, ed. Agostino Ziino (Quaderni di San Maurizio, 3; Lucca: Libreria Musicale Italiana, 1992), 105–17.

—— *Western Plainchant: A Handbook* (Oxford: Clarendon Press, 1993).

—— 'Das Wolfgang-Offizium des Hermannus Contractus – Zum Wechselspiel von Modustheorie und Gesangspraxis in der Mitte des XI. Jahrhunderts', in Berschin and Hiley (eds), *Die Offizien des Mittelalters*, 129–42.

Hintze, Gisa, *Das byzantinische Prokeimena-Repertoire: Untersuchungen und kritische Edition* (Hamburg: Verlag der Musikalienhandlung Wagner, 1973).
Historia monachorum in Aegypto, ed. André Marie Jean Festugière (Subsidia hagiographica, 53; Brussels: Société des Bollandistes, 1971).
Hofmann-Brandt, Helma, *Die Tropen zu den Responsorien des Officiums*, 2 vols (diss., University of Erlangen, 1971).
Hohler, Christopher, 'The Durham Services in Honour of St. Cuthbert', in C. F. Battiscombe (ed.), *The Relics of Saint Cuthbert* (Oxford: Oxford University Press for the Dean and Chapter of Durham Cathedral, 1956), 157–91.
—— 'Reflections on Some Manuscripts Containing 13th-Century Polyphony', *PMM* 1 (1978), 2–38.
Holl, K., 'Die Ursprung des Epiphaniefestes', in *Sitzungsberichte der Preussischen Akademie der Wissenschaften* (1971), 402–38.
Holman, Hans-Jörgen, 'Melismatic Tropes in the Responsories for Matins', *JAMS* 16 (1963), 36–46.
Holtz, Louis, *Donat et la tradition de l'enseignement grammatical* (Paris: Centre National de la Recherche Scientifique, 1981).
Holschneider, Andreas, *Die Organa von Winchester: Studien zum ältesten Repertoire polyphoner Musik* (Hildesheim: Olms, 1968).
Hourlier, Jacques, Review of Alejandro Planchart, *The Repertory of Tropes at Winchester*, in *Etudes grégoriennes*, 17 (1978), 231–2.
Hucbald, Guido, and John on Music: Three Medieval Treatises, trans. Warren Babb, ed. Claude V. Palisca (Music Theory Translation Series, 3; New Haven: Yale University Press, 1978).
Hucke, Helmut, 'Gregorianische Fragen', *Musikforschung,* 41 (1988), 304–30.
—— 'Das Responsorium', in Wulf Arlt, Ernst Lichtenhahn and Hans Oesch (eds), *Gattungen der Musik in Einzeldarstellungen: Gedenkschrift Leo Schrade* (Bern: Francke, 1973), 144–91.
—— 'Toward a New Historical View of Gregorian Chant', *JAMS* 33 (1980), 437–67.
Hugh of St. Victor, *The Didascalicon of Hugh of St. Victor: A Medieval Guide to the Arts*, trans. J. Taylor (Records of Western Civilization; New York: Columbia University Press, 1961).
Hughes, David G., 'Evidence for the Traditional View of the Transmission of Gregorian Chant', *JAMS* 40 (1987), 377–404. See also 'Communications' in *JAMS* 41 (1988), 566–78; 42 (1989), 432–4; and 44 (1991), 517–25.
—— 'Music for St. Stephen at Laon', in Laurence Berman (ed.), *Words and Music: The Scholar's View. A Medley of Problems and Solutions Compiled in Honor of A. Tillman Merritt By Sundry Hands* (Cambridge, Mass.: Harvard University Press, 1972), 137–59.
—— 'Parisian Sanctorals of the Late Middle Ages', in Gillingham and Merkley (eds), *Chant and its Peripheries*, 277–309.
—— 'The Sources of *Christus manens*', in Jan LaRue et al. (eds), *Aspects of Medieval and Renaissance Music: A Birthday Offering to Gustave Reese* (New York: Norton, 1966), 423–34.
Huglo, Michel, 'Antifone antiche per la "fractio panis"', *Ambrosius*, 31 (1955), 85–95.

Hugло, Michel, 'Le Chant "vieux-romain": liste des manuscrits et témoins indirects', *Sacris erudiri*, 6 (1954), 96–124.
—— 'Le *De musica* des Etymologies de saint Isidore de Séville d'après le manuscrit de Silos', *Revista de musicología*, 15 (1992), 565–78.
—— 'Le Développement du vocabulaire de l'*Ars musica* à l'époque carolingienne', *Latomus*, 34 (1975), 131–51.
—— 'Les Diagrammes d'harmonique interpolés dans les manuscrits hispaniques de la *Musica Isidori*', *Scriptorium*, 48 (1994), 171–86.
—— 'Die *Musica Isidori* nach den Handschriften des deutschen Sprachgebietes', in Walter Pass and Alexander Rausch (eds), *Mittelalterliche Musiktheorie in Zentraleuropa* (Musica mediaevalis Europae occidentalis, 4; Tutzing: Hans Schneider, 1998), 79–86.
—— 'Notated Performance Practices in Parisian Chant Manuscripts of the Thirteenth Century', in Thomas Forrest Kelly (ed.), *Plainsong in the Age of Polyphony* (Cambridge Studies in Performance Practice, 2; Cambridge: Cambridge University Press, 1992).
—— 'Les *Preces* des graduels aquitains empruntées à la liturgie hispanique', *Hispania sacra*, 8 (1955), 361–83.
—— 'La Réception de Calcidius et des *Commentarii* de Macrobe', *Scriptorium*, 44 (1990), 15–17.
—— *Les Tonaires: inventaire, analyse, comparison* (Publications de la Société française de musicologie, 3rd ser., 2 [Paris: Société française de musicologie, 1971].
—— 'Tradition orale et tradition écrite dans la transmission des mélodies grégoriennes', in Hans Heinrich Eggebrecht and Max Lütolff (eds), *Studien zur Tradition in der Musik: Kurt von Fischer zum 60. Geburtstag* (Munich: Musikverlag Katzbichler, 1973), 31–42.
—— et al. (eds), *Fonti e paleografia del canto ambrosiano* (Archivio ambrosiano, 7; Milan: [Scuola tip. San Benedetto], 1956).
Hüls, Rudolf, *Kardinäle, Klerus und Kirchen Roms, 1049–1130* (Bibliothek des Deutschen Historischen Instituts in Rom, 48; Tübingen: Niemeyer, 1977).
Hülsen, Christian C. F., *Le chiese di Roma nel Medio Evo: cataloghi ed appunti* (Florence: L. S. Olschki, 1927; repr. Hildesheim: G. Olms, 1975).
Husmann, Heinrich, *Tropen- und Sequenzenhandschriften* (RISM B V/1; Munich-Duisberg: Henle Verlag, 1964).
Iamblicus, *De vita pythagorica liber*, ed. Ludovicus Deubner, rev. Uldaricus Klein (Leipzig: B.G. Teubner, 1975).
Introitus Tropen, i: *Das Repertoire der südfranzösischer Tropare des 10. und 11. Jahrhunderts*, ed. Günther Weiss (MMMA 3; Kassel: Bärenreiter, 1970).
Isidore of Seville, *Isidori Etymologiae: Codex Toletanus (nunc matritensis) 15, 8 phototypice editus*, ed. Rudolf Beer (Codices Graeci et Latini photographice depicti, 13; Leiden: A. W. Sijthoff, 1909).
—— *Isidori Hispalensis episcopi Etymologiarum sive Originum libri XX*, ed. Wallace Martin Lindsay, 2 vols. (Scriptorum classicorum bibliotheca Oxoniensis; Oxford: Clarendon Press, 1911).
—— *Sancti Isidori Episcopi Hispalensis De ecclesiasticis officiis*, ed. Christopher M. Lawson (CCSL 113; Turnhout: Brepols, 1989).

Itinerarium Burdigalense, ed. P. Geyer and O. Cunz, in *Itineraria et alia geographica* (CCSL 175–6; Turnhout: Brepols, 1965), 1–26.

Jacques de Liège, *Speculum musicae*, ed. Roger Bragard, 7 vols. in 8 (Corpus scriptorum de musica, 3; Rome: American Institute of Musicology, 1955–73).

Jammers, Ewald, 'Studien zu Neumenschriften, Neumenhandschriften und neumierter Musik', *Bibliothek und Wissenschaft*, 2 (1965), 85–161.

Jeffery, Peter, 'The Earliest Christian Chant Repertory Recovered: The Georgian Witnesses to Jerusalem Chant', *JAMS* 47 (1994), 1–39.

—— 'Eastern and Western Elements in the Irish Monastic Prayer of the Hours', in Margot Fasler and Rebecca Baltzer (eds), *The Divine Office in the Latin Middle Ages: Methodology and Source Studies, Regional Developments, Hagiography, Written in Honor of Professor Ruth Steiner* (New York: Oxford University Press, 2000), 99–143.

—— 'The Introduction of Psalmody into the Roman Mass by Pope Celestine I (422–432), Reinterpreting a Passage in the *Liber Pontificalis*', *AfLw* 26 (1984), 147–65.

—— 'The Lost Chant Tradition of Early Christian Jerusalem: Some Possible Melodic Survivals in the Byzantine and Latin Chant Repertories', *EMH* 11 (1992), 151–90.

—— *A New Commandment: Toward a Renewed Rite for the Washing of Feet* (Collegeville, Minn.: Liturgical Press, 1992).

—— *Re-envisioning Past Musical Cultures: Ethnomusicology in the Study of Gregorian Chant* (Chicago: University of Chicago Press, 1992).

—— 'Rome and Jerusalem: From Oral Tradition to Written Repertory in Two Ancient Liturgical Centers', in Boone (ed.), *Essays on Medieval Music in Honor of David G. Hughes*, 207–47.

Jounel, Pierre, *Le Culte des saints dans les basiliques du Latran et du Vatican au douzième siècle* (Collection de l'Ecole Française de Rome, 26; Rome: Ecole Française de Rome, 1977).

Jülicher, Adolf, *Itala: Das neue Testament in altlateinischer Überlieferung* (Berlin: Walter de Gruyter, 1954).

Karp, Theodore, *Aspects of Orality and Formularity in Gregorian Chant* (Evanston, Ill.: Northwestern University Press, 1998).

—— 'Performing from the Graduale triplex', in Gillingham and Merkley, *Chant and its Peripheries*, 12–36.

—— 'An Unknown Late Medieval Fragment', in *Cantus Planus, Papers Read at the 9th Meeting, Esztergom and Visegrád, 1998* (Budapest: Hungarian Academy of Sciences Institute for Musicology, 2001), 173–88.

Kasch, Elisabeth, *Das liturgische Vokabular der frühen lateinischen Mönchsregeln* (Regulae Benedicti Studia, Supplementa, 1; Hildesheim: Gerstenberg, 1974).

Kelly, J. N. D., *The Oxford Dictionary of Popes* (Oxford: Oxford University Press, 1986).

Kelly, Thomas Forrest, *The Beneventan Chant* (Cambridge: Cambridge University Press, 1989).

Kelly, Thomas Forrest, 'Melisma and Prosula: The Performance of Responsory Tropes', in *Liturgische Tropen: Referate zweier Colloquien des Corpus Troporum in München (1983) und Canterbury (1984)*, ed. Gabriel Silagi (Munich: Arbeo, 1985), 163–80.

—— 'Melodic Elaboration in Responsory Melismas', *JAMS* 27 (1974), 461–74.

—— 'Neuma Triplex', *Acta musicologica*, 60 (1988), 1–30.

—— 'New Music from Old: The Structuring of Responsory Prosas', *JAMS* 30 (1977), 366–90.

—— 'Responsory Tropes' (Ph.D. diss., Harvard University, 1973).

—— 'Texts Related to the Exultet at Rome', unpublished text accompanying a lecture, 'The Exultet at Rome', at Royaumont, 20 September 1993.

Klauser, Theodor, *Das römische Capitulare Evangeliorum* (2nd edn; Liturgiewissenschaftliche Quellen und Forschungen, 28; Munster: Aschendorff, 1972).

Klewitz, Hans-Walter, *Reformpapsttum und Kardinalkolleg: Die Entstehung des Kardinalkollegiums. Studien über die Wiederherstellung der römischen Kirche in Suditalien durch das Reformpapsttum. Das Ende des Reformpapsttum* (Darmstadt: H. Gentner, 1957).

Klingshirn, William E., *Caesarius of Arles: The Making of a Christian Community in Late Antique Gaul* (Cambridge Studies in Medieval Life and Thought, Fourth Series; Cambridge: Cambridge University Press, 1994).

Kohrs, Klaus Heinrich, *Die aparallelen Sequenzen: Repertoire, liturgische Ordnung, musikalischer Stil* (Beiträge zur Musikforschung, 6; Munich: Musikverlag Katzbichler, 1978).

Kok, Frans, 'L'Office pachômien: *psallere, orare, legere*', *Ecclesia orans*, 9 (1992), 70–95.

Konkler, Paul J., 'Unceasing Prayer' (Thesis, Jesuit School of Theology at Berkeley, 1977).

Kornmüller, Utto, 'Der heilige Wolfgang als Beförderer des Kirchengesanges', in Johann Baptist Mehler (ed.), *Der heilige Wolfgang – Bischof von Regensburg – Jubiläumsschrift 994–1894* (Regensburg: F. Pustet, 1894), 140–62.

Kozachek, Thomas Davies, 'The Repertory of Chant for Dedicating Churches in the Middle Ages' (Ph.D. diss., Harvard University, 1995).

Krautheimer, Richard, et al., *Corpus Basilicarum Christianarum Romae*, 5 vols. (Monumenti di antichità cristiana, 2. ser.; Vatican City: Pontificio Istituto di Archeologia Cristiana, 1937–77).

Kruckenberg-Goldenstein, Lori Ann, 'The Sequence from 1050–1150: Study of a Genre in Change' (Ph.D. diss., University of Iowa, 1997).

Laistner, M. L. W., *Thought and Letters in Western Europe, A.D. 500 to 900* (Ithaca: Cornell University Press, 1931; repr. 1966).

Lami, Giovanni, *Catalogus codicum manuscriptorum qui in Bibliotheca Riccardiana adservantur* (Livorno: Antonii Sanctinii & sociorum, 1756).

Lawless, George, *Augustine of Hippo and his Monastic Rule* (Oxford: Clarendon Press, 1987).

Leclercq, Jean, 'Culte liturgique et prière intime dans le monachisme au moyen âge', *La maison-Dieu*, 69 (1962), 39–55.

Le Lectionnaire de la semaine sainte: texte copte édité avec traduction française d'après le manuscrit Add. 5997 du British Museum, ed. Oswald Hugh Ewart Burmester (PO 24, fasc. 2; 25, fasc. 2; Paris: Firmin-Didot, 1933, 1939).

Le Lectionnaire de Luxeuil (Paris, ms. lat. 9427), édition et étude comparative, ed. Pierre Salmon, 2 vols. (Collectanea Biblica Latina, 7, 9; Rome: Abbaye Saint-Jérome; Vatican City: Libreria Editrice Vaticana, 1944, 1953).

Leeb, Helmut, *Die Psalmodie bei Ambrosius* (Wiener Beitrage zur Theologie, 18; Vienna: Herder, 1967).

Lehmann, Paul, *Mittelalterliche Bibliothekskataloge Deutschlands und der Schweiz*, i (Munich: Beck, 1918).

Lentini, Anselmo, *Il ritmo prosaico nella regola di S. Benedetto* (Miscellanea Cassinese, 23; Montecassino, 1942).

[Leo I, Pope], *Sancti Leonis Magni Romani Pontificis Tractatus septem et nonaginta*, i, ed. Antoine Chavasse (CCSL 138; Turnhout: Brepols, 1973).

Leonardi, Claudio, 'I Codici di Marziano Capella', *Aevum*, 33 (1959), 443–89; 34 (1960), 1–99, 411–524.

Levy, Kenneth, 'Charlemagne's Archetype of Gregorian Chant', *JAMS* 40 (1987), 1–30.

—— *Gregorian Chant and the Carolingians* (Princeton: Princeton University Press, 1998).

—— 'The Italian Neophytes' Chants', *JAMS* 23 (1970), 181–227.

—— 'Latin Chant Outside the Roman Tradition', in *NOHM*, ii: *The Early Middle Ages to 1300*, ed. Richard Crocker and David Hiley (Oxford: Oxford University Press, 1990), 93–101.

—— '*Lux de luce*: The Origin of an Italian Sequence', *MQ* 57 (1971), 40–61.

—— 'A New Look at Old Roman Chant', *EMH* 19 (2000), 81–104.

—— 'A New Look at Old Roman Chant - II', *EMH* 20 (2001), 173–97.

—— 'On Gregorian Orality', *JAMS* 43 (1990), 185–227.

—— 'On the Origin of Neumes', *EMH* 7 (1987), 59–90.

—— 'Toledo, Rome, and the Legacy of Gaul', *EMH* 4 (1984), 49–99.

Lewis, Naphtali, *Life in Egypt under Roman Rule* (Oxford: Clarendon Press, 1983).

Liber misticus de cuaresma y pascua (Cod. Toledo, Bibl. Capit. 35,5), ed. José Janini (Serie liturgica, Fuentes 2; Toledo: Instituto de Estudios Visigótico-Mozárabes, 1980).

Liber responsorialis (Solesmes: Abbaye Saint-Pierre, 1895).

Liber sacramentorum Romanae aeclesiae ordinis anni circuli (Cod. Vat. Reg. lat. 316 / Paris Bibl. nat. 7193, 41/56), Sacramentarium Gelasianum, ed. Leo Cunibert Mohlberg, Leo Eizenhöfer and Petrus Siffrin (Rerum ecclesiasticarum documenta, Series maior; Fontes, 4; Rome: Herder, 1960).

Lindsay, Wallace Martin, *The Latin Language: An Historical Account of Latin Sounds, Stems, and Flexions* (Oxford: Clarendon Press, 1894).

Loriquet, Henri, *Le Graduel de l'église cathédrale de Rouen au XIIIe siècle*, 2 vols. (Rouen: J. Lecerf, 1907).

Lowe, E. A., *Codices Latini antiquiores: A Palaeographical Guide to Latin Manuscripts Prior to the Ninth Century*, 12 vols. (Oxford: Clarendon Press, 1934–66).

Lubac, Henri de, *Exégèse médiévale: les quatre sens de l'écriture*, 2 vols. in 4 (Théologie, 41, 42, 59; Paris: Aubier, 1959–64). Translated by Mark Sebanc and E. M. Macierowski as *Medieval Exegesis: The Four Senses of Scripture*, 2 vols. (Grand Rapids, Mich.: William B. Eerdmans; Edinburgh: T. & T. Clark, 1998–2000).

Lutz, Cora, 'Martianus Capella: 1. Martinus Laudunensis', in *CTC*, ii, 370–71.

MacCormack, Sabine, *The Shadows of Poetry: Vergil in the Mind of Augustine* (The Transformation of the Classical Heritage, 26; Berkeley: University of California Press, 1998).

Mallet, Jean, and Thibaut, André, *Les Manuscrits en écriture bénéventaine de la Bibliothèque Capitulare de Bénévent* (Documents, études, et repertoires, 71/1–2; Paris: Editions du Centre National de la Recherche Scientifique, 1984–97).

Mano-Zissi, Djordje, 'La Question des différents écoles de mosaïques gréco-romaines de Yougoslavie et essai d'une esquisse de leur évolution', in *La Mosaïque gréco-romaine, Paris 29 août – 3 septembre 1963* (Colloques internationaux du Centre Nationale de la Recherche Scientifique, Sciences humaines; Paris: Editions du Centre Nationale de la Recherche Scientifique, 1965), 287–95.

Mantello, Frank Anthony Carl, and Rigg., A. G., *Medieval Latin: An Introduction and Bibliographical Guide* (Washington, DC: Catholic University of America Press, 1996).

Manuale Ambrosianum ex codice saec. XI olim in usum canonicae vallis Travaliae, ii: *Officia totius anni et alii ordines*, ed. Marco Magistretti (Monumenta veteris liturgiae Ambrosianae, 3; Milan: Ulrico Hoepli, 1904; repr. Nendeln, Liechtenstein: Kraus Reprint, 1971).

Le Manuscrit du Mont-Renaud, Xe siècle: graduel et antiphonaire de Noyon (*PM* 16; Solesmes: Abbaye Saint-Pierre, 1955–6).

Le Manuscript 807, Universitätsbibliothek Graz (XIIe siècle): Graduel de Klosterneuburg, ed. Jacques Froger (PM 19; Bern, 1974).

Marosszéki, Solutor Rodolphe, *Les Origines du chant cistercien: recherches sur les réformes du plain-chant cistercien au XIIe siècle* (Analecta sacri ordinis cisterciensis, annus 8, fasc. 1–2; Vatican City: Tip. poliglotta vaticana, 1952).

Martianus Capella, ed. Adolph Dick (Leipzig: Teubner, 1925; repr. 1978).

Martianus Capella, ed. James Willis (Leipzig: Teubner, 1983).

Martimort, Aimé-Georges, et al. (eds), *The Church at Prayer: An Introduction to the Liturgy*, iv: *The Liturgy and Time* (new edn, Collegeville, Minn.: Liturgical Press, 1983).

—— 'La Lecture patristique dans la liturgie des heures', in Giustino Farnedi (ed.), *Traditio et progessio: studi liturgici in onore del Prof. Adrien Nocent, OSB* (Studia Anselmiana, 95; Analecta liturgica, 12; Rome: Pontificio Ateneo S. Anselmo, 1988), 311–31.

Marx, Michael, 'Incessant Prayer in Ancient Monastic Literature' (diss., Rome: Facultas theologica S. Anselmi de Urbe, 1946).

Maschke, Timothy, 'St. Augustine's Theology of Prayer: Gracious Conformation', in Joseph T. Lienhardt et al. (eds), *Augustine: Presbyter Factus Sum* (Collectanea Augustiniana; New York: Peter Lang, 1993), 431–46.

Mateos, Juan, *La Célébration de la parole dans la liturgie byzantine: étude historique* (OCA 191; Rome: Pontificium Institutum Studiorum Orientalium, 1971).
—— 'L'Office monastique à la fin du IVe siècle', *Oriens Christianus*, 47 (1963), 53–88.
Mathiesen, Thomas, *Apollo's Lyre: Greek Music and Music Theory in Antiquity and the Middle Ages* (Publications of the Center for the History of Music Theory and Literature, 2; Lincoln, Neb.: University of Nebraska Press, 1999).
McClure, J., 'Gregory the Great: Exegesis and Audience' (D.Phil. diss., Oxford University, 1979).
McGee, Timothy J., *Medieval Instrumental Dances* (Music: Scholarship and Performance; Bloomington: Indiana University Press, 1989).
McGinn, Bernard, *The Presence of God: A History of Western Christian Mysticism*, i: *The Foundations of Mysticism* (New York: Crossroad, 1991).
McKinnon, James, *The Advent Project: The Later-Seventh-Century Creation of the Roman Mass Proper* (Berkeley: University of California Press, 2000).
—— 'Antoine Chavasse and the Dating of Early Chant', *PMM* 2 (1992), 123–47.
—— 'The Book of Psalms, Monasticism, and the Western Liturgy', in Nancy van Deusen (ed.), *The Place of the Psalms in the Intellectual Culture of the Middle Ages* (SUNY Series in Medieval Studies; Albany: State University of New York Press, 1999), 43–58.
—— 'Desert Monasticism and the Later Fourth-Century Psalmodic Movement', *M&L* 75 (1994), 505–21.
—— 'The Eighth-Century Frankish-Roman Communion Cycle', *JAMS* 45 (1992), 179–227.
—— 'The Emergence of Gregorian Chant in the Carolingian Era', in id. (ed.), *Antiquity and the Middle Ages from Ancient Greece to the Fifteenth Century* (London: Macmillan, 1990), 88–119.
—— 'Festival, Text and Melody: Chronological Stages in the Life of a Chant', in Gillingham and Merkley (eds), *Chant and its Peripheries*, 1–11.
—— 'The Fourth-Century Origin of the Gradual', *EMH* 7 (1987), 91–106.
—— 'Lector Chant versus Schola Chant', in Janka Szendrei and David Hiley (eds), *Laborare fratres in unum: Festschrift László Dobszay zum 60. Geburtstag* (Hildesheim: Weidmann, 1995), 201–11.
—— 'Liturgical Psalmody in the Sermons of St. Augustine', in Peter Jeffery (ed.), *The Study of Medieval Chant, Paths and Bridges, East and West: In Honor of Kenneth Levy* (Rochester, NY: Boydell & Brewer, 2001), 7–24.
—— 'Musical Instruments in Medieval Psalm Commentaries and Psalters', *JAMS* 21 (1968), 3–70.
—— 'The Origins of the Western Office', in Margot Fassler and Rebecca Baltzer (eds), *The Divine Office in the Latin Middle Ages: Methodology and Source Studies, Regional Developments, Hagiography, Written in Honor of Professor Ruth Steiner* (New York: Oxford University Press, 2000), 63–73.
—— 'The Patristic Jubilus and the Alleluia of the Mass', in *Cantus Planus: Papers read at the Third Meeting of the International Musicological Society*

Study Group, Tihany, Hungary, 19–24 September 1988, ed. László Dobszay et al. (Budapest: Hungarian Academy of Sciences Institute for Musicology, 1990), 61–70.

McKinnon, James, 'Preface to the Study of the Alleluia', *EMH* 15 (1996), 213–49.

—— 'Properization: The Roman Mass', in *Cantus Planus: Papers Read at the Sixth Meeting of the International Musicological Society Study Group, Eger, Hungary, 1993*, ed. László Dobszay (Budapest: Hungarian Academy of Sciences Institute for Musicology, 1994), 15–22.

—— 'The Roman Post-Pentecostal Communion Series', in *Cantus Planus: Papers Read at the Fourth Meeting of the International Musicological Society Study Group, Pécs, Hungary, 1990*, ed. László Dobszay (Budapest: Hungarian Academy of Sciences Institute for Musicology, 1992), 175–86.

—— *The Temple, the Church Fathers, and Early Western Chant* (Variorum Collected Studies Series; Aldershot: Ashgate Variorum, 1998).

—— 'Vaticana Latina 5319 as a Witness to the Eighth-Century Roman Proper of the Mass', in *Cantus Planus: Papers Read at the Seventh Meeting of the International Musicological Society Study Group, Sopron, Hungary, 1995*, ed. László Dobszay (Budapest: Hungarian Academy of Sciences Institute for Musicology, 1998), 401–11.

—— (ed.), *Music in Early Christian Literature* (Cambridge Readings in the Literature of Music; Cambridge: Cambridge University Press, 1987).

McManus, Frederick R., 'From the *Rubricae Generales* and *Ritus Servandus* of 1570 to the *Institutio Generalis* of 1969', in Kathleen Hughes (ed.), *Finding Voice to Give God Praise: Essays in the Many Languages of the Liturgy* (Collegeville, Minn.: Liturgical Press, 1998), 214–42.

Mearns, James, *The Canticles of the Christian Church Eastern and Western in Early and Medieval Times* (Cambridge: Cambridge University Press, 1914).

Meiming, Odilo (ed.), *Das Sacramentarium Triplex: Die Handschrift C 43 der Zentralbibliothek Zürich* (Corpus ambrosianum liturgicum, 1; Liturgiewissenschaftliche Quellen und Forschungen, 49; Munster: Aschendorff, 1968).

Merton, Thomas, *The Climate of Monastic Prayer* (Cistercian Studies Series, 1; Shannon Irish University Press, 1969).

Metzger, Bruce, *Manuscripts of the Greek Bible: An Introduction to Greek Palaeography* (New York: Oxford University Press, 1981).

—— *The Text of the New Testament: Its Transmission, Corruption, and Restoration* (3rd enlarged edn, New York: Oxford University Press, 1992).

Millares-Carlo, Agustín, *Corpus de códices visigóticos*, 2 vols. (Las Palmas de Gran Canaria: Universidad Nacional de Educación a Distancia, Centro Asociado de Las Palmas de Gran Canaria, Gobierno de Canarias, 1999).

Milne, Herbert John Mansfield, 'Early Psalms and Lections for Lent', *Journal of Egyptian Archaeology*, 10 (1924), 278–82.

Missale Gothicum (Vat. Reg. Lat. 317), ed. Leo Cunibert Mohlberg (Rerum ecclesiasticarum documenta, Series maior, Fontes, 5; Rome: Herder, 1961).

Mohrmann, Christine, 'A propos des collectes du psautier', *Vigiliae Christianae*, 6 (1952), 1–19; repr. in ead., *Etudes sur le latin des chrétiens*, iii: *Latin chrétien et liturgique* (Rome: Edizioni de storia e letteratura, 1965), 245–63.

Mommsen, Theodor, 'Die Einführung des asianischen Kalendars', in *Gesammelte Schriften*, 8 vols. (Berlin: Weidmann, 1905), v, 518–31.

Moneta Caglio, E., 'I responsori "cum infantibus" nella liturgia ambrosiana', in *Studi in onore di Carlo Castiglioni prefetto dell'Ambrosiana* (Fontes Ambrosiani, in lucem editi cura et studio Bibliothecae Ambrosianae, 32; Milan: A. Giuffre, 1957), 481–578.

Moolan, John, *The Period of Annunciation–Nativity in the East Syrian Calendar: Its Background Place in the Liturgical Year* (Pontifical Oriental Institute of Religious Studies, India Series, 90; Kottayam, Kerala: Paurastya Vidyapitham, 1985).

Moosburger Graduale: München, Universitätsbibliothek, 2° Cod. ms. 156, ed. David Hiley (Veröffentlichungen der Gesellschaft für Bayerische Musikgeschichte; Tutzing: Hans Schneider, 1996).

Moran, Neil K., *The Ordinary Chants of the Byzantine Mass*, 2 vols. (Hamburg: Karl Dieter Wagner, 1975).

Morin, Germain, *Etudes, textes, découvertes: contributions à la littérature et à l'histoire des douze premiers siècles* (Anecdota Maredsolana, 2nd ser., 1; Maredsous: Abbaye de Maredsous, and Paris: A. Picard, 1913).

—— 'Liturgie et basiliques de Rome au milieu du VIIe siècle', *Révue bénédictine*, 28 (1911), 296–330.

—— 'L'Ordre des heures canoniales dans les monastères de Cassiodore', *Revue bénédictine*, 43 (1931), 145–52.

Müller, Hans, *Die Musik Wilhelms von Hirschau: Wiederherstellung, Übersetzung und Erklärung seines musik-theoretischen Werkes* (Frankfurt: [n. pub.], 1883).

Murethach [Muridac]: In Donati Artem maiorem, ed. Louis Holtz (CCCM 50; Turnhout: Brepols, 1977).

Murphy, Joseph M., 'The Communions of the Old Roman Chant' (Ph.D. diss., University of Pennsylvania, 1977).

Musica enchiriadis and Scolica enchiriadis, trans. Raymond Erickson (Music Theory Translation Series; New Haven: Yale University Press, 1995).

Musici scriptores graeci, ed. Karl van Jan (Leipzig: Teubner, 1895–9; repr. Hildesheim: Olms, 1962).

Myers, Walter Neidig, 'The Hymns of Saint Hilary of Poitiers in the Codex Aretinus: An Edition, with Introduction, Translation, and Notes' (Ph.D. diss., University of Pennsylvania, 1928).

Nau, F., 'Les Plérophories de Jean évêque de Maiouma', *Revue de l'Orient chrétien*, 3 (1898), 232 ff.

Negro, Francesca, 'Le sequenze della tradizione liturgica padovana', in Giulio Cattin and Antonio Lovato (eds), *Contributi per la storia della musica sacra a Padova* (Fonti e ricerche de storia ecclesiastica padovana, 24; Padua: Istituto per la storia ecclesiastica padovana, 1992).

Neunheuser, Burckhard, 'The Relation of Priest and Faithful in the Liturgies of Pius V and Paul VI', in *Roles in the Liturgical Assembly* (New York: Pueblo, 1981), 207–19.

The New Jerome Biblical Commentary, ed. Raymond E. Brown, Joseph A. Fitzmyer and Roland E. Murphy (Englewood Cliffs, NJ: Prentice Hall, 1990).

Nikolasch, Franz, 'Zur Ursprung des Epiphaniefestes', *EL* 83 (1968), 393–429.

Nocent, Adrien, *The Liturgical Year*, ii: *Lent*, trans. Matthew J. O'Connell (Collegeville, Minn.: Liturgical Press, 1977).

—— 'La Semaine sainte dans la liturgie romaine', in Anthony George Kollamparampil et al. (eds), *Hebdomadae sanctae celebratio: conspectus historicus comparativus* (Bibliotheca Ephemerides liturgicae, Subsidia, 93; Rome: CLV, 1997), 277–310.

Noel, William, *The Harley Psalter* (Cambridge Studies in Palaeography and Codicology, 4; Cambridge: Cambridge University Press, 1995).

Novum Testamentum Domini Nostri Iesu Christi Latine, ed. John Wordsworth and Henry White (Oxford: Clarendon Press, 1889–98).

Nowacki, Edward, 'Chant Research at the Turn of the Century', *PMM* 7 (1998), 47–71.

—— 'Constantinople–Aachen–Rome: The Transmission *of Veterem hominem*', in Cahn and Heiner (eds), *De musica et cantu*, 95–115.

—— 'The Gregorian Office Antiphons and the Comparative Method', *JM* 4 (1985), 243–75.

—— 'The Modes of the Old Roman Mass Proper: What Kind of Glue?', in *Papers Read at Cantus Planus, Visegrád, 1998* (Budapest: Hungarian Academy of Sciences, 2001), 431–48.

—— 'Studies on the Office Antiphons of the Old Roman Manuscripts' (Ph.D. diss., Brandeis University, 1980).

Nussbaum, Martha Craven, *The Therapy of Desire: Theory and Practice in Hellenistic Ethics* (Martin Classical Lectures, New Series, 2; Princeton: Princeton University Press, 1994).

Oakeshott, Walter, *The Mosaics of Rome from the Third to the Fourteenth Centuries* (Greenwich, Conn.: NY Graphic Society, 1967).

O'Daly, Gerard, *Augustine's Philosophy of Mind* (London: Duckworth, 1987).

O'Donnell, James J., *Cassiodorus* (Berkeley: University of California Press, 1979).

Oesch, Hans, *Berno und Hermann von Reichenau als Musiktheoretiker* (Publikationen der Schweizerischen Musikforschenden Gesellschaft, Series 2, 9; Bern: P. Haupt, 1961).

Offertoriale sive versus offertoriorum, ed. Carolus Ott (Paris: Desclée, 1935); repr. with additions as *Offertoires neumés* (Solesmes: Abbaye Saint-Pierre, 1978).

Omont, Henri Auguste, 'Manuscrits illustrés de l'Apocalypse au IXe et Xe siècles', *Bulletin de la Société française de reproductions de manuscrits à peintures*, 6 (1922), 80 ff.

O'Neill, J. C., 'The Origins of Monasticism', in Rowan Williams (ed.), *The Making of Orthodoxy: Essays in Honour of Henry Chadwick* (Cambridge: Cambridge University Press, 1989), 270–87.

Ordinary Chants and Tropes for the Mass from Southern Italy, A.D. 1000–1250: Pt. 1, Kyrie eleison; Pt. 2, Gloria in excelsis; Pt. 3, Preface Chants and Sanctus, ed. John Boe and Alejandro Enrique Planchart (Beneventanum troporum corpus, 2; Recent Researches in the Music of the Middle Ages and Early Renaissance, 19–28; Madison, Wis.: A-R Editions, 1994–6).

Ordo antiquus gallicanus: Der gallikanische Messritus des 6. Jahrhunderts, ed. Klaus Gamber (Textus patristici et liturgici, fasc. 3; Regensburg: F. Pustet, 1965).

Oury, Guy Marie, 'Formulaires anciens pour la messe de Saint Martin', *Etudes grégoriennes*, 7 (1967), 21–40.

Pachomian Koinonia, ed. and trans. Armand Veilleux, 3 vols. (Cistercian Studies Series, 45–7; Kalamazoo, Mich.: Cistercian Publications, 1980–82).

Palladius, *The Lausiac History*, trans. Robert Meyer (Ancient Christian Writers, 34; Westminster, Md.: Newman Press, 1965).

—— *The Lausiac History of Palladius*, ed. Joseph Armitage Robinson, 2 vols. (Texts and Studies, Contributions to Biblical and Patristic Literature, 6/1–2; Cambridge: Cambridge University Press, 1898).

Paverd, Frans van de, *Zur Geschichte der Messliturgie in Antiocheia und Konstantinopel gegen Ende des vierten Jahrhunderts: Analyse der Quellen bei Johannes Chrysostomos* (OCA 187; Rome: Pontificium Institutum Studiorum Orientalium, 1970).

Penco, G., 'La preghiera presso il monachesimo occidentale del secolo VI', in Vagaggini (ed.), *La preghiera*, 469–512.

Pifarré, Cebrià, *Arnobio el Joven y la cristología del 'Conflictus'* (Scripta et documenta, 35; Montserrat: Publicacions de l'Abadia de Montserrat, 1988).

Planchart, Alejandro Enrique, 'An Aquitanian *Sequentia* in Italian Sources', in *Corpus troporum*, viii: *Recherches nouvelles sur les tropes liturgiques* ['Huglo Festschrift'], ed. Wulf Arlt (Acta universitatis stockholmiensis, Studia latina stockholmiensis, 36; Stockholm: Almqvist & Wiksell, 1993), 371–94.

—— 'Fragments, Palimpsests, and Marginalia', *JM* 6 (1988), 293–339.

—— 'Italian Tropes', *Mosaic*, 18/4 (1985), 11–32.

—— 'Notes on the Tropes in Manuscripts of the Rite of Aquileia', in Boone (ed.), *Essays on Medieval Music in Honor of David G. Hughes*, 333–69.

—— 'On the Nature of Transmission and Change in Trope Repertories', *JAMS* 41 (1988), 215–49.

—— *The Repertory of Tropes at Winchester*, 2 vols. (Princeton: Princeton University Press, 1977).

Plato, *The Collected Dialogues of Plato including the Letters*, trans. Edith Hamilton and Huntington Cairns (New York: Pantheon, 1961, repr. Princeton: Princeton University Press, 1980).

—— *Œuvres complètes*, x: *Timée, Critias*, ed. Albert Rivaud, 4th rev. edn (Paris: Société d'édition Les Belles Lettres, 1963).

—— *Timaeus a Calcidio translatus commentarioque instructus*, ed. Jan Hendrik Waszink (Plato Latinus, 4; London: Warburg Institute, 1962; 2nd edn, London: E. J. Brill, 1975).

Plutarch, *Moralia*, xiii, pt. 1: *De animae procreatione in Timaeo*, ed. Harold Cherniss (Cambridge, Mass.: Harvard University Press, 1976).

Poisson, Léonard, *Nouvelle méthode: ou Traité théorique et pratique du plain-chant* (Paris: P. N. Lottin & J. H. Butard, 1745).

Le Pontifical romain au moyen âge, i: *Le pontifical romain du XIIe siècle*, ed. Michel Andrieu (Studi e testi, 86; Vatican City: Biblioteca Apostolica Vaticana, 1938).

Le Pontifical romano-germanique du dixième siècle, ii, ed. Cyrille Vogel and Reinhard Elze (Studi e testi, 227; Vatican City: Biblioteca Apostolica Vaticana, 1963).

Porphyry, *In Platonis Timaeum commentariorum fragmenta*, ed. Angelo Raffaele Sodano (Naples: [n. pub.], 1964)

—— *Kommentar zur Harmonielehre des Ptolemaios*, ed. Ingemar Düring (Göteborg: Elanders boktryckeri aktiebolag, 1932).

Pothier, Joseph. 'Ex ejus tumba', *RCG* 9 (1900–1), 49–52.

—— 'Inviolata', *RCG* 2 (1893–4), 19–22.

Pouderoijen, Kees, 'Die melodische Gestalt der Communio "Videns Dominus"', in *Cantando praedicare: Godehard Joppich zum 60. Geburtstag* (Beiträge zur Gregorianik, 13–14; Regensburg: G. Bosse, 1992), 129–55.

Préaux, Jean G., 'Le Commentaire de Martin de Laon sur l'œuvre de Martianus Capella', *Latomus*, 12 (1953), 437–59.

Processional, Graduel, Antiphonaire et Psautier à l'usage de l'église primatiale et métropolitaine de Sens (Sens: Thomas-Malvin, 1844).

Prier au moyen âge: pratiques et expériences (V^e–XVe siècles): textes traduits et commentés, ed. Nicole Bériou, Jacques Berlioz and Jean Longère (Témoins de notre histoire; Turnhout: Brepols, 1991).

Proclus, *Commentaire sur le Timée*, ed. André Marie Jean Festugière (Paris: Les belles lettres, 1967).

—— *In Platonis Timaeum commentaria*, ed. Ernst Diehl, 3 vols. (Bibliotheca scriptorum Graecorum et Romanorum Teubneriana; Leipzig: B. G. Teubner, 1903–6).

Prophetologium, ed. Carsten Höeg and Günther Zuntz (Monumenta musicae Byzantinae, Lectionaria, 1; Copenhagen: Munksgaard, 1939–81).

Prosopographie chrétienne du bas-empire, ii: *Prosopographie de l'Italie chrétienne (313–604)*, ed. Charles Pietri and Luce Pietri (Rome: Ecole française, 2000).

Le Psautier chez les Pères (Cahiers de Biblia Patristica, 4; Strasbourg: Centre d'Analyse et de Documentation Patristiques, 1994.)

Le Psautier romain et les autres anciens psautiers latins, ed. Robert Weber (Collectanea Biblica Latina, 10; Rome: Abbaye Saint-Jérôme; Vatican City: Libreria Vaticana, 1953).

Puech, H. C., 'Le Cerf et le serpent: note sur le symbolisme de la mosaïque découverte au baptistère d'Enchir-Messaouda', *Cahiers archéologiques*, 4 (1949), 17–60.

Quasten, Johannes, *Expositio antiquae liturgiae gallicanae* (Opuscula et textus, Series liturgica, 3; Munster: Aschendorff, 934).

—— *Music and Worship in Pagan and Christian Antiquity*, trans. Boniface Ramsey (NPM Studies in Church Music and Liturgy; Washington, DC: National Association of Pastoral Musicians, 1983).

—— *Patrology*, i: *The Beginnings of Patristic Literature*; ii: *The Ante-Nicene Literature after Irenaeus*; iii: *The Golden Age of Greek Patristic Literature* (Utrecht: Newman Press, 1950–66).

Questions d'un païen à un chrétien: Consultationes Zacchaei christiani et Apollonii philosophi, ed. and trans. J. L. Feiertag, 2 vols. (SC 401–2; Paris: Editions du Cerf, 1994).

Quintilianus, M. Fabius, *Institutionis oratoriae libri XII*, ed. L. Radermacher (Leipzig: Teubner, 1965).

Raasted, Jürgen, *Intonation Formulas and Modal Signatures in Byzantine Musical Manuscripts* (Monumenta musicae Byzantinae, 7; Copenhagen: Munksgaard, 1966).

—— 'Die Jubili Finales und die Verwendung von interkalierten Vokalisen in der Gesangspraxis der Byzantiner', in *Griechische Musik und Europa: Antike – Byzanz – Volksmusik der Neuzeit, im Gedenken an Samuel Baud-Bovy. Symposion: Die Beziehung der griechischen Musik zur europäischen Musiktradition, vom 9.–11. Mai 1986 in Würzburg*, ed. Rudolf M. Brandl and Evangelos Konstantinou (Orbis musicarum, 3; Aachen: Alano Verlag, Edition Herodot, 1988), 67–80.

—— 'The "Laetantis adverbia" of Aurelian's Greek Informant', in *Aspects de la musique liturgique au Moyen Age: Actes des colloques de Royaumont de 1986, 1987, et 1988*, ed. Christian Meyer (Paris: Editions Créaphis, 1991), 55–66.

Rajeczky, Benjamin, 'Gregorianik und Volksgesang', in *Handbuch des Volksliedes*, ed. Rolf Wilhelm Brednich, Lutz Röhrich and Wolfgang Suppan (Munich: Wilhelm Fink Verlag, 1975), ii, 393–405.

Ramackers, Johannes, 'Die Weihe des Domes von Sorrent am 16 März 1113 durch Kardinal-Bischof Richard von Albano', in Clemens Bauer, Laetitia Boehm and Max Muller (eds), *Speculum Historiale: Geschichte im Spiegel von Geschichtsschreibung und Geschichtsdeutung; Johannes Sporl aus Anlass seines 60.Geburtstag, dargebracht von Weggenossen, Freunden, und Schulen* (Freiburg and Munich: Alber, 1965), 578–89.

Randel, Don Michael, *An Index to the Chant of the Mozarabic Rite* (Princeton Studies in Music, 6; Princeton: Princeton University Press, 1973).

Raugel, Felix, 'Saint-Césaire, précepteur du Chant gallican', in *International Musicological Society: Bericht über den siebenten Internationalen musikwissenschaftlichen Kongress Köln 1958*, ed. Gerald Abraham et al. (Kassel: Bärenreiter, 1959), 217–18.

RB 1980: The Rule of St. Benedict in Latin and English with Notes, ed. Timothy Fry et al. (Collegeville, Minn.: Liturgical Press, 1981).

La Règle de saint Augustin, i: *Tradition manuscrite*, ed. Luc Verheijen (Paris: Etudes augustiniennes, 1967).

La Règle de saint Benoît, ed. Adalbert de Vogüé and Jean Neufville, 7 vols. (SC 181–6; Paris: Editions du Cerf, 1971–7).

La Règle du Maître, ed. Adalbert de Vogüé, 3 vols. (SC 105–7; Paris: Editions du Cerf, 1964–5).

Les Règles des Saints Pères, ed. Adalbert de Vogüé, 2 vols. (SC 297–8; Paris: Editions du Cerf, 1992).

Regnault, Lucien, 'Les Apophtegmes en Palestine au Ve–VIe siècles', *Irénikon*, 54 (1981), 320–30; repr. in Regnault, *Les Pères du désert: à travers leurs apophtegmes* (Sablé-sur-Sarthe: Abbaye Saint-Pierre de Solesmes, 1987).

Regula Pauli et Stephani: Edició crítica i comentari, ed. J. Evangelista M. Vilanova (Scripta et documenta, 11; Montserrat: Abadia de Montserrat, 1959).

Remigius of Auxerre, *Commentum in Martianum Capellam*, ed. Cora Lutz (Leiden: E. J. Brill, 1962).

Reydellet, Marc, 'La Diffusion des "Origines" d'Isidore de Séville au haut Moyen Age', *Mélanges de l'Ecole française de Rome*, 78 (1966), 383–437.

Riché, Pierre, *Ecoles et enseignement dans le haut Moyen Age: fin du ve siècle–milieu du xie siècle* (Paris: Picard, 1989).

Robertson, Anne Walters, 'The Reconstruction of the Abbey Church at St-Denis (1231–81)', *EMH* 5 (1985), 205–31.

—— *The Service Books of the Royal Abbey of Saint-Denis: Images of Ritual and Music in the Middle Ages* (Oxford: Clarendon Press, 1991).

Roezter, Wunibald, *Des heiligen Augustinus Schriften als liturgiegeschichtliche Quellen* (Munich: M. Hueber, 1930).

Rollason, David W., 'St Cuthbert and Wessex: The Evidence of Cambridge, Corpus Christi College MS 183', in Gerald Bonner, David W. Rollason and Clare Stancliffe (eds), *St. Cuthbert, his Cult and his Community to AD 1200* (Woodbridge, Suffolk: Boydell Press, 1989), 413–24.

Rondeau, Marie-Josèphe, *Les Commentaires patristiques du psautier (IIIe–Ve siècles)*, 2 vols. (OCA 219–20; Rome: Pontificium Institutum Studiorum Orientalium, 1982, 1985).

—— 'L'Epître à Marcellinus sur les psaumes', *Vigiliae Christianae*, 22 (1968), 176–97.

Rose, André, '"Attollite portas, principes, vestras": aperçus sur la lecture chrétienne du Ps. 24 (23)', in *Miscellanea liturgica in onore di Sua Eminenza il Cardinale Giacomo Lercaro, arcivescovo di Bologna, presidente del 'Consilium' per l'applicazione della costituzione sulla sacra liturgia*, 2 vols. (Rome: Desclée, 1966), 453–78.

—— 'Les Psaumes de l'initiation chrétienne I. Les psaumes ou versets psalmiques utilisés dans l'église occidentale', *Questions liturgiques et paroissiales*, 47 (1966), 279–92; 48 (1967), 111–20.

—— *Les Psaumes: voix du Christ et de l'église* (Paris: P. Lethielleux, 1981).

Rossi, Giovanni Battista de, *Mosaici cristiani: saggi dei pavimenti delle chiese di Roma anteriori al secolo XV* (Rome: [n. pub.], 1899).

Rousseau, Philip, *Pachomius: The Making of a Community in Fourth-Century Egypt* (Transformation of the Classical Heritage, 6; Berkeley: University of California Press, 1985).

Rücker, A., 'Die wechselnden Gesangstücke der ostsyrischen Messe', *Jahrbuch für Liturgiewissenschaft*, 1 (1921), 61–86.

The Rule of the Master, trans. Luke Eberle and Charles Philippi (Cistercian Studies, 6; Kalamazoo, Mich.: Cistercian Publications, 1977).

Ruppert, Fidelis. 'Meditatio – ruminatio: Zu einem Grundbegriff christlicher Meditation', *Erbe und Auftrag*, 53 (1977), 83–93.

Russell, Norman (trans.), *The Lives of the Desert Fathers: The Historia monachorum in Aegypto* (Cistercian Studies Series, 34; Kalamazoo, Mich.: Cistercian Publications, 1981).

Rutgers, Leonard Victor, *The Jews in Late Ancient Rome: Evidence of Cultural Interaction in the Roman Diaspora* (Religions in the Graeco-Roman World, 126; Leiden: E. J. Brill, 1995).

Das Sacramentarium Triplex: Die Handschrift C 43 der Zentralbibliothek Zürich, ed. Odilo Heimig (Liturgiewissenschaftliche Quellen und Forschungen, 49; Corpus Ambrosiano-Liturgicum, 1; Münster: Aschendorff, 1968).

Salmon, Pierre, *Les 'Tituli Psalmorum' des manuscrits latins* (Collectanea Biblica Latina, 12; Rome: Abbaye Saint-Jérôme; Vatican City: Libreria Vaticana, 1959).

The Sayings of the Desert Fathers: The Alphabetical Collection, ed. and trans. Benedicta Ward (Cistercian Studies Series, 59; Kalamazoo, Mich.: Cistercian Publications, 1975).

Schattauer, Thomas H., 'The Koinonicon of the Byzantine Liturgy: An Historical Study', *Orientalia Christiana Periodica*, 49 (1983), 91–129.

Schier, Volker, 'Propriumstropen in der Würzburger Domliturgie', *Kirchenmusikalisches Jahrbuch*, 76 (1992), 3–43.

Schlager, Karl-Heinz, *Thematischer Katalog der ältesten Alleluia-Melodien aus Handschriften des 10. und 11. Jahrhunderts, ausgenommen das ambrosianische, alt-römische und alt-spanische Repertoire* (Erlanger Arbeiten zur Musikwissenschaft, 2; Munich: W. Ricke, 1965).

—— and Wohnhaas, Theodor, 'Zeugnisse der Afra-Verehrung im mittelalterlichen Choral', *Jahrbuch des Vereins für Augsburger Bistumsgeschichte*, 18 (1984), 199–226.

Schlieben, Reinhard, *Cassiodors Psalmenexegese: Eine Analyse ihrer Methoden als Beitrag zur Untersuchung der Geschichte der Bibelauslegung der Kirchenväter und der Verbindung christlicher Theologie mit antiker Schulwissenschaft* (Göppinger Akademische Beiträge, 110; Göppingen: Kümmerle, 1979).

Schoell, Fritz, 'De accentu linguae Latinae', *Acta Societatis Philologiae Lipsiensis*, 6; Leipzig: Teubner, 1876).

Schubiger, Anselm, *Die Sängerschule St. Gallens vom achten bis zwölften Jahrhundert: Ein Beitrag zur Gesanggeschichte des Mittelalters* (Einsiedeln: K. & N. Benziger, 1858).

Schwartz, Eduard, 'Zum Decretum Gelasianum', *Zeitschrift für neutestamentliche Wissenschaft*, 29 (1930), 161–8.

Scriptores ecclesiastici de musica sacra potissimum, ed. Martin Gerbert, 3 vols. (St. Blasien, 1784; repr. Milan: Bollettino Bibliografico Musicale, 1931).

Scriptorum de musica medii aevi nova series, ed. Edmond de Coussemaker, 4 vols (Paris: Durand, 1864–76).

Sedulius Scottus, *In Donati Artem maiorem*, ed. Bengt Löfstedt (CCCM 40B: Grammatici Hibernici Carolini aevi, pars III, 1; Turnhout: Brepols, 1977).

Seebass, Tilman, *Musikdarstellung und Psalterillustration im früheren Mittelalter: Studien, ausgehend von einer Ikonologie der Handschrift Paris, Bibliothèque nationale, fonds latin 1118,* 2 vols. (Bern: Francke, 1973).

Septuaginta 10: *Psalmi cum Odis*, ed. Alfred Rahlfs (Göttingen: Vandenhoeck & Ruprecht, 1931).

Serbat, Guy, *Les Structures du latin: le système de la langue classique* (Paris: A. & J. Picard, 1975).

Servatius, Carlo, *Paschalis II (1099–1118): Studien zu seiner Person und seiner Politik* (Papste und Papsttum, 14; Stuttgart: Hiersemann, 1979).

Servius, *Commentarius in Artem Donati*, in *Grammatici Latini*, iv, ed. H. Keil (Leipzig: Teubner, 1868; repr. 1961).
Severus, Emmanuel von, 'Das Wort "Meditari" im Sprachgebrauch der Heiligen Schrift', *Geist und Leben*, 26 (1953), 365–75.
Sextus Empiricus, *Against the Musicians*, ed. and trans. Denise Davidson Greaves (Greek and Latin Music Theory; Lincoln: University of Nebraska Press, 1986).
Sidler, Hubert, *Studien zu den alten Offertorien mit ihren Versen* (Veröffentlichungen der Gregorianischen Akademie zu Freiburg, 1; Reihe der Veröffentlichungen des Musikwissenschaftlichen Instituts der Universität Freiburg i. d. Schweiz, 20; Fribourg: Verlag des Musikwissenschaftlichen Instituts der Universität, 1939).
Siguinis, Magister, *Ars lectoria*, ed. C. H. Kneepkens and H. F. Reijnders (Leiden: E. J. Brill, 1979).
Sillem, Aelred, 'St Benedict (ca. 480–ca. 550)', in David Hugh Farmer (ed.), *Benedict's Disciples* (Leominster: Gracewing, 1980; repr. 1995), 21–40.
Slocum, Kay Brainerd, 'Prosas for Saint Thomas Becket', *PMM* 8 (1999), 39–54.
Sole, Laura M., 'Some Anglo-Saxon Cuthbert *Liturgica*: The Manuscript Evidence', *Revue bénédictine*, 108 (1998), 104–44.
Sottocornola, Franco, *L'anno liturgico nei sermoni di Pietro Crisologo: ricerca storico-critica sulla liturgia di Ravenna antica* (Studia Ravennatensia, 1; Cesena: Centro studi e ricerche sulla antica provincia ecclesiastica ravennate, 1973).
Špidlík, Tomas, Michelina Tenace, and Richard Cemus, *Questions monastiques en Orient* (OCA 259; Rome: Pontificium Institutum Studiorum Orientalium, 1999).
Stäblein, Bruno, 'Die Sequenzmelodie "Concordia" und ihr geschichtlicher Hintergrund', in Horst Heussner (ed.), *Festschrift Hans Engel zum siebzigsten Geburtstag* (Kassel: Bärenreiter, 1964), 364–92.
—— 'Zur Frühgeschichte der Sequenz', *AfMw* 28 (1961), 4–7.
Stein, Franz A., 'Das ältere Offizium des hl. Wolfgang in der Handschrift Clm 14872 aus St. Emmeram zu Regensburg in der Bayerischen Staatsbibliothek München', in id. (ed.), *Sacerdos et cantus Gregoriani magister: Festschrift Ferdinand Haberl zum 70. Geburtstag* (Regensburg: Bosse, 1977), 279–302.
Steinen, Wolfram von den, *Notker der Dichter und seine geistige Welt*, 2 vols. (Bern: A. Francke, 1948; repr. 1978).
Steiner, Ruth, 'The Gregorian Chant Melismas for Christmas Matins', in Jerald C. Graue (ed.), *Essays on Music for Charles Warren Fox* (Rochester: Eastman School of Music, 1979), 241–53.
—— '*Holocausta medullata*: An Offertory for St. Saturninus', in Cahn and Heimer (eds), *De musica et cantu*, 263–74.
—— 'On the Verses for the Offertory *Elegerunt*', in Peter Jeffrey (ed.), *The Study of Medieval Chant, Paths and Bridges, East and West: In Honor of Kenneth Levy* (Rochester, NY: Boydell & Brewer, 2001), 283–301.
—— 'The Prosulae of the MS Paris BN lat. 1118', *JAMS* 22 (1969), 367–93.
—— 'The Responsories and Prosula for St. Stephen's Day at Salisbury', *MQ* 56 (1970), 162–82.

—— 'Some Melismas for Office Responsories', *JAMS* 26 (1973), 108–31.
—— *Studies in Gregorian Chant* (Aldershot: Ashgate Publishing, 1999).
Stewart, Columba, *Cassian the Monk* (Oxford Studies in Historical Theology; New York: Oxford University Press, 1998).
Stiftsbibliothek Sankt Gallen Codices 484 & 381: Kommentiert und in Faksimile, ed. Wulf Arlt, Susan Rankin and Cristina Hospenthal (Winterthur: Amadeus, 1996).
Stock, Brian, *Augustine the Reader: Meditation, Self-Knowledge, and the Ethics of Interpretation* (Cambridge, Mass.: Belknap Press of Harvard University Press, 1996).
Strobel, August, *Ursprung und Geschichte des frühchristlichen Osterkalenders* (Texte und Untersuchungen zur Geschichte der altchristlichen Literatur, 121; Berlin: Akademie-Verlag, 1977).
The Stowe Missal, ed. George F. Warner, ii (Henry Bradshaw Society, 32; London: Harrison & Sons, 1915).
Strunk, Oliver, 'The Latin Antiphons for the Octave of the Epiphany', in *Essays on Music in the Byzantine World* (New York: Norton, 1977), 208–19.
—— *Source Readings in Music History*, ii: *The Early Christian Period and the Latin Middle Ages,* rev. edn, ed. James McKinnon (New York: Norton, 1998).
Sulpicius Severus, et al., *The Western Fathers*, ed. F. R. Hoare (London: Sheed & Ward, 1954; repr. New York: Harper, 965).
Supino Martini, Paola. *Roma e l'area grafica romanesca (secoli X–XII)* (Biblioteca di scrittura e civiltà, 1; Alessandria: Edizioni dell'Orso, 1987).
Szendrei, Janka, László Dobszay and Benjamin Rajeczky, *XVI–XVII. századi dallamaink a népi emlékezetben* [Tunes in Folk Memory of the 16th and 17th Centuries], i–ii (Budapest: Akadémiai Kiadó, 1979).
Taft, Robert F., *The Great Entrance: A History of the Transfer of Gifts and other Pre-Anaphoral Rites* (OCA 200; Rome: Pontificium Institutum Studiorum Orientalium, 1978).
—— *The Liturgy of the Hours in East and West: The Origins of the Divine Office and its Meaning for Today* (Collegeville, Minn.: Liturgical Press, 1986; 2nd rev. edn, Collegeville, Minn.: Liturgical Press, 1993).
—— 'Praise in the Desert: The Coptic Monastic Office Yesterday and Today', *Worship*, 56 (1982), 513–36.
Talley, Thomas, *The Origins of the Liturgical Year* (2nd emended edn, Collegeville, Minn.: Liturgical Press, 1991).
Tax, Peter W., *Notker Latinus: Die Quellen zu den Psalmen, Psalm 1–150*, 3 vols (Altdeutsche Textbibliothek, 74–5, 90; Die Werke Notkers des Deutschen, 8A–10A; Tubingen: M. Niemeyer, 1972–5).
Teeuwen, Mariken, 'Harmony and the Music of the Spheres: The *Ars musica* in Ninth-Century Commentaries on Martianus Capella' (Ph.D. diss., University of Utrecht, 2000).
Les Témoins manuscrits du chant bénéventain, ed. Thomas Forrest Kelly (PM 21; Solesmes: Abbaye Saint-Pierre, 1992).
Theon of Smyrna, *Theonis Smyrnaei philosophi Platonici expositio rerum mathematicarum ad legendum Platonem utilium*, ed. Eduard Hiller

(Bibliotheca scriptorum Graecorum et Romanorum Teubneriana; Leipzig: B. G. Teubner, 1878).
Thompson, Edward Maunde, *An Introduction to Greek and Latin Paleography* (Oxford: Clarendon Press, 1912).
Treitler, Leo, 'Centonate Chant: Übles Flickwerk or E pluribus unus?' *JAMS*, 28 (1975), 1–23.
—— 'Reading and Singing: On the Genesis of Occidental Music-Writing', *EMH* 4 (1984), 135–208.
—— 'Homer and Gregory: The Transmission of Epic Poetry and Plainchant', *MQ* 60 (1974), 333–72.
—— 'Oral, Written and Literate Process in the Transmission of Medieval Music', *Speculum*, 56 (1981), 202–11.
Troparium, Sequentiarium, Nonantulanum. Cod. Casanat. 1741, ed. Giuseppe Vecchi (Monumenta lyrica medii aevi italica, 1; Latina, 1; Modena: Academia Scientiarum Litterarum Artium, 1955).
Tropes of the Proper of the Mass from Southern Italy, A.D. 1000–1250; ii: *Ordinary Chants and Tropes for the Mass from Southern Italy, A.D. 1000–1250: Pt. 1, Kyrie eleison; Pt. 2, Gloria in excelsis; Pt. 3, Preface Chants and Sanctus*, ed. John Boe and Alejandro Enrique Planchart (Beneventanum troporum corpus, 1; Recent Researches in the Music of the Middle Ages and Early Renaissance, 16–18; Madison, Wis.: A-R Editions, 1994–6).
Le Typicon de la Grande Eglise: Ms. Saint-Croix no 40, Xe siècle, ed. Juan Mateos, 2 vols. (OCA 165–6; Rome: Pontificium Institutum Studiorum Orientalium, 1962–3).
'Τυπικὸν τῆς ἐν Ἱεροσολύμοις Εκκλῃσιας', [Typikon of the Church in Jerusalem] Ἀνάλεκτα Ἱεροσολυμιτικῆς Σταχυιλαγοας' [Collections of Gleanings from Jerusalem], ed. A. Papadopoulos-Keramefs (St. Petersburg: B. Kirschbaum, 1894; repr. Brussels: Culture et Civilisation, 1963).
The Utrecht Prosarium: liber sequentiarum ecclesiae capitularis Sanctae Mariae Ultraiectensis saeculi XIII, Codex Ultraiectensis, universitatis bibliotheca 417, ed. N. de Goede (Monumenta musica Neerlandica, 6; Amsterdam: Vereniging voor Nederlandse Muziekgeschiedenis, 1965).
Vagaggini, Cipriano (ed.), *La preghiera nella bibbia e nella tradizione patristica e monastica* (2nd edn, Milan: Edizioni Paoline, 1988).
Variae preces (Solesmes: Abbaye Saint-Pierre, 1888).
Varro, *On the Latin Language*, trans. Roland G. Kent (Cambridge, Mass.: Harvard University Press, 1938).
Väterlein, Christian (ed.), *Graduale Pataviense: Wien 1511: Faksimile* (Das Erbe deutscher Musik, 87; Kassel: Bärenreiter, 1982).
Veilleux, Armand, *La Liturgie dans le cénobitisme pachômien au quatrième siècle* (Studia Anselmiana philosophica theologica, 57; Rome: Herder, 1968).
Velimirovic, Milos, 'Christian Chant in Syria, Armenia, Egypt, and Ethiopia', in *NOHM*, ii: *The Early Middle Ages to 1300*, ed. Richard Crocker and David Hiley (Oxford: Oxford University Press, 1990).
Verbraken, Pierre-Patrick, 'Le Psautier des tropistes', in Gunilla Iversen (ed.), *Research on Tropes* (Konferenser Kungliga Vitterhets, Historie och Antikvitets Akademien, 8; Stockholm: Almqvist & Wiksell, 1983).

Villetard, Henri, *Office de Pierre de Corbeil (Office de la circoncision) improprement appelé 'Office des fous'* (Bibliothèque musicologique, 4; Paris: A. Picard, 1907).

—— *Office de Saint Savinien et de Saint Potentien, premiers évèques de Sens* (Bibliothèque musicologique, 5; Paris: Picard, [1956]).

Vogüé, Adalbert de, 'The Cenobitic Rules of the West', *Cistercian Studies*, 12 (1977), 175–83.

—— *De saint Pachôme à Jean Cassien: études littéraires et doctrinales sur le monachisme égyptien à ses débuts* (Rome: Cento Studi S. Anselmo, 1996).

—— 'Les Deux fonctions de la méditation dans les Règles monastiques anciennes', *Revue d'histoire de la spiritualité*, 51 (1975), 3–16.

—— 'La *Glossa Ordinaria* et le commentaire des rois attribué à Grégoire le Grand', *Révue bénédictine*, 108 (1998), 58–60.

—— *Histoire littéraire du mouvement monastique dans l'antiquité*, 5 vols. (Paris: Editions du Cerf, 1991–).

—— 'Lectiones sanctas libenter audire": silence, lecture et prière chez Saint Benoît', *Benedictina*, 27 (1980), 11–26.

—— *Le Maître, Eugippe et Saint Benoît: recueil d'articles* (Regulae Benedicti Studia, Supplementa, 17; Hildesheim: Gerstenberg, 1984).

—— 'Psalmodier n'est pas prier', *Ecclesia orans*, 6 (1989), 7–32.

—— 'Le Psaume et l'oraison: nouveau florilège', *Ecclesia orans*, 12 (1995), 325–49.

—— *La Règle de Saint Benoît*, v: *Commentaire doctrinal et spirituel* (SC 185; Paris: Editions du Cerf, 1971).

—— *La Règle de Saint Benoît*, vii: *Commentaire doctrinal et spirituel* (Paris: Editions du Cerf, 1977). Translated by John Baptist Hasbrouck in *The Rule of Saint Benedict: A Doctrinal and Spiritual Commentary* (Cistercian Studies Series, 54; Kalamazoo, Mich.: Cistercian Publications, 1983).

—— *Les Règles monastiques anciennes (400–700)* (Typologie des sources du Moyen Age occidental, 46; Turnhout: Brepols, 1985).

—— 'Les Sources des quatres premiers livres des Institutions de Jean Cassien: introduction aux recherches sur les anciennes règles monastiques latines', in *De saint Pachôme à Jean Cassien*, 373–456.

Waddell, Helen, *The Desert Fathers* (London: Constable, 1936).

Wagner, Peter, *Einführung in die gregorianische Melodien: Ein Handbuch der Choralwissenschaft*, 3 vols. (2nd edn, Leipzig: Breitkopf & Härtel, 1911–21).

Ward, Benedicta, *The Wisdom of the Desert Fathers: The Apophthegmata Patrum* (Fairacres Publication, 48; Oxford: S. L. G. Press, 1975).

Weakland, Rembert, 'The Compositions of Hucbald', *Etudes grégoriennes*, 3 (1959), 155–62.

Wellesz, Egon, *A History of Byzantine Music and Hymnography* (2nd edn, Oxford: Clarendon Press, 1961).

Werf, Hendrik van der, *The Emergence of Gregorian Chant: A Comparative Study of Ambrosian, Roman, and Gregorian Chant. I–II* (Rochester, NY: [the author], 1983).

Wessely, Otto, 'Die Musikanschauung des Abtes Pambo', *Anzeiger der Österreichischen Akademie der Wissenschaften, Philosophisch-historische Klasse*, 89 (1953), 42–62.

Whealey, Alice, 'Prologues on the Psalms: Origen, Hippolytus, Eusebius', *Révue bénédictine*, 106 (1996), 234–45.

Wilhelm of Hirsau, *Musica*, ed. Denis Harbinson (Corpus scriptorum de musica, 23; Rome: American Institute of Musicology, 1975).

Wilmart, André, *Analecta reginensia: extraits des manuscrits latins de la reine Christine conservés au Vatican* (Studi e testi, 59; Vatican City: Biblioteca Apostolica Vaticana, 1933; repr. 1966).

—— *The Psalter Collects from V–VIth Century Sources (Three Series)*, ed. Louis Brou (Henry Bradshaw Society, 83; London: Harrison & Sons, 1949).

Wolf, Gerhard, *Salus Populi Romani: Die Geschichte römischer Kultbilder im Mittelalter* (Weinheim: VCH, Acta humaniora, 1990).

Wood, Susan K., *Spiritual Exegesis and the Church in the Theology of Henri de Lubac* (Grand Rapids, Mich.: William B. Eerdmans; Edinburgh: T. & T. Clark, 1998).

Woodruff, Paul, 'Rhetoric and Relativism: Protagoras and Gorgias', in *The Cambridge Companion to Early Greek Philosophy*, ed. A. A. Long (Cambridge: Cambridge University Press, 1999), 290–301.

Yarnold, Edward, *The Awe-Inspiring Rites of Initiation: The Origins of the R[ite of] C[hristian] I[nitiation of] A[dults]* (2nd edn, Collegeville, Minn.: Liturgical Press, 1994).

Zaminer, Frider, 'Pythagoras und die Anfänge des musiktheoretischen Denkens bei den Griechen', *Jahrbuch des Staatlichen Instituts für Musikforschung Preussischer Kulturbesitz*, 1979–80, 203–11.

Index of Manuscripts

Incipits Index

[Page numbers in **bold** denote musical examples]

General Index